English Language Learner and Diversity Manual

Second Custom Edition for Azusa Pacific University

Taken from:

Differentiated Early Literacy for English Language Learners: Practical Strategies
by Paul Boyd-Batstone

The Crosscultural Language and Academic Development Handbook:
A Complete K-12 Reference Guide, Fourth Edition
by Lynne T. Díaz-Rico and Kathryn Z. Weed

Fifty Strategies for Teaching English Language Learners, Third Edition
by Adrienne L. Herrell and Michael Jordan

Effective Teaching Strategies That Accommodate Diverse Learners, Third Edition
by Michael D. Coyne, Edward J. Kame'enui, and Douglas W. Carnine

A Course for Teaching English Learners
by Lynne T. Díaz-Rico

Special Populations in Gifted Education: Working with Diverse Gifted Learners
by Jaime A. Castellano

The Foundations of Dual Language Instruction, Fifth Edition
by Judith Lessow-Hurley

Bridging Multiple Worlds: Case Studies of Diverse Educational Communities, Second Edition
by Lorraine S. Taylor and Catharine R. Whittaker

Learning Solutions

New York   Boston   San Francisco
London   Toronto   Sydney   Tokyo   Singapore   Madrid
Mexico City   Munich   Paris   Cape Town   Hong Kong   Montreal

ISBN 10: 0-558-65557-2
ISBN 13: 978-0-558-65557-0

CONTENTS

INTRODUCTION

by Nilsa J. Thorsos, Ph.D.

Teacher Education Programs in California are designed to prepare new teachers to work with diverse populations. In order to obtain a teaching credential in California, teacher candidates are extensively educated to be culturally competent. The Teacher Education Program (TEP) at Azusa Pacific University (APU) helps develop competency, both in teaching diverse populations and in supporting English language learners (ELL) who speak English as a second language. Our teacher candidates learn to identify and recognize the vast richness of our diverse student population. Our goal in TEP is to prepare new teachers to be highly effective and skilled in working with K–12 students from a multitude of cultural, socioeconomic, and linguistic backgrounds.

A critical factor that impacts the issue of diversity and ELL in California's classrooms can be found in the demographics reported for California. According to the 2000 Census, most of California's population growth in the past few decades has occurred among Hispanics and Asians. Projections for the future suggest that strong growth among California's Hispanic and Asian populations will continue well into the 21st century and that by the year 2025, Hispanics will be the largest ethnic group in the state (Public Policy Institute of California, 2001). Families representing this increasing number of students are immigrant English language learners from diverse religious backgrounds. In addition, a growing number of students are identified as having a disability or exceptionality. Teacher candidates need to develop competence for working with students from diverse backgrounds and with exceptionalities to ensure that all students have equal access to the curriculum and equal opportunities to learn.

The Teacher Education Program acknowledges diversity as defined in the National Council of Accreditation for Teacher Education (NCATE) Standards, which delineates the following definition: Differences among groups of people and individuals based on ethnicity, race, socioeconomic status, gender, exceptionalities, language, religion, sexual orientation, and geographical area (2002, p. 53). Varying aspects of diversity are described in the NCATE Standards and can be illustrated with different scenarios typical for teacher candidates at APU. Our teacher candidates work in a variety of settings in many districts throughout Southern California. For example, interns are currently working with ELL students, as well as with the broadest range of diverse students in K–12 settings, ranging from the suburbs to rural areas and from wealthy areas to those representing the poorer inner city schools. Candidates are also found teaching in both traditional and nontraditional settings, including charter schools and private Christian schools. Given the circumstances of the different teaching environments, teacher candidates may not have ELL or diverse students in their classrooms in a given time. Regardless of whether the teacher candidates live in areas of great or low diversity settings, they must be prepared to help all students learn and to teach from multicultural and global perspectives. Candidates must also be able to respectfully draw on the histories, experiences, and representations of students from diverse cultural backgrounds. Candidates must also be able to provide successful learning experiences for those students with exceptionalities who are included in regular education classrooms, and to also accommodate any gender differences and the impact on learning (http://www.ncate.org/2000/2000stds).

Our School of Education reaffirms our focus on preparing teachers who make a difference in today's society through the unit's conceptual framework, which includes the preparation of: (a) ethical professionals who are committed to diversity, equity, and social justice within their school communities; (b) responsive professionals who practice reflective critical thinking in their engagements with diverse communities of learners; and (c) informed professionals who are dedicated to collaboration and lifelong learning to support the diverse needs of all students (Institutional Report for NCATE, Standard 4, 2007).

In response to the need for a consistent and broad theoretical foundation, we have created a custom, departmental handbook, which includes the best chapters from ten cutting-edge textbooks into one manual that will serve as a foundational ELL companion text throughout all credential programs. Each selection was carefully chosen to address the many components required to ensure teacher candidates have access to current ELL theories, history of bilingual education, and models of bilingual education programs, as well as classroom-friendly strategies, techniques, and applications. Additionally, candidates will extend their knowledge base to incorporate the broadest interpretation of diversity in California schools.

It is the intention of the department of TEP that teacher candidates using this manual will find themselves well prepared to meet the challenges and experience the success of helping K–12 students learn. Those teachers who are well educated in working with diverse students are most likely to make significant, life-long contributions to our children and youth—as well as to society in general.

Nilsa J. Thorsos, Ph.D.
Director Special Education Department Chair
Special Education Programs
Azusa Pacific University

INTRODUCTION

by Ivy Yee-Sakamoto, Ph.D.

This customized text, *English Language Learner and Diversity Manual,* and accompanying DVD were designed for use in the Azusa Pacific University teaching credential preparation programs. Whether you are planning to teach at elementary or secondary level, or with learners with special needs, your credential preparation must address the issues and needs of culturally and linguistically diverse learner populations. Each of the credential program courses is designed so you can build your knowledge base about diverse populations while developing the skills and dispositions to make you a sensitive and responsive educator. The custom text is a compilation of outstanding chapters from nine different texts and is designed for use throughout your credential program as a companion piece to the other required texts and resources. You will master three domains of knowledge so you can earn your English Learner Authorization in California: (1) culture, cultural diversity, and providing culturally responsive instruction, (2) language structure and first and second language development, and (3) theory and method of bilingual instruction, instruction for English language development (ELD), specially designed academic instruction delivered in English (SDAIE), and language and content area assessment.

The first section of this text addresses the first domain of knowledge. It includes Parts Four and Five of Diaz-Rico and Weed's book, *The Crosscultural Language and Academic Development Handbook: A Complete K–12 Reference Guide.* In Chapters 1 through 3, the authors present an overview of cultural diversity in the United States, the intercultural educator, and culturally responsive schooling. Chapter 1 addresses historical and legal perspectives of culture and immigration, the impact of culture, and the current status of minority groups and English language learners. Chapter 2, with its focus on the intercultural educator, presents the key concepts of culture and the need to learn about ourselves and our students as cultural beings as a key factor in achieving equity in schooling for all students. In Chapter 3 the emphasis is on the critical role sensitive and informed educators can play in bridging the home and school and reducing culture shock between those two worlds. More importantly, the authors argue that teachers who understand cultural diversity become engaged in the struggle for equity and the promotion of academic success for all students. In Chapters 4 and 5, Diaz-Rico and Weed address the role of educators in language planning and policy. They present it as a professional responsibility, an imperative which when denied, is an abdication of authority. Also discussed are the needs of culturally and linguistically diverse learners with special needs and perspectives and strategies for the design and delivery of instruction appropriate for meeting their needs.

In the second section of this text, Chapters 6 and 7 come from Diaz-Rico's *A Course for Teaching English Learners* and Lessow and Hurley's *Foundations of Dual Language Instruction.* These chapters provide the history and theory for instructing English learners, dual language program models for English language learners, language structure, and first and second language development which address the second domain of knowledge. Chapter 8 is Taylor and Whitaker's work from *Bridging Multiple Worlds: Case Studies of Diverse Educational Communities,* which presents an overview on the changing pattern of immigration.

The third section of this book focuses on strategies for ELD, SDAIE, and assessment which comprise the third domain of knowledge. Here, chapters from Boyd-Batstone's *Differentiated Early Literacy for English Language Learners: Practical Strategies,* Coyne, et al's book, *Effective Teaching Strategies that Accommodate Diverse Learners,* and Herrell and Jordan's *50 Strategies for Teaching English Language Learners* provide you with strategies for differentiated instruction so whether you are teaching language arts, mathematics, science, social studies, the visual and performing arts, or any other content area, your instruction will be designed and delivered effectively for culturally and linguistically diverse learners.

In the final section of this text special issues are addressed. Castellano's [ldquo]Casting a Wider Net: Linking Bilingual and Gifted Education" and [ldquo]ESL Students in Gifted Education" provides a special focus on the gifted bilingual and English language learner. Finally, there is Nworie's chapter on gay, lesbian, bisexual, and transgender (GLBT) learners followed by [ldquo]Counseling Queer Youth: Preventing Another Matthew Shepard Story" authored by Fernando J. Gutiérrez, from *Youth at Risk,* which addresses the issue of working with gay and lesbian students. Each of these chapters have been included for their reminder that there are populations which can be easily overlooked and underserved, thus compromising our efforts to teach all students.

Finally, there is a DVD included with this text which was designed to accompany Herrell and Jordan's *50 Strategies for Teaching English Language Learners.* This resource is to be used in concert with the chapters from the Herrell and Jordan text so you can see the strategies being described. This DVD can be easily referenced time and again when you are constructing lessons for your classes.

The scholarly work in the areas of culture, linguistic and academic development has compounded rapidly such that this knowledge base makes customizing a text from the many available texts a daunting task. However, the design team for this custom text is pleased to present you with this text which would not have been possible if it had not been for the collaborative efforts of dedicated faculty members (Nancy Contrucci, Ann Hagmaier, Greg Kaiser, Bennett Nworie, Gail Reeder, Ann Test, Nilsa Thorsos, Ivy Yee-Sakamoto) and the representatives of Pearson-Allyn and Bacon and Pearson-Merrill Prentice Hall (Arthur Garcia, Elizabeth Kaster, Christine Nguyen, Robin Russo). We are more than grateful for each person's contributions.

Ivy Yee-Sakamoto, Ph.D.
Azusa Pacific University
ELL/CLAD Certificate Coordinator
Teacher Education Program Leadership Team

CULTURE, CULTURAL DIVERSITY, AND CULTURALLY RESPONSIVE INSTRUCTION

CHAPTER

CULTURAL DIVERSITY

Immigration has brought the world into U.S. schools.

Before I came to America I had dreams of life here. I thought about tall Anglos, big buildings, and houses with lawns. I was surprised when I arrived to see so many kinds of people—Black people, Asians. I found people from Korea and Cambodia and Mexico. In California I found not just America, I found the world.

—Mexican immigrant student (Olsen, 1988, p. 10)

They still come—a medical student from India who remains in Knoxville to set up a practice; a Danish au pair worker who meets a U.S. college student and extends her work visa; a Vietnamese grandmother who follows her daughter, who followed her teenage sons; a Mexican lawyer who sets up an import–export practice in Tijuana and San Diego; Romanian orphans brought to the United States through an adoption service; a Hong Kong capitalist who settles his family in San José while he commutes by jet to maintain his businesses. The immigration that has enriched the United States shows little sign of abating.

Each successive wave of immigration has had unique characteristics and a distinct impact on U.S. education. Whether attracted to the United States or forced here from their native country, immigrants have brought with them cultural, political, religious, and economic values, along with multiple tongues and various skills. Whether legally or illegally residing in the United States, immigrants contribute material aspects of their culture (crafts, foods, technology) as well as nonmaterial aspects (family values, spiritual beliefs, medical practices). During the process of settlement, these immigrants require social and educational services to help them adapt to their new environment.

The extent of immigration and the policies that shape it have been controversial issues since the founding of this country. This great experiment—the United States of America—has required the innovation, fabrication, and synthesis of whole new patterns of existence. Those who have participated in this great cultural amalgamation have been themselves transformed. This transformation has not ended and will not end in the foreseeable future. Not only do we need to live with it, but we also have the unique opportunity to enjoy and value it.

HISTORICAL PERSPECTIVES

The North American continent has received people from all over the world. Diverse ethnic groups have arrived on both coasts and have caused continuous intermingling and confrontation with indigenous populations and among themselves. In what was to become the United States, these contacts began when the Europeans arrived in the original thirteen colonies and met the many cultures of the Native Americans. Later, the colonists imported African slaves, who brought with them the various cultures of West Africa. Then, as settlers moved toward the interior, they encountered different native groups in the plains and pueblos. In the mid-nineteenth century, English-speaking Americans expanded into the Southwest, home to Native Americans as well as the Spanish-speaking heirs of land grants dating back to the sixteenth century. Finally, in the nineteenth and twentieth centuries, immigrant groups from all over the world poured into the United States, coming into contact with the descendants of all earlier groups.

From this contact came the expectation that these many cultures would merge into a homogeneous, shared national culture. The idea that the United States was a "melting pot" generated pressure on newcomers to conform in thought and behavior—and if this were not possible, pressure for the children of these newcomers to assimilate. For some, assimilation was easier than for others, and language, clothing, and other forms of distinction were easy to erase. For others, however, discarding traditions was not so easy. The Hassidic Jews, the Amish, the Hopi, the Navajo—those clinging to religious rites, lifestyles, or property without choosing to compromise—resisted assimilation pressures (Rubel & Kupferer, 1973). These groups and others have created a more modern metaphor, that of the salad bowl: a mix in which the individual ingredients are not melted but, rather, retain their flavor and texture.

Another powerful metaphor is that of the kaleidoscope, in which the shifting patterns of culture, language, and race combine and recombine ceaselessly, yet are bound together by an idea: that in the United States, diverse peoples are held together through common ideals. The contributions of different ethnic cultures to the United States cannot be underestimated, yet the picture is not uniformly sunny. Dark and sordid episodes of conflict between, and discrimination against, various groups cloud the history of this nation. Minorities have systematically been denied opportunities and rights accorded the more privileged. Those groups that are least similar to the original European-American immigrants have suffered exploitation and, in some cases, linguistic, racial, or cultural genocide. Despite the hardships many have endured, ethnic groups in this country have become inseparable threads in the cultural tapestry of the United States.

Contributions

The North American continent had a myriad of indigenous cultures characterized by high levels of civilization before the European invasion began. These civilizations were either obliterated or they accommodated the arrival of new cultures through the creation of a hybrid New World. The result has been a broad mix of lifestyles and contributions of both artifacts and patterns that reflect life in contemporary North America. For the most part, European invaders attempted to replicate the life they had lived in the Old World, and those who were not a part of this mainstream of culture had the choice of assimilating or leading a separate existence. Assimilation was never intended for everyone. Those who could not assimilate were largely left alone to carry on their linguistic and cultural traditions, albeit often treated as outsiders.

Many contributions of nonmainstream peoples remained just beneath the surface of the American dream—in some cases, *too* far beneath to influence the main paths of culture. For example, the spiritual heritage of the Native Americans—the deep and abiding respect for nature—has not had the impact on the dominant culture that may be necessary for the survival of the flora and fauna of the continent.

Native Americans. In many ways, the indigenous civilizations of precolonial North America were more highly developed than European cultures. The cities and roads of the Aztec culture astounded the European conquerors. The agricultural systems featured advanced forms of irrigation, with the cultivation of foods that were unknown to the Old World. Some of these foods (potato, corn, peanuts, and other grains) were later to provide 60 percent of Europe's diet and were responsible for the greatest explosion of population since the Neolithic Age (Feagin & Feagin, 1993). Substances from the New World (cocoa, tobacco, coca) were to provide Europeans with exhilarating addictions in the centuries to come.

Did You Know?

According to author Kay Porterfield (2002), "Ancient American Indians were building pyramids before the Egyptians. They domesticated corn from a wild grass. They performed complicated surgeries. They also knew how to work with platinum and how to vulcanize rubber, two things Europeans could not do until the 1800s" (p. 1).

FIND OUT MORE ABOUT . . .

Native-American Contributions

Porterfield, K., & Keoke, E. (2003). *American Indian Contributions to the World: 15,000 Years of Invention and Innovation.* New York: Checkmark Books.
> This reference contains approximately 450 entries that detail and document the inventiveness of North, Meso-, and South American Indians.

Porterfield, K., & Keoke, E. (2005). *American Indian Contributions to the World: 15,000 Years of Invention and Innovation, Grades 4–9.*
> A five-volume collection that introduces young readers to the advances that American Indians have made throughout history. Volumes include Food, Farming, and Hunting; Buildings, Clothing, and Art; Trade, Transportation, and Warfare; Medicine and Health; Science and Technology. (To order, visit www.factsonfile.com/newfacts/FactsHome. asp).

Medicinal products from the Americas revolutionized the treatment of disease in Europe and still fascinate pharmacologists with as yet untapped treasures. The political systems of native peoples ranged from the religious theocracies in Mexico, sources of advanced astronomical and mathematical achievement unparalleled in the world of that day, to the democratic councils of the Algonquin, Iroquois, and other nations that were much admired by Benjamin Franklin and Thomas Jefferson (Hardt, 1992).

African Americans. The culture of African Americans has evolved from an African base that survived despite harshly limiting circumstances: Slaves could bring little or none of the material aspects of African culture with them. The aspects that survived did so in the hearts and minds of those who were forcibly moved to the New World. The present-day legacies of the African past are evident not only in the dance, music, literature, and religion of contemporary African Americans, but also in the sheer power of the patterns of everyday life and language that were strong enough to survive despite centuries of oppression. Ironically, the genre of music most associated with the United States—jazz— is permeated with African-American influence. One could argue that the music of the United States would not exist in its current form without this influence. Even today the endlessly mutating forms of African-American culture constitute an ongoing avant-garde (Criston, 1993), aspects of which are alternately embraced and denigrated by the wider society (some say, appropriated and abused by European-American performers and producers—see Dyson, 1996).

Did You Know?

Although African Americans comprise 12 percent of the U.S. population, they account for more than 42 percent of all students enrolled in public schools (Russell, 2008). The fact that only 2.4 percent of teachers are African-American men and 5.6 percent are African-American women leaves a racial and cultural gap in the preparation of African American teachers. In the top twenty urban school districts in America (with a total enrollment of 5 million students), over 80 percent of the students are African-American, yet over 70 percent of teachers in urban schools are European American.

Despite substantial discrimination, a long line of African-American writers, such as James Weldon Johnson, Claude McKay, Richard Wright, Ralph Ellison, James Baldwin, Imamu Baraka (LeRoi Jones), Maya Angelou, Toni Morrison, and Langston Hughes, have enriched U.S. literature and inspired new generations of poets, writers, and rappers. The religion of Black America has been a source of sustenance to African Americans since the arrival of the first slaves and has played a major role in fomenting protest for social justice. The nonviolent civil disobedience movement from the mid-1950s to the 1970s had religious underpinnings, with prominent minister-leaders such as the Reverend Martin Luther King Jr.

FIND OUT MORE ABOUT . . .

African-American Contributions in the Arts

African-American Contributions to Theatrical Dance www.theatredance.com
> This Website lists the characteristics of African dance that have contributed to various dance movements. Different types of dances are described.

The Nathaniel C. Standifer Video Archive of Oral History: Black American Musicians www.umich.edu/~/afroammu/standifer.html
> This collection was begun in 1968 and contains approximately 150 videotaped interviews, primarily with black musicians who have made highly significant contributions to musical genres of African-American origin or influence.

Did You Know?

Over his lifetime, Elijah McCoy was granted fifty-two patents, most of which were for improvements in steam engines, although he did patent a folding ironing board and self-propelled lawn sprinkler. In 1916 he patented what he described as his greatest invention, the "graphite lubricator," which used powdered graphite suspended in oil to lubricate cylinders of "superheater" train engines. Others tried to copy his oil-dripping cup but none was as successful, prompting McCoy's customers to ask for "the real McCoy"—hence the expression (http://teacher.scholastic.com/activities/bhistory/inventors/mccoy.htm).

FIND OUT MORE ABOUT . . .

African-American Inventors

The Top 10 African-American Inventors
http://teacher.scholastic.com/activities/bhistory/inventors/ index.htm
This teacher- and student-friendly Website provides short introductions to ten African-American inventors and links to other sites with further information.

American Chemical Society (ACS). (1994). *Inventing the Future: African-American Contributions to Scientific Discovery and Invention.* Washington, DC: Author.
This series of videotapes features highlights from the careers of many African-American scientists and inventors who have contributed to science and technology in the United States. Provided with the videotape is a teacher's guide that contains facts about each of the scientists and that includes hands-on activities for grades 3 through 6 that relate to the scientific fields practiced by the featured scientists and inventors.

African Americans have made substantial contributions to science. In the years preceding 1900, more than 1,000 patents were awarded to African-American inventors, despite the fact that slaves were barred from applying for patents. For example, Jo Anderson, a slave in the Cyrus McCormick household, was the coinventor of the McCormick reaper. A slave of Jefferson Davis, president of the Confederate States of America, invented a boat propeller but was unable to patent the device. In the twentieth century, major scientists were active in such fields as aviation; electrical, mechanical, and construction engineering; rocketry; and many others. African Americans who have contributed in social science and philosophy include W. E. B. DuBois, Marcus Garvey, Elijah Muhammad, Frederick Douglass, E. Franklin Frazier, Oliver C. Cox, and Malcolm X (Appiah & Gates, 2003).

The story of Ernest E. Just illustrates the difficulties faced by African-American scientists in their ascent to prominence. Just, a marine biologist, rose to become vice president of the American Society of Zoologists but was once refused admittance to Rockefeller Institute. Although Just authored over sixty scholarly papers and was a leading authority on egg fertilization, artificial parthenogenesis, and cell division, he was never appointed to a European-American university. By contrast, George Washington Carver never aspired to take his place alongside European-American scientists in their well-equipped, well-financed research facilities but revolutionized the agronomy of the peanut working in his small laboratory in Tuskegee.

EXAMPLE OF CONCEPT

An African-American History Curriculum

A partnership between the Baltimore City School System, the Reginald F. Lewis Museum, and local businesses has resulted in a new curriculum of forty-three lessons for elementary- and middle-school students grades 4–8 that features African-American history. Field trips, primary-source reading materials, audio and video clips, and activities that provide for a variety of learning styles make history come alive for Baltimore's students. As of 2008, more than 1,400 students have visited local sites of importance to African-American history (Weber, 2008).

Hispanics/Latinos. Hispanic contributions, which predate the landing of the Pilgrims at Plymouth Rock, have also been significant. Hispanic settlers in the Southwest helped lay the foundations for the agricultural, mining, and cattle industries on which early city and state economies were built (Hispanic Concerns Study Committee, 1987). This influence continues today. With the influx of Cubans during the 1960s, Miami was transformed, becoming a vibrant international and bicultural metropolis. New York and its environs contain more Puerto Ricans than the island of Puerto Rico. Los Angeles is now the second-largest Latin-American city in the world.

Although Hispanics living in the United States can trace their roots to several different countries, a common denominator of Hispanic culture in the United States includes language, religious beliefs and practices, holidays, and life patterns. Values shared among Hispanics include the importance of interdependence and cooperation of the immediate and extended family and the importance of emotional relationships. As the mainstream culture comes into more contact with the Hispanic culture, it is beginning to recognize the importance of these family values.

In politics, Hispanic Americans have influenced urban life and education. The political impetus behind bilingual education stems from the culmination of Cuban immigrant pressure in Florida and the "Chicano Power" movement of the 1960s. A lasting contribution of this bilingual legislation may be current attempts to preserve the "small incidence" languages of Native Americans and Micronesia, linguistic resources that are endangered. Thus, Hispanic leadership has helped to preserve cultural resources in unforeseen ways.

In literature and the other arts, Hispanic Americans have made significant contributions. An impressive folk tradition of Spanish songs and ballads has maintained a musical current containing the history, joys, and sorrows of the Mexican-American, Puerto Rican, and Cuban experiences. Spanish radio and television stations and newspapers have played a major role in sustaining the language and reinforcing the values of Spanish America.

Did You Know?

The Spanish governor of the Louisiana Territory, Bernardo de Galvez, provided the armies of General George Washington and General George Rogers Clarke with gunpowder, rifles, bullets, blankets, medicine, and supplies. Once Spain entered the Revolutionary War on the side of the Americans, Galvez raised an army of Spanish and Cuban soldiers, Choctaw Indians, and black former slaves that beat off the British attack in 1780 and gained control of the Mississippi River, thus frustrating a British plan to encircle the American colonies. After the war, because of the generous assistance that Galvez gave some European Americans who wanted to settle Texas, they named their city after him, Galveston (Padilla, 1998).

FIND OUT MORE ABOUT . . .

Hispanic-American Contributions

Contributions of Americans of Hispanic Heritage
www.neta.com/f~Istbooks/dod2.htm
> An excellent site that provides a historical account of Hispanic contributions as well as an annotated list of important Hispanics in fields such as politics, entertainment, sports, business, and the military.

Impacto, Influencia, Cambio
www.smithsonianeducation.org/scitech/ impacto/graphic/index.html
> This site highlights the lives and accomplishments of inventors, aviators, astronauts, and the everyday people of Latin America and the southwestern United States who have affected science and technology.

Spanish words have enriched the minds and tongues of North Americans. Fiction and poetry, in both languages, affirm Hispanic heritage and identity. Puerto Rican and Mexican-American theater has dramatized the struggles for a voice. The public art of Mexico is a centuries-old tradition, with the colorful *steles* of the Aztecs and Mayans resonating through time and reappearing in the murals of the barrios and the public art of cities throughout the Southwest. Art, to the Hispanic, is a breath of culture, and artists, like intellectuals, are esteemed as cultural leaders. The culinary contributions of Hispanics are legion and include enchiladas from Mexico, black beans from Cuba, *mangú* from the Dominican Republic, and *pasteles* from Puerto Rico.

Asian Americans. Contributions of the Pacific Rim peoples to the United States will be of increasing importance in the twenty-first century. The economic power of Asian capital stems not only from Japanese post–World War II efforts but also from the Chinese diaspora that has provided capital for economic investment in much of Southeast Asia, Indonesia, Australia, and California. Although Chinese and Japanese immigration to western America was severely curtailed throughout the history of the United States, through sheer force of numbers and the volume of international trade, Asian economic and cultural influences on the United States have been consistent.

The cultures of Asia, characterized by unparalleled continuity from ancient times to the present, have contributed to Western culture in innumerable ways. The U.S. fascination with Asian cultures has included the martial arts, Eastern spiritual philosophies, fireworks, acupuncture, and Asian food, décor, and gardening.

Did You Know?

A Chinese-American horticulturist helped to develop Florida's frost-resistant citrus fruit and paved the way for the state to compete in the citrus industry against California. Another Chinese American patented the process to make evaporated milk. There are Chinese-American astronauts who go into space, and a Chinese-American scientist helped to develop the fabric to make the space suits.

Source: Lin (2002, pp. 2–3).

The chief stumbling block to greater acceptance of Asian influences in the United States is the perceived linguistic barrier. The fact that more Asians speak English than the reverse closes the doors to a deeper knowledge of Asian cultures for many Americans. Perhaps the current generation of high-school students will begin to bridge this gap; Japanese is now taught in 563 U.S. schools, approximately 125 of which are in Hawaii, and Chinese in 85, of which almost half are in Washington state (Center for Advanced Research on Language Acquisition, 2001). Table 1.1 offers a variety of Web-based resources for promoting the Educational success of Asian Americans.

Arab Americans. Other groups as well have been ignored or remain invisible in the mainstream literature and education. However, events can propel a particular group to the forefront. Such is the case of Arab Americans, who are suddenly the object of much media attention. Because words such as *terrorism* and *anti-Americanism* arise, the ELD teacher may need to help students fight stereotypes and misinformation about this group.

Several waves of immigrants from Arabic-speaking countries have been settling in the United States since the 1880s. Unlike the previously mentioned groups, most Arab Americans have been able to assimilate into American life, and 80 percent of them are American citizens. They work in all sectors of society; are leaders in many professions and organizations; have a strong commitment to family, economic, and educational achievements; and are making contributions to all aspects of American life (Arab American Institute Foundation, n.d.).

Among other impressive contributions include those of surgeon Michael DeBakey, who invented the heart pump; comedian and actor Danny Thomas, the founder of St. Jude's Children's Research

Table 1.1   Websites with Resources for Teaching Asian Americans

www.asianamericanbooks.com	K–12 books and materials for Asian-American cultural awareness
www.teachingforchange.org	Books, DVDs, CDs, and videos on the Asian-American experience
www.chabotcollege.edu/Library/subjectindex/ AsianAmericanStudies.htm	Asian-Americans/Pacific Islanders Studies Website index and list of reference books
www.csun.edu/asianamericanstudies	Resources for community activism, speakers' bureau
www.cetel.org/res.html	Gateway to online exploration of Asian-American history, culture, media, and curricular resources
http://sun3.lib.uci.edu/~dfsang/aas2.htm	A comprehensive guide to information about Asian Americans and Pacific Islanders
http://falcon.jmu.edu/~/ramseyil/asiabio.htm	Links to noteworthy Asian Americans in ten different fields as well as related sites about Asian Americans
http://inventors.about.com/od/astartinventor/a/Asia Inventors.htm	A brief description of the inventions of Asian Americans with links to more detailed sites

Did You Know?

In the summer of 1895, Kahlil Gibran arrived in New York from a small village in Lebanon. He became a well-known painter and writer. His most famous book, *The Prophet,* remains a bestseller sixty-two years after his death.

FIND OUT MORE ABOUT . . .

Arab-American Contributions

Arab Americans: Making a Difference
www.aaiusa.org
   Divided into areas such as military, politics, sports, activism, business, law, entertainment, education, art and literature, fashion, and science and medicine, this Website lists and briefly describes leading Arab Americans in the above fields.

Hospital; and lawyer Edward Masry, who, along with Erin Brockovich, filed a class action lawsuit against Pacific Gas and Electric for polluting the drinking water of Hinkley, California. Through their efforts, PG&E paid out the largest toxic tort injury settlement in U.S. history, $333 million in damages (Suleiman, 1999).

Exploitation

The contributions of minorities to the cultural mainstream have not consistently been valued. On the contrary, many peoples in the cultural mix have been exploited. Their labor, their art, and their votes have been used and abused without adequate compensation.

From the beginning, European settlers exploited others. Many indentured servants worked at low wages for years to repay their passage to the New World. Native Americans brought food to the starving colonists and, in return, saw their fertile coastal lands taken away. Westward expansion features many a sordid tale of killing and robbery on the part of European settlers (Eckert, 1992). On the West Coast, Spanish missionaries also colonized native peoples, with somewhat more pious motives but a similar result. The Hispanic settlers in the West were in turn exploited by European Americans. Although superior firearms still carried the day, legal manipulations carried out in the English language systematically disenfranchised Hispanic settlers and caused a vast number of them to lose their property and water rights. Chinese settlers who were permitted into the West during the nineteenth century found that their labor was valued only in the meanest way, and the jobs available constituted "woman's work" such as laundry and cooking. And the story of exploitation of Africans brought to the New World is a tale of tears mixed with genocide and forced miscegenation.

In many cases, this exploitation continues to this day as the underclass of the United States, whether white, brown, or black, is inadequately paid and undereducated, forced to live without health benefits or adequate housing (see Table 1.2). Temporary jobs without benefits are the hallmark of the crueler, harsher world of the twenty-first century as economic and political forces polarize society.

The most difficult piece of the puzzle is the challenge of population growth. Creating jobs for a burgeoning population that will provide the financial means for the purchase of health care, education, housing, and an adequate diet is the issue. The population in 2050 is projected to consist largely of developing nations' peoples. The challenge is evident. Wrongs from the past cannot be righted, but present and future citizens can avoid those wrongs by understanding exploitative measures and working for change.

Table 1.2 Poverty Rates, Educational Attainment, Average Earnings, and Health Insurance by Race and Origin

Race and Origin	Poverty Rates (3-year average 2001–2003)	Educational Attainment (high-school graduate or more)	Average Earnings in 2002 for All Workers, 18 Years and Older			Health Insurance People without Coverage (3-year average 2001–2003)
			Total	Not High-School Graduate	High-School Graduate	
White	10.2%	85.1%	$37,376	$19,264	$28,145	14.2%
Non-Hispanic White	8.2%	89.45%	$39,220	$19,423	$28,756	10.6%
Black	23.7%	80.0%	$28,179	$16,516	$22,823	19.6%
American Indian/ Alaska Native	23.2%	—	—	—	—	27.5%
Asian	10.7%	87.6%	$40,793	$16,746	$24,900	18.5%
Asian and/or Native Hawaiian and other Pacific Islanders	10.8%	—	—	—	—	18.6%
Hispanic origin (of any race)	21.9%	57.0%	$25,827	$18,981	$24,163	32.8%

Source: Adapted from U.S. Census Bureau (2004a, 2004b, 2004c).

THE IMPACT OF A CHANGING POPULATION

By the year 2010, one of every three Americans will be either African American, Hispanic American, or Asian American. This represents a dramatic change from the image of the United States throughout its history. In the past, when Americans have looked in the mirror, they have seen a largely European-American reflection. Immigration, together with differing birthrates among various populations, is responsible for this demographic shift. Along with the change in racial and ethnic composition has come a dramatic change in the languages spoken in the United States and the languages spoken in U.S. schools.

In the midst of the changing demographics in the United States, two minority groups—immigrants and economically disadvantaged minorities within the country—face similar challenges. Both immigrants and indigenous minorities must adjust to the demands of modern technological societies and must redefine their cultural self-identity. Economic and educational achievement is not equally accessible to these minorities.

Poverty among Minority Groups

A key difficulty for many minorities is that of poverty. Almost one-quarter (24 percent) of African Americans and over one-fifth (22 percent) of Hispanic Americans live in poverty (U.S. Census Bureau, 2004c). Worse, Blacks and Hispanics are even more likely not to be simply poor, but to be *extremely* poor—with incomes under half the poverty level of Whites. In fact, at 16.1 percent, the share of the Black population that is extremely poor is over four times that of non-Hispanic Whites (3.7 percent), and well above that of Hispanics (10.5 percent) (Henwood, 1997).

Poverty is associated with a host of difficulties, such as underemployment, homelessness, educational deprivation, single-parent homes, and other types of instability. However, not all poverty can be linked to these difficulties; some minorities continue in poverty because of social and political factors in the country at large, such as racism and discrimination. Poverty hits minority children particularly hard.

The number of children living in poverty in the United States has grown by 11.3 percent to approach 13 million (Reid, 2006). Although the vast majority of the poor are non-Latino Whites (4.3 million), since 2000, more than 600,000 Latino children have fallen into poverty; and in 2005, one in every three Black children living in America was poor.

Since 2002, for every five children who fell into poverty, four fell into extreme poverty (living with an annual income below $7,412 for a family of three, $18,660 for a family of four). Unfortunately the number of children in extreme poverty grew 11.5 percent, almost twice as fast as the 6.0 percent rate of increase for child poverty overall (Children's Defense Fund, 2004c).

Contrary to popular perceptions about poor families, 70 percent of children in poverty lived in a family in which someone worked full- or part-time for at least part of the year. Almost one in three poor children (31.4 percent) lived with a full-time year-round worker. One of the results of poverty, according to the Department of Agriculture, is that poor households are "food insecure" (without enough food to fully meet basic needs at all times due to lack of financial resources). This was the case for one out of every six households with children in 2002 (Children's Defense Fund, 2004a).

Poverty does not mean merely inadequate income; rather, it engenders a host of issues, including insufficient income and jobs with limited opportunity, lack of health insurance, inadequate education, and poor nutrition. Poor children are more likely to die in infancy, have a low birth weight, and lack health care, housing, and adequate food (Children's Defense Fund, 2004b). Poor children are at least twice as likely as nonpoor children to suffer stunted growth or lead poisoning or to be kept back in school. They score significantly lower on reading, math, and vocabulary tests when compared with similar nonpoor children (Children's Defense Fund, 2004c). Table 1.3 lists outcomes of health and education and the risk incurred by low-income children.

Among people living below the poverty line, 56 percent speak a language other than English, compared with 41 percent for those above the poverty line (Gorman & Pierson, 2007). English learners often face severe educational shortfalls, as one researcher noted: "Compared with affluent schools, ELs attend schools which are likely to experience higher teacher turnover, allocate fewer resources to classrooms, and face more challenging conditions overall" (Merino, 2007, p. 1).

Table 1.3 Why Poverty Matters

Outcomes	Low-Income Children's Higher Risk
Health	
Death in infancy	1.6 times as likely
Premature birth (under 37 weeks)	1.8 times as likely
Low birth weight	1.9 times as likely
No regular source of health care	2.7 times as likely
Inadequate prenatal care	2.8 times as likely
Family had too little food sometime in the last 4 months	8 times as likely
Education	
Math scores at ages 7 to 8	5 test points lower
Reading scores at ages 7 to 8	4 test points lower
Repeated a grade	2 times as likely
Expelled from school	3.4 times as likely
Being a dropout at ages 16 to 24	3.5 times as likely
Finishing a four-year college	Half as likely

Source: Children's Defense Fund (2004a). Reprinted with permission.

Did You Know?

Each day in the United States . . .

	Among All Children	Among White Children	Among Black Children	Among Latino Children	Among Asian Children	Among Native American Children
Babies die before their first birthdays	76	36	22	13	3	1
Babies are born to mothers who received late or no prenatal care	390	139	98	128	18	9
Babies are born at low birth weight	860	434	216	157	45	8
Babies are born without health insurance	1,707	526	378	820	—	—
Babies are born into poverty	2,171	762	659	711	36	40
High-school students drop out	2,539	1,072	489	689	94	—

Source: Adapted from Children's Defense Fund (2004b).

Poverty plays a large role in the education of America's youth. It affects the ability of the family to devote resources to educational effort. This situation, coupled with social and political factors that affect minority children in schools, stacks the deck against minority-student success. Demographic trends ensure that this will be a continuing problem in the United States.

Almost three-quarters (74 percent) of the Hispanic population are under thirty-five years of age, compared with a little more than half (51.7 percent) of the non-Hispanic White population. Hispanics were more than two and a half times more likely to live in families of five or more people than were non-Hispanic Whites (26.5 percent versus 10.8). Only 25.9 percent of Hispanic families consist of two people, whereas 48.7 percent of White families do (U.S. Census Bureau, 2003a). The average Hispanic female is well within childbearing age, and Hispanic children constitute the largest growing school population. Therefore, the educational achievement of Hispanic children is of particular concern.

The Education of Minorities

The economy of the United States in the future will rest more on Asian-American and Hispanic-American workers than at present. As a consequence, the education of these populations will become increasingly important. Consider that in 2000, 38.8 percent of students enrolled in public elementary and secondary schools were minorities—an increase of 30 percent from 1986, largely due to the growth in the Hispanic population (NCES, 2002). Of these minorities, 87.6 percent of Asian Americans have a high-school diploma and 49.8 percent have bachelor degrees. In contrast, only 57 percent of Hispanics have high-school diplomas and 11.4 percent have college degrees. Eighty-five percent of non-Hispanic Whites, on the other hand, have high-school diplomas and over a quarter (27.6 percent) have bachelor degrees (U.S. Census Bureau, 2004a). The extent of the problem becomes clearer.

Minority students typically live in racially isolated neighborhoods and are more likely to attend segregated schools. Over one-third (38 percent) of Hispanic students and Black students (37 percent) attended schools with minority enrollments of 90 to 100 percent. Seventy-seven percent of Hispanics and 71 percent of Blacks were enrolled in schools where minorities constitute 50 percent or more of the population.

In addition, minority children are overrepresented in compensatory programs in schools. In the 1999–2000 school year, 15 percent of Black and 14 percent of Native-American students were enrolled in special education, a significantly higher proportion than White and Hispanic (11 percent) and Asian/Pacific Islander students (6 percent) (NCES, 2003a, 2003b; University of Texas at Austin, 1991).

Thus, nearly a half-century after *Brown v. Board of Education*, a student who is Black, Latino, or Native American remains much less likely to succeed in school. A major factor is a disparity of resources—inner-city schools with large minority populations have been found to have higher percentages of first-year teachers, higher enrollments, fewer library resources, and less in-school parental involvement, characteristics that have been shown to relate to school success (U.S. Government Accounting Office, 2002).

The conclusion is inescapable: The educational system of the United States has been fundamentally weak in serving the fastest growing school-age populations. Today's minority students are entering school with significantly different social and economic backgrounds from those of previous student populations and therefore require educators to modify their teaching approaches to ensure that these students have access to the American dream.

Second-Language-Speaking Minority Populations

Many minority students come to school with home languages other than English. According to the 2000 census, one American in five, 47 million, speaks a language other than English at home. Almost 3 million school-age children spoke Spanish as a native language—more than three-quarters (76.9 percent) of English learners in schools. No other native language exceeded 3 percent. The five most common languages after Spanish were Vietnamese (2.4 percent), Hmong (1.8 percent), Korean (1.2 percent), Arabic (1.2 percent), and Haitian Creole (1.1 percent) (Hopstock & Stephenson, 2003).

How is the impact of these large numbers of students with English-learning needs felt in schools? Districts find themselves scrambling for teachers and staff with second-language competencies and for those knowledgeable about language, culture, and academic development for English learners; for primary-language as well as appropriate English-language materials; and for ways of working with and involving parents.

IMMIGRATION AND MIGRATION

The United States has historically been a nation of immigrants, but the nature and causes of immigration have changed over time. The earliest settlers to the east coast of North America came from England and Holland, whereas those to the South and West came mainly from Spain. In the early eighteenth century, these settlers were joined by involuntary immigrants from Africa. Subsequent waves of immigrants came from Scotland, Ireland, and Germany, and later from central and eastern Europe. Immigration from the Pacific Rim countries was constrained by severe immigration restrictions until the last decades of the twentieth century.

Did You Know?

The number of foreign-born people in the United States is now, in absolute numbers, at its highest point in history—representing about 10 percent of the population. According to U.S. Census Bureau 2000 data, approximately 51 percent are from Latin America, 25.7 percent from Asia, 15.2 percent from Europe, and 8.1 percent from other regions such as Africa and Oceania (Migration Policy Institute, 2004).

However, imperialistic policies of the United States, primarily the conquest of the Philippines, Puerto Rico, Hawaii, and the Pacific Islands, caused large influxes of these populations throughout the twentieth century. The wars in southeast Asia and Central America throughout the 1970s and 1980s led to increased emigration from these areas. In the 1990s, immigrants arrived from all over the world. In 2000, 40 percent of all legal immigrants came from just five countries—Mexico, China, the Philippines, India, and Vietnam (Migration Policy Institute, 2004).

Immigrants have come to the United States for a variety of reasons. The earliest immigration was prompted by the desire for adventure and economic gain in a new world combined with the desire to flee religious and political persecution. These factors provided both attractive forces (pull) and expulsive forces (push). Later, U.S. foreign policy created connections with populations abroad that pulled certain groups to the United States. For example, the conquest of the Philippines at the turn of the century eventually resulted in significant Philippine immigration to the United States.

Once in the United States, both immigrants and natives have historically been restless populations. Much of the history of the United States consists of the migration of groups from one part of the country to another.

Causes of Immigration

Migration is an international phenomenon. Throughout the world, populations are dislocated by wars, famine, civil strife, economic changes, persecution, and other factors. The United States has been a magnet for immigrants seeking greater opportunity and economic stability. The social upheavals and overpopulation that characterized nineteenth-century Europe and Asia brought more than 14 million immigrants to the United States in the forty-year period between 1860 and 1900. A century later this phenomenon can be witnessed along the border between the United States and Mexico. Politics and religion as well as economics provide reasons for emigration. U.S. domestic and foreign policies affect the way in which groups of foreigners are accepted. Changes in immigration policy, such as amnesty, affect the number of immigrants who enter the country each year.

Economic Factors in Immigration. The great disparity in the standard of living attainable in the United States compared to that of many developing countries makes immigration attractive. Self-advancement is uppermost in the minds of many immigrants and acts as a strong incentive despite the economic exploitation often extended to immigrants (e.g., lower wages, exclusion from desirable jobs).

FIND OUT MORE ABOUT . . .

Economic Factors

U.S. Immigration Facts
www.rapidimmigration.com/usa/1_eng_immigration_facts.html
This site provides general facts about recent U.S. immigration and then discusses immigrant entrepreneurs and economic characteristics of immigrants.

Immigration policy has corresponded with the cycles of boom and bust in the U.S. economy; the Chinese Exclusion Act of 1882 stopped immigration from China to the United States because of the concern that Chinese labor would flood the market. The labor shortage in the western United States resulting from excluding the Chinese had the effect of welcoming Japanese immigrants who were good farm laborers. Later, during the Great Depression of the 1930s, with a vast labor surplus in the United States, the U.S. Congress severely restricted Philippine immigration, and policies were initiated to "repatriate" Mexicans back across the border.

When World War II transformed the labor surplus of the 1930s into a severe worker shortage, the United States and Mexico established the Bracero Program, a bilateral agreement allowing Mexicans to cross the border to work on U.S. farms and railroads. The border was virtually left open during the war years (Wollenberg, 1989). However, despite the economic attractiveness of the United States, now, as then, most newcomers to this society experience a period of economic hardship.

Political Factors in Immigration. Repression, civil war, and change in government create a "push" for emigration from foreign countries, whereas political factors within the United States create a climate of acceptance for some political refugees and not for others. After the Vietnam War, many refugees were displaced in southeast Asia. Some sense of responsibility for their plight caused the U.S. government to accept many of these people into the United States. For example, Cambodians who cooperated with the U.S. military immigrated to the United States in waves: first, a group including 6,300 Khmer in 1975; second, 10,000 Cambodians in 1979; third, 60,000 Cambodians between 1980 and 1982 (Gillett, 1989a).

The decade of the 1980s was likewise one of political instability and civil war in many Central American countries, resulting in massive civilian casualties. In El Salvador, for example, such instabilities caused the displacement of 600,000 Salvadorans who lived as refugees outside their country (Gillett, 1989b). Through the Deferred Enforced Departure program of the U.S. government, nearly 200,000 Salvadoran immigrants were given the right to live and work legally in the United States.

Other populations, such as Haitians claiming political persecution, have been turned away from U.S. borders. U.S. policy did not consider them to be victims of political repression, but rather of economic hardship—a fine distinction, in many cases, and here one might suspect that racial issues in the United States make it more difficult for them to immigrate. It would seem, then, that the grounds for political asylum—race, religion, nationality, membership in a particular social group, political opinion—can be clouded by confounding factors.

In sum, people are pushed to the United States because of political instability or political policies unfavorable to them in their home countries. Political conditions within the United States affect whether immigrants are accepted or denied.

Religious Factors in Immigration. Many of the early English settlers in North America came to the New World to found colonies in which they would be free to establish or practice their form of religious belief. Later, Irish Catholics left Ireland in droves because their lands were taken by Protestants. Many eastern European Jews, forced to emigrate because of anti-Semitic pogroms in the nineteenth century, came to the United States in great numbers. Current immigration policies permit refugees to be accepted on the basis of religion if the applicant can prove that persecution comes from the government or is motivated by the government (Siskind Susser, n.d.).

Family Unification. The risks associated with travel to the New World have made immigration a male-dominated activity since the early settlement of North America. In some cases, such as that of the Chinese in the nineteenth century, immigration laws permitted only young men to enter. Initial Japanese immigration, which was not restricted as severely as Chinese, involved predominantly young men between the ages of twenty and forty. Similarly, today's Mexican immigrant population consists largely of young men who have come to the United States to work and send money home. Once settled, these immigrants seek to bring family members to the United States. Family unification is a primary motivation for many applications to the Bureau of Citizenship and Immigration Services (BCIS) in the Department of Homeland Security.

Unfortunately, too often the mainstream media in the United States focus on anti-immigration stories, particularly against Mexicans. Rarely featured in the media, however, are analyses of the reasons behind persistent Mexican emigration attempts: Today, the majority of Mexicans are poorer and more economically insecure that they were just a few years ago (Bigelow, 2007). Under the North American Free Trade Agreement (NAFTA), manufacturing wages in Mexico declined 9 percent between 1994 and 2004, poverty in rural areas increased from 54 percent to 81 percent, and almost 1.5 million Mexican farmers lost their land because of cheap corn imports from the United States. These facts argue for a more compassionate stance toward Mexican English learners who are recent immigrants.

Migration

Americans have always been restless. Historically, crowding and the promise of greater economic freedom were reasons for moving west. The gold rush attracted, for the most part, English-speaking European Americans from the eastern United States, but other minority groups and immigrants were also drawn to the search for instant wealth. Miners from Mexico, Peru, and Chile increased California's Latino population; Greeks, Portuguese, Russians, Poles, Armenians, and Italians flocked to the San Francisco Bay area. During the Depression, many of these populations migrated once again to California's central valley to find work as farm laborers (Wollenberg, 1989). With the rise of cities, rural populations sought economic advancement in urban environments. Many African Americans migrated to northern cities after World War I to escape prejudice and discrimination.

Today, many immigrants are sponsored by special-interest groups such as churches and civic organizations that invite them to reside in the local community. Once here, however, some groups find conditions too foreign to their former lives and eventually migrate to another part of the United States. For example, a group of Hmong families sponsored by Lutheran charities spent two years in the severe winter climate of the Minneapolis area before resettling in California. Hispanics, on the other hand, are migrating from cities in the Southwest, New York, and Miami toward destinations in the Midwest and middle South (Wilson, 1984).

Based on the 2000 census, Americans continue to move. The most mobile population between 1995 and 2000 was Hispanics (56 percent), followed by Asians (54 percent), Native Americans and Alaska Natives (50 percent), and Blacks (49 percent). The least mobile population was non-Hispanic Whites (43 percent). Of the regions in the United States, the South had the highest level of net domestic immigration of non-Hispanic Whites, Blacks, Asians, and Hispanics. Of the states, Nevada had the largest gain in numbers of Asians, Florida in numbers of Hispanics, and Georgia in numbers of Blacks (Schachter, 2003).

For newly arriving immigrants, historical patterns are also changing. California, which had attracted 33 percent of these immigrants, recently has only received 22 percent. Newer immigrants are settling in states such as Oregon, Arizona, Iowa, Arkansas, Georgia, North Carolina, Kentucky, Tennessee, and Virginia (Migration Policy Institute, 2004).

Immigration Laws and Policies

Economic cycles in the United States have affected immigration policies, liberalizing them when workers were needed and restricting immigration when jobs were scarce. These restrictive immigration policies were often justified with overtly racist arguments. Asian immigration was targeted for specific quotas. The first Asian population that was specifically excluded was the Chinese (the

Did You Know?

Although Hispanics are the most urbanized ethnic/racial group in the United States (90 percent living in metropolitan areas in 2000), the nonmetro Hispanic population is now the most rapidly growing demographic group in rural and small-town America. By 2000, half of all nonmetro Hispanics lived outside traditional southwest cities. Many of these Hispanics are newly arrived undocumented young men from rural, depressed areas of Mexico. In spite of their relatively low education levels and weak English skills, employment rates exceeded those of all other nonmetro Hispanics and non-Hispanic Whites.

Source: Adapted from Kandel and Cromartie (2004).

Chinese Exclusion Act of 1882), but the growth of Japanese immigration as a result of this quota prompted Congress to extend the concept of Chinese exclusion to Japan (1908) and the rest of Asia. The immigration laws of the 1920s (the National Origins Acts of 1924 and 1929) banned most Asian immigration and established quotas that favored northwestern European immigrants. The quota system, however, did not apply to Mexico and the rest of the Western Hemisphere. In 1943, Congress symbolically ended the Asian exclusion policy by granting ethnic Chinese a token quota of 100 immigrants a year. The Philippines and Japan received similar tiny quotas after the war.

U.S. Foreign Policy. As the United States grew as a capitalist nation, economic forces had a great influence on U.S. foreign policy. In the early growth of commercial capitalism from 1600 to 1865, new settlers were a source of labor; Africans were enslaved to provide plantation labor, and poor Europeans such as Irish Catholics were recruited abroad for low-wage jobs in transportation and construction. In the phase of industrial capitalism (1865–1920), U.S. treaties with Europe and intervention in European affairs (World War I) maintained the labor supply until the 1924 Immigration Act, which provided overall limits on immigration (favoring immigrants from Europe over other regions of the world). U.S. imperialist policies in Asia (conquest of the Philippines and Hawaii) ensured a supply of raw materials and a home for U.S. military bases in the Pacific, but immigration policy denied access to the United States for the majority of Asians.

The Immigration and Nationality Act Amendments of 1965 brought about vast changes in immigration policy by abolishing the national origins quota system and replacing it with a seven-category preference system for allocating immigrant visas—a system that emphasizes family ties and occupation. Although there is a per-country limit for these preference immigrants, certain countries—People's Republic of China, India, Mexico, and the Philippines—are "oversubscribed," and hopeful immigrants are on long waiting lists, some extending for as many as twelve years (U.S. Department of State, 2004).

An additional provision in the 1965 act is the diversity immigrant category, in which 55,000 immigrant visas can be awarded each fiscal year to permit immigration opportunities for persons from countries other than the principal sources of current immigration to the United States. No one country can receive more than 7 percent of the available diversity visas in any one year (U.S. Department of State, 2004).

The Refugee Act of 1980 expanded the number of persons considered refugees, again allowing more immigrants to enter the United States under this category. As a result of these policy changes, immigrants from Latin America and Asia began to enter the United States in unprecedented numbers, eclipsing the previous dominance of Europeans.

Legal Status. Many immigrants are *documented*—legal residents who have entered the United States officially and live under the protection of legal immigration status. Some of these are officially designated *refugees,* with transitional support services and assistance provided by the U.S. government. Most immigrants from Cambodia, Laos, Vietnam, and Thailand have been granted refugee status. *Undocumented* immigrants are residents without any documentation who live in fear of being identified and deported.

FIND OUT MORE ABOUT . . .

U.S. Immigration Policy

U.S. Department of State, Bureau of Consular Affairs, Visa Bulletin
http://travel.state.gov/visa/frvi/bulletin/bulletin_ 1360.html
   The Visa Bulletin, updated monthly, provides information about immigrant numbers and eligibility criteria for various categories.

United States Immigration Policy
www.cbo.gov/doc.crfm?index-7051
   This paper, written in 2007, provides an overview of U.S. immigration policy, a summary of current U.S. immigration law, statistics, enforcement efforts, and requirements for naturalization.

Being in the United States illegally brings increased instability, fear, and insecurity to school-age children because they and their families are living without the protection, social services, and assistance available to most immigrants. With the passage of the Immigration Reform and Control Act in 1986, however, undocumented children are legally entitled to public education. Often they and their families are unclear about this right, and school staff and authorities sometimes worsen the situation by illegally asking for immigration papers when children are being registered (Olsen, 1988).

Resources Available to Immigrants. The Emergency Immigrant Education Program (EIEP; No Child Left Behind, Title III, subpart 4) provides assistance to school districts whose enrollment is affected by immigrants. The purpose of the program is to provide high-quality instruction to immigrant children and youth, to help them with their transition into U.S. society, and to help them meet the same challenging academic content and student academic achievement standards as all children are expected to meet (NCLB, Sec. 3241). School districts and county offices of education qualify for EIEP funding if they have an enrollment of at least 500 eligible immigrant pupils and/or if the enrollment of eligible immigrant pupils represents at least 3 percent of the total enrollment.

How far have we come? The Puritans brought to New England a religion based on a monochromatic worldview. They outlawed Christmas and disapproved of celebration. The United States of America has struggled with this severe cultural reductionism since its founding. As the splendor and the celebratory spirit of the Native-American and immigrant cultures have been recognized, the people of the United States have opened up to accept the beauty and brilliant hues that Native-Americans and immigrants have contributed. As more and more diverse groups settle and resettle throughout the continent, customs and traditions mingle to create an ever-new mix. The salad bowl, the kaleidoscope—these are metaphors for diversity in taste, in pattern, and in lifestyle. The American portrait is still being painted, in ever-brighter hues.

LEARNING MORE

Further Reading

Lies My Teacher Told Me by J. Loewen (1995) is a fascinating book that questions many of the "facts" presented in U.S. history textbooks. According to the author, "African American, Native American, and Latino students view history with a special dislike" (p. 12). Perhaps the Eurocentric every-problem-is-solved approach in the texts deadens students to the true nature of the controversies and to the richness of the stories of history.

Web Search

Using a search engine (Google, for example), enter "contributions of _____" (the group of students who are most represented in your school). Based on what you find, share your findings with the school staff and then prepare a lesson (with the help of the students and their parents) that highlights the contributions of the group.

Exploration

Visit a local school district office (or use the Internet) to find out which ethnic groups are represented in your state and school district. Prepare a presentation for the staff at your school and brainstorm how you can be more proactive in including these groups in the curriculum.

Collaboration

Determine what school-site activities involve minority groups. Are the activities confined to flags, food, and fiestas? Are the activities confined to specific months (e.g., African Americans discussed only during Black History Month)? Work with other teachers to develop an overall year plan that incorporates contributions of various groups to the richness of the United States.

Multicultural Education

Administrators from Hans Christian Andersen School discuss their conceptions of multicultural education. They also deal with issues of evaluating students' and their own performances. They share their thoughts about political correctness.

To access the video, go to MyEducationLab (www.myeducationlab.com), choose the Díaz-Rico and Weed text, and log in to MyEducationLab for English Language Learners. Select the topic Cultural-Based Instruction, and watch the video entitled "Multicultural Education."

Answer the following questions:

1. What advantages of a multicultural curriculum are discussed? What do these administrators mean when they say that schools are desegregated but not integrated?
2. What is meant in this video by "politically correct"?
3. Several administrators describe students' pride in their cultural heritage. How does this relate to students' pride in being a successful student? Discuss the differences in the definition of a "successful student." How does one define success?

CHAPTER 2

THE INTERCULTURAL EDUCATOR

Teachers who take the time to chat with students can learn about their cultures, homes, and family lives.

Unlike my grandmother, the teacher did not have pretty brown skin and a colorful dress. She wasn't plump and friendly. Her clothes were of one color and drab. Her pale and skinny form made me worry that she was very ill. . . . The teacher's odor took some getting used to also. Later I learned from the girls this smell was something she wore called perfume. The classroom . . . was terribly huge and smelled of medicine like the village clinic I feared so much. Those fluorescent light tubes made an eerie drone. Our confinement to rows of desks was another unnatural demand made on our active little bodies. . . . We all went home for lunch since we lived a short walk from the school. It took coaxing, and sometimes bribing, to get me to return and complete the remainder of the school day.

—Joe Suina (1985, writing his impressions on entering school at age 6)

The narrative of this Pueblo youth illustrates two cultural systems in contact. Neither is right or wrong, good or bad, superior or inferior. Suina was experiencing a natural human reaction that occurs when a person moves into a new cultural situation—culture shock. He had grown up in an environment that had subtly, through every part of his life, taught him appropriate ways of behavior—for example, how people looked (their color, their size, their dress, their ways of interacting) and how space was structured (the sizes of rooms, the types of lighting, the arrangement of furniture). His culture had taught him what was important and valuable. The culture Suina grew up in totally enveloped him and gave him a way to understand life. It provided him with a frame of reference through which he made sense of the world.

Culture is so pervasive that often people perceive other cultures as strange and foreign without realizing that their own culture may be equally mystifying to others. Culture, though largely invisible, influences instruction, policy, and learning in schools. Members of the educational community accept the organization, teaching and learning styles, and curricula of the schools as natural and right, without realizing that these patterns are cultural. And the schools *are* natural and right for members of the culture that created them. As children of nondominant cultures enter the schools, however, they may find the organization, teaching and learning styles, and curricula to be alien, incomprehensible, and exclusionary.

Unfortunately, teachers—who, with parents, are the prime acculturators of society—often have little training regarding the key role of culture in teaching and learning. Too often, culture is incorporated into classroom activities in superficial ways—as a group of artifacts (baskets, masks, distinctive clothing), as celebrations of holidays (Cinco de Mayo, Martin Luther King Jr. Day), or as a laundry list of stereotypes and facts (Asians are quiet; Hispanics are family-oriented; Arabs are Muslims). Teachers who have a more insightful view of culture and cultural processes are able to use their understanding to move beyond the superficial and to recognize that people live in characteristic ways. They understand that the observable manifestations of culture are but one aspect of the cultural web—the intricate pattern that weaves and binds a people together. Knowing that culture provides the lens through which people view the world, teachers can look at the "what" of a culture—the artifacts, celebrations, traits, and facts—and ask "why."

Teachers in the twenty-first century face a diverse student population that demands a complicated set of skills to promote achievement for all students. As intercultural educators, teachers understand cultural diversity and can adapt instruction accordingly. Table 2.1 outlines the skills and responsibilities of the intercultural educator. This chapter addresses cultural diversity and the struggle to achieve equity in schooling. Chapter 3 focuses on using culturally responsive pedagogy to promote student achievement.

Table 2.1   The Skills and Responsibilities of the Intercultural Educator

Understand Culture and Cultural Diversity

Explore key concepts about culture.

Investigate ourselves as cultural beings.

Learn about students' cultures.

Recognize how cultural adaptation affects learning.

Strive for Equity in Schooling

Detect unfair privilege.

Combat prejudice in ourselves and others.

Fight for fairness and equal opportunity.

Promote Achievement

Respect students' diversity.

Work with culturally supported facilitating or limiting attitudes and abilities.

Sustain high expectations for all students.

Marshal parental and community support for schooling.

Source: Díaz-Rico (2000).

UNDERSTANDING CULTURAL DIVERSITY

As an initial step in learning about the complexity of culture and how the culture embodied within the school affects diverse students, the following sections examine the nature of culture. Knowledge of the deeper elements of culture—beyond superficial aspects such as food, clothing, holidays, and celebrations—can give teachers a crosscultural perspective that allows them to educate students to the greatest extent possible. These deeper elements include values, belief systems, family structures and child-rearing practices, language and nonverbal communication, expectations, gender roles, and biases—all the fundamentals of life that affect learning.

The Nature of Culture

Does a fish understand water? Do people understand their own culture? Teachers are responsible for helping to pass on cultural knowledge through the schooling process. Can teachers step outside their own culture long enough to see how it operates and to understand its effects on culturally diverse students? A way to begin is to define culture.

The term *culture* is used in many ways. It can refer to activities such as art, drama, and ballet or to items such as pop music, mass media entertainment, and comic books. The term *culture* can be used for distinctive groups in society, such as adolescents and their culture. It can be used as a general term for a society, such as the "French culture." Such uses do not, however, define what a culture is. As a field of study, culture is conceptualized in various ways (see Table 2.2).

Table 2.2 Definitions of Culture

Definition	Source
The sum total of a way of life of a people; patterns experienced by individuals as normal ways of acting, feeling, and being	Hall (1959)
That complex whole that includes knowledge, belief, art, morals, law, and custom, and any other capabilities acquired by humans as members of society	Tylor (in Pearson, 1974)
A dynamic system of symbols and meanings that involves an ongoing, dialectic process in which past experience influences meaning, which in turn affects future experience, which in turn affects subsequent meaning, and so on	Robinson (1985)
Mental constructs in three basic categories: *shared knowledge* (information known in common by members of the group), *shared views* (beliefs and values shared by members of a group), and *shared patterns* (habits and norms in the ways members of a group organize their behavior, interaction, and communication)	Snow (1996)
Partial solutions to previous problems that humans create in joint mediated activity; the social inheritance embodied in artifacts and material constituents of culture as well as in practices and ideal symbolic forms; semi-organized hodgepodge of human inheritance. Culture is exteriorized mind and mind is interiorized culture	Cole (1998)
Frames (nationality, gender, ethnicity, religion) carried by each individual that are internalized, individuated, and emerge in interactions	Smith, Paige, and Steglitz (1998)

The definitions in Table 2.2 have common factors but vary in emphasis. The following definition of culture combines the ideas in Table 2.2:

> Culture is the explicit and implicit patterns for living, the dynamic system of commonly agreed-upon symbols and meanings, knowledge, belief, art, morals, law, customs, behaviors, traditions, and/or habits that are shared and make up the total way of life of a people, as negotiated by individuals in the process of constructing a personal identity.

The important idea is that culture involves both observable behaviors and intangibles such as beliefs and values, rhythms, rules, and roles. The concept of culture has evolved over the last fifty years away from the idea of culture as an invisible, patterning force to that of culture as an active tension between the social "shortcuts" that make consensual society possible and the contributions and construction that each individual creates while living in society. Culture is not only the filter through which people see the world but also the raw dough from which each person fashions a life that is individual and satisfying.

Because culture is all-inclusive, it includes all aspects of life. Snow (1996) listed a host of components (see Table 2.3).

Table 2.3 Components of Culture

Daily Life

Animals	Hobbies	Medical care	Sports
Clothing	Housing	Plants	Time
Daily schedule	Hygiene	Recreation	Traffic and transport
Food	Identification	Shopping	Travel
Games	Jobs	Space	Weather

The Cycle of Life

Birth	Divorce	Rites of passage
Children	Friends	Men and women
Dating/mating	Old age	
Marriage	Funerals	

Interacting

Chatting	Functions in communication	Parties
Eating	Gifts	Politeness
Drinking	Language learning	Problem solving

Society

Business	Education	Government and politics	Science
Cities	Farming	Languages and dialects	Social problems
Economy	Industry	Law and order	

The Nation

Holidays	Cultural borrowing	National issues
Geography	Famous people	Stereotypes
History		

Creative Arts

Arts	Genres	Music
Entertainment	Literature	Television

Philosophy, Religion, and Values

Source: Adapted from Snow (1996).

Cultures are more than the mere sum of their traits. There is a wholeness about cultures, an integration of the various responses to human needs. Cultures cannot be taught merely by examining external features such as art and artifacts. For example, a teacher who travels to Japan may return laden with kimonos and chopsticks, hoping these objects will document Japanese culture. But to understand the culture, that teacher must examine the living patterns and values of the culture that those artifacts represent.

Key Concepts about Culture

Despite the evolving definitions of culture, theorists agree on a few central ideas. These concepts are first summarized here and then treated with more depth.

Culture Is Universal. Everyone in the world belongs to one or more cultures. Each culture provides templates for the rituals of daily interaction: the way food is served, the way children are spoken to, the way needs are met. These templates are an internalized way to organize and interpret experience. All cultures share some universal characteristics. The manner in which these needs are met differs.

Culture Simplifies Living. Social behaviors and customs offer structure to daily life that minimizes interpersonal stress. Cultural patterns are routines that free humans from endless negotiation about each detail of living. Cultural influences help unify a society by providing a common base of communication and common social customs.

Culture Is Learned in a Process of Deep Conditioning. Cultural patterns are absorbed unconsciously from birth, as well as explicitly taught by other members. Culture dictates how and what people see, hear, smell, taste, and feel, and how people and events are evaluated. Cultural patterns are so familiar that members of a culture find it difficult to accept that other ways can be right. As cultural patterns are learned or acquired through observation and language, seldom are alternatives given. The fact that cultural patterns are deep makes it difficult for the members of a given culture to see their own culture as learned behavior.

Culture Is Demonstrated in Values. Every culture deems some beliefs and behaviors more desirable than others, whether these be about nature, human character, material possessions, or other aspects of the human condition. Members of the culture reward individuals who exemplify these values with prestige or approval.

Culture Is Expressed Both Verbally and Nonverbally. Although language and culture are closely identified, the nonverbal components of culture are equally powerful means of communication about cultural beliefs, behaviors, and values. Witness the strong communicative potential of the obscene gesture! In the classroom, teachers may misunderstand a student's intent if nonverbal communication is misinterpreted.

EXAMPLE OF CONCEPT

Nonverbal Miscommunication

Ming was taught at home to sit quietly when she was finished with a task and wait for her mother to praise her. As a newcomer in the third grade, she waited quietly when finished with her reading assignment. Mrs. Wakefield impatiently reminded Ming to take out a book and read or start another assignment when she completed her work. She made a mental note: "Ming lacks initiative."

Societies Represent a Mix of Cultures. The patterns that dominate a society form the *macroculture* of that society. In the United States, European-American traditions and cultural patterns have largely determined the social behaviors and norms of formal institutions. Within the macroculture, a variety of *microcultures* coexist, distinguished by characteristics such as gender, socioeconomic status, ethnicity, geographical location, social identification, and language use.

Did You Know?

The first generation of Japanese immigrants, who often referred to themselves as issei, or first generation, came to the United States starting about 1900 and consisted, for the most part, of young men who became agricultural laborers or skilled craftsmen. Often seen as a threat by European Americans, these immigrants were often the target of discrimination, which peaked after the attack on Pearl Harbor. The issei were divested of their property and removed to relocation camps. Their children, the nisei generation, are often considered to have a very low ethnic profile, perhaps as a response to the treatment given to their parents (Leathers, 1967).

Generational experiences can cause the formation of microcultures. For example, the children of Vietnamese who immigrated to the United States after the Vietnam War often became native speakers of English, separating the two generations by language. Similarly, Mexicans who migrate to the United States may find that their children born in the United States consider themselves "Chicanos."

Individuals who grow up within a macroculture and never leave it may act on the assumption that their values are the norm. When encountering microcultures, they may be unable or unwilling to recognize that alternative beliefs and behaviors are legitimate within the larger society.

Culture Is Both Dynamic and Persistent. Human cultures are a paradox—some features are flexible and responsive to change, and other features last thousands of years without changing. Values and customs relating to birth, marriage, medicine, education, and death seem to be the most persistent, for humans seem to be deeply reluctant to alter those cultural elements that influence labor and delivery, marital happiness, health, life success, and eternal rest.

Culture Is a Mix of Rational and Nonrational Elements. Much as individuals living in western European post-Enlightenment societies may believe that reason should govern human behavior, many cultural patterns are passed on through habit rather than reason. People who bring a real tree into their houses in December—despite the mess it creates—do so because of centuries-old Yule customs.

Did You Know?

The Persistence of Cultural Values

The Sarmatians, like their neighbors the Scythians, were nomadic people who lived just north of the Black Sea in ancient times. They had one outstanding trait in particular—a unique love of their horses, such that graves were almost always found with horse bones, bridles, and other accoutrements buried next to the human remains. Thousands of years later, in the twentieth century, their descendants, the Ossetians, waged a fierce cultural skirmish with government officials of the Union of Soviet Socialist Republics (USSR). The issue? The Ossetians insisted on killing a man's horse when he died and burying it with the corpse. The Soviets mandated that it was a crime to waste the People's resources. For many years, subterfuge persisted—a deceased man's horse mysteriously would become sick or disabled and had to be shot, and graves would be reopened in the dead of night to accommodate one more body. (More information at www.ossetians.com/eng.)

Did You Know?

Extreme dedication to the concept of standardized testing is deeply ingrained in Chinese parents. "In China, an examination system to qualify candidates for higher education was established as early as 206 B.C. During the Tang Dynasty, 618 A.D. to 907 A.D., the examination system began to be used to select government officials. The extreme difficulty of the examinations required candidates to study for many years. There were three levels of examinations, with the second-level examination lasting for 9 days. During the 9-day written examination, the candidate lived in a small cell that provided no room for sleeping" (Spring, 2001, www.mhhe.com/socscience/education/spring/commentary.mhtml, paragraph 5).

Similarly, carving a face on a hollow pumpkin is not a rational idea. Those who create elaborate altars in their homes or take food to the grave of a loved one for the Mexican celebration of Day of the Dead do so because of spiritual beliefs.

Cultures Represent Different Values. The fact that each culture possesses its own particular traditions, values, and ideals means that the culture of a society provides judgments that may differ from those of other cultures about what actions are deemed right or wrong for its members. Actions can be judged only in relation to the cultural setting in which they occur. This point of view has been called *cultural relativism*. In general, the primary values of human nature are universal—for example, few societies condone murder. However, sanctions relating to actions may differ. The Native-American cultures of California before contact with Europeans were pacifists to the extent that someone who took the life of another would be ostracized from the tribe. In contrast, the U.S. macroculture accepts as heroes soldiers who have killed in the context of war (for example, Andrew Jackson and Ulysses S. Grant).

Attempting to impose "international" standards on diverse peoples with different cultural traditions causes problems. This means that some cardinal values held by teachers in the United States are not cultural universals but instead are values that may not be shared by students and their families. For example, not all families value children's spending time reading fiction; some may see this as a waste of time. Some families may not see value in algebra or higher mathematics; others might consider art in the classroom to be unimportant.

Did You Know?

Various cultures set differing value on the idea that academic activities should be based on competition or that children are expected to work on their own. In U.S. schools, many instructional activities are based on the cultural values of competition and individualization (for example, spelling contests, computer-assisted instruction, independent study projects). Students who come from cooperative, group-conforming cultures, in which it is permissible and even desirable to work together and in which it is abhorrent to display knowledge individually, may find themselves negatively evaluated because of their different value systems, not because of any academic shortcomings.

Diverse Societies Have a Mainstream Culture. The term *mainstream culture* refers to those individuals or groups who share values of the dominant macroculture. In the United States, this dominant or core culture is primarily shared by members of the middle class. Mainstream American culture is characterized by the following values (Gollnick & Chinn, 2006):

- Individualism and privacy
- Independence and self-reliance

- Equality
- Ambition and industriousness
- Competitiveness
- Appreciation of the good life
- Perception that humans are separate from and superior to nature

Culture Affects People's Attitudes toward Schooling. For many individuals, educational aspiration affects the attitude they have toward schooling: what future job or profession they desire, the importance parents ascribe to education, and the investment in education that is valued in their culture. The son of blue-collar workers, for example, may not value a college education because his parents, who have not attained such an education, have nevertheless prospered, whereas the daughter of a recent, low-wage immigrant may work industriously in school to pursue higher education and a well-paid job.

Cultural values also affect the extent to which families are involved in their children's schooling and the forms this involvement takes. Family involvement is discussed in Chapter 3.

ADAPTED INSTRUCTION

Working with Attitudes toward Schooling

In working with diverse students, teachers will want to know:

- What educational level the student, family, and community desire for the student
- What degree of assimilation to the dominant culture (and to English) is expected and desired

Culture Governs the Way People Learn. Any learning that takes place is built on previous learning. Students have learned the basic patterns of living in the context of their families. They have learned the verbal and nonverbal behaviors appropriate for their gender and age and have observed their family members in various occupations and activities. The family has taught them about love and about relations between friends, kin, and community members. They have observed community members cooperating to learn in a variety of methods and modes. Their families have given them a feeling for music and art and have shown them what is beautiful and what is not. Finally, they have learned to use language in the context of their homes and communities. They have learned when questions can be asked and when silence is required. They have used language to learn to share feelings and knowledge and beliefs. Indeed, they are native speakers of the home language by the age of five, and can express their needs and delights.

The culture that students bring from the home is the foundation for their learning. Although certain communities exist in relative poverty—that is, they are not equipped with middle-class resources—poverty should not be equated with cultural deprivation. Every community's culture incorporates vast knowledge about successful living. Teachers can utilize this cultural knowledge to organize students' learning in schools.

Culture appears to influence learning styles, the way individuals select strategies and approach learning (Shade & New, 1993). For example, students who live in a farming community may have sensitive and subtle knowledge about weather patterns, knowledge that is essential to the economic survival of their family. This type of knowledge may predispose students to value learning in the classroom that helps them better understand natural processes like climate. These students may prefer kinesthetic learning activities that build on the same kind of learning that has made it possible for them to sense subtleties of weather. In a similar manner, Mexican-American children from traditional families who are encouraged to view themselves as an integral part of the family may prefer social learning activities.

EXAMPLE OF CONCEPT

Culturally Specific Learning Styles

Students can acquire knowledge by means of various learning modalities, which are often expressed in culturally specific ways. The Navajo child is often taught by first observing and listening, and then taking over parts of the task in cooperation with and under the supervision of an adult. In this way, the child gradually learns all the requisite skills. Finally, the child tests himself or herself privately—failure is not seen by others, whereas success is brought back and shared. The use of speech in this learning process is minimal (Phillips, 1978).

In contrast, acting and performing are the focus of learning for many African-American children. Children observe other individuals to determine appropriate behavior and to appreciate the performance of others. In this case, observing and listening culminates in an individual's performance before others (Heath, 1983b). Reading and writing may be primary learning modes for other cultures such as traditionally educated Asian students.

ADAPTED INSTRUCTION

Learning Modalities

- Observe students learning from one another in a natural, unstructured setting to determine their culturally preferred modalities of learning. For example, have students make a small beaded leather shield to celebrate Native American Day (the last Friday in September). By making beads and leather available—without tightly structuring the activity—you can see how students organize materials, teach, cooperate, or compete with one another.
- At a family conference, ask family members what kind of work is done at home and how the child participates.

INVESTIGATING OURSELVES AS CULTURAL BEINGS

The Personal Dimension. For intercultural educators, self-reflection is vital. By examining their own attitudes, beliefs, and culturally derived beliefs and behaviors, teachers begin to discover what has influenced their value systems. Villegas and Lucas (2002) summarized this self-reflection in eight components (see Table 2.4).

Self-Study. Self-study is a powerful tool for understanding culture. A way to begin a culture inquiry is by investigating one's personal name. For example, ask, "Where did I get my name? Who am I named for? In which culture did the name originate? What does the name mean?" Continue the self-examination by reviewing favorite cultural customs—such as holiday traditions, home décor, and favorite recipes. More difficult self-examination questions address the mainstream U.S. values of individual freedom, self-reliance, competition, individualism, and the value of hard work. Ask, "If someone in authority tells me to do something, do I move quickly or slowly? If someone says, 'Do you need any help?' do I usually say, 'No, thanks. I can do it myself'? Am I comfortable promoting myself (for example, talking about my achievements in a performance review)? Do I prefer to work by myself or on a team? Do I prefer to associate with high achievers and avoid spending much time with people who do not work hard?" These and other introspective questions help to pinpoint

Table 2.4 Components of the Personal Dimension of Intercultural Education

Component	Description
Engage in reflective thinking and writing.	Awareness of one's actions, interactions, beliefs, and motivations—or racism—can catalyze behavioral change.
Explore personal and family histories by interviewing family members.	Exploring early cultural experiences can help teachers better relate to individuals with different backgrounds.
Acknowledge group membership.	Teachers who acknowledge their affiliation with various groups in society can assess how this influences views of, and relationships with, other groups.
Learn about the experiences of diverse groups by reading or personal interaction.	Learning about the histories of diverse groups—from their perspectives—highlights value differences.
Visit students' families and communities.	Students' home environments offer views of students' connections to complex cultural networks.
Visit or read about successful teachers.	Successful teachers of children from diverse backgrounds provide exemplary role models.
Appreciate diversity.	Seeing difference as the norm in society reduces ethnocentrism.
Participate in reforming schools.	Teachers can help reform monocultural institutions.

Source: Adapted from Villegas and Lucas (2002).

CULTURAL SELF-STUDY

Self-Exploration Questions

- Describe yourself as a preschool child. Were you compliant, curious, adventuresome, goody-goody, physically active, nature loving? Have you observed your parents with other children? Do they encourage open-ended exploration, or would they prefer children to play quietly with approved toys? Do they encourage initiative?
- What was the knowledge environment like in your home? What type of reading did your father and mother do? Was there a time when the members of the family had discussions about current events or ideas and issues? How much dissent was tolerated from parental viewpoints? Were children encouraged to question the status quo? What was it like to learn to talk and think in your family?
- What kind of a grade-school pupil were you? What is your best memory from elementary school? What was your favorite teacher like? Were you an avid reader? How would you characterize your cognitive style and learning style preferences? Was the school you attended ethnically diverse? What about your secondary school experience? Did you have a diverse group of friends in high school?
- What is your ethnic group? What symbols or traditions did you participate in that derived from this group? What do you like about your ethnic identity? Is there a time now when your group celebrates its traditions together? What was the neighborhood or community like in which you grew up?
- What was your experience with ethnic diversity? What were your first images of race or color? Was there a time in your life when you sought out diverse contacts to expand your experience?
- What contact do you have now with people of dissimilar racial or ethnic backgrounds? How would you characterize your desire to learn more? Given your learning style preferences, how would you go about this?

cultural attitudes. Without a firm knowledge of one's own beliefs and behaviors, it is difficult to contrast the cultural behaviors of others. However, the self-examination process is challenging and ongoing. It is difficult to observe one's own culture.

LEARNING ABOUT STUDENTS' CULTURES

Teachers can use printed, electronic, and video materials, books, and magazines to help students learn about other cultures. However, the richest source of information is local—the life of the community. Students, parents, and community members can provide insights about values, attitudes, and habits. One method of learning about students and their families, ethnographic study, has proved useful in learning about the ways that students' experiences in the home and community compare with the culture of the schools.

Ethnographic Techniques

Ethnography is an inquiry process that seeks to provide cultural explanations for behavior and attitudes. Culture is described from the insider's point of view, as the classroom teacher becomes not only an observer of the students' cultures but also an active participant (Erickson, 1977; Robinson, 1985). Parents and community members, as well as students, become sources for the gradual growth of understanding on the part of the teacher.

For the classroom teacher, ethnography involves gathering data in order to understand two distinct cultures: the culture of the students' communities and the culture of the classroom. To understand the home and community environment, teachers may observe and participate in community life, interview community members, and visit students' homes. To understand the school culture, teachers may observe in a variety of classrooms, have visitors observe in their own classrooms, audio- and videotape classroom interaction, and interview other teachers and administrators.

Observations. Initial observations of other cultures must be carried out, ideally, with the perspective that one is seeing the culture from the point of view of a complete outsider. Observers need to be descriptive and objective and make explicit their own attitudes and values in order to overcome hidden sources of bias. This requires practice and, ideally, some training. However, the classroom teacher can begin to observe and participate in the students' cultures, writing up field notes after participating and perhaps summing up the insights gained in an ongoing diary that can be shared with colleagues. Such observation can document children's use of language within the community; etiquettes of speaking, listening, writing, greeting, and getting or giving information; values and aspirations; and norms of communication.

When analyzing the culture of the classroom, teachers might look at classroom management and routines; affective factors (students' attitudes toward activities, teachers' attitudes toward students); classroom talk in general; and nonverbal behaviors and communication. In addition to the raw data of behavior, the thoughts and intentions of the participants can also be documented.

Interviews. Interviews can be divided into two types: structured and unstructured. Structured interviews use a set of predetermined questions to gain specific kinds of information. Unstructured interviews are more like conversations in that they can range over a wide variety of topics, many of which the interviewer would not necessarily have anticipated. As an outsider learning about a new culture, the classroom teacher would be better served initially using an unstructured interview, beginning with general questions and being guided in follow-up questions by the interviewee's responses. The result of the initial interview may in turn provide a structure for learning more about the culture during a second interview or conversation. A very readable book about ethnography and interviewing is *The Professional Stranger: An Informal Introduction to Ethnography* (Agar, 1980).

Home Visits. Home visits are one of the best ways in which teachers can learn what is familiar and important to their students. The home visit can be a social call or a brief report on the student's progress that enhances rapport with students and parents. Scheduling an appointment ahead of time is a courtesy that some cultures may require and provides a means for the teacher to ascertain if home visits are welcome. Dress should be professional. The visit should be short (twenty to thirty minutes) and the conversation positive, especially about the student's schoolwork. Viewing the child in the context of the home provides a look at the parent–child interaction, the resources of the home, and the child's role in the family. One teacher announces to the class at the beginning of the year that she is available on Friday nights to be invited to dinner. Knowing in advance that their invitation is welcomed, parents and children are proud to act as hosts.

EXAMPLE OF CONCEPT

A Home Visit

Home visits can be an effective way for a teacher not only to demonstrate accessibility and interest to students and their families, but also to learn about the family and the context in which the student lives, as seen in this story from Hughes:

> Years ago a child named Nai persuaded her parents to let me visit them. Many people lived in the small apartment. One of the men spoke a little English as I tried a few Mien phrases that drew chuckles and good will. I ate with them. Recently a community college student dropped in at our school. "Nai!" I cried, delighted. . . . "How's your family?" "They OK." "I enjoyed my visit with them," I said. She smiled. "My parents . . . they talk still about 'that teacher,' they call you." (Hughes, 2004, p. 10)

Students as Sources of Information. Students generally provide teachers with their initial contact with other cultures. Through observations, one-on-one interaction, and group participatory processes, teachers gain understanding about various individuals and their cultural repertoire. Teachers who are good listeners offer students time for shared conversations by lingering after school or opening the classroom during lunchtime. Teachers may find it useful to ask students to map their own neighborhood. This is a source of knowledge from the students' perspectives about the boundaries of the neighborhood and surrounding areas.

Parents as Sources of Information. Parents can be sources of information in much the same way as their children. Rather than scheduling one or two formal conferences, PTA open house events, and gala performances, the school may encourage parent participation by opening the library once a week after school. This offers a predictable time during which parents and teachers can casually meet and chat. Parents can also be the source for information that can form the basis for classroom writing. Using the Language Experience Approach, teachers can ask students to interview their parents about common topics such as work, interests, and family history. In this way, students and parents together can supply knowledge about community life.

Community Members as Sources of Information. Community members are an equally rich source of cultural knowledge. Much can be learned about a community by walking or driving through it, or stopping to make a purchase in local stores and markets. One teacher arranged to walk through the neighborhood with a doctor whose office was located there. Other teachers may ask older students to act as tour guides. During these visits, the people of the neighborhood can be sources of knowledge about housing, places where children and teenagers play, places where adults gather, and sources of food, furniture, and services.

Through community representatives, teachers can begin to know about important living patterns of a community. A respected elder can provide information about the family and which members constitute a family. A community leader may be able to contrast the community political system with the city or state system. A religious leader can explain the importance of religion in community life. Teachers can also attend local ceremonies and activities to learn more about community dynamics.

The Internet. Websites proliferate that introduce the curious to other cultures. Webcrawler programs assist the user to explore cultural content using keyword prompts.

Participating in Growth Relationships. Self-study is only one means of attaining self-knowledge. Teachers who form relationships with individuals whose backgrounds differ from their own, whether teacher colleagues or community members, can benefit from honest feedback and discussions that help to expand self-awareness. Intercultural educators are not free from making mistakes when dealing with students, family and community members, and colleagues whose culture differs from their own. The only lasting error is not learning from these missteps or misunderstandings.

Sociocultural Consciousness. Villegas and Lucas (2007) invite teachers who were raised in middle-class, monolingual communities to develop a "sociocultural consciousness" (p. 31) that impels them to examine the role of schools in both perpetuating and challenging social inequities. Understanding the role that differential distribution of wealth and power plays in school success helps teachers to commit to the ethical obligation of helping all students learn.

How Cultural Adaptation Affects Learning

As immigrants enter American life, they make conscious or unconscious choices about which aspects of their culture to preserve and which to modify. These decisions affect learning. We cannot know all things about all cultures, but it is possible to understand what happens when the home culture comes into contact with the school culture and how this contact affects schooling. When cultures meet, they affect each other. Cultures can be swallowed up (*assimilation*), one culture may adapt to a second (*acculturation*), both may adapt to each other (*accommodation*), or they may coexist (*pluralism* or *biculturalism*). When an individual comes in contact with another culture, there are characteristic responses, usually stages, an individual goes through in adapting to the new situation. Contact between cultures is often not a benign process. It may be fraught with issues of prejudice, discrimination, and misunderstanding. Means of mediation or resolution must be found to alleviate cultural conflict, particularly in classrooms.

Since the 1980s, an unprecedented flow of immigrants and refugees has entered the United States. One of the impacts of this immigration is that many school districts not only have three or more languages spoken in a single classroom, but they also have students who speak the same non-English language but who come from different cultures. These demographic issues pose a number of questions about cultures in contact. Are there characteristic differences in the patterns of adaptation to schooling among individuals from various cultures? Can we understand how to increase the school success of all students by studying the process of cultural contact?

Fears about Cultural Adaptation. Pryor (2002) captured the nature of immigrant parents' concerns about their children's adjustment to life in the United States:

> In the United States, some immigrant parents live in fear that their children will be corrupted by what they believe to be the materialistic and individualistic dominant culture, become alienated from their families, and fall prey to drugs and promiscuity. Their fears are not unfounded, as research shows that the longer that immigrants live in the United States, the worse their physical and mental health becomes. . . . One Jordanian mother stated, "I tell my son (who is 8 years old) not to use the restroom in school. I tell him he might catch germs there that he could bring home, and make the whole family ill. I really am afraid he may get drugs from other kids in the restroom." (p. 187)

Many immigrant parents are overwhelmed with personal, financial, and work-related problems; they may miss their homelands and family members abroad and have few resources to which to turn for help. In the process of coming to terms with life in a foreign country, they may be at odds with the assimilation or acculturation processes their children are experiencing, causing family conflict.

Assimilation. When members of an ethnic group are absorbed into the dominant culture and their culture gradually disappears in the process, they are said to assimilate. For assimilation to be complete, there must be both cultural and structural assimilation (Gordon, 1964). *Cultural assimilation* is the process by which individuals adopt the behaviors, values, beliefs, and lifestyle of the dominant culture. *Structural assimilation* is participation in the social, political, and economic institutions and organizations of mainstream society. It is structural assimilation that has been problematic for many immigrants. Gordon found that only limited structural assimilation occurred for groups other than White Protestant immigrants from northern and western Europe.

Individuals may make a choice concerning their degree of cultural assimilation. However, the dominant society determines the extent of structural assimilation. These two related but different concepts have important consequences in classrooms. Teachers may strive to have students assimilate but be blind to the fact that some of their students will not succeed because of attitudes and structures of the dominant society.

Acculturation. When individuals adapt effectively to the mainstream culture, they are said to *acculturate*. This concept should be distinguished from *enculturation,* the process through which individuals learn the patterns of their own culture. To acculturate is to adapt to a second culture without necessarily giving up one's first culture. It is an additive process in which individuals' right to participate in their own heritage is preserved (Finnan, 1987). Some researchers have emphasized the importance of acculturation for success in school. For example, Schumann (1978a) claims that the greater the level of acculturation in a particular individual, the greater the second-language learning will be for that individual.

Schools are the primary places in which children of various cultures learn about the mainstream culture. Sometimes culture is taught explicitly as a part of the ELD curriculum (Seelye, 1984). According to Cortés (1993):

> Acculturation . . . should be a primary goal of education. Schools have an obligation to help students acculturate because additive acculturation contributes to individual empowerment and expanded life choices. But schools should not seek subtractive assimilation, which can lead to personal and cultural disempowerment by eroding students' multicultural abilities to function effectively both within the mainstream and within their own ethnic milieus. . . . In our increasingly multicultural society, even traditional additive acculturation is not the only acculturation goal. Education for the twenty-first century should embrace what I call "multiculturation," the blending of *multiple* and *acculturation*. (p. 4)

Accommodation. A two-way process, accommodation happens when members of the mainstream culture change in adapting to a minority culture, the members of which in turn accept some cultural change as they adapt to the mainstream. Thus, accommodation is a mutual process. To make accommodation a viable alternative in schools, teachers need to demonstrate that they are receptive to learning from the diverse cultures in their midst, and they also need to teach majority students the value of "interethnic reciprocal learning" (Gibson, 1991).

EXAMPLE OF CONCEPT
Accommodating Students' Culture

[I]n non-Indian classes students are given opportunities to ask the teacher questions in front of the class, and do so. Indian students are given fewer opportunities for this because when they do have the opportunity, they don't use it. Rather, the teacher of Indians allows more periods in which she is available for individual students to approach her alone and ask their questions where no one else can hear them. (Philips, 1972, p. 383)

Pluralism. Assimilation, not acculturation, was the aim of many immigrants who sought to become part of the melting pot. More recently, minority groups and their advocates have begun to assert that minority and ethnic groups have a right, if not a responsibility, to maintain valued elements of their ethnic cultures (Kopan, 1974). This *pluralist* position is that coexistence of multicultural traditions within a single society provides a variety of alternatives that enrich life in the United States. Pluralism is the condition in which members of diverse cultural groups have equal opportunities for success, in which cultural similarities and differences are valued, and in which students are provided cultural alternatives.

But does pluralism endanger society, as cultural purists have charged, by heightening ethnic group identity, leading to separatism and intergroup antagonism? In a healthy society, these groups may sometimes clash in the process of coexistence, but the strength of the society is founded on a basic willingness to work together to resolve conflicts. According to Bennett (2003), schools can evince *integrated pluralism* (actively trying to foster interaction between different groups) or *pluralistic coexistence* (different racial or ethnic groups informally resegregate). Integration creates the conditions for cultural pluralism. Merely mixing formerly isolated ethnic groups does not go far enough, because groups rapidly unmix and resegregate.

Biculturalism. Being able to function successfully in two cultures constitutes biculturalism. Darder (1991) defined *biculturalism* as

> a process wherein individuals learn to function in two distinct sociocultural environments: their primary culture, and that of the dominant mainstream culture of the society in which they live. It represents the process by which bicultural human beings mediate between the dominant discourse of educational institutions and the realities they must face as members of subordinate cultures. (pp. 48–49)

Everyone is to some extent bicultural. Every pluralistic society (take, for example, life in New York City) contains individuals who become a part of more than one culture. At a minimum level, everyone who works outside the home functions daily in two cultures—personal (home) and professional (work). For some individuals, the distance between the cultures of work and home are almost indistinguishable, whereas for others the distance is great. For example, Native-American children who were sent to Bureau of Indian Affairs boarding schools often experienced great difficulties in adjusting to the disparate cultures of home and school.

What is it like to be bicultural in the United States? Bicultural people are sometimes viewed with distrust. An example is the suspicion toward Japanese Americans during World War II and the resulting internment. Parents may also feel threatened by their bicultural children. Appalachian families who moved to large cities to obtain work often pressured their children to maintain an agrarian, preindustrial lifestyle, a culture that is in many ways inconsistent with urban environments (Pasternak, 1994). Similarly, families from rural Mexico may seek to maintain traditional values after immigrating to the United States even as their children adopt behaviors from the U.S. macroculture. The process of becoming bicultural is not without stress, especially for students who are expected to internalize dissimilar, perhaps conflicting, values.

Cultural Congruence. In U.S. schools, the contact of cultures occurs daily. In this contact, the congruence or lack thereof between mainstream and minority cultures has lasting effects on students. Students from families whose cultural values are similar to those of the European-American mainstream culture may be relatively advantaged in schools, such as children from those Asian cultures who are taught that students sit quietly and attentively. In contrast, African-American students who learn at home to project their personalities and call attention to their individual attributes (Gay, 1975) may be punished for efforts to call attention to themselves during class.

Teachers, who have the responsibility to educate students from diverse cultures, find it relatively easy to help students whose values, beliefs, and behaviors are congruent with U.S. schooling but often find it difficult to work with others. The teacher who can find a common ground with diverse students will promote their further education. Relationships between individuals or groups of different cultures are built through commitment, a tolerance for diversity, and a willingness to communicate. The teacher acting as intercultural educator accepts and promotes cultural content in the classroom as a valid and vital component of the instructional process and helps students to achieve within the cultural context of the school.

Stages of Individual Cultural Contact. Experiencing a second culture causes emotional ups and downs. Reactions to a new culture vary, but there are distinct stages in the process of experiencing a different culture (Brown, 2000). The stages are characterized by typical emotions and behaviors beginning with elation or excitement, moving to anxiety or disorientation, and culminating in some degree of adjustment (Levine & Adelman, 1982). These same emotional stages can occur for students. The intensity will vary depending on the degree of similarity between home and school culture, the individual child, and the teacher.

The first state, *euphoria,* may result from the excitement of experiencing new customs, foods, and sights. This may be a "honeymoon" period in which the newcomer is fascinated and stimulated by experiencing a new culture.

The next stage, *culture shock,* may follow euphoria as cultural differences begin to intrude. The newcomer is increasingly aware of being different and may be disoriented by cultural cues that result in frustration. Deprivation of the familiar may cause a loss of self-esteem. Depression, anger, or withdrawal may result. The severity of this shock will vary as a function of the personality of the individual, the emotional support available, and the perceived or actual differences between the two cultures.

The final stage, *adaptation to the new culture,* may take several months to several years. Some initial adjustment takes place when everyday activities such as housing and shopping are no longer a problem. Long-term adjustment can take several forms. Ideally, the newcomer accepts some degree of routine in the new culture with habits, customs, and characteristics borrowed from the host culture. This results in a feeling of comfort with friends and associates, and the newcomer feels capable of negotiating most new and different situations. On the other hand, individuals who do not adjust as well may feel lonely and frustrated. A loss of self-confidence may result. Certain aspects of the new culture may be actively rejected. Eventually, successful adaptation results in newcomers finding value and significance in the differences and similarities between cultures and in being able to actively express themselves and to create a full range of meaning in the situation.

EXAMPLE OF CONCEPT

Language and Culture Shock

Zacharian (2004b) related the story of one student experiencing language and culture shock and the effect it had on his personality: "One student, whom I'll call Jin, shared some powerful feelings with his classmates. Through his tutor, he stated that he had been very popular in China, made friends easily, and loved to be with his friends. However, after a few weeks of attempting to ask short questions in English and not being able to understand the responses he received he had found it increasingly painful and frustrating to try to speak English. 'From being popular and having a lot of friends,' Jin stated through his translator, 'to being silenced by my lack of English is terrible for me'" (pp. 12–13).

ADAPTED INSTRUCTION

Students in Culture Shock

In the classroom, some students may show culture shock as withdrawal, depression, or anger. Mental fatigue may result from continually straining to comprehend the new culture. Individuals may need time to process personal and emotional as well as academic experiences. Teachers must take great care not to belittle or reject students who are experiencing culture shock.

ACHIEVING EQUITY IN SCHOOLING

Teachers who were themselves primarily socialized in mainstream American culture may not be aware of the challenges faced by individuals from nondominant cultures as they strive to succeed in U.S. schools. Bonilla-Silva (2003) contended that European Americans have developed powerful rationalizations and justifications for contemporary racial inequality that exculpate them from responsibility for the status of people of color. This constitutes a new racial ideology he called "color-blind racism" (p. 2), which is a way of committing or participating in racist practices while not believing that oneself is racist (also called "racism without racists" [p. 1] and "new racism" [p. 3]).

To create school environments that are fair for all students, teachers need to achieve clarity of vision (Balderrama & Díaz-Rico, 2005) about the social forces that advantage some members of society and disadvantage others. This work entails recognizing that society is becoming increasingly polarized, moving toward a vast separation between the rich and the poor. Class and racial privilege, prejudice, and unequal opportunity are barriers to success. Awareness of unfair practices is the first step toward remedy.

Detecting Unfair Privilege

For European-American middle-class teachers to accept the work of achieving equity in education, they must at some point examine their own complicity in the privileges of being white and middle class in a society predicated on inequity. *Privilege* is defined as the state of benefiting from special advantages, favors, or rights accorded to some, to the exclusion of others. Although no one likes to think that one person's advantage is another person's disadvantage, in effect, the middle class is a socially privileged position, one that directly or indirectly benefits from the discomfort of others who are lower on the economic scale.

McIntosh's (1996) article "White Privilege and Male Privilege" is a useful tool for exploring the advantage experienced by those who are white, male, or middle-class in order to become aware of the many social advantages they have reaped at the expense of those who are nonwhite, non-middle-class, or female. According to McIntosh, the privileges of being male, white, and middle-class function as an invisible backpack, full of advantages that those in these categories can build on—but that are not available to those outside these categories, giving them an unfair handicap. Figure 2.1 presents some of the privileges that the dominant race/class/gender enjoys.

I can rent or purchase housing in an affordable, desirable area, with neighbors who will be neutral or pleasant to me.

My children will see their race represented in curricular materials.

When I purchase, my skin color does not suggest financial instability.

I can criticize our government without being seen as a cultural outsider.

"The person in charge" is usually a person of my race.

Traffic cops do not single me out because of my race.

My behavior is not taken as a reflection on my race.

If my day is going badly, I need not suspect racial overtones in each negative situation.

I can imagine many options—social, political, or professional—without wondering if a person of my race would be allowed to do what I want to do.

Figure 2.1 The Privileges of the Dominant Race/Class/Gender

Source: Adapted from McIntosh (1996).

Fighting for Fairness and Equal Opportunity

Schools in the United States have not been level playing fields for those of nonmainstream cultures. Teachers can remedy this in both academic and extracurricular areas. According to Manning (2002), teachers should

> consider that all learners deserve, ethically and legally, equal access to curricular activities (i.e., higher-level mathematics and science subjects) and opportunities to participate in all athletic activities (i.e., rather than assuming all students of one race will play on the basketball team and all students of another race will play on the tennis or golfing teams). (p. 207)

Cultural fairness can extend to the social and interpersonal lives of students, those daily details and microinteractions that also fall within the domain of culture. Manning (2002) emphasized that listening to students' voices and requesting input on their concerns leads to fairness. For instance, is there only one kind of music played at school dances? Do teachers or administrators appear to show bias toward certain groups over others? Teachers who invest time to get to know their students, as individuals as well as cultural beings, address issues of fairness through a personal commitment to equality of treatment and opportunity.

Combating Prejudice in Ourselves and Others

If diversity is recognized as a strength, educators will "avoid basing decisions about learners on inaccurate or stereotypical generalizations" (Manning, 2002, p. 207). Misperceptions about diversity often stem from prejudice.

The Dynamics of Prejudice. One factor that inhibits cultural adaptation is prejudice. Although prejudice can include favorable feelings, it is generally used in a negative sense.

Prejudice takes various forms: excessive pride in one's own ethnic heritage, country, or culture so that others are viewed negatively; *ethnocentrism*, in which the world revolves around oneself and one's own culture; a prejudice against members of a certain racial group; and stereotypes that label all or most members of a group. All humans are prejudiced to some degree, but it is when people act on those prejudices that discriminatory practices and inequalities result. A simple explanation for prejudice is that it is based on fear—fear of the unknown, fear of engulfment by foreigners, or fear of contamination from dissimilar beliefs or values.

A closer look at various forms of prejudice, such as racism and stereotyping, as well as resulting discriminatory practices can lead to an understanding of these issues. Teachers can then be in a position to adopt educational methods that are most likely to reduce prejudice.

EXAMPLE OF CONCEPT

Xenophobia in U.S. History

Sutherland (1989) described the Centennial of 1876, which was held in Philadelphia:

> [T]he Centennial impressed everyone. Its 167 buildings and 30,000 exhibits covered 236 acres in Fairmount Park. The Main Exhibition Building, housing the principal exhibits of manufactured products and scientific achievements, measured 1,800 feet long and 464 feet wide, the largest building in the world. . . . [A] total of thirty-five foreign nations provided exhibits or entertainment in one form or another. . . . [W]herever they went on the fairgrounds, visitors saw and heard xenophobic expressions of prejudice. Foreign-looking people of all races and nationalities, were they Orientals, Turks, Slavs, Egyptians, or Spaniards, were "followed by large crowds of idle boys, and men, who hooted and shouted at them as if they had been animals of a strange species." (pp. 263, 264, 268)

Racism. Racism is the view that a person's race determines psychological and cultural traits—and, moreover, that one race is superior to another. Racism can also be cultural when one believes that the traditions, beliefs, languages, artifacts, music, and art of other cultures are inferior. On the basis of such beliefs, racists justify discriminating against or scapegoating other groups. As important as is the facet of symbolic violence that racism represents, of equal importance is the fact that goods and services are distributed in accordance with such judgments of unequal worth.

Racism is often expressed in hate crimes, which are public expressions of hostility directed at specific groups or individuals. These may take the form of harassment (scrawling graffiti on people's homes; pelting houses with eggs; burning crosses on lawns; children playing in yards being subjected to verbal taunts; hate-filled e-mails sent to individuals or groups; swastikas carved into public text-books, school desks, or other property; etc.) or, at the extreme, assaults and murder directed toward minorities. At present, data show that 60 percent of hate crimes are directed toward African Americans.

Youth at the Edge, a report from the Southern Poverty Law Center (1999), described a new underclass of disenchanted youth in the United States who are susceptible to hate groups. Perhaps due to feelings of frustration at social and economic forces they cannot control, those who are marginally employed and poorly educated often seek out scapegoats to harass. Too often, the targets are immigrants, particularly those of color. The availability of information on the Internet has unfortunately encouraged a resurgence of hate groups worldwide. Over 250 Internet sites foment white supremacy and other forms of racial hatred. Schools are often prime sites in which hate crimes are committed. This fact underscores the urgency of educators' efforts to understand and combat racism.

Stereotypes. Often resulting from racist beliefs, stereotypes are preconceived and oversimplified generalizations about a particular ethnic or religious group, race, or gender. The danger of stereotyping is that people are not considered as individuals but are categorized with all other members of a group. A stereotype can be favorable or unfavorable, but, whether it is positive or negative, the results are negative: The perspective on an entire group of people is distorted.

EXAMPLE OF CONCEPT
Comparisons within a Cultural Group

Mrs. Abboushi, a third-grade teacher, discovers that her students hold many misconceptions about the Arab people. Her goal becomes to present them with an accurate and more rounded view of the Arab world. She builds background information by using a world map on which the students identify the countries featured in the three books they will read: *Ibrahim* (Sales, 1989), *The Day of Ahmed's Secret* (Heide & Gilliland, 1990), and *Nadia, the Willful* (Alexander, 1983).

After reading and interactively discussing the books, students are divided into groups of four, each receiving a copy of one of the books. Students prepare a Cultural Feature Analysis chart that includes the cultural features, setting, character and traits, family relationships, and message. Groups share their information and Mrs. Abboushi records the information on a large chart. During the follow-up discussion, students discover that not all Arabs live the same way, dress the same way, or look the same way. They recognize the merging of traditional and modern worlds, the variability in living conditions, customs and values, architecture, clothing, and modes of transportation (Diamond & Moore, 1995, pp. 229–230).

Teaching against Racism. Students and teachers alike must raise awareness of racism in the attempt to achieve racial equality and justice. Actively listening to students in open discussion about racism, prejudice, and stereotyping can increase teachers' understanding of how students perceive and are affected by these concepts. School curricula can be used to help students be aware of the existence

ADAPTED INSTRUCTION

Antiracist Activities and Discussion Topics

- Recognize racist history and its impact on oppressors and victims.
- Understand the origins of racism and why people hold racial prejudices and stereotypes.
- Be able to identify racist images in the language and illustrations of books, films, television, news media, and advertising.
- Identify specific ways of developing positive interracial contact experiences.
- Extend the fight against racism into a broader fight for universal human rights and respect for human dignity.

Source: Bennett (2003, pp. 370–373).

and impact of racism. Science and health teachers can debunk myths surrounding the concept of race. Content-area teachers can help students develop skills in detecting bias.

Programs to Combat Prejudice and Racism. The Southern Poverty Law Center distributes *Teaching Tolerance* magazine, a free resource sent to over 600,000 educators twice a year that provides antibias strategies for K–12 teachers. Carnuccio (2004) describes the Tolerance.org Website, a Web project of the Southern Poverty Law Center (available at www.splcenter.org), as an "extremely informative resource":

> The project has done an excellent job of collecting and disseminating information on the advantages of diversity. . . . The site features pages designed specifically for children, teens, teachers, and parents. *Planet Tolerance* has stories for children to read and listen to and games for them to play. Teens can find ideas on how to bring diverse groups together in their schools. Teachers' pages feature articles, films and books to order, lesson ideas, and a forum in which to share ideas with other teachers. The pamphlet *101 Tools for Tolerance* suggests a variety of ideas for community, workplace, school, and home settings. *Parenting for Tolerance* offers ways for parents to guide their children to develop into tolerant adults. (p. 59)

Institutional Racism. "[T]hose laws, customs, and practices that systematically reflect and produce racial inequalities in American society" (Jones, 1981) constitute institutional racism. Classroom teaching that aims at detecting and reducing racism may be a futile exercise when the institution itself—the school—promotes racism through its policies and practices, such as underreferral of minority students to programs for gifted students or failing to hire minority teachers in classrooms where children are predominantly of minority background.

Classism. In the United States, racism is compounded with classism, the distaste of the middle and upper classes for the lifestyles and perceived values of the lower classes. Although this classism is often directed against linguistic and cultural minorities—a typical poor person in the American imagination is urban, black, and young, either a single teen mother or her offspring—portraying poverty that way makes it easier to stigmatize the poor (Henwood, 1997).

Classism has engendered its own stereotype against poor European Americans—for example, the stereotyped European-American indigent who is called, among other things, "White trash" (Wray & Newitz, 1997). The distaste for "White trash" on the part of the U.S. middle class is compounded in part by ignorance and frustration. According to Wray and Newitz, "Americans love to hate the poor. . . . [I]n a country as steeped in the myth of classlessness, we are often at a loss to explain or understand poverty. The White trash stereotype serves as a useful way of blaming the poor for being poor" (p. 1). Often, middle-class teachers view the poor as unwilling or unable to devote resources to schooling. Ogbu (1978) postulated that indigenous minorities may be unable to accept the belief in the power of education to elevate individuals to middle-class status. Poor whites, who outnumber poor minorities, may bear the brunt of a "castelike" status in the United States as much as linguistic and cultural minorities do.

Discrimination. Discrimination refers to actions that limit the social, political, or economic opportunities of particular groups. Discriminatory practices tend to legitimize the unequal distribution of power and resources between groups defined by such factors as race, language, culture, gender, and/or social class. Blatant discrimination, in which differential education for minorities is legally sanctioned, may be a thing of the past, but discrimination persists. De facto segregation continues; most students of color are still found in substandard schools. Schools with a high percentage of minority enrollment tend to employ faculty who have less experience and academic preparation. Teachers who do not share the ethnic background of their students may not communicate well with their students or may tend to avoid interaction, including eye and physical contact. Teachers may communicate low expectations to minority students. The "hidden curriculum" of tracking and differential treatment results in schools that perpetuate the structural inequities of society. Thus, school becomes a continuation of the discrimination experienced by minorities in other institutions in society (Grant & Sleeter, 1986).

In the past, those in power often used physical force to discriminate. Those who did not go along were physically punished for speaking their language or adhering to their own cultural or ethnic customs. With the spread of literacy, the trend moved away from the use of physical force toward the use of shame and guilt. The school plays a part in this process. The values, norms, and ideology of those in power are taught in the school. Skutnabb-Kangas (1981, 1993) called this *symbolic-structural violence.* Direct punishment is replaced by self-punishment, and the group discriminated against internalizes shame associated with cultural differences. The emotional and intellectual bonds of internalized injustice make the situation of minorities more difficult.

Skutnabb-Kangas (1981) cited a variety of examples of discrimination that has taken place against minority students in Swedish and Norwegian schools. These examples demonstrate the internalization of shame.

> The headmaster said, "You have a name which is difficult for us Swedes to pronounce. Can't we change it? . . . And besides, perhaps some nasty person will make fun of your name." "Well, I suppose I'd better change it," I thought. (p. 316)

> I love my parents and I respect them but what they are and everything they know count for nothing. . . . Like lots of Turkish children here, [my parents] know lots about farming and farm animals, . . . but when is a Turkish child given the task at school of describing the cultivation of vines? (p. 317)

Reducing Interethnic Conflict

Students experiencing cultural conflict may meet racism and anti-immigration sentiment from others in their environment. Subtle incidents occur every day across campuses in the United States. Verbal abuse, threats, and physical violence, motivated by negative feelings and opinions, are all too common. The scope of these incidents, together with the increasing involvement of young adults, is a disturbing trend on today's campuses. Schools are crucial to the resolution of hate crime because the young are perpetrators and the schools are staging grounds. Policies, curricula, and antiracism programs are needed to prevent and control hate crimes.

 EXAMPLE OF CONCEPT

Cultural Conflicts

A Latina elementary teacher had this to say about cultural conflicts in the schools:

> I am sensitive to cultural barriers that exist among educators. These barriers are created by lack of communication between people coming from different backgrounds and cultures. Unfortunately, we don't discuss cultural conflicts openly. We have learned that conflicts are negative and produce racial disharmony when, in fact, the opposite is true. (Institute for Education in Transformation, 1992, p. 12)

The Culturally Receptive School. In general, research suggests that substantive changes in attitudes, behaviors, and achievement occur only when the entire school environment changes to demonstrate a multicultural atmosphere. Parents are welcomed in the school; counselors, teachers, and other staff implement culturally compatible practices; and programs are instituted that permit interactions between students of different backgrounds. In such schools, all students learn to understand cultures different from their own. Minority students do not internalize negativity about their culture and customs. Cooperative learning groups and programs that allow interaction between students of diverse backgrounds usually result in fewer incidents of name-calling and ethnic slurs as well as in improved academic achievement (Nieto & Bode, 2008).

It is not easy for culturally and linguistically diverse (CLD) students to maintain pride in their cultures if these cultures suffer low status in the majority culture. Students feel conflict in this pride if their culture is devalued. When the languages and cultures of students are highly evident in their schools and teachers refer to them explicitly, they gain status. Schools that convey the message that all cultures are of value—by displaying explicit welcome signs in many languages, by attempts to involve parents, by a deliberate curriculum of inclusion, and by using affirmative action to promote hiring of a diverse faculty—help to maintain an atmosphere that reduces interethnic conflict.

Strategies for Conflict Resolution. If interethnic conflict occurs, taking immediate, proactive steps to resolve the conflict is necessary. Table 2.5 presents a scenario in which conflict resolution is needed and describes a twelve-skill approach to mediation.

EXAMPLE OF CONCEPT

Conflict Resolution in New Jersey

Real estate development in the West Windsor–Plainsboro School District in the 1980s and 1990s brought into one rural area a population that was diverse in income, culture, race, and ethnicity. Increasing incidents of racial unrest in the schools and in the community at large caused school administrators to set into motion a program of conflict resolution in K–12 classrooms. Among its components were the following:

- A peacemaking program at the elementary level to teach children how to solve problems without resorting to aggression
- Training for middle school students in facilitating positive human relations
- A ninth-grade elective course in conflict resolution
- An elective course for grade 11 and 12 students to prepare student mediators for a peer-mediation center
- An annual "human relations" retreat for student leaders and teachers that encouraged frank and open conversations about interpersonal and race relations
- A planned welcome program for newcomers at the school to overcome feelings of isolation
- A minority recruitment program for teachers
- Elimination of watered-down, nonrigorous academic courses in lieu of challenging courses, accompanied by a tutoring program for academically underprepared high-school students

Within three years, the number of incidences of vandalism, violence, and substance abuse in the school district was reduced considerably. The people of West Windsor and Plainsboro "accomplished much in their quest to rise out of the degradation of bigotry" (Bandlow, 2002, pp. 91–92; Prothrow-Smith, 1994).

Table 2.5 Applying a Twelve-Skill Approach to Interethnic Conflict

Scenario: A group of four European-American girls in tenth grade had been making fun of Irena and three of her friends, all of whom were U.S.-born Mexican Americans. One afternoon Irena missed her bus home from high school, and the four girls surrounded her when she was putting books in her locker. One girl shoved a book out of the stack in her hands. Irena shoved her back. Just then, a teacher came around the corner and took Irena to the office for discipline. The assistant principal, Ms. Nava, interviewed Irena to gain some background about the situation. Rather than dealing with Irena in isolation, Ms. Nava waited until the next day, called all eight of the girls into her office, and applied the twelve-skill approach to conflict resolution.

Skill	Application of Skills to Scenario
1. The win–win approach: Identify attitude shifts to respect all parties' needs.	Ms. Nava asked each girl to write down what the ideal outcome of the situation would be. Comparing notes, three of the girls had written "respect." Ms. Nava decided to use this as a win–win theme.
2. Creative response: Transform problems into creative opportunities.	Each girl was asked to write the name of an adult who respected her and how she knew it was genuine respect.
3. Empathy: Develop communication tools to build rapport. Use listening to clarify understanding.	In turn, each girl described what she had written above. The other girls had to listen, using eye contact to show attentiveness.
4. Appropriate assertiveness: Apply strategies to attack the problem not the person.	Ms. Nava offered an opportunity for members of the group to join the schools' Conflict Resolution Task Force. She also warned the group that another incident between them would result in suspension.
5. Cooperative power: Eliminate "power over" to build "power with" others.	Each girl was paired with a girl from the "other side" (cross-group pair) to brainstorm ways in which teens show respect for one another.
6. Managing emotions: Express fear, anger, hurt, and frustration wisely to effect change.	Ms. Nava then asked Irena and the girl who pushed her book to tell their side of the incident without name-calling.
7. Willingness to resolve: Name personal issues that cloud the picture.	Each girl was asked to name one underlying issue between the groups that this incident represented.
8. Mapping the conflict: Define the issues needed to chart common needs and concerns.	Ms. Nava mapped the issues by writing them on a wall chart as they were brought forth.
9. Development of options: Design creative solutions together.	Still in the cross-group pairs from step 5 above, each pair was asked to design a solution for one of the issues mapped.
10. Introduction to negotiation: Plan and apply effective strategies to reach agreement.	Ms. Nava called the girls into her office for a second day. They reviewed the solutions that were designed and made a group plan for improved behavior.
11. Introduction to mediation: Help conflicting parties to move toward solutions.	Each cross-group pair generated two ideas for repair if the above plan failed.
12. Broadening perspectives: Evaluate the problem in its broader context.	The eight girls were asked if racial conflict occurred outside their group. Ms. Nava asked for discussion: Were the same issues they generated responsible for this conflict?

Source: Adapted from www.crnhq.org.

Johnson and Johnson (1979, 1994, 1995) emphasized the usefulness of cooperative, heterogeneous grouping in the classroom in the resolution of classroom conflict. Explicit training for elementary students in negotiation and mediation procedures has proved effective in managing conflict, especially when such programs focus on safely expressing feelings, taking the perspective of the other, and providing the rationale for diverse points of view (Johnson, Johnson, Dudley, & Acikgoz, 1994).

Especially critical is the role of a mediator in establishing and maintaining a balance of power between two parties in a dispute, protecting the weaker party from intimidation, and ensuring that both parties have a stake in the process and the outcome of mediation. In contrast, those programs that teach about "group differences," involve exhortation or mere verbal learning, or are designed directly for "prejudice reduction" are usually not effective.

Educators should not assume that cultural contact entails cultural conflict. Perhaps the best way to prevent conflict is to include a variety of cultural content and make sure the school recognizes and values cultural diversity. If conflict does occur, however, there are means to prevent its escalation. Teachers should be aware of conflict resolution techniques before they are actually needed.

ADAPTED INSTRUCTION

Resolving Conflicts in the Classroom

- Resolve to be calm in the face of verbalized anger and hostility.
- To defuse a problem, talk to students privately, encouraging the sharing of perceptions on volatile issues. Communicate expectations that students will be able to resolve their differences.
- If confrontation occurs, set aside a brief period for verbal expression. Allow students to vent feelings as a group.
- Do not tolerate violence or personal attacks.

This chapter has emphasized the profound influence of culture on people's perceptions, feelings, and actions, and the variety of ways in which individuals experience contact with other cultures. Let us revisit briefly Joe Suina, the Pueblo youth whose contact with school created cultural conflict for him. How could the school have been more accommodating? Ideally, Suina's teacher would be a Pueblo Indian and would share his culture. Classrooms in a Pueblo school would resemble the home, with intimate spaces and furniture designed for student comfort. If these conditions are not feasible, a non-Pueblo teacher would accommodate to the ways of the students in the same way that students are expected to accommodate to the school. Actually, students of any culture would appreciate schools that were more comfortable and less institutional, wouldn't they?

LEARNING MORE

Further Reading

Victor Villaseñor's *Rain of Gold* (1992) is a fascinating history of his family's experience as Mexican immigrants to southern California. Read the book and identify passages that illustrate the following Mexican values: the importance of religion, the woman as center of home and family, respect for the mother, protection of women's virtue, the ideal woman as pure, how to be a man, the role of the man as protector of the family, the importance of tradition, respect for life, death as a part of life, respect for work, respect for learning, importance of honor, and acceptance of passion as a part of life.

Web Search

Explore the Southern Poverty Law Center's Website at www.splcenter.org. The most current issue of *Teaching Tolerance,* the organization's magazine for teachers, is available to read online, and by clicking other buttons you can discover ideas and resources for teachers, parents, teens, and children. Also investigate www.tolerance.org. This site also provides invaluable information for teachers, parents, teens, and children. Share your findings with your colleagues and plan how to incorporate some of the lessons and ideas from this site into your overall school plan.

Exploration

Ask your parent or grandparent about a favorite family holiday. How was it celebrated differently in "the old days"? What aspects have changed? How might your family's favorite holiday be celebrated (if at all) by other groups? What holidays are favorites among the other teachers, and among your students? How are the celebrations different and the same?

Collaboration

With a colleague, enroll in a training program to acquire conflict-resolution skills. Compare what you learn with the needs of a nearby school. Discuss with your colleague how the program or skills you acquired could be useful.

Incorporating the Home Experience of Culturally Diverse Students into the Classroom, Part 2

In this video segment, we recognize that all students have experiences, yet not all of these experiences are acknowledged in schools. Oftentimes these behaviors conflict with the ideologies and norms of the schools and of teachers. As you are viewing this clip, try to recognize how biases of teachers can often be problematic for culturally diverse students. Try to identify how different cultural behaviors of students are unaccepted by teachers.

To access the video, go to MyEducationLab (www.myeducationlab.com), choose the Díaz-Rico and Weed text, and log in to MyEducationLab for English Language Learners. Select the topic Cultural-Based Instruction, and watch the video entitled "Incorporating the Home Experience of Culturally Diverse Students into the Classroom, Part 2."

Answer the following questions:

1. Explain at least two different types of cultural behaviors students may exhibit in the classroom that may not be tolerated by the teacher as stated in the video clip. How can a teacher be better prepared to handle these types of cultural differences?
2. What is the role of an ethnographer?
3. Students of culturally diverse backgrounds have
   a. varied experiences.
   b. experiences that may not be acknowledged in schools.
   c. demonstrated behaviors that may conflict with the norms of the school.
   d. all of the above.

CHAPTER 3

CULTURALLY RESPONSIVE SCHOOLING

Multicultural festivals encourage students to share their cultures with others.

"Teacher," Maria said to me as the students went out for recess. "Yes, Maria?" I smiled at this lively Venezuelan student, and we launched into conversation. The contents of this talk are now lost on me, but not the actions. For as we talked, we slowly moved, she forward, me backward, until I was jammed up against the chalkboard. And there I remained for the rest of the conversation, feeling more and more agitated. She was simply too close. . . .

I did not ascribe any negative or aggressive tendencies to her. But knowing the difference in personal space requirements between my culture and hers did not lessen my anxiety. What it afforded me was the knowledge that we were behaving differently and that such differences were normal for our respective groups.

—**Kathryn Z. Weed**

Culture influences every aspect of school life. Becoming an active member of a classroom learning community requires specific cultural knowledge. Students from a nonmainstream culture are acquiring a mainstream classroom culture that may differ markedly from their home culture.

Intercultural educators who understand students' cultures can design instruction to meet children's learning needs. They invite students to learn by welcoming them, making them feel that they belong, and presenting learning as a task at which students can succeed. Teachers and students do not necessarily share the same perceptions of what is acceptable behavior and what is relevant learning. Teaching styles, interaction patterns, classroom organization, curricula, and involvement with parents and the community are factors within the teacher's power to adapt.

The skills and responsibilities of the intercultural educator include understanding cultural diversity and striving to achieve equity in schooling (see Chapter 2). In addition, the intercultural educator uses culturally responsive schooling practices to promote the school success of culturally and linguistically diverse (CLD) students. As Richards, Brown, and Forde (2004) stated, "In a culturally responsive classroom, effective teaching and learning occur in a culturally supported, learner-centered context, whereby the strengths students bring to school are identified, nurtured, and utilized to promote student achievement" (n.p.).

The four major components of culturally responsive schooling that promote achievement (see Table 2.1 on page 22) are as follows.

- Respect students' diversity.
- Work with culturally supported facilitating or limiting attitudes and abilities.
- Sustain high expectations for all students.
- Marshal parental and community support for schooling.

This chapter examines each of these components in turn.

RESPECTING STUDENTS' DIVERSITY

Traditionally, educators have used the word *diversity* to denote racial differences. However, today's school population is diverse in a number of ways: academic ability, multiple intelligences, learning styles, thinking styles, gender, attitudes, culture and ethnicity, socioeconomic status, home language, and developmental readiness (Kagan, 2007). Differentiated instruction has come to mean the responsibility that teachers must assume in diversifying classroom practices to ensure that individual students will succeed.

Differentiated instruction involves first assessing students to get to know them in a variety of ways. Then, instructional components must be diversified (see Table 3.1). Differentiated instruction

Table 3.1 Components of Differentiated Instruction

Component to Be Varied	Examples
Instructional strategies	Direct instruction, learning centers, Internet discovery, individual task cards
Instructional resources	Almanacs, computer software, magazines, manipulatives, research, films
Student support	Aides, specialists, tutors, classroom volunteers
Time and workload	More/fewer problems, more time to think, alternative tasks
Difficulty	Tiers and levels for projects, vary the required level of thinking skill, more/less modeling
Products and presentations	Individual oral presentations, team presentations, written reports, exhibits, demonstrations
Types of assessment	Portfolios, work samples, discussions, behavioral observation

Source: Kagan (2007).

is an approach in which teachers assess students to determine how they differ on an array of characteristics and then modify instruction to honor that diversity. Ongoing assessment helps teachers maintain a flexible understanding of students' needs, whether it be for solitary versus group learning experiences, preference for visual versus auditory channels, wholistic versus linear-sequential learning, or other personal qualities.

Teachers who are members of the mainstream culture and who have an accommodating vision of cultural diversity recognize that they need to adapt culturally to culturally and linguistically diverse (CLD) students, just as these individuals, in turn, accept some cultural change as they adapt to the mainstream. In this mutual process, teachers who model receptiveness to learning from the diverse cultures in their midst help students to see this diversity as a resource. The first step toward communicating this vision is for teachers to build awareness and celebration of diversity into daily practice.

Acknowledging Students' Differences

Imagine a classroom of thirty students, each with just one unique fact, value, or belief on the more than fifty categories presented in Table 2.3 ("Components of Culture," p. 24). Yet this dizzying array of uniqueness is only the tip of the iceberg, because within each of these categories individuals can differ. Take, for example, the category "Food" under "Daily Life" in Table 2.3. Each student in a classroom of thirty knows a lot about food. What they know, however, depends largely on what they eat every day.

EXAMPLE OF CONCEPT

Students Have Diverse Facts

When I first arrived in Puerto Rico to live, I thought I knew a lot about fruits. But Leo and Alejandro, the children who lived next door, knew so much that I didn't know! The fat, green fruit with the clawlike barbs on the skin and the milky white flesh with big brown seeds was a *guanábana.* The small bananalike fruits were finger bananas, *deditos.* The *quenepa,* a small fruit that appears in the summer, looks like bunches of large, green grapes. The *acerola* is tart and stains the fingers red. The *pepino* is a large, oval melon. . . . There was so much new to learn. And all from our back patios! (Díaz-Rico, n.d.)

Culture includes diversity in values, social customs, rituals, work and leisure activities, health and educational practices, and many other aspects of life. Each of these can affect schooling and are discussed in the following sections, including ways that teachers can respond to these differences in adapting instruction.

Values, Beliefs, and Practices. Values are "beliefs about how one ought or ought not to behave or about some end state of existence worth or not worth attaining" (Bennett, 2003, p. 64). Values are particularly important to people when they educate their young, because education is a primary means of transmitting cultural knowledge.

All the influences that contribute to the cultural profile of the family and community affect the students' reactions to classroom practices. Different cultures organize individual and community behavior in radically different ways—ways that, on the surface, may not seem compatible with school practices and beliefs. To understand these differences is to be able to mediate for the students by helping them bridge relevant differences between the home and the school cultures.

EXAMPLE OF CONCEPT

Values Affect Schooling

Some student populations have very different cultures despite a shared ethnic background. Such is the case at Montebello High School in the Los Angeles area:

> Students at Montebello . . . may look to outsiders as a mostly homogenous population— 93 percent Latino, 70 percent low income—but the 2,974 Latino students are split between those who are connected to their recent immigrant roots and those who are more Americanized. In the "TJ" (for Tijuana) side of the campus, students speak Spanish, take ESL classes, and participate in soccer, *folklorico* dancing, and the Spanish club. On the other side of campus, students speak mostly English, play football and basketball, and participate in student government. The two groups are not [mutually] hostile . . . but, as senior Lucia Rios says, "it's like two countries." The difference in values between the two groups stems from their families' values—the recent immigrants are focused on economic survival and do not have the cash to pay for extracurricular activities. . . . Another difference is musical taste (soccer players listen to Spanish music in the locker room, whereas football players listen to heavy metal and rap). (Hayasaki, 2004, pp. A1, A36–A37)

Social Customs. Cultures cause people to lead very different daily lives. These customs are paced and structured by deep habits of using time and space. For example, time is organized in culturally specific ways.

EXAMPLE OF CONCEPT

Cultural Conceptions about Time

Adela, a Mexican-American first-grade girl, arrived at school about twenty minutes late every day. Her teacher was at first irritated and gradually exasperated. In a parent conference, Adela's mother explained that braiding her daughter's hair each morning was an important time for the two of them to be together, even if it meant being slightly late to school. This family time presented a value conflict with the school's time norm.

Other conflicts may arise when teachers demand abrupt endings to activities in which children are deeply engaged or when events are scheduled in a strict sequence. In fact, schools in the United States are often paced very strictly by clock time, whereas family life in various cultures is not regulated in the same manner. Moreover, teachers often equate speed of performance with intelligence, and standardized tests are often a test of rapidity. Many teachers find themselves in the role of "time mediator"—helping the class to adhere to the school's time schedule while working with individual students to help them meet their learning needs within the time allotted.

ADAPTED INSTRUCTION

Accommodating Different Concepts of Time and Work Rhythms

- Provide students with choices about their work time and observe how time spent on various subjects accords with students' aptitudes and interests.
- If a student is a slow worker, analyze the work rhythms. Slow yet methodically accurate work deserves respect; slow and disorganized work may require a peer helper.
- If students are chronically late to school, ask the school counselor to meet with the responsible family member to discuss a change in morning routines.

Space is another aspect about which social customs differ according to cultural experience. Personal space varies: In some cultures, individuals touch one another frequently and maintain high degrees of physical contact; in other cultures, touch and proximity cause feelings of tension and embarrassment. The organization of the space in the classroom sends messages to students: how free they are to move about the classroom, how much of the classroom they "own," how the desks are arranged. Both the expectations of the students and the needs of the teacher can be negotiated to provide a classroom setting in which space is shared.

Some *symbolic systems* are external, such as dress and personal appearance. For example, a third-grade girl wearing makeup is communicating a message that some teachers may consider an inappropriate indicator of premature sexuality, although makeup on a young girl may be acceptable in some cultures. Other symbolic systems are internal, such as beliefs about natural phenomena, luck and fate, vocational expectations, and so forth.

ADAPTED INSTRUCTION

Accommodating Different Concepts of Personal Space

- If students from the same culture and gender (one with a close personal space) have a high degree of physical contact and neither seems bothered by this, the teacher does not have to intervene.
- The wise teacher accords the same personal space to students no matter what their culture (e.g., does not touch minority students more or less than mainstream students).

EXAMPLE OF CONCEPT

Beliefs about Natural Occurrences

One teacher noticed during a strong earthquake that the Mexican-American students seemed much less perturbed than their European-American peers. In succeeding days, several of the European-American children were referred to the school counselor because of anxiety, but the Mexican-American children showed no signs of anxiety. The principal attributed this difference to the Mexican-Americans' cultural belief that nature is powerful and that humans must accept this power. In contrast, most European-American cultures include the view that nature is something to be conquered. When natural forces are greater than human control, anxiety results. Thus, the students' different behavior during earthquakes is a result of different symbolic systems—beliefs—about nature.

ADAPTED INSTRUCTION

Culturally Influenced School Dress Codes

- Boys and men in some cultures (rural Mexico, for example) wear hats; classrooms need to have a place for these hats during class time and provision for wearing the hats during recess.
- Schools that forbid "gang attire" yet permit privileged students to wear student council insignia (sweaters with embroidered names, for instance) should forbid clique-related attire for all.
- A family–school council with representatives from various cultures should be responsible for reviewing the school dress code on a yearly basis to see if it meets the needs of various cultures.

Rites, Rituals, and Ceremonies. Each culture incorporates expectations about the proper ways to carry out formal events. School ceremonies—for example, assemblies that begin with formal markers such as the Pledge of Allegiance and a flag salute—should have nonstigmatizing alternatives for those whose culture does not permit participation.

Rituals in some elementary classrooms in the United States are relatively informal. For example, students can enter freely before school and take their seats or go to a reading corner or activity center. Students from other cultures may find this confusing if they are accustomed to lining up in the courtyard, being formally greeted by the principal or head teacher, and then accompanied in their lines as they enter their respective classrooms.

ADAPTED INSTRUCTION

Accommodating School Rituals

- Teachers might welcome newcomers with a brief explanation of the degree of formality expected of students.
- School seasonal celebrations are increasingly devoid of political and religious content. The school may, however, permit school clubs to honor events with extracurricular rituals.
- Teachers might observe colleagues from different cultures to view the rituals of family–teacher conferences and adapt their behavior accordingly to address families' cultural expectations.

Rituals are also involved in parent conferences. Greeting and welcome behaviors, for example, vary across cultures. The sensitive teacher understands how parents expect to be greeted and incorporates some of these behaviors in the exchange.

Work and Leisure Systems. Crosscultural variation in work and leisure activities is a frequently discussed value difference. Many members of mainstream U.S. cultures value work over play; that is, one's status is directly related to one's productivity, salary, or job description. Play, rather than being an end in itself, is often used in ways that reinforce the status achieved through work, and one's work status governs who is invited to attend leisure-time events.

Young people, particularly those in the middle class, are trained to use specific tools of play, and their time is structured to attain skills (e.g., organized sports, music lessons). In contrast, other cultures do not afford children any structured time to play but instead expect children to engage in adult-type labor at work or in the home. In still other cultures, such as that of the Hopi Nation in Arizona, children's playtime is relatively unstructured, and parents do not interfere with play. Cultures also vary in the typical work and play activities expected of girls and of boys. All these values have obvious influence on the ways children work and play at school (Schultz & Theophano, 1987).

Did You Know?

In Japan, individuals compete fiercely for admission to prestigious universities, but accompanying this individual effort is a sense that one must establish oneself within a group. Competition in the Japanese classroom is not realized in the same way as in U.S. schools; being singled out for attention or praise by teachers may result in embarrassment (Furey, 1986).

Medicine, Health, and Hygiene. Health and medicine practices involve deep-seated beliefs, because the stakes are high: life and death. When students come to school with health issues, teachers need to react in culturally compatible ways. Miscommunication and noncooperation can result when teachers and the family view health and disease differently. For example, community health practices,

ADAPTED INSTRUCTION

Accommodating Diverse Ideas about Work and Play

- Many high-school students arrange class schedules in order to work part time. If a student appears chronically tired, a family–teacher conference may be needed to review priorities.
- Many students are overcommitted to extracurricular activities. If grades suffer, students may be well advised to reduce activities to regain an academic focus.
- Plagiarism in student work may be due to unclear conceptions about the permissability of shared work.
- Out-of-school play activities such as birthday parties should not be organized at the school site, such as passing out invitations that exclude some students.

such as the Cambodian tradition of coining (in which a coin is dipped in oil and then rubbed on a sick person's back, chest, and neck), can be misinterpreted by school officials who, seeing marks on the child, call Child Protective Services.

ADAPTED INSTRUCTION

Health and Hygiene Practices

- Families who send sick children to school or, conversely, keep children home at the slightest ache may benefit from a conference with the school nurse.
- All students can profit from explicit instruction in home and school hygiene.

Institutional Influences: Economic, Legal, Political, and Religious. The institutions that support and govern family and community life have an influence on behavior and beliefs and, in turn, are constituted in accordance with these behaviors and beliefs. These institutions influence daily life in the United States by means of a complex web of law, custom, and regulation that provides the economic and legal infrastructure of the dominant culture.

Interwoven into this rich cultural–economic–political–legal texture are religious beliefs and practices. In the United States, religious practices are heavily embedded but formally bounded: witness the controversy over Christmas trees in schools but the almost universal cultural and economic necessity for increased consumer spending at the close of the calendar year.

Teacher Judy Haynes (2007) discusses the "December dilemma":

The biggest issue of the December [holiday] wars is the traditional school concert that is at the heart of the celebration of Christmas. The dilemma arises when deciding what music to sing. The question is whether a school concert can include religious Christmas music without promoting a particular belief. The courts have decreed that some religious music may be included if the purpose is to teach about a particular religion and the program is balanced (Anti-Defamation League, 2004).

I think the onus should be taken off December. Let's solve the December dilemma by learning about Diwali and Ramadan in September, Rosh Hashanah in October, and Christmas in December. We should not overemphasize one particular holiday. (pp. 6–7)

Religious beliefs underlie other cultures even more fundamentally. Immigrants with Confucian religious and philosophical beliefs, for example, subscribe to values that mandate a highly ordered society and family through the maintenance of proper social relationships. In Islamic traditions, the Koran prescribes proper social relationships and roles for members of society. When immigrants with these religious beliefs encounter the largely secular U.S. institutions, the result may be that customs and cultural patterns are challenged, fade away, or cause conflict within the family.

ADAPTED INSTRUCTION

Economic, Legal, Political, and Religious Practices

- On a rotating basis, teachers could be paid to supervise after-school homework sessions for students whose parents are working multiple jobs.
- Schools can legally resist any attempts to identify families whose immigration status is undocumented.
- Permission for religious garb or appearance (e.g., Islamic head scarves, Sikh ritual knives, Hassidic dress) should be a part of the school dress code.

Educational Expectations. In the past, educational systems were designed to pass on cultural knowledge and traditions, much the same learning that parents taught their children. However, in the increasingly complex society of the United States, schools have shifted their emphasis to teaching unforeseen kinds of content, including science and technology and multicultural education.

This shift affects all students but is particularly troublesome for children whose parents teach them differently than the school does. Students come to school already steeped in the learning practices of their own family and community. They come with expectations about learning and generally expect that they will continue to learn in school. Many of the organizational and teaching practices of the school may not support the type of learning to which students are accustomed. For immigrant children with previous schooling, experience in U.S. classrooms may create severe conflicts. Teachers who can accommodate students' proclivities can gradually introduce student-centered practices while supporting an initial dependence on the teacher's direction.

Did You Know?

Polynesian students coming from the South Pacific may have experienced classroom learning as a relatively passive activity. They expect teachers to give explicit instruction about what to learn and how to learn it and to carefully scrutinize homework daily. When these students arrive in the United States and encounter teachers who value creativity and student-centered learning, they may appear passive as they wait to be told what to do (Funaki & Burnett, 1993).

Teachers who seek to understand the value of education within the community can interview parents or community members.

ADAPTED INSTRUCTION

Accommodating Culturally Based Educational Expectations

- Classroom guests from the community can share methods for teaching and learning that are used in the home (e.g., modeling and imitation, didactic stories and proverbs, direct verbal instruction).
- Children from cultures that expect passive interaction with teachers (observing only) can be paired with more participatory peers to learn to ask questions and volunteer.

Roles and Status. Cultures differ in the roles people play in society and the status accorded to these roles. For example, in the Vietnamese culture, profoundly influenced by Confucianism, authority figures are ranked in the following manner: The father ranks below the teacher, who ranks only below the king. Such a high status is not accorded to teachers in U.S. society, where, instead, medical doctors enjoy this type of prestige. Such factors as gender, social class, age, occupation, and education level influence the manner in which status is accorded to various roles. Students' perceptions about the roles possible for them in their culture affect their school performance.

Gender. Immigrants to the United States often come from cultures in which men and women have rigid and highly differentiated gender roles. The gender equality that is an ostensible goal in classrooms in the United States may be difficult for students of these cultures. For example, parents may spend much time correcting their sons' homework while ascribing little importance to their daughters' schoolwork.

Sexual identification is also a part of gender issues. Gay, lesbian, or bisexual adolescents who face a hostile school climate or undergo harassment, and/or verbal or physical abuse may become truant, drop out, or resort to suicide or substance abuse (Nichols, 1999).

ADAPTED INSTRUCTION

Gender-Role Expectations

- Monitor tasks performed by boys and girls to ensure they are the same.
- Make sure that boys and girls perform equal leadership roles in cooperative groups.
- If families in a given community provide little support for the scholastic achievement of girls, a systematic effort on the part of school counselors and administrators may be needed to help families accommodate their beliefs to a more proactive support for women.

Social Class. Stratification by social class differs across cultures. Cultures that are rigidly stratified, such as India's caste system, differ from cultures that are not as rigid or that, in some cases, border on the anarchic, such as continuously war-torn countries. The belief that education can enhance economic status is widespread in the dominant culture of the United States, but individuals in other cultures may not have similar beliefs.

In general, individuals and families at the upper-socioeconomic-status levels are able to exert power by sitting on college, university, and local school boards and thus determining who receives benefits and rewards through schooling. However, middle-class values are those that are generally incorporated in the culture of schooling. The social class values that children learn in their homes largely influence not only their belief in schooling but also their routines and habits in the classroom.

ADAPTED INSTRUCTION

The Influence of Social Class on Schooling

- Students who are extremely poor or homeless may need help from the teacher to store possessions at school.
- A teacher who receives an expensive gift should consult the school district's ethics policies.
- A high grade on a school assignment or project should not depend on extensive family financial resources.

Age-Appropriate Activities. Age interacts with culture, socioeconomic status, gender, and other factors to influence an individual's behavior and attitudes. In various cultures, expectations about appropriate activities for children and the purpose of those activities differ. Middle-class European Americans expect children to spend much of their time playing and attending school rather than performing tasks similar to those of adults. Cree Indian children, on the other hand, are expected from an early age to learn adult roles, including contributing food to the family. Parents may criticize schools for involving children in tasks that are not related to their future participation in Cree society (Sindell, 1988).

Cultures also differ in their criteria for moving through the various (culturally defined) life cycle changes. An important stage in any culture is the move into adulthood, but the age at which this occurs and the criteria necessary for attaining adulthood vary according to what *adulthood* means in a particular culture.

ADAPTED INSTRUCTION

Accommodating Beliefs about Age-Appropriate Activities

- Child labor laws in the United States forbid students from working for pay before a given age. However, few laws govern children working in family businesses. If a child appears chronically tired, the school counselor may need to discuss the child's involvement in the family business with a responsible family member.
- Cultural groups in which girls are expected to marry and have children at the age of fifteen or sixteen (e.g., Hmong) may need access to alternative schools.

Occupation. In the United States, occupation very often determines income, which in turn is a chief determinant of prestige in the culture. Prestige is one factor in occupational choices. Other factors can include cultural acceptance of the occupation, educational requirements, gender, and attainability. Students thus may not see all occupations as desirable for them or even available to them and may have mixed views about the role education plays in their future occupation.

Some cultural groups in the United States are engaged in a voluntary way of life that does not require prolonged schooling (e.g., the Amish). Other groups may be involuntarily incorporated into U.S. society and relegated to menial occupations and ways of life that do not reward and require school success (e.g., Hispanics in the Southwest). As a result, they may not apply academic effort (Ogbu & Matute-Bianchi, 1986).

EXAMPLE OF CONCEPT

Collaborative Relationships

Conchas (2006) studied the Medical Academy at Baldwin High School (California), a school-within-a-school that prepares students for careers in health-related occupations. A positive learning environment connected students and teachers across race, gender, and class differences. Both immigrant and U.S.-born Latinos formed a strong sense of belonging and identification with other students in the program; strong collaborative relationships led to academic success.

ADAPTED INSTRUCTION

Occupational Aspirations

- At all grade levels, school subjects should be connected with future vocations.
- Teachers should make available at every grade an extensive set of books on occupations and their requirements, and discuss these with students.
- Role models from minority communities can visit the classroom to recount stories of their success. Successful professionals and businesspeople can visit and explain how cultural diversity is supported in their place of work.

Child-Rearing Practices. The way in which families raise their children has wide implications for schools. Factors such as who takes care of children, how much supervision they receive, how much freedom they have, who speaks to them and how often, and what they are expected to do affect their behavior on entering schools. Many of the misunderstandings that occur between teachers and students arise because of different expectations about behavior, and these different expectations stem from early, ingrained child-rearing practices.

Because the largest group of English learners in California is of Mexican ancestry, teachers who take the time to learn about child-rearing practices among Mexican immigrants can help students adjust to schooling practices in the United States. An excellent source for this cultural study is *Crossing Cultural Borders* (Delgado-Gaitan & Trueba, 1991).

Food Preferences. As the numbers of school-provided breakfasts and lunches increase, food preferences are an important consideration. Furthermore, teachers who are knowledgeable about students' dietary practices can incorporate their students' background knowledge into health and nutrition instruction.

Did You Know?

Students from Korean-American backgrounds may be accustomed to an authoritarian discipline style in the home. These parents often seek to influence their children's behavior by expecting reciprocity for the sacrifices made for them. Decision-making strategies reward conformity and obedience, and teachers are expected to reinforce this. An egalitarian classroom atmosphere may create conflicts for Korean-American students between the pressures they experience in their families and the school environment (CDE, 1992).

Besides customs of what and when to eat, eating habits vary widely across cultures, and "good" manners at the table in some cultures are inappropriate or rude in others. For example, Indochinese consider burping, lip smacking, and soup slurping to be common behaviors during meals, even complimentary to hosts. Cultural relativity is not, however, an excuse for poor or unhygienic eating, and teachers do need to teach students the behaviors that are considered good food manners in the U.S. mainstream context.

ADAPTED INSTRUCTION

Dealing with Food Preferences

- In addition to knowing in general what foods are eaten at home, teachers will want to find out about students' favorite foods, taboo foods, and typical foods.
- Eating lunch with students—even on a by-invitation basis—can provide the opportunity to learn about students' habits.
- If a student's eating habits alienate peers, the teacher may need to discuss appropriate behaviors.

Humanities and the Arts. In many cultures, crafts performed at home—such as food preparation; sewing and weaving; carpentry; home building and decoration; religious and ritual artistry for holy days, holidays, and entertaining—are an important part of the culture that is transmitted within the home. Parents also provide an important means of access to the humanities and the visual and performing arts of their cultures. Often, if immigrant students are to gain an appreciation of the great works of art, architecture, music, and dance that have been achieved by their native culture, it is the classroom teacher who must provide this experience and awareness by drawing on the resources of the community and then sharing these with all the members of the classroom.

Educating Students about Diversity

Both mainstream students and CLD students benefit from education about diversity, not only cultural diversity but also diversity in ability, gender preference, and human nature in general. This engenders pride in cultural identity, expands the students' perspectives, and adds cultural insight, information, and experiences to the curriculum.

Did You Know?

James Banks (1994) explained the difference between studying the cultures of other countries and the cultures within the United States. According to Banks, teachers may implement a unit on the country of Japan but avoid teaching about Japanese internment in the United States during World War II (Brandt, 1994).

Global and Multicultural Education. ELD teachers—and mainstream teachers who teach English learners—can bring a global and multicultural perspective to their classes.

> Language teachers, like teachers in all other areas of the curriculum, have a responsibility to plan lessons with sensitivity to the racial and ethnic diversity present in their classrooms and in the world in which their students live. . . . [Students] can learn to value the points of view of many others whose life experiences are different from their own. (Curtain & Dahlberg, 2004, p. 244)

Table 3.2 lists some cultural activities that Curtain and Dahlberg recommended for adding cultural content to the curriculum.

The goal of multicultural education is to help students "develop cross-cultural competence within the American national culture, with their own subculture and within and across different subsocieties and cultures" (Banks, 1994, p. 9). Banks introduced a model of multicultural education that has proved to be a useful way of assessing the approach taken in pedagogy and curricula. The model has four levels, represented in Table 3.3 with a critique of strengths and shortcomings taken from Jenks, Lee, and Kanpol (2002).

There is a clear distinction between multiculturalism and globalism, although both are important features of the school curriculum: "Globalism emphasizes the cultures and peoples of other lands, and multiculturalism deals with ethnic diversity within the United States" (Ukpokodu, 2002, pp. 7–8).

Table 3.2 Sample Cultural Activities for Multicultural Education

Activity	Suggested Implementation
Visitors and guest speakers	Guests can share their experiences on a variety of topics, using visuals, slides, and hands-on materials.
Folk dances, singing games, and other kinds of games	Many cultures can be represented; cultural informants can help.
Field trips	Students can visit neighborhoods, restaurants, museums, or stores that feature cultural materials.
Show-and-tell	Students can bring items from home to share with the class.
Read books about other cultures	Age-appropriate fiction or nonfiction books can be obtained with the help of the school or public librarian.
Crosscultural e-mail contacts	Students can exchange cultural information and get to know peers from other lands.

Source: Curtain and Dahlberg (2004).

Table 3.3 Banks's Levels of Multicultural Education, with Critique

Level	Description	Strengths	Shortcomings
Contributions	Emphasizes what minority groups have contributed to society (e.g., International Food Day, bulletin board display for Black History Month).	Attempts to sensitize the majority white culture to some understanding of minority groups' history.	May amount to "cosmetic" multiculturalism in which no discussion takes place about issues of power and disenfranchisement.
Additive	Adding material to the curriculum to address what has been omitted (reading *The Color Purple* in English class).	Adds to a fuller coverage of the American experience, when sufficient curricular time is allotted.	May be an insincere effort if dealt with superficially.
Transformative	An expanded perspective is taken that deals with issues of historic, ethnic, cultural, and linguistic injustice and equality as a part of the American experience.	Students learn to be reflective and develop a critical perspective.	Incorporates the liberal fallacy that discussion alone changes society.
Social action	Extension of the transformative approach to add students' research/action projects to initiate change in society.	Students learn to question the status quo and the commitment of the dominant culture to equality and social justice.	Middle-class communities may not accept the teacher's role, considering it as provoking students to "radical" positions.

Sources: Model based on Banks (1994); strengths and shortcomings based on Jenks, Lee, and Kanpol (2002).

Nieto and Bode (2008) make the point that multicultural education does more than merely celebrate diversity:

> [M]ulticultural education does not simply involve the affirmation of language and culture. Multicultural education confronts not only issues of difference but also issues of power and privilege in society. This means challenging racism and other biases as well as the inequitable structures, policies, and practices of schools and, ultimately, of society itself. Affirming language and culture can help students become successful and well-adjusted learners, but unless language and cultural issues are viewed critically through the lens of equity and social justices, they are unlikely to have a lasting impact in promoting real change. (pp. 4–5)

Similar to Banks's superficial-to-transformative continuum is that of Morey and Kilano (1997). Their three-level framework for incorporating diversity identifies as "exclusive" the stereotypical focus on external aspects of diversity (what they called the four *f*'s: food, folklore, fun, and fashion); "inclusive," the addition of diversity into a curriculum that, although enriched, is fundamentally the same structure; and "transformed," the curriculum that is built on diverse perspectives, equity in participation, and critical problem solving. Howard (2007) has suggested that a transformative approach to diversity has five basic phases: building trust, engaging personal culture, confronting issues of social dominance and social justice, transforming educational practices, and engaging the entire school community. Thus, it is clear that pouring new wine—diversity—into old bottles—teacher-centered, one-size-fits-all instruction—is not transformative.

EXAMPLE OF CONCEPT

Action Research for Curricular Change

Diane Red and Amy Warner are two fourth-grade teachers who are dissatisfied with the four-week unit on "Explorers" in the social studies curriculum. They were concerned that the unit was too focused on the European viewpoint and did not adequately represent the perspectives of the indigenous people of the Americas. They modified the readings to include books that presented a range of perspectives on Columbus. In an action research project, they asked students to tally the number of times in each book that Europeans were pictured versus the native Tainos or Caribs from the islands where Columbus landed, and used the tallies as data in their research. In the modified lessons, they used K-W-L charts, and included many opportunities for discussion. Their "action research" focused on gathering evidence to evaluate the success of their "renovated" approach.

Source: Nolan and Hoover (2008).

Validating Students' Cultural Identity. "An affirming attitude toward students from culturally diverse backgrounds significantly impacts their learning, belief in self, and overall academic performance" (Villegas & Lucas, 2002, p. 23). Cultural identity—that is, having a positive self-concept or evaluation of oneself and one's culture—promotes self-esteem. Students who feel proud of their successes and abilities, self-knowledge, and self-expression, and who have enhanced images of self, family, and culture, are better learners.

Oakes and Lipton (2007) believe that students should view their cultural identities as integral to their school success, not as something they must "overcome":

> Perhaps schools' greatest challenge is to create a school culture that supports college attendance for students whose lives do not conform to [the profile of a person with high scores on standardized tests, whose parents went to college, whose main language is mainstream, unaccented English, and who have middle-class perspectives and financial support]. The school culture must position college success as expected and inevitable not just for students who change [identities] or for students who are exceptions to stereotypes, but for students who have no need or no intention to slight their family's background and culture as they acquire skills and knowledge that are genuinely useful for college success. (p. 354)

Of course, the most powerful sense of self-esteem is the result not solely of one's beliefs about oneself but also of successful learning experiences. Practices of schooling that damage self-esteem, such as tracking and competitive grading, undermine authentic cooperation and sense of accomplishment on the part of English learners.

Classroom Practices That Validate Identity. Díaz-Rico (2008) suggested that through observations, shared conversations during lunchtime or before or after school, and group participation, teachers can gain understanding about various individuals and their cultures. Teachers can also ask students to interview their parents about common topics such as work, interests, and family history and then add a reflective element about their relationship and identification with these aspects of their parents' lives.

Adolescents acquire identities through sociocultural groups, such as language and cultural groups, as well as through activities in which they engage (athletics, band, computers, gangsta, goth). They are also labeled by schools (students in honors or special education, English learners, "at-risk," "leaders"). These identities may influence school behavior, as some groups pressure members not to invest in school success, but rather to adopt resistance or apathetic attitudes.

Instructional Materials That Validate Identity. Classroom texts are available that offer literature and anecdotal readings aimed at the enhancement of identity and self-esteem. *Identities: Readings from Contemporary Culture* (Raimes, 1996) includes readings grouped into chapters titled "Name,"

EXAMPLE OF CONCEPT

A Cultural Heritage Project

Promoting research projects is a way for students to participate in school in ways related to their personal identities. One teacher based a unit plan on this standard from the Michigan Curriculum Standard from Social Studies: *Students will gain knowledge about the past to construct meaningful understandings of our diverse cultural heritage.* In this unit, students were to compare two aspects of cultural heritage from information obtained from the Internet, culminating in an individual report on a favorite artist or inventor as well as a group PowerPoint presentation and simulated interview with the historical figure.

The Puerto Rican group compared Ladislao Martinez and Alvin Medina, one traditional and one contemporary cuatro (folk guitar) player. They contrasted the two players, drawing on sound clips that included current musical favorites. A rich context of time and place gave each participant a personal connection to the topic (Conley, 2008).

"Appearance, Age, and Abilities," "Ethnic Affiliation and Class," "Family Ties," and so forth. The readings contain authentic text and may be best used in middle- or high-school classes.

The use of multicultural literature may enhance cultural and ethnic identity, but this is not always the case. In 1976 a committee of Asian-American book reviewers evaluated books to identify those that could be used effectively in educational programs. When they had evaluated a total of sixty-four books related to Asian-American issues or characters, they concluded that most of the existing literature was "racist, sexist, and elitist and that the image of Asian Americans [the books] present is grossly misleading" (Aoki, 1992, p. 133). The challenge, then, is to represent ethnic characters in a more realistic way.

A book that is useful for a comparison of Asian cultural values with those of mainstream American culture is Kim's (2001) *The Yin and Yang of American Culture.* This book presents a view of American culture—its virtues and vices—from an Eastern perspective and may stimulate discussion on the part of students. *Exploring Culturally Diverse Literature for Children and Adolescents* (Henderson & May, 2005) helps readers understand how stories are tied to specific cultural and sociopolitical histories, opening readers' minds to literature written from the "insider's" versus the "outsider's" point of view.

Promoting Mutual Respect among Students

The ways in which we organize classroom life should make children feel significant and cared about—by the teacher and by one another. Classroom life should, to the greatest extent possible, prefigure the kind of democratic and just society we envision and thus contribute to building that society. Together, students and teachers can create a "community of conscience," as educators Asa Hillard and George Pine call it (Christensen, 2000, p. 18).

Mutual respect is promoted when the curriculum includes multiple points of view and when students are given the chance to genuinely talk to one another about topics that concern them. The instructional conversation is a discourse format that encourages in-depth conversation.

ADAPTING TO STUDENTS' CULTURALLY SUPPORTED FACILITATING OR LIMITING ATTITUDES AND ABILITIES

A skilled intercultural educator recognizes that each culture supports distinct attitudes, values, and abilities. These may facilitate or limit the learning situation in U.S. public schools. For example, the cultures of Japan, China, and Korea, which promote high academic achievement, may foster facilitating behaviors, such as the ability to listen and follow directions; attitudes favoring education and respect for teachers and authorities; attitudes toward discipline as guidance; and high-achievement motivation. However, other culturally supported traits may hinder adjustment to the U.S. school, such as lack of experience participating in discussions; little experience with independent thinking; strong preference for conformity, which inhibits divergent thinking; and distinct sex-role differentiation, with males more dominant.

EXAMPLE OF CONCEPT
Overcoming Reluctance to Participate Orally

Asian students are more likely to speak up in class when the participation is structured, such as in a debate that has definite rules for whose turn it is to talk. Unstructured class discussions in which one must aggressively promote one's turn may make many Asian students feel anxious and uncomfortable, because this does not mirror the home environment, where often students speak only when requested to do so by a parental authority (Tateishi, 2007–2008). Small-group discussion with leaders whose task is to involve all members can be a means of conducting classroom talk.

Similarly, African-American family and cultural values that encourage independent action, self-sufficiency, and imagination and humor may facilitate adjustment to the classroom, but dialect speakers with limited experiences with various types of Standard English patterns may be hindered. The Mexican-American cultural values that encourage cooperation; affectionate and demonstrative parental relationships; children assuming mature social responsibilities such as child care and translating family matters from English to Spanish; and eagerness to try out new ideas may facilitate classroom success. On the other hand, such attitudes as depreciating education after high school, especially for women; explicit sex-role stereotyping favoring limited vocational roles for women; and dislike of competition may go against classroom practices and hinder classroom success (Clark, 1983).

Cooperation versus Competition

Triandis (1995) stated that the most important difference between cultures that can be identified in schools is the contrast between individualist and collectivist value systems. Traditional U.S. classrooms mirror middle-class European-American values of competition: Students are expected to do their own work; are rewarded publicly through star charts, posted grades, and academic honors; and are admonished to do their individual best. In the Cree Indian culture, however, children are raised in a cooperative atmosphere, with siblings, parents, and other kin sharing food as well as labor (Sindell, 1988). In the Mexican-American culture, interdependence is a strength; individuals have a commitment to others, and all decisions are made together. Those who are successful have a responsibility to others to help them succeed.

Because about 70 percent of the world's population lives in a collectivist culture (including Native Americans, Native Hawaiians, Latin American, African Americans, Asians, and Arab groups), according to Tileston and Darling (2008), it is probably wiser for teachers to emphasize interdependence among students rather than aggressive and competitive competition. Some balance must be achieved in the classroom between the individual competitive culture of the dominant U.S. culture and the collaborative preferences of students from group-oriented, cooperative cultures.

Developing cooperative skills requires a focus in the classroom on communication and teamwork. Kluge (1999) emphasized the following elements:

- *Positive interdependence:* Members of a group depend on one another, and no one is exploited or left out.
- *Face-to-face interaction:* Students work in proximity to one another.

- *Individual accountability:* Each group member bears full responsibility for the work performed by the group.
- *Social skills training:* The teacher explicitly explains and models the kind of communication and cooperation that is desired.
- *Group processing:* The teacher makes time for reflection on how the group is working together and helps the group set goals for improvement.

The Use of Language

In learning a second language, students (and teachers) often focus on the form. Frequently ignored are the ways in which that second language is used. The culture that underlies each language prescribes distinct patterns and conventions about when, where, and how to use the language (see Labov, 1972). Heath's (1983b) *Ways with Words* noted that children in "Trackton," an isolated African-American community in the South, were encouraged to use spontaneous verbal play, rich with metaphor, simile, and allusion. In contrast, the children of "Roadville," a lower-middle-class European-American community in the South, used language in more restricted ways, perhaps because of habits encouraged by a fundamentalist religious culture. Heath contrasted language usage in these two cultures: verbal and nonverbal communication (the "said" and the "unsaid"), the use of silence, discourse styles, the nature of questions, and the use of oral versus written genres.

Social Functions of Language. Using language to satisfy material needs, control the behavior of others, get along with others, express one's personality, find out about the world, create an imaginative world, or communicate information seems to be universal among language users. How these social functions are accomplished, however, varies greatly among cultures. For example, when accidentally bumping someone, Americans, Japanese, Koreans, and Filipinos would say "excuse me" or "pardon me." The Chinese, however, would give an apologetic look.

Verbal and Nonverbal Expression. Both verbal and nonverbal means are used to communicate a language function. Educators are oriented toward verbal means of expression and are less likely to accord importance to the "silent language." However, more than 65 percent of the social meaning of a typical two-person exchange is carried by nonverbal cues (Birdwhistell, 1974). *Kinesic* behavior, including facial expressions, body movements, postures, and gestures, can enhance a message or constitute a message in itself. *Physical appearance* is an important dimension of the nonverbal code during initial encounters. *Paralanguage*—the nonverbal elements of the voice—is an important aspect of speech that can affirm or belie a verbal message. *Proxemics,* the communication of interpersonal distance, varies widely across cultures. Last but not least, *olfactics*—the study of interpersonal communication by means of smell—constitutes a factor that is powerful yet often overlooked.

The Role of Silence. People throughout the world employ silence in communicating. Silence can in fact speak loudly and eloquently. As with other language uses, however, silence differs dramatically across cultures. In the United States, silence is interpreted as expressing embarrassment, regret, obligation, criticism, or sorrow (Wayne in Ishii & Bruneau, 1991). In Asian cultures, silence is a token of respect. Particularly in the presence of the elderly, being quiet honors their wisdom and expertise. Silence can also be a marker of personal power. In many Native-American cultures, silence is used to create and communicate rapport in ways that language cannot.

The Nature of Questions. Intercultural differences exist in asking and answering questions. In middle-class European-American culture, children are exposed early on to their parents' questioning. While taking a walk, for example, a mother will ask, "See the squirrel?" and, later, "Is that a squirrel? Where did that squirrel go?" It is obvious to both parent and child that the adult knows the answer to these questions. The questions are asked to stimulate conversation and to train children to focus attention and display knowledge. In the Inuit culture, on the other hand, adults do not question children or call their attention to objects and events in order to name them (Crago, 1993).

Did You Know?

Heath (1983b) described differences in questions that adults ask children between the Road-ville (lower-middle-class European-American community) and the Trackton African-American community. Roadville parents used questions to ask their children to display knowledge ("What is three plus three?"). In contrast, Trackton adults challenged the child to display creative thinking: "What's that like?"

Responses to questioning differ across cultures. Students from non-Western cultures may be reluctant to attempt an answer to a question if they do not feel they can answer absolutely correctly. Students do not share the European-American value of answering questions to the best of their ability regardless of whether that "best" answer is absolutely correct or not.

Discourse Styles. Cultures may differ in ways that influence conversations: the way conversations open and close, the way people take turns, the way messages are repaired to make them understandable, and the way in which parts of the text are set aside. These differences in discourse are stressful for second-language learners. Multiply this stress by the long hours children spend in school, and it is no wonder that English learners may feel subjected to prolonged pressure.

EXAMPLE OF CONCEPT

Classroom Discourse Patterns

Discourse in the classroom can be organized in ways that involve children positively, in ways that are culturally compatible. A group of Hawaiian children, with the help of an encouraging and participating adult, produced group discourse that was co-narrated, complex, lively, imaginative, and well connected. Group work featured twenty-minute discussions of text in which the teacher and students mutually participated in overlapping, volunteered speech and in joint narration (Au & Jordan, 1981). In contrast, Navajo children in a discussion group patterned their discourse after the adults of their culture. Each Navajo student spoke for an extended period with a fully expressed statement, and other students waited courteously until a clear end was communicated. Then another took a similar turn. In both communities, children tended to connect discourse with peers rather than with the teacher functioning as a central "switchboard." If the teacher acted as a central director, students often responded with silence (Tharp, 1989a).

Oral versus Written Language. Orality is the foundation of languages. Written expression is a later development. In fact, of the thousands of reported languages in use, only seventy-eight have a written literature (Edmonson, 1971). Research has suggested that acquiring literacy involves more than learning to read and write. Thinking patterns, perception, cultural values, communication style, and social organization can be affected by literacy (Ong, 1982; Scribner & Cole, 1978).

In studying oral societies, researchers have noted that the structure and content of messages tend to be narrative, situational, and oriented toward activity or deeds, although abstract ideas such as moral values are often implicit. In contrast, the style of literacy is conceptual rather than situational. Words are separate from the social context of deeds and events, and abstract ideas can be extracted from written texts. In an oral society, learning takes place in groups because narration must have an audience. This contrasts with a literate society, in which reading and writing can be solitary experiences. In an oral society, much reliance is placed on memory, as this is the principal means of preserving practices and traditions (Ong, 1982).

ADAPTED INSTRUCTION

How Students Tell You They Don't Understand

Arabic (men): *Mish fahem*
Arabic (women): *Mish fahmeh*
Armenian: *Yes chem huskenur*
Chinese (Cantonese): *Ngoh m-ming*
Chinese (Mandarin): *Wo bu dung*
Persian: *Man ne'me fah'mam*
Japanese: *Wakarimasen*
Korean: *Juh-neun eehae-haji mot haget-ssum-nida*
Russian: *Ya nye ponimayu*
Spanish: *No comprendo*
Vietnamese: *Toi khong hieu*
Yiddish: *Ikh veys nikht*

In addition to ways to say "I don't understand" in 230 languages, J. Runner's Webpage has translations in many languages for the following phrases: "Hello, how are you?" "Welcome," "Good-bye," "Please," "Thank you," "What is your name?" "My name is . . . ," "Do you speak English?" "Yes," and "No." There is also a link to Internet Language Resources; see www.elite.net/~runner/jennifers/understa.htm.

Source: Runner (2000).

EXAMPLE OF CONCEPT

Characteristics of One Oral Culture

Hmong immigrants in the United States demonstrate the comparative disadvantage faced by individuals from an oral culture when expected to perform in a literate environment. Hmong individuals may become frustrated in the abstract world of school. The very concept of independent study is alien to this culture because learning always occurs in community groups. Learning among strangers and doing homework, a solitary endeavor, run counter to traditional group practices and may distance children from their families. As Hmong children become literate and engage in independent study, parents may become disturbed over the loss of centrality and power in their children's lives, which may produce family tension (Shuter, 1991).

Participation Styles

The way teachers are taught to teach is a reflection of the expectations of U.S. culture. Teachers raised in a mainstream culture have elements of that culture embedded in their personal teaching approach. The selection of a particular teaching method reflects cultural values more than it argues for the superiority of the method. Some of these elements may need to be modified to meet the needs of students from other cultures. The accompanying Example of Concept illustrates the way the culturally preferred participation style of one group of students differed from their teachers'.

Even in monocultural classrooms, the teacher's style is more in accordance with some students than with others. Flexibility becomes a key in reaching more students. In a multicultural classroom, this flexibility is even more crucial. With knowledge of various teaching styles, teachers can examine

EXAMPLE OF CONCEPT
Culturally Preferred Participation Styles

In classrooms on the Warm Springs (Oregon) Reservation, teacher-controlled activity dominated. All the social and spatial arrangements were created by the teacher: where and when movement took place; where desks were placed and even what furniture was present in the room; and who talked, when, and with whom. For the Warm Springs students, this socialization was difficult. They preferred to wander to various parts of the room, away from the lesson; to talk to other students while the teacher was talking; and to "bid" for one another's attention rather than that of the teacher.

For the Native-American children, the small-reading-group structure in which participation is mandatory, individual, and oral was particularly ill fitting. They frequently refused to read aloud, did not utter a word when called on, or spoke too softly to be audible. On the other hand, when students controlled and directed interaction in small-group projects, they were much more fully involved. They concentrated completely on their work until it was completed and talked a great deal to one another in the group. Very little time was spent disagreeing or arguing about how to go about a task. There was, however, explicit competition with other groups.

A look at the daily life of the Warm Springs children revealed several factors that would account for their willingness to work together and their resistance to teacher-directed activity. First, they spend much time in the company of peers with little disciplinary control from older relatives. They also spend time in silence, observing their elders and listening without verbal participation. Speech seems to be an optional response rather than a typical or mandatory feature of interaction. One last characteristic of community life is the accessibility and openness of community-wide celebrations. No single individual directs and controls all activity, and there is no sharp distinction between audience and performer. Individuals are permitted to choose for themselves the degree of participation in an activity. Schooling became more successful for these students when they were able to take a more active part.

Source: Adapted from Philips (1972, pp. 370–394).

their own style, observe students' reactions to that style, ask questions about a teacher's expected role and style in the community, and modify their style as necessary.

Teacher–Student Interactions

The teacher–student relationship is culturally mandated in general ways, although individual relationships vary. Teacher–student interaction may derive from parent–child relationships or from values transmitted by the parent toward teachers and schooling. Students who have immigrated may bring with them varying notions of teacher–student interactions. For example, in some cultures, learning takes place in an absolutely quiet classroom where the teacher is in complete control and authority is never questioned. In other cultures, students talk among themselves and are able to engage with teachers in cooperative planning. Attitudes toward authority, teacher–student relationships, and teacher expectations of student achievement vary widely. Yet the heart of the educational process is in the interaction between teacher and student. This determines the quality of education the student receives.

ADAPTED INSTRUCTION

Encouraging Positive Relationships

Although it may appear daunting to be able to accommodate the various teacher–student relations represented by different cultural groups in a classroom, there are several ways teachers can learn about their students to provide a learning environment.

- Express care and respect equally to all students.
- Openly communicate acceptance of students and be accessible to them.
- In classroom discussions and in private, encourage students to talk about their expectations for learning.
- Be sensitive to home conditions and try to make students' class experiences positive.
- Welcome and respect parents in classrooms.
- Understand that you are not only helping students academically but that you may also be helping families adjust.

Source: Adapted from Lemberger (1999).

Power and Authority. Most students expect power and authority to be vested in the teacher, and teachers expect respect from students. Respect is communicated verbally and nonverbally and is vulnerable to cultural misunderstanding. In the United States, respect is shown to teachers by looking at them, but in some cultures looking directly at the teacher is a sign of disrespect. Moreover, students are expected to raise their hands in North-American classrooms if they wish to ask or answer a question. In general, one must not conclude that a particular behavior is disrespectful; it may be that the child has learned different customs for communicating with those in authority.

ADAPTED INSTRUCTION

Understanding Behaviors Related to Power and Authority

- Seek alternative explanations to unexpected behavior rather than interpreting the behavior according to your own cultural framework.
- Ask "Why is this behavior occurring?" rather than "What is the matter with this child?"

Source: Adapted from Cushner (1999, p. 75).

Teacher–Student Relationships. The relationships that are possible between teachers and students also show cultural influences. The role of teachers in multicultural classrooms is to make explicit their understandings of the teacher–student relationship and to build a mutually satisfying classroom community. Sometimes this means going that extra mile to sustain a relationship that is at risk.

Kottler (1997) proposed that teachers take a cultural view when learning about students, asking these reflective questions:

- How are my cultural values and biases getting in the way of honoring those among my students who are different from what I am used to?
- What is it that I do not know or understand about this child's background that might help me to make sense of what is happening?
- What is it about where this student comes from that leads him or her to respond to others the way he or she does?
- How might I investigate further the customs of this child's family? (p. 98)

EXAMPLE OF CONCEPT

"Retooling" to Improve Teacher–Student Relationships

Even teachers of color find they need to "retool" their practice when assigned to a classroom of culturally and linguistically diverse students. An African-American teacher who taught for many years in a predominantly white suburban school said, "When I first found myself teaching classes of mostly black kids, I went home frustrated every night because I knew I wasn't getting through to them, and they were giving me a hard time. It only started getting better when I finally figured out that I had to re-examine everything I was doing" (Howard, 2007, p. 17).

Classroom Organization

The typical organization of U.S. classrooms is that of a teacher-leader who gives assignments or demonstrates to the students, who act as audience. Teacher presentations are usually followed by some form of individual study. Learning is then assessed through recitation, quizzes, or some other performance. Small-group work, individual projects, or paired learning require distinct participation structures, ways of behaving and speaking. Learning how to behave in these settings may require explicit cultural adaptation. Many students new to U.S. classrooms have never before taken part in group problem solving, story retelling, or class discussion. Such activities entail social as well as linguistic challenges. Teachers can help students by providing clear instructions and ample models, by calling on more self-confident students first, and by assigning self-conscious students minor roles at first in order not to embarrass them.

The ability to ask for help when needed involves cultural norms and discourse competence. The common practice in teacher-directed classrooms is for students to bid to answer a teacher's question or for the teacher to call on a specific individual. Both procedures can be problematic for English learners, who may be reluctant to bring attention to themselves, either because they see such an action as incompatible with group cohesiveness and cultural norms or because they may be reluctant to display knowledge in front of others. Teachers who are sensitive to varying cultural styles organize other means for students to demonstrate language and content knowledge, and they act as observers and guides rather than directors or controllers of student activity.

EXAMPLE OF CONCEPT

Class Discussions

A Vietnamese student who moved to the United States describes his reaction to a class discussion:

> As a student in Vietnam, I learned not to ask questions, not to raise my hand, or to have much contact with the teacher. I listened, took notes, and memorized the material. The teacher was always right. Imagine my surprise when I entered a U.S. classroom and listened as my classmates talked, argued, and discussed! The teacher encouraged discussion and even listened to what the students had to say. This felt very different to me.

Source: Dresser (1993, p. 120).

The explicit cultural knowledge needed to function well in a classroom is evident when students first encounter school, in preschool or kindergarten. For the children in two communities studied by Heath (1983b), those from Roadville were able to comply with teachers' rules for various activity centers (block building, reading, playing with puzzles). They had learned in their homes to play only certain kinds of games in certain areas and to put away their toys when finished. Children from Trackton did not confine toys to specific areas but instead were creative and improvised new and flexible functions for the toys, often mixing items from different parts of the room. A puzzle piece that looked like a shovel, for example, was taken outside to the sandbox. As Heath points out:

> [These] children . . . were accustomed to playing with toys outdoors almost all of the time and they insisted on taking the school's "indoor toys" outside; at home, almost all their toys stayed outside, under the porch, or wherever they were left when play ended. Moreover, at home, they were accustomed to using toys for purposes they created, not necessarily those which the toy manufacturer had envisioned. (p. 275)

Thus, the differences in the home culture created differences in the way the students played at school. This, in turn, was noted by teachers as they formed judgments about which students were more academically capable than others.

Curriculum

Many aspects of the school curriculum are highly abstract and contain themes and activities for which many CLD students have little referent. Some teachers, rather than finding ways in which students can become familiar with academically challenging content, are quick to devise alternative activities of lower academic worth. Research on Alaska Native education suggests a number of abuses perpetrated in the name of "being sensitive to children's cultural backgrounds." Teachers often exempt Alaska Native students from standards applicable to other students. For example, they assign an essay on "Coming to the City from the Village" as a substitute for a research paper. They justify the lack of challenging courses with comments such as, "Well, they are going home to live in their village. What do they need algebra for anyway?" Too many lessons are created featuring stereotypic content (kayaks and caribou) that demonstrates a shallow cultural relevance (Kleinfeld, 1988).

Teachers who lack a solid foundation of cultural knowledge are often guilty of trivializing the cultural content of the curriculum. The sole cultural reference maybe to holidays or food, or they may have "ethnic" bulletin boards only during certain times of the year (e.g., Black History Month). People from cultures outside the United States are shown only in "traditional" dress and rural settings or, if they are people of color, are always shown as poor. Native Americans may be represented as peoples from the past. Moreover, students' cultures are misrepresented if pictures and books about Mexico, for example, are used to teach about Mexican Americans or books about Africa are used to teach about African Americans (Derman-Sparks and Anti-Bias Curriculum Task Force, 1988).

Avoiding bias means more than using "politically correct" terminology that does not incorporate prejudice. It also means protecting the authenticity of sources. Reese (2007) comments on the distortions often displayed when children are presented with literature about Native Americans: Indians are portrayed either as savages, or on the other extreme, as poetic, romantic figures with a message about living in harmony with the earth. Reese, a Pueblo Indian, calls for literature that reflects the

EXAMPLE OF CONCEPT

The Eurocentric Curriculum

What is a Eurocentric perspective, and why is that limiting for today's students? Because the United States began as a set of British colonies, many perspectives published even in contemporary textbooks reflect a European point of view. For example, in geography, Europe and the United States are centered side-by-side, with the rest of the world at the margins. Parts of the world are named according to their position relative to Europe, for example, the "Middle East" (Hernandez, 2001). World capitals are named in English rather than using their indigenous names ("Moscow" rather than "Moscova"). Students may become depressed when their native countries and regions play so small a role in the curricula and texts, and the world of information does not include their issues and perspectives.

heterogeneity of the Native-American experience in ways that counter culturally and historically inaccurate mythmaking. She offers valuable guidelines for evaluating and selecting Native-American literature for classroom use, especially featuring markers of cultural authenticity.

ADAPTED INSTRUCTION

Assessing Ethnic, Linguistic, and Gender Biases in the Curriculum

The following checklist can help teachers assess the extent to which ethnic, linguistic, and gender biases exist in the curriculum:

- What groups are represented in texts, discussion, and bulletin board displays? Are certain groups invisible?
- Are the roles of minorities and women presented in a separate manner from other content, isolated or treated as a distinct topic?
- Are minorities (and women) treated in a positive, diversified manner, or stereotyped into traditional or rigid roles?
- Are the problems faced by minorities presented in a realistic fashion, with a problem-solving orientation?
- Is the language used in the materials inclusive, or are biased terms used, such as masculine forms (*mankind, mailman*)?
- Does the curriculum foster appreciation of cultural diversity?
- Are experiences and activities other than those common to middle-class European-American culture included?

In her article "Educating Teachers for Cultural and Linguistic Diversity: A Model for All Teachers," Parla (1994) discussed issues related to the multicultural classroom and includes information on cultural sensitivity, linguistic diversity, and teaching strategies that can help teachers grow in their understanding of cultural issues and translate that understanding into classroom practice. The article can be found at www.ncela.gwu.edu/pubs/nysabe/vol9/model.htm.

SUSTAINING HIGH EXPECTATIONS FOR ALL STUDENTS

Jussim (1986) offered a general framework for the relationship between teacher expectations and student achievement. Teachers develop initial expectations based on a student's reputation, on previous classroom performance, or on stereotypes about racial, cultural, and linguistic groups. These expectations, which often resist change despite evidence to the contrary, form the basis for differential treatment of students and for the rationalization for such treatment. Students, in turn, react to this differential treatment in ways that confirm the teacher's expectations. Thus, teachers have a high degree of effect on student achievement: Student effort and persistence are shaped, in part, by students' perception of the teacher's expectations.

Teachers' expectations for student performance are culturally based, as are their criteria for evaluation. Pedagogical training can enable teachers to organize instruction that more accurately allows diverse students access to the curriculum.

Expecting high achievement from English learners and communicating these expectations require specific educational programs that draw attention to the hidden curriculum of the school, quality of interaction between teachers and students, diverse learning styles, the use of the community as a resource, and a commitment to democratic ideals in the classroom (Gollnick & Chinn, 2006). Overall, the effect of teacher expectations amounts to a continuous, de facto, day-to-day assessment of students' worth and capabilities.

Assessing Students' Ability and Achievement Validly

A major responsibility of the intercultural educator is to ensure that students' abilities are truly developed by instructional experiences. Many students' abilities are underestimated because their second-language skills do not adequately convey their talents. Sometimes unfamiliarity with the students' culture compounds the language barrier.

Challenging Students to Strive for Excellence as Defined by Their Potential

Teachers tread a fine line between expecting too much of their students, causing frustration on students' part through stress and overwork, and expecting too little by watering down the curriculum, leading to boredom and low academic achievement. Ongoing formative assessment, combined with a sensitive awareness of students' needs and a willingness to be flexible, helps the teacher to monitor and adjust the instructional level to students' abilities.

Teachers' behavior varies with the level of expectation held about the students. Students of whom much is expected are given more frequent cues and prompts to respond to, are asked more and harder questions, are given a longer time to respond, are encouraged to provide more elaborate answers, and are interrupted less often (Good & Brophy, 1984). Teachers tend to be encouraging toward students for whom they have high expectations. They smile at these students more often and show greater warmth through nonverbal responses such as leaning toward the students and nodding their heads as students speak (Woolfolk & Brooks, 1985). The online report *Expectations and Student Outcomes* (Cotton, 1989) is a useful resource in learning about how expectations are communicated to students.

Students' responses to teacher expectations seem to be highly influenced by cultural background and home discourse patterns. Some cultures encourage students to set internal standards of worth, and peer pressure devalues dependence on teachers for approval.

Motivating Students to Become Active Participants in Their Learning

Learner autonomy is a key element of constructivist learning—teachers help students to construct new knowledge, providing scaffolds between what students already know and what they need to learn. Learner autonomy occurs when learners feel that studying is taking place due to their own volition. This autonomy is the basis for self-managed, self-motivated instruction. Such autonomy must be supported in a systematic way by the teacher and curriculum in order for the learner to benefit.

Educators acknowledge that it is impossible to teach learners everything they need to know while they are in class. Therefore, a major aim of classroom instruction should be to equip learners with learning skills they can employ on their own. These include the following:

- Efficient learning strategies
- Identification of their preferred ways of learning
- Skills needed to negotiate the curriculum
- Encouragement to set their own learning objectives
- Support for learners to set realistic goals and time frames
- Skills in self-evaluation (Nunan, 1989, p. 3)

Student autonomy is at risk in the climate of coercive adherence to standardized test scores as the sole criterion of effective instruction. Certainly there is a place for choice in topics and freedom to voice divergent views as the core of democratic schooling (see Giroux & McLaren, 1996).

Encouraging Students to Think Critically

An important aspect of schooling in a democracy is the ability to think for oneself, analyze ideas, separate fact from opinion, support opinions from reading, make inferences, and solve problems. The ability to think critically can enhance self-understanding and help students approach significant issues in life with analytical skills. This includes critical thinking, preparing students to be problem solvers who can analyze, evaluate, synthesize, and design when offered real-life situations—students who can make connections between divergent ideas and face the world with compassion and empathy (Mintz & Yun, 1999). An organized introduction to this complex field, presenting lesson plans that have been remodeled to include critical thinking strategies, is available from www.criticalthinking .org/resources/articles under "Sample Teaching Strategies for K–12 Teachers."

Critical thinking includes the ability to look for underlying assumptions in statements, to detect bias, to identify illogical connections between ideas, and to recognize attempts to influence opinion by means of propaganda. These skills are fundamental to the clear thinking required of autonomous citizens in a democracy.

Helping Students Become Socially and Politically Conscious

"Sociocultural consciousness means understanding that one's way of thinking, behaving, and being is influenced by race, ethnicity, social class, and language" (Kea, Campbell-Whatley, & Richards, 2004, p. 4). Students as well as teachers need to have clarity of vision about their sociocultural identities and their role in the institutions that maintain social and economic distinctions based on social class and skin color.

Political and social consciousness is hard-won. It requires teachers to offer students a forum in which to discuss social and political events without partisan rancor; to investigate issues in the national and local press that have possible multiple perspectives; and to find a way to support students' voices about their lives and feelings. Bulletin boards on which student writing can be posted, weekly current event discussions, and class newsletters are projects that can encourage autonomous student thinking, writing, and discussion.

MARSHALING FAMILY AND COMMUNITY SUPPORT FOR SCHOOLING

Family and community involvement supports and encourages students and provides opportunities for families and educators to work together in educating students. Families need to become involved in different settings and at different levels of the educational process. Family members can help teachers to establish a genuine respect for their children and the strengths they bring to the classroom. They can work with their own children at home or serve on school committees. Collaborative involvement in school restructuring includes family and community members who help to set goals and allocate resources.

Parental involvement in the school is influenced by cultural beliefs. The U.S. system was developed from small, relatively homogeneous local schools with considerable community and parental control. The pattern of community and parental involvement continues today with school boards, PTAs, and parent volunteers in the schools. This pattern is not universal outside the United States. In cultures in which teachers are accorded high status, parents may consider it improper to discuss educational matters or bring up issues that concern their children. Many Asian-American parents, for example, have high expectations for their children's academic success, but are reluctant to become involved in the classroom, believing education is the responsibility of the school (Fuller & Olson, 1998).

Other factors that make family involvement difficult are school procedures such as restrictive scheduling for family–teacher conferences and notification to parents that students' siblings are not welcome at school for conferences and other events. These procedures tend to divide families and exclude parents. School staffs can involve the community by talking with parents and community liaisons to work out procedures that are compatible with cultural practices.

It is important that parents not be used in a compensatory manner or given the message that they need to work to bring their children "up" to the level of an idealized norm. This approach often makes parents feel that they are the cause of their children's failure in school. Attributing students' lack of success to parental failure does not recognize that the school itself may be the culprit by failing to meet students' needs.

EXAMPLE OF CONCEPT

A Parent Fosters Cultural Pride

One Chinese-American parent successfully intervened in a school situation to the benefit of her daughter and her classmates:

> After my daughter was teased by her peers because of her Chinese name, I gave a presentation to her class on the origin of Chinese names, the naming of children in China, and Chinese calligraphy. My daughter has had no more problems about her name. What is more, she no longer complains about her unusual name, and she is proud of her cultural heritage. (Yao, 1988, p. 224)

Whether parents are willing to come to school is largely dependent on their attitude toward school, a result in part of the parents' own school experiences. This attitude is also a result of the extent to which they are made welcome by the schools. Invitational barriers can exclude parents as well as students. On the other hand, teachers who are willing to reach out to parents and actively solicit information from them about their children and their hopes for their children's schooling are rewarded with a richer understanding of students' potential.

EXAMPLE OF CONCEPT

Cultural Differences in Parent Involvement

A major difference between Russian parents and those from other cultural groups is the assertive way in which Russian parents often approach classroom teachers to inquire about their children's academic progress. Russian parents also approach teachers even though they do not speak English very fluently. The children translate for them as they inquire about homework or progress in class (Gaitan, 2006, p. 60).

ADAPTED INSTRUCTION

Involving Parents as Cultural Mediators

Parents can act as cultural mediators in several ways:

- Establish an explicit open-door policy so parents will know they are welcome.
- Send written information home about classroom assignments and goals, and encourage parents to reply.
- Call parents periodically when things are going well and let them know when they can call you.
- Suggest specific ways parents can help in assignments.
- Get to know the community by visiting the community, and letting parents know when you are available to visit homes or talk at some other location.
- Arrange several parent conferences a year and let parents talk about their child's achievement.
- Solicit parents' views on education through a simple questionnaire, telephone interviews, or student or parent interviews.

Source: Adapted from Banks (2004).

EXAMPLE OF CONCEPT

Parent Training Sessions

Parents of kindergarten English learners at Lillian Elementary School in Los Angeles were invited to two Saturday workshops in October and two more in December, where they were taught by teachers how to help their children learn to recognize alphabet letters and learn sight words such as *here* and *the*.

In a math lesson, teacher Gloria Sigala urged parents to teach their children the concept of a pair, or circles, triangles, and rectangles. Even though many parents are immigrants who work long hours to support their families, educators are seeing that time parents spend helping their children pays off. Teachers say that the kindergarteners are more confident and attentive in class (Quinones, 2008).

Parents and older siblings can be encouraged to work with preschool and school-age children in a variety of activities. Rather than recommending that parents speak English more at home, teachers can encourage parents to verbalize in their home language with children in ways that build underlying cognitive skills. Parents can sit with the child to look at a book, pointing to pictures and asking questions; they can read a few lines and let the child fill in the rest or let the child retell a familiar story. Children can listen to adults discuss something or observe reading and writing in the primary language. Schools can assist communities with implementing literacy or cultural classes or producing a community primary-language newspaper. The school can also educate students and parents on the benefits of learning the home language of the parents and can find ways to make dual-language proficiency a means of gaining prestige at school.

EXAMPLE OF CONCEPT

Home and School Connection

Here one teacher describes the success of a nonfiction publishing party hosted by the students:

> Parents and many extended family members came, as did neighbors and youth organization leaders with whom the students were involved. At various places around the room, reports were visible with yellow comment sheets. Visitors could sit at a desk or table, read, and comment on what they had read.
>
> Language was not a barrier: Many parents encouraged their children to read to them in English and translate the stories into the native language. They were proud of the English that their child had learned and proud that the child remembered the native language well enough to translate. Many students encouraged their parents to try saying the name of the objects in the pictures that accompanied many of the reports in English. Everywhere I looked, I saw proud children beaming as they showed their work off to the people they cared about and who cared about them. (Cho Bassoff, 2004, para. 9 and 10)

This chapter has emphasized the important role that teachers can play in learning about their students' communities and cultures and in reducing the culture shock between home and school by working actively toward the creation of culturally responsive instruction. The best way for a teacher to understand culture is first to understand himself or herself and the extent to which mainstream U.S. cultural values are explicitly or implicitly enforced during instruction. A teacher who understands his or her own teaching and learning styles can then ask to what extent each student is similar or dissimilar. This goes a long way toward understanding individual differences.

An understanding of cultural diversity leads to engagement in the struggle for equity and then to a commitment to promoting educational achievement for all students. A variety of activities—ones that appeal to different students in turn—may be the most effective approach. The observation cycle continues as teachers watch students to see *which* approaches meet *whose* needs. The key for the intercultural educator is to be sensitive, flexible, and open.

LEARNING MORE

Further Reading

Order a catalog online from the multicultural literature source www.Shens.com. How many cross-cultural versions of the Cinderella story do they sell?

Web Search

Using a Webcrawler or a search engine, enter the terms *parent involvement* or *family–school connections*. Make a list of helpful suggestions from the most professional Websites on this topic.

Exploration

Ask several educators how they celebrate the birthday of Dr. Martin Luther King Jr. on the legal holiday of his birth. Find a commemoration in your area and attend. How does this stimulate you to follow the ideals of Dr. King?

Collaboration

View the movie *Stand and Deliver,* which is about the success of Jaime Escalante, the outstanding mathematics teacher at Garfield High School in Los Angeles. Watch the scene two or three times in which a grandmother comes to Escalante's house. Role-play with a friend the elaborate greeting ritual with which Mr. Escalante warmly welcomes the elderly woman. Discuss with a friend or classmate a form of greeting that might be appropriate for an elderly family member who visits a classroom.

PEARSON
myeducationlab
The Power of Classroom Practice
www.myeducationlab.com

The Importance of Culture

In this video, teachers and other English-learner education experts discuss the role of culture in the process of second language acquisition, especially as it plays out in classroom interactions among students and teachers. Various aspects of culture are highlighted, including what people do, think, and believe about what constitutes appropriate ways to interact in the classroom; cultural norms concerning the meaning of eye contact, gestures, and facial expressions; and how much distance to maintain from others during conversations. The importance of learning about and validating students' home cultures is emphasized.

To access the video, go to MyEducationLab (www.myeducationlab.com), choose the Díaz-Rico and Weed text, and log in to MyEducationLab for English Language Learners. Select the topic Diversity, and watch the video entitled "The Importance of Culture."

(continued)

Answer the following questions:

1. How would you define "culture"? Provide three examples of how it applies to classroom interactions and student learning.

2. The video emphasizes learning about and validating students' home cultures. Describe several ways you can modify instruction to better involve students' families and their resources.

3. In the video, mention is made of the friction and emotional stress that may occur when cultural norms are violated. Identify one specific cultural aspect that might be a source of friction or stress due to differences between home and school norms. How might you resolve the issue while at the same time respecting the home culture?

4. How can teachers promote tolerance by integrating home and school learning experiences? How can teachers solicit the help of parents as cultural mediators (see the section "Marshaling Family and Community Support for Schooling")?

CHAPTER 4

THE ROLE OF EDUCATORS IN LANGUAGE POLICY

Interacting with the community brings recognition to the student as well as the school.

The teacher had a new student who came from Ethiopia and spoke no English. She could not speak the student's language . . . but rather than allowing him to languish, she chose to allow him to teach the class enough of his native language so that they could all communicate a little bit. . . . The children got excited about discovering a new language. This led to the teacher doing a unit on Africa complete with a wall-size relief mural of the entire continent. The end result was that the Ethiopian student was treated as a valued part of the class. He was able to contribute the richness of his culture while learning about his new home.

—Yvonne and David Freeman (1998, p. 124)

Teachers have a significant influence over the daily lives of students in their classroom. They can actively create a climate of warmth and acceptance for culturally and linguistically diverse (CLD) learners, supporting the home language while fostering the growth of a second language. Conversely, they can allow policies of the school to benefit only the students whose language and culture are in the majority by, for example, condoning the exclusive use of the dominant language. This permits majority-language students to gain advantage at the expense of those students who speak minority languages. Teachers make policy day by day, by the actions they take in the classroom, by the professional commitments they honor, and by the stance they take on the importance of their students' primary languages.

Policies about language—and, to a lesser extent, about culture (lesser only because the cultural patterns of schooling are less obvious)—determine the organization and management of schooling. Such factors as class size, allocation of classrooms, availability of primary-language instruction, availability of support services for CLD learners, and funds for curricular materials are determined by policies that are made by decisions at the federal, state, local, or school level. The questions of *who makes policy* and *who influences policy* are important. Can teachers influence policy on a scale larger than their single classroom—on a schoolwide level, on a districtwide level, on the level of a community as a whole, on a statewide or national basis? Or are policy decisions too remote from the daily life of classrooms for teachers to be influential?

Policies can be formal and official, or they can be informal, such as efforts to create and manipulate attitudes toward languages and language variations (Corson, 1990). Both formal and informal policies have an impact on second-language teaching. Like it or not, teachers work under conditions that are highly affected by social and political conditions. Ideally, teachers' decisions further the academic success of English learners. If this is not the case, the academic future of these students is undermined or undone.

This chapter focuses on policy in language matters rather than on the more pervasive topic of cultural matters for two reasons. First, language policy is a current zone of contention for educators, and thus awareness in this area is urgent. Second, cultural patterns of schooling are more difficult to examine and, although equally important to the day-to-day lives of students and teachers alike, are not the subject of current controversy to the extent of such topics as bilingual education. However, the role of teachers in creating and executing policy in this area is also crucial.

A CRITICAL APPROACH TO LANGUAGE POLICY

Several sociologists and social philosophers who study language and society have urged a wider perspective on the social tensions that underlie arguments about the language(s) used in schooling. A critical perspective, one that looks at broad social issues of dual-language proficiency and language policy, has developed from the work of five theorists in particular: James Tollefson, Michel Foucault, Norman Fairclough, Pierre Bourdieu, and Jim Cummins.

Tollefson: Power and Inequality in Language Education

Tollefson (1995) has examined issues of language equity—the social policies and practices that lead to inequity for non-native language speakers—in various international contexts and laid the foundation for a worldwide vision of language equity issues. He contrasted two ways to study language behavior: *descriptive* and *evaluative* (Tollefson, 1991). A descriptive approach seeks to understand the relationship of language behavior and social participation. It examines such linguistic phenomena as *diglossia* (why low-status versus high-status language is used in various contexts); *code shifting* (why bilingual speakers choose one language over another in social contexts); *relations of dominance* (how language is used to establish and maintain social position); and *register shifts* (how the formality/informality of language shapes rules and norms of interaction).

An evaluative approach, on the other hand, looks at such language policy issues as efforts to *standardize* or *purify language,* attempts to *preserve* or *revive endangered languages,* and movements to *establish national languages* or *legislate language usage.* In these separate domains of inquiry, those who study language descriptively focus on language as it is actually used, and those who take an evaluative perspective describe shaping or changing language behavior.

Language diversity can be seen as a problem, as a right, or as a resource (Galindo, 1997; Ruíz, 1984). The view that dual-language proficiency is a *problem* that must be remedied is, at best, socially and economically shortsighted—and, at worst, the foundation for linguistic genocide (defined by Skutnabb-Kangas, 1993, as "systematic extermination of a minority language"; see also Skutnabb-Knagas, 2000). The position that language diversity is a *right* has been the basis for the court cases and congressional mandates that have created bilingual education; however, these movements have probably been successful because of the emphasis on transitional efforts, with bilingual education seen as a right that expires when a student makes the shift into English.

The idea that language diversity is a *resource,* that dual-language proficiency is a valuable asset, is gaining some adherents in the United States, particularly among those who do business with second-language populations in the United States and abroad. Unfortunately, current policy allows a young child's primary language to wither and die and then attempts to create foreign-language proficiency within a three-year high-school program. Many citizens maintain conversational proficiency in a primary language but do not attain a high level of cognitive academic proficiency either in the primary language or in English. The work of Tollefson and his colleagues (see Pennycook, 1994; Skutnabb-Kangas, 2000) has documented that fights for language equity have profound ramifications for social as well as economic policy on a worldwide basis.

Tollefson's work in providing a larger context for viewing the struggles of minority-language speakers is useful in policy settings in which an economic argument is made for English-only schooling (that English-only schooling furthers economic success for English learners). Ironically, English-only schooling will not be as valuable as dual-language proficiency—attaining advanced skills in more than one language—as the source of employment advancement for most job seekers in the coming global economy.

Foucault: The Power of Discursive Practices

Foucault, a twentieth-century social historian, traced the spread of power relations in the modern world, relations that are sustained by means of networks shaped largely by language practices. In several important treatises, Foucault outlined the links between power and language. He documented ways in which authorities have used language to repress, dominate, and disempower social groups in favor of social norms that are favorable to those in power; yet conversely, certain social groups have appropriated or acquired language practices that mimic those in power and thus have shaped power to their own ends. Foucault (1979, 1980) emphasized that the struggle for power is "a struggle for the control of discourses" (Corson, 1999, p. 15). In this same vein, Gramsci (1971) conceptualized social power as hegemonic; that is, people are influenced to follow invisible norms and forms of cultural power, even when it is not to their advantage to do so. Thus, the forms of power that benefit the dominant class influence and shape the behavior of subordinated classes, sometimes to their detriment.

Foucault's contribution to the study of language policy, although indirect, is profound. He has shown that language is not neutral; discursive practices are inseparable from the workings of power, and in fact are the direct vehicle for the circulation of power. Power, however, is neutral; it can be a creative force for those who use discourse masterfully, as well as a destructive force that excludes those without effective language practices.

Fairclough: Critical Language Analysis

Although Foucault laid the foundation for the study of the role of language in the workings of power, Fairclough (1989, 1997) has offered a structured means to analyze linguistic features of discourse in order to discover the power messages that are conveyed. Fairclough conceives of discourse as a nested set of boxes: first, the text itself that constitutes the message; second, the institutional influence on the message; and third, the social/cultural influence on the message. Any text, whether spoken or written, has features at these three levels. These levels constitute the power that the message carries. Fairclough's critical language analysis (CLA) offers tools to tease out the hidden messages of power in a discourse (Table 4.1).

Table 4.1 Fairclough's Critical Language Analysis

Box Level	Description	Questions to Ask
First (innermost)	Describe features of the text	In order to read the message "between the lines," ask the following:
		What is the style of writing, level of vocabulary, complexity of syntax, and tone of the message?
		What is assumed that the reader knows?
		What features of gendered language are noticeable?
		Who is responsible for the actions, opinions, or stance taken in the text?
		Where did the text originate?
		What interaction generated it?
		What is said?
		What is unsaid but implied?
		What is the tone of the message?
Second (middle layer)	Probes the institutional influence on the text	To interpret this influence, ask:
		What social group or agency (a school, television, schooling, friendship, etc.) supplied the context for the message?
		What was the institutional origin of the message?
		Who supplied the platform, the paper, the computer, or the microphone?
		Who stands to benefit from the message?
		How was the text influenced by an institution?
Third (outermost layer)	Examines the sociocultural context	What sociocultural factors came into play?
		How did society's attitudes/treatment of age, gender, culture influence the text?
		How might the text have been different had its origin been a person of different culture, gender, or age?
		What hidden messages can be understood about this message knowing its social origin?

Source: Adapted from Fairclough (1989).

CLA can be used to scrutinize a parent newsletter sent home from an elementary school to Spanish-speaking parents. The intent of the newsletter is to explain to parents how to help their child with homework:

- At the level of text, the newsletter appears to be a word-for-word translation of the reverse side, a letter to English-speaking parents. The text has been written on a word processor, in dual columns like a newspaper. There are no illustrations—merely a page full of text. The content has ten paragraphs, each explaining a different feature of "homework tips."
- At the institutional level, the sheet is part of a "School Open House" packet distributed with about six other papers, some of which are in Spanish and some of which are not. The text was written by an assistant principal and translated by an aide.

- At the sociocultural level, the text assumes that the parents welcome the advice of the school authorities and that the parents' role is to help the students complete the assignments sent home by the teachers. There is no mention of a role for parents as collaborating with the teacher to determine the worth or value of the assignments.

In contrast, another teacher works with students to write a "Homework Help" manual, a six-page "little book" composed by students themselves in cooperative groups. Each group decides on a title for their book and brainstorms the book's content. Will it include recommendations of a special place to study at home? Will it mention adequate lighting? Will it discuss how to deal with the distractions of television or of siblings? Will it advise students how to solicit help from parents? Will it advise parents how to communicate to teachers the comparative worth of different types of assignments? Will the book be in more than one language? Each group adds the ideas that the members choose. When the books are ready, the teacher asks each student to take the book home, discuss it with the family, and then come back to class with feedback about whether the suggestions are apt.

Examined with the analytical tools of CLA, these little books are a very different product from the parent newsletter previously described.

- At the level of text, this effort is an individual product, with personalized artwork, student-generated ideas, and student-generated language that is understandable to family members.
- At the institutional level, both the existing habits of the family and the needs of the school are respected, and communication between home and school is built into the project.
- At the sociocultural level, the student is positioned as a consultant on the family's habits and values, and family is positioned as a valued partner in teaching and learning.

Thus, CLA, a structured means of creating awareness of hidden levels of language, can be used to examine assumptions that lie beneath schooling practices. This awareness operates unconsciously but smoothly in skilled power players but is useful as a conscious tool for those who could benefit from an increased understanding of power, particularly as it operates at the institutional and sociocultural levels. As an analytic tool, it is simple yet easy enough to teach to children as they become aware of what is said—and not said—in discourse.

Bourdieu: Language as Social Capital

The French anthropologist Bourdieu considered language to be *cultural capital*—that is, a part of the social "goods" that people accumulate and use to assert power and social class advantage. In a capitalist society, those who are native speakers of a high-status language have cultural capital, whereas those who speak a lower-status language must work hard to overcome the lack of such capital. *Social capital* is a major form of cultural capital. Social capital for children in most middle-class families includes being provided transportation to public libraries, buying additional school-related materials, visiting museums, being given music or art lessons, traveling, having homework supervised, benefitting from tutors, attending school functions, and even moving into the best school districts (Chang, 2005).

Bourdieu (1977) emphasized that schools act as agents of an economic system to reproduce the existing distribution of capital. Schools permit the "haves" (those already possessing cultural capital) to succeed at the expense of the "have-nots," those who are comparatively lacking in the linguistic skills, prior knowledge, or other social resources to succeed. Education plays a key role in the determination of social success, and permits further understanding of the challenges faced by those whose language skills are not deemed of social importance.

The unique contribution of Bourdieu was his recognition that language, along with other intangible social factors, is an asset, as are physical resources. In a classroom, a teacher's predilection is to be attracted toward social capital—to those children who already appear to be successful—and to shun those who appear to lack this attraction. One might also deduce that a teacher's attention, admiration, and reinforcement are therefore aspects of a teacher's social capital that he or she can deploy at will. Bourdieu placed schooling, with its behaviors and practices, squarely in the center of the surrounding economic reality, with policies that act as currency—currency that functions every bit as powerfully as does hard cash.

Cummins: Language Policies as Emancipatory

Cummins (2001) clearly delineated educational practices that function as collaborative relations of power and set these against counterpractices that are coercive in nature. Cummins cautioned that children who enter schools in which diversity is *not* affirmed soon grasp that their "difference" is not honored but, rather, is suspect. If students are not encouraged to think critically, to reflect, and to solve problems, they are being submitted to a "transmission model" of pedagogy. The resulting sense of reduced worth undermines achievement. Pressuring students to conform, or to participate in schooling practices that are unfair or discriminatory, causes them to lose their identity as human beings: They are subjected to what Cummins (1989) called "identity eradication." To counteract this devaluation of students, teachers' and students' roles must be redefined.

Cummins thus took a critical pedagogy stance, in line with Paulo Freire's (1985) call for a liberating education of "transforming action," in which teachers are dedicated to social change. Unfortunately, many teachers are unaware of the power practices that either help students to develop or hinder them from developing a sense of control over their own lives. They are equally unaware of the ways in which spoken and unspoken language can circulate messages of dominance or subordination—features of institutional racism and disempowerment. Cummins's work, together with the work of other critical pedagogists, highlights the need for structural changes within schools that support positive attitudes, strong personal and social identities on the part of English learners, and academic success.

To summarize the contributions of the critical language theorists, power relations hidden within language issues are a characteristic of societies around the world. The tools of the social language critic work to clarify and reveal the covert power relations that language enables. Language is a chief vehicle for deploying power, whether constructively or destructively. The power potential of any message, verbal or nonverbal, can be systematically analyzed. Language is a kind of social asset, and schools are agencies through which language is used to benefit or to detract from the accrual of social wealth. Schooling practices can empower or disempower, depending on the language and cultural policies within the school.

FIND OUT MORE ABOUT . . .

Language Policy in the United States and the World

Language Policy
http://ourworld.compuserve.com/homepages/JWCRAWFORD/langpol.htm
> This article begins with a dictionary definition of language policy and then reviews language policy in the United States historically. The author, J. W. Crawford, ends the article with his opinion ("Today, in my view, the central question of U.S. language policy is how we should respond to demographic changes in ways that serve the national interest and uphold our democratic traditions") followed by three questions. The rest of the site provides links to issues in U.S. language policy and to articles and other sites that treat language policy.

Language Policies in Education: Critical Issues
www-writing.berkeley.edu/TESI-EJ/ej20/r11html
> This is an online review of the 2002 book edited by J. W. Tollefson. The initial chapters are described and the four articles that treat language education issues in Asia are examined. Because the book ranges the world, U.S. educators can view language policies in their schools from a broader perspective.

LANGUAGE POLICY: THE CLASSROOM

Teachers *can* influence language policy, and those who are experts on the education of English learners *should* be influential. If teachers do not influence policy, decisions will be made by others: by the force of popular opinion, by politicians, by bureaucrats, by demagogues. The influence of teachers will not be felt, however, by wishing or hoping. Teachers need to examine closely the possibilities that exist for influence on policy and then work hard to make this influence a reality. This influence can be wielded by teachers in different ways in various social and political arenas: by monitoring procedures and curricula within the classroom itself, at the school level, and at the level of the local school district; by encouraging support within the community; by working within state commissions and professional organizations; and by lobbying for federal policies that benefit English learners. As Villegas and Lucas (2007) note: "Teaching is an ethical activity, and teachers have an ethical obligation to help all students learn. To meet this obligation, teachers need to serve as advocates for their students, especially those who have been traditionally marginalized in schools" (p. 32).

Educational Equity in Everyday Practices

Equitable educational practices require discipline and vigilant self-observation on the part of classroom teachers (Tollefson, 1991). Practicing gender, socioeconomic, racial, and cultural equity means that males and females from minority and majority races and cultures, whether rich or poor, receive equal opportunity to participate, such as being given equally difficult questions to answer during class discussion, along with adequate verbal and nonverbal support.

Cultural equity calls for teachers to accept students' personalization of instruction; to use multicultural examples to illustrate points of instruction; to listen carefully to the stories and voices of the students from various cultures; and to tie together home and school for the benefit of the students. Issues of socioeconomic equity arise, for example, when assignments for at-home projects are evaluated more highly when they incorporate a wealth of resources that some families can provide and others cannot.

In a democratic classroom, even the teacher must not play an autocratic role, usurping the rights of others to be treated fairly and with respect. As Faltis and Coulter (2008) explain, students must be taught the interpersonal skills they need to solve problems that interfere with learning. In this way, the classroom functions smoothly and the focus is on learning.

Teachers must endeavor to extend the rich, close relationship of mentor and protégé to all students. Referrals to special education on the one hand, and to gifted or enriched instruction on the other, should not unfairly favor or target students of one gender, race, or culture. (If school site or district criteria result in de facto lack of equity in these areas, teachers may need to ask for a review of the criteria.) Practicing "everyday equity" ensures the possibility of equal opportunity for all. The following classroom policies promote inclusion for students:

- Teachers value the experiences of culturally different children.
- The primary language is seen as a worthy subject for instruction and as a means by which students can acquire knowledge.
- Classroom strategies guarantee boys and girls equal access to the teacher's attention.

Marshall and Oliva (2006) sum up the role of socially conscious educators:

School leaders sometimes do equity work when they implement equity-related policies. . . . Some go further, demanding better than the letter of the law, for example, by joining in political coalitions or in legal actions for school finance equity, for the preservation of bilingual programs, and the like. However, the activist, interventionist stance of social justice leadership goes even further, inspired not just by an intellectual ideal, but also by moral outrage at the unmet needs of students and a desire for a caring community where relationships matter. . . . Social justice leadership reconnects with emotional and idealistic stances. It supports leaders' . . . efforts to conceptualize and articulate models of leadership that incorporate democratic community engagement, spirituality and emotion, and caring and compassion. (pp. 7–8)

The Social Environment of the Classroom

Students come to school for social as well as academic reasons. School practices in noncurricular areas, such as discipline, and in extracurricular activities, such as school clubs, should be nondiscriminatory. These activities provide ways in which the school climate can foster or retard students' multicultural competence (Bennett, 2003). If the school climate is accepting of the linguistic and cultural identities of students, these identities will develop in ways that are consonant with an academic environment. If not, a resistance culture may develop that rejects schooling, with outcomes such as high dropout rates and high incidences of school vandalism. The formal and the hidden curriculum of a school need to be consistent with each other so that they support diversity and achievement. The social climate of the school can be one of acceptance for all students in the following ways:

- Culturally and linguistically diverse students are grouped heterogeneously.
- Children and staff learn about the cultural practices of the families represented in the school.
- Students can win prestige positions in extracurricular activities regardless of their ethnic or cultural background.
- Dress codes do not discriminate against some subcultures while allowing others to dress as they wish.
- School staff members (e.g., office personnel) are equally courteous to all students and visitors.

The Policies Embodied in Teachers' Plans

Teachers can be explicit about issues of equity and multicultural inclusion in planning yearly units and daily lessons. Teachers are responsible for obtaining materials that are nonbiased and promote positive role models from a variety of ethnic groups and for designing and planning instruction that makes success possible for all students (see Díaz-Rico, 1993). This responsibility cannot be transferred to other decision-making bodies. Materials are readily available that describe multicultural education (see Bennett, 2003; Harris, 1997; Nieto & Bode, 2008). Teachers can plan for culturally and linguistically fair instruction in the following ways:

- Students' interests and backgrounds are taken into consideration when planning instruction.
- Materials depict individuals of both genders and of various races and cultures in ways that suggest success.
- Materials for bilingual and multicultural instruction receive equitable share of budgeted resources.
- Daily plans include adequate time for development of primary-language skills.

POLICY AT THE SCHOOL LEVEL

An exemplary teacher's greatest contribution at the school site may be the positive outcomes evident throughout the school as that teacher's students provide leadership, goodwill, and academic models for other students. However, a school site can be the setting for scores of such students when school personnel take explicit roles in school-site decision making.

Collaboration with Colleagues

Schools can benefit greatly when teachers work together. Sharing resources, working together to plan instruction, and teaching with one another add insight and vitality to a job that is often isolating. It is vital that personal relations be established and maintained with all colleagues at a school site to ensure that the staff are not polarized along lines of cultural, linguistic, or philosophical differences. Decisions that are often made collaboratively are the following:

- Extra-duty assignments are adjusted for teachers who must translate letters sent home to parents or develop primary-language materials.

- Primary-language materials and other materials are freely shared among professional staff.
- Primary-language instructors are socially integrated with the mainstream staff.

School-Site Leadership

School authorities, particularly principals, can support ELD and bilingual instruction in many ways. Often, principals are the leading advocates for funding increases at the district level. Principals can work with teachers to configure classes and class sizes to the benefit of English learners. Appointing a lead or mentor teacher can help new teachers adjust to and meet the needs of English learners. Lead teachers may be able to develop professional presentations that showcase student abilities or program features. Districtwide principals' meetings or school board meetings may be venues where these presentations can be seen and heard. By communicating to others about students' abilities as well as innovative program structures for English learners, principals begin to develop a climate of acceptance for linguistic and cultural diversity. This can be accomplished in the following ways:

- Marking policies are monitored to ensure that all students have equal opportunity to receive high grades.
- Staff members who have expertise in English-language development or expertise in primary-language instruction are given time to be of assistance to other teachers.
- Teachers with English-language development or primary-language assignments are given an equal share of mentoring and supervisory assistance.
- Leaders in the school set an example of respect and encouragement for diverse language abilities and cultures within the school.

FIND OUT MORE ABOUT . . .

School-Site Leadership

Professional Development for Teachers in Culturally Diverse Schools
www.cal.org/resources/digest/profdvpt.html
> A digest that describes a set of necessary conditions concerning school and district policies in order for teachers to effectively teach second-language learners. In addition, it documents several schools that have successfully restructured their academic programs to include all students.

Leading for Diversity: How School Leaders Can Improve Interethnic Relations
www.cal.org/crede/pubs/edpractice/EPR7.htm
> A report based on case studies of twenty-one schools across the United States in which the leadership had taken proactive steps to improve relations between the varying student groups. It provides two sample dilemmas and discusses how to assess the school context, set priorities, and develop a plan.

The Academic Ambiance of the School

Schools that are noted for academic excellence attract community attention because of the success of their students and alumni. Academic competitions outside of schools are one way in which certain schools garner academic laurels and gain the reputation for an academic ambiance. The better examples of this type of competition tend to promote problem solving rather than simple recall skills. Competitions that require inventive thinking are also available, and the fact that these are less language dependent may be more attractive to English learners. Schools can foster an academic ambiance in a variety of ways:

- Teachers who sponsor academically oriented extracurricular activities are given extra pay, just as athletic coaches are.

- Funds are available for students to travel to intellectual competitions.
- Individuals from diverse cultural and linguistic backgrounds are actively solicited for teams that compete for academic awards.
- Some intellectual activities such as contests are held in the primary language.

Involving Parents/Families

Encouraging parents and families to participate in school activities is vital. The extra step of sending families letters, reports, and notices in their home language helps to build rapport and extend a welcome to the school. These language policies constitute the daily message that home languages are important and valued. Families can receive the message that they are valued in many ways:

- Representative family committees can advise and consent on practices that involve CLD students.
- Parents/guardians can use the school library to check out books with their children.
- School facilities can be made available for meetings of community groups.

EXAMPLE OF CONCEPT

Involving Families and Communities

A simple invitation invited families, school district employees, local businesses, and community members to Community Literacy Day at the new elementary school in town. Each individual was asked to bring a favorite book to share. A table of book choices was available with volunteers to help match volunteer, book, and grade level. The program was a huge success. Each classroom had several readers, and some visitors went to more than one class (Guth, 2002).

FIND OUT MORE ABOUT . . .

Parental Involvement

Parental Involvement: Title I, Part A
www.ed.gov/programs/titleiparta/parentinvguid.doc
> This guidance document from the U.S. Department of Education explains the parental involvement responsibilities of the state and local education agencies and the school under the No Child Left Behind legislation.

POLICY IN LOCAL SCHOOL DISTRICTS

The policies of local school districts are shaped by the values of the community. This may create frustration for teachers who feel that educational decisions are not in the hands of educators. On the other hand, teachers who take responsibility for helping to shape the community's beliefs and values may find that their leadership as teachers is very welcome.

Professional Growth and Service

Serving on district curriculum adoption committees is one way in which teachers can share and contribute their expertise. Teacher-led presentations to other teachers, staff, or community members are also important contributions. These activities deliver the message that teachers are knowledgeable and interested in the community at large. Consider the following ideas for teacher involvement:

- Teachers' opinions are consulted for materials purchased by school district and community libraries.
- Teachers participate in leadership training for English-language-development programs.

The School Board

Teachers are very much aware that school policies are determined by the beliefs of school board members as well as by legal precedents set by state and federal laws and court decisions. Part of the

FIND OUT MORE ABOUT . . .

Professional Development

Professional Development for Language Teachers
www.cal.org/resources/digest/0303diaz.html
This digest discusses professional development and lists six strategies for teachers to help them with their development.

advocacy position suggested by Cazden (1986) is the need for teachers to espouse and support appropriate program for English learners before local boards. In cooperation with parent groups, teachers can be effective in marshaling support for programs designed for language-minority groups. School board policies can be influenced in positive ways:

- Policy committees can place recommendations before the school board in a timely manner, with clear, concise, well-researched presentations.
- Frequent attendance at school board meetings sends the message that the meetings are monitored by those who support language-minority students' achievement.

COMMUNITY SUPPORT FOR ENGLISH LEARNERS

A supportive community offers a home for linguistic and cultural diversity. This support takes many forms: affirming variety in neighbors' lifestyles, patronizing minority businesses, fund-raising for college scholarships for English learners, and providing community services that are user-friendly for all.

The Public Forum

Communities accept other languages being spoken in the community if there is little fear of economic or political encroachment by immigrants. By supporting English learners and their rights, teachers can see that situations such as that which occurred in Monterey Park, California, do not recur. A Monterey Park city council member led a fight to halt the use of public funds for the purchase of Chinese-language books for the city's library. The criticism was that these books solely benefit the Chinese community. Those who supported the initiative did not recognize that the Chinese population has as much right to be supported by the government as any other group and that English-speaking Americans studying Chinese might benefit from these books (Dicker, 1992). In this case, local policy was being affected by the linguistic chauvinism of one community leader.

Policies of community agencies such as the library can be influenced by the following teacher-led activities:

- Librarians can file teachers' lesson plans in the library and make specific materials accessible to students.
- Teachers can justify to librarians the need for primary-language materials.
- Teachers can conduct classes open to parents in community arenas, including the library.
- Schools can work together with parents to encourage the use of community resources such as libraries.

Community Organizations

Service organizations are often run by community leaders who set the tone for the community and who are a source of employment for workers. Business leaders sometimes have strong ideas about education. They usually enjoy dialogue with professional educators and seek to be updated on current beliefs and practices. It is in this dialogue that professional educators need to present the foundation for current pedagogy. The leaders of community organizations want to help schools improve so that their children and their workers will be productive. Obtaining this help is easier when requests are concrete and the justification is strong. Ways in which community organizations can interact with schools include the following:

- Sending representatives to school career days to talk about the importance of more than one language in the workplace.
- Establishing partnerships with schools to support activities such as student internships, tutoring, and mentoring.
- Establishing partnerships with school districts to help finance language programs.

STATE COMMISSIONS AND PROFESSIONAL ORGANIZATIONS

Outside the immediate community, a larger community awaits. Statewide commissions or state boards of education are opportunities for teachers to be involved in writing statewide curricula, adopting textbooks, and serving on advisory boards. National professional organizations often have state counterparts. Joining Teachers of English to Speakers of Other Languages (TESOL) or the National Association for Bilingual Education (NABE) puts educators in contact with language development specialists nationally and internationally. These organizations' publications carry news from state affiliates, and newsletters from the state organizations carry news of local associations. If there is no local organization, why not start one?

The Voice of the Expert

Attending district or regional professional conferences is a beginning step toward developing one's own expertise on linguistic and cultural issues and teaching practices. Successful teachers may be able to join with colleagues to develop school-level or district-level presentations about a particular area of instruction. Reading articles in professional magazines and journals helps to develop particular expertise, as does advanced university course work. Some journals, such as TESOL's *Essential Teacher* (see www.tesol.org for submission guidelines), and publishers solicit publications from teachers. This is one way to share successful classroom practices.

Professional Leadership Roles

A career is developed over a lifetime. Expertise in particular areas continues to grow along with teaching experience. One can envision a more just and equitable society thirty years from now as today's new teachers reap the harvest of the support for linguistic and cultural diversity that they have promoted. Those who are willing to take responsibility within professional organizations by serving on committees, drafting proposals, attending meetings, calling members, stuffing envelopes, and other activities are those who can be called on to serve in leadership positions. Leadership roles can come in various forms:

- Mentors and other experienced teachers can invite beginning teachers to professional meetings so the organizations can benefit from fresh energy.
- Teachers can start a local affiliation of a national organization.

Legislation and Public Opinion

State and national legislators are responsive to popular opinion as expressed by letters of support and phone calls on controversial issues. Bilingual education and language issues often arouse strong emotions, perhaps because language itself is so closely connected to the soul of a person or because language policies affect the criteria for employment vital to economic survival and success in the United States (Heath, 1983a). Legislators need to hear from professionals in the field to balance the effect of those who perceive language and cultural diversity as a threat. The debate that takes place within a legislature brings to public attention the issues involved in any complex area of public life and allows a public forum for criticizing government policies (Jewell, 1976). The strong backing of professional organizations supports legislators who have the courage to promote dual-language education. Public policy can be supported in the following ways:

- Organizations can send subscriptions to professional magazines to legislative libraries.
- Teachers and parents can organize letter-writing campaigns and visit legislators personally to convey interest in language-minority issues.

INFLUENCING FEDERAL POLICIES

In countries where more than one language is spoken, rarely do these languages share an equal social status. Speakers of the dominant language are those who make social policy, including language policy. These policies can range from support for the subordinate language, to benign neglect, to overt language suppression. Decisions are primarily made on political and economic grounds and reflect the values of those in political power (Bratt Paulston, 1992). Citizens have a duty to affect these policies.

Federal Funds for Innovation

The U.S. Department of Education provides billions of dollars in grants to states and school districts to improve elementary and secondary schools. With the help of these monies, numerous schools have restructured using dual-language and other enrichment models that actively engage CLD and mainstream students.

Notices about competitions for funds and special programs are usually available from state and county offices of education. By working with district grant specialists, teachers can write successful grant proposals. Individuals who have competed successfully for funding may be willing to offer workshops for others to increase the general expertise in such areas.

Federal Legislation

Programs such as Title III of the No Child Left Behind Act originate in Congress. Part of the Elementary and Secondary Education Act, this legislation must be reauthorized periodically. At such intervals, public opinion plays a large role in determining the continuation of programs that benefit English learners. When bills are introduced that commit federal funds on a large scale to minorities, conservative forces within Congress often target these programs for extinction. At these times, lobbying efforts are needed to communicate the need for these programs.

- Teachers can request that professional organizations send cards and letters to congressional representatives.
- E-mail campaigns can bring critical aspects of pending legislation to the attention of congressional leaders.

The National Spirit

A national spirit is created in part by individuals who voice their opinions freely. A national magazine, for example, offers a platform to writers whose opinions can be influential. Teachers need to exercise their writing skills frequently and at length in order to participate in national arguments that are rehearsed in the media.

Controversial actions and media figures also shape the national spirit. When demagogues arise who voice reactionary or incendiary viewpoints, the population at large must take steps to defuse their voices. Letters to national networks voicing opposition to and distaste for antiminority or racist viewpoints, for example, are necessary in order that these media do not glorify controversial figures and give them undue voice. The United States operates on a system of checks and balances. Those who oppose racism or bigotry must speak up and must speak as loudly as the voices of separation

FIND OUT MORE ABOUT . . .

Grant Proposals and Exemplary Programs

U.S. Department of Education
www.ed.gov/fund/landing.jhtml
> Provides links to sites that answer questions about the grant process, enables a search of the Department of Education's programs by topic (for example, English Language Acquisition), and makes available application packages along with information about deadlines and contacts.

School Reform and Student Diversity: Case Studies of Exemplary Practices for LEP Students
www.ncela.gwu.edu/pubs/schoolreform
> This article describes programs in eight schools that "have created exemplary learning environments for language-minority students who have limited English proficiency" (Introduction, para. 4). All of them combine LEP program features with more general restructuring.

and intolerance. Often, teachers of English learners must become advocates for their concerns until the voices of the minority community become skilled enough to speak for themselves and powerful enough to be heard. Teachers who share the culture and language of the minority community have a natural function as community leaders.

- Teachers can make policymakers aware of the need for workers proficient in more than one language.
- With school administrators, teachers can generate community support to advocate for programs for CLD students.

In a nation consisting of more than 300 million people, the majority of whom share English as the language of daily interchange, the language skills and rights of minorities are a fragile resource. Social and political forces on a national scale may seem overwhelming. Indeed, as much as individualism is a part of the national mythology of the United States, by working together with colleagues and district personnel, by joining and becoming leaders in professional organizations, teachers can exert national influence for constructive change in the education of CLD learners. This constructive change is possible at every level from the national to the local by the use of appropriate professional activities.

At the classroom level where teachers are most comfortable, language policy means creating an educational and social climate that makes school a place where all students are comfortable, where all students meet success in learning. The days are past when the failure of large numbers of CLD learners can be blamed on students' personal shortcomings or supposed deficiencies in family background. When students fail to learn, schools and teachers have failed.

If teachers are willing to step outside the confines of the classroom to help students be successful, then it is time to learn how to influence policy on a larger scale. The belief that teachers have no role in language planning and language politics is a denial of professional responsibility, an abdication of authority. A teacher who believes in the potential for success of CLD learners is in a strong position to fight for the recognition of their rights and the allocation of resources that make educational success possible.

LEARNING MORE

Further Reading

Rebecca Freeman's (2004) *Building on Community Bilingualism* demonstrates how schools that serve bilingual communities can promote English-language development, academic achievement, *and* expertise in other languages. Through an ethnographic account of bilingualism and education in the Puerto Rican community in Philadelphia, she shows how individual teachers and teams of educators have organized their policies, programs, and practices to promote bilingualism through schooling on the local school and school district levels. The book concludes by outlining how educators working in other contexts can develop language policies, programs, and practices that address the needs of the students and communities they serve.

Web Search

The Center for Applied Linguistics' Website (www.cal.org) provides several links to other organizations that deal with public policy and language issues (go to www.cal.org/links/policy.html). In addition, several language policy and planning digests provide insights into what teachers can do (www.cal.org/resources/digest/subject.html).

Exploration

The case studies of the eight exemplary schools in the School Reform and Student Diversity document (www.ncela.gwu.edu/pubs/schoolreform) are divided into the following sections: school and community context; learning environment; curriculum and instructional strategies; program for LEP students; school structure; and district support. Choose one of these areas and examine your school and district according to the model from the article.

Collaboration

Based on your exploration, work with colleagues and your administration to implement some of your findings. Conversely, collaborate with your district grant specialist to work on funding for a program at your site.

Community Support for Culturally Diverse Students and Families

In this video, Christine Slater expresses the need for pre-service teachers to bridge the gap between the school and the community. She discusses the importance of understanding the implications of a network of adults who are associated with each child.

> To access the video, go to MyEducationLab (www.myeducationlab.com), choose the Díaz-Rico and Weed text, and log in to MyEducationLab for English Language Learners. Select the topic Diversity, and watch the video entitled "Community Support for Culturally Diverse Students and Families."

Answer the following questions:

1. It is often a preconceived notion for teachers that mothers and fathers are the only adults in contact with their students. Explain how a community can provide a network of adults that provide support for children.
2. In what ways does the support community impact academic achievement for children learning English as a second language?
3. How can a teacher help to align community and schooling in a more coherent way?

CHAPTER 5

CULTURALLY AND LINGUISTICALLY DIVERSE LEARNERS AND SPECIAL EDUCATION

English learners who are blind can achieve communicative competence by interacting with mainstream peers.

Srinivasa Ramanujan was born in 1887 in Erode, a town in southern India. . . . At the age of fifteen, he obtained a copy of Carr's *Synopsis of Elementary Results in Pure and Applied Mathematics,* a collection of 6,000 mathematical theorems. By himself, he verified the results of the 6,000 theorems and began to develop his own. . . . Through private correspondence with a leading mathematician of the time, he obtained a position as a visiting scholar at Cambridge. . . . He published brilliant papers in English and European journals and became the first Indian elected to the Royal Society of London. He died at the age of thirty-three from tuberculosis he contracted in London. . . . [H]e is recognized by mathematicians as one of the most phenomenal geniuses of all time. . . .

If [Ramanujan] had been in a U.S. school as an English learner, would his teacher have referred him to education designated for the gifted and talented?

—James R. Newman (1956)

Culturally and linguistically diverse (CLD) learners, as any other cross-section of today's learners, may need special education services. Often, mainstream classroom teachers find themselves responsible for teaching students with special education needs who also need to acquire English. A consultation model introduces constructive ways for teachers of CLD learners and other certified personnel to collaborate in order to meet the needs of such special learners.

> Given the rapid demographic changes that have occurred in schools, communities, and workplaces, a major concern in the field of special education and rehabilitation today is the provision of effective services to multilingual/multicultural diverse populations. . . . [C]hildren and youth of these diverse groups will form a major part of the future workforce in this country. Therefore, the services provided in schools as well as in rehabilitation play an important role in strengthening this workforce for our society. (Chang, 2005)

This chapter includes such topics as identifying CLD learners with special instructional needs, teaming with resource or special education teachers, and teaching strategies for inclusion. The emphasis will be on students who need additional instructional mediation, because those students' needs tend to surface in an obvious way. However, similar principles—if not strategies—can be applied to CLD learners who are gifted and talented.

Researchers who have looked at the special education services available to English learners (e.g., Baca & Cervantes, 1984; Figueroa, 1993; González, 1994) have found a host of issues, including cultural differences as well as language issues.

Both special education and special education–CLD learner interface have come under attack from those who criticize the current models of service delivery. Sleeter (1986) believed that the process that labels certain students as "handicapped" without a critical look at the social and cultural conditions of regular schooling needed to be examined. Stainback and Stainback (1984) advocated that special education and regular education be merged and that all students receive individualized education. Others (Artiles & Trent, 1994; Bernstein, 1989; Figueroa, Fradd, & Correa, 1989) have addressed the over- or underrepresentation of CLD students in special education. Few believe, however, that the current special education system, including the treatment of CLD learners within that system, will undergo vast systemic reform in the near future.

Jesness (2004) outlines the complexity of the situation when special education and ELD are mixed: "Placing learning disabled children in classes designed for English learners is as unethical and harmful as placing English learners in classes meant to serve the learning disabled and mentally challenged" (p. 82). Certainly those who have been educated in English for only a short time deserve an adequate period of adjustment. However, the Individuals with Disabilities Education Act (IDEA) specifically allows referral and placement for English learners and young children with developmental delays, which may include language acquisition.

In their call for a restructuring of bilingual special education, Baca and de Valenzuela (1994) offered three primary goals: (1) Classrooms should conform to the needs of students rather than students conforming to the classroom; (2) efforts should be made to increase the academic performance of CLD special education students; and (3) teachers should be actively involved throughout the assessment process, with assessment-based curricular adaptations becoming a major part of the intervention process before a student is referred for special education services, and a diagnostic teaching model put in place instead of a remedial approach. These goals provide a direction for the efforts to augment and improve the overall delivery of education to CLD learners. But first, who are these learners? What educational and policy issues does their education raise?

SCENARIOS AND ISSUES

The issues surrounding culture, learning, and second-language acquisition are complex. The needs of many students can be addressed only with the aid of careful diagnostic work and documentation of student progress. However, many cases involve similar situations and evoke consistent fundamental questions.

Who Are CLD Learners with Special Needs?

Because of the complexity of the issues that underlie special educational services for CLD learners, both personal and academic, it is helpful to personalize these issues with cases drawn from the field. Each scenario does not represent any student in particular but rather a composite of several students created from similar circumstances.

Elisa's Memory. Elisa's third-grade teacher, Stephanie Robinson, is wondering if Elisa has a memory problem. She did not attend kindergarten, and in first grade the instruction was primarily in Spanish. In second grade, the only class taught in English was social studies. Now that she is being asked to learn to read in English, Elisa doesn't seem to remember words that she has read before. When she reads aloud, she can decode most new words adequately but acts as though each word is new each time—there is little sense of recognition or increase in comprehension when she reencounters a word. Mrs. Robinson is just about to make a referral to special education. Does she have adequate grounds for referral?

Losing ELD Services after Referral. Alsumana comes from a family that recently emigrated from Papua New Guinea. His mainstream classroom teacher has successfully made a case for referral to testing, but Ron Patton, his pull-out ELD teacher, is not supportive of this referral because in the past, when a student was placed into a special education environment, that student lost access to ELD services. Because, in Ron's opinion, success in school ultimately depends on the child's acquisition of English, he would like to ensure that CLD learners are not deprived of any other services that would help them. How can he remain involved if Alsumana is placed in special education?

Conflict over Referral. Mrs. Espinoza, the fourth-grade classroom teacher, is struggling with Luke. Luke's parents emigrated from Romania and settled in a rural area in the school district. Luke attends school only reluctantly and says that he would rather be working with his father outdoors. Mrs. Espinoza insists his poor performance in school is due to his attitude toward schooling and not to a learning disability. The school social worker, however, has advocated all year for Luke to be referred for a special education evaluation. During this time, he has made little academic progress. Should he be referred to special education?

Social and Emotional Adjustment. New arrivals are "fresh meat" for the gangs in the area around Bud Kaylor's elementary school. Bud has taught ELD and fifth grade for six years, and although he finds rewards in the challenges of an urban school, he sees the fear and threats that students experience outside the school environment as detrimental to their learning. One student, José Luis, seems overcome by fear in the school setting and never speaks a word. Bud feels that psychological counseling could be a way to deal with the social and emotional problems José Luis seems to be experiencing. Should he refer José Luis for help?

Sonia Doesn't Read. Fifth-grader Sonia is a native-Spanish speaker from the Dominican Republic. She did not attend school until the second grade. She was taught to read in Spanish, but now that she does not have access to Spanish reading instruction, she is falling behind. She attends a resource program, but the resource teacher sees that the problems that show up in English (poor oral language, limited vocabulary development, difficulties with writing, and poor comprehension) limit Sonia's progress. Should Sonia be referred to special education?

Tran the Troubled. Tran is a new student in the fourth grade. His family lives a fairly isolated life in a community of immigrants from Vietnam, but his parents want Tran to grow up speaking English, so they speak to his sister and him in English. However, because the parents both work, they leave Tran for long periods with his grandmother, who speaks only Vietnamese. Tran acts like a dual personality. In class, his performance is uneven; he does not volunteer and does not complete work, yet he seeks constant attention and approval from his teacher. On the playground, his teacher sees in Tran a quick intelligence that comes out when he interacts with the other boys. The teacher is

Table 5.1   Scenarios and Issues in Special Educational Services for English Learners

Scenario	Issues
Elisa's Memory. Does Elisa, a third-grade student who demonstrates low English reading skills, have a memory problem connected with a learning disability?	At what point is a learning problem considered a language-acquisition delay and not a learning disability?
Losing ELD Services after Referral. Will Alsumana, a recent immigrant, be deprived of ELD services if he is placed in special education?	Should ELD services be available to special education students?
Conflict over Referral. Does Luke's poor performance in school indicate a learning disability, or is it due to his low academic motivation?	What role do family attitudes and values play in the issue of special education referral?
Social and Emotional Adjustment. Should his teacher refer José Luis to psychological counseling to deal with his social and emotional problems in an urban school?	What is the role of psychological counseling in second-language acquisition?
Sonia Doesn't Read. Should Sonia, a fifth-grader with limited prior schooling experience and low English skills, be referred to special education?	What is the role of special education for immigrant students with little prior literacy experience?
Tran the Troubled. Tran's quick intelligence shines on the playground but not in the classroom. Is he learning disabled?	What role does cultural difference play in a case in which a student has classroom learning problems?

unsure how to handle Tran; he may have a learning disability, but his school problems may be due to extreme cultural differences between home and school. Does she have adequate grounds for referral for psychological testing?

Issues Underlying the Scenarios

Each of these scenarios reflects a particular aspect of the relationship between three distinct domains—learning, second-language acquisition, and special education services in the schools—and these domains are set in a background of cultural issues. Table 5.1 outlines the relationships between the scenarios and underlying issues.

These scenarios and the issues surrounding the education of CLD learners are centered on two basic questions: How can these students' language acquisition, cultural adjustment, and emotional/motivational difficulties be distinguished from learning problems? And how can these issues best be addressed? Special education–CLD learner issues are complex, yet a central dilemma focuses the essential debate: How can a school district avoid inappropriate referrals and placements yet ensure access for CLD learners who are learning disabled? The ELD–special education interface brings with it a set of collaboration issues. What is the role of the ESL specialist (or the CLAD teacher) in referral, assessment, and subsequent services to students who may be placed in special education?

PRINCIPLES FOR THE EDUCATION OF CLD–SPECIAL EDUCATION STUDENTS

Several basic principles characterize fair and effective processes for determining the educational services appropriate for the CLD learner who may be experiencing learning difficulties. These principles may be used to guide initial identification and early intervention, diagnostic evaluation and testing, and, if necessary, placement in a special education learning environment. The principles address five

Table 5.2 Principles for the Education of English-Learning Special Education Students

Domain	Principle
Responsibility of students for learning	English learners need to become self-responsible, active students who know how to learn. They need linguistic and nonlinguistic strategies, including metalinguistic and metacognitive, that may be generalizable across learning contexts.
Students' need for self-knowledge	Students need to understand their own learning styles and preferences, as well as discover their intrapersonal strengths and weaknesses in a variety of areas, including both linguistic and nonlinguistic (logical-mathematical, musical, and spatial) domains.
Goals for instruction	Students need meaningful and relevant language and academic goals that promote effective communication and learning, in social as well as academic domains.
Relationship of educational services to mainstream instruction	Any education setting must provide educational content and approaches that facilitate students' abilities to make smooth transitions to mainstream instruction.
Need for informed decision making	Educational decisions concerning CLD learners should involve ELD specialists, parents, and other professionals making collaborative, informed judgments that are based on a thorough, fair assessment of the child's language acquisition stage, culture, and individual needs and talents.

Source: Adapted from Wallach and Miller (1988).

domains: the responsibility of students for learning, students' need for self-knowledge, goals for instruction, relationship of educational services to mainstream instruction, and the need for informed decision making. Table 5.2 presents each of these five domains and its accompanying principle.

THE DISPROPORTIONATE REPRESENTATION OF CULTURALLY AND LINGUISTICALLY DIVERSE CHILDREN IN SPECIAL EDUCATION

The Individual with Disabilities Education Act (IDEA) entitles all individuals with disabilities to a free, appropriate public education (FAPE) and mandates nondiscriminatory assessment, identification, and placement of children with disabilities. The law stipulates that children not be labeled "disabled" if their poor school achievement is due to ethnic, linguistic, or racial difference. Currently, the assessment and placement of CLD students have become major issues in special education (Burnette, 2000), including overidentification (i.e., students are classified into a disability category when they do not have genuine disabilities); underidentification (i.e., students' disabilities are overlooked and not addressed in their educational programs); and misidentification (i.e., students' disabilities are assigned to inappropriate disability categories) (Brusca-Vega, 2002).

Overrepresentation in Disability Programs

In the United States, some ethnic groups continue to be overrepresented in programs for those who are mildly mentally retarded (MMR) or seriously emotionally disturbed (SED). Overrepresentation of CLD learners in MMR programs was the basis for litigation in a number of court cases in the 1970s.

The cases addressed the lack of due-process procedural safeguards, improper intelligence testing in the student's second language, and inadequate training of evaluators and special educators, resulting in mandated remedies in these areas (Coutinho & Oswald, 2004).

If the proportion of special education students of a given ethnic background exceeds the proportion of this group in the general population, then overrepresentation is a problem because the educational treatment that students receive is not equivalent to that received by the general student population (Macmillan & Reschly, 1998); because disproportionate placement in special education settings can segregate students by race; and because being labeled as a special education student has potentially negative effects on students' self-esteem and on teachers' perception of students (Valles, 1998).

Although the court cases of the 1970s helped to reduce the number of CLD students being sent into special education classes, recent expansion of disability categories to include mild learning disabilities and developmental delays has resulted in an increase in the number of bilingual students being served in remedial education classes (Connor & Boskin, 2001). Some researchers have cautioned that aptitude (or lack of it) is a cultural construction—cultural groups differ in what is considered a disability. For example, when students do not use expected classroom discourse rules, the teacher may judge them to be disabled.

EXAMPLE OF CONCEPT

Misunderstanding Is Construed as Disability

Mrs. Patterson asked a "known-answer" question to the class to see who had read the science pages assigned as homework. "Who can tell me, in what system is 100 degrees the boiling point of water?" Mario looked down, but Mrs. Patterson was eager to have him participate. "Mario?" she asked. Mario looked up and squinted. "Metr?" he answered softly. Mrs. Patterson shook her head and asked, "Who can help Mario? Is it Fahrenheit or centigrade?" (She thought sadly, *Mario never knows the answer. Maybe he has a learning disability.* But Mario thought, puzzled, *What was wrong with "metric"?*)

Underrepresentation in Gifted Programs

Conversely, CLD students are underrepresented in gifted education with the exception of Asian-American students, who are overrepresented in proportion to the general population in the United States. According to Ryan (2008), African-American, Latino, and Native-American students have been historically underrepresented in gifted programs. These students may be underrepresented by as much as 30 to 70 percent (p. 53). Ford (1998) suggested that the issue of underrepresentation of Hispanic and African-American students is compounded by several problems: the widely differing definitions of *gifted* across the school districts of the United States, the inadequacy of relying solely on standardized tests for admission to such programs, the lack of training on the part of teachers to recognize diverse talents as they nominate students, the confusing nature of the nomination process for minority parents, the lack of self-nomination on the part of minority students, lack of diversity on the part of selection panels, and inadequate training of assessment personnel who act as gatekeepers for gifted programs. The following list provides recommended remediation for underrepresentation (Ford, 1998):

- Use valid identification instruments (for example, Raven's Matrices instead of the Wechsler Scale for Children–Revised).
- Collect multiple types of information from various sources (including both descriptive and quantitative data).
- Provide support services prior to identification (such as help with study skills and time management).

- Train teachers and school personnel on culturally derived learning styles.
- Increase family involvement in identification and support.
- Increase awareness of research on giftedness in minorities.

Identification, Referral, and Early Intervention

Classroom teachers, along with parents and other school-site personnel, are responsible for identifying CLD learners with special instructional needs. When a classroom teacher initially identifies a student who may need additional mediation, a phase of intensive focus begins that may, or may not, result in a placement in special education.

Typically, the most common reasons for referral to special education for English learners are the "high-incidence" diagnoses: learning disability (LD), mild cognitive delays, speech and language delays and disorders, attention-deficit/hyperactivity disorder (ADHD), and/or emotional or behavior disorders (EBD; De la Paz, 2007). However, lack of understanding of cultural and language issues has led some educators to be overly cautious about referring English learners for special education services (Echevarria & Graves, 2007).

The Referral Process: The Roles of the Classroom Teacher and the ELD Specialist

The School Screen Team or otherwise-named entity is a school-site committee that bears responsibility for receiving and acting on an initial referral by the classroom teacher for a student who is in need of additional mediation in learning. The team not only reviews the classroom teacher's specific concerns about the student but also makes suggestions for modifying the learning environment for the student within the regular classroom and provides guidance, training, and assistance in implementing *initial interventions* that may prove helpful in educating the student in question.

How can the classroom teacher decide if a student might have a disability requiring referral to special education? Friend and Bursuck (2006) offered these questions to assist in the decision-making process:

- What are specific examples of a student's needs that are as yet unmet in the regular classroom?
- Is there a chronic pattern that negatively affects learning? Or, conversely, does the difficulty follow no clear pattern?
- Is the student's unmet need becoming more serious as time passes?
- Is the student's functioning significantly different from that of classmates?
- Do you discover that you cannot find a pattern?

One last consideration is the discrepancy between the student's performance in the first and second languages. If the problem does not occur when the child receives instruction in the primary language, it is likely that the situation has resulted from second-language acquisition rather than from a learning disability.

After receiving a referral from the classroom teacher, the school ELD or bilingual specialist, as a member of the team, may be asked to fill out a data sheet containing test data, school history, language preferences, and other information about the student. Thus, this person plays an important role in investigating the following aspects of the CLD learner's case.

Background Experience and Previous School Settings. Does the student have a previous history of difficulty? In this case, contacting a previous teacher and checking records from previously attended schools can provide important background information. A file containing the history of special education services, if it exists, is not routinely transferred with a student unless specifically requested by the receiving school personnel.

Response to the Classroom Environment. Does the student seem uncomfortable or unaccustomed to a classroom environment? A history of previous schooling may uncover evidence of little or no prior schooling.

Cultural and Linguistic Background. The home language survey given on entering a school should properly identify the home language. If the home culture of the CLD learner is new to the classroom teacher, it may be useful to perform an ethnographic study of that culture.

Level of Acculturation. Contacting parents to determine the degree of acculturative stress that the family of the student is experiencing can provide important insights. Observing the student interacting with other students, staff, and parents in the home, school, and community can help the specialist identify possible acculturation problems.

Learning Styles. Observation of the student across a variety of academic tasks and content areas may show the need for curricular interventions that provide instructional variety.

Physical Health. The school nurse may provide or obtain a student's health record and developmental history, as well as a record of vision and hearing examinations and determination of overall physical health and diet.

Academic and Learning Problems That CLD Learners May Experience

CLD learners and students with learning disabilities may experience similar difficulties. This creates a challenge to determine whether a learning impairment is due to the students' second-language-acquisition process or to an underlying learning disability that warrants a special education placement. Gopaul-McNicol and Thomas-Presswood (1998) noted the following possible characteristics of CLD learners that may overlap with those of students with learning disabilities.

- *Discrepancies between verbal and nonverbal learning.* Exposure to enriching and meaningful linguistic experiences and activities may have been limited in a student's culture. Nonetheless, the student may have skills in nonlinguistic domains.
- *Perceptual disorders.* If a CLD student's home language is nonalphabetic, he or she may have difficulty with alphabetic letters. If a student was not literate in L1, he or she may have difficulty with sound–symbol relationships.
- *Language disorders.* A student may experience difficulty processing language, following directions, and understanding complex language.
- *Metacognitive deficits.* CLD learners without CALP may process information slowly. If from a nonliterate background, the student may lack preliteracy behaviors and strategies, such as regulatory mechanisms (planning, evaluating, monitoring, and remediating difficulties), or not know when to ask for help.
- *Memory difficulties.* Lack of transfer between the first and second language or limited information retention in the second language may be present.
- *Motor disorders.* Cultural differences and lack of previous education can influence motor performance such as graphomotor (pencil) skills.
- *Social–emotional functioning.* CLD learners may experience academic frustration and low self-esteem. This may lead to self-defeating behaviors such as learned helplessness. Limited second-language skills may influence social skills, friendships, and teacher–student relationships.
- *Difficulty attending and focusing.* CLD learners may exhibit behavior such as distractibility, short attention span, impulsivity, or high motor level (e.g., finger tapping, excessive talking, fidgeting, inability to remain seated). These may stem from cognitive overload when immersed in a second language for a long period of time.
- *Culture/language shock.* Students experiencing culture or language shock may show uneven performance, not volunteer, not complete work, or seek constant attention and approval from the teacher. The emotional reactions to long-term acculturation stress may lead to withdrawal, anger, or a pervasive sense of sadness.
- *Reading dysfunctions.* CLD learners may exhibit a variety of reading problems. These problems may include slow rate of oral or silent reading (using excessive lip movement or vocalization in silent reading); short perceptual span (reading word by word rather than in phrases);

mispronunciation, omission, insertion, substitutions, reversals, or repetition of words or groups of words in oral reading; lack of comprehension; and inability to remember what has been read.

- *Written expression skill deficits.* Writing may present an additional area of difficulty for CLD learners, at the level of grammar and usage or at the level of content. Teachers often judge writing as "poor" if it lacks the following characteristics: variety in sentence patterns; variety in vocabulary (choosing correct words and using synonyms); coherent structure in paragraphs and themes; control over usage, such as punctuation, capitalization, and spelling; and evidence that the writer can detect and correct his or her own errors.

One cannot expect a newcomer to English to demonstrate proficiency in these skills immediately. Some writing skills may not be a part of the student's native culture, and thus acquiring these requires acculturation as well as second-language acquisition.

Similarities between Ethnic Language Variations and Learning Disability Symptoms

A systematic analysis of three sets of language users (native-English speakers, CLD learners, and students with learning disabilities) reveals similarities in abilities and dysfunctions between CLD learners and students who are learning disabled. This overlap in language characteristics highlights the difficulty in identifying an English learner as possibly learning disabled. Table 5.3 illustrates the three sets of language abilities and disabilities according to five language components: pragmatics, prosody, phonology, syntax, and semantics.

Early Intervention

The classroom teacher's primary concern is to determine if a student's academic or behavioral difficulties reflect factors other than disabilities, including inappropriate or inadequate instruction. If a student is not responsive to alternative instructional or behavioral interventions over a period of several weeks or months, there is more of a chance that a placement in special education will be necessary (García & Ortiz, 2004; Ortiz, 2002).

The School Screen Team works with the classroom teacher to design intervention strategies that address the CLD learner's second-language-acquisition, language development, and acculturation needs, and decides if formal referral to testing is warranted.

ADAPTED INSTRUCTION

Instructional Modifications for CLD Students

Although many of the strategies recommended below are appropriate for all students, they are particularly critical for CLD students suspected of a learning disability:

- Use reality-based or experiential models that feature visual, auditory, and tactile modeling.
- Teach skills and strategies explicitly (a direct instruction model in conjunction with an experiential approach).
- Focus on content over form.
- Provide understandable input and check frequently for understanding.
- Monitor the student for fatigue.
- Provide "wait time" and "think time."
- Respond positively to communication attempts.
- Use questions appropriate to students' second-language-acquisition stage.
- Explain behavioral expectations.

Source: Adapted from Nemmer-Fanta (2002).

Table 5.3 Similarity in Language Abilities and Disabilities among Standard American English Speakers, English Learners, and Students with Learning Disabilities

Component of Oral Language	Definition	Expectations for Native Speakers of English	English Learners Often . . .	Learning Disabled Students May . . .
Pragmatics	The ability to use and manipulate language (including nonverbal language) in a given context	Know how to use language in a social context and to behave nonverbally with language	Use nonverbal language in a way that they learn from their native culture (e.g., eye contact)	Have difficulties with social rules in communicative exchanges (e.g., turn taking, reading social cues)
Prosody	An understanding of the correct use of rhythm, intonation, and stress patterns of a language	Understand and use different intonation to convey information	Use the intonation curves of sentences in L1 when attempting L2	Have prosodic difficulties such as ambiguous intonation
Phonology	The speech sounds that constitute spoken language and the pronunciation rules	Produce and comprehend phonemes normally	Have difficulty with certain L2 phonemes that are not present in their L1	Have difficulty articulating or differentiating language sounds
Syntax	How words are organized to produce meaningful phrases and sentences	Use appropriate sentence structure	Have difficulty with articles, word order in sentences, noun–verb agreement, negation, and verb tenses	Have difficulty in sentence-level comprehension or understanding verb aspects such as mood
Semantics	The meaning of words and sentences	Use words that mean what they want to say	Have difficulties with connotation and denotation of words, as well as understanding be verbs	Have difficulty understanding multiple meanings of words or figurative language

Source: Adapted from Gopaul-McNicol and Thomas-Presswood (1998).

A key to the diagnosis of language-related disorders is the presence of similar patterns in both the primary and the secondary languages. The classroom teacher adopts an experimental attitude, implementing strategies over a period of time and documenting the effect these innovations have on the student in question.

The Web resource ldonline (www.ldonline.org/indepth/bilingual) provides suggestions for teaching English learners with learning disabilities. In addition, other checklists (Aladjem, 2000, www.ncela.gwu.edu/pubs/voices) assist in the initial intervention process. They include, among others, ways to ensure that the prereferral process fits the needs of bilingual learners, that initial assessment has taken place in the students' primary language, that family members have been adequately involved, and that any tests or alternative assessments that have been used are fair and free from linguistic or cultural bias.

Roles of Classroom Teachers and ELD Teachers during the Process of Determining Eligibility for Additional Services

Both classroom teachers and the ELD teacher may play a variety of roles during the process of determining a student's eligibility for additional services:

- *Organizer.* The classroom teacher, with the help of the ELD teacher, organizes student records, records of interventions attempted and the relative success thereof, records of parent contact, and records of contact with other community agencies.
- *Instructor.* The ELD teacher may be able to advise the classroom teacher about adapting learning environments to greater diversity in students' learning styles, devising initial intervention strategies, and using curriculum-based assessment to document student achievement.
- *Investigator.* The ELD teacher or a bilingual paraprofessional may accomplish preliminary testing in the student's L1, study students' culture and language, and interview parents.
- *Mentor to students.* The classroom and ELD teacher may get to know the student and family, suggest a testing environment compatible with the student's culture, and prepare the student for the evaluation process.
- *Colleague.* The ELD teacher and the classroom teacher act as helpful colleagues, sharing expertise about L2 acquisition effects, potential crosscultural misunderstandings, and possible effects of racism or discrimination on CLD learners and families. They collaborate to resolve conflicts, work with translators, and draw on community members for information, additional resources, and parental support. This collaboration is discussed later in this chapter.

TESTING FOR SPECIAL EDUCATION

The School Screen Team, after reviewing the evidence provided by the classroom teacher and analysis of the early intervention accommodations, approves or denies the request for special education testing. If approved, such testing will take place only after parental approval has been secured in writing. A school psychologist or licensed professional evaluator performs the testing. Figueroa (1989) and the American Psychological Association's Office of Ethnic and Minority Affairs (1991) provided guidelines for the testing of ethnic, linguistic, and culturally diverse populations. Figure 5.1 offers some fundamentals that must be in place to ensure the validity of such testing.

Bilingual students must be tested in both languages to qualify for special education services. The most difficult students to refer to testing are those who may have language delay or mild learning disabilities, aggravated by the need to acquire English (Jesness, 2004). Some students may have had their prior schooling interrupted, making assessment of their ability a confusing process. The most important figure in this quandary is the bilingual psychologist, who can administer dual-language evaluation and make a reasoned determination for the student as to what kind of educational program is most appropriate.

1. The person administering testing is licensed and certified, and has adequate training concerning the following:
   - Administration, scoring, and interpretation of the test
   - Pitfalls and limitations of a particular test
   - Capability to establish rapport and understand the nonverbal language and cultural beliefs/practices of the person being tested
   - Oral ability in the language of the person or provision made for a trained interpreter

2. Instruments chosen for assessment have norms that represent the population group of the individual being tested.

3. The person being tested understands the words used and can operate from a worldview that understands what is expected from the testing situation.

4. Behavior sampled is an adequate measure of the individual's abilities.

Some caveats about the above assumptions:

1. Translated tests may not be equivalent to their English forms in areas such as content validity and the amount of verbalization that can be expected from different cultures. Even having discrete norms for different languages may not provide norms for different cultures.

2. Many individuals do not have testing experience or experience with test materials, such as blocks or puzzles. Conversely, what they do have expertise in may not be measured in the test. The individual's learning style or problem-solving strategies can be culturally bound.

3. Individuals who have the following characteristics will do well on tests. These are consistent with the dominant U.S. American mainstream culture and may not be present, or may be present to a limited degree, in an individual from another culture:
   - Monochronic orientation: focus on one task at a time
   - Close proximity: can tolerate small interpersonal space
   - Frequent and sustained eye contact
   - Flexibility in response to male or female examiner
   - Individual orientation: motivated to perform well in testing situation
   - Understanding of verbal and nonverbal aspects of majority culture
   - Internal locus of control: taking responsibility for one's own success
   - Field-independent cognitive style: can perceive details apart from the whole
   - Reflective, methodological, analytical cognitive style

Figure 5.1 Assumptions in Psychological Testing

Source: Adapted from Gopaul-McNicol and Thomas-Presswood (1998, pp. 46–50).

The Descriptive Assessment Process

Evaluating CLD learners for possible placement in a special education classroom involves attention to linguistic and cultural factors that may impede the school success of the student. A *descriptive assessment* (Jitendra & Rohena-Díaz, 1996) process in three phases takes these factors into account.

The first phase is descriptive analysis, in which an oral monologue, an oral dialogue, and observation of the student in class are used together to ascertain if the student has a communicative proficiency problem. If this is the case, the assessment may end, and the student may be referred to a speech/language therapist for additional mediation in language development. Alternatively, the student may be referred for additional mediation in language development *and* the evaluation process may continue, indicating that the student has a communicative proficiency problem as well as other problems.

If there is evidence of some other learning problem, the second phase begins—explanatory analysis. The assessor examines extrinsic factors, such as cultural or ethnic background or level of acculturation, that determine if normal second-language-acquisition or crosscultural phenomena can account for the student's learning difficulties. If these factors do not account for the described difficulties, the examination continues to the third phase: assessment for the presence of intrinsic factors, such as a learning disability. This three-phase evaluation process helps to ensure that linguistic and cultural differences receive thoughtful consideration in the overall picture of the student's academic progress.

Family Support for Evaluation

During the evaluation process, the classroom teacher who keeps the family informed about the process reaps the benefit of knowing that family members understand the need for professional assessment and support the student's need for additional mediation of learning. Teacher–family conferences play an important part in sustaining support.

EXAMPLE OF CONCEPT

Helping the Family Understand Their Child's Level of Achievement

Mrs. Said keeps three demonstration portfolio folders for use during family conferences. One folder displays average work for the grade level (all names have been removed from such work samples), one folder displays superior work, and a third folder contains work samples that are below grade level. During conferences, family members compare their child's work with these samples to gain a context for achievement at that grade level. If their child's performance is not at grade level, they often are more willing to support the provision of additional help for their child.

COLLABORATION AMONG ESL–ELD RESOURCE TEACHERS AND SPECIAL EDUCATORS

Organizing a collaborative program requires cooperation between professionals who are concerned for the welfare of the student. Teachers can play a variety of collaborative and consultative roles within school contexts, using a variety of problem-solving strategies to design successful ways to create student success.

Definition and Principles of Collaboration

Collaboration is "a style for direct interaction between at least two coequal parties voluntarily engaged in shared decision making as they work toward a common goal" (Friend & Cook, 1996, p. 6). This definition pinpoints several necessary principles: Professionals must treat one another as equals; collaboration is voluntary; a goal is shared (that of finding the most effective classroom setting for the student under consideration); and responsibility is shared for participation, decision making, and resources, as well as accountability for outcomes. These are predicated on a collegial working environment of mutual respect and trust.

Collaboration among Professionals

In a well-designed program for educating English learners, much collaborative planning takes place among staff members. If there is an ELD specialist in the school, that professional often engages in planning with content teachers to integrate content instruction with language-development objectives; with classroom/mainstream teachers in grade-level team meetings; with bilingual teachers to choose complementary materials in the first and second languages; with resource teachers to share diagnostic tools and other forms of assessment; with program, school, and district administrators to design and implement services, offer in-service workshops, and set policies for grading, record keeping, and redesignation; and with curriculum coordinators to create model units of instruction that incorporate content and English-language-development standards (TESOL, 2006).

English-language-development services, whether delivered by the classroom teacher or by an ELD resource teacher, should continue during the period of referral and testing, and then continue if a student receives special education services.

Working with an Interpreter

Teachers who do not share a primary language with the student under consideration may benefit from collaborative relations with an interpreter. However, instructional aides who are hired as teaching assistants should not be automatically pressed into service as translators or interpreters. Interpretation is a professional service that should be provided by trained and certified personnel. Figure 5.2 gives guidelines for successful cooperative relations with interpreters.

Relationship of Continued ELD with Other Services

English-language-development services are a continuing resource for students throughout the initial intervention, testing, and recommendation phases of special education referral. An ELD teacher may work with the student directly, continuing to implement early intervention strategies, or help the student indirectly by working with other teachers, parents, and peers.

Direct Services. Working directly with the student, the ELD teacher may tutor or test the child in the curricular material used in the classroom, or chart daily measures of the child's performance to see if skills are being mastered. The ELD teacher may work specifically on those areas in which the student requires additional mediation or continue to teach the student as a part of an ELD group in the regular classroom.

---

1. Meet regularly with the interpreter to facilitate communication, particularly before meeting with a student or parent.

2. Encourage the interpreter to chat with the client before the interview to help determine the appropriate depth and type of communication.

3. Speak simply, avoiding technical terms, abbreviations, professional jargon, idioms, and slang.

4. Encourage the interpreter to translate the client's own words as much as possible to give a sense of the client's concepts, emotional state, and other important information. Encourage the interpreter to refrain from inserting his or her own ideas or interpretations, or from omitting information.

5. During the interaction, look at and speak directly to the client. Listen to clients and watch their nonverbal, affective response by observing facial expressions, voice intonations, and body movements.

6. Be patient. An interpreted interview takes longer.

Figure 5.2 How to Work with an Interpreter

Source: Adapted from Lopez (2002).

Indirect Services. Supplementing the classroom teacher's role, the ELD teacher may consult with other teachers on instructional interventions; devise tests based on the classroom curricula and give instruction on how to develop and use them; show how to take daily measures of a child's academic and social behavior; establish parent groups for discussion of and help with issues of concern; train older peers, parent volunteers, and teacher aides to work with younger children as tutors; and offer in-service workshops for teachers that focus on special interest areas such as curriculum-based assessments, cultural understanding, and second-language-acquisition issues (West & Idol, 1990).

If the evaluation process results in the recommendation of special education services, the ELD teacher helps write the student's individual educational plan (IEP). Collaboration between ELD, special educators, the classroom teacher, parents, and the student is vital to the drafting and approval of an IEP that will result in academic success. The plan for continued ELD services are a part of the document.

TEACHING STRATEGIES FOR THE CLD SPECIAL LEARNER

Modified instruction can accommodate different instructional needs within the classroom and foster learning across academic content areas. *Inclusion* is a term often used to describe the provision of instruction within the conventional/mainstream classroom for students with special needs or talents. Although primarily associated with the education of exceptional students, this term has also been used for the varying degrees of inclusion of CLD learners in the mainstream classroom (Florida Department of Education, 2003). The use of this term should not, however, be interpreted as encouraging an indiscriminate overlap of the instruction recommended for CLD learners and that of special education students.

The mainstream classroom of an included student is a rich, nonrestrictive setting for content instruction and language development activities. The three components of an exemplary program for CLD learners—comprehensible instruction in the content areas using primary language and SDAIE, language arts instruction in English, and heritage (primary) language maintenance or development—are present.

The teacher makes every effort for the student to be "as dynamically a part of the class as any student that is perceived as routinely belonging to that class" (Florida Department of Education, 2003, n.p.). Overall, teaching for inclusion features teaching practices that showcase learners' strong points and support the areas in which they may struggle. By using a variety of interactive strategies, teachers have ample opportunity to discover which methods and activities correspond to student success.

The task for the teacher becomes more complex as the increasingly varied needs of students—those who are mainstream (non-CLD/non-special-education), mainstream special education, CLD learner, CLD learner–special education—are mixed in the same classroom. Such complexity would argue that an inclusive classroom be equipped with additional educational resources, such as teaching assistants, lower student to teacher ratio, and augmented budget for instructional materials. The chief resource in any classroom, however, is the breadth and variety of instructional strategies on which the experienced teacher can draw. The following sections suggest multiple strategies in the areas of listening skills, reading, and writing.

Adapting Listening Tasks

Techniques to teach listening skills have been grouped in Table 5.4 into the three phases of the listening process (before listening, during listening, and after listening).

Adapting Reading Tasks

Reading assignments for inclusion students, listed in Table 5.5, follow the three-part division of the reading process (before reading, during reading, and after reading, alternatively named "into," "through," and "beyond").

Table 5.4 Strategies for Additional Mediation for Included Students According to the Listening Process

Phase	Strategies
Before listening	• Directly instruct listening strategies. • Arrange information in short, logical, well-organized segments. • Preview ways to pay attention. • Preview the content with questions that require critical thinking. • Establish a listening goal for the lesson. • Provide prompts indicating that the information about to be presented is important enough to remember or write down.
During listening	• Actively involve students in rehearsing, summarizing, and taking notes. • Use purposeful, curriculum-related listening activities. • Model listening behavior and use peer models. • Teach students to attend to teacher cues and nonverbal signs that denote important information. • Use verbal, pictorial, or written prelistening organizers to cue students to important information. • Teach students to self-monitor their listening behavior using self-questioning techniques and visual imagery while listening.
After listening	• Discuss content. Use teacher questions and prompts to cue student response (e.g., "Tell me more"). • Integrate other language arts and content activities with listening as a follow-up.

Source: Adapted from Mandlebaum and Wilson (1989).

Table 5.5 Strategies for Additional Mediation for Included Students According to the Reading Process

Phase	Strategies
Before/into reading	• Preview reading materials to assist students with establishing purpose, activating prior knowledge, budgeting time, and focusing attention. • Explain how new content to be learned relates to content previously learned. • Create vocabulary lists and teach these words before the lesson to ensure that students know these vocabulary words rather than just recognize them. • Ensure that readability levels of the textbooks and trade books used in class are commensurate with the student's language level. • Locate lower-reading-level supplements in the same topic so that tasks can be adapted to be multilevel and multimaterial. • Rewrite material (or solicit staff or volunteers to do so) to simplify the reading level, or provide chapter outlines or summaries. • Tape text reading or have it read orally to a student. Consider the use of peers, volunteers, and/or paraprofessionals in this process.
During/through reading	• Highlight key words, phrases, and concepts with outlines or study guides. • Reduce extraneous noise. • Use visual aids (e.g., charts and graphs) to supplement reading tasks.
After/beyond reading	• When discussing stories, paraphrase material to clarify content. • Encourage feedback from students to check for understanding. • Reteach vocabulary to ensure retention. • Provide the page numbers where specific answers can be found in a reading comprehension/content assignment. • Use brief individual conferences with students to verify comprehension.

Source: Adapted from Smith, Polloway, Patton, and Dowdy (2003).

Adapting Writing Tasks

Writing is used in two main ways in classrooms: to capture and demonstrate content knowledge (taking notes, writing answers on assignments or tests) and to express creative purposes. If the acquisition of content knowledge is the goal, students can often use a variety of alternatives to writing that avoid large amounts of written work (both in class and homework). In general, teachers of students with special needs in inclusive settings change the response mode to oral when appropriate (Smith, Polloway, Patton, & Dowdy, 2003).

ADAPTED INSTRUCTION

Strategies for Content Writing

- Provide a written outline of key content from lecture notes to reduce the amount of board copying.
- Allow group written responses through projects or reports, with the understanding that each member takes an equal turn in writing.

A Focus on Self-Expression. When students write for self-expression, they should follow a well-defined writing process, with provision for generating ideas, drafting, and peer editing. Students can use a stamp that indicates "first draft" to distinguish drafts from polished, or recopied, versions; this helps to honor rough drafts as well as completed writing.

ADAPTED INSTRUCTION

Strategies for Writing Conventions

- To help CLD learners with spelling, display a word bank on a classroom wall with commonly used words that native speakers would already know.
- Help students select the most comfortable method of writing (i.e., cursive or manuscript).
- For the purpose of improving handwriting, make available an optional calligraphy center where students can practice elegant forms of handwriting, with correct models available of cursive styles.

Adapting Homework Tasks

Special education students, like English learners, may need homework to be adapted to fit their needs:

- Adapted format—shorter assignments, alternative response formats (e.g., oral rather than written)
- Adapted expectations for performance—longer time until due date, grade based on effort rather than performance, provision for extra credit opportunities
- Scaffolded performance—arrangements made for teacher, aide, peer tutor, or study group assistance; auxiliary learning aids sent home with student (calculator, study guides)
- Monitored performance—student checks in frequently with teacher or parent (Hibbard & Moutes, 2006, p. 95)

EXAMPLE OF CONCEPT

Adapting to a Student's Learning Style

Amber, a student in an inclusion classroom, describes what teachers have done to help her learn: "I am a relater and a visual learner. So I get along better if I work in groups, relate ideas, and make pictures of what I learn. After I read a chapter or listen to a lecture, I use something we call 'pegs'—to draw pictures. . . . [W]hen we studied the Bill of Rights, I used it to remember each of the Rights. For example, the first one is a picture of a Jewish man holding a pen. That kicks off peg 1 and reminds me of freedom of religion" (Sands, Kozleski, & French, 2000).

ASSESSING STUDENT PERFORMANCE IN THE MAINSTREAM CLASSROOM

A key feature of instruction for inclusion is continuous student assessment. Ongoing assessment accomplishes three purposes: It evaluates the curriculum using immediate, measurable results; diagnoses which instructional tasks and strategies are responsible for student success; and provides a basis for communicating this success to the student, parents, and collaborating team members. A variety of means are available to assess the success of the student in response to the curriculum, instructional strategies, and psychosocial aspects of the inclusion environment, and to judge if the inclusion placement of the student is appropriate.

Methods of Assessing the Success of Included Students

Direct observation and *analysis of student products* are two ways to assess the success of included students. Direct observation, by the teacher or by a collaborating team member, can determine if the student has opportunities to speak in class, has enough academic engaged time and time to complete assigned tasks, and is receiving teacher feedback that communicates high expectations and immediate contingencies for completion or noncompletion of work, correct responding, or misbehavior.

Analysis of student products can help team members determine which instructional activities have been successful and which may need to be modified. Throughout this process, formative assessment gives students feedback about their performance and ways they can improve.

Assessing Students' Work

For students who need a significantly modified curriculum, the issue of assigning grades should be addressed before the individualized education plan (IEP) is approved. The grading system used for included students should not differ significantly from that used for other students, although alternative grading systems are appropriate as long as the school district ensures that the grading practices and policies are not discriminatory. Teachers working together in the classroom collaborate to establish guidelines for achievement and assign grades. The grading process may include teachers' writing descriptive comments that offer examples of student performance or of certain instructional approaches or strategies that have proven successful, or observations about students' learning styles, skills, effort, and attitude.

The widespread emphasis on standards-based instruction means that grades should reflect student mastery of required material. A nationwide study (Bursuck, Polloway, Plante, Epstein, Jayanthi, & McConeghy, 1996) found that teachers were concerned about grading practices for special education students who are mainstreamed in regular classrooms. Most teachers found pass–fail and checklist-type grades more helpful for students with disabilities than letter and number grades; yet 80 percent of school districts mandate letter grades on report cards. This results in a high percentage of low grades given to included students. Bursuck et al. (1996) recommend that school districts allow multiple grades or multiple coding systems to be used with students who have learning disabilities (i.e., progress reports, grades for effort), perhaps modifying the modality depending on the recipient of the report (parents versus administrators, for example).

Using the Results of Assessment

Ongoing assessment monitors the extent to which the student's IEP is being fulfilled. Assessment activities should be detailed to the greatest extent possible when the IEP is approved so that all members of the collaborating team are aware of their roles and responsibilities. In this way, the results of assessment are immediately compared to the performance stipulated in the IEP and progress is ensured.

Keeping parents informed as full participating members of the collaborating team ensures that they know what they can do at home to assist their child. Persistence and positive feedback in this effort help parents stay motivated and engaged.

UNIVERSAL DESIGN FOR SPECIAL POPULATIONS OF ENGLISH LEARNERS

English learners with special needs include those with learning disabilities and vision, hearing, health, and mobility impairments. These conditions add complexity to the second-language-acquisition challenges these learners face. Educators have begun to view the education of these learners from a unified perspective: Universal Instructional Design (UID), which is based on Universal Design (UD).

Principles of Universal Design, a model from the field of architecture and design, have been used to make products and environments "usable by all people, to the greatest extent possible, without the need for adaptation or specialized design" (Connell, Jones, Mace, Mueller, Mullick, Ostroff, Sanford, Steinfield, Story, & Vanderheiden, 1997, p. 1). The seven principles of Universal Design are as follows:

1. Equitable use (useful to people with diverse abilities)
2. Flexibility in use (accommodates individual preferences and abilities)
3. Simple and intuitive use (easy to understand, regardless of the user's experience, knowledge, language skills, or current concentration level)
4. Perceptible information (necessary information is communicated effectively to the user, regardless of ambient conditions or the user's sensory abilities)
5. Tolerance for error (adverse consequences of accidental or unintended actions are minimized)
6. Low physical effort (efficient, comfortable, and relatively effortless)
7. Size and space for approach and use (affords approach, reach, and manipulation regardless of user's body size, posture, or mobility)

Universal Instructional Design

With an augmented emphasis on learning styles and other learner differences, UD, now called *Universal Instructional Design,* has moved into education. Application of UID goes beyond merely physical access for all students (e.g., wheelchair ramps and sign language translators), ensuring access to information, resources, and tools for students with a wide range of abilities, disabilities, ethnic backgrounds, language skills, and learning styles. Burgstahler (2008) noted that

Universal Instructional Design principles . . . give each student meaningful access to the curriculum by assuring access to the environment as well as multiple means of representation, expression, and engagement. (p. 1)

Table 5.6 Principles of Universal Instructional Design Applied to English Learners with Special Needs

Principle	Definition	Application
Inclusiveness	A classroom climate that communicates respect for varying abilities	Use bilingual signage and Braille bilingual materials; welcome and respect aides and assistants; supply multiple reading levels of texts.
Physical access	Equipment and activities that minimize sustained physical effort, provide options for participation, and accommodate those with limited physical abilities	Use assistive technologies such as screen readers and online dictionaries; make online chatrooms available for deaf and hearing-impaired students.
Delivery methods	Content is delivered in multiple modes so it is accessible to students with a wide range of abilities, disabilities, interests, and previous experiences	Employ a full range of audiovisual enhancement, including wireless headsets and captioned video; build in redundant modes (e.g., audiotaped read-along books, typed lecture notes, and study guides).
Information access	Use of captioned videos and accessible electronic formats; in printed work, use of simple, intuitive, and consistent formats	Ensure that information is both understandable and complete; reduce unnecessary complexity; highlight essential text; give clear criteria for tests and assignments.
Interaction	Accessible to everyone, without accommodation; use of multiple ways for students to participate	Set up both heterogeneous groups (across second-language ability levels) and homogeneous groups (same language-ability level); instruct students on how to secure a conversational turn.
Feedback	Effective prompting during an activity and constructive comments after the assignment is complete	Employ formative assessment for ongoing feedback.
Demonstration of knowledge	Provision for multiple ways students demonstrate knowledge—group work, demonstrations, portfolios, and presentations	Offer different modes to all students so that special-needs students are not the only ones with alternatives.

Source: Adapted from Burgstahler (2002), Egbert (2004), and Strehorn (2001).

Table 5.6 offers an overview of the principles of UID and some suggested applications of these principles in the education of English learners with special needs. UID does not imply that one universal size fits all but rather that a diversity of opportunities will work for many different students.

TEACHING BLIND ENGLISH LEARNERS

Because 80 percent of learning is visual (Seng, 2005), blind English learners are a special concern. Table 5.7 offers considerations to help teachers who are not trained to teach the blind so they can deliver effective instruction to these students.

Table 5.7 Addressing the Needs of Blind Students

Aspects of Concern	Questions and Suggestions
Understanding degrees of blindness	Is the student partially or totally blind? Residual vision should be used to the maximum extent possible.
Understanding the background	How and when did the student become blind—at the age of eight or nine (certain visual memory will be retained) or blind at birth (ideas and images will be conceived differently)?
Setting up a readers service	Textbooks are usually translated into Braille one chapter at a time, but a pool of volunteers can read to blind students or tape-record books.
Technological help	Computer software can download material and transcribe it into Braille dots. Blind students can use the computer sound synthesis software such as text to speech and voice recognition—some software can be downloaded for free.
In the classroom	Because the blind student cannot see the classroom board, the teacher has to be more vocal and repeat every word put on the board. When plans or diagrams are used, they can be embossed by sticking string to cardboard.
Reactions of other students	Many sighted students come forward willingly to help their blind classmates both in the classroom and in the community.
Teaching tips	Use talking books and taped dialogues for reading comprehension lessons; use real objects in lessons; and use field trips to bring culture, exposure, and experiences to the blind students.

ADAPTED INSTRUCTION

Assistive Technology for the Visually Impaired

Reese (2006) describes many ways that ELD programs can accommodate the visually impaired with assistive technology; audio books; and magnifiers, large print, print-enlarging devices, or Braille for written materials. For accessing materials at a distance such as a chalkboard, mildly impaired students can use monocular telescopes or bioptic lenses.

TEACHING ENGLISH LEARNERS WITH HEARING IMPAIRMENTS

Over 40 percent of school-age deaf and hard-of-hearing students are from ethnically and racially diverse families (Schildroth & Hotto, 1994). Deaf students in the public school setting face the challenge of three different cultures: their own ethnic background, the Deaf community, and that of mainstream hearing people (Qualls-Mitchell, 2008). Working with such cultural diversity, it is helpful to encourage students to appreciate and respect one another's differences, and to develop an awareness of the needs of others. Using signing, multimodal presentation of information, imagery, and highly motivating materials helps deaf students become active learners. Biographies that represent role models are motivating for all students. Qualls-Mitchell (2008) presents 15 different resources for teachers of hearing-impaired students, including Moore and Panara's (1996) *Great Deaf Americans,* a source book for biographies representing diverse populations.

Hearing loss can be *conductive* (damage or obstruction in the outer or middle ear), *sensorineural* (damage to the inner ear), *mixed* (both of previous), or *central* (involving the central nervous system and/or brain). Each type of hearing loss requires distinct intervention, conductive damage being the easiest to remediate using a hearing aid. Table 5.8 features teaching strategies for those with hearing impairments.

Table 5.8   Instructional Strategies for Students with Hearing Impairments

Services Available

- Speech/language training from a specialist
- Amplification systems
- Interpreter using sign language
- Captioned videotapes and television
- Note-taking assistance
- Instruction for teachers and peers in sign language
- Counseling
- Increased use of visual materials

Classroom Management

- Arrange desks in a semicircle to facilitate speech-reading.
- Reduce distracting ambient noise.
- Speak clearly, with good enunciation.
- Use gestures to facilitate understanding when speaking.

Student–Teacher Interaction

- Seat the student close to the teacher and face the student when talking.
- Speak face to face, using natural speech.

Academic Assistance

- List key points on the chalkboard.
- Use several forms of communication.
- Give short, concise instructions and have the student repeat key points privately to ensure comprehension.
- Appoint a peer buddy to help the student stay abreast of the class during oral reading.

Social Skills Development

- Create opportunities for group work.
- Model patience and respect during communication.
- Teach social cues and unspoken rules of conversation if the student seems to make inappropriate interactions.

Source: Adapted from Pierangelo and Giuliani (2001).

Teaching CLD learners in U.S. classrooms is a challenge on a scale without precedent in modern education. As the social and economic stakes are raised, students who fail to reach their potential represent a loss to society as a whole. Each student—including those with special needs, whether for additional mediation or acceleration of instruction—is a treasure box, with his or her individual and specific talents, cultural background, and life experiences locked inside. Opening this treasure chest and releasing these talents to the world is an educational adventure of the highest order. The teacher with crosscultural, language, and academic development training holds the key.

LEARNING MORE

Further Reading

Ask your school or local public librarian for a list of biographies, autobiographies, or other genres that will raise your awareness of a specific disability: autism, attention-deficit/hyperactivity disorder, or a physical, emotional, or learning disability.

Web Search

Go online to see if the following organizations' Websites offer specific suggestions for the education of CLD students:

- Alexander Graham Bell Association for the Deaf
- American Association for the Deaf-Blind
- American Association on Mental Retardation
- American Council of the Blind
- American Society for Deaf Children
- Autism Society of America, Inc.
- Beach Center on Families and Disability
- Challenge (Attention Deficit Disorder Association)
- Children with Attention Deficit Disorders (ChADD)

Exploration

Visit a special education classroom in which instruction takes place in one or more primary languages. Discuss with the teacher the availability of special education materials in the language(s).

Experiment

Try "Second-Language Lead Me Blindfolded," a variation of the "Lead Me Blindfolded" game, in which a partner leads you around the block blindfolded and you must rely on that partner for cues. Choose a partner who will speak to you only in a foreign language with which you are not familiar as you are led around.

The Inclusive Classroom

With inclusion, students of all abilities are educated together in the general education classroom. Children with special needs are not isolated, but are involved in all aspects of the classroom, curriculum, and learning activities. The classroom diversity that results requires that the teacher function as part of a cooperative team that includes specialists that offer special services.

To access the video, go to MyEducationLab (www.myeducationlab.com), choose the Díaz-Rico and Weed text, and log in to MyEducationLab for English Language Learners. Select the topic Special Needs and Inclusion, and watch the video entitled "The Inclusive Classroom."

Answer the following questions:
1. What are the elements of an effective inclusive classroom for English learners?
2. What can the teacher of culturally and linguistically diverse (CLD) students do to create an effective inclusive classroom?
3. The inclusion of children with special needs adds to the diversity of the classroom. Evaluate the rewards and challenges of an inclusive classroom for culturally and linguistically diverse (CLD) students. Explain your answer.

LANGUAGE STRUCTURE, AND FIRST AND SECOND LANGUAGE DEVELOPMENT

CHAPTER 6

PROGRAMS FOR ENGLISH LEARNERS

English learners enter schooling fluent in a primary language other than English, a proficiency that can function as a resource. In many parts of the world, including Canada, second-language instruction is considered either a widely accepted component of being well educated or a legal mandate in an officially bilingual country. Acquiring a second language is not easy, especially to the level of using that language to succeed in postsecondary education. English learners face that challenge daily.

A growing number of schools in the United States offer two-way immersion programs that help English learners develop academic competence in their heritage language while acquiring fluency and literacy in English—while at the same time native-English-speaking students develop speaking fluency and academic competence in the home language of the English learners. These programs showcase the idea that *multicompetent language use* (Cook, 1999, p. 190) is a valuable skill. Proficiency in multiple languages is also a career enhancement in the modern world of global commerce.

The classrooms of the United States are increasingly diverse, with students coming from many countries of the world. The challenge to any English-language development program is to cherish and preserve the rich cultural and linguistic heritage of the students as they acquire English.

This chapter addresses the history, legality, and design of program models that induct speakers of other languages into English instruction. Although most of these programs take place at the elementary level, an increasing number of students immigrate to the United States at the middle and high school levels, and programs must be designed to meet their needs as well. The program models presented in this chapter vary greatly on one key dimension—how much encouragement is offered to students to maintain their primary language and how much instructional support they receive to accomplish this.

THE HISTORY OF MULTILINGUAL COMPETENCY IN THE UNITED STATES

Bilingualism has existed in the United States since the colonial period, but over the more than two centuries of American history it has been alternately embraced and rejected. The immigrant languages and cultures in North America have enriched the lives of the people in American communities, yet periodic waves of language restrictionism have virtually eradicated the capacity of many U.S. residents to speak a foreign or second language, even those who are born into families with a heritage language other than English. For English learners, English-only schooling has often brought difficulties, cultural suppression, and discrimination even as English has been touted as the key to patriotism and success. This section traces the origin and development of, and support for, language services for English learners in the United States.

Early Bilingualism in the United States

At the time of the nation's founding, at least twenty languages could be heard in the American colonies, including Dutch, French, German, and numerous Native-American languages. In 1664 at least eighteen colonial languages were spoken on Manhattan Island. Bilingualism was common among both the working and educated classes, and schools were established to preserve the linguistic heritage of new arrivals. The Continental Congress published many official documents in German and French as well as in English. German schools were operating as early as 1694 in Philadelphia, and by 1900 more than 4 percent of the United States' elementary school population was receiving instruction either partially or exclusively in German. In 1847, Louisiana authorized instruction in French, English, or both at the request of parents. The Territory of New Mexico authorized Spanish–English bilingual education in 1850 (Crawford, 1999). Table 6.1 surveys the early history of language use and policy in America.

Although there were several such pockets of acceptance for bilingual education, other areas of the country effectively restricted or even attempted to eradicate immigrant and minority languages. In 1879, however, the federal government forced Native-American children to attend off-reservation, English-only schools where they were punished for using their native language. In the East, as large numbers of Eastern Europeans immigrated, descendants of the English settlers began to harbor resentment against these newcomers. New waves of Mexican and Asian immigration in the West brought renewed fear of non-English influences (Crawford, 1999).

BEST PRACTICE

Early Cherokee Language Rights

Under an 1828 treaty, the U.S. government recognized the language rights of the Cherokee tribe. Eventually, the Cherokees established a twenty-one-school educational system that used the Cherokee syllabary to achieve a 90 percent literacy rate in the native language. About 350,000 Aniyunwiya (Cherokee) people currently live primarily in Oklahoma and North Carolina, and about 22,000 speak the language (which today is known as Isalagi) (www.native-languages.org/cherokee.htm)

The Struggles for Language Education Rights in the Twentieth Century

World War I brought anti-German hysteria, and various states began to criminalize the use of German in all areas of public life. Subsequently, fifteen states legislated English as the basic language of instruction. This repressive policy continued during World War II, when Japanese-language schools were closed. Until the late 1960s, "Spanish detention"—being kept after school for using Spanish—remained a formal punishment in the Rio Grande Valley of Texas, where using a language other than English as a medium of public instruction was a crime (Crawford, 1999).

Although the U.S. Supreme Court, in the *Meyer v. Nebraska* case (1923), extended the protection of the Constitution to everyday speech and prohibited coercive language restriction on the part of states, the "frenzy of Americanization" (Crawford, 1999) had fundamentally changed public attitudes toward learning in other languages. European immigrant groups felt strong pressures to assimilate, and bilingual instruction by the late 1930s was virtually eradicated throughout the United States. This assimilationist mentality worked best with northern European immigrants. For other language minorities, especially those with dark complexions, English-only schooling brought difficulties. Discrimination and cultural repression became associated with linguistic repression.

After World War II, writers began to speak of language-minority children as being "culturally deprived" and "linguistically disabled." The cultural deprivation theory pointed to such environmental factors as inadequate English-language skills, lower-class values, and parental failure to stress educational attainment. On the basis of their performance on IQ tests administered in English, a disproportionate number of English learners ended up in special classes for the educationally handicapped.

Bilingual education was reborn in the early 1960s in Dade County, Florida, as Cuban immigrants, fleeing the 1959 revolution, requested bilingual schooling for their children. The first program at the Coral Way Elementary School was open to both English and Spanish speakers. The objective was fluency and literacy in both languages. Subsequent evaluations of this bilingual program showed success both for English-speaking students in English and for Spanish-speaking students in Spanish and English. Hakuta (1986) reported that by 1974 there were 3,683 students in bilingual programs in the elementary schools nationwide and approximately 2,000 in the secondary schools.

Table 6.1 Early History of Language Use and Policy in America

Date	Event	Significance
Pre-1492	North America is rich in indigenous languages.	Linguistic diversity is a type of biodiversity, encoding millennia of information about the physical and social environment.
16th century	Spain establishes missions in what is now California.	Spanish rulers decree the replacement of indigenous languages by Spanish.
1781	U.S. Articles of Confederation are written in English, French, and German.	Early acknowledgment of U.S. multilingualism on the part of the Founding Fathers.
1800s	European Americans settle Western U.S.	Mexicans and Indians are excluded from whites-only schools.
1828	U.S. government signs a treaty with Cherokee tribes.	The U.S. government recognizes the language rights of the Cherokee tribes. Eventually, a 21-school educational system achieves a 90% literacy rate in Cherokee.
1839	Ohio adopts bilingual education.	Schools could operate in German and English at request of parent.
1848	Mexican territory is annexed to the United States in the Treaty of Guadalupe Hidalgo.	Mexican residents of appropriated territory in what are now California, Arizona, New Mexico, Texas, Utah, and Nevada are promised the right to use Spanish in schools, courts of law, employment, and everyday life.
1864	The federal government forces Native-American children to attend off-reservation schools.	Schools are English only. Native Americans are punished for using their native language.
1888	First antibilingual education legislation is passed.	Wisconsin and Illinois attempt to institute English-only schooling.
1898	U.S. wins Spanish–American War and colonizes Puerto Rico and the Philippines.	Public and private schools are forced to use English as the language of instruction. Submersion in English is a sustained policy in Puerto Rican schools until the 1950s.

Legal and Legislative Mandates Supporting Language Education Rights

Progress in English-language development services in the United States has taken place on three fronts: cultural, legislative, and judicial. Culturally, the people of the United States have seemed to accept bilingualism when it has been economically useful and to reject it when immigrants were seen as a threat. Legislative and judicial mandates have reflected this ambivalence.

After the civil rights era, the provision of services for English learners has been viewed as a right. This is consonant with the Universal Declaration of Linguistic Rights signed in Barcelona in June 1996, the 1948 Universal Declaration of Human Rights, and the Declaration on the Rights of Persons Belonging to National, Ethnic, Religious and Linguistic Minorities of the General Assembly of the United Nations (1992). The May 25 Memorandum from the Office for Civil Rights (also called the Lau Remedies) mandated that school districts with more than 5 percent national-origin minority children must offer special language instruction for students with a limited command of English. It prohibited the assignment of students to classes for the handicapped on the basis of their English-language skills, prohibited placing such students in vocational tracks instead of teaching them

English, and mandated that administrators communicate with parents in a language parents can understand.

Because the states reserve the right to dictate educational policy, services for English learners have depended on the vagaries of state law. When the U.S. Congress enacted legislation to begin Title VII of the Elementary and Secondary Education Act, federal funding became available for bilingual education programs. Almost simultaneously, the courts began to rule that students deprived of bilingual education must receive compensatory services. Together, the historical precedents, federal legislative initiatives, and judicial fiats combined to establish bilingual education in the United States (see Tables 6.2 and 6.3).

Table 6.2   The Early Twentieth Century: Language Use and Policy Are Contested in the United States

Date	Event	Significance
1906	Congress passes English requirement for naturalized citizenship.	First national English-language requirement
1917–1918	The governor of Iowa bans the use of any foreign language in public; Ohio passes legislation to remove all uses of German from the state's elementary schools.	With German speakers as the target, mobs raid schools and burn German textbooks. Subsequently, 15 states legislate English as the basic language of instruction.
1920s–1970s	Ku Klux Klan members in Maine, numbering 150,141 in 1925, burn crosses in hostility to French Americans.	French is forbidden to be spoken in schools in Maine.
1923	*Meyer v. Nebraska*	The Supreme Court bans an English-only law in a case brought by German Americans.
1930	*Del Rio Independent School District v. Salvatierra*	A Texas superior court finds that the Del Rio Independent school district cannot segregate Mexican students, but a higher court rules that the segregation is necessary to teach English to Mexican students.
1931	*Lemon Grove v. Álvarez*	A state superior court rules that school segregation is against the law in California.
1936	Massive IQ testing of Puerto Ricans in New York is used to justify widespread school placement of Spanish-speaking children 2–3 years below grade level.	Thousands of New York Puerto Ricans launch a campaign for bilingual education.
1941	Japanese-language schools are closed.	Japanese are incarcerated in internment camps with English-only schools.
1946, 1947	*Méndez v. Westminster School District*	The U.S. Ninth District Court applies the 14th Amendment to schools, insisting "schools must be open to all children . . . regardless of lineage."
1961	Immigrants fleeing the Cuban revolution demand Spanish-language schooling.	Dade County, Florida, implements Spanish–English bilingual education.
1968	10,000 Chicanos boycott schools in Los Angeles demanding bilingual education and more Latino teachers; boycotts spread across U.S.	Leaders of Los Angeles boycott are arrested; two years later charges against them are declared unconstitutional.

Table 6.3 Key Legislation and Court Cases in the Struggle for English Learners' Language Rights

Date	Event	Significance
1964	The Civil Rights Act: Title VI	Prohibits denial of equal access to education on the basis of race, color, national origin, or limited proficiency in English in the operation of a federally assisted program. Compliance is enforced through the United States Office for Civil Rights.
1968	ESEA Title VII offers funding for bilingual education programs.	First bilingual kindergarten in New York City; first bilingual education major at Brooklyn College.
Early 1970s	Bilingual programs reach only one out of every forty Mexican-American students in the Southwest.	Based on these data, the U.S. Office of Civil Rights begins enforcing compliance with judicial mandates.
1972	*Serna v. Portales Municipal Schools*	The first federal court enforcement of Title VI of the Civil Rights Act. A federal judge orders instruction in native language and culture as part of a desegregation plan.
1973	*Keyes v. School District No. 1, Denver, Colorado*	Latinos must be covered by *Brown v. Board of Education*—Mexicans cannot be labeled "white" and used to create falsely desegregated schools containing only blacks and Latinos.
1974	The Equal Education Opportunities Act (EEOA) (U.S. Congress)	"No state shall deny equal educational opportunities to an individual on account of his or her race, color, sex, or national origin by the failure of an educational agency to take appropriate action to overcome language barriers that impede equal participation by its students in its instructional programs."
1974	*Lau v. Nichols* (414 U.S. 563)	U.S. Supreme Court establishes the right of students to differential treatment based on their language minority status, but it does not specify a particular instructional approach.
1975	Lau Remedies—guidelines from the U.S. Commissioner of Education	Standardized requirements for identification, testing, and placement into bilingual programs. Districts are told how to identify and evaluate children with limited English skills, what instructional treatments to use, when to transfer children to all-English classrooms, and what professional standards teachers need to meet.
1977	*Ríos v. Read*	A federal court rules that a bilingual program must include a cultural component.
1981	*Castañeda v. Pickard*	The Fifth Circuit Court tests the 1974 EEOA statute, outlining three criteria for programs serving EL students: District programs must be: (1) based on "sound educational theory," (2) "implemented effectively" through adequately trained personnel and sufficient resources, and (3) evaluated as effective in overcoming language barriers. Qualified bilingual teachers must be employed, and children are not to be placed on the basis of English-language achievement tests.
1983	*Keyes v. School District #1*	Due process is established for remedies of EEOA matters.
1987	*Gómez v. Illinois State Board of Education*	State school boards can enforce state and federal compliance with EEOA regulations. Districts must properly serve students who are limited in English.

(continued)

Table 6.3 *(continued)*

Date	Event	Significance
1992	*Plyler v. Doe*	The U.S. Supreme Court decides that a state's statute that denies school enrollment to children of illegal immigrants "violates the Equal Protection Clause of the Fourteenth Amendment."
1994	California passes Proposition 187, which makes it illegal to provide public education to illegal immigrants.	Proposition is overturned in the courts because it violates *Plyler v. Doe*.
1998	California voters approve Unz Initiative Proposition 227 (ED Code 300–340).	Requires that K–12 instruction be overwhelmingly in English, restricting use of primary language as a means of instruction. Subsequent measures pass in Arizona and Massachusetts, but French speakers vote down similar initiative in Maine.
2001	No Child Left Behind Act, Title III	Federal funding is available to support schools in educating English learners.
2004	Individuals with Disabilities Education Improvement Act of 2004 (IDEA), Public Law 108–446	Congress aligns education of children with disabilities with NCLB to mandate equity and accountability.
2004	*Williams v. State of California*	California schools must provide equitable access to textbooks, facilities, and teaching staffs, including teachers of English learners.

* See also Crawford (2004, pp. 96–97) for expanded timeline, "Linguistic Diversity in America."

Sources: Cockcroft, 1995; Wiese & García, 1998; Crawford, 1999.

BEST PRACTICE

Indigenous Language Rights

Times have changed for, Native-American language speakers. In the United States, 281,990 families speak an American-Indian home language (www.infoplease.com/ipa/A0192523.html). The most-spoken Native-American language is Navajo, with 150,000 speakers. In 1990 the U.S. Congress passed Public Law 101-477, which sustains the right of Native Americans to express themselves through the use of Native-American languages in any public proceeding, including publicly supported education programs. Among the goals of this law are the following.

- Preserve, protect, and promote the rights and freedom of Native Americans to use, practice, and develop Native American languages
- Increase student success and performance
- Increase students awareness and knowledge of their culture and history
- Increase student and community pride

FEDERAL AND STATE REQUIREMENTS FOR ELD SERVICES

Successive authorizations of the federal Elementary and Secondary Education Act in 1968, 1974, 1978, 1988, and 1989 incorporated federal recognition of the unique educational disadvantages faced by non-English-speaking students. In 1968, Congress authorized $7.5 million to finance seventy-six bilingual education projects serving 27,000 children. In 1974, Congress specifically linked equal educational opportunity to bilingual education, allowing Native-American and English-speaking children to enroll in bilingual education programs, and funding programs for teacher training, technical assistance for program development, and development and dissemination of instructional materials.

In 1978, Congress added to the definition of bilingual education, stipulating that instruction in English should "allow a child to achieve competence in the English language." Additionally, parents were included in program planning, and personnel in bilingual programs were to be proficient in the language of instruction and English. In 1988, Congress increased funding to state education agencies, placed a three-year limit on participation in transitional bilingual programs, and created fellowship programs for professional training. Developmental bilingual programs were expanded to maintain the native language of students in the reauthorization of 1989.

When the Elementary and Secondary Education Act of 1965 was amended and reauthorized in 1994, it was within the framework of Goals 2000, with the goal to "educate limited-English-proficient children and youth to meet the same rigorous standards for academic achievement expected of all children and youth" ([7102] [b]). This emphasis on standards was the linchpin of the 2001 reauthorization, the No Child Left Behind Act, in which all schools are required to provide qualified teachers, and all students are required to pass standardized tests.

No Child Left Behind

Under the No Child Left Behind Act, states must measure student progress on statewide achievement tests. Title III of this act, titled "Language Instruction for Limited English Proficient and Immigrant Students," proposes to measure the progress of English learners against common expectations for student academic achievement by aligning academic assessments, teacher preparation and training, curriculum, instructional materials, and state academic standards.

The purpose of Title III is to upgrade schooling for low-achieving children in highest-poverty schools, including limited-English-proficient children. The goal is to hold schools, local educational agencies, and states accountable for improving the academic achievement of all students, potentially by closing underperforming schools or providing high-quality educational alternatives to students in such schools.

Because English learners must be tested annually after thirty months of schooling (with few exceptions), and because the continued existence of the school is predicated on annual improvement, English learners experience high-stakes pressure to test well. No second-language acquisition theory in existence makes the claim that the high anxiety of testing furthers language learning. Often, "teaching to the test" leaves little room for teaching English. NCLB, then, appears to be an unfortunate fit with what is known about effective second-language learning.

Proposition 227

In 1998, California, with a school enrollment of approximately 1.4 million limited-English-proficient children, passed Proposition 227, a measure rejecting bilingual education. The proposition stipulates that

> all children in California public schools shall be taught English by being taught in English. In particular, this shall require that all children be placed in English language classrooms. Children who are English learners shall be educated through sheltered English immersion during a temporary transition period not normally intended to exceed one year . . . . Once English learners have acquired a good working knowledge of English, they shall be transferred to English language mainstream classrooms. (California State Code of Regulations [CSCR], 1998, Article 2,305)

Article 3, Provision 310 of the CSCR provided parents with waiver possibilities if their children met criteria spelled out in the law: "Under such parental waiver conditions, children may be transferred to classes where they are taught English and other subjects through bilingual education techniques or other generally recognized educational methodologies permitted by law." Before parents can ask for a waiver, however, a student must sit through thirty days of structured English immersion (SEI). Potentially one-ninth of a school year could pass before an English learner at the beginning level could comprehend instruction. Unfortunately, expecting children to learn English (along with academic subjects) in a single year flies in the face of contemporary research on language acquisition (Collier, 1987).

Empirical evidence is lacking that indicates any benefit to language-minority students from passage of Proposition 227. A summary of findings from ten studies conducted by research institutes and scholars affiliated with major California universities found that Proposition 227 had demonstrated considerable disruption to the education of language-minority students with no demonstrable benefits in terms of improved teaching and learning conditions or academic achievement (Garcia, 2000).

A study released by the University of California's Linguistic Minority Research Institute (Gándara, Maxwell-Jolly, García, Asato, Gutiérrez, Stritkus, & Curry, 2000) described the implementation of Proposition 227 in sixteen school districts and twenty-five schools throughout the state. The report documents wide variation in the ways school districts have interpreted 227's requirements. School districts with a strong English-only stance before passage showed a mean decrease in primary-language instruction from 17 percent in 1998 to 2 percent in 1999. In contrast, districts with strong primary-language instruction programs experienced only a 2 percent lower rate of use of Spanish, from 33 to 31 percent, because parents applied for and were granted waivers.

Williams et al. v. State of California. In 2000, in a class action lawsuit, a group of plaintiffs, including Eliezer Williams, represented by the Mexican American Legal Defense and Educational Fund (MALDEF) sued the State of California, the California Department of Education, the California Board of Education, and the California Superintendent of Public Instruction of behalf of 75,000 public school students, alleging that substandard conditions in California schools were causing deprivation in violation of the equal protection clauses of the California Constitution. The lawsuit claimed that the students in question had suffered from poorly trained teachers, serious overcrowding, inadequate physical conditions for schooling (filthy bathrooms, leaky roofs, and nonfunctioning heating and cooling systems), and insufficient or outdated textbooks.

A settlement was reached requiring the State of California to pass legislation requiring that every school district provide a uniform complaint process for complaints regarding insufficient instructional materials, unsafe or unhealthy facility conditions, and teacher vacancies and misassignments. Such a law was signed into effect in 2004. Funding was also provided for facilities repair, new instructional materials, upgraded education for teachers of English learners, and phasing out of multitrack schools in the lowest-performing schools. In return for these provisions, the plaintiffs in *Williams v. California* agreed not to initiate lawsuits for redress until a period of four years had elapsed.

This lawsuit should inaugurate a renewed emphasis on the preparation of teachers for classrooms of English learners, as well as improve the learning conditions in California's underperforming schools.

Lau v. Nichols. In 1973 a group of non-English-speaking Chinese students sued San Francisco Unified School District officials, claiming that "sink or swim" instruction (denial of language development services) was a violation of their civil rights under Title VI of the Civil Rights Act of 1964. Lower federal courts had absolved the school district of any responsibility for minority children's "language deficiency." But a unanimous Supreme Court ruled as follows: "There is no equality of treatment merely by providing students with the same facilities, textbooks, teachers, and curriculum, for students who do not understand English are effectively foreclosed from any meaningful education"—essentially stating that imposing the requirement that a child must have basic skills in English before effectively participating in the educational program is "to make a mockery of public education" (414 U.S. 563).

Although *Lau v. Nichols* did not specify what type of program a school district must offer, the Chinese parents who sued the San Francisco Unified School District formed an advisory committee, and eventually a program emerged that satisfied the requirements set forth by the court. In 1975 the so-called Lau Remedies published by the U.S. Commissioner for Education provided standardized requirements for identifying and evaluating children with limited English skills, for the instructional treatments to use, for procedures to transfer children to all-English classrooms, and for professional standards teachers need to meet. To be in compliance with *Lau v. Nichols*, the Lau Remedies are still used as the required elements in most states.

THE POLITICS OF BILINGUAL EDUCATION

Perceptive teachers realize that the topic of provision of services for English learners is surrounded by political debate. Given the fact that few Americans engage in controversy about second-language acquisition, it is obvious that the underlying arguments for or against bilingual education probably have to do with attitudes about immigration and the role of language in public life. This controversy will continue as Spanish speakers surpass African Americans as the largest minority population in the United States. These arguments treat three main topics: the wisdom of supporting heritage-language proficiency, the role of the native English speaker in bilingual education, and the movement to establish governmental English-only policies.

Support for Heritage-Language Proficiency

Developmental bilingual programs are designed for students who enter schooling with a primary language other than English. The goals of developmental bilingual programs are maintenance and full development of the student's primary language; full proficiency in all aspects of English; grade-appropriate achievement in all domains of academic study; integration into all-English-language classrooms; and positive identification with both the culture of the primary-and the majority-language group (Cloud et al., 2000).

Monolingual English voters outnumber bilingual voters—for example, 61 percent of voters in California are white (presumably monolingual), whereas only 16 percent of voters are Hispanic, despite the fact that Hispanics make up 30 percent of the population. Changing the political climate from its current position of hostility to bilingual education will take a commitment on the part of English-only voters to foster heritage-language skills. Many heritage-language speakers enjoy and seek to preserve their primary language as a cultural and economic resource. Because Spanish is the third most widely spoken language in the world, Spanish–English bilingualism is a distinct competitive advantage in the local and global marketplace, a valuable asset not only for bilingual individuals but also for society as a whole.

Support for Two-Way (Dual) Immersion

For parents of English speakers to start their child's second-language instruction in elementary school, they must seek to maintain or establish two-way immersion (TWI) language programs in conjunction with parents of language-minority students. In this model, English learners from a single language background are taught in the same classroom with approximately equal numbers of English-speaking students. Grade-level-approximate curriculum is provided in both languages. Speakers of each language develop proficiency in both their native and second language, achieve academically through and in two languages, and come to appreciate each others' languages and cultures (Lindholm, 1994).

One advocate of TWI found that this model promises "mutual learning, enrichment, and respect"; is "the best possible vehicle for integration of language minority students, since these students are grouped with English-speakers for natural and equal exchange of skills"; and is "particularly appealing because it not only enhances the prestige of the minority language but also offers a rich opportunity for expanding genuine bilingualism to the majority population" (Porter, 1990, p. 154). Cummins (2000a) argued that "a major advantage of two-way bilingual programs . . . is that they overcome segregation in a planned program that aims to enrich the learning opportunities of both minority- and majority-language students" (p. 142).

The politics of TWI are such that two distinct types of parents have sought and attained such programs in their communities. The first are the liberal, middle-class whites who have seen the success of Canadian schools in promoting dual-language competence in English and French and have forged alliances with Spanish-speaking parents (for example, in Long Beach, California; Evanston, Illinois; and Alexandria, Virginia) or French-speaking parents (in the International School of Tucson French Program). The second group comprises parents who are not heritage speakers of a language but who want their children to regain the heritage language (for example, Spanish in Ontario-Montclair School District, California, or in San Antonio, Texas; Cantonese in San Francisco; or Navajo in Chinle, Arizona).

Parents of native-English-speaking children who advocate for the establishment of such a program for their children become advocates for language maintenance on the part of English learners. These parents see advantages in their children learning academic and social skills in two languages, and parents of English learners see that the home language is valued.

English-Only Efforts

The politics of the U.S. English-only movement are driven by an assimilationist model in the belief that for many immigrants the ability to speak English is a necessity for access to the American middle class. However, as Mora (2002) noted, "this outdated image of the assimilation process ignores the multiple patterns of acculturation for different ethnic groups, many of whom enjoy and preserve their bilingualism as an important cultural and economic resource" (n.p.). Therefore, the idea that the majority should enforce monolingualism on a linguistic minority amounts to linguistic authoritarianism.

English-only bills in the U.S. Congress have repeatedly been defeated. Crawford (2006) described English-only efforts as the politics of fear:

> English Only has always been about fear. Fear of demographic and cultural change, as American communities are transformed by immigrants. Fear of strangers speaking Spanish in public places or posting business signs in Chinese. Fear among Anglos about losing their majority status and, with it, their political dominance. Fear of "the other." (n.p.)

Evidence has shown repeatedly that English learners are more successful when given a firm foundation in their primary language (c.f. Ramírez, 1992) and that bilingualism offers a cognitive advantage (Cummins, 1976). To insist that the United States revert to an outmoded model of monolingualism is to attempt to turn back the clock to an era of language restrictionism, a poor move in a world in which bilingual skills are in increasing demand.

What Is "Fully Qualified" under NCLB?

It is imperative that teachers are able to understand fundamental principles about second-language acquisition and to communicate, to some degree, with those students acquiring English. Therefore, for teachers to be fully qualified as required by the No Child Left Behind legislation, one might ask, "To be considered 'fully qualified' should teachers acquire at least a basic linguistic competency in the languages that students speak?"

The convenient and widely accepted mythology in the United States that a person can be well educated and remain monolingual is questionable with regard to being "fully qualified." The Hispanic population has become the largest minority in the United States, and educators who are able to augment their teaching using both second-language acquisition principles and Spanish-language skills are increasingly needed. Furthermore, teachers with linguistic competence can enhance the stature of the U.S. educational system in the eyes of the world, as U.S. citizens will no longer be viewed by linguistically multicompetent world citizens as being linguistically handicapped by monolingualism.

EMPOWERMENT ISSUES RELATED TO ENGLISH LEARNERS

Despite the fact that research has shown the effectiveness of educational programs that support and develop a student's primary language, very few students have ever been fully served with bilingual education programs; for example, in California only 8 percent of students received bilingual education services before Proposition 227 (Mora, 2002). Therefore, one must ask, in a social climate that does not support primary-language programs for students, how can English learners nonetheless be supported? How can communities empower themselves to ensure that language-minority students receive educational equity?

One answer—equivalent to the real estate mantra "location, location, location"—is politics' mantra "lawyers, lawyers, lawyers." MALDEF's victory in *Williams et al. v. State of California* has provided school district–based means for families to submit grievances about poor facilities and resources. Moreover, authorities can respect parent program choices by encouraging parents to seek out primary-language maintenance programs and by staffing such programs in each neighborhood school rather than forcing families to bus their children to magnet programs.

In addition to supporting families in gaining access to equivalent resources by means of the *Williams v. California* remedies, school authorities can do much to create a positive affective environment for all students, including English learners, in the classroom and the school. The positive involvement of family and community members does much to communicate that school and the family are partners in education.

Cummins (1989, 1996) contrasted educational practices that serve as *collaborative* relations of power with those that are *coercive*. Cummins cautioned that children who enter schools in which diversity is *not* affirmed soon perceive that their "difference" is not honored. Often English learners are not encouraged to think critically, to reflect, and to solve problems. This attitude on the part of teachers communicates a sense of reduced worth, resulting in poor motivation to achieve.

Pressuring students to conform to schooling practices that are unfair or discriminatory results in a loss of their identity as human beings. Teachers who are dedicated to social change must help students develop the confidence and motivation to succeed academically; they must also be aware of the ways in which spoken and unspoken language can encourage positive attitudes, building strong personal and social identities.

EQUITY AND POLICY ISSUES RELATED TO ENGLISH LEARNERS

Achieving high-quality education for English learners has been a centuries-long struggle in the United States. Judging from many measures (e.g., achievement gap, dropout rates, expulsion and detention rates, retention/promotion, tracking, access to AP classes, segregation, length of program, special education placements, gifted education placements, teacher qualifications, teacher retention, and funding and resources), the struggle is by no means over (Rumbaut, 1995; Donato, 1997; Mora, 2000).

Among the indicators that language-minority students have not done well in schools is the fact that nationally Latino students (30.3 percent of whom are limited-English-speaking) are behind their peers in grades 4 and 8, with more than 50 percent below the basic level in reading and math. Latino students are being taught by less qualified teachers, have less access to high-level rigorous classes, are enrolled in fewer college prep courses, and receive fewer state and local funds. More than 40 percent of the teachers teaching English-as-a-second language/bilingual classes are not certified to teach bilingual education or ESL (Gutierrez & Rodríguez, 2005). Only 9.9 percent of Hispanics/Latinos have a college degree, and 48.5 percent do not have a high school diploma. The average income is $14,000 (www.asian-nation.org/demographics.shtml).

Statistics show poor progress as well for Cambodian, Hmong, and Laotian students (44.3 percent of whom are limited-English-speaking); 52.7 percent of this population have no high school diploma and have a median personal income of $16,000. Pacific Islanders also show poor school achievement—13.6 percent have a college degree (compared with 25.3 percent for Whites). The Vietnamese have a 40.4 percent rate of "not English proficient" and have a 13.8 percent rate of attaining a college degree, while 37.8 percent lack a high school diploma (www.asian-nation.org/demographics.shtml).

However, not all language minorities in the United States have done poorly in school. Available data show that 31.3 percent of Chinese are not proficient in English, yet 46.3 percent have college degrees; 32.9 percent of Koreans are not proficient in English yet have a 43.6 percent rate of attaining a college degree (www.asian-nation.org/demographics.shtml).

There is no question that the public climate of support affects the supply of teachers with expertise in educating English learners. Gándara and colleagues (2000) found that between 1997–98 and 1998–99, the year of implementation of Proposition 227 in California, the number of credentialed bilingual teachers in California using their bilingual credential in a teaching assignment with language-minority students dropped by 32 percent. In 1998, 10,894 teacher candidates had bilingual certification;

in 1999, that number was reduced to 5,670. The number of teacher candidates earning a credential with a crosscultural, language, and academic development (CLAD) endorsement, meanwhile, rose only 11 percent (Gándara et al., 2000). This does not bode well for staffing the classrooms of English learners, at least in California.

COMPONENTS OF ELD PROGRAMS

In the widely varied climate of support from area to area in the United States, educational programs range from those that promote additive bilingualism to those that in effect eradicate primary-language proficiency. At the same time as learning English, the language-minority student must gain adequate access to academic content, so a comprehensive program must make provisions for both English and academic learning (and, ideally, a primary-language maintenance component to ensure content and language development in L1). A representative set of the main program types is offered as follows, with the acknowledgment that local implementations might result in a mix of program models, or in outcomes that are not optimal.

Dual-Language Development Programs (Additive Bilingualism)

In two-way immersion classrooms (also called two-way maintenance bilingual classrooms), English learners from a single language background are grouped in the same classroom with approximately equal numbers of English-speaking students. Grade-level-approximate curriculum is provided in both languages. Speakers of each language develop proficiency in both their native and second language, achieve academically through and in two languages, and come to appreciate each other's languages and cultures (Lindholm, 1994). This enhances the status of the students' primary language, promoting self-esteem and increased cultural pride (Lindholm-Leary, 2000), leading to increased motivation.

Dual-language programs encourage students from two different languages to teach one another their languages.

Two-way immersion programs had been implemented in 329 schools in the United States by 2006 (www.cal.org/twi/directory/), with the number of schools growing yearly. Sites were located in twenty-nine states ranging from Alaska to Florida, with the largest numbers in California and New York. Nearly all schools (308) are Spanish–English in design, although other schools immersed students in Cantonese–English, Japanese–English, Navajo–English, Mandarin–English, and German–English. The grade levels served were predominantly K–6, but thirty-four of these schools are middle schools and nine are high schools.

Careful attention to a high-quality bilingual program in the context of primary-language maintenance is key to the success of dual immersion programs (Veeder & Tramutt, 2000). The National Clearinghouse for English Language Acquisition has a wealth of information about two-way programs at www.ncela.gwu.edu, as does a website from the California Department of Education (www.cde.ca.gov/sp/el/ip/faq.asp).

BEST PRACTICE

Two-Way Immersion

An example of a highly successful dual-language program is that in the Valley Center–Pauma Joint Unified School District in Valley Center, California, a program in existence for over twenty years that promotes language proficiency in English and Spanish. The schools with the program are those with very high populations of English learners (ranging from 25 to 50 percent). Both English learners and Spanish learners are held to the same high standards of achievement, and in fact students in the program have an 80 percent pass rate on the California high school exit examination.

"Project FLUENT focuses on the development of Spanish as a second language utilizing rich activities which incorporate the National Foreign Language Standards K–8th grade and effective use of age-appropriate computerized curriculum and a focus on careers in Mass Communications and Technology." (www.languagepolicy.org/flap04.html)

TWI is predicated on beginning literacy instruction for students in both languages. Reading in a foreign language above the level of emergent literacy takes place by using both literature and subject area content, following many of the same principles as reading in the native language. Time is given in class for reading so that students working in groups can facilitate one another's comprehension. To appeal to students' varied interests, all types of content are used (magazines, newspapers, plays, novels, stories, and poems), depending also on the proficiency level of students and the level of language studied. In this way, students are assured of receiving a challenging academic program in both languages.

Critics have alleged that TWI delays English learning and that these programs fail to teach English to English learners. Amselle (1999) argued, "dual immersion programs are really nothing more than Spanish immersion, with Hispanic children used as teaching tools for English-speaking children" (p. 8). Experts concede that the greatest challenge in two-way bilingual programs is to "reduce the gap" between the language abilities of the two groups (English learners and second-language learners [SLLs]). This gap appears when content classes in English are modified (slowed down) for English learners to "catch up," or when content delivery in the primary language is slowed for SSLs. Table 6.4 features program elements of two-way immersion programs.

Not all primary-language maintenance programs are two-way immersion, but two-way immersion programs featuring native English speakers often enjoy more community support. The following vignette illustrates the public pressure faced by one such school that offers primary-language maintenance.

Transitional Bilingual Education

Transitional bilingual education (TBE) programs support the use of students' home language in academic settings only during the period in which they acquire enough English proficiency to make the transition into English-only education. This supports a subtractive view of bilingualism, in effect

Table 6.4 Program Components of Two-Way Immersion

Program Elements	Program Features
Philosophy	Bilingualism as a resource
Goal	Additive bilingualism for English learners and native English speakers
Purpose	Cognitive academic language proficiency achieved through grade-level-appropriate instruction in both languages
Ideal Outcome	Additive bilingualism for English learners and native English speakers
Grade/Proficiency Level(s)	Usually begins in kindergarten, with cohort staying together throughout elementary or middle school
Placement Criteria	Parental exemption waiver
Exit Criteria	Parental choice
Program Length	Parent choice (usually K–6)
Class Composition	Ideally, 50/50 English native speaker and English learner
Language Components	English-language development and primary-language maintenance for English learners; English language arts (ELA) and primary-language-as-a-second-language instruction for native English speakers
Limitations	ELD and ELA must be taught separately, as must primary-language maintenance versus primary-language-as-a-second-language instruction for native English speakers, or both groups will be slowed in achievement in their native languages

CLASSROOM GLIMPSE: Semillas del Pueblo

A primary-language maintenance chapter school in El Sereno (part of Los Angeles), Academia Semillas del Pueblo, found itself in the center of controversy when a local talk radio station and a conservative Internet blog made assertions that the school espoused a covert separatist ethos. Principal Minnie Ferguson said that despite low test scores, other measures of achievement are more encouraging, showing Semillas del Pueblo students advancing to English fluency at a greater rate than Los Angeles Unified students overall.

The Academia held an open house in June, during which groups of children in brightly colored red and yellow shirts sat in circles and played games as others listened intently to teachers reading history lessons in Spanish or sang songs in Mandarin. The curricular emphasis is on multicultural values, with enrollment in 2005–06 that included White, Black, Latino, Asian-American, American-Indian, and native Hawai'ian or Pacific Islander children. (Rivera, 2006)

requiring that English learners discontinue the use of their native language as they increase their fluency in English (Nieto, 2004). In these programs, students receive initial instruction in most, if not all, content areas in their home language while they are being taught English.

There are numerous problems with a TBE program. It may be perceived as a remedial program or another form of segregated, compensatory education. TBE rests on the common misconception that two or three years is sufficient time to learn a second language for schooling purposes, but in fact this is not long enough for students to build cognitive academic language proficiency (CALP) either in their native tongue or in English. As a consequence, they may not be able to carry out cognitively demanding tasks in English or their home language.

Another shortcoming of transitional bilingual education is the effect that English-only schooling has on home-language use. After transition to English, students frequently switch to English as their primary language of communication, and conversational fluency in the home language tends to erode. This retards rather than expedites academic progress in English, primarily because children

Table 6.5 Program Components of Transitional Bilingual Education

Program Elements	Program Features
Philosophy	Bilingualism as a bridge to English proficiency
Goal	Bilingualism for English learners only until replaced by English as the language of instruction
Purpose	Cognitive academic language proficiency achieved through grade-level-appropriate instruction in English
Ideal Outcome	Educational parity for English learners and native English speakers
Grade/Proficiency Level(s)	Usually K–2, from beginning through advanced proficiency
Placement Criteria	Parental exemption waiver
Exit Criteria	(See on Reclassification.)
Program Length	Usually three years (K–2)
Class Composition	Usually Spanish-speaking, but in California bilingual teachers have been certified in twenty languages
Language Components	Content instruction in the primary languages, combined with ELD instruction
Limitations	Lack of programmatic support after transition often leads to subtractive bilingualism

and parents lose the benefit of a shared language for such purposes as homework help. For these and other reasons, TBE programs have not led to school success for many students (see Medina & Escamilla, 1992) (see Table 6.5).

Structured English Immersion

Structured English immersion (SEI) programs are those in which students are taught solely in English supplemented with strategies designed to increase their understanding of the content, and teachers are not necessarily fluent in the L1 of the students. Many of the teaching techniques used for SEI programs were developed for use in multilingual, often urban, classes where there is not a single primary language shared by the learners. In these classes, the use of L1 was not feasible, or was strongly discouraged because of the belief that L1 would interfere with learning L2.

SEI programs are designed to address the learning needs of English learners whose English is at the intermediate level of fluency or above. Unfortunately, this approach is too often used for beginning English learners. The chief element of "structure" built into these programs is the use of Specially Designed Academic Instruction in English (SDAIE), also called "sheltered instruction." SDAIE incorporates specific teaching (not language) modifications to make a lesson understandable to students.

Students obtain access to core curriculum subjects when the content is modified using SDAIE, and thus they can maintain parity with native-English-speaking classmates. Even literature classes can be modified with SDAIE so that English learners are not relegated to ELD programs whose course credits may not be considered college preparatory in nature. However, teachers need to be trained in SDAIE techniques.

SEI programs have one key advantage: All teachers are responsible for the education of English learners and must be knowledgeable about language development issues and techniques. Students are not linguistically segregated, which too often occurs in secondary school settings.

Although supporters of SEI programs promote increased time spent immersed in English as a way to increase classroom learning, SEI is based on an erroneous assumption: that more time spent immersed in a foreign language will somehow compensate for a lack of comprehension. Even with an elaborate set of SDAIE techniques designed to augment—in reality, substitute for—verbal explanation, few experts would agree that a student subjected to SEI achieves the same level of comprehension that same student would achieve if taught in the primary language.

Table 6.6 Program Components of Structured English Immersion

Program Elements	Program Features
Philosophy	Bilingualism as a bridge to English proficiency
Goal	Bilingualism for English learners only until replaced by English as the language of instruction
Purpose	Cognitive academic language proficiency achieved through grade-level-appropriate instruction in English
Ideal Outcome	Educational parity for English learners and native English speakers
Grade/Proficiency Level(s)	Possibility for all grades, all CELDT levels
Placement Criteria	CELDT score level of beginner through advanced
Exit Criteria	(See on Reclassification.)
Program Length	Varies depending on individual progress
Class Composition	Mixed CELDT levels.
Language Components	Content instruction in SDAIE-enhanced English combined with ELD instruction
Limitations	Access to core academic content depends on SDAIE skills of teachers

A key factor is missing in the SEI approach—the opportunity is lost for additive bilingualism. The same drawbacks that can be identified in the TBE model also hold true for SEI programs: There is no development of the primary language, resulting in subtractive bilinguality (see Table 6.6).

Newcomer (Front-Loaded) English

The goal of newcomer programs is to foster in recent immigrants rapid English learning during the period of early acculturation (Short & Boyson, 2004). Newcomer centers, like Newcomer High School in San Francisco, are more common at the secondary level than in the elementary grades. Newcomer programs may be organized as centers, as separate programs in their own locations, or as programs within a school (Genesee, 1999).

The chief rationale for newcomer programs is that students must learn English before they can be educated in English. A second rationale is that students need social and emotional support during the time in which they may experience culture shock. A third rationale is that there are not enough teachers for the number of English learners, so they must be grouped for educational services.

Programs vary in length of day; some are full day, in which students have various content courses along with ELD, whereas others are half-day or after school. Students may be enrolled for a year, four years, or only one semester (Short, 1998). The curriculum is designed to help students move into the regular language support program as soon as possible while helping them gain an understanding of U.S. schools and educational expectations. SDAIE techniques predominate in content classes, if offered. Increasingly, however, the newcomer model is called "front-loading." This means that only English-language development is offered, on an intensive basis, during the newcomer period, with students' having limited access to the core curriculum during this time.

However, research has repeatedly cast doubt on the argument that students must learn English before they can be educated in English. Major disadvantages of the newcomer approach are, first, the idea that newcomers should be separated from the mainstream, English-speaking population during their period of early adjustment. The U.S. Supreme Court, in the ruling *Brown v. Board of Education* (1954), has ruled that separate educational programs, however well meaning, are inherently unequal in implementation. The idea that immigrants should be educated separately—at any stage—promotes segregation in a nation whose school facilities are increasingly ethnically separate (Orfield & Lee, 2005).

A second drawback is that the newcomer approach is based on subtractive bilingual education. Academic support in the primary language is seldom offered, much less primary-language development. It is probably helpful for students to receive counseling and other assistance to help with culture

Table 6.7 Program Components of Newcomer (Front-Loaded) Programs

Program Elements	Program Features
Philosophy	Intensive English is the key to English proficiency
Goal	Intensive English for English learners must take place before English can be used as the language of instruction
Purpose	Cognitive academic language proficiency achieved through grade-level-appropriate instruction in English
Ideal Outcome	English learners can participate in SDAIE-enhanced content instruction.
Grade/Proficiency Level(s)	Newcomer programs are usually implemented in secondary schools, but front-loading can be done at any grade or level, beginning through intermediate proficiency
Placement Criteria	Varies—CELDT score level of beginner or early intermediate plus parental choice
Exit Criteria	(See on Reclassification.)
Program Length	Varies
Class Composition	Mixed CELDT levels
Language Components	Content instruction in SDAIE-enhanced English combined with ELD instruction
Limitations	Access to core academic content depends on SDAIE skills of teachers; segregative

shock, but no amount of humanistic socioemotional "support" in English during students' adjustment period can realistically take the place of genuine support—receiving mediation in the primary language.

A third drawback is that content vocabulary cannot be learned effectively in a front-loaded manner because it is an integral part of learning content concepts. Unfortunately, students are inevitably slowed in their educational advancement when forced to halt academic learning until their English is developed to some arbitrary point. Moreover, if basic interpersonal skills take two years of exposure to English to develop, and cognitive academic language takes five or more years to develop (Cummins, 1981a; Hakuta et al., 2000), then theoretically two to five years of "boot camp" English would be required, an inordinate amount of time for newcomers to be segregated. Thus, the newcomer, or front-loading, model is ill advised (see Table 6.7).

English-Language Development Programs

English is taught to English learners in a variety of ways, and studies have shown varying degrees of student success depending on the program model (Thomas & Collier, 1997). Whereas it may be true that extensive exposure to a high-quality English-language development program is a necessity, it is a fallacy to believe that total immersion in English is effective. When students are provided with a solid foundation in their primary language, faster English acquisition takes place. The following four models are the norm for teaching English to English learners.

Pull-Out ELD. When English learners must leave their home classroom and receive instruction in vocabulary, grammar, oral language, or spelling for separate half-hour to one-hour-a-day classes with a trained ELD teacher, they are said to be "pulled out." Such instruction rarely is integrated with the regular classroom program, and when students return to the home classroom, they usually are not instructed on curriculum they missed while they were gone. This lack only exacerbates an already difficult learning situation. Of the various program models, ELD pull-out is the most expensive to operate because it requires hiring an extra resource teacher (Chambers & Parrish, 1992). It has, however, been the most implemented, despite being the least effective model (Thomas & Collier, 1997).

ELD Class Period.   Although pull-out ELD is normally found at the elementary level, students in the secondary school often have separate ELD classes that help them with their English skills. Unfortunately, these classes often focus entirely on the English language and do not help students with their academic subjects. Moreover, in some school districts students who are placed in separate ELD classes at the high school level do not receive college-entrance-applicable credits for these classes. In other words, to be placed in an ELD class is to be denied the chance for college admission. This unfortunate policy is avoided if students are placed in SDAIE-enhanced high school English classes that do bear college-entry credit value.

Content-Based ELD.   Although content-based ELD classes are still separate and contain only English learners, students learn English through academic content in a curriculum organized around grade-level academic objectives. The most effective of these models is when the ELD teacher collaborates with content area teachers to organize learning objectives around academic subjects in order to prepare students to master grade-level curricula (Ovando & Collier, 1998). Content-based ELD classes develop not only language proficiency but also content knowledge, cognitive strategies, and study skills. Teachers familiarize students with the difference in the style and structure of texts and the type of vocabulary featured in the particular discipline.

Content-based instruction can be of great benefit if content instructors and language teachers work together to provide learners with comprehensible input, as well as to design tasks that are both comprehensible and important. Systematic, planned instruction must present vocabulary, concepts, and structures that are required for mastery of the content (Snow, 1993). The content to be taught, general instructional goals, and time available for instruction are negotiated with the content teacher.

Learning English through content is a worldwide means of English instruction (Brinton & Master, 1997), whether for purposes of business, engineering, medicine, or science. It is most effective when content teachers take an interest in language development and ELD teachers take more responsibility for content.

Universal Access to the Language Arts Curriculum.   As described in the goal of ELD programs is for English learners to make the transition from the ELD standards to the standards outlined in the *Reading/Language Arts Framework* and the ELA standards so they can be instructed in a mainstream classroom. This is accomplished through implementing principles of Universal Instructional Design (UID).

With an augmented emphasis on learning styles and other learner differences, UID promotes access to information, resources, and tools for students with a wide range of abilities, disabilities, ethnic backgrounds, language skills, and learning styles. Burgstahler (2002) noted that "Universal Instructional Design principles . . . give each student meaningful access to the curriculum by assuring access to the environment as well as multiple means of representation, expression, and engagement" (p. 1).

Table 6.8 offers an overview of the principles of UID and some suggested applications of these principles in the education of English learners. UID does not imply that one universal strategy fits all but rather that a diversity of opportunities will work for many different students.

The recommended model for delivery of ELD is that it be integrated with content instruction in a classroom in which the English learner has access to native speakers of English as language models. However, because the English learner is still acquiring basic English skills, ELD instruction cannot provide grade-level-appropriate content. To accomplish this, academic instruction and ELD must go hand in hand.

ENGLISH-LANGUAGE DEVELOPMENT AND ACADEMIC INSTRUCTION

English learners can succeed in content area classes taught in English. If they can follow and understand a lesson, they can learn content material, and the content area instruction—if modified to include English-language development—becomes the means for acquiring English. Basically, SDAIE

Table 6.8 Principles of Universal Instructional Design Applied to English Learners

Principle	Definition	Application
Inclusiveness	A classroom climate that communicates respect for varying abilities	Use bilingual signage and materials; welcome and respect aides and assistants; supply multiple reading levels of texts.
Physical access	Equipment and activities that minimize sustained physical effort, provide options for participation, and accommodate those with limited physical abilities	Use assistive technologies such as screen readers and online dictionaries to assist in translation; make online chatrooms available for students in two languages.
Delivery methods	Content is delivered in multiple modes so it is accessible to students with a wide range of abilities, interests, and previous experiences.	Employ a full range of audiovisual enhancement, including wireless headsets and captioned video; build in redundant modes (e.g., audiotaped read-along books, typed lecture notes, and study guides).
Information access	Use of captioned videos and accessible electronic formats; in printed work, use of simple, intuitive, and consistent formats	Ensure that information is both understandable and complete; reduce unnecessary complexity; highlight essential text; give clear criteria for tests and assignments.
Interaction	Accessible to everyone, without accommodation; use of multiple ways for students to participate	Set up both heterogeneous groups (across second-language ability levels) and homogeneous groups (same language-ability level); instruct students on how to secure a conversational turn.
Feedback	Effective prompting during an activity and constructive comments after the assignment is complete	Employ formative assessment for ongoing feedback.
Demonstration of knowledge	Provision for multiple ways students demonstrate knowledge—group work, demonstrations, portfolios, and presentations	Offer different modes to all students so that English learners are not the only ones with alternatives.

Source: Adapted from Burgstahler (2002), Egbert (2004), & Strehorn (2001).

addresses the following needs of English learners: (1) to learn grade-appropriate content, (2) to master English vocabulary and grammar, (3) to learn "academic" English, and (4) to develop strategies for learning how to learn.

The SDAIE-Enhanced Content Classroom

Specially designed academic instruction in English combines second-language acquisition principles with those elements of quality teaching that make a lesson understandable to students. SDAIE is, ideally, one component in a program for English learners that includes ELD instruction, primary-language instruction in content areas (so that students continue at grade level as they learn English), and content-based ESL classes.

An SDAIE classroom has content objectives identical to those of a mainstream classroom in the same subject but, in addition, includes language and learning strategy objectives. Instruction is modified for greater comprehensibility. The distinction between SDAIE and content-based ELD instruction is that SDAIE features content instruction taught by content area teachers with English-language support. Content-based ELD, taught by ELD teachers, features the use of content area materials as texts for ELD lessons.

A Model for SDAIE

A model for SDAIE originally developed at the Los Angeles Unified School District in 1993 had four components—content, connections, comprehensibility, and interaction. Often, however, teachers could be technically proficient in many of the SDAIE elements yet not be successful with English learners. Discussion and observation revealed that the teacher's attitude played such a critical part in the success of the class that it needed to be explicitly incorporated into the model. Therefore, teacher attitude was added as an overarching component (see Figure 6.1).

Depending on their assessed English level, students can participate in SDAIE-enhanced content lessons.

Figure 6.1 A Model of the Components of Successful SDAIE Instruction

Teacher Attitude

The teacher is open and willing to learn from students.

Content

Lessons include subject, language, and learning-strategy objectives.

Material is selected, adapted, and organized with language learners in mind.

Comprehensibility

Lessons include explicit strategies that aid understanding:
- Contextualization
- Modeling
- Teacher speech adjustment
- Frequent comprehension checks through strategies and appropriate questioning
- Repetition and paraphrase

Connections

Curriculum is connected to students' background and experiences.

Interaction

Students have frequent opportunities to
- Talk about lesson content
- Clarify concepts in their home language
- Represent learning through a variety of ways

Teachers often find that they do not use every aspect of the model in every lesson, but by working within the overall frame they are more assured of providing appropriate learning opportunities for their English learners. The following sections explain and illustrate each of the five SDAIE components.

Teacher Attitude. Teachers are no different from the rest of the population when faced with something new or different. Many recoil, dig in their heels, and refuse to change. But teachers have also chosen to work with people, and they frequently find delight and satisfaction in their students' work, behavior, and learning. It is this sense of delight that is important to capture in working with all learners, particularly English learners.

Three aspects characterize a successful attitude in working with second-language learners:

- Teachers believe that all students can learn.
- Teachers are willing to nurture language development.
- Teachers recognize that a person's self-concept is involved in his or her own language and that at times students need to use that language.

BEST PRACTICE

Positive Teacher Attitudes

An ELD teacher observed and interviewed her colleagues at her school. She discovered that accomplished teachers set up effective learning environments for the English learners. They understood the needs of their culturally and linguistically diverse students and created an atmosphere in the classroom that helped newly arrived students integrate into the life of the school. For example they would pair each English learner with buddy. They encouraged friendships by asking a classmate to stay with the English learner at lunch. They provided appropriate instruction for their English learners and applauded their successes. This environment helped relieve much of the beginners anxiety (Haynes, 2004)

Content. *Content objectives* are necessary to guide teaching. A lesson with a clear objective focuses the instruction by concentrating on a particular goal and guides the teacher to select learning activities that accomplish the goal. Teachers may have to be selective in choosing only the most essential content standards to address in the time allotted.

BEST PRACTICE

Organizing Content for the Theme of "Acculturation"

Content materials for the social studies theme "acculturation" might include primary documents, personal histories and literature. Students who research specific concepts related to acculturation, such as immigration assimilation, culture shock, job opportunities or naturalization, may find that each document features a unique voice. A government document presents a formal, official point of view, whereas a personal or family story conveys the subject from a different, more intimate perspective. In addition, numerous pieces of literature, such as Eve Bunting's *How Many Days to America?* (1988) or Laurence Yep's *Dragonwings* (1975), offer yet other points of view.

Connections. Students engage in learning when they recognize a connection between what they know and the learning experience. Therefore, a critical element of the SDAIE lesson is the deliberate plan on the teacher's part to elicit information from and help make connections for the students. This can be accomplished in several ways: through *bridging*—linking concepts and skills to student experiences or eliciting/using examples from students' lives—and by *schema building*—using scaffolding strategies to link new learning to old.

Table 6.9 Media, Realia, Manipulatives, and Human Resources to Contextualize Lessons

Object Resources	Human Resources
Picture files	Cooperative groups
Maps and globes	Pairs
Charts and posters	Cross-age tutors
Printed material:	Heterogeneous groups
Illustrated books	Community resource people
Pamphlets	School resource people
News articles	Parents
Catalogs	Pen pals (adult and child)
Magazines	Keypals
Puzzles	
Science equipment	
Manipulatives:	
M&Ms	
Buttons	
Tongue depressors	
Gummy bears	
Costumes	
Computer software	
Internet	

Comprehensibility. A key factor in learning is being able to understand. Through all phases of a lesson, the teacher ensures that students have plenty of clues to understanding. This is one of the aspects of SDAIE that makes it different from mainstream instruction. Teachers are aware that they need to present concepts in a variety of ways. They increase the comprehensibility of lessons in four ways: *contextualization* (strategies that augment speech and/or text through pictures, realia, dramatizations, etc.); *modeling* (demonstration of the skill or concept to be learned); *speech adjustment* (strategies to adjust speech from the customary native speech patterns); and *comprehension checks* (strategies to monitor listening and reading comprehension). Table 6.9 provides a list of both object and human resources that can help contextualize classroom content.

Interaction. The organization of discourse is important for language acquisition in content classes. In "teacher-fronted" classrooms (Harel, 1992), the teacher takes the central role in controlling the flow of information, and students compete for the teacher's attention and for permission to speak. More recent research (Gass, 2000), however, points to the role of the learner in negotiating, managing, even manipulating conversations to receive more comprehensible input. Instead of English learners being dependent on their ability to understand the teacher's explanations and directions, classrooms that feature flexible grouping patterns permit students to have greater access to the flow of information.

The teacher orchestrates tasks so that students use language in academic ways. Students are placed in different groups for different activities. Teachers themselves work with small groups to achieve specific instructional objectives.

In planning for interaction in the SDAIE lesson, the teacher considers opportunities for students to talk about key concepts, expects that students may clarify the concepts in their primary language, and allows a variety of means through which students can demonstrate their understanding.

SDAIE offers English learners an important intermediate step between content instruction in the primary language, an environment in which they may not advance in English skills, and a "sink-or-swim" immersion, in which they may not learn key content-related concepts. In most effective

CLASSROOM GLIMPSE: Interaction

In one fifth-grade class, the students produced a news program with a U.S. Civil War setting. The program included the show's anchors; reporters in the field interviewing generals, soldiers, and citizens; a weather report; and reports on sports, economics, and political conditions. There were even commercial breaks. The students engaged in much research in order to be historically accurate, but enthusiasm was high as they shared their knowledge in a format they knew and understood. In addition, students were able to work in the area of their particular interest.

instruction for English learners, ELD methods and SDAIE are used together to provide language development and achievement of core content standards for English learners, depending on the program model used and the specific needs of the students.

PARENTAL RIGHTS AND COMMUNICATING WITH FAMILIES

"Strong parent involvement is one factor that research has shown time and time again to have positive effects on academic achievement and school attitudes" (Ovando & Collier, 1998, p. 270). Yet, for various reasons on the part of both schools and communities, parent involvement has sometimes been an elusive goal. The growing number of English learners in the school system, however, clearly requires that efforts continue to establish communication, develop partnerships, and involve parents, families, and communities. Fortunately, over the past decade successful programs have developed and various guidelines are available to help school personnel, parents, and communities work together to ensure parental rights, parental involvement, successful programs, and school–community partnerships that benefit students.

Parental Rights

Parents have numerous rights that educators must respect and honor in spite of the challenges they may present to the school. These include (1) the right of their children to a free, appropriate public education; (2) the right to receive information concerning education decisions and actions in the language parents comprehend; (3) the right to make informed decisions and to authorize consent before changes in educational placement occur; (4) the right to be included in discussions and plans concerning disciplinary action toward their children; (5) the right to appeal actions when they do not agree; and (6) the right to participate in meetings organized for public and parent information (Young & Helvie, 1996).

Parents have the right to choose in which language development program options their child will participate (e.g., waiver process) and have the right to be contacted about such rights in an appropriate and effective medium (e.g., bilingual phone calls, home visits, primary-language materials, videos). The *Williams et al. v. State of California* remedies offer several mechanisms by which parents can exert more influence on school procedures.

A fundamental right that all parents have is support in school for the home language. To deny access to native-language literacy exploits minorities (Cummings, 1989). It is important that teachers help families understand the advantages that bilingualism provides to the individual, connecting students to their heritage culture; adding a cognitive dimension by expanding and deepening students' thinking; and, later in life, expanding career opportunities. Family support for bilingualism helps to establish expectations for high academic performance in two languages (Molina, Hanson, & Siegel, 1997).

School–Community Partnerships

In addition to developing partnerships with parents, schools are reaching toward communities for help in educating all children. Community-based organizations (CBOs)—groups committed to helping people obtain health, education, and other basic human services—are assisting students in ways that go beyond traditional schooling. Adger (2000) found that school–CBO partnerships support students' academic achievement by working with parents and families, tutoring students in their first language, developing students' leadership skills and higher education goals, and providing information and support on issues such as health care, pregnancy, gang involvement, and so on.

Communities can foster a climate of support for English learners by featuring articles in local newspapers and newsletters about these students' achievements in the schools and prizes they have won, by sponsoring literature and art exhibitions that feature students' work, and by publishing their stories written in both languages. Students can be invited to the local library to offer their stories, books, and poetry to other students, again in both English and the primary language. In this way, support for bilingualism and bilingual education programs is orchestrated in the community at large.

Many people feel that any tolerance of linguistic diversity undermines national unity. However, others hold the view of the United States as a "salad bowl," which features a mixture of distinct textures and tastes, instead of a "melting pot," in which cultural and linguistic diversity is melted into one collective culture and language. The best educational programs for English learners are explicitly bicultural as well so that students' native cultures as well as heritage languages can be fostered. With these programs in place, the United States will benefit from the rich language resources of all its people.

VIDEO WORKSHOP: "A Bilingual Navajo School"

Rockpoint Community School is a bilingual school with a large Navajo population. In this video, a school administrator discusses why it is important for his students to learn in both English and Navajo, and then we see an elementary teacher teach a lesson in English.

To access the video, log on to MyLabSchool at www.mylabschool.com, enter Assignment ID **ENV2** into the **Assignment Finder,** and select the video entitled "A Bilingual Navajo School." Watch the video, complete the questions that follow, and e-mail your responses to your professor for credit.

CHAPTER 7

DUAL LANGUAGE PROGRAM MODELS

Simply stated, *dual language instruction* is an educational program offered in two languages. This definition is straightforward but lacks specificity. Dual language instruction can be offered in a variety of formats or models, depending on the goals of a program and the population it serves.

Some programs, for example, are designed to promote bilingualism and biliteracy for students. Others use a primary or home language as a bridge to assist students while they learn the dominant mainstream language.

This chapter will explain the concept of a program model and describe various types of programs currently in use in the United States. It will also present an overview of the competencies that teachers must have to provide instruction in dual language classrooms.

WHAT IS A PROGRAM MODEL?

If you were to visit a dual language classroom you might note several features, including the functional use of each language and the methodology for distributing the languages in the curriculum. You would also notice the amount of time each language is used. In a particular classroom, you might observe that Spanish is used for instruction 50 percent of the day. Such an observation, however, takes on meaning only in the context of a program model. A *program model* refers to the span of language use and distribution toward a goal for a specific population, across the grades.

If, for example, the classroom you have visited is a Spanish–English -bilingual kindergarten, it would be important to know whether the 50-50 time distribution of languages continues in first grade, or whether the use of Spanish diminishes as children progress, to 40 percent in the first grade and 30 percent in the second, so that children move toward a situation where no Spanish is used at all. Such a program model differs significantly from one where the 50-50 ratio is maintained throughout all grades and both languages are maintained and developed.

Dual language instructional models have been described in a number of ways, some far more complex than others. One theorist cross-referenced the learner, the languages, the community, and the curriculum to arrive at 90 different possible kinds of programs (Mackey, 1972). A simpler typology, based on philosophical rather than linguistic factors, distinguishes between assimilationist and pluralistic program models. Assimilationist programs aim at moving ethnic minority children into the mainstream (dominant) culture. In contrast, pluralistic program models are those that support minority languages and cultures (Kjolseth, 1976).

TRANSITIONAL BILINGUAL PROGRAMS

Which Students Do Transitional Programs Serve?

Transitional programs serve students who are limited English proficient (LEP). For general purposes, we can define LEP students as those who have been determined to have insufficient English to function academically in an English language classroom where instruction is designed for native English speakers. Which students are actually designated as LEP may vary from state to state or even from district to district within a state, because tests and testing procedures are not uniform.

It should be noted that the labels we use are significant and shape and reflect how we respond to the world around us. *Limited English proficient* is a deficit-based term—it identifies students by what they can't do, and sets us up to consider serving them in a remedial or compensatory mode. Today, educators generally refer to English language learners, a serviceable and fairly neutral term.

What Is the Goal of a Transitional Program?

The goal of transitional programs is to develop a student's proficiency in English. In a transitional program, the primary language is used for instructional support until students have reached satisfactory levels of English proficiency, usually as defined by a process involving test scores and teacher observations. Students are expected to move out of a transitional program when they are capable of functioning in an English-only classroom. In many programs, the expectation is that children will be ready to make the change after a period of approximately three years.

U.S. government policy tends to favor transitional programs—by far the most common models in use today. There are a number of problems inherent in transitional bilingual programs:

- They foster subtractive, rather than additive, bilingualism.
- They are compensatory and do not involve the monolingual English-speaking community.
- Exit assessments may measure students' face-to-face language skills and fail to consider the specialized language skills needed for academic success. Placement in English-only classrooms on the basis of such programs can lead to academic failure.
- It is unrealistic to expect all children to master a second language in a three-year period.

Transitional Programs: A Lot Better than Nothing

In 1988, the California Association for Bilingual Education published *On Course: Bilingual Education's Success in California* (Krashen & Biber, 1988), a summary and analysis of data from eight programs across the state, including transitional programs. The Eastman Avenue School in Los Angeles reported an increase in the California Assessment Program (CAP) scores for students who participated in a carefully structured transitional program. More recently, a study that looked at the achievement of English learners over eight years and across content areas (CREDE, 2003) concludes that English language learners who attended mainstream programs with no primary language support "showed large decreases in reading and math achievement by Grade 5 when compared to students who participated in language support programs" (p.3).

Ultimately, we have to think back to the concept of "program." Villarreal points out that effective programs must have enthusiastic leaders who are committed to supporting dedicated, qualified teachers. Effective programs, transitional or otherwise, provide a supportive climate and an instructional program that is both accessible and challenging, built on the linguistic and cultural resources of students, their families, and their communities (Villarreal, 1999). A carefully modeled transitional program that meets those criteria, while not the best of all worlds, offers meaningful support for English language learners and is undoubtedly better than submersion.

LANGUAGE MAINTENANCE PROGRAMS

Language maintenance programs are pluralistic and promote bilingualism and biliteracy for language minority students. Maintenance programs may be the most effective means of promoting English proficiency for limited English proficient students because:

- Concepts and skills learned in a student's first language transfer to the second language.
- A strong base in a first language facilitates second language acquisition.
- Support for home language and culture builds self-esteem and enhances achievement (Hakuta & Gould, 1987).

In other words, maintenance bilingual education, which is additive rather than subtractive, leads to academic success and also facilitates the acquisition of English skills for the language minority student.

ENRICHMENT PROGRAMS

Efforts were made in the late 1960s and early 1970s to provide dual language instructional programs for both language minority children and monolingual English children. The need, however, for language support for limited English proficient children has been overwhelming. In the face of limited resources and staffing, the response has been largely compensatory in nature. The tendency to view dual language instruction as compensatory education has eroded the political base necessary to assure services for language minority students and has denied access to bilingual education for monolingual English-speaking children as well.

Educators have begun to reconsider enrichment or two-way bilingual instruction, which provides dual language instruction for all students. Two-way programs are becoming increasingly popular in areas where magnet schools have been established to facilitate desegregation. Problems in implementing enrichment programs arise from a lack of qualified staff, constant pressure to meet the needs of increasing numbers of non-English speakers, and lack of community understanding and support for dual language instruction.

IMMERSION PROGRAMS

Beginning in 1965 with the now famous Saint-Lambert experiment, success in Canada has inspired a strong interest in immersion programs. In an immersion program all the usual curricular areas are taught in a second language—this language being the medium, rather than the object, of instruction. Immersion instruction should not be confused with submersion or "sink-or-swim" instruction, where non-English-speaking children are mainstreamed in English-only classrooms without assistance and expected to keep the pace. In an immersion classroom:

- Grouping is homogeneous, and second language learners are not competing with native speakers.
- The teacher speaks the child's first language and can respond to student needs.
- Children are not expected to function immediately in their second language and can express themselves in their first.
- First language support is offered in the form of language arts instruction.
- Instruction is delivered in the second language, but is carefully structured so as to maximize comprehension for students.

The Results of Immersion: The Canadian Experience

The implementation of carefully structured additive immersion programs may provide useful educational services to both limited English proficient and monolingual English students in the United States. Results of research and evaluation studies of French early immersion programs in Canada indicate that students:

- Achieve at levels comparable to those of comparison groups who received all instruction in English.
- Fall behind comparison groups initially in English literacy skills, but catch up to and even surpass those groups once English instruction begins.
- Achieve higher levels of proficiency in the second language than students who study it as an isolated subject.

- Attain native-like receptive skills in their second language and, while their productive skills fall short of native proficiency, are quite capable of expressing themselves in the second language.
- Have heightened sensitivity to social and cultural aspects of their second culture (Cummins & Swain, 1986).

The Canadian experience with immersion instruction suggests that the model works best with children from a dominant language group who are not at risk of losing their first language since it is readily available in the environment beyond the school. In other words, immersion programs are most effective when they are linguistically and culturally additive.

Immersion Programs in the United States

There are several immersion program models currently operating in the United States. Enrichment, two-way, and English immersion programs will be described in the following pages.

Enrichment Immersion Programs. These programs, like the Canadian programs that inspired them, immerse monolingual English speakers in a second language. The Culver City Spanish Immersion Program in California, started in 1971, is the oldest example of a replication of the Canadian model in the United States. Enrichment immersion programs have been used as "magnets" in voluntary desegregation efforts. Such efforts expand participation in enrichment immersion programs beyond middle-class white students to working-class and black students and provide opportunities for research on the effects of immersion on speakers of nonstandard varieties of English (Genesee, 1987).

Two-Way Immersion Programs. In these innovative programs, sometimes called *developmental* or *bilingual immersion programs,* monolingual English-speaking children are immersed in a second language alongside limited English proficient children who are native speakers of the second language. English is introduced gradually until it comprises about 50 percent of the curriculum. The model is actually a combination of maintenance bilingual instruction for LEP students and immersion instruction for monolingual English speakers. The strength of this approach is that it aims at additive bilingualism for all the students involved. The goals of a two-way immersion program are bilingualism and biliteracy for all students.

According to Thomas and Collier (1997), the following factors are present in successful two-way immersion programs:

- Students participate for at least six years.
- The ratio of speakers of each language is balanced.
- Languages are carefully separated.
- The minority language is emphasized in the early grades.
- Instruction is excellent and emphasizes core academics.
- Parents have a strong, positive relationship with the school.

The two-way immersion model was first implemented in San Diego, California, in 1975, and has been replicated nationwide. At River Glen Elementary School in northern California, a linguistically heterogeneous group of kindergarten children starts school each year in a classroom where Spanish is used 90 percent of the time and English 10 percent of the time. By fifth grade, English and Spanish are each used 50 percent of the time in class. The program at River Glen was started as part of a magnet school desegregation program and has been extremely successful in attracting an ethnically diverse student population.

Two-way immersion programs address an issue that has surfaced in research on traditional programs. In traditional programs, the teacher is the only native speaker in the classroom. Native-like language input is therefore somewhat limited, and students in interaction with each other tend to develop what might be characterized as a classroom pidgin of the target language (Higgs, 1991; Swain, 1991). Because two-way immersion classrooms mix students from both language groups, all students have many opportunities to interact with native speakers, which enhances their chances to develop native-like proficiency in their new language.

According to a directory published by the Center for Applied Linguistics (2007), as of November 2006 there were 338 two-way immersion programs in the United States. All programs pair English with another language, most commonly Spanish, which is offered in 316 schools. The other languages offered are scattered among French, Cantonese, Korean, Navajo, Japanese, Mandarin and German. California has the greatest number of schools offering two-way immersion programs, but programs exist in 29 states and the District of Columbia.

A web search indicates that interest in Mandarin is surfacing in many areas. For example, Iowa, which does not appear in the CAL data as of this writing, is using newly available federal funds to begin two-way immersion programs in both Spanish and Mandarin (Iowa State University, 2006).

Bilingual immersion supports the primary language of language minority students, and offers an enrichment program to English speakers. Results of longitudinal studies indicate that students in these programs achieve high levels of bilingualism as well as high levels of academic competence in their subject areas (Lindholm & Molina, 1998). Another important outcome of two-way immersion programs is that students not only speak each other's languages, they learn to appreciate and respect each other's culture (Guido, 1995; Lindholm, 1994).

English Immersion

Political pressure in the United States to move away from primary language instruction has resulted in experimentation with English immersion programs, sometimes called *structured immersion,* for minority students (see Table 7.1). One important longitudinal study of English immersion indicates that it is less successful for minority language students than bilingual education with native language support (Ramírez et al., 1991).

MODELS AND REALITIES: WHAT DOES BILINGUAL EDUCATION LOOK LIKE IN PRACTICE?

Description of program models doesn't always capture the reality of bilingual program implementation. In real schools, educators must deal with the realities of resources, staffing, and the variety of needs that children bring. A report commissioned by the U.S. Department of Education (Fleischman & Staples-Said, 1994) describes ten programs nationwide in districts that range from small to quite large, from rural to urban, serving children from a wide variety of backgrounds and languages.

Table 7.1 Program Models, Goals, and Outcome

Program Model	Goal	Outcome
Transitional	Proficiency in L2 for language minority students (assimilationist)	Subtractive bilingualism
Maintenance	Bilingualism and biliteracy for language minority students (pluralist)	Additive bilingualism
Enrichment/Two-way	Bilingualism and biliteracy for language minority and language majority students (pluralist)	Additive bilingualism
Immersion		
1. Enrichment	Bilingualism and biliteracy for language majority students (pluralist)	Additive bilingualism
2. Two-way	Bilingualism and biliteracy for language minority and language majority students (pluralist)	Additive bilingualism
3. English immersion	Proficiency in English for language minority students (assimilationist)	Subtractive bilingualism

Note: L1 = first language; L2 = second language. For language minority students in the United States, L2 = English.

Newcomer Programs

The challenges of providing appropriate schooling for second language learners are complicated at the secondary level by a number of factors. The structure of secondary schools themselves, with multiple course offerings and tracks, makes it difficult to offer a consistent program for second language learners without restricting choices of electives and limiting their high school experience. Also, even though older students with first language literacy learn English quickly, they may encounter difficulties with advanced high school curricula. For students who aren't literate, the challenge is clear, and materials and methods for meeting their needs are not readily available.

Beyond the demands of classes and assignments, newly arrived students who have had no schooling in their home countries and even those who have are likely to have little knowledge of the way we "do" high school in the United States. Think, for example, about the way bells ring to signal the change of classes. If you grew up and went to school in the United States, that probably seems quite ordinary—so ordinary that you probably barely notice it. If you didn't grow up here, and you were new to this country, daily procedures like the bells in a U.S. school might be perplexing, even overwhelming.

Finally, newly arrived students may have needs associated with the pain of leaving their home countries or adjusting to U.S. society. Some of them may be refugees, some may have left parents and other family behind, and some may have suffered the deprivations and horrors of war.

In an effort to help newly arrived students adjust to the experience and expectations of U.S. schools, some districts have created newcomer programs. Newcomer programs take a number of forms, from an orientation class to a freestanding school, but they generally attempt to assist students to:

- Overcome the trauma of relocation.
- Develop familiarity with the customs and culture of U.S. schooling.
- Develop English proficiency.
- Adapt to U.S. society in general.
- Succeed in their transition to mainstream schools.

Until recently, there was little research on newcomer programs, but the need for such programs and interest in them is growing. Additional information about newcomer programs is available on the web at www.ncela.gwu.edu and www.cal.org.

The smallest of these, a southwestern rural district with a total population of 165, supports 31 LEP migrant farmwork students with an ESL pull-out program. The ESL teacher is Spanish-speaking and uses primary language to assist students in developing primary language literacy skills. The largest district described in the report is urban and located in the Southeast. The district's total enrollment is about 300,000 students, 15 percent of whom are LEP. Of the 45,000 LEP students, most are Spanish speaking, 12 percent speak Haitian Creole, and a small number speak other languages. Where language concentrations make it practicable, the district offers primary language instruction in core curriculum classes. All LEP students receive English as a second language (ESL) instruction in a pull-out program. A newcomer program serves LEP middle and high school age students who need to develop primary language literacy skills to facilitate their transition to English.

Despite the very different qualities of all the districts described in the report, and the variety of populations they serve, all the teachers interviewed for the report expressed concerns about the need for support and understanding from their colleagues and administrators. Another area of concern was the need for services for parents who themselves do not speak English and are often undereducated as well as overwhelmed by the demands of working several jobs.

Teachers expressed similar concerns in interviews conducted by Lemberger (1997). Her analysis of eight teachers' narratives reinforces the idea that consistent leadership and administrative support are essential to program success.

Also, schools must be responsive to the needs of language minority parents. Traditional forms of parent involvement may not be effective, and schools have to devise innovative, creative approaches to outreach and involvement. All the teachers in Lemberger's study expressed frustration with the limited availability of materials in both native and second languages. This is especially important because LEP students may not have access to many books at home (Krashen, 1997/1998).

It should be noted once again that many "programs" are not programs at all, lacking a consensual set of goals and consistent approaches to reaching them. Lemberger (1997) comments: "A teacher could never be sure that what she taught in one grade would be followed up by another colleague. Native language development might not be supported and built upon from year to year depending on whether the receiving teacher understood the value of maintaining and using the native language" (pp.147–148).

Critics of bilingual education often overstate the extent of services to LEP students. Many LEP students, however, are not served by any program at all. The Council of Chief State School Officers reports (1990) that in 20 of the 48 states that responded to a survey on services to LEP students at least 25 percent receive no services. Four states responded that they fail to serve 60 percent of their LEP student populations. The report characterizes the current state of service to LEP students as "an abdication of legal responsibility as well as social responsibility" (p.22).

DUAL LANGUAGE INSTRUCTION IN PRIVATE SCHOOLS

Professional attention generally focuses on dual language instruction in public school settings. Despite current interest in two-way and enrichment programs, most address the needs of limited English proficient children. Bilingualism, however, is widely considered the hallmark of an educated person, and dual language instruction has found outlets in the private school arena as well.

Dual language instruction for privileged sectors of society has been available in the United States for quite some time. For example, Bryn Mawr School in Baltimore, Maryland, established in 1885, offers French, Latin, Greek, German, and Spanish as enrichment for students in kindergarten through fifth grade (Tomlinson & Eastwick, 1980).

According to one comprehensive report, there are approximately 6,500 private schools in the United States that provide some form of education in a language other than English. At the time the study was completed, the Jewish community accounted for nearly half that number, providing schooling in both Hebrew and Yiddish, but at least 108 languages were represented in private schools (Fishman, 1985).

It would be difficult to estimate the number of such schools at the present time, but there are revealing examples. For instance, the Association of Northern California Chinese Schools lists 84 member schools (ANCCS, 2003). Some of them enroll upwards of a thousand students. These are generally "Saturday" schools, offering Chinese instruction on weekends only. Note that children who attend these schools develop language and literacy in two languages. In other words, they actually receive a bilingual education—it just happens under more than one roof.

As part of a federal project on bilingual education, researchers made site visits to 24 private schools that had dual language instructional programs. They found that private schools use many of the same methods as public schools for providing dual language instruction. Despite the lack of innovation, private dual language programs are distinguished by their emphasis on the value of knowing two languages (Elford & Woodford, 1982). This emphasis appears to persist, even in the current political climate. For example, the International School of the Peninsula in Palo Alto, California, offers a full curriculum in both Mandarin Chinese and French to approximately 500 students, many of whom are American-born English speakers. In its mission, the school states: "We are committed to developing well-rounded individuals with a broad international awareness and the ability to communicate in at least two languages" (International School of the Peninsula, 2003).

Reports in the popular press indicate that demand for second language instruction has spread to include private preschools (Wells, 1986). The value placed on bilingualism by those who can afford to pay for private schooling raises an important issue: Why is dual language instruction desirable for a socioeconomic elite but undesirable for minority language groups? Despite the current lack of government support for bilingual programs and public misconceptions about their value, perhaps two-way enrichment programs will change attitudes about bilingualism and dual language instruction.

BILINGUAL TEACHERS

All too often lay people, and even some professionals, assume that bilingual teachers are teachers whose only qualification is that they speak two languages. That would be the same as assuming that an English teacher is any person who speaks, reads, and writes English! A good bilingual teacher, like all good teachers, has attitudes, knowledge, and skills that are particular to the students and the subject matter. What good teachers do, and what they need to know to do it, is the subject of ongoing conversation among professionals at every level.

Clearly, bilingual teachers need to be bilingual and biliterate in English and in the language of their students. But they need other competencies as well. They need to understand the nature of language and how languages are learned so they can create appropriate learning environments for second language learners.

In addition, they must understand their students' culture in ways that transcend surface culture and address the values and beliefs underlying the ways their students act in and out of classrooms. Understanding of culture, combined with awareness of the social contexts of their students, allows effective bilingual teachers to reach out and connect with the families and communities of the students they serve. Understanding the historical and political contexts of bilingual education and of their students supports teachers' abilities to advocate for their students' needs in a climate increasingly characterized by hostility toward newcomers and diversity.

Finally, like all teachers, bilingual teachers must be skilled at assessing students' needs, as well as planning appropriate goals, objectives, and activities to meet those needs and gathering evaluative data on an ongoing basis as students grow and change. Bilingual teachers plan and prepare in more than one language, and strive to meet multiple content and language objectives as students learn two languages through bilingual instruction. Currently, 44 states and the District of Columbia offer certification for teachers of English as a second language, and 28 certify bilingual teachers. Seventeen states require that teachers placed in bilingual classrooms have the appropriate certification (NCELA, 2007).

SUMMARY

Dual language instruction may be transitional or maintenance-oriented. Immersion models have received attention recently because they have proven effective in Canada for teaching minority languages to majority children. A variety of immersion designs are currently being tried in the United States. Enrichment programs that provide second language instruction for monolingual English speakers are increasing in popularity. Dual language programs are available in private schools as well. Teachers who work in dual language instructional settings need specialized training in both bilingual and multicultural education.

QUESTIONS TO THINK ABOUT AND DISCUSS

1. If you were going to build a program that served English language learners from the ground up, what would it look like? What outcomes would you try to achieve? To meet those goals, what kind of program model would you implement? What competencies would you expect teachers to have?
2. Consider your own teacher preparation program: Does it adequately prepare you to meet the needs of second language learners? If so, how, and if not, what experiences and expectations would you choose to add or improve?

ACTIVITIES

1. Visit a public dual language instructional program. Interview a program administrator, a teacher, a parent, and a student enrolled in the program. Find out what they perceive the goals of the program to be. Analyze the program design. Does the program model fit the goals that the participants envision?
2. Visit a private school that offers dual language instruction. What program model is in use? What are the goals of administrators, teachers, parents, and students in this school? Describe the student population of the school.

SUGGESTIONS FOR FURTHER READING

Cummins, J. (1989). *Empowering minority students*. Sacramento: California Association for Bilingual Education.
This book examines the relationship between minority students' experience of schooling and the sociopolitical context of education. Language and bilingual education are explored from the perspective of critical pedagogy, and programs that have been successful for language minority students are described.

Cummins, J. (1996). *Negotiating identities: Education for empowerment in a diverse society*. Ontario, CA: California Association for Bilingual Education.
Negotiating Identities is more a simple update of Empowering Minority Students. *Cummins expands on the notion that bilingual education cannot be thought of simply in terms of language, and this book guides the reader to think about language and schooling in terms of power relations and the impact of social and political contexts on the relationships of students and their teachers.*

Cummins, J., & Swain, M. (1986). *Bilingualism in education*. London: Longman.
This book explores the nature of bilingual proficiency and suggests that positive linguistic, cognitive, and academic consequences result from high levels of proficiency in two languages. Results of research and evaluation studies related to Canadian French immersion programs are described in detail.

Frederickson, J. (1995). *Reclaiming our voices: Bilingual education, critical pedagogy & praxis*. Los Angeles: California Association for Bilingual Education.
Critical pedagogy creates a classroom world wherein students can find their own voices, engage in creative dialogue, and transform their lives and their worlds. This collection of articles brings the reader into the conversation about critical theory and pedagogy tied directly to considerations of language, culture, bilingualism, and biculturalism.

Genesee, F. (1987). *Learning through two languages: Studies of immersion and bilingual education*. Rowley, MA: Newbury House.
An examination of immersion programs for majority students in Canada and bilingual programs for minority language students in the United States. A chapter on immersion in the United States details programs in California, Maryland, and Ohio.

Genesee, F. (Ed.). (1994). *Educating second language children: The whole child, the whole curriculum, the whole community*. Cambridge, UK: The Cambridge University Press.
This collection of articles links schools, families, and communities, and addresses the second language learner's experience in all those contexts, reaching beyond language to incorporate social and cultural dimensions as well.

Krashen, S., & Biber, D. (1988). *On course: Bilingual education's success in California.* Sacramento: California Association for Bilingual Education.

Following a summary of a rationale for primary language instruction, this book provides descriptions of bilingual programs in California that have been successful in improving student achievement.

Lemberger, N. (1997). *Bilingual education: Teachers' narratives.* Mahwah, NJ: Lawrence Erlbaum Associates.

The author interviewed eight bilingual teachers from a variety of backgrounds who teach in a variety of settings. The book includes the teachers' own stories, as well as an analysis of the issues and themes that emerge. No book to date better captures the on-the-ground experience of teachers in bilingual classrooms.

Office of Bilingual Bicultural Education, California State Department of Education. (1984). *Studies on immersion education: A collection for United States educators.* Sacramento: California State Department of Education.

The first section of this book presents an overview of major issues related to immersion programs. The second section includes descriptions of programs in Canada. Section three looks at immersion education in the United States.

Olsen, L. et al. (1994). *The unfinished journey: Restructuring schools in a diverse society.* San Francisco: California Tomorrow.

Using descriptions of a number of programs currently in place, this report shows how schools can effectively restructure to meet the needs of diverse student populations.

Skutnabb-Kangas, T. (1981). *Bilingualism or not: The education of minorities.* Clevedon, UK: Multilingual Matters.

Far more than a simple discussion of program models, this book provides an insightful analysis of bilingualism and the education of minorities from a broad political perspective. Included are discussions of bilingualism of children from a variety of language backgrounds, the neuro-linguistic and cognitive aspects of bilingualism, the impact of social and educational policy on immigrant children, and a typology of dual language programs accounting for differences between majority and minority students.

CHAPTER 8

THE CHANGING PATTERN OF IMMIGRATION

Immigrants have been a primary source of population growth and cultural changes throughout our history. They have come to enjoy political freedom, religious tolerance, economic opportunities, and family reunification. They came through forced immigration in the case of slavery. Recent data on immigration show consistent trends and new patterns. One consistent trend is that of immigration from Mexico, which became one of the top five countries of origin for immigrants to the United States in 1921 (U.S. Department of Justice, 1994). It became the leading country in 1961 and that trend continued until 2005, the most recent data available (Tables 8.1 and 8.2).

The recent patterns have contributed to the increasing diversity of our population. Immigrants from Asia, Africa, and Central and South America have largely replaced those of Western Europe. As we continue to receive immigrants whose cultures, languages, races and ethnicities, and religions differ from those of the dominant U.S. mainstream, it will be essential to help all children acquire the knowledge, understanding, attitudes, and skills to live and work together for the common good. We hope that the content of this text will aid teachers and others who work with children in achieving these goals.

Table 8.1 Immigrants by Continent of Origin 1961–2000

	1961–1970	1971–1980	1981–1990	1991–2000
Europe	1,238,600	801,300	705,601	1,309,106
Asia	445,300	1,633,800	2,817,381	2,890,153
Africa	39,300	91,500	192,293	382,520
Oceania	NA	NA	NA	47,926
North America	1,351,100	1,645,000	3,124,958	3,910,082
Mexico	443,300	637,200	1,653,268	2,250,497
South America	228,300	284,400	455,919	539,330

Source: U.S. Department of Homeland Security, Office of Immigration Statistics, *2005 Yearbook of Immigration Statistics.*

Table 8.2 Immigrants by Continent of Origin 2000–2005

	2000	2001	2002	2003	2004	2005
Europe	130,996	174,411	173,524	100,434	133,181	176,569
Asia	264,413	348,256	340,494	243,918	334,540	400,135
Africa	44,534	53,731	60,101	48,642	66,422	85,102
Oceania	5,105	6,071	5,515	4,351	5,985	6,546
North America	338,959	405,638	402,049	249,968	342,468	345,575
Mexico	173,493	205,560	218,822	115,585	175,411	161,445
South America	55,823	68,484	74,151	55,028	72,060	103,243

Source: U.S. Department of Homeland Security, Office of Immigration Statistics, *2005 Yearbook of Immigration Statistics.*

HISTORICAL OVERVIEW

Although Mexico has been one of the major sources of immigrants to the United States since 1920, in every decade between 1880 and 1924, 13 million immigrants from Southern Europe, on average, came to the United States (U.S. Department of Justice, 1994). This massive, predominantly European immigration ended in the mid-1920s during an isolationist period of anti-Jewish, anti-Catholic sentiment when laws restricting immigration were passed (Jacobson, 1996).

Quotas restricted the numbers and were lowest for those from countries labeled "undesirable," a category in which the countries change periodically depending on U.S. attitudes regarding race and social class. For example, the Chinese Exclusion Act of 1882 reduced the number of Chinese immigrants to the United States. Chinese laborers had been imported to build the transcontinental railroad that would connect San Francisco to the Atlantic states and cultivate the rich soil of California (Takaki, 1989). Palmer commented in 1848, "No people in all the East are so well adapted for clearing wild lands and raising every species of agricultural products as the Chinese" (cited in Takaki, 1989, p. 22). Although the Chinese constituted only 0.002 percent of the U.S. population in 1880, the passage of the act was a response to the class tensions and conflict within white society during a time of economic crisis (Takaki, 1989). Thus, "Congress voted to make it unlawful for Chinese laborers to enter the United States for the next ten years and denied naturalized citizenship to the Chinese already here" (Takaki, 1989, p. 111). The prohibition that was initially directed at Chinese laborers was broadened to include all Chinese in 1888 (Takaki, 1989).

Changes in the immigrant population also occurred from 1841 to 1861 when France, Canada, Norway, and Sweden were added to the list of dominant sending countries and from 1901 to 1920 when Italy moved to the top of the list, followed by Austria-Hungary, the Soviet Union, Canada, and England. Important changes were seen again from 1921 to 1940 when Mexico became one of the top sending countries. In fact, during the 1920s, immigration from Mexico increased significantly when both families and single men crossed the border in search of work and in 1942 when an emergency wartime agreement between the United States and Mexico allowed the legal entry of temporary agricultural workers known as the *braceros*. This arrangement lasted for twenty-two years until 1964.

Amendments to the U.S. immigration laws in 1965 resulted in higher immigration rates than at any time since the early 1920s (Jacobson, 1996). During the 1960s, Asia, Central and South America, and Mexico became the predominant countries of origin for the majority of immigrants. By 1994 the top five sending countries were Mexico, the Philippines, China, Korea, and Vietnam, and from 1995 to 1998 Mexico continued to lead all countries in the number of immigrants to the United States, followed by China, India, and the Philippines.

The dominance of Asians and Latin Americans in the recent immigrant population is due to family unity–based selection priorities, which favor newer immigrant groups, and a shift in the demand for immigration to the less developed regions of the world (Meissner, Hormats, Walker, & Ogata, 1993). As Pastor (1983) noted, people of the Caribbean Basin, for example, pull up their roots for a new land for two "of the elemental human instincts, hope or fear, and in some cases, both" (p. 98).

The 1990s revealed an economic gap between "relatively few, but mostly very rich, developed countries of Europe, North America, Australia and Japan on the one hand, and on the other, the very many countries, mostly, but by no means all, poor, developing countries of the Third World, where more than three quarters of the world's population live" (Gould & Findlay, 1994, p. 23). Large, economic disparities among countries are the root cause of most international migration (United Nations, 1999). However, migration is also driven by (1) internal and international conflicts, (2) the failure of governments to respect the rights of minorities, (3) the lack of good governance, which includes the collapse of the state, and (4) the lack of security in terms of basic necessities, the environment, or human rights (United Nations, 1999). To some extent, the interaction of race and the push to emigrate is another factor. Citizens of Cuba and Haiti, for example, who have attempted to flee poverty and persecution have not received equal treatment in their pleas. The "asylum" explanation has apparently worked for Cubans fleeing Castro's communist regime, while it has not worked for Haitians.

Other incentives for migration have arisen from the advent of global media and multinational corporations that initiate international transfers of employees, as well as from the collapse of internal controls in former Eastern Bloc countries, more accessible means for migration, and "brain drain" migration from countries where young, well-educated persons cannot find suitable employment. Calls for temporary labor in agriculture have also contributed to the intense pressure for migration in developing countries in the 1990s (Gould & Findlay, 1994).

The United Nations has been very involved in human rights and other issues regarding international migration. Thus, international protection for those who emigrate from one country to another is embodied in certain agreements and conventions of the United Nations. For example, the 1975 Helsinki Accords required countries to lower the barriers to free movement of people and ideas, and the Refugee Act of 1980 made countries more open to the claims of refugees (Sassen, 1996). Second, The International Convention, adopted by the United Nations in December 1990, protects the rights of all migrant workers and members of their families. Courts have blocked the attempts by several countries to limit family reunification based upon that Convention (Sassen, 1996). The Programme of Action of the International Conference on Population and Development in 1999 called for cooperation between governments of origin and countries of destination. In response, the governments of Canada, Mexico, the United States, and each of the Central American countries have set up a consultation mechanism known as the Puebla Process (United Nations, 1999). This process involves a multilateral mechanism to coordinate the policies, actions, and objectives agreed to by participating countries. This process, also known as the Regional Conference on Migration, is important, because it provides a focus on effective responses to problems arising in the area of migration (International Organization for Migration, 1999). Countries participating in the process include Belize, Canada, Costa Rica, Dominican Republic, El Salvador, Guatemala, Honduras, Mexico, Nicaragua, Panama, and the United States.

Finally, the 1999 United Nations Conference on Population and Development focused on the need to ensure protection against racism, ethnocentrism, xenophobia, and physical harm for both documented, or legal, immigrants and undocumented, or illegal, immigrants (United Nations, 1999). In fact, Sassen (1996) has noted that "there is a shift to the rights of the individual regardless of nationality, and respect for international human rights codes" (p. 95).

LEGISLATION

Important national legislation has also affected the flow of immigrants to the United States. Immigration law in the United States began with World War I when fears regarding the arrival of enemy spies encouraged Congress to pass a law in 1917 that introduced literacy requirements, banned "Asiatic" immigrants, and required all arrivals to have a passport (Harris, 1995). This law was superseded by legislation in 1921 and 1924, which introduced immigrant quotas in proportion to the national origins of the U.S. population (Harris, 1995).

After World War II, the U.S. Congress conducted a review of the country's immigration policies and passed new legislation, the Immigration and Nationality Act, also known as the McCarran–Walter Act. This legislation, in effect since 1952, continues as the basic immigration law (United Nations, 1998). The McCarran–Walter Act eliminated previous racial exclusions, but retained the national origins formula of the Quota Act of 1924 (United Nations, 1998). It allocated visas according to nationalities already represented in the U.S. population. The McCarran–Walter Act also gave preference to relatives of American citizens and skilled workers.

As mentioned earlier, in 1965, during the Kennedy administration, Amendments to the Quota Act abolished quotas based on national origins, fixed a ceiling on Western Hemisphere immigration, and devised a preference system favoring close relatives of U.S. residents and citizens; those with needed occupational skills, abilities, or training; and refugees (Fuchs, 2000). Other aspects of the amendments allocated visas on a first-come, first-served basis and placed no numerical limit on immediate relatives of U.S. citizens (Fuchs, 2000). The 1965 legislation resulted in a great shift in the nationality of immigrants and, by 1985, 46.4 percent of immigrants to the United States came from Asia (United Nations, 1998).

Illegal Immigrants: Facts

- Only a small percentage work in agriculture.
- About 20 percent work in construction.
- About 17 percent work in leisure and hospitality industries.
- About 14 percent work in manufacturing.
- About 11 percent work in the wholesale and retail trades.
- Pay rates are commonly in the range of $10 to $20 per hour.
- It seems likely that there are about 8 million illegal immigrants with jobs now. (Based upon the Center's figures).

Source: Passel, Pew Hispanic Research Center, 2005.

The Refugee Act of 1980 provided that refugee admissions would be a permanent component of immigration. In addition, the Immigration Reform and Control Act (IRCA) of 1986 legalized the status of many illegal aliens, most of whom were from Mexico and had lived in the United States continuously since 1982. In the amendments of the IRCA, family reunification is a high priority, which has led to a tremendous increase in immigration and a change in the ethnic composition of the immigrant population. Nevertheless, the number of illegal immigrants has continued to increase due to both regional and global changes.

Subsequently, the Immigration Act of 1990, which provided the first major change in immigration legislation in twenty-five years, changed the quota preference system to allow an increase in skilled workers, reduce the delay in the admission of immigration-eligible family members, and provide greater diversity in the sending countries (Meissner et al., 1993; United Nations, 1998). The IMMACT (Immigration Act of 1990), in fact, established annual overall limits on total legal immigration; created a guaranteed minimum number of visas for close family members; increased the number of persons admitted for employment reasons, with higher priority for professionals and highly skilled persons; and created a diversity class of admissions for persons from nations that had not recently sent many immigrants to the United States (U.S. Commission on Immigration Reform, 1997). Diversity admissions refers to provisions in the IMMACT to increase national diversity in the immigrant population by widening access for immigrants from underrepresented countries whose citizens have neither strong family nor job ties to the United States (U.S. Commission on Immigration Reform, 1997).

Thus, in recent years the percentage of foreign-born persons in the general U.S. population increased from a total of 5.4 percent in 1960 to 86 percent in 1993. About 68 percent of immigrants in 1993 came from only fifteen countries (Jacobson, 1996), and immigrants are most concentrated in six states: California, New York, Texas, Florida, New Jersey, and Illinois (U.S. Department of Homeland Security, 2004).

The Illegal Immigration Reform and Immigrant Responsibility Act of 1996 is the most recent U.S. legislation. This act was designed to provide increased funds to apprehend, detain, and deport illegal aliens. Rules were severely tightened for those claiming asylum and for illegal aliens who tried to prevent their deportation to avoid severe hardship (Fuchs, 2000).

ILLEGAL IMMIGRATION

The aftermath of 9/11, in addition to the marked increase in international acts of terrorism, has caused a renewed national interest in immigration, particularly illegal immigration. The economic, social, and political aspects of immigration have created controversy in the Congress and across the country. Similarly, the impact of population growth in view of the current rate is a concern of environmentalists and others. The population is projected to increase from 288 million in 1996 to 400 million in 2050 (Center for Immigration Studies, 2006). The question is whether a population of 350 or 400 million will be beneficial or harmful to the future of the country (Bouvier, 2007).

Illegal immigration has dominated the national debate, although the exact number of illegal immigrants can only be estimated. The U.S. Government Accountability Office (GAO) (2006) estimates that between 400,000 and 700,000 illegal immigrants have entered the United States each year since 1992. From Pew Hispanic Center Report 20, Mexicans make up about 57 percent of illegal immigrants, Latin and Central Americans about 25 percent, about 9 percent from Asia, 6 percent from Europe and Canada combined, and 4 percent from the rest of the world (Passel, 2005).

Immigrants can become illegal when they (1) cross the U.S. borders without authorization or inspection, (2) stay beyond the authorized period after they enter legally, and (3) violate terms of their legal entry. A substantial portion of the estimated 400,000 to 700,000 who enter illegally do so by crossing the U.S.-Mexico border or the U.S.-Canada border (U.S. GAO, 2006). In fact, border control has become a major issue throughout the country, especially in those states and cities close to our borders.

Some immigrants overstay the amount of time permitted by their visas after entering the United States legally. In other cases, immigrants enter the United States using a Border Crossing Card and then violate the restrictions imposed on the cardholders. The Border Crossing Card is a laminated, credit-card type document with many security features and a ten-year validity (U.S. Department of State, 2002). In order to track visa overstayers, the new U.S. Visit program collects and retains biographic, travel, and biometric information, such as photographs and fingerprints of foreign nationals seeking entry into the United States (Passel, 2005). The third type of illegal immigration into the United States involves violation of the terms of legal entry. Accepting unauthorized employment is an example of violating terms of entry. Another example is coming to the United States on a student visa and not attending school or not leaving after finishing school. The introduction of the Student and Exchange Visitor Information System (SEVIS) by which universities are required to report electronically any "no-shows" or irregularities to the U.S. Immigration and Customs Enforcement (ICE), has somewhat curtailed the student visa problem.

CURRENT ISSUES

Current issues include the problem of what is to be done with illegal immigrants already in this country. One of the most controversial solutions suggested is granting amnesty or "guest worker" status. While many employers who need low-wage workers are in favor of this solution, many citizens and members of Congress are opposed. In fact, the President proposed a guest worker program in 2004 that failed to be enacted by Congress.

Another issue involves "birthright citizenship." The Fourteenth Amendment has been interpreted by the U.S. Supreme Court to grant citizenship to nearly every child born in the United States, regardless of the citizenship of the parents, with the exception of children of diplomats and children born to enemy forces in hostile occupation of the United States. Thus, children of illegal immigrants have the same rights to a free, public education as other U.S. children (Mexican American Legal Defense and Education Fund, 2007).

The Supreme Court ruled in 1982, in the case of *Plyer v. Doe,* that undocumented children have the same right as U.S. citizens and legal permanent residents to receive a free, public education. The underlying rationale is that deprivation of public education punishes a class of individuals not responsible for their legal status. However, legal custody and residence within the school district are required.

The issue of border control has been equally divisive. Falfurrias, a small town in Texas, has one of the traffic checkpoints that serves as a "strategic enforcement lay" of the approach by the Customs and Border patrol (PCB) for border security. Agents check the immigration status of the occupants of every car. When they spot something, or if a canine alerts, they send the vehicle to a secondary site for more complete inspection (Kane, 2007). At the Falfurrias checkpoint, the highest rate of seizure exists (Kane, 2007). In 2006 the Falfurrias checkpoint apprehended almost four times as many illegal aliens as residents (Kane, 2007). In this area, which includes some of the largest ranches in the country, ranchers help by providing extra eyes and ears for the agents.

In Cochise County, Arizona, agents have reported that not only Mexicans are involved in the smuggling traffic. Central and South Americans, Asians, and Middle Easterners attempt to enter the United States by crossing the border there. Even illegal immigrants from countries such as Egypt and Yemen have been caught. The San Diego *Tribune* reported that after 9/11 attacks, an anonymous caller led Mexican immigration agents to forty-one undocumented Iraqis waiting to cross into the United States. Thus, potential terrorists are well aware that the 4,000-mile border between the United States and Mexico is easy to cross, with vast, unmonitored stretches (Walley, 2007). The possibility of potential terrorists illegally crossing the border had been predicted before 9/11.

PROPOSED LEGISLATION

In both the U.S. House and Senate, a significant amount of legislation has been introduced to reform immigration laws. Legislation has been proposed by the 109th (2005–2006) and the 110th (2007) Congresses. Bills in the Senate have included legislation designed to increase border control, organize illegal immigrants in a three-tiered system, develop a temporary worker program, and offer legal residence to children of illegal immigrants. Similar bills have been introduced in the House of Representatives. Bills to increase the screening and tracking of aliens; to remove alien terrorists, criminals, and human rights violators; and to expedite removal proceedings have been proposed in the House (Republican National Hispanic Assembly, 2007).

Other bills introduced have proposed more drastic changes: a moratorium on immigration until the government can effectively reduce illegal immigration, a reduction in the quota of family-sponsored immigrants to zero, the ending of birthright citizenship, elimination of the Visa Lottery Program, lowering all levels of legal immigration, repealing some visa categories, and creating a massive agricultural guest worker amnesty (Republication National Hispanic Assembly, 2007).

A comprehensive immigration bill that received the agreement of a bipartisan group was recently introduced in the Senate. Although the bill addressed all of the previously identified issues, it was defeated in the final Senate vote.

On a recent White House website, a series of possible reforms that the President will pursue are listed. The reforms address a broad range of current issues including those of immigration (The White House, 2007).

ASSIMILATION AND ACCULTURATION

Immigrants to the United States have historically assimilated, adopting the new culture and language as their own. In fact, according to Horace Mann (cited in Salins, 1997), public schools were necessary, above all, to ensure the assimilation of immigrants. Salins (1997) has described assimilation "American style":

> Assimilation American style set out a simple contract between the existing settlers and all newcomers. Immigrants would be welcome as full members of the American family if they agreed to abide by three simple precepts: First, they had to accept English as the national language. Second, they were expected to take pride in their American identity and believe in America's liberal democratic and egalitarian principles. Third, they were expected to live by the protestant ethic—to be self-reliant, hardworking, and morally upright (Salins, 1997, p. 6).

Assimilation occurs when an individual or group does not maintain its own culture when in contact with other cultures or social environments. Mrs. Lee, for example, emigrated from Taiwan 50 years ago. She commented to one of the authors that she had been so eager to "fit in" the mainstream that she never taught her children the language or the culture of Taiwan. She wanted them to learn only English. When her daughter was 18 years old, she bitterly complained that she "really didn't know who she was." She wanted to go to Taiwan to learn about her background and language (S. Tung, personal communication, 1995).

A somewhat different perspective appeared in a campus memo at San Francisco State University where Linda Juang (2003) wrote about the cultural differences that sometimes created differences in the family. She had to explain to her friends that a young woman would never keep late hours in the culture of her Taiwanese parents, even at 21. She also noted that "in many Chinese American homes with parents who grew up with traditional Chinese values and behaviors, children are often pulled in two directions—being Chinese and being American" (Juang, 2003, p. 1).

Thus, assimilation in the twenty-first century has become a controversial concept. In the view of Renshon (2005),

> it carries with it the implication that there is a national American identity and culture. It also carries the implication that immigrants choosing to come here should, in good faith, try to embrace it. (p. 84)

Renshon also points out that assimilation is now being contested by many multiculturists as "stripping immigrants of their identity" (p. 84). For Renshon, as for many who oppose *multiculturalism*, immigrants come to the United States not to express their ethnicity but to seek political and economic freedom.

Yet, when we listen to people like Mrs. Lee's daughter above, it is easy to appreciate her longing for the identity to be found in knowledge of Taiwan, its history, language, and culture. However, in his book, *The 50% American*, Renshon (2005) disagrees with the view of many people that "we can encourage and integrate millions of new immigrants who have come to our country by encouraging their emotional, political, and economic ties to their home country" (p. 1).

He describes national identity and the need for elements that constitute the "core foundations of American society—our psychology, emotional attachments to our country, our values and ideals, and the institutions that reflect and encourage them to fit together" (p. 1). However, Renshon is most concerned about dual citizenship (the meaning of his book's title), which allows a person to have many of the rights and responsibilities inherent in citizenship in each country of which he or she is a citizen. He describes it as "encouraging or resulting in shallower attachments to the American national community." In a world threatened by terrorism, national unity and loyalty are urgently needed, in his view. Many Americans agree, for example, as Katel writes:

> In small communities experiencing unprecedented waves of new immigrants, many residents say that Mexican immigrants—perhaps because they need only walk across the border to return home—stick to themselves and refuse to learn English or to assimilate (Katel, 2005, p. 17).

Support for Renshon's point of view is implied in the following comments expressed by The Center for Immigration Studies (2006):

> Though most immigrants will undergo a superficial assimilation, however broken our immigration policy is, there is more to Americanization than learning English and getting a job. The development of a visceral, emotional attachment to America and its history, or "patriotic assimilation," is increasingly unlikely when the schools and culture at large are skeptical, even hostile to patriotism (p. 1).

In contrast to assimilation, acculturation involves the process of learning a second culture while maintaining one's culture of origin. Indicators of acculturation include language usage, media behavior (television programs watched in the first language, for example), ties to one's country of origin, length of time in the United States, values expressed, and the composition of one's interpersonal network (Korzenny, 1998).

Both behavioral and attitudinal changes that may be superficial, intermediate, or significant occur in the acculturation process (Casas & Pytluk, 1995; Marin, 1992). Whereas superficial changes may only involve learning and forgetting cultural facts and traditions, significant changes involve alterations in one's beliefs, values, and norms (Marin, 1992).

Both assimilation and acculturation are gradual processes, and different individuals may be at different points in the process at any given time (Korzenny, 1998). However, either process can be prevented when immigrants are marginalized as barriers to participation in the new culture are erected.

Acculturation is in practice at a charter school in Minnesota where the cultures of diverse students are respected as they acquire language and customs of the United States.

DEMOGRAPHIC CHANGES IN THE SCHOOLS

Statistics show that foreign-born immigrants continue to cluster into a handful of metropolitan areas. According to Frey and DeVol (2000), "just 10 metropolitan areas house 58 percent of the U.S. Hispanic population and ten metropolitan areas, led by Los Angeles, New York, and San Francisco, house 61 percent of all U.S. Asians" (p. 3).

The increased number of ethnically and linguistically diverse immigrants in the central cities, which are densely populated centers of a metropolitan area with a concentration of cultural and commercial facilities and a disproportionately high population of disadvantaged persons, and metropolitan areas of major cities has also affected the school population. Furthermore, in many central cities and metropolitan regions, the population of African American and Hispanic students may be close to 100 percent due to hypersegregation (excessive segregation) or resegregation by which a school previously desegregated becomes segregated again through practices such as tracking, bias in the identification and placement of gifted students and those with disabilities, advanced placement courses that screen out certain groups of students, and biased counseling or guidance.

The most recent data on the school-aged population reflects the national, regional, and local changes in the general population. Indian/Alaskan Natives comprise 1.2 percent; Asian/Pacific Islanders, 4.2 percent; Hispanic, 15.4 percent; Black-non-Hispanic, 16.4 percent; and White-non-Hispanic, 63.3 percent (U.S. Census Bureau, 2000).

While the population of culturally diverse students in the schools is changing dramatically, the characteristics of teachers and administrators remain largely homogeneous. From 1971 to 1991, 88.3 to 88.8 percent of public school teachers were White (National Education Association, 1993). The most recent data show a slight decrease to 80.5 percent for White teachers, 9 percent for African American teachers, and 5 percent for Hispanic teachers (Yasin, 1999). School principals are also predominately White, approximately 84 percent in the 1993–1994 school year and 82.2 percent in 2003–2004 ("Characteristics of Elementary School Principals," 2006).

The implications for teachers are obvious. Even in areas of the country that remain predominately White, it is essential that teachers learn about the cultures and languages of many children who are arriving in greater numbers and entering their schools for the first time. Furthermore, many of the jobs available in the next decade will be in urban areas where the population is likely to be more diverse. All children will need to work and live harmoniously with members of many diverse groups. Teachers will need to develop the knowledge, skills, and attitudes necessary to prepare a diverse population of students for success in the mainstream, while also respecting their cultures and languages of origin.

Geographic variations exist in the diversity of the school-aged population among states, as well as among urban, suburban, and rural areas of the country. For example, comparisons between California and South Dakota show that California has many students in each of the racial or ethnic groups identified, while South Dakota has relatively few (Table 8.3). Language diversity may also be a challenge because in some locations there will be more English language learners than in others. The need for translators and interpreters will vary accordingly.

Table 8.3 Public School Membership, by Race/Ethnicity and State: School Year 2001–02

State	Students reported[1]	American Indian/ Alaska Native	Asian/Pacific Islander	Hispanic	Black non-Hispanic
United States	47,440,514	561,799	2,010,685	8,103,281	8,152,385
Alabama	725,349[1]	5,357	5,869	11,108	264,506
Alaska	134,358	34,210	7,870	4,812	6,254
Arizona	922,180	60,404	19,361	325,661	43,551
Arkansas	449,805	2,300	4,159	18,672	104,951
California	6,108,071[1]	53,314	686,074	2,717,602	512,996
Colorado	742,145	8,710	22,131	172,940	42,361

State	Students reported[1]	American Indian/ Alaska Native	Asian/Pacific Islander	Hispanic	Black non-Hispanic
Connecticut	570,228	1,677	16,878	77,966	78,826
Delaware	115,555	325	2,807	7,600	35,900
District of Columbia	68,449[1]	32	1,121	6,427	57,751
Florida	2,500,478	6,916	48,079	511,247	621,569
Georgia	1,470,634	2,437	34,812	80,776	561,354
Hawaii	184,546	794	133,408	8,384	4,469
Idaho	246,521	3,238	3,279	27,633	1,908
Illinois	2,071,391	3,535	71,667	335,535	439,478
Indiana	996,133	2,388	10,212	38,943	117,857
Iowa	485,932	2,638	8,344	19,523	19,955
Kansas	470,205	6,286	10,316	45,929	42,023
Kentucky	621,956[1]	1,312	4,287	6,920	63,808
Louisiana	731,328	4,765	9,311	11,358	349,550
Maine	205,586	1,373	2,279	1,324	2,826
Maryland	860,640	3,111	39,401	46,251	320,489
Massachusetts	973,140	3,165	44,148	105,053	83,642
Michigan	1,730,668	18,014	34,493	62,754	345,575
Minnesota	851,384	17,145	44,273	31,935	59,924
Mississippi	493,507	769	3,566	4,208	251,728
Missouri	909,792	2,948	11,100	18,337	159,059
Montana	151,947	16,121	1,560	2,835	962
Nebraska	285,095	4,452	4,502	23,459	19,594
Nevada	356,814	6,158	21,648	97,782	36,737
New Hampshire	206,847	505	3,016	4,255	2,539
New Jersey	1,341,656	2,390	88,558	214,546	239,554
New Mexico	320,260	36,137	3,413	163,378	7,534
New York	2,872,132	12,461	178,495	534,527	571,850
North Carolina	1,315,363	19,336	25,245	68,957	412,192
North Dakota	106,047	8,587	872	1,431	1,138
Ohio	1,804,123[1]	2,382	21,429	33,447	301,480
Oklahoma	622,139	108,800	9,051	40,373	67,334
Oregon	540,813[1]	11,707	22,641	62,392	16,061
Pennsylvania	1,821,627	2,386	37,945	87,219	279,256
Rhode Island	158,046	897	5,098	23,336	12,782
South Carolina	688,258[1]	1,674	6,879	16,187	286,819
South Dakota	127,542	13,004	1,256	1,744	1,635
Tennessee	909,856[1]	1,487	10,575	18,940	225,717
Texas	4,163,447	12,776	116,229	1,735,040	598,223
Utah	484,677	7,456	13,646	47,940	4,934
Vermont	101,179	556	1,524	1,013	1,166
Virginia	1,163,091	3,261	50,094	63,950	315,105

(continued)

Table 8.3 *Continued*

State	Students reported[1]	American Indian/ Alaska Native	Asian/Pacific Islander	Hispanic	Black non-Hispanic
Washington	1,009,200	26,452	75,916	110,468	54,589
West Virginia	282,885	297	1,567	1,173	12,386
Wisconsin	879,361	12,520	29,488	43,621	89,293
Wyoming	88,128	2,834	793	6,370	1,195

Outlying Areas, DoD Dependents Schools, and Bureau of Indian Affairs

State	Students reported[1]	American Indian/ Alaska Native	Asian/Pacific Islander	Hispanic	Black non-Hispanic
Bureau of Indian Affairs[2]	46,476	46,476	0	0	0
DoDDS: DoDs Overseas	56,571[1]	547	5,131	5,262	10,809
DDESS: DoDs Domestic	27,741[1]	170	965	5,137	7,158
American Samoa[2]	15,897	0	15,897	0	0
Guam	31,992	20	31,310	75	104
Northern Marianas	10,479	0	10,429	0	6
Puerto Rico[2]	604,177	0	0	604,177	0
Virgin Islands	18,780	—	—	—	—

— Not available.

[1]Totals exclude students for whom race/ethnicity was not reported.

[2]American Samoa, Puerto Rico, and the BIA reported all of their students in one category of race/ethnicity.

Source: U.S. Department of Education, National Center for Education Statistics, Common Core of Data, "State Nonfiscal Survey Public Elementary/Secondary Education."

REFERENCES

Bouvier, L. (2007). *Population growth and immigration.* Washington, DC: Center for Immigration Studies.

Casas, M. J., & Pytluk, S.D. (1995). Hispanic identity development: Implications for research and practice. In J.G. Ponterotto, J. Manuel Casas, L.A. Suzuki, & C.M. Alexander (Eds.), *Handbook of multicultural counseling* (pp. 155–180). Thousand Oaks, CA: Sage.

Center for Immigration Studies. (2006). Immigration from Mexico: Costs and benefits for the United States. Washington, DC: Author.

Characteristics of elementary school principals. (2006) *Principal, 86*(1), 42–47.

Frey, W., & Devol, R. (2000). *America's demography in the new century: Aging baby boomers and new immigrants as major players.* Milliken Institute Policy Brief. Santa Monica, CA: Milken Institute.

Gould, W. T. S., & Findlay, A. M. (1994). *Population and the changing world order.* New York: Wiley.

Harris, N. (1995). *The new untouchables: Immigration and the new world order.* London: J.B. Taurus Publishers.

International Organization for Migration (1999). Retrieved December, 2001, from: http://www.iom.int/

Jacobson, D. (1996). *Rights across the borders: Immigration and the decline of citizenship.* Baltimore: Johns Hopkins University Press.

Juang, L. (2003). Understanding culture and adolescents. *Campus Memo, 5*(15). San Francisco: San Francisco State University.

Kane, L. (2007 April/May). Falfurrias, Texas—a "star" border control checkpoint. Washington, DC: U.S. Customs and Border Protection. In *Today* newsletter.

Katel, P. (2005). Illegal immigration. *CQ Researcher*, 15, 393–420. Retrieved August 6, 2007, from *CQ Researcher Online*, http://library.cqpress.com/cqresearcher/cqresrre2005050600.

Korzenny, F. (1998). *Acculturation: Conceptualization and measurement*. Retrieved July 2007, from: http:// www.cheskin.com/assets/hispanicacculturation/measurement.pdf.

Larsen, L. J. (2004). *Foreign born population in the United States, 2003*. Washington, DC: U.S. Department of Commerce, Economics, and Statistics Administration, U.S. Census Bureau.

Mexican American Legal Defense and Education Fund (2007). The rights of immigrant children. Retrieved July 2007, from http://isbe.state.il.us/bilingual/pdfs/rights.

Marin, G. (1992). Extreme response style and acquiescence among Hispanics: The role of acculturation and education. *Journal of Cross-Cultural Psychology, 23*(4), 498–509.

Meissner, D., Homats, R., Walker, A.G., & Ogata, S. (1993). *International migration challenges in a new era*. New York: The Trilateral Commission.

Merriam-Webster Online dictionary. Retrieved December 2006, from http://www.M-W.com

National Education Association. (1993). *The status of the American public school teacher 1961–1991*. Washington, DC: Author.

Passel, J. (2005). Estimates of the size and characteristics of the undocumented population. Pew Hispanic Center, March 21, 2005. Retrieved July 20, 2007 from http://www.Pew Hispanic Center.org.

Pastor, R. (1983). Migration in the Caribbean Basin: The need for an approach as dynamic as the phenomenon. In M.M. Kritz (Ed.), *U.S. immigration and refugee policy: Global and domestic issues*. Washington, DC: Georgetown University Press.

Renshon, S.A. (2005). *The 50% American: Immigration and national identity in an age of terror*. Washington, DC: Georgetown University Press.

Republican National Hispanic Assembly (2007). *Immigration Reform Now*. A project of the Republican National Hispanic Assembly. Retrieved May 4, 2007 from http://www.immigrationreformnow.org/Bills.htm.

Salins, P. D. (1997). *Assimilation American style: An impassioned defense of immigration and assimilation as the foundation of American greatness and the American dream*. New York: Basic Books.

Sassen, S. (1996). *Losing control: Sovereignty in an age of globalization*. New York: Columbia University Press.

Takaki, R. (1989). *Strangers from a different shore*. Boston: Little Brown.

United Nations. (1997). *International migration and development: The concise report*. New York: Author.

United Nations. (1998). *International migration policies*. New York: United Nations, Department of Economic and Social Affairs Population Division.

United Nations. (1999). *Review and appraisal of the progress made in achieving the goals and Objectives of the Programme of Action of the International Conference on Population and Development*.

U.S. Census Bureau (2000, October). *Current population survey*.

U.S. Commission on Immigration Reform. (1997). Immigration Act of 1990. Washington, DC: General Accounting Office.

U.S. Department of Education (2001–2002). National Center for Educational Statistics. Common Core of Data. "State Nonfiscal Survey Public Elementary/Secondary Education."

U.S. Department of Homeland Security (2004). Yearbook of immigration statistics, 2003. Washington, DC: U.S. Government Printing Office. Retrieved November 17, 2007 from: http://xlibraryassets/statistics/yearbook/2003/2003imm.pdf.

U.S. Department of Justice. (1994). *Statistical yearbook of the Immigration and Naturalization Service*. Washington, DC: Author.

U.S. Office of Homeland security.

Walley, J. Z. (2007). Arab terrorists crossing border: Middle Eastern illegals find easy entrance into U.S. from Mexico. Retrieved July 2007, from http://worldnetdaily.com.

The White House (2007). Retrieved August 31, 2007, from http://www.whitehouse.gov/infocus/immigration.

Yasin, S. (1999). The supply and demand of elementary school teachers in the United States. Washington, DC: ERIC Clearinghouse on Teaching and Teacher Education (ERIC Document Reproduction Services No. ED436529).

STRATEGIES FOR ELD, SDAIE, AND ASSESSMENT

CHAPTER 9

DIFFERENTIATED EARLY LITERACY FOR ENGLISH LANGUAGE LEARNERS

INTRODUCTION

Imagine a typical elementary school classroom in an urban setting in the United States. Chances are there are a significant number of English Language Learners (ELLs) in the classroom. Current federal estimates indicate five to six million ELLs in public schools (No Child Left Behind, 2002). Yet one student may be a new arrival with little knowledge of the English language. Another student might have arrived six months earlier and is beginning to respond to open-ended questions. Another ELL might write fluently with many errors in English. And another might be mistaken for a native speaker except when discussing new topics. Each one of these students may be classified as an ELL, yet their instructional needs are diverse.

Early literacy at elementary grades for English Language Learners is a significant focus of No Child Left Behind (NCLB). The broad purpose of the legislation stated in the text of the law is to ". . . ensure that all children have a fair, equal, and significant opportunity to obtain a high-quality education and reach, at a minimum, proficiency on challenging State academic achievement standards . . ." (No Child Left Behind, 2002). Use of national and state standards dictate a degree of uniformity of instruction; ELLs, however, are not a uniform group. They are from unique cultural, linguistic, and socioeconomic backgrounds, are of all ages and grade levels, and are placed in classrooms based on a variety of proficiency levels in English. Furthermore, much of the NCLB discussion about early literacy is defined by the following five components of reading instruction: phonemic awareness, phonics, vocabulary development, fluency, and comprehension. This book, however, is not a reading text. Differentiated instruction in early literacy for English Language Learners is the focus. Even though there is some overlap with the five reading components, the purpose of this book is to address a differentiated perspective of language arts in literacy development with the prospective and practicing teacher in mind. The book is designed to meet the demands of NCLB and to reference national Teachers of English to Speakers of Other Languages (TESOL) standards, while providing instructional strategies and activities that match levels of language proficiency.

ENGLISH LANGUAGE LEARNERS AND STANDARDS

Snow (2000) advocated the use of English as a Second Language (ESL) standards to help teachers implement effective instructional practice for English Language Learners. Hakuta (2001) argued that academic standards designed for ELLs contributed to accurately evaluating academic progress, particularly in the ELLs' initial years of schooling. Others have described ways to implement ESL standards in classroom practice (Herrell & Jordan, 2004; Agor, 2000; Irujo, 2000; Samway 2000; Smallwood, 2000).

At first glance, referring to standards and differentiation in the same sentence might appear to be an oxymoron. But standards provide a framework on which to create differentiated instruction. I like the image of an Olympic diver using the structure of a diving board to launch herself into a spectacular series of twists and flips to execute the perfect dive. It is the structure underneath that supports the unique creative effort of the diver. In much the same way, the standards form the structure underneath. They do not dictate specific instructional tasks, which may vary infinitely, but they inform and support instructional decisions.

Lachat (1998) documented several benefits to using standards to inform instructional practice for ELLs. He noted that standards reverse the tendency to provide less challenging curriculum for ELLs, that standards fostered higher expectations particularly when they matched instructional practice to the process of acquiring a second language. The development of standards for ESL instruction was initially undertaken by the Teachers of English to Speakers of Other Languages (TESOL, 1997), a professional organization that established standards around three fundamental goals: 1) to use English to communicate in social settings, 2) to use English to achieve academically in all content areas, and 3) to use English in socially and culturally appropriate ways. A total of nine standards (see below), three assigned to each goal, attempt to inform all aspects of learning another language. TESOL standards provide valuable insight into ESL instruction. As the TESOL standards are virtually the only nationally accepted standards for ELLs at this time, they will be referenced throughout this book.

Even though TESOL standards are embraced on a national level, they do pose some implementation problems for elementary school teachers of ELLs. The broad categories and organization of the TESOL standards can be unspecific and insufficient to inform current NCLB instructional priorities. TESOL standards, for instance, do not differentiate between levels of language proficiency. There is no distinction between a beginning or an advanced ELL. The assumption is that the instructional needs of all ELLs are uniform, like using a one-size-fits-all approach to teaching. Examples of a uniform approach to teaching ELLs with early literacy can be found in Tomkins (1997). Conversely, the English Language Development (ELD) content standards (1999), compiled at the state level in California, applied five levels of proficiency, three basic levels and two sub-levels using the term [ldquo]early": beginning, early intermediate, intermediate, early advanced, and advanced. This differentiated approach to standards fosters greater accuracy in assessment and encourages differentiated instruction for ELLs.

TESOL standards do have indicators for pre-K to third grade and fourth to eighth grade levels, but the organization of the standards is not mirrored in the early literacy priority set forth by NCLB and the National Reading Panel (2000). Early literacy is a prominent area of focus that frames instructional design in elementary school classrooms for both English-only speakers and ELLs. For example, August (2002) found that oral English proficiency is predictive of early reading success. This finding has also been linked to ELLs (Baker & Gersten, 1997; Garcia, 2000; Gersten & Geva, 2003). Therefore, elementary school classrooms tend to be structured around early literacy programs. TESOL Goal 1, however, addresses communicative competence in a variety of social settings. Social settings for children tend to be pretty narrow, so creating a variety of social settings in which to practice English is much more in line with secondary- or adult-level ESL instruction. Further, although TESOL Goal 2 addresses academic areas, three standards are insufficient to guide listening, speaking, understanding, reading, and writing in all their forms.

True, TESOL standards are beneficial for instruction and assessment of ELLs, but as argued above, they also pose certain problems for the diverse elementary school classroom. The solution, then, is to utilize and reference the informed ESL perspective of the nationally accepted TESOL standards. However, the difference is to maintain an early literacy focus with an eye to differentiating strategies and activities across levels of English proficiency. In this book, prospective and practicing elementary school teachers of ELLs will find practical ways to teach across levels of proficiency. Key areas include standards-based strategies and activities for early literacy that are differentiated to the appropriate levels of English proficiency, a range of assessment tools to document academic progress, and ideas for increased parental involvement in keeping with the demands of No Child Left Behind.

TIPS FOR INCREASING PARENTAL INVOLVEMENT

Throughout the book the reader will find tips for involving parents. According to Purcell-Gates (2000), family literacy was identified as foundational for learning. Additionally, programs that targeted specific literacy strategies for parents were found to be effective in improving academic achievement. Literacy development areas in which parents can help their children include vocabulary development, reading fluency, and process writing.

Vocabulary instruction is key to English language development and has a significant impact on achievement in reading and writing skills (Blanchowicz & Fisher, 2000). Parents, even though they are limited English speakers themselves, can assist in vocabulary development on two levels. The first is in providing primary language (L1) support. Berndhart and Kamil (1995) documented that language development in L1 contributed to and supported language development in L2. Another way that parents assist vocabulary development is by facilitating reading at home. Considering that some parents may be illiterate or minimally literate, facilitating reading at home may require creative alternatives to directly reading to their children. Alternative ways to provide support at home may include taking children to the public library, utilizing audio-recorded books, sitting with the children as they read and asking strategic questions about the reading, and listening for fluency as their children read aloud. Specific tasks that foster language development at home are detailed throughout the book.

STRATEGIES AND ACTIVITIES THAT FIT

The use of strategies is universal. In every facet of life, we employ a broad array of strategies. Whether it is fixing a car, cooking a meal, playing a sport, or teaching English Language Learners, each arena of life requires strategies to solve problems. Applying strategies that fit, though, requires being responsive to the complex needs at hand. Research on the use of strategies by ELLs (Chamot, Barnhardt, El-Dinary, & Robbins, 1999; Gu, Hu, & Zhang 2003) suggests that academically successful ELLs not only orchestrate a wide range of learning strategies, but they also monitor and select which ones are most useful for a given situation.

Literacy development with ELLs poses multiple situations for using strategies. The instructional needs of ELLs are as diverse as the languages they speak at home, the literacy levels they have attained, and the sociocultural backgrounds they bring to the classroom. Addressing linguistic needs requires differentiating instruction to match levels of proficiency. It also requires strategies that are situational (Lave & Wenger, 1991), and that provide ELLs with the means to explore their own identities (Toohey, 2000) and to utilize expressions of their own culturally grounded knowledge (Moll, Amanti, & Gonzalez, 1992).

Think about teaching the writing process to a group of fourth-grade ELLs. One student may be a new arrival with little education in his own language, another may come from a language group that uses non-Western script, and still another may be quite literate in her own language with a high level of proficiency in English. Certainly, an insightful teacher would not presume to teach each student in the same way. The teaching strategies used must fit the child. Matching strategies that fit the needs of the child is essentially response-oriented instruction with a focus on the ELL.

The strategies in the following chapters are designed to respond to the ELL's level of proficiency and personal perspective. Rosenblatt (1938/1986; 1978), the seminal theorist for response-oriented pedagogy, advanced the idea of exploration of aesthetic experiences in the language arts. Bahktin (1981) argued that words by themselves are lifeless, but that languages come alive when they are uttered in the context of one's experience. On a predominantly linguistic level, the strategies and activities in this book are designed to match levels of proficiency in English. Yet, on a more global level, the strategies are also designed to address the situational interests and needs of ELLs. The selected strategies and activities invite exploration of one's experience and expression of one's knowledge while learning English.

HOW TO USE THESE CHAPTERS

The following chapters work best as a reference guide rather than as a text one would read cover to cover. Book chapters address areas of early literacy development with strategies and activities arranged according to levels of proficiency. Levels of proficiency are divided into three basic groupings: beginning, intermediate, and advanced. In cases that require a finer degree of differentiation, additional levels of early intermediate and early advanced are used. These distinctions help the teacher decide which strategies would best apply to a given ELL.

The following chapters address a variety of aspects of the language arts: identification of levels of proficiency, questioning strategies, vocabulary development strategies, reading strategies, writing strategies, and the mechanics of handwriting, grammar, and spelling. This is by no means a comprehensive listing of all available strategies and activities. The selected strategies and activities were included because of their high degree of success with ELLs in the context of the classroom, and because they are easily implemented with a minimum of preparation and/or materials development.

A brief overview is as follows. In Chapter 10, identification of levels of proficiency does not presume to replace the complex normative measures of English language development. Nevertheless, teachers need a way to quickly assess a student's level of proficiency. Often a student arrives in a classroom with little to no background information. It may take weeks for the assessment data to be made available. Using a simple quick assessment tool, the teacher can begin to provide instruction that is appropriate for the ELL's level of proficiency. Beyond the quick assessment tool are more in-depth descriptors for each level of proficiency according to listening, speaking, reading, and writing domains of language arts. The TESOL standards are adapted to create a summative assessment with a differentiated perspective as well. The chapter finishes with a sample profile of an ELL with matching strategies to address strengths and needs.

In Chapter 11, questioning strategies address oral language development. Students' oral responses can range from silent gestures to wordy narratives depending on their levels of proficiency. Included in the chapter are a number of ways to use appropriate questions and also to frame response opportunities.

In Chapter 12, the mechanics of writing—specifically handwriting, grammar, and spelling—are addressed. A unique feature is the use of total physical response for each letter of the alphabet, upper and lower case, to teach handwriting. Selected grammar teaching strategies are provided. The spelling strategies draw on stages of developmental spelling and ELD techniques. Additionally, the chapter describes ten of the most baffling spelling rules that ELLs experience.

In Chapter 13, vocabulary development is discussed as a key to language learning. ELLs do not perceive words the same way that literate adults do. Literate adults tend to see words as inherently meaningful. The reality is that words in isolation are abstract representations of meaning. Teaching vocabulary at a more concrete level is key to making words meaningful.

In Chapter 14, reading is taught explicitly and implicitly. Since there are numerous texts on reading which address phonemic awareness and phonics, this chapter addresses reading in the long run as a way of organizing instruction in the classroom that provides explicit instruction, but structures time for independent reading that fosters a rhythm of lifelong reading. The strategies are selected to allow students to formulate their own interpretations and to explore their ideas as they read.

In Chapter 15, process-writing instruction is differentiated to accommodate the needs of specific ELLs. The strategies are selected to teach the entire writing process no matter the level of proficiency. The intention is to equip the ELL with the tools to write to a variety of genres. Included in the chapter are genre-specific rubrics for each level of student.

Matching instruction to the child with a differentiated approach is the surest way to meet broad legislative reforms. Margaret Taylor Stewart (2004) reminds us that, in light of sweeping national reforms of NCLB, it is still the classrooms teacher that makes the difference. "Whatever else is mandated, teachers must create time in classrooms to attend to the needs of individual learners. Knowledgeable, caring teachers are key to implementing NCLB in ways that help children experience learning success and become lifelong learners who choose to read and write in their daily lives" (p. 740). This applies to teachers of all learners, but particularly to those prospective and practicing teachers working to meet the diverse needs of ELLs.

APPENDIX: TESOL GOALS AND STANDARDS (1997)

Goal 1: To use English to communicate in social settings

Standard 1: Students will use English to participate in social interactions

Standard 2: Students will interact in, through, and with spoken and written English for personal expression and enjoyment

Standard 3: Students will use learning strategies to extend their communicative competence

Goal 2: To use English to achieve academically in all content areas

Standard 1: Students will use English to interact in the classroom

Standard 2: Students will use English to obtain, process, construct, and provide subject matter information in spoken and written form

Standard 3: Students will use appropriate learning strategies to construct and apply academic knowledge

Goal 3: To use English in socially and culturally appropriate ways

Standard 1: Students will use the appropriate language variety, register, and genre according to audience, purpose, and setting

Standard 2: Students will use nonverbal communication appropriate to audience, purpose, and setting

Standard 3: Students will use appropriate learning strategies to extend their sociolinguistic and sociocultural competence

REFERENCES

Agor, B. (Ed.) (2000). *Integrating the ESL standards into classroom practice: Grades 9–12*. Alexandria, VA: TESOL.

August, D. (2002). *English as a second language instruction: Best practices to support the development of literacy for English language learners*. Baltimore: Johns Hopkins University, Center for Research on the Education of Students Placed at Risk.

Bahktin, M. M. (1981). The dialogic imagination. Austin, TX: University of Texas Press.

Baker, S., & Gersten, R. (1997). *Exploratory meta-analysis of instructional practices for English language learners.* (Tech Rep. No. 97–01). Eugene, OR: Eugene Research Institute.

Bernhardt, E. B., & Kamil, M. L. (1995). Interpreting relationships between L1 and L2 reading: Consolidating the linguistic threshold and the linguistic interdependence hypotheses. *Applied Linguistics,* 16, 15–34.

Blanchowicz, C., & Fisher, P. (2000). *Vocabulary instruction.* In M. L. Kamil, P. B. Mosenthal, P. D. Pearson, & R. Barr (Eds), *Handbook of reading research,* Vol III (pp. 503–523). Mahwah, NJ: Erlbaum.

California Department of Education. (1999). *English-Language Development Standards for California Public Schools.* Sacramento, CA: California Department of Education.

Chamot, A. U., Barnhardt, S., El-Dinary, P. B., & Robbins, J. (1999). *The learning strategies handbook.* White Plains, NY: Longman.

Garcia, G. (2000). Bilingual children's reading. In M. L. Kamil, P. B. Mosenthal, P. D. Pearson, & R. Barr (Eds.), *Handbook of reading research,* Vol. III (pp. 813–834). Mahwah, NJ: Erlbaum.

Gersten, R., & Geva, E. (2003). Teaching reading to early language learners. *Educational Leadership, 60* (8), 44–49.

Gu, Y., Hu, G., & Zhang, L. J. (2003). *Eliciting learning strategies from lower primary school students in Singapore.* Paper presented at the ERAS Conference, Singapore.

Hakuta, K. (2001). *The education of language minority students.* Testimony to the U. S. Commission on Civil Rights, April 13, 2001 [online]. Available: www.stanford.edu/~hakuta/Docs/Civil-RightsCommission.htm.

Herrell, A., & Jordan, M. (2004). *Fifty strategies for teaching English language learners.* (2nd ed.) Upper Saddle River, NJ: Merrill/Prentice Hall.

Irujo, S. (Ed.) (2000). *Integrating the ESL standards into classroom practice: Grades 6–8.* Alexandria, VA: TESOL.

Lachat, M. A. (1998). *Shifting to standards-based learning. What does it mean for schools, teachers, and students? Educating linguistically and culturally diverse students: An ASCD professional inquiry kit.* Alexandria, VA: Association for Supervision and Curriculum Development.

Lave, J., & Wenger, E. (1991). *Situated learning: Legitimate peripheral participation.* Cambridge, England: Cambridge University Press.

Moll, L. C., Amanti, C., & Gonzalez, N. (1992). Funds of knowledge for teaching: Using a qualitative approach to connect homes: and classrooms. *Theory Into Practice, 31 (2),* 132–141.

National Reading Panel. (2000). *Teaching children to read: An evidence-based assessment of the scientific research literature on reading and its implications for reading instruction.* Rockville, MD: National Institute of Child Health and Human Development.

No Child Left Behind Act of 2001, Pub. L. No. 107–110, 1001, 115 Stat. 1439. (2002). Retrieved May 29, 2002 from http://edworkforce.house.gov/issues/107th/education/nclb/nclb.htm.

Purcell-Gates, V. (2000). *Family literacy.* In M. L. Kamil, P. B. Mosenthal, P. D. Pearson, & R. Barr (Eds), *Handbook of reading research,* Vol. III (pp. 853–870). Mahwah, NJ: Erlbaum.

Rosenblatt, L. (1938/1986). *Literature as exploration.* New York: MLA.

Rosenblatt, L. (1978). *The reader, the text, the poem.* Carbondale and Edwardsville, IL: Southern Illinois University Press.

Samway, K. (Ed.) (2000). *Integrating the ESL standards into classroom practice: Grades 3–5.* Alexandria, VA: TESOL.

Smallwood, B. (Ed.) (2000). *Integrating the ESL standards into classroom practice: Grades pre-K–2.* Alexandria, VA: TESOL.

Snow, M. (Ed.) (2000). *Implementing the ESL standards for pre K–12 students through teacher education.* Alexandria, VA: TESOL.

Stewart, M. T. (May 2004). Early literacy instruction in the climate of No Child Left Behind. *Reading Teacher, 57*(8), 732–743.

TESOL (1997). *ESL standards for pre-K–12 students.* Alexandria, VA: TESOL.

Tomkins, G. E. (1997). *Literacy for the twenty-first century: A balanced approach.* Upper Saddle River, NJ: Merrill/Prentice Hall.

Toohey, K. (2000). *Learning English at school: Identity, social relations, and classroom practice.* Clevedon, England: Multilingual Matters.

CHAPTER 10

IDENTIFYING PROFICIENCY LEVELS

MATCHING INSTRUCTIONAL STRATEGIES AND STUDENT ACTIVITIES

Differentiated instruction assumes that one size does *not* fit all. Prior to selecting appropriate English Language Development (ELD) strategies and activities, it is vital to identify the level of language proficiency the student has achieved in order to provide matching instructional strategies. In this chapter, assessment tools for identification of an English Language Learner's proficiency level are presented. The tools are as follows: 1) Quick Assessment of ELD Levels of Proficiency for initial identification of language level, 2) ELD Behavioral Indicators across reading/language arts domains, and 3) a reference table for teacher strategies and student activities across reading/language arts domains.

There are formal means for assessing levels of proficiency. The assessment process, however, is time consuming and requires a specialized examiner to administer a test, and in many cases there is a delay of several months between taking the initial assessment and receiving the results. Nevertheless, the teacher must begin instruction as soon as the ELL enters the classroom. The teacher needs a quick assessment of proficiency levels based upon characteristic behaviors for each level and a ready reference for which strategies and activities would be appropriate for instruction.

The TESOL standards (1997) inform assessment, yet they do not differentiate levels of English language proficiency. The way to deal with this situation is to borrow the structure from the English Language Development Standards (1999), which are divided into five basic levels of proficiency: beginning, early intermediate, intermediate, early advanced, and advanced. Each level is numbered as a stage from 1 to 5, with 1 corresponding to beginning and 5 corresponding to advanced.

THE KEY TO DIFFERENTIATED ELD

Herein lies the key to differentiated English Language Development. One set of strategies does not meet the needs of all ELLs. Identifying the appropriate level of proficiency generates a range of specific strategies and activities.

There are a number of "universal" behaviors, however, that can be attributed to ELLs at various stages of proficiency. Knowing these allows the teacher to quickly provide a rough assessment in order to accommodate instruction appropriately. I have developed a quick reference (see Table 10.1). To use this quick assessment, observe the student as he participates in classroom activities, and compare the behaviors listed in the table with the kinds of behaviors the student exhibits. I have also developed a summative tool, discussed later in this chapter, that can be used to evaluate levels of language proficiency based on the descriptors for each TESOL standard and the five levels of proficiency.

Several factors come into play when assessing language levels. First of all, one must ask, is the ELL literate in his/her native language? Initial literacy assumes phonemic awareness, knowledge of concepts about print, and decoding skills. If the ELL is not literate in the primary language, then those areas must be taught. If the ELL is literate in the primary language, then grade level considerations come into play.

Table 10.1   Quick Assessment of ELD Levels of Proficiency

Level	Stage	Duration	Student Behaviors
1	Beginning	<6 months	• May remain silent/active listening • Uses gestures to convey a message • Yes/No responses predominantly • Gives 1- to 2-word expressions • Follows oral directions when modeled
2	Early Intermediate	3 months to 1 year	• Speaks simple sentences (limited to simple present and past tense) • Responds to an open-ended question • Retells events (from personal experience or in stories) • Reads basic vocabulary • May read simple sentences • Frequent grammatical errors in speech (confuses he/she, him/her; infrequent use of irregular verbs)
3	Intermediate	2 to 3 years	• Retells events using descriptive vocabulary • Summarizes narrative accounts • Identifies main ideas • Provides details orally • Makes comparisons • Identifies and defines new vocabulary orally • Relies on illustrations for reading context clues • Writes simple sentences using high-frequency words
4	Early Advanced	3 to 4 years	• Appears to be orally fluent • Begins to use discipline-specific, academic terminology (e.g., math: numerator/denominator) • Near grade level proficiency in academic areas • Comprehends grade level texts with assistance • Writes fluently with spelling and grammatical errors
5	Advanced	>3 years	• Paraphrases/synthesizes content material • Generates discussions • Socially comfortable • Understands and makes plays on words • Reads/writes at grade level

Tip for Parent Involvement

Parents are stake holders in the assessment process. Include them in assessment by taking time to describe levels of proficiency and expected ELL behaviors for each level. Verify your, assessment, with their in sight into how their end uses language at home.

LEVELS OF PROFICIENCY

Level	Stage	Duration	Student Behaviors
1	Beginning	<6 months	• May remain silent/active listening • Uses gestures to convey a message • Gives Yes/No responses predominantly • 1- to 2-word expressions • Follows oral directions when modeled

Level 1, the Beginning Stage

When considering working with a beginning level student, I think of a traveler who is feeling lost in another country. The traveler intently looks for signs that can give direction, and makes one- to two-word utterances coupled with gestures to indicate meaning. Similarly, beginning students are easily identifiable due to their absence of a working vocabulary in English. Attempting to force a student to speak at this stage is futile and can lead to frustration for both the student and the teacher. Teachers can expect an ELL to be at this stage for a few weeks to as long as six months. Characteristic behaviors include staying silent, while actively listening for something that makes sense. A student at this level will use and respond to gestures to convey meaning. (One of the first gestures I teach beginning students is a hand sign for the bathroom.) A common behavior of nodding the head in the affirmative or shaking it to say "no" gives insight into how a teacher can communicate with a beginning student.

Key Strategies.   Teachers should frame Yes/No questions and model meaningful gestures to facilitate communication. Beginning students follow oral directions, such as "sit" "stand," or "raise your hand," particularly if they are modeled by the teacher or another student. (See Total Physical Response in Chapter 12.) Extensive use of visuals, models, and real objects to make communication meaningful is strongly encouraged.

Level	Stage	Duration	Student Behaviors
2	Early Intermediate	3 months to 1 year	• Speaks simple sentences (limited to simple present and past tense) • Responds to an open-ended question • Retells events (from personal experience or in stories) • Reads basic vocabulary • May read simple sentences • Frequent grammatical errors in speech (confuses he/she, him/her; infrequent use of irregular verbs)

Level 2, the Early Intermediate Stage

As a teacher, I always knew when a student moved from level 1 to level 2 by "The Tattletale Test." The moment the beginning student would come running up to me at recess and begin to tattle on another student, I would say, "Congratulations! You've achieved early intermediate fluency." Achieving this level of proficiency can take as little as three months or in some cases up to a year. In my experience, the cases that took up to a year were due in large part to lack of literacy in the home or emotional trauma related to refugee circumstances. In a caring social environment, however, it is amazing how quickly an ELL moves to early intermediate fluency.

Students at this stage begin to speak in complete, yet simple, sentences. Beginning students tell about their own experiences, and consequently, are able to retell events in order from a story that has been read to them. They can respond orally to open-ended questions such as, "What are you doing?" or "How do you feel?" Early intermediate students begin to read simple, predictable books with vivid illustrations. They can recognize key vocabulary in a sentence. They also commonly misapply gender with nouns, pronouns, and titles (he/she, him/her, Mr./Mrs.) Irregular verbs are problematic in cases such as "She *brang* (brought) it to school."

Key Strategies.   These behaviors invite a variety of instructional strategies including those already mentioned for Level 1. Valuable strategies for classroom teachers with students at this stage include collaborative chart stories (see Chapter 14), selecting books with vivid illustrations to enhance meaning, and providing simple books with predictable sentence patterns (see Chapter 13). Interactive journal writing allows the teacher to label student drawings and model writing using the student's own words (see Chapter 14). Another efficient teaching strategy is direct instruction of key vocabulary in stories and content area lessons (see Chapter 12).

Level	State	Duration	Student Behaviors
3	Intermediate	2 to 3 years	• Retells events using descriptive vocabulary • Summarizes narrative accounts • Identifies main ideas • Provides details orally • Makes comparisons • Identifies and defines new vocabulary orally • Relies on illustrations for reading context clues • Writes simple sentences using high-frequency words

Level 3, the Intermediate Stage

When I hear a student describe a story character with words like "delighted" or "nasty," rather than the ubiquitous "happy/sad" descriptors, I see them achieving the intermediate stage. Beyond using simple vocabulary and just retelling events, intermediate-stage students use richer vocabulary and expand on their thinking. Students at this level of proficiency begin to use language to apply higher-order thinking skills to learning. They will summarize events and main ideas. They will make comparisons to other stories or prior experiences, and will actively inquire about words they don't know and pursue definitions. When reading they look to story illustrations to provide context clues. Their writing may appear to be fluent, but upon review, high-frequency words are used extensively. Because students at this stage are working to deepen their proficiency with language, it takes time to advance to the next level, as much as two to three years.

Key Strategies.   The kinds of strategies that benefit an intermediate student include creating illustrated thesauruses to expand vocabulary, word study of etymologies, and use of cognates (see Chapter 12); teaching study skills like note taking, double-entry journals for citing important story parts and reflecting on the meaning, and using picture walks prior to reading (see Chapter 13); using graphic organizers to facilitate organizing ideas, exploring figurative language and employing process writing to expand simple sentences, and facilitating writing with presentation software that utilizes hypermedia (see Chapter 14).

Level	Stage	Duration	Student Behaviors
4	Early Advanced	3 to 4 years	• Appears to be orally fluent • Begins to use discipline-specific, academic terminology (e.g., math: numerator/denominator) • Near grade level proficiency in academic areas • Comprehends grade level texts with assistance • Writes fluently with spelling and grammatical errors

Level 4, the Early Advanced Stage

Students often appear to languish in intermediate and early advanced stages due to the time it actually takes to develop a deep understanding of and fluency in English. In some cases it can take as long as four years to advance to the next level. Students who are readers and writers move forward in a predictable amount of time, but those who struggle with literacy progress at much slower rates. At these levels, the differences are not readily apparent. Just listening for oral language usage is insufficient. What distinguishes each level is literacy in subject matter instruction at appropriate grade levels of complexity. A practical indicator that a student has achieved early advanced proficiency is when the student argues about a concept in a subject area using subject-specific terminology with specific references to a text. It requires literacy as well as fluency to correctly state a case and substantiate one's ideas with textual references.

Characteristic behaviors unique to the early advanced stage include oral fluency in English with few spoken grammatical errors and near grade level proficiency in academic areas. Students at this level readily learn and use terminology specific to various academic disciplines. They write with a high degree of fluency, but commonly make errors of spelling and grammar.

Key Strategies. Appropriate strategies for students at this level include using comic strips or a "joke of the day" to give students the opportunity to explore wordplay with humor—when students laugh, you know they understood the language. Direct instruction of formulating questions of who, what, where, and why addresses oral ways to seek answers. Students at this level need content area vocabulary development and assistance with reading grade level textbooks. Grouping strategies with reading material that is divided up in a "jigsaw" format is helpful. Note-taking and prewriting skills are essential at this stage to aid recording and organizing thoughts in content areas.

Level	Stage	Duration	Student Behavior
5	Advanced	>3 years	• Paraphrases/synthesizes content material • Generates discussions • Socially comfortable • Understands and makes plays on words • Reads/writes at grade level

Level 5, the Advanced Stage

What sometimes causes confusion is the assumption that the behaviors of a student at the advanced stage are essentially the same as those of a native speaker. An advanced student may still have gaps in specialized areas. For example, a student may struggle in explaining to the school nurse the exact location of physical discomfort. Or the student might feel out of place in certain culturally embedded situations such as knowing how to behave on an obscure holiday. But many of these situations can be addressed easily with a brief word of explanation because the student is so fluent in English.

A student at the advanced stage comprehends and discusses content area material with relative ease. A quick check for this stage is to ask the student to read a short selection from a grade level text and then write a brief synopsis. The ability to paraphrase and synthesize content area material distinguishes the advanced student. One should also expect the student to appear socially comfortable within a group of native speakers. A sure indicator of comfort level is to what extent the student understands a play on words. Laughter at appropriate times is a good sign of comprehension. Finally, a writing sample that demonstrates grade level proficiency is a strong indicator that the student is at an advanced level. Attaining this level may take as long as three years.

Key Strategies. Fostering social interactive situations such as group projects and/or presentations addresses the social comfort level of the advanced student. Taking time to paraphrase textual material and to summarize the thoughts of another student are essential to working in content areas. Studying figurative language and plays on words in order to write limericks, joke books, and humorous stories gives the opportunity to explore nuance in the language. Advanced organizers for lectures and content reading help clarify difficult concepts.

INDICATORS OF ELD ACROSS LANGUAGE ARTS DOMAINS

The above quick assessment of levels of proficiency is a blunt tool that provides rapid identification. The following tool looks at indicators of English Language Development across the language arts domains of listening, speaking, reading, and writing (see Table 10.2). Again, by observing the student

Table 10.2 ELD Behavioral Indicators across Reading/Language Arts Domains

Level/Stage	Listening	Speaking	Reading	Writing
1 **Beginning**	• May remain silent/ active listening • Follows oral directions when modeled	• Uses gestures to convey a message • Yes/No responses predominantly • Gives 1- to 2-word expressions	• May have concepts about print • Follows picture books	• May write name
2 **Early Intermediate**	• Follows oral directions without modeling • Responds to an open-ended question	• Speaks simple sentences (limited to simple present and past tense) • Retells events (from personal experience on in stories) • Frequent grammatical errors in speech (confuses he/she, him/ her; infrequent use of irregular verbs)	• Reads basic vocabulary • May read simple sentences • May read picture books • May read pattern books	• Copies words or simple sentences • May label items in a drawing
3 **Intermediate**	• Relies on illustrations for reading context clues • After hearing a story can recall events in order • Asks questions	• Retells events using descriptive vocabulary • Provides details orally • Makes comparisons	• Reads simple stories with illustrations • Follows written directions • Identifies and defines new vocabulary orally • Identifies main ideas • Summarizes narrative accounts	• Writes simple sentences using high-frequency words
4 **Early Advanced**	• Laughs at funny stories of jokes • Formulates what, where, how, why questions • Asks clarifying questions	• Appears to be orally fluent • Begins to use discipline-specific, academic terminology (e.g. math: numerator/ denominator)	• Near grade level proficiency in academic areas • Comprehends grade level texts with assistance	• Writes fluently with spelling and grammatical errors
5 **Advanced**	• Paraphrases content material • Understands and makes plays on words • Poses higher-order questions	• Generates discussions • Socially comfortable • Formulates wordplay	• Reads at grade level	• Writes at grade level

and matching indicators of English Language Development, the teacher can identify areas of strengths and needs in specific domains. Simply draw a large "X" through the box that matches the student's behaviors. This tool is followed by reference tables of teacher strategies and student activities that apply to each domain and each language level.

REFERENCE GUIDE FOR TEACHER STRATEGIES AND STUDENT ACTIVITIES

Referring to Table 10.2, imagine a student who relies on pictures to derive meaning from reading (listening/level 3), retells events from stories but does not use expanded vocabulary (speaking/level 2), reads simple picture and pattern books with some fluency (reading/level 2), and writes simple sentences using high-frequency words (writing/level 3). Recognizing those behaviors gives the teacher initial indications of strengths and needs according to language arts domains. This is the beginning of developing a personal profile for the student with recommended teacher strategies and student activities (see Table 10.8 for a sample profile).

The following is a reference section of strategies and activities appropriate for levels of proficiency of English Language Development. *Strategies* refer to what teachers do and the approaches they take for instructional purposes. *Activities* refer to what students do naturally at a given level of proficiency and what they are able to learn to do given their identified level. They are ordered according to the domains of language arts and can be used to generate instruction tailored to each ELL.

TESOL Summative Assessment Tool

I developed the following assessment tool for the purpose of generating a summative evaluation of a student's English language proficiency according to the TESOL standards and descriptors. The assessment tool generates a quantitative measure that can be useful for making larger-scale reports of yearly progress toward advanced proficiency in English.

Goal #1, TESOL Standards and Descriptors Assessment
Scoring: 1 = Beginning (little to no communication); 2 = Early Intermediate (some communication, short phrases); 3 = Intermediate (fluent communication, frequent errors); 4 = Early Advanced (very fluent communication, some errors); 5 = Advanced (highly fluent communication, few to no errors)

Goal 1, Standard 1
To use English to communicate in social settings: Students will use English to participate in social interactions

Descriptors	1	2	3	4	5
1. Sharing and requesting information					
2. Expressing needs, feelings, and ideas					
3. Using nonverbal communication in social interactions					
4. Getting personal needs met					
5. Engaging in conversations					
6. Conducting transactions					
Subtotals					
Total					
Average Score (Total/6)					

Goal 1, Standard 2

To use English to communicate in social settings: Students will interact in, through, and with spoken and written English for personal expression and enjoyment

Descriptors	1	2	3	4	5
1. Describing, reading about, or participating in a favorite activity					
2. Sharing social and cultural traditions and values					
3. Expressing personal needs, feelings, and ideas					
4. Participating in popular cultural events					
Subtotals					
Total					
Average Score (Total/4)					

Goal 1, Standard 3

To use English to communicate in social settings: Students will use learning strategies to extend their communicative competence

Descriptors	1	2	3	4	5
1. Testing hypotheses about language					
2. Listening to and imitating how others use English					
3. Exploring alternative ways of saying things					
4. Focusing attention selectively					
5. Seeking support and feedback from others					
6. Comparing nonverbal and verbal cues					
7. Self-monitoring and self-evaluating language development					
8. Using the primary language to ask for clarification					
9. Learning and using language "chunks"					
10. Selecting different media to help understand language					
11. Practicing new language					
12. Using context to construct meaning					
Subtotals					
Total					
Average Score (Total/12)					
Standard Score (Sum of Average Scores/3)					

Note high and low extreme scores as benchmark indicators of strengths or needs.

Goal #2, TESOL Standards and Descriptors Assessment

Scoring: 1 = Beginning (little to no communication); 2 = Early Intermediate (some communication, short phrases); 3 = Intermediate (fluent communication, frequent errors); 4 = Early Advanced (very fluent communication, some errors); 5 = Advanced (highly fluent communication, few to no errors)

Goal 2, Standard 1

To use English to achieve academically in all content areas: Students will use English to interact in the classroom

Descriptors	1	2	3	4	5
1. Following oral and written directions, implicit and explicit					
2. Requesting and providing clarification					
3. Participating in full class, group, and pair discussions					
4. Asking and answering questions					
5. Requesting information and assistance					
6. Negotiating and managing interactions to accomplish task					
7. Explaining actions					
8. Elaborating and extending other people's ideas and words					
9. Expressing likes, dislikes, and needs					
Subtotals					
Total					
Average Score (Total/9)					

Goal 2, Standard 2

To use English to achieve academically in all content areas: Students will use English to obtain, process, construct, and provide subject matter information in spoken and written form

Descriptors	1	2	3	4	5
1. Comparing and contrasting information					
2. Persuading, arguing, negotiating, evaluating, and justifying					
3. Listening to, speaking, reading, and writing subject matter information					
4. Gathering information orally and in writing					
5. Retelling information					
6. Selecting, connecting, and explaining information					
7. Analyzing, synthesizing, and inferring from information					
8. Responding to the work of peers and others					
9. Representing information visually and interpreting information presented visually					
10. Hypothesizing and predicting					
11. Formulating and asking questions					
12. Understanding and producing technical vocabulary and text features according to content area					
13. Demonstrating knowledge through application in a variety of contexts					
Subtotals					
Total					
Average Score (Total/13)					

Goal 2, Standard 3

To use English to achieve academically in all content areas: Students will use appropriate learning strategies to construct and apply academic knowledge

Descriptors	1	2	3	4	5
1. Focusing attention selectively					
2. Applying basic reading comprehension skills: skimming, scanning, previewing, and reviewing text					
3. Using context to construct meaning					
4. Taking notes to record important information and aid one's own learning					
5. Applying self-monitoring and self-corrective strategies to build and expand a knowledge base					
6. Determining and establishing the conditions that help one become an effective learner					
7. Planning how and when to use cognitive strategies and applying them appropriately to a learning task					
8. Actively connecting new information to information previously learned					
9. Evaluating one's own success in a completed learning task					
10. Recognizing the need for and seeking assistance appropriately from others					
11. Imitating the behaviors of native English speakers to complete tasks successfully					
12. Knowing when to use native language resources to promote understanding					
Subtotals					
Total					
Average Score (Total/12)					
Standard Score (Sume of Average Scores/3)					

Note high and low extreme scores as benchmark indicators of strengths or needs.

Goal #3, TESOL Standards and Descriptors Assessment

Scoring: 1 = Beginning (little to no communication); 2 = Early Intermediate (some communication, short phrases); 3 = Intermediate (fluent communication, frequent errors); 4 = Early Advanced (very fluent communication, some errors); 5 = Advanced (highly fluent communication, few to no errors)

Goal 3, Standard 1

To use English in socially and culturally appropriate ways: Students will use the appropriate language variety, register, and genre according to audience, purpose, and setting

Descriptors	1	2	3	4	5
1. Using the appropriate degree of formality with different audiences and settings					
2. Recognizing and using standard English and vernacular dialects appropriately					
3. Using a variety of writing styles appropriate for different audiences, purposes, and settings					

Descriptors	1	2	3	4	5
4. Responding to and using slang appropriately					
5. Responding to and using idioms appropriately					
6. Responding to and using humor appropriately					
7. Determining when it is appropriate to use a language other than English					
8. Determining appropriate topics for interaction					
Subtotals					
Total					
Average Score (Total/8)					

Goal 3, Standard 2

To use English in socially and culturally appropriate ways: Students will use nonverbal communication appropriate to audience, purpose, and setting

Descriptors	1	2	3	4	5
1. Interpreting and responding appropriately to nonverbal cues and body language					
2. Demonstrating knowledge of acceptable nonverbal classroom behaviors					
3. Using acceptable tone, volume, stress, and intonation in various social settings					
4. Recognizing and adjusting behavior in response to nonverbal cues					
Subtotals					
Total					
Average Score (Total/6)					

Goal 3, Standard 3

To use English in socially and culturally appropriate ways: Students will use appropriate learning strategies to extend their sociolinguistic and sociocultural competence

Descriptors	1	2	3	4	5
1. Observing and modeling how others speak and behave in a particular situation or setting					
2. Experimenting with variations of language in social and academic settings					
3. Seeking information about appropriate language use and behavior					
4. Self-monitoring and self-evaluating language use according to setting and audience					
5. Analyzing the social context to determine appropriate language use					
6. Rehearsing variations for language in different social and academic settings					
7. Deciding when use of slang is appropriate					
Subtotals					
Total					
Average Score (Total/7)					
Standard Score (Sum of Average Scores/3)					

Note high and low extreme scores as benchmark indicators of strengths or needs.

Sample English Language Learner Profile

Utilizing Tables 10.3 through 10.7 and the Summative Assessment Tool, the teacher can quickly generate an individual profile of an English Language Learner with recommended strategies and activities for instruction. Another use of generating the profile is to group students with like strengths and needs for more efficient instruction at appropriate levels. Table 10.8 shows a sample profile that details a student's domains of strengths and needs.

Table 10.3   Beginning Level

Reading/Language Arts Domains	Teacher Strategies	Student Activities
Listening	• Provide realia and visuals, model gestures • Total Physical Response	• May remain silent/active listening • Follow oral directions when modeled
Speaking	• Do not force speech • Ask Yes/No questions • Use simple speech, caretaker speech	• Use gestures to convey a message • Yes/No responses • Make lists of items to categorize & sort
Reading	• Read to student • Show stories on video • Supply picture books • Teach letter and word recognition • Label pictures	• Listen to story • Select picture books to read • Categorize and sort letters, items, or pictures
Writing	• Model and illustrate writing on charts • Provide journals for writing and drawing	• May write name • Trace letters and simple words • Draw pictures

Table 10.4   Early Intermediate Level

Reading/Language Arts Domains	Teacher Strategies	Student Activities
Listening	• Write directions on charts Ask students to model written directions • Provide a variety of hand signals to check for understanding	• Follows oral directions with and without modeling • Use hand signals to indicate understanding
Speaking	• Ask cloze questions • Ask open-ended questions • Conduct collaborative interviews • Tap prior knowledge and experience • Model appropriate speech • Mirror speech back to students • Provide interactive word games to develop fluency	• Give short answers • Respond to an open-ended question • Discuss story events and character traits • Compare story to prior experiences • Play interactive word games to develop fluency

(continued)

Table 10.4   (continued)

Reading/Language Arts Domains	Teacher Strategies	Student Activities
Reading	• Provide buddy readers or cross-age readers • Conduct word sorting • Supply simple picture and pattern books • Choral read chart stories • Recite chart poems • Sing charted songs • Repeated reading for fluency development • Make big books • Teach vocabulary with visuals/realia/models	• Listen to cross-age readers • Read with a partner • Read picture books • Read pattern books • Match word cards to pictures • Sort word families • Practice repeated reading • Read big books • Study vocabulary
Writing	• Interactive journal writing • Encourage invented spelling • Language Experience Approach	• Copy words or simple sentences • Label items in a drawing • Participate in collaborative chart stories • Make pattern books • Make big books

Table 10.5   Intermediate Level

Reading/Language Arts Domains	Teacher Strategies	Student Activities
Listening	• Take book walks and picture walks • Teach basic story elements • Use story pictures to sequence events in order • Teach questioning • Ask students to paraphrase directions	• Preview pictures in stories • After hearing a story, recall events in order • Ask questions • Paraphrase oral directions
Speaking	• Ask cloze questions • Ask open-ended questions • Conduct collaborative interviews • Tap prior knowledge and experience • Model appropriate speech • Mirror speech back to students • Provide interactive word games to develop fluency	• Retell events using descriptive vocabulary • Make comparisons • Make and maintain a personal dictionary and thesaurus
Reading	• Teach literary analysis • Facilitate literary response • Use reference materials (dictionaries, thesaurus, encyclopedia) • Teach reading fluency • Guide discussions of reading • Teach genres	• Read simple stories with illustrations • Follow written directions • Identify and define new vocabulary orally • Identify main ideas • Summarize narrative accounts • Identify genres

(continued)

Table 10.5   *(continued)*

Reading/Language Arts Domains	Teacher Strategies	Student Activities
Writing	• Employ double-entry journals • Teach process writing • Use graphic organizers for prewriting • Use word banks and writing frames • Encourage expanded vocabulary use • Analyze genres of writing • Use rubric assessment	• Cite and comment on important passages in double-entry journals • Prewrite using a graphic organizer • Access reference materials • Create word banks and writing frames • Differentiate narrative from informational writing • Learn/practice rubric criteria

Table 10.6   Early Advanced Level

Reading/Language Arts Domains	Teacher Strategies	Student Activities
Listening	• Tell a joke of the day • Use comic strips • Teach *Wh* questions • Call for students to formulate questions	• Respond to funny stories or jokes • Formulate what, where, how, why questions • Ask clarifying questions
Speaking	• Teach content ELD • Preview key terminology with content area instruction • Study word origins • Practice fluency development with interactive games such as charades, lingo bingo, who am I?	• Begin to use discipline-specific, academic terminology (e.g. math: numerator/denominator) • Give oral presentations • Practice fluency with word games
Reading	• Guide content reading • Jigsaw lengthy textual material • Provide advanced organizers of reading material • Read to learn information • Provide reference material	• Read grade level texts with assistance • Cooperative groups for reading • Outline informational reading • Look up key words in reference material
Writing	• Provide instruction of grammar rules • Teach spelling rules • Teach note taking • Use prewriting graphic organizers • Teach outlining	• Practice editing common grammatical errors • Write notes from lectures, videos, texts • Outline readings • Use graphic organizers for writing • Write in all genres

Table 10.7 Advanced Level

Reading/Language Arts Domains	Teacher Strategies	Student Activities
Listening	• Ask students to paraphrase • Practice wordplay • Teach higher-order questioning	• Paraphrase content material • Make plays on words • Pose higher-order questions
Speaking	• Assign leadership roles in cooperative groups • Establish a rubric for oral presentations	• Generate discussions • Organize group presentations of student work • Produce video programs
Reading	• Literature circle • Encourage personal responses to literature • Supply a wide range of books in literature and content areas	• Grade level literary analysis • Grade level literary response • Select books from all genres • Maintain individual reading log
Writing	• Teach writing multifaceted projects • Provide research tools • Provide computer technology • Teach presentation software	• Produce complex writing projects • Use word processing tools • Create multimedia presentations

Table 10.8 Sample English Language Learner Profile

Strengths	Needs
Level: 3/Listening and Writing	**Level:** 2/Speaking and Reading
Listening: relies on pictures to derive meaning from reading	**Speaking:** retells personal and events from stories but does not use expanded vocabulary
Writing: writes simple sentences using high-frequency words	**Reading:** reads simple picture and pattern books with some fluency

Recommended Instructional Strategies and Student Activities

Listening

Strategies:
• Take book walks and picture walks
• Teach basic story elements
• Use story pictures to sequence events in order
• Teach questioning
• Ask student to paraphrase directions

Activities:
• Preview pictures in stories
• After hearing a story can recall events in order
• Ask questions
• Paraphrase oral directions

Speaking

Strategies:
• Ask cloze questions
• Ask open-ended questions
• Conduct collaborative interviews
• Tap prior knowledge and experience
• Model appropriate speech
• Mirror speech back to student
• Provide interactive word games to develop fluency

Activities:
• Give short answers
• Respond to an open-ended question
• Discuss story events and character traits
• Compare story to prior experiences
• Play interactive word games to develop fluency

(continued)

Table 10.8 *(continued)*

Strengths	Needs
Writing	*Reading*
Strategies:	*Strategies:*
• Employ double-entry journals	• Provide buddy readers or cross-age readers
• Teach process writing	• Conduct word sorting
• Use graphic organizers for prewriting	• Supply simple picture and pattern books
• Use word banks and writing frames	• Choral read chart stories
• Encourage expanded vocabulary use	• Recite chart poems
• Analyze genres of writing	• Sing charted songs
• Use rubric assessment	• Repeated reading for fluency development
	• Teach vocabulary with visuals/realia/models
Activities:	*Activities:*
• Cite and comment on important passages in double-entry journals	• Listen to cross-age readers
• Prewrite using a graphic organizer	• Read with a partner
• Access reference materials	• Read picture books
• Create word banks and writing frames	• Read pattern books
• Differentiate narrative from informational writing	• Match word cards to pictures
• Learn/practice rubric criteria	• Sort word families
	• Practice repeated reading for fluency
	• Read big books
	• Study vocabulary

REFERENCES

California Department of Education. (1999). *English-Language Development Standards for California Public Schools*. Sacramento, CA: California Department of Education.

O'Malley, J. M., & Valdez-Pierce, L. (1996). *Authentic assessment for English Language Learners: Practical approaches for teachers*. White Plains, NY: Addison Wesley Longman.

TESOL (1997). *ESL standards for pre-K-12 students*. Alexandria, VA: TESOL.

C H A P T E R

11

STRATEGIES TO DEVELOP LISTENING AND SPEAKING

Listening and speaking are foundational domains of language. There are numerous ways to embed instructional strategies that target these domains. In this chapter, I will discuss accommodating teacher talk to facilitate listening and speaking; the use and management of Total Physical Response for students at early levels of fluency; facilitating student interaction with grouping strategies; the use of humor and wordplay to enhance social interaction; and questioning strategies to foster higher-order thinking, listening, and speaking.

TEACHER TALK

The teacher of ELLs must employ mental discipline when speaking. Two useful strategies to accommodate teacher talk are mirroring speech and adjusting pacing.

Mirroring Speech

Mirroring speech means responding to a student's question or statement by using that student's words, but modeling the appropriate use of terminology, grammar, and syntax. This technique allows the teacher to address miscues without putting the ELL on the spot. The ELL student risks embarrassment when speaking up in class. Correcting a syntax error or an error of noun–verb agreement in front of the class may only result in silencing the student. Mirrored responses show the student conventional speech indirectly. It also establishes that the content of what the student wanted to say is important.

When mirroring speech, keep in mind the following:

- If the student employs syntax that is reflective of his/her native language, to the degree possible, use the student's choice of words, but in conventional order according to English. For example:

ELL: I see the *balloon red*.
T: A red balloon? Where do you see a red balloon?

- Avoid criticizing the language usage of the student. This is no time to risk embarrassing the student and thus silencing her attempts at speaking in front of a group of peers. There is simply no benefit to saying, "That's not how you say it. You should say . . ."
- Be prepared to negotiate the student's intended meaning. As you rephrase the student's words, ask clarifying questions such as: Did you mean . . .? or Would you say . . .?

Adjusting Pacing

In our fast-paced environment, there is a tendency to want to cover the content as quickly as possible. However, keep in mind this mantra: Speed Kills! Fast-paced speech on the part of the teacher will only lead to confusion and frustration on the part of the ELL. "Slow and steady" will enhance the comfort level of students and increase their ability to comprehend. Bill Cosby, comedian and educator, exemplified pacing. As you listen to his early comedy routines, you hear him talking extremely fast as if he is racing to pack as many jokes in as possible. As he matured, his pacing slowed and his routines became funnier and much more poignant. In much the same way, a classroom teacher must speak with intention at a slightly slower pace.

TOTAL PHYSICAL RESPONSE: INSTRUCTIONAL TECHNIQUES AND MANAGEMENT STRATEGIES

James Asher (1982) conceived of Total Physical Response (TPR) as a strategic way to teach language. In brief, TPR is modeling physical movements to convey meaning on a nonverbal level. The technique was developed originally to help patients of brain trauma recover speech, and it has found broad application with instruction for ELLs as well. TPR is especially strategic for beginners and early intermediate students.

In one case, Asher asked a Japanese teacher to demonstrated TPR with the Japanese word *kobe*. Rather than writing the definition of the word and asking students to use it in a sentence, he held hands with two students and walked three steps, counting "one, two, three." On the third step, they jumped

Key Ways to Facilitate Pacing

- Plan ahead. Outline the lesson content. Be able to summarize the main points of your lesson in a few bullet statements.
- Differentiate teachable moments, mini-lessons, full lesson plans, and multiday plans.
- Stick to your agenda. Avoid getting derailed from the lesson plan. If a student brings up an interesting idea that would move the discussion elsewhere, note the insightful comment and suggest a later time to explore the issue. Pull the group back on track with a brief summary of what was discussed up to that point.
- Pause after you finish a main point. Check for understanding by asking students to paraphrase to each other what you just said.
- Learn to anticipate the clock. Good teachers have a highly developed sense of how long an activity will take. In other words be a clock watcher.
- When asking a question, wait for students to process. Count to ten silently. (To ensure wait time, I hold my hands behind my back and physically count using my fingers while waiting for students to respond.)
- Get used to moments of silence as students ponder what you just said.

into the air as the teacher said "kobe!" They repeated the action several times. As the students performed the action, they learned that *kobe* means "jump". It was a total physical experience of meaning.

Prior to discussing the strategy itself, a word must be said about meaning and nonverbal experiences in language development. Whether we realize it or not, meaning is predominantly nonverbal. We understand much about the world around us before we have conventional labels, or names, for objects and concepts. Think for a moment about how a baby understands "hug" and "caress" long before he knows the word or is even able to articulate the word. As adults, we can enjoy a flowering plant before we know its name. The point is what comes first. A meaningful experience precedes a name or a label for it. TPR provides meaningful, nonverbal experiences of movement and then labels the experience. The verbal experience (spoken and written words) follows the nonverbal experience.

Think of TPR as a series of commands given by the teacher, who models the action for students to perform in turn. Some have equated TPR with the popular children's game "Simon Says." Whereas with "Simon Says" you are trying to catch someone off-guard and eliminate them from the group, TPR seeks to make commands for actions comprehensible to all learners. This is not a competition; it is an effort to create a meaningful experience. A typical TPR lesson might look like the following:

Total Physical Response Lesson

Theme: Drawing a Face
Materials or props: Paper, pencils
Series of Commands:

1. You are going to draw a face.
2. Draw an oval shape for the head.
3. Make an *L* shape for the nose in the middle.
4. Trace the letter *C* on either side for ears.
5. Don't forget to flip the letter *C* on the right side.
6. Draw a small circle above the nose on either side for the eyes.
7. Scribble eyebrows over each eye.
8. Rub your finger over the eyebrows to smear the lines.
9. Spike hair on the top of the head.
10. Use a half-circle to make the mouth smile.

Target Vocabulary

Commands (Verbs)	Facial Parts (Nouns)	Shapes (Nouns)	Positions (Prepositional phrases)
draw	face	oval	in the middle
make	head	L shape	on either side
trace	nose	the letter *C*	on the right side
flip	ears	small circle	above
scribble	eyes	half-circle	over
rub	eyebrows		on the top
smear	hair		
spike	mouth		
use	smile		

Tip for Parent Involvement

Once the student learns the series of commands for a given TPR lesson, send home a one-page sheet with the TPR commands. The child can practice being the teacher and give the commands to members of the family. This will have the added effect of fostering reading.

Key Points with Using TPR

- Write the commands in large letters on chart paper. This gives students something to refer to and establishes basic reading skills such as concepts about print and word recognition.
- Number each command for quick reference.
- Highlight the verb in each command in a different color for easy recognition.
- Be sure to physically model the actions written on the chart paper. Simply giving commands without demonstration does not convey nonverbal meaning.
- Use a prop to help convey meaning (For example, use a scarf to demonstrate prepositional phrases such as "wave it over your head "hold it below your waist," and so forth.)
- Draw illustrations on the chart of the key prop as well as the actions.
- Begin a unit with a TPR lesson to help establish a theme for the instruction. Start off each day with a sequence of TPR commands.

How to conduct a TPR lesson:

1. Begin the lesson by displaying the chart of commands and showing the object(s), if any, that will be used as props.
2. Point to #1 with your finger as you read and demonstrate the command.
3. Ask all students to follow the command.
4. Point to #2 with your finger and, as above, read and demonstrate the command. (Continue with each command written on the chart.)
5. Call on volunteer students to help model the actions for the entire class.
6. Next time you teach the lesson, divide the students into small groups and assign a student to be the group leader. Have the group leader model the commands, either as the teacher reads aloud, or as a more fluent student reads aloud the commands to the class.
7. Keep the current TPR chart on display so that students can practice with a partner during a centers time or during a free time.

Assessment of TPR

Total Physical Response is a matter of student performance. Performance is appropriately assessed by using a rubric. It is possible to assess TPR with a simple rubric: 4 = Follows all commands; 3 = Follows most commands; 2 = Follows few commands; 1 = Follows no commands. A more detailed rubric format allows the teacher to assess the degree to which the student performs according to specified line items. It recognizes the qualitative difference between following, identifying, and reading the charted commands in the TPR lesson (see example below). I prefer to use a line item rubric format because it allows the teacher to differentiate areas of strength and need. The line item rubric provides a rapid way to check off ratings of the student's performance. There is also a space to include brief observational comments.

TPR Rubric Criteria	**4** **all**	**3** **most**	**2** **few**	**1** **none**	**Comments**
• Followed modeled commands					
• Identified key verbs by gesture and action					
• Read commands accurately					

Interpreting The Rubric

The four-point rating system permits the evaluator to readily assess attainment of the criteria. In a four-point system there is no middle ground. It forces the evaluator to decide whether or not the student met the criteria. This system makes for a clear evaluation of the student's performance. A rating of 3 or 4 would mean attaining the criteria, while a rating of 1 or 2 would mean not meeting the criteria.

The three criteria statements establish a graded level of difficulty. In other words, the first criterion statement, in terms of language usage, is easier to attain than the next. "Followed modeled commands" means conducting the action dictated by the written commands as modeled by the teacher. "Identified key verbs by gesture and action" refers to the student being able to point to the appropriate verb in a written command and do the applicable action. "Read commands accurately" refers to reading the written commands fluently from the chart.

Beginning students would be expected to follow modeled commands to a certain degree, but would not be expected to identify the key verbs in each command. Nor would they be expected to read the written commands. Early intermediate students should be able to identify key verbs and read some commands. Intermediate students should be able to attain a rating of 3 or 4 for each rubric criterion.

GROUPING STRATEGIES FOR STUDENT INTERACTION

As a teacher educator, I observe teachers on a weekly basis. Quality teachers recognize the benefit of student-to-student interaction. Language is developed in socially interactive environments. A key strategy for facilitating social interaction is to arrange the classroom for listening and speaking purposes. Several considerations about grouping students come into play: grouping students according to language level; building flexibility into student groups; and forming questions to maximize student interaction.

Grouping Students According to Language Level

Conventional wisdom would place beginning-level students at the front of the room followed by more proficient students, with the most proficient at the back of the room. The thinking here assumes that the room is arranged in straight rows and that the teacher delivery is basically lecture/discussion mode. Since it is easier to hear in the front of the room, placing the beginner ELLs in front appears to make sense. The problem with this approach, however, is that when it comes time for students to interact, the more advanced students at the back will talk, but the less advanced students at the front will remain silent. The beginner ELLs are all grouped together and have a limited capacity to interact. In reality, they provide each other little, if any, accurate modeling for conventional English.

A much better approach would be to form heterogeneous table groups with a mixture of language levels in each table group. In the reality of the classroom, it is impractical to try to maintain a mathematically perfect balance of each language level; nevertheless, mixing students across language levels ensures that a stronger English model is within listening/speaking distance of every beginner ELL.

Grouping students for interaction means setting up table with an even number of students at each table for partnering. If at all possible avoid setting up a table with an odd number of students, to lessen the chance that someone will be left out.

Using Humor and Wordplay to Facilitate Social Interaction

Malcolm Douglass (1989) posed a problem regarding the assessment of comprehension. How can one really know if a listener actually understood what was said? One solution he posited was humor. If the listener laughs at a joke, one can assume that comprehension has been demonstrated. If the listener responds otherwise, one can assume that it is either a bad joke or there was no comprehension.

The premise appears to make sense; but, oh, if it were all that simple. I will never forget checking the aural comprehension of a first grader, a new arrival from El Salvador. He spoke Spanish and a little English. He had a charming smile and enthusiasm about responding to questions. The conversation went something like this:

Me:	"I'm going to ask you something funny. Do you have three ears?"
Student:	Giggling and smiling confidently, "No."
Me:	"That's right, you know you don't have three ears. How many ears do you have?"
Student:	Again smiling confidently, "Six."

What I first imagined was having a conversation with a child with six ears; but I came to realize that the student, being six years old, was hearing the question according to Spanish syntax. In Spanish, ¿ *Cuántos años tienes?* literally reads, "How many *years* do you have?" He thought I was joking about his age. What the above scenario suggests is that humor can be a complex matter. Laughing at a joke does not necessarily equate to comprehension.

Tip for Parent Involvement

As a homework assignment, have students collect jokes from family members. Compile the jokes into a joke book that can be read at home.

There is a wonderful place for jokes and humor in learning English, though. Using jokes strategically requires matching levels of proficiency to types of jokes:

1. Beginning and early intermediate fluency: Funny scenario
2. Intermediate fluency and above: Mixing homophones
3. Intermediate fluency and above: Comic strip bubbles
4. Early advanced fluency and above: Wordplay

Funny scenario. Years ago, I was traveling in La Paz, Bolivia. I had only recently arrived there. At a local restaurant, I ordered a meal with several items. What I did not realize was the quantity of each item I ordered. When the food arrived, my solo meal was enough to feed a banquet of ten people. All I could do was laugh. Reenacting that kind of scenario has universal appeal. With very few words, an ELL can demonstrate meaningful humor. If the teacher acts as the director for the scenario by calling out a list of commands, it complements Total Physical Response. Think of the universal appeal of Punch and Judy, puppets that date back to medieval times. The humor is basically a funny scenario of two puppets and slapstick. Although I am not advocating having students perform slapstick with each other, I am suggesting that reenacting a funny scenario with puppets or people is a meaningful way to insert humor into instruction.

The following are possible scenarios to reenact:

- Ordering an item at a restaurant which turns out to be too much, or too little, or other than what was ordered
- Losing your glasses and finding them on your face
- Bumping into an acquaintance and forgetting her name
- Getting the wrong directions to school

With each of the above scenarios, the instructor is teaching questioning strategies. At the restaurant, one is playing a waiter taking orders and inquiring about each item. The other is playing the restaurant patron who is asking about the food selection. With losing your glasses, imagine one student wearing a pair of glasses and going around the room asking other students, "Have you seen my glasses?" "Where are my glasses?" While others respond with, "Have you checked your face?" or "I don't know." In the scenario of the acquaintance, one party chitchats while the other tries to find out the name of the person without asking right out, "What is your name?" Getting lost and having to ask directions again is a repetitive way to practice asking directions.

The way one produces a funny scenario for instructional purposes is to create a script chart. A script chart is a two-column chart in large print so that all can see. In the left column are the directions to be read aloud and modeled by the instructor. In the right column are the corresponding words, phrases, or sentences that the student will be saying.

Sample Scenario: *"Getting the wrong directions to school"*
Cast: *Student, friend #1, friend #2, friend #3.*
Props: *A school sign*

Actions	Lines
1. Walk to the right. 2. Point to the right.	Student: "Which way to school?" Friend #1: "Walk right down this street."
3. Continue to walk to the right. 4. Point to the left.	Student: "Where is the school?" Friend #2: "Walk to the left, down this street."
5. Walk to the left. 6. Point to the right.	Student: "How do I get to school?" Friend #3: "Walk right down this street."
7. Walk to the right. Shake your head left to right. 8. Turn around.	Student: "Do you know where the school is?" Friend #4: "It's behind you."

Notice the various conceptual and language instructions the above scenario presents. First, the actions dictate directionality. Second, notice that each question asks the same thing, while providing the ELL with a repertoire of questions to use.

Mixing Homophones. Mixing homophone pairs (words that sound alike, but are written differently and have different meanings) is an appropriate strategy for students at the intermediate level because it requires a level of vocabulary development prior to participation. Students must also be able to visualize the difference between paired homophones.

Prior to creating humorous pairings of homophones, students need to establish a homophone picture bank. A picture bank is created simply by folding a piece of paper in half lengthwise to make left- and right-hand sides of the paper. Write in the homophone pair, one word on each side. For example, use the word pair "hair/hare." Write "hair" on the left side of the fold and "hare" on the right side of the fold.

hair	hare

Then ask students to illustrate each word on the corresponding side. Students who do not like to draw can cut and glue magazine pictures, or utilize computer clip art. (When searching on-line for child-friendly clip art selections, I prefer to use a children's search engine like www.yahooligans.com.)

For the picture bank, collect a wide range of homophone pairs with their accompanying illustrations. Post the various illustrated pairs on a bulletin board or on a large sheet of chart paper. Display the picture bank for children to use as a quick reference for their humorous writing.

Next, select a homophone pair from the picture bank to use in a humorous way. Note how one of the words is used, and then substitute its homophone pair. For example, let's look at "hair styling." Now substitute the homophone "hare" to produce "hare styling." Imagine how a picture of "hare styling" would look. I imagine a rabbit going into a beauty parlor, or better yet, one exiting a beauty parlor with a fancy hairdo. Or should I say, "hare-do."

Begin by modeling the substitution of homophone pairs and the students will get the idea. The illustration is the key to the process. Give them time to think about combinations of images first, then follow with appropriate words. Remember that the image drives the humor; the nonverbal aspect of the meaning is the funny part of the exercise. This tells us that meaning takes place predominantly at a nonverbal level.

Comic Strip Bubbles. Using images to generate humorous language play is vital to making language development meaningful for ELLs. For students who are able to write in English at the intermediate level or above, filling in cartoon bubbles is an excellent exercise. This activity is ideal for a learning center activity.

Comic strip bubbles are the rounded shapes in comic strips where dialog or thoughts appear. Having students supply their own words for the pictures is an easy and meaningful way to use written language. Simply cut out your favorite comic strip from the newspaper. (Black and white comics work better for this activity.) Use liquid "white-out" to blank out the words in the bubbles. Then photocopy the comic strip with blank cartoon bubbles. You may need to enlarge the image so that there will be room to write in words. Next ask the students to fill in the comic strip bubbles with their own dialog. It is that simple. Remember that this is used strictly for educational purposes.

Several things to remember: 1) Prior to writing in the bubbles, ask the students to write and edit their words on a separate sheet of paper. This also gives the writer an indication of the space and the size of the letters to use. 2) You are appropriating published material for educational purposes only. Do not publish the work in a school newsletter, or other publication, without obtaining written permission from the publisher. 3) As a follow-up activity, students can create their own comic strips based on their own original drawings.

Wordplay. The most open-ended strategy for injecting humor into language development is wordplay; thus it is best done by more advanced ELLs. In other words, the more words students know the more they can play with. Nevertheless, all students may participate to the extent that they are able. When you want to have some fun with words, play one of the following games with your students.

Team Webbing: A word webbing activity in a team/competitive setting

---

Purpose: To generate as many word associations as possible related to a core word in just five minutes.
Materials: Core word cards, blank paper and pencils.
Preparation: Write selected words on word cards in two-inch letters. These will be the "core words" for the game. The core words can be any words you choose. I recommend that they be words from a spelling list, or from an instructional unit in a subject area.

Directions:

1. Divide the class into teams with two students on a team.
2. Hand each team a piece of blank paper to share.
3. In the center of the paper, ask one member of each team to draw an oval large enough to accommodate a core word.
4. Show the first core word card so that all can see it.
5. Ask the second member of each team to copy the word in the oval in the center of the piece of paper.
6. At the command, "Go!", team members take turns drawing a line from the center and writing a word that is associated with the core word.
7. You may draw a line from a new word associated with the core word and write another association, thus expanding the web.
8. After five minutes, all teams stop writing.
9. Words are then counted on the webs and verified for spelling and justifiable associations.
10. The team with the most verified words on the web wins.

Rules:

1. One pencil per team.
2. Team members must take turns writing associated words. No pencil hogging.
3. All words must be spelled correctly to be included in the web.
4. Random words or words with dubious associations will not be counted.
5. Opponents can challenge words that do not appear to have a meaningful association.
6. The writer of a word being challenged must justify her word to the referee.
7. The teacher or designee acts as a referee.
8. The web with the most correctly spelled, verified words wins.

Variation of the game: Use plastic transparencies with water-soluble writing pens in lieu of paper. These are reusable, and allow the class to see a completed web all at once as it is projected on a screen using an overhead projector. This will lead to lively discussion and challenges from the class, resulting in whole class teachable moments.

Hot Words: A variation of that old familiar game, hot potato, but with words

Purpose: To generate as many words as possible of like initial letters from a key word in a set period of time.

Materials: An egg timer, a set of word cards in the shape of a potato.

Preparation: Cut brown tagboard into potatolike shapes. Write selected words on the cards to be used in the game.

Directions:

1. Form circle groups of approximately six to eight participants.
2. Set an egg timer for three minutes.
3. Give a player in the circle a potato word card.
4. At the command, "Hot Word, Go!" the first player reads the word and then says another word with the same initial letter. (For example: If the potato word is "barrel," then the player would need to say another word beginning with *b,* such as "bitter.")
5. After successfully saying a word of like initial letter, the player passes the potato word card to any other player in the circle.
6. The next player to receive the potato word card must then state another word beginning with the same initial letter.
7. Continue passing the potato word card and generating same initial letter words.
8. When a player is unable to think of a new word—one that has not already been used—that player is out of the round.
9. Play resumes until no more words can be generated and/or one player is left.
10. Once the timer sounds, a new word is thrown into the circle and the old word is removed.
11. The round is over when only one player is left.

Rules:

1. Generated words must match the initial letter in the potato word card.
2. A player is out if he cannot think of a word with the appropriate initial letter or if he states a word that has already been used.
3. Players must make good passes of the potato word card to other players.
4. The winner is the last player left in the circle.

Variations of the game: Play with the letters of the potato word card in sequence so that the first player uses the initial letter, the second player must think of a word that begins with the second letter, the next uses the third letter, and so forth.

> *Telephone Picture Tag: A variation of the game telephone, in which a message is passed from one player to another. At the end the various changes in the message are shared. This is noncompetitive language play.*

Purpose: To represent a message by a drawing and then to attempt to figure out the message based on the drawing.

Materials: Sufficient number of pencils for all players, a stack of three-inch paper squares for each player. The number of paper squares in each stack must correspond to the number of players in the game.

Preparation: Cut blank paper into three-inch squares. Ascertain the number of players there will be in a round of play. If there are nine players, then each player must have a stack of nine squares (a total of eighty-one squares would be needed to play the game). Supply pencils for each player.

Directions:

1. Players sit around a table. Although there is technically no limit to the number of players, the game works best with six to ten participants.
2. Once all players have paper and pencil, the group takes a few moments to think of a short famous quotation or title of a book, movie, or song.
3. Write the quote or title on the top square of paper.
4. At the command, "Ready, Pass!", each player passes the entire stack of papers with the quote or title to the person on their right.
5. After receiving a new stack, players should read the quote or title silently to themselves. (It is essential to read silently so as not to tip off other players about the quote or title.)
6. Place the quote or title on the bottom of the stack.
7. Draw a picture that represents what the quote or title means.
8. At the command, "Ready, Pass!", each player passes the entire stack of papers to the person on their right. This time, the paper square on top is the picture.
9. Look only at the picture and try to figure out what it represents. Do not look at the other papers for clues.
10. Place the picture on the bottom of the stack.
11. Each player writes the words that tell, to the best of their ability, what the picture represented.
12. Each time the stack is passed, the play alternates between writing words and drawing pictures.
13. Continue to play until each stack of paper squares returns to the original player.
14. Finish the game by having each player share the original message and the various drawings and permutations of the original quote or title. The fun is in seeing the crazy way the message was changed.

Rules:

1. Keep all stacks of paper together and moving in the same direction.
2. Avoid taking too much time to write or draw.
3. No peeking at the words or pictures within a stack until the end of the game.

Variations of the game: Specify at the outset of the game a category for a round of play, such as "song titles." Another approach would be to limit the category to a specific area of study, such as "U.S. History: Civil War Period."

In the movie *Dead Poets Society,* John Keating, the English teacher played by Robin Williams, asks the students, "What is the purpose of learning language and poetry?" After the students make several nominal attempts to respond to his question, he provides a comical answer, ". . . to woo women." A decidedly chauvinistic comment; but the point to note here is that language by its very nature is social-interactive. Using wordplay and humor emphasizes the social-interactive aspect of language usage. Social interaction is a key pedagogical component to language development. Helping ELLs develop language requires creating situations in which they can interact with one another according to their level of proficiency.

MATCHING QUESTIONS AND RESPONSES TO LEVELS OF PROFICIENCY

As instructional strategies, questioning and responding date back to antiquity; however, for ELLs to develop listening and speaking skills teachers need to form appropriate questions and frame responses to match levels of proficiency. Questions have been ordered in a hierarchy according to cognitive levels. One of the most common ways to order questions is according to Bloom's (1968) taxonomy of higher-order thinking. Ideally, as teachers, we seek to move students from responding to simple factual information to synthesis. The challenge that arises is that in order to respond appropriately to higher-order questions, conventional wisdom dictates that the ELL needs to be more fluent in English. The problem that this creates is the false impression that until ELLs are fluent, they cannot participate in higher-order thinking. If the ELL is only able to speak in one- to two-word phrases, an open-ended question is not appropriate. Consequently, the ELL is not asked to consider higher-order questions. The truth is, however, that there are ways to structure questions and responses that encourage higher-order thinking.

Think about Bloom's taxonomy for a moment. Synthesis, the highest level of question according to Bloom, actually requires very few words. In the same way that a newspaper headline can synthesize a lengthy article, a student can synthesize a concept, a story, or an article. Synthesis can be demonstrated by a phrase with as few as one to three words. What this means is that higher-order thinking can take place even though the ELL is at a lower level of fluency. What the teacher must provide is an accessible way for the student to respond.

Here are three ways to help ELLs respond to a synthesis question: highlighting key words; creating a synthesis word bank; and inviting students to talk among themselves in their primary language.

Highlighting Key Words

A simple way to facilitate synthesis is to ask ELLs to highlight key words in a story or article. Key words would be the words that appear to be the most meaningful. Key words can be highlighted by using a marking pen or colored pencil, or by simply copying them on a separate piece of paper. Collect the highlighted words and write them on a chart. Then ask the students to pick three words that embody the message of the story or article.

Generating a Synthesis Word Bank

Another way to facilitate synthesis is to generate a word bank. Prior to asking a synthesizing question, solicit descriptive phrases from the entire class. Write the various random phrases on the board or on chart paper, to make a word bank. Then ask the synthesizing question and let students use the word bank to formulate written responses of their syntheses. The basis for this strategy is that each classroom contains a range of students at various levels of English proficiency; a word bank strategy draws on the knowledge and fluency of the entire group. Students at lower levels of proficiency can utilize the words that were generated by more proficient English speakers.

Inviting Primary Language Discussion

This strategy is simple in that it requires no special preparation. It is just a matter of inviting students at selected points in a lesson to talk to their same-language neighbor to paraphrase the learning thus far. Then follow by asking those who are able to translate their thinking into English for the whole group.

Tip for Parent Involvement

Encourage students to interview family members regularly about subjects being taught at school. Provide basic interview questions that match the topic. Have the students take notes like a reporter and report back to class the following day.

Just because a student is unable to discuss a concept in depth in English does not mean that she is unable to conceptualize it in her primary language. The fundamental notion here is that thinking is not bound by a specific language. Could you imagine someone claiming that you can only solve math problems in English? It sounds ludicrous. Conversely, have you ever noticed a bilingual person switching to a dominant language to work out a complex problem? The same thinking applies to this strategy. Rather than seeing language diversity as a "barrier," begin to see other languages as different paths to knowledge and understanding.

REFERENCES

Asher, J. (1982). *Learning another language through actions: The complete teacher's guidebook.* Los Gatos, CA: Sky Oaks.

Bloom, B. (1968). Learning for mastery. *Evaluation Comment, 1*(2). Los Angeles, CA: University of California, Los Angeles Center for the Study of Evaluation and Instructional Programs.

Douglass, M. (1989). *The reading process.* New York: Teachers College Press.

TEACHING THE MECHANICS OF HANDWRITING, GRAMMAR, AND SPELLING

TESOL Goals and Standards

Goal 2: To use English to achieve academically in all content areas	Standard 2: Students will use English to obtain, process, contruct, and provide subject matter information in spoken and written form
Standard 1: Students will use English to interact in the classroom	

One might ask, when is it appropriate to teach handwriting, grammar, and spelling? A more precise question is the following: What strategies help English Language Learners learn handwriting, grammar, and spelling at beginning, intermediate, and advanced stages? Fundamentally, instructional strategies must take into account the proficiency level of the student as well utilize the student's words as a starting point before moving to more abstract approaches (see Table 12.1).

Table 12.1 Language Mechanics across Levels of Proficiency

Conventions	Beginning and Early Intermediate	Intermediate	Early Advanced/ Advanced
Handwriting	• Modeling	• When to use uppercase • Sort letters by shape • Total Physical Response	• Font selection and lowercase
Grammar	• Modeling grammar in context	• The world's shortest sentences	• Prepositional phrases • Color-coded word walls
Spelling	• Letter and word recognition	• Word sorts and word building	• Word study

HANDWRITING

Handwriting is composed of various elements. According to Barbe, Wasylyk, Hackney, and Braun (1984), the elements are letter formation, size and proportion, spacing, slant, alignment, and line quality. There is also a sequence to letter formation. Generally letters are formed from top to bottom and left to right. Although teaching handwriting takes place in the primary grades, some newly arrived immigrant students at any grade level may not be familiar with Western script. They may need to be taught handwriting as part of letter recognition and formation.

Sort Letters By Shape

Rather than teach handwriting in alphabetical order, sort the letters by shape for lower- and upper-case. When the letters are sorted by shape, they become grouped according to similar strokes. This facilitates teaching letter formation. Note that there are basically lines, circles, curves, angles, and various combinations thereof. Also note the differences when sorting by lower- and uppercase. Some letters change their shape combinations.

Begin by teaching the straight-lined letters. It is an easy adjustment for students to follow with angled letters. Then teach circle-based letters, and then curves.

Letters Sorted by Shape and Case

Fundamental Letter Shape	Lowercase	Uppercase
Line	l t i	L T I E F H
Angle	v w x y k z	A M N V W X Y K Z
Circle/Line	o a b d p q	O Q
Open circle	c e	C G
Line/Half-circle		B D P R
Curved	h m n u	U
Partial curve	f r j g	J
S-curve	s	S

Use of Total Physical Response

Total Physical Response (TPR) is very useful for teaching letter shapes. TPR relies on physical actions in the form of demonstrated commands to orient oneself to letter formation.

Imagine the dotted line in the middle of a writing line (see illustration) as your belt, or waistline, with the top line across your forehead, and the bottom line at your feet. Using the body to orient the writing space on the paper, the teacher can give TPR commands to actively demonstrate letter formation. Give TPR commands that draw an imaginary line from head to toe. For example, for a lowercase "1," say, "Touch your head. Reach for your toes."

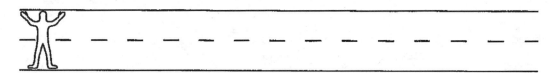

Begin each handwriting lesson with a TPR activity to actively demonstrate letter formation. Keep in mind that block print letters are generally formed from top to bottom and left to right. Write the TPR commands on charts to display on the walls with the proper formation of each letter. The following commands are grouped according to the fundamental shapes of the lower- and uppercase letters as illustrated above.

Tip for Parent Involvement

Show parents the following TPR commands to practice at home with their children. Make letter cards with the TPR commands on the opposite side. Use the cards like a game. Show a letter card and ask the child to demonstrate the actions.

Total Physical Response Commands for Straight-Lined Letters

Lowercase

1: Touch your head.
  Reach for your shoes.

t: Touch your head.
  Cross at the shoulders.

i: Touch your belt.
  Reach for your shoes.
  Dot it above the belt.

Uppercase

L: Touch your left ear.
  Reach for your left shoe.

  Cross to the right at your toes.

T: Touch your head.
  Reach, down the middle, for your toes.
  Cross at your head.

I: Touch your head.
  Reach for your toes.

E: Touch your left ear.
  Reach for your left shoe.
  Touch your left ear.
  Cross to the right.
  Touch your left side.
  Cross to the right.
  Touch your left shoe.
  Cross to the right.

F: Touch your left ear.
  Reach for your left shoe.
  Touch your left ear.
  Cross to the right.
  Touch your left side.
  Cross to the right.

H: Stand with feet apart.
  Touch your left ear.
  Reach for your left shoe.
  Touch your right ear.
  Reach for your right shoe.
  Cross it at the belt.

Total Physical Response Commands for Angled Letters

Lowercase

k: Stand with feet apart.
  Touch your left ear.
  Reach for your left shoe.
  Touch your right shoulder.
  Reach for your left side.
  Reach for your right shoe.

w: Touch your left side.
  Reach for your left foot.
  Touch your belt.
  Reach for your right shoe.
  Touch your right side.
  Reach for your right shoe.

v: Stand with feet together.
  Touch your left side.
  Reach between your shoe.
  Touch your right side.
  Reach for the ground.

x: Stand with feet apart.
  Touch your left side.
  Cross over to reach for your right foot.
  Touch your right side.
  Cross over to reach for your left foot.

z: Stand with feet apart.
  Touch your left side.
  Cross it at the belt.
  Cross over to reach for your left shoe.
  Cross it to right at your shoes.

y: Stand with feet together.
  Touch your left side.
  Reach for your shoes.
  Touch your right side.
  Reach below your shoes.

Uppercase

A: Stand with feet apart.
  Touch the top of your head.
  Reach for your left shoe.
  Touch the top of your head.
  Reach for your right shoe.
  Cross it at the belt.

N: Stand with feet apart.
  Touch your left ear. Reach for your left foot.
  Touch your left ear again.
  Cross over to your right foot.
  Touch your right ear.
  Reach for your right foot.

X: Stand wit feet apart.
  Touch your left ear.
  Cross over to reach your right shoe.
  Touch your right ear.
  Cross over to reach your left shoe.

K: Stand with feet apart.
  Touch your left ear.
  Reach to your left shoe.
  Touch your right ear.
  Reach to your left side.
  Reach from your left side to your right shoe.

V: Stand with feet together.
  Touch your left ear.
  Reach for the middle, between your shoes.
  Touch your right ear.
  Reach for the middle, between your shoes.

Y: Stand with feet together.
  Touch your left ear.
  Cross over to the middle of your belt.
  Touch your right ear.
  Cross over to the middle of your belt.
  Reach from your belt to your shoes.

M: Stand with feet apart.
Touch your left ear.
Reach for your left shoe.
Touch your left ear.
Reach for the middle,
between your shoes.
Touch your right ear.
Reach for the middle,
between your shoes.
Touch your right ear.
Reach for your right shoe.

W: Stand with feet slightly apart.
Touch your left ear.
Reach for your left shoe.
Touch the top of your head.
Reach for your left shoe again
Touch the top of your head.
Reach for your right shoe.
Touch your right ear.
Reach your right shoe.

Z: Stand wit feet apart.
Touch your left ear.
Cross to the right ear.
Cross over to your
left shoe.
Cross to your right shoe.

Total Physical Response Commands for Circle/Line Letters

Lowercase

o: Touch your belt in the middle.
Reach down to make a circle
to the left.
Touch your shoes before
curving up to the belt.

a: Touch your belt in the middle.
Reach down to make a circle
to the left.
Touch your shoes before curving
up to the belt.
Touch your right side.
Reach to your right shoe.

b: Touch your left ear.
Reach for your left shoe.
Touch your belt in the
middle.
Reach down to make a
circle to the left.
Touch your shoes before
curving up to the belt.

d: Touch your belt in
the middle.
Reach down to make a
circle to the left.
Touch your shoes before
curving up to the belt.
Touch your right ear.
Reach for your right shoe.

p: Touch your left side.
Reach down below your
left shoe.
Touch your belt in the middle.
Reach down to make a circle
to the left.
Touch your shoes before curving
up to the belt.

q: Touch your belt in the
middle.
Reach down to make a
circle to the left.
Touch your shoes before
curving up to the belt.
Touch your right side.
Reach down below your
right shoe.

Uppercase

O: Touch the top of your head.
Curve a circle to the left
Touch your shoes before curving
up to your head.

Q: Touch the top of your head.
Curve a circle to the left.
Touch your shoes before curving up to your head.
Touch your belt in the middle.
Squiggle a line to your right shoe.

Total Physical Response Commands for Open Circle Letters

Lowercase

c: Touch your right leg just above the knee.
Curve around to the left.
Touch your shoes.
Stop the curve just before your right knee.

e: Touch your right leg just above the knee.
Curve to the left around at the belt.
Curve down and touch your shoes.
Stop the curve just before your right knee.
Cross to the left.
Stop at your left leg.

Uppercase

C: Touch your right shoulder.
Curve up to the left.
Touch the top of your head.

G: Touch your right shoulder.
Curve up to the left.
Touch the top of your head.

Touch your left side.
Touch your shoes.
Stop at your right knee.

Touch your left side.
Touch your shoes.
Stop at your right side.
Cross to the left at the belt.

Total Physical Response Commands for Curved Letters

Lowercase

h: Stand with feet apart.
   Touch your left ear.
   Reach to your left shoe.
   Touch your left side just below the belt.
   Curve up to the right.
   Touch the belt.
   Curve down to your right shoe.

m: Stand with feet apart.
   Touch your left side at the belt.
   Reach down to your left shoe.
   Curve up and touch your belt.
   Curve to the middle between your shoes.
   Curve up to your belt.
   Curve down to your right shoe.

n: Stand with feet apart.
   Touch your left side at the belt.
   Reach down to your left shoe.
   Curve up and touch your belt.
   Reach down to your right shoe.

u: Stand with feet apart.
   Touch your left side at the belt.
   Reach down to your left shoe.
   Curve over to your right shoe.
   Reach up to your right side at the belt.
   Reach back down to your right shoe.

Uppercase

U: Touch your left ear.
   Reach down to your left shoe.
   Curve over to your right shoe.
   Reach up to your right ear.

Total Physical Response Commands for Letters Formed from Lines and Half-Circles

Uppercase (only)

B: Touch your left ear.
   Reach down to your left shoe.
   Touch your left ear again.
   Curve down to the right.
   Cross at the belt.
   Curve down to the right from the belt.
   Cross your shoes.
   Stop at your left shoe.

D: Touch your left ear.
   Reach down to your left shoe.
   Touch your left ear again.
   Make a big curve to the right.
   Cross your shoes.
   Stop at your left shoe.

P: Touch your left ear.
   Reach down to your left shoe.
   Touch your left ear again.
   Curve down to the right.
   Cross at the belt.

R: Touch your left ear.
   Reach down to your left shoe.
   Touch your left ear again.
   Curve down to the right.
   Cross at the belt.
   Cross over from the belt to your right shoe.

Total Physical Response Commands for Partially Curved Letters

Lowercase

f: Start at the middle, above the belt.
   Curve down to the left shoe.
   Cross at the belt.

r: Touch your left side.
   Reach down to your left shoe.
   Touch the belt at the middle.
   Curve down to the left side.

j: Start at the middle of your belt.
   Reach down below your shoes and curve to the left.
   Dot it in the middle above the belt.

g: Touch your belt in the middle.
   Reach down to make a circle to the left.
   Touch your shoes before curving up to the belt.
   Touch your right side.
   Reach below your shoes.
   Curve to the left below your shoes.

Uppercase

J: Touch your right ear.
   Reach down to your shoes.
   Curve up to the left.
   Stop at your knee.

Total Physical Response Commands for the S-Curve Letters

Lowercase

s: Start on your right side, just below the belt.
   Curve up across the belt.
   Curve down across the knees.
   Touch your right shoe.
   Curve up across your shoes.
   Stop at the knees.

Uppercase

S: Touch your right ear.
   Curve over your head to the left.
   Touch your left shoulder.
   Curve down to the right across your belt.
   Curve down to your right knee.
   Curve to the left across your shoes.
   Stop at your left knee.

GRAMMAR

There is a strong connection between oral and written language; however, the two are not entirely synonymous. According to King and Rentel (1981), children in grades one through four tended to write in much the same way that they spoke. With ELLs the use of primary language syntax in English is prevalent. Sulzby and Teale (2003) argued that instruction of conventional grammar in written language is required to help children sort out the differences between oral and written language.

The World's Shortest Sentence

Using hyperbole with regard to writing can illustrate a fundamental aspect about grammar, that a sentence is composed of a noun phrase + verb phrase.
   Directions:

1. Divide the class into small groups of four students each.
2. Ask each group to compose and write down the shortest sentence that they can possibly think of.
3. Allow two to three minutes for the group work.
4. As groups compose their sentences, have them write them on the board. (This gives the whole class a small number of sentences to analyze, yet each member of the class has provided input.)
5. Ask every student to write down the sentences as they appear on the board.

6. Begin to analyze the sentences:
   - Which one is the shortest?
   - Is it a complete sentence? Explain your understanding of a complete sentence.
   - What words can be taken out to make it shorter, yet still complete?
7. Once you analyze and shorten a sentence as a whole group, ask the students to shorten the other sentences. Challenge them to get the sentences down to two words.
8. Ultimately, students will pare them down to sentences as short as "She ran." At this point, ask students the following: What are the components of a complete sentence? (Be prepared for the students that form a command such as "Go!" Ask them if it is a complete sentence and to explain their thinking as to why it is complete or not.)
9. As students will soon discover, a sentence is composed of a noun phrase plus a verb phrase. This simple discovery raises their level of awareness about the make-up of a sentence fragment or a complete sentence.
10. Now ask them to identify the noun phrase and verb phrase in other sentences.

Color Code Parts of Speech

When developing a word wall for a classroom, consider color coding parts of speech. Use different colored word cards for each part of speech. For example, display nouns on yellow cards, verbs on blue, adjectives on red, and adverbs on green. Make a legend for the color coding to be displayed next to the word wall.

Tip for Parent Involvement

Make up color-coded noun phrase cards and verb phrase cards. Ask parents to play a game with the cards by combining noun and verb phrases to make complete sentences. Also color code parts of speech cards to combine words into complete sentences.

Teach Prepositions as Phrases

Think about the baffling nature of prepositions. We ride *in* a car, but *on* an airplane. Teaching prepositions in isolation does not account for their situational usage; teaching prepositions in a phrase does not necessarily explain why we use them in a particular way, but it provides some contextual usage.

SPELLING

Spelling in English poses many problems. Conventional spelling is determined by social and historical factors rather than by a prescribed system of logical rules. Nevertheless, there are certain ways to understand the acquisition of spelling proficiency as a developmental process. Gentry (1987) posited an organization of spelling in developmental stages. This organization provides a way to understand how students will spell a word like "monster" as representational scribble and pictures, as a collection of consonants like *mtr*, as an idiosyncratic invention like *munstr* or *mostar*, or finally as a conventionally accepted norm *monster*.

The developmental stages for spelling according to Gentry (1987) are precommunicative, semiphonetic, phonetic, transitional, conventional, and morphemic/syntactic. Briefly, the precommunicative stage is characterized by representational scribble and drawings of caricatures. Semiphonetic spellings include letters that indicate dominant sounds in words. Phonetic spellings use a vowel in each syllable, but are idiosyncratic, inventive spellings. Transitional spellings are characterized by misspellings that do not have a phonetic quality. Conventional spellings are those agreed upon by our culture as normative. Finally, morphemic/syntactic spellers master the language to the point where they can manipulate words accurately for their own intentions.

Table 12.2 shows the various stages of developmental spelling and how the stages map on to corresponding levels of English Language Development (ELD) with appropriate strategies for each level.

Table 12.2   The stages of Developmental Spelling and Levels of English Language Development

Developmental Stage	Descriptors	Examples	Corresponding ELD Level (Recommended Strategies)
Precommunicative	• Scribbling can be representational • Understands speech can be written • Lacks concept of a word • Makes letterlike shapes • May write name	(random scribbles, marks, or drawings)	**Beginning** (Strategies: letter and word recognition)
Semiphonetic (*Rule of thumb:* Not a plausible word structure in English: e.g. CCC)	• Spells few words correctly but knows letters make words • Still invents symbols for letters and words • Makes 1- to 3-letter representations of words, usually consonants • Has more control over beginnings and endings of words • Predicts words auditorially in frequently occurring patterns	*mtr*	**Beginning, Early Intermediate** (Strategies: letter and word recognition, word sorting)
Phonetic (*Rule of thumb:* Plausible structure for a word in English: e.g. CVCV)	• Spellings include all sound features of words as heard. • Invents system of phonetic spelling that is consistent • Understands relationship of sounds in speech to symbols in writing • Spelling can be read by others	*mostar* *monstr*	**Early Intermediate, Intermediate** (Strategies: word sorts, identify structural patterns, word families)
Transitional (*Rule of thumb:* May appear as a typo; no auditory distinction)	• Begins to spell conventionally and knows it is necessary for others to read their writing • Uses knowledge of how words look as well as sound and applies this to other words • Includes vowels in every syllable • Uses familiar spelling patterns. • Intersperses conventional spelling with invented spelling	*monstar* *monstur* *monstir* *monstor*	**Early Advanced** (Strategies: continue word sorts, patterns, families; add word study, systematic rule building)

(continued)

Table 12.2 *(continued)*

Developmental Stage	Descriptors	Examples	Corresponding ELD Level (Recommended Strategres)
Conventional	• Begins to spell correctly • Has mastered root words, past tense, and short vowels • Still struggles with consonant doubling, letter position, and word affixes • Has growing knowledge of word meanings and complicated vowel patterns	*monster*	**Early Advanced, Advanced** (Strategies: word study, systematic rule building, etymologies, roots, parts of speech)
Morphemic/ Syntactic	• Increasingly understands how meaning and grammatical structure control spelling • Adds morphemic and syntactic knowledge to phonological knowledge • Is better at doubling consonants spelling alternative forms of words, and word endings • Conducts wordplay in creative ways	"Monster, schmonster, it doesn't scare me."	**Advanced** (Strategies: same as above; encourage word play)

Rules of Thumb

At first, it may appear difficult to differentiate semiphonetic, phonetic, and transitional spellings. Use the following guidelines to help identify unique features of the spellings. For semiphonetic spellings, the rule of thumb is that it is not a plausible structure of a word in English. For example, many semiphonetic spellings are a collection of consonants with no vowels, as in *mtr* for monster. No plausible word in English will have three consonants without vowels in between; in English each syllable needs a vowel.

For phonetic spelling, conversely, the rule of thumb is that the spelling has a plausible structure of a word in English, such as CVCV. The phonetic spellings are not conventional, but they are decodable. Phonetic spellers will spell multisyllabic words in creative ways; for example, the word *attention* might be spelled *atenshun*. There is a certain logic to phonetic spelling. The spelling follows a conventional structure, but the spelling is invented. Each syllable will have a vowel sound, although final consonants that have a vowel quality such as *r* or *l* may not carry a vowel. Examples of this are *monstr* for monster or *lidl* for little.

For transitional spelling, the rule of thumb it that it looks like a typo (a single letter misplaced) and that the variance is not phonetic or auditory. Generally speaking, transitional spellers use conventional spelling for most words; however, double consonants, silent *e*, *wh-*, and homophones are particularly problematic. Examples of transitional spellings are as follows: double consonants, *little/little*; silent *e, time/tim* or *with/withe*; words using *wh, which/wich*; homophones, *right/write*. In each example the variance is not attributed to an auditory feature of the word. One does not hear a consonant doubled in medial position, a silent *e*, the *h* in *which*, or the difference between *right* and *write*. These are characteristics that need to be recognized by sight.

Activities to Address Spelling

The following spelling activities are arranged to correspond to stages of developmental spelling and ELD levels of fluency. Note that there is some overlap between the two systems.

Letter/Word Recognition.   (Spelling stages: precommunicative/semiphonetic; ELD levels: beginning/early intermediate)

Match Picture Cards with Letters in Initial Position.   Develop a picture card file. Order the file according to the alphabet. On one side of the cards glue pictures cut from magazines. You can even have the students help by selecting pictures to cut out and glue. On the other side, write the initial letter that represents the picture with the word. File the pictures in a box with dividers for each letter of the alphabet.

Make an accompanying set of letter cards and word cards that match the pictures in the file. Students can either look for pictures that match a specific letter or find the right letter to match the picture.

Use a sand tray to give students the opportunity to practice writing upper- and lowercase letters that match the pictures in the file. A sand tray is simply a rectangular tray like a cookie sheet. Pour an even layer of fine grain sand (salt can be substituted) in the tray. Allow students to finger-spell letters and words. Follow the finger-spelling with a practice writing activity on lined paper.

Word Sorts.   (Spelling stages: phonetic/early transitional; ELD levels: early intermediate/intermediate)

Use a word wall to list words according to the same initial letter.   Make the word wall with a large wall space and yarn. Use the yarn to lay out a grid for each letter of the alphabet. Configure the grid as a five-row, five-column square, and then add one more space for *z*.

Each time the group learns a new word, ask a student to make a word for the word wall. Allow the student the opportunity to figure out the appropriate space on the word wall for the card. Consider making a poster-sized word wall grid. Give the students a stack of high-frequency words and ask them to place them in the appropriate spaces on the grid.

Alpha strips for alphabetizing words.   To help beginning or early intermediate students, have them make their own alpha strips. Give each student a tag board strip, twenty-six inches long, with inch marks. Direct the students to fill in the letters in the right order, one per inch.

Give students a stack of word cards to place in alphabetical order. Begin with initial letters and then make the alpha sorting more complex with words that have the same initial letter so that the students will have to refer to the second, third, or fourth letter.

Word search for common structures.   Make up a series of cards that represent common word structures using arrangements of consonants and vowels, for example, CVC, CVCV, CCVC, and so forth. Create a table with multiple columns. Label each column with a different common structure. Give the students a selected text to conduct a word search.

Hold up one of the cards, such as CVC, and ask the students to read through the selected text to find as many words as possible that have that structure (e.g., cat, bat, log, jog). To add motivation and fun, establish teams and a time limit. See which team can find the most words according to the stated structures. Record the findings on the table under the appropriate subheading.

A variation of this activity is to ask students to make up what they think are plausible structures of words in English using the C-V coding. Ask teams to challenge one another to find the "hidden" word(s) in the text that use that structure.

Tip for Parent Involvement

Give parents a list of English word structures using the C. V. coding. Ask them to search through a newspaper and clip out the words that match each structure.

Word families with r-controlled vowels (-ar, -er, -ir, -or, -ur). Create cluster maps to identify words that belong in the same r-controlled vowel group.

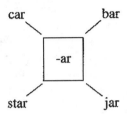

Word Building. (Spelling stages: phonetic/early transitional; ELD levels: early intermediate/intermediate)

Word-building activities put together whole or parts of words to form new words. There are limitless possibilities, but the following activities are some that will be used frequently.

Onsets and rimes. Forming onsets and rimes is another way to explore word families. A very common word family is made from the rime *-ake.* A wide variety of onsets can be placed in front of *-ake* to form words with similar structure such as *bake, cake, fake, Jake.*

A way to give students the opportunity to explore onsets and rimes is to make a vertical strip with the alphabet written sequentially from top to bottom. Then make a series of cards with rimes. For the rime cards, you can simply leave a space for the onset (vertical alphabet strip) or you can cut a window in the card for the onset to pass through. Either way, students will line up the vertical alphabet strip against a rime card and begin to form words. Some of the words will be nonsense words; for example, the onset *z-* and the rime *-ake* makes the nonsense word *zake.* To deal with nonsense words as opposed to actual words, make a T-graph as a comparative table to record them.

Add to the activity by making vertical strips with consonant blend onsets such as *ch-, sh-, bl-,* and *gr-.* Ask students to create their own vertical onset strips and rime cards. Again, compare plausible structures with ones that never occur in English.

Prefix, root, and suffix guided construction. This activity addresses the relationship of prefixes, roots, and suffixes. It requires a three-column table and three sets of word cards. First make a three-column table with the headings of prefix, root, and suffix.

Prefix	Root	Suffix

Make a series of prefix cards. On one side write the prefix, such as pre-. On the opposite side of the card write the definition of the prefix, such as *"pre- means before."* You can get a comprehensive listing of prefixes from any quality dictionary.

Make a series of root word cards. Write cards in lowercase letters because you will be affixing word parts to the front of the roots. On one side, write the root word. On the opposite side, write the definition and include a sketch when appropriate.

The difficult task with this activity is to make the suffix cards. The reason is that affixing suffixes sometimes requires a change in the spelling of the root word. (See the spelling rules below for some of the changes.) In making the suffix cards, you will need to include all the variations of a particular suffix, for example-*ion, -tion, -sion,* and so forth. Like the prefixes, look up suffix in a quality dictionary to get a comprehensive list.

Once the table and card sets are made, students can use the materials to build words. At first, it is highly recommended that this be a guided activity because so many of the suffix conversions are not intuitive. Another reason for guiding the exploration with this activity is that the meanings of the words will change considerably with affixes. Initially the teacher may need to clarify the meaning of words and also explain which are actual words in the lexicon and which are created by the exploratory activity.

Word Study.   (Spelling stages: transitional/conventional/morphemic-syntactic; ELD levels: early advanced/advanced)

Teaching explicit spelling rules.   Viswamohan (2004) identified ten spelling rules that are particularly baffling to English learners. It is probably safe to say that they are baffling to native English speakers as well. These rules need to be taught explicitly because they are not intuitive and defy logical patterns. The ten rules are as follows:

1. What comes first, *i* or *e?* The common rule "i before e, except after c" has almost as many exceptions as words that follow the rule. For example achieve, deceive, heinous, protein, fief, receive. There are two ways to approach this rule. One is to simply teach the *ei* words as a word family. The other way is to conduct word searches in context for examples of *ei* or *ie* words.

2. Replace *y* with *i* or *e* when a word ends in a consonant plus *y.* Two aspects govern this rule: the part of speech and the specific inflected ending of the word. Inflected endings are *-s, -ly, -er, -est, -ed.* Create a table to show the relationships among parts of speech, inflections, and rules.

Part of Speech and Inflection	*Retain -y-*	*Change to -i-*	*Change to -ie-*	*Change -ie-to -y-*
Nouns **-s**	Plurals after a vowel: survey > surveys		Plurals after a consonant: baby > babies	
Adjectives **-er** **-est**		Comparatives: early > earlier, earliest		
Adverbs **-ly**		Adverbs formed from adjectives: busy > busily		
Verbs **-ed** **-ing**	Before -ing: copy > copying	Past-tense ending with a consonant +y: cry > cried		Before -ing: die > dying

3. Silent -*e* in final position indicates a "long" vowel sound. Examples are *made, theme, time, lode,* and *cute*. There are numerous exceptions to this rule, however. Some exceptions are words ending in -*nse* or -*nce* such as *tense* or *mince*. One of the best ways to teach this rule is to have students conduct a word search in a selected text to find as many examples of silent -*e* as possible. Use a T-table to note words that follow the rule and those that are exceptions.

4. The reasons for consonant doubling. Essentially consonant doubling is to indicate the vowel sound as follows: a long vowel with a single consonant, as in "hoping," and a short vowel sound with consonant doubling, as in "hopping." It also indicates stress on a syllable such as with "recur" and "recurrence." Also, the letters *y, w,* and *x* are not doubled.

Consonant doubling is confusing because of the way we describe vowels as long or short. "Long and short vowels" do not refer to the length of a sound. They are arbitrary descriptors at best and are inaccurate ways to describe vowel sounds. More accurately, the stress on a syllable describes the length of the sound. Say the word "forbidden" aloud. Note that the stress is on the second syllable "for-*bid*-den." You can accentuate the stress by saying the word slowly, "for-r-*BID*-den." When you say it slowly, note how the stressed syllable is actually longer in duration than the other syllables. Making this distinction will help students understand the function of the double consonant to indicate stress.

To help students visualize the stress on a syllable, use a gesture. Touch your hands together at the fingertips. Speak a word aloud and slowly. As you say a stressed syllable in the word, pull your hands apart to indicate the length of the stress. Try it with the following words: *MAR*-ket (market), for-*GET*-ting. pre-*FERRED*.

5. The emergence of the schwa in medial position. A feature unique to English that poses problems for transitional spellers is the placement of appropriate vowels in the middle of a multisyllabic words. In English speech with multisyllabic words, medial vowels convert, by default, to a schwa sound. The schwa sound has been described as *uh,* like a cartoon caveman saying, *"ugh."* This *uh* sound is evident in two syllable words like *"butter,"* three syllable words such as *"realize,"* and in words with more syllables such as "char*a*cterize." No matter the spelling, the schwa sound emerges in the middle of words. The specific letters used for conventional spelling do not necessarily correspond to the letter sound. Therefore, transitional spellers will often misplace a vowel in multisyllabic words.

An activity that Viswamohan (2004) suggested is to use clue words to help identify the appropriate spelling of potentially problematic words.

Problem Word	Clue Word	Hidden Vowel
defin_te	definition	i
rep_tition	repeat	e
exam_nation	examine	i

6. Using the right suffix, -*able* or -*ible*. As a general rule, a word like "adaptable" can stand on its own if the suffix -*able* is removed; while the word "feasible" is not a free standing word once the suffix -*ible* is removed. To teach the rule, therefore, is to ask the students to play with the morphology of the words and to break them into parts to test if they require -*able* or -*ible*.

7. Using -*ous* or -*us*. The schwa factor comes into play here. The two structures sound alike because they default to a schwa sound. The key is to teach parts of speech in conjunction with these word endings. Create a T-table showing adjectives and nouns. Also, the adjectives are complete words without the suffix -*ous*, whereas -*us* on the nouns is part of the word.

Adjectives	Nouns
amorous	fungus
dangerous	status
hazardous	nexus

8. Using -*er* or -*or*. The r-controlled schwa poses problems for all spellers. As an aside, it seems like the Russians solved this problem by eliminating the vowel in words like "Petr." Alas, in English we have to use more complex means to spell verbs and nouns. But the rule only works most of the time.

-or Rule

Verbs	Nouns
create	creator
terminate	terminator
indicate	indicator
survey	surveyor
collect	collector
govern	governor

-er Exceptions

Verbs	Nouns
design	designer
mine	miner
sing	singer

9. Use of *-ion* at the end of a word in its various forms. This complex structure cannot be written as a rule. It is best to display a chart as a reminder to students. Remember that the purpose of the *-ion* suffix is to change a verb to a noun.

Types of word structures	Variation of -ion	Examples of verb > noun change with -ion
Verbs ending in *-t* or *-ct*	*-ion*	edit > edition, direct > direction
Verbs with the suffix *-ate*	*-tion*	migrate > migration
Verbs ending in *-mit, -ede, -eed, -ss, -rt, -end*	*-ssion* or *-sion*	transmit > transmission, concede > consession, succeed, succession, obsess > obsession, convert > conversion, comprehend > comprehension
Verbs ending in *-firm* or *-form*	*-ation*	confirm > confirmation, inform > information
Verbs with suffix *-fy* or *-ly*	*-ication*	glorify > glorification, imply > implication
Verbs with an *-ei-* pattern	*-eption*	receive > reception
Verbs ending in *-uce*	*-uction*	reduce > reduction
Verbs ending in *-ume*	*-umption*	consume > consumption
Verbs with suffix *-scribe*	*-ription*	inscribe > inscription

10. Silent consonants *h, p, g, n, k,* and *b,* at first glance, appear to have no function. To understand the use of silent consonants, it is vital to know the etymologies of the words that utilize these problematic structures. Many of our silent consonants are derived from Latin, Greek, and/or Norse roots. But sometimes the use of the silent consonant can only be explained as a phonological device that makes pronunciation less awkward.

The use of a silent *h* is the least problematic for Spanish speakers because of the same function in Spanish. Words with silent *h* like *honor* and *honest* correspond to cognates due to the Latin roots.

Greek roots utilize a silent *p* in words *like psychology, pneumonia,* and *pterodactyl.*

The use of silent *p* in the noun adjunct *cupboard,* however, simply reduces the awkwardness of trying to pronounce a *p* followed by a *b* in the same word. Notice the position of your lips as you speak. The *p* and *b* are the same position, which means you would have to pronounce the *p,* then open and close your mouth again to pronounce the *b.*

Other Greek-loaned silent letters are the *m* in the *mneumonic* and the *g* in *sign, gnat, gnome, phlegm,* and *foreign.* Curiously the *n* in final position is silent when proceeded by an *m* in words such as *solemn, autumn* and *condemn,* but when the words are used in a different form, the *n* is pronounced as in *condemnation.*

Norse influence in the language gives us a silent *k* when coupled with an *n* in initial position. Examples of this are *knot, knife, knuckle, knight, knead*, and *knee*. Approximately a half-dozen words in the entire English lexicon have this structure; therefore, it does not require a rule.

The silent *b* appears when it follows *m* in final position. Examples of silent *b* after *m* are *comb, numb, lamb*, and *tomb*. Note that the rule breaks down when *-er* is at the end. While *beachcomber* and *plumber* maintain a silent *b*, *amber* and *slumber* do not.

Create a personal thesaurus to explore multiple meanings (u/you/ewe). Creating a personal thesaurus gives the students the benefits of a personal dictionary, yet it is a living document. With a personal dictionary, once the definition is recorded a word is complete. With a personal thesaurus, the associations can grow as the student develops greater knowledge of the language.

To initiate a personal thesaurus, provide each student with a loose-leaf binder. Each page should begin as an empty cluster map. Have the student write a key word in the center of the cluster map. Around the center of the cluster-mapped key word, add words with related meanings.

Each week provide students with one or two key words for the center of the cluster maps. Also, give the students a blank cluster map page with the instructions that they are to find a key word to develop. Set aside a thesaurus development time each week and encourage students to read to find new words to add to the thesaurus. Encourage them also to compare notes with classmates to come up with other meanings to include. The cluster map format, being nonlinear, allows for numerous additions.

Tip for Parent Involvement

As part of a regular homework routine, ask parents to work with their child on developing their personal thesaurus. Begin the thesaurus at school, but once a week send it home. Use the same guidelines as above. Target words that are especially difficult for ELLs to spell.

Illustrate homophone pairs (sale/sail). Have students illustrate homophone pairs to differentiate them. Decorate the classroom with the illustrations, or bind them in a homophone pair picture book.

Illustrating homophone pairs is as simple as folding a piece of paper in half. Partner students by homophone pairs and give each one a word to illustrate.

Another approach to using illustrated homophone pairs is to play a mix and matching game. Once a student has illustrated a word, she must mingle with classmates to find the matching pair.

REFERENCES

Barbe, W. B., Wasylyk, T. M., Hackney, C. S., & Braun, L. A. (1984). Zaner-Bloser creative growth in handwriting (grades K-8). Columbus, OH: Zaner-Bloser.

Gentry, J. R. (1987). *Spel . . . is a four-letter word*. Portsmouth, NH: Heinemann.

King, M., & Rentel, V. (1981). *How children learn to write: A longitudinal study*. (Final report to the National Institute of Education, RF Project 761861/71238 & 765512/711748). Columbus, OH: Ohio State University Research Foundation.

Sulzby, E., & Teale, W. H. (2003). The development of the young child and the emergence of literacy. In J. Flood, D. Lapp, J. R. Squire, & J. M. Jensen (Eds.). *Handbook of research on teaching the English Language Arts*. (2nd ed.) (pp. 300–313). Mahwah, NJ: Erlbaum.

Viswamohan, A. (May 2004). Putting students under the spell. *Language Magazine, 3*(9), pp. 14–17.

CHAPTER 13

VOCABULARY DEVELOPMENT

Have you ever noticed that we tend to teach vocabulary the way we were taught in school? Unfortunately, many of us were taught vocabulary in a very passive and abstract way. As students, we were asked to look up new terms in the glossary at the back of the text, or told to copy definitions from the dictionary and then memorize them. By the same token, I have yet to meet a person who enjoyed learning vocabulary by looking up glossary terms. As an initial approach to teaching English Language Learners, asking them to use glossaries or dictionary definitions is ineffective for vocabulary instruction. Teaching vocabulary to ELLs at early levels of fluency is even more challenging, and calls for a more strategic approach.

In this chapter, prior to looking at strategies, we must first understand vocabulary development from the perspective of the ELL. We will look at vocabulary as concrete, symbolic representational, and abstract and explore ways to provide instruction at each level. Abstraction poses unique challenges to teaching ELLs; therefore, we will also look at ways to "unpack" the meaning in abstract words. Finally, we will examine ways to develop fluency with vocabulary once the meaning is established, with interactive games to develop fluency, digital flash cards using presentation software to practice high-frequency words, and developing descriptive continua.

UNDERSTANDING VOCABULARY DEVELOPMENT FROM AN ENGLISH LANGUAGE LEARNER'S PERSPECTIVE

In order to effectively teach vocabulary, it is helpful to understand how the unique perspective of the ELL calls for a range of strategies. First let's consider how literate, English-speaking adults perceive words in significantly different ways from ELLs. As literate adults, when we see a word such as *brilliant*, the word by itself appears to be quite meaningful. We see the combination of letters as meaningful because we involuntarily call to mind what the word represents. "Brilliant" conjures up images of light, intelligence, brightness, intense color, and so forth. In other words, literate, English-speaking adults automatically see words as inherently meaningful because they already know what the word means. Conversely, an ELL may look at the same combination of letters and see only letters without perceiving the images that give it meaning. The letter combinations by themselves are essentially abstract.

Meaning, therefore, is something apart from combining letters in a conventional sequence. Meaning is experiential, sensorial, and image driven. It is nonverbal. To illustrate, think of how a baby learns a word such as *hug*. A baby does not learn the word "hug" from a word card or glossary. A baby learns it through a concrete experience of hugging. In other words, the experience of meaning is initially nonverbal; the verbal label of "hug" is applied after the experience has taken place.

In much the same way, an ELL initially learns vocabulary through the senses. This is easily seen when we look at languages that use nonalphabetic systems. If you do not read Japanese, for instance, the characters appear to be abstract, random, and meaningless. Obviously, it would not be helpful to look at Japanese word cards in order to find meaning. To understand the meaning of the word in Japanese requires a demonstration or a meaningful experience first.

Curiously, some teachers begin vocabulary instruction in very abstract ways with word cards, glossaries, and so forth, thus assuming that looking at a word by itself is meaningful. However, teaching vocabulary from an abstraction without grounding it in a meaningful experience is ineffective teaching.

This is not to excoriate the use of word cards, but by themselves word cards cannot provide a meaningful experience. A more strategic use for word cards is to follow the experience as a label. Again, what comes first? The experience? Or its label? Remember the rule of thumb: "Show first; tell second."

A RANGE OF STRATEGIES FOR MAKING VOCABULARY AND CONCEPTS COMPREHENSIBLE

Learning from a concrete experience is not a new idea. It can be attributed to Dewey (1902) and Piaget (1926), and more recent work with vocabulary development strategies has been done by Chamot and O'Mally (1987). We learn by doing, by experiencing meaning. Based on an adaptation of Piagetian categories, items and techniques for teaching vocabulary instruction can be organized across a developmental continuum of three groupings: concrete, symbolic/representational, and abstract.

Concrete	Symbolic/ Representational	Abstract
Real objects (realia)	Pictures	Word cards
Meaningful Movement (TPR)	Symbols, icons	Sentence strips
Actual experiences	Visual aids	Oral explanations (w/o modeling)
Experiments	Maps	Theoretical discussion
Performance	Models	Decontextualized print
Demonstration/modeling	Semantic maps	
	Flowcharts	
	Illustrated books	

Concrete

Concrete techniques provide actual experiences of learning with the real object of study. These include providing real objects, or realia, that students can handle and explore with their senses. For example, a trip outside the classroom doors to a eucalyptus tree, to touch its shedding bark, smell its aromatic leaves, hear it creak in the wind, and see its height from different perspectives, teaches the word "eucalyptus" in a profound way. Nouns are taught with concrete objects, yet verbs are taught by meaningful actions. Total Physical Response (TPR), discussed in the previous chapter, gives students a concrete experience with verbs.

Although concrete instruction of vocabulary is extremely effective, the difficulty with concrete/experiential teaching is that sometimes it is impossible to provide the real object. For example, you are not going to bring a live cow into a classroom to teach the word "Holstein." Nor is it possible to go back in time to see real events in history as they unfolded. In those cases, it is helpful to utilize the symbolic level of teaching vocabulary.

Symbolic/Representational

Strategies on the symbolic level involve providing representations of the word to be taught: providing visuals to illustrate the meaning of a word, or a short digital video clip to supply more visual context. When real objects are not available or practical to utilize, provide a model. Some possible models include masks of historical or story characters, anatomical models (e.g. heart), layered models to show the atmosphere or the make-up of a planet, landscapes, cityscapes, or scenescapes.

Abstract

Abstraction is a strategy in language employed to conceptualize complex ideas, or to combine a variety of concepts into a key term for theory development. For example, when describing similar events in history, we label them as a trend. The function of the abstraction is that it allow one to discuss the multiple events using a single word. The prerequisite for abstraction is that all parties know what the term means. Therefore, it is incumbent upon the teacher to use concrete and symbolic strategies prior to moving into abstraction.

When and How to Use Word Cards.   Imagine a teacher holding up a word card without context clues and saying, "What do you think this means?" The fact that the question is raised, probably means that the students don't know what it means. So why ask the question?

STRATEGIES FOR VOCABULARY DEVELOPMENT ACROSS LEVELS OF PROFICIENCY

Choosing a Strategy

Although beginning English Language Learners will benefit from predominantly concrete instruction, this does not mean that they cannot understand abstract words. Conversely, advanced-level ELLs benefit significantly from concrete instruction. Choosing the appropriate strategy involves more than matching levels of proficiency. Judging the appropriateness of using concrete, symbolic, or abstract strategies requires knowing what to do with a particular word. Some words lend themselves to the use of realia, while others do not. There are words in which a visual is the most appropriate strategy available. Additionally, there are words that are more conceptually abstract that can be "unpacked" in order to find their meaning at a concrete or representational level. Unpacking a conceptual word means exploring its multiple meanings and/or word origins to get to a more grounded understanding of its meaning. For example, in literary analysis, if one is teaching the term *denouement,* knowing its etymology is essential to illustrating the meaning. The word comes from the French term for untying a knot. The etymology provides a visual way to understand the term of how a plot is being disentangled.

Knowing a word, therefore, dictates the strategy. Here is a three-point test for a word in order to determine the appropriate strategy.

1. How can a real object or experience be used to teach the word?
2. How can a visual or model be used to teach the word?
3. Is the word conceptual or abstract? If so, select one or more unpacking strategies:
   - Check the etymology
   - Explore related roots
   - Discuss cognates
   - Provide primary language support
   - Use similes and metaphorical thinking with word study charts

Consider the range of strategies from concrete to abstract as building a foundation for meaning. To the extent possible, begin with concrete objects and experiences, follow with visuals or models, and then address the abstraction. The broader and deeper the concrete experience, the greater the degree of abstraction that can be attained in the long run. For example, a highly fluent ELL may have knowledge gaps in a specific subject area such as marine science; therefore, it would be appropriate to use realia and visuals as materials for instruction such as supplying pieces of coral or shells, or showing visuals such as a video to develop meaning. The concrete and visual instruction enhances instruction for all parties. Now that some background has been established, we will look at how the strategies are applied to specific words and across levels of fluency.

How Can a Real Object or Experience Be Used to Teach the Word?

Use of Realia. Imagine that you are teaching vocabulary from the book, *The Tale of Peter Rabbit* by Beatrix Potter. Chamomile tea was an important part of the story. You may recall at the end of the story Peter's mother sent him to bed and gave him chamomile tea to restore him back to health. The word "chamomile" (although spelled "chamomile" in the original version) poses several problems for ELLs because of its unique sound/symbol correspondence with a hard /k/ sound written as a *ch* and a silent *e* at the end.

So how can the words "chamomile tea" best be taught? If the words are taught by giving students an experience, a deeper learning takes hold. Begin by teaching "chamomile tea" with a taste of the tea (use iced tea, rather than hot, in classroom situations, with individual paper cups); tear open chamomile tea bags for the students to touch and smell. With the actual tea, the students are using multiple senses (sight, smell, taste, touch) to construct meaning of the words. Once the experience has established the meaning of chamomile tea, follow with a word card as its label.

While students are exploring the realia, record their observations on a sense chart. Make a four-column chart with the four senses. (Taste is not included because we do not want to encourage children to place objects in their mouths, particularly objects being handled by others or objects that can cause choking.)

Sense Chart for Chamomile Tea

Smell	Touch	Sight	Sound
spicy	like dry leaves	yellow/green color	only when you slurp
like chewing gum	wet and cool	like dirty water	

Providing Actual Experience. There are several ways of providing meaningful experiences to teach vocabulary. A walk in a park to name various shrubs and trees, or to identify bird life, is meaningful and memorable. But when teaching selected verbs, Total Physical Response (TPR) (Asher, 1982) is an ideal strategy. An effective use of TPR would be to conduct a directed drawing activity to teach the terminology of various drawing techniques, or to identify parts of face.

Asking if a word can be made meaningful with the concrete object or experience is fundamental. The first line of strategy is to look for how to use realia. If that is not possible or practical, move to the use of visuals or models.

How can a visual, or model, be used to teach the word?

Using Visuals. Teaching the word *metamorphosis* takes a considerable amount of time using realia. Teachers bring a collection of moths or tadpoles to the classroom and record the physical changes the creatures go through during their life cycles. Of course the concrete experience provides the deepest level of instruction, but one can also use pictures, or a model. There are numerous picture books, card sets, and Internet resources available with sequential pictures of metamorphosis (try www.yahooligans.com for child-secure Internet pictures). I recommend the following ways in particular to use the pictures: 1) Provide multiple pictures of the same term so that students can see diverse examples. 2) Display the pictures along with the term as a semantic map in either a cluster format (surround the term with the various pictures that represent the meaning) or as a tree map (arrange the pictures below the term in a hierarchy according to subcategories). Involve the students in preparing the map by having them position and glue the pictures in relation to the core term. 3) Once students have seen pictures, have them draw their pictures of the term to be included for display. The use of display provides a continual classroom reminder of the meaning of key terms and involves the students in active construction of meaning.

Tip for Parent Involvement

It takes a wide range of objects, models, and pictures to make vocabulary comprehensible. Make a list of the items you need, and ask parents to help supply the items.

Using Models. The use of a model is sometimes very effective for teaching vocabulary because you can teach multiple terms from a single model. For example, in geography, when teaching land forms a single model of painted papier-mâché on a cardboard base can be constructed to teach an array of terms (island, peninsula, estuary, intertidal zone, and so forth). Having small groups of students create the models for labeling and display in the classroom actively involves the students and makes the classroom come alive with meaningful representations of what the students are learning.

Use of Total Physical Response. Here is another way to use Total Physical Response to represent vocabulary. Imagine that you are listening to a lecture on the nervous system and the lecturer says the following: "Before we get to the lecture, I want to preview some of the key terms that I will be using. In order to do this, please follow my directions. One: Hold up your hand with the fingers spread apart. This is roughly the shape of a 'dendrite.' Dendrites extend from nerve endings and attach to one another. Two: Touch your two thumbs together to imagine two dendrites connecting. This connection is called a 'synapse.' Three: Reach out to a neighbor and touch your fingers with theirs. When multiple synapses are made among several dendrites, it is called a 'ganglia.' A ganglia is a clump of nerve endings knotted together."

Notice how this strategy allows the instructor to use high-level terminology in an illustrative way without giving short shrift to the content. The use of gestures is not realia, but a representational way to understand the meaning of the words. Thinking creatively about how to apply meaningful actions and gestures can greatly serve instruction. A wonderful resource for meaningful gestures are teachers of deaf and hard-of-hearing students. Their fluency with sign language makes them skilled users of meaningful gestures.

Instructional Diagrams and Flowcharts for a Pictorial Thesaurus. Related to using pictures and creating models is having students create instructional diagrams that label key terms from a particular subject area. For example, in teaching the systems of the human body, you could use a model of the body to show each of the systems; however, if the students were divided into groups according to each system (circulatory system, gastrointestinal system, nervous system, and so forth), each group could be responsible for drawing and labeling the essential components of their assigned system to present to the class and display in the room. The value of this kind of teaching is that the students are the ones doing the work. They are making it meaningful for themselves and teaching each other content vocabulary.

Flowcharts can be helpful to show relationships and to visually outline processes. A good use of a flowchart is in comparing the words *revolution* and *evolution*. A significant difference between the two words is the flow of events over time. Revolution would be drawn as a series of events leading to a capitulation, whereas evolution would be a gradual change in adaptations over time.

Students might also create a pictorial thesaurus using a semantic map cluster on each page. A thesaurus page would include a core word at the center. Around the word would be other words with similar meanings and pictures to depict their meanings. Students might draw pictures, cut pictures from magazines or newspapers, or use computer clip art. The key is to keep it simple and to take class time to develop pages on an ongoing basis. Allow time each day to work on thesaurus pages.

A wonderful computer software tool for generating semantic maps, tree maps, instructional diagrams, and flowcharts is a program called Inspiration. There is also a program for younger children called Kidspiration. This very intuitive program allows the user to select from a large library of clip art and to arrange the pictures semantically in cluster format or in a tree map hierarchy. Pictures can also be imported from the Web or from a scanner. The tool has several amazing features. While students are selecting pictures and arranging them on the screen, the labels for the pictures are placed automatically on the screen. Further, the program is designed to generate a linear outline of the semantic map. It also allows the user to insert notes that are placed in the auto-generated outline.

Is the Word Conceptual or Abstract? Use Unpacking Strategies

Vocabulary that is abstract poses special challenges to teaching ELLs. I use the term "unpacking" in reference to teaching abstract words because their meaning is not readily apparent, or cannot be represented by realia or a visual. Before meaningful instruction can take place a teacher must do some background work. There are a number of strategies that will help make words meaningful; but nothing replaces knowing the word thoroughly. This may sound unnecessary to emphasize, but let me illustrate with a common word that we all use.

The word *color* is easy to recognize, but surprisingly complex to define. Color can be defined as a range of hue, value, and intensity. Hue is a continuum of colors related to temperatures from cold to hot, value a continuum from light to dark, and intensity a continuum from bright to dull. These continua are also referred to as spectra. Of course, this does not deal with the concept of primary, secondary, and tertiary colors. The point is that some words pack multiple meanings which need to be "unpacked" before teaching can occur. To teach color without exploring hue, value, and intensity does not do justice to understanding the word. Knowing the word requires developing background knowledge. The first place to go for background knowledge is to check the word's etymology.

Check the Etymology. Etymology is the study of word origins. There are several reasons for studying a word's etymology. Knowing an etymology tells the story of a word. It reminds us that words are organic rather than fixed, that words change over time, and that they are used for a variety of intentions. Studying etymology exposes a word's roots and derivations. Etymologies also get to the grounded meaning of a word which often provides a visual for teaching the word.

Look at the word *spirit,* for example. After studying its etymology, one sees that the word's original meaning is "breath"; it has the same root as the words "respiration," re-breathing, and "conspiracy," a kind of breathing or whispering together. Knowing the root and related meaning of "spirit" as breathing dictates a simple shared experience in teaching the word's meaning. The teacher might simply have students experience breathing as a way to begin to understand and remember "spirit."

At times, studying etymologies can seem like being a detective uncovering the truth about a word. Any quality dictionary will supply etymologies; but it may require some digging to find the meaning of root words. Several Internet resources are of great help in studying etymologies. One free resource is www.dictionary.com. A paid subscriber resource is from the Oxford English Dictionary, www.oed.com. Web-based resources make finding etymologies tremendously easy and a task that students at the intermediate level of fluency and above can do for themselves with relative ease.

Explore Related Roots. Related to researching etymologies is looking at related words in order to get to a grounded understanding of a word's meaning. When one looks at a range of words that share the same root meaning, it reinforces the meaning of the word in question. This can be illustrated by looking at words related to the word *static,* as in static electricity. The meaning of *static* may not be readily apparent. However, if you ask a group of students to find other words that begin with *sta-,* the meaning comes to light. Although there are numerous words beginning with *sta-,* you can expect students to suggest common words such as stay, stand, station.

Static electricity, in other words, is the kind of electricity that stays, stands, or stations itself on the surface of an object. Exploring related roots provides visual insight into the word's meaning.

A picture of static can now be formed, whereas before looking at related roots, the word appeared to be more abstract.

Use of Cognates. Once when I was working with a group of Khmer-speaking Cambodian students, I was surprised to learn that the Khmer word for whale is *baleen*. The Spanish word for whale is *ballena*. In English, we refer to baleen whales as those without teeth, that use long strands of baleen to literally strain the water out of their catch of tiny krill to eat. Obviously, the word is an example of a cognate from Romance language roots. Although Khmer is not a Romance language, it acquired the word, one would suspect, several centuries ago when European whalers sailed into port. One would not expect English to share cognates with an Asian language; in this case, however, a cognate is like a bridge or touch point between the two languages.

Tip for Parent Involvement

Parents can help identify cognates. Ask them to highlight words in the English text that are similar in Spanish. In the classroom, create a cognate word wall based on the highlighted words found by the parents.

It takes specialized knowledge of languages to use cognates. Knowing when a word is a cognate is important. Some words that are spelled similarly may not share the same meaning; these are called false cognates. Spanish shares many cognates with English and is a language that is used by a great number of students in our schools. Rodriguez (2001) has provided some insights into using cognates with Spanish. Tables 13.1 and 13.2 can help understand the nature of Spanish cognates and which ones can be readily applied to instruction.

Primary Language Support

Although it appears counterintuitive at first glance, using a student's primary language (home language) as a means to introduce vocabulary and content instruction is a very efficient way to teach English. A simple yet effective way to provide primary language support is called preview/review (Lessow-Hurley, 1990).

Have you ever found yourself in the following situation? You are in the middle of teaching a lesson. You think you are making perfect sense; but then, you suddenly realize that the class is staring at you blankly. The students had quit following what you were saying about five minutes earlier, but

Table 13.1 Spanish Cognates

Type	Identical Cognates	Similar Spelling Cognates	Spelling Less Apparent	Oral Cognates	Partial Meaning Cognate	Root Cognates Cognates	False
English	fatal hotel actor	contami- nation evidence castigate	sport perilous	pleasure peace	letter (alphabet, correspon- dence)	disappear appear	bigot embar- rassed
Spanish	*fatal hotel actor*	*contami- nación evidencia castigar*	*deporte peligroso*	*placer paz*	*letra, carta*	*desaparecer aparecer*	*bigote (moustache) embarazada (pregnant)*

Source: T. A. Rodgriguez (2001). "Teaching ideas: From the known to the unknown: Using cognates to teach English to Spanish literates:". *Reading Teacher 54*(8), 744–746.

Table 13.2 Other Common Cognates

English	Spanish	English	Spanish
	Writing		**Book Terms**
alphabet	*alfabeto*	appendix	*apéndice*
punctuation	*puntuación*	atlas	*atlas*
initials	*initials*	volume	*volumen*
letter	*letra*	page	*página*
symbol	*símbolo*	introduction	*introducción*
comma	*coma*	title	*título*
	Math		**Science**
decimal	*decimal*	hypothesis	*hipótesis*
double	*doble*	acid	*ácido*
fraction	*fracción*	metal	*metal*
dozen	*docena*	ozone	*ozono*
circle	*círculo*	corrosion	*corrosión*
equal	*igual*	plastics	*plásticos*
	History		**Animals**
civilization	*civilización*	animal(s)	*animal(es)*
history	*historia*	human	*humano*
past	*pasado*	kangaroo	*canguro*
pioneer	*pionero*	elephant	*elefante*
colonial	*colonial*	dinosaur	*dinosaurio*
diary	*diario*	eagle	*águila*
	Common Words		**Your Own List**
action	*acción*		
group	*grupo*		
program	*programa*		
opportunity	*oportunidad*		
popular	*popular*		
family	*familia*		

Source: R. Nash (1997). *NTC's dictionary of Spanish cognates.* Chicago: NTC Publishing Group.

did not stop to tell you so. In the middle of the lesson, then, you halt, back up, and define key terms and review main points for the class. All at once you hear the group say, "Oh, so that's what you're talking about."

There are a number of reasons why the above scenario takes place. One is that key terms and essential concepts were not previewed prior to presenting the body of instruction, or that key terms were not meaningful to the students when they were being previewed. Another possible reason is that the key terms were so new and unfamiliar that the students promptly forgot what they meant.

Meaningfully previewing key vocabulary and essential content is an effective way to conduct instruction. Previewing vocabulary and essential content in the student's primary language can be even more effective, ensuring greater understanding for teaching the lesson in English. Once students have a grasp of the meaning of key vocabulary, a working knowledge of their usage, and an outline of essential concepts in their own language, the lesson in English can flow without being interrupted at midpoint by lengthy explanations of misunderstood words or ideas. Finishing a lesson with a brief review of the key terms and essential content in the primary language reinforces the meaning. To take it a step further, use the review time at the end of the lesson to engage students in primary-language discussions about their learning. Ask students to paraphrase the learning in their own words and raise questions that they were unable to formulate in English.

Preview/review actually creates language zones in classroom instruction. The key for the teacher is to teach as a language model. In the preview section, the teacher is a Spanish model on proper use and pronunciation of the vocabulary while also providing a logical sequence of the lesson. Then, the teacher switches to English instruction to create, in effect, an English zone where English is maintained as a model. Even though students may raise questions or have comments in another language, the teacher maintains English as a model of conventional usage. This requires mental discipline on the part of the teacher. The teacher does not discourage the use of another language, but remains a model for proper use of English. Often, the teacher will rephrase a student's question or comment using conventional English as part of a language teaching strategy. At the end of the lesson, the language zone shifts back to the primary language for review and discussion.

Tip for Parent Involvement

If you are literate in the child's home language, extend the concept of preview/review to the home. Provide an advanced organizer for content instruction in the home language at the beginning of the week with instructions to review the essential lesson concepts and vocabulary. Follow up with a homework assignment to discuss the learning and vocabulary with family members later on in the week.

The use of preview/review raises frequently asked questions (FAQs). The following are some FAQs about preview/review.

What if the teacher does not speak the students' primary language? It takes a highly qualified teacher who is literate in the students' primary language to expertly use preview/review; however, some teachers are fortunate to work with bilingual teacher aides who can provide preview/review for the class while the teacher teaches the body of the lesson in English. In some cases, peer tutors can help provide preview/review instruction.

What if the administration does not allow anything but English instruction? Know the education code for your state and district. Go to your administrator for authorization and be sure you know the policies prior to using another language for instruction. It is also important to inform parents about your classroom practice. Invite them to observe the quality of your instruction. Dual-language instruction has a controversial history. Although preview/review pedagogically is a highly sound instructional practice, it may not be perceived that way by uninformed individuals. Therefore, be advised to employ primary-language support within your educational system's guidelines in consultation with knowledgeable practitioners.

What if there are multiple languages in the classroom? Preview/review was designed to work in a classroom setting with two languages, although variations can be made to accommodate other languages. Pairing students according to language groups can facilitate using preview/review. If students have access to dual-language dictionaries in their own primary language and English, they can look up words prior to instruction. The teacher can preview the terms and then ask students to paraphrase the vocabulary definitions and lesson outline in their own words. After instruction in English, they can review the instruction in the primary language as well.

Use Similes and Metaphorical Thinking with Word Study Charts

Another strategy for exploring the meaning of words that do not initially lend themselves to realia or showing a visual is to apply similes and metaphorical thinking with word study charts. A simple way to initiate similes and metaphorical thinking is to ask, "What do you think it is like?" Earlier in the chapter, I referred to the word *brilliant*. Again let me raise the question: What is "brilliant" like? There are two directions to go with this word: one is the realm of light and brightness; the other is the realm of intelligence and genius. To illustrate those realms of meaning, make a semantic map that includes pictures and words arranged around the core word, showing on one side brightness and on the other side intelligence. Include questions on the chart such as, What is "brilliant" like? What are examples of "brilliant" around us?

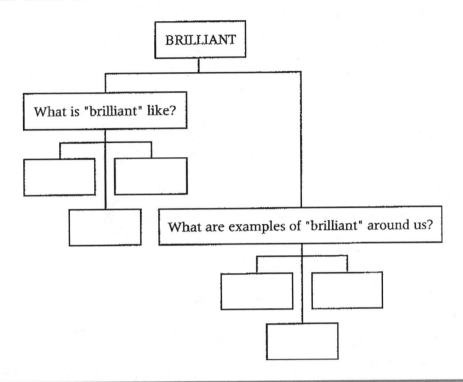

Tip for Parent Involvement

Send home a word study chart that is partially complete. Ask parents to help find magazine or newspaper pictures to complete the chart.

DEVELOPING FLUENCY

Understanding the meaning of vocabulary words is vital to learning. Students also need to put the words to use immediately in order to develop fluency with the terms. Developing fluency has several benefits. Fluent use of a new word ensures retention of the word in the future and in other contexts. Embedding fluency development in the lesson also provides a check for conventional usage, pronunciation, and spelling. The following section shows how to develop fluency with interactive games, digital flash cards, and developing descriptive vocabulary.

Interactive Games to Develop Fluency with New Vocabulary

One of the easiest ways to embed fluency development in a lesson is to play a game. The higher the level of social interaction in the game, the greater the opportunity to use the word multiple times, which results in fluency development. The following is a list of games with simple directions that are highly interactive and provide students with practice of new terminology to develop fluency.

Tip for Parent Involvement

Send word cards home with children along with directions for a specific fluency game. Families can play the games at home and reinforce vocabulary development.

1. **Sentence line-ups**
   - Provide a variety of word cards color coded and organized according to nouns, verbs, adjectives, adverbs, prepositions, and articles (one to two cards per student).
   - Form small groups.
   - Ask students to form coherent sentences about a specific topic by lining up the word cards.
   - The rest of the class must read the sentence line-up.
2. **Who am I? Or What am I?**
   - Tape a name card or word card to the back of each student.
   - Given a set amount of time (three to five minutes), the students must ask yes/no questions to find out who or what the card represents.
3. **Concentration**
   - Make up a set of card pairs, each matching a word to a picture.
   - Place all cards in an array facedown on a table.
   - Students must match a picture card to a word card in order to obtain points.
   - The student with the most paired cards wins.
4. **Adaptation of the Dictionary game**
   - Use key vocabulary words.
   - Divide students into teams.
   - One student will have the correct definition, others will have to make up a plausible definition to bluff opponents.
   - Team that guesses the correct definition receives a point.
5. **Charades**
   - Using key vocabulary, ask one or more students to act out a word.
   - Other students must guess what word is being acted out.
6. **Adaptation of picture definition game**
   - Students are asked to draw a picture representing a key vocabulary word.
   - Other students try to guess what word is being drawn.
   - May be played in teams or pairs.
7. **Crossword puzzles** (Avoid solitary work. Have students work in pairs.)
   - Have students make their own crossword puzzles, using quarter-inch-square grid paper.
   - Tell students to input key vocabulary words.
   - They may try out the crossword puzzles on each other.

Developing Descriptive Vocabulary

A significant way to foster encountering meaning is to develop descriptive vocabulary. Think about how a wine connoisseur describes wine. At first it appears that the taster has a vivid imagination with descriptions of "herbaceous" or "fruity." What really is at play is the setting of two descriptors against each other at opposite ends of a continuum. Some examples are sweet versus sour or weak versus strong. The use of a continuum to clarify descriptions is directly applicable to teaching students how to articulate their own perceptions of experience. Here are some continua that are simple and can be used to help students describe words or experiences.

Rough	←	TEXTURE	→	Smooth
Hard	←	TEXTURE	→	Soft
Light	←	VALUES	→	Dark
Hot	←	TEMPERATURE	→	Cold
Bright	←	INTENSITY	→	Dull
Sweet	←	TASTE or SMELL	→	Sour
Bland	←	TASTE or SMELL	→	Spicy
Accurate	←	ON TARGET	→	Inaccurate
Distant/Far	←	PROXIMITY	→	Close by/Near

Tall	←	HEIGHT	→	Short
Heavy	←	WEIGHT	→	Light
Large	←	SIZE	→	Small
Strong	←	STRENGTH	→	Weak
Sad	←	EMOTIONS	→	Happy
Exciting	←	EXPERIENCES	→	Boring

If you insert graded words into each continuum, such as "very/highly" or "a little/somewhat," you add range to the descriptors. Now you can describe a wide variety of items with appropriate descriptors such as "highly accurate" or "somewhat inaccurate," "very rough" or "a little rough." By displaying these terms on a chart in the classroom, students have a quick reference for making appropriate descriptions. Descriptive continua can be applied across the curriculum in the following ways: Literary Analysis: character study; Math/Statistics: describing a frequency table; Science: describing experimental phenomena.

APPENDIX: HELPFUL COMPUTER SOFTWARE: WEB BUILDING WITH INSPIRATION

Getting Started with Inspiration

(See www.Inspiration.com for a free trial version)

Toolbar

Outline: Generates an outline of your tree chart diagram.
New Look: Previews default picture/symbols for the diagram.
Rapid Fire: Shortcut to entering extensive ideas related to a symbol.
Link: Creates a link between symbols displayed by an arrow.
Add Note: Creates a text box for additional information related to a symbol.
Create: Positions a new symbol in either a horizontal, vertical, or diagonal direction.
Position: Used to grasp and move the entire diagram.
Arrange: Provides a variety of display formats for the diagram.
Spell: Checks spelling.
Library Box: Displays a wide range of pictorial libraries to use to make symbols. (Left/right arrows shuttle through libraries; down arrow displays available topics.)

Task #1: The Main Idea Symbol

1. The program opens with a "Main Idea" symbol. This is the starting point and cannot be deleted.
2. Double-click on the symbol. In the text box below the icon, highlight "Main Idea" and write over it the word "Weather."
3. Click the down arrow in the library box. Select "Science." Select "Weather."
4. At the top of the weather library, choose a text box symbol (oval, shadow box, rounded corner box, basic box, cloud, or off-set box). Click on your choice.
5. The symbol you have selected is now the main idea "Weather" symbol in your diagram.
6. Click once on the symbol to highlight it. Highlighting is noted by a red square surrounding the symbol.
7. Click and hold down the mouse button, and drag a corner of the red box to size your symbol.

Task #2: Create a Diagram

1. Click once on the main idea "Weather" symbol.
2. Move the cursor to the tool bar button, "Create"—refrain from clicking.

3. Note that the arrows light up blue to designate the position of a new symbol in a horizontal, vertical, or diagonal direction. Each time you want to create a new symbol, decide the position of the new symbol, then click on the "Create" button.
4. Click once on the main idea symbol each time you wish to create a new related symbol.
5. Repeat the process with each new symbol.
6. Create four new symbols linked to and surrounding the main idea "Weather" symbol.
7. Click on a new symbol once. Select a picture from the weather library to represent your idea. Repeat the process until each new symbol has a unique picture displayed.
8. Double-click on each new symbol to write in the white box the label for that symbol.
9. You may also wish to click and drag a symbol to reposition it.

Task #3: Add Notes/Rapid Fire

1. Click once on a new symbol surrounding the main idea.
2. On the toolbar, select "Add Notes" and a text box will appear.
3. Write a more detailed explanation of your symbol.
4. Click on the background to close the note.
5. You may also click on "Rapid Fire" as a shortcut to adding information to a symbol.
6. The information that you have written appears in the outline.

Task #4: Automatic Outlining

1. Select the "Outline" button on the tool bar.
2. Your diagram is automatically outlined.
3. You may even change the order of your outline by simply clicking and dragging the outline statement to the position you choose.
4. Return to the diagram by selecting the "Diagram" button on the tool bar.

Task #5: Arranging a Tree Chart

1. Select the "Arrange" button on the tool bar. A menu box will appear with a variety of diagram arrangements to choose from.
2. Pick a new arrangement for your diagram. Click on "OK."
3. View your new diagram arrangement.

REFERENCES

Chamot, A., & O'Mally, J. (1987). The cognitive academic language learning approach: A bridge to the mainstream. *TESOL Quarterly, 21,* 227–249.

Dewey, J. (1902). *The child and the curriculum.* Chicago, IL: University of Chicago Press.

Lessow-Hurley, J. (1990). *The foundations of dual language instruction.* White Plains, NY: Longman.

Nash, R. (1997). *NTC's dictionary of Spanish cognates.* Chicago, IL: NTC Publishing Group.

Piaget, J. (1926). *The language and thought of a child.* New York: Harcourt, Brace and World.

Rodgriguez, T. A. (2001). "Teaching ideas: From the known to the unknown: Using cognates to teach English to Spanish literates." *Reading Teacher 54(8),* 744–746.

CHAPTER 14

SUPPORTING READING INSTRUCTION

TESOL Goals and Standards

Goal 1: To use English to communicate in social settings

   Standard 3: Students will use learning strategies to extend their communicative competence

Goal 2: To use English to achieve academically in all content areas

   Standard 1: Students will use English to interact in the classroom

Standard 2: Students with use English to obtain, process construet and provide subject matter information in spoken and written form

Standard 3: Students will use appropriate learning strategies to construct and apply academic knowledge

READING IN THE LONG RUN

In a review of effective reading programs for ELLs, Slavin and Cheung (2003) found that many of the same components in comprehensive reading programs for English-only speakers were helpful for Spanish bilingual students. Evidence from the reviewed studies also favored high-quality programs that used bilingual approaches for reading instruction. This concurs with other research evidence that found children's reading proficiency in their first language to be a strong predictor of reading performance in English (Garcia, 2000; Reese, Garnier, Gallimore, & Goldenberg, 2000). Although establishing a bilingual reading program at a school site is beyond the scope of this book, the practice is highly recommended. The strategies and activities found in this chapter work with both English-only and ELL students. What is unique is that the strategies and activities are differentiated to match the level of the reader.

I use the phrase "reading in the long run" because, as a long-distance runner, I find certain parallels between running and reading. They are tasks for both purpose and pleasure. They require regular practice to develop proficiency. For some, the task is easier to perform than for others. But one does not need to be the fastest to get enjoyment out of the activity.

Other specific parallels exist between running and reading that give insight into generating lifelong readers. These parallels are warming up, rhythm/fluency, strength training/word power, speed and pacing, visualizing/imagining, independent/shared activity, developing a love for the task, and recording progress. All these contribute to persistence and focus for the long run. Let's look more closely at the parallels.

Warming Up

Just as with running, reading benefits from warm-up activities. There are many ways to warm up to reading. For the purposes of this book, we will look at five different ways and how they vary across levels of fluency for ELLs. Be reminded that a teacher would only use one of the warm-up strategies a day. Trying to do several warm-up strategies at a time would risk frustrating the reader. Also keep in mind that a warm-up activity should not take longer than five to ten minutes.

Tip for Parent Involvement

Demonstrate to parents how to walk through a book prior to reading. Show how to hold the book while reading so that all can see. Teach parents to ask predicting questions as they read to their children.

Book Walks. There are essentially four elements to a book walk: book orientation, predicting questions, story overview, and highlights. Let's look at how to address these across levels of fluency. There is very little difference in how one would approach a book walk for early intermediate to intermediate and early advanced to advanced, so those levels are grouped together in two headings (see Table 14.1).

Table 14.1 Book Walks

	Beginning	**Early Intermediate and Intermediate**	**Early Advanced and Advanced**
Book Orientation	• Preview front/back cover art • Identify title • Identify author and illustrator (show pictures obtained from author's Web site)	(Same as prior level) • Note publisher, date • Dedication • Note author and illustrator information on overleaf	(Same as prior level) • Review Library of Congress information
Predicting Questions	• Ask yes/no questions: "Do you think that this will happen next?" • Call for gestures: "Point to the next action." • Draw a picture of what you think will happen next	• Ask either/or questions: "How will Peter escape? By losing his jacket or by tearing off a button?" • Ask open-ended questions: "What do you think will happen next?" • Tell your neighbor what will happen	• Think of two possible actions that could happen • Discuss your ideas with your neighbor • Summarize what your neighbor thought might happen • Write down the best possible outcome from those you've discussed
Story Overview	• Conduct a picture walk through the story Identify settings, characters, and events • Provide a pictorial storyboard to order events	(Same as prior level) • Summarize the main events of the story • Use a graphic organizer to map the story events	(Same as prior level) • Outline story events • Create your own flowchart of story events
Highlights	• Read a selection of a favorite part • Point to your favorite part of the story • Note other books by the same author for free reading at another time	(Same as prior level) • Tell your neighbor about your favorite part of the story • Note descriptive text of setting, characters, events	(Same as prior level) • Create a digital book walk for other students using presentation software (See *end of chapter for details.*)

Context Development.   Warming up to read means giving students background information. Depending on the story selection, the context development may vary. Five areas of context development are other stories by the same author, geographical location, historical setting, key aspects of the story, and character traits and motivations. How you approach these across fluency levels is relatively consistent. A key strategy is to make the process as visual as possible. Web-based graphics are essential to developing context. Web sites like www.yahooligans.com are very helpful as well as the author's personal website (see Table 14.2).

Mini-Lessons.   Mini-lesson formats fit nicely with the warm-up metaphor for reading instruction. Taking a few minutes for instruction of key vocabulary, word analysis, grammar/punctuation conventions, story grammar, or genre will help the ELL read through difficult passages and increase comprehension. Note the difference between vocabulary development and word analysis. Vocabulary development focuses primarily on meaning whereas word analysis attends to linguistic features of words. Similarly, note that grammar/punctuation conventions refers to grammatical features of sentences, paragraphs, punctuation marks and so forth, while story grammar refers to the structure of a type of story. Table 14.3 describes what to do for each level of fluency.

Table 14.2   Context Development

	Beginning	Early Intermediate and Intermediate	Early Advanced and Advanced
Other stories by the same author	• Display an array of books by the same author • Preview each book • Make them available for free reading	• Identify and describe settings, events, and characters from other stories by the same author stories by other authors	• Identify other authors with similar stories • Compare and contrast settings, events, and characters from other
Geographical location and/or interior settings	• Provide pictures of the location • Locate setting on a pictorial map • Use play furniture to arrange interior settings	• Trace events on a map • Picture search the geographical location • Draw room arrangements for interior settings	• Conduct Internet research of geographical location
Historical setting	• Display pictures that depict the time period of the story • Note clothing, architecture, transportation, etc.	• Note key events of the time period that influence the events of the story	• Find newspaper articles from the time period via the Internet • Identify major events of the day • Discuss changes over time
Key aspects of the story	• Show pictures of the story's climax • Identify major events in the story	• Create a story ladder of events leading to a climax	• Identify cause and effect of major events in the story • Use a highlighter to mark key events in a story
Character traits and/or motivations	• Make a semantic map of random traits of a selected main character	• Order random character traits into a tee map organizer	• Identify flat characters who do not change • Identify protagonist(s) and antagonist(s) • Discuss character motivations

Table 14.3 Mini-lessons

	Beginning	Early Intermediate and Intermediate	Early Advanced and Advanced
Key Vocabulary	• For verbs, use meaningful actions • For nouns, use realia, visuals, models • Create a thesaurus with pictures labeled • Display a pictorial word bank on a wall chart • Explain meanings of words in the students' primary language	• Create a personal thesaurus with a key word at the center of a semantic cluster map of other words with similar meanings (see directions below under Strength Training/Word Power) • Highlight key words when they appear in the story	• Look up words using an Internet source such as www.dictionary.com
Word Analysis	• Identify letters in initial, medial, and final position • Identify letter-sound correspondence • Segment words into syllables • Identify consonant blends • Note function of certain words as "helping words," "sight words," etc.	• Arrange words in family groups (-ar, -er, -ir, -or, -ur) • Analyze vowel digraphs • Note homophones and homographs • Build words with roots, prefixes, infixes, suffixes • Analyze inflected endings (-ed, -s, -ing) • Analyze contractions	• Trace word origins • Study root meanings • Compare multiple meanings • Identify use of slang and idiomatic expressions • Study cultural influences on words • Identify Latin, Greek, Middle English, etc. roots
Grammar/ Punctuation Conventions	• Syntax: Use word cards to create sentence line-ups of selected sentences • Identify ending punctuation • Note paragraph indents	• Parts of speech: color code words as nouns, adjectives, adverbs • Compose Cinquain poetry • Identify unique constructions in a story • Build sentences with parts of speech • Introduce use and function of quotation marks, comma, semicolon, colon	• Compare selected sentences used in story texts • Diagram sentences • Peer editing
Story Grammar	• Identify beginning, middle, and end of story • Describe setting and characters • Identify problem/solution	• Identify and describe story elements: conflict, key events, climax, denouement • Highlight shifts in the storyline • Create a wall chart of similar stories to detail setting, characters, problem/solution	• Compare conflict, key events, climax and denouement with similar stories • Outline the story
Genre	• Identify fiction versus nonfiction	• Study unique features of each genre category • Sort and label stories according to appropriate genre	• Compare key features of selected stories that place them in certain genres

Tip for Parent Involvement

Encourage parents to share with the their children their own experiences that have a connection with the story. For example, if the story is set on the coast, share prior experiences at the beach.

Responding to Reading.   Literary response occurs involuntarily when one is reading a story. Readers cannot help but picture events or feel emotion evoked by a good story. Responding to reading can be an individual experience or shared. Shared experiences give insight into the way a reader perceives and interprets the meaning of the story. Cultural nuance and individual difference in understanding can be explored with literary response. Table 14.4 shows ways to respond to reading individually and as a shared experience according to levels of fluency.

Tip for Parent Involvement

Practice asking questions about stories, such as the following

- What were you thinking as you read the story?
- Have you ever felt like the character?
- What would you do if you were in that situation?
- How would you change the story?
- Even parents who are illiterate can ask these questions as they listen to their child read and discuss the story.

Table 14.4   Responding to Reading

	Beginning	**Early Intermediate and Intermediate**	**Early Advanced and Advanced**
Individual Experience	• Draw a picture of a favorite part of the story • Describe the picture to a literate adult to transcribe in a journal • Draw yourself into the story (Where are you? Who are you? What are you doing?)	• Write about your favorite part of the story in a journal • Picture yourself at various places in the story (outside as a spectator, next door as a neighbor, side by side as a friend, as the main character)	• Maintain a two-column journal. Cite special sections in the left column and write responses in the right column.
Shared Experience	• Listen to a proficient reader read the story • Use a face chart showing a range of emotions to identify how the story made the student feel • Create a chart story in a small group • Illustrate the chart story • Copy the chart story in a journal	• Discuss the following questions: "What did you see in your mind as you read the story? If you were the main character, how would you feel?" • Collaborate with a partner to compose a description of what was visualized by reading the story	• Write a review/critique of the in your mind as you read the story to publish in a classroom newsletter • Compose poetry or songs in response to the story

Rhythm/Fluency

Developing rhythm and pacing in running parallels fluency in reading in that they both require practice on a regular basis. Running is only developed by getting out and running. You can look at videos about running, study form, and plan a running schedule; but without stepping out on the track or the road, one cannot develop the rhythm to have stamina to run. This does not mean running hard every day, though, which leads to burnout and injury. It means running easy some days, fast on other days, long on other days, with warm-ups and speed and strength training inserted. A running program would build to a point each week for a long run. The distance and the time for each session would progressively increase by 1 to 5 percent increments, and the location and terrain for each run would vary. A simplistic version of a regular running program would look something like the following:

Day 1: Warm-up/Very easy run/Strength training
Day 2: Warm-up/Easy run
Day 3: Warm-up/Tempo training
Day 4: Warm-up/Easy run
Day 5: Long, slowly paced run (no need for warm-up due to the slow pace)
Day 6: Rest
Day 7: Warm-up/Easy run

Now, think of a weekly classroom reading program that asks students to read at a variety of levels, times, and durations with vocabulary development built in and even a rest day once a week. Just as with running, a warm-up time is provided. But with reading, the warm-up would take various forms to preview the reading or highlight certain aspects of reading. Picture a weekly classroom reading program like this:

Day 1: Warm-up (book walk)/Easy read/Vocabulary development for word power
Day 2: Warm-up (context development)/Normal reading
Day 3: Warm-up (mini-lessons/word analysis)/Tempo reading for fluency training
Day 4: Warm-up (vocabulary check)/Normal reading
Day 5: Long read (extended continuous read time for 30 minutes or more)/Literary response
Day 6: Rest
Day 7: Warm-up (reader responses)/Easy read

Each week the length of reading time would be increased by a few minutes and the warm-up activities would vary to meet the observed needs of the students. Now let's break down each component according to levels of English language proficiency. For example, the way an advanced ELL would warm up with a book walk would vary from the way a book walk would be conducted with a beginning-level ELL.

Tip for Parent Involvement

Ask parents to have their child read a short story or poem several times to develop fluency.

Strength Training/Word Power

Strength training in running parallels word power in reading. The primary way to develop vocabulary is through reading. There are a number of strategies to develop vocabulary. The following are strategies that empower the students to develop vocabulary knowledge for themselves. The first strategy is to initiate a personal thesaurus. The second is to use Web-based resources.

A Personal Thesaurus. One would think that a student should first initiate a personal dictionary; however, a thesaurus can provide the definition function of a dictionary while being more flexible and easier to develop and maintain.

- Start the personal thesaurus with a loose-leaf binder and several pages of paper.
- In the center of each page, draw a diagram of a cluster map, sometimes called a word web. (A cluster map is basically a circle with branches reaching out from the center like wagon-wheel spokes.)
- Write a generative word in the center of each of the clusters. (Use key vocabulary words from your reading selection.)
- As students encounter a word with a similar meaning to the word in the center, they can add it to the cluster by writing it at the end of one of the branches.
- When appropriate, include a drawing of the key word or one of the branched-off words.
- Add a page each time you want to include a new key word.
- Encourage students to add key words to their thesaurus.
- As a spelling activity, students can take spelling lists and include the words in their the saurus. This requires them to think if the word is an alternate meaning of a key word already included or if they need to start a new page.
- Review each thesaurus on a periodic basis (once a week or every other week).

If students have access to individual computers, they can develop a personal thesaurus using Inspiration software (www.Inspiration.com). This intuitive program fosters creating word webs and includes an extensive clip art library that lets the user illustrate each word.

Web-based Resources. Although there are numerous sites available, the following two sites have proven to be extremely helpful particularly for vocabulary development.

An easily accessible resource that includes a variety of useful tools is www.dictionary.com. It combines a number of search engines for words, including words in other languages such as Spanish, German, or French. A given word search provides a pronunciation key, a brief etymology, and multiple definitions. It also includes links to other dictionary programs and search engines.

An excellent child-protected search engine that provides educational resources across subject areas is www.yahooligans.com. It is a wonderful resource for pictures as well as educational text material.

Tempo and Pacing/Fluency

Although it is important, speed is not the primary goal of reading. Sure there remain speed-reading courses on the market, but reading in the long run, for information or pleasure, is more a matter of reading at an appropriate pace that allows for clear comprehension. (Imagine comparing speed reading to "speed watching." Given a prescribed speed-watching course you can watch five movies in only forty-five minutes. Speed becomes ludicrous in such a scenario.) Fluency is a more appropriate way to express this idea. Fluency does involve the speed and pacing that the reader adopts. More efficient readers tend to read at a more rapid rate when appropriate. More efficient readers do several tasks as they read. They preview what they are about to read, and they do not read word for word but read groups of meaningful word clusters. They also read regularly and they reread. The following are strategies to enhance fluency. Some involve speed, others pacing; but ultimately, fluency is dictated by comprehension at an appropriate rate.

Digital Flash Cards (Part 1). Use presentation software to practice high-frequency words. Here's an idea to improve upon the old flash card concept. Use media presentation software like Power-Point to create flash cards for high-frequency words. (Instructions for using PowerPoint are given at the end of this chapter.) Select a two-column slide and type in the high-frequency words you wish to have students practice. Type in four words in each column for a total of eight words on a slide. Then animate the words to appear in a sequential order. You can use the "Rehearse Timings" menu option to adjust the duration of time each word appears. In a short period of time, you can create a wide range of slides that provide students with practice in reading key words fluently. For fun, finish with applause from the auditory menu options.

Digital flash cards (Part 2).   Use presentation software to practice reading meaningful clusters of words at a glance. Based on the same idea as above, create a PowerPoint presentation that shows in succession noun phrases and verb phrases. This will give the students individual practice in looking for meaning in sets of words as opposed to reading word for word.

Repetitive reading for time.   Each week give the students a selected text to read and reread for practice. For the first read-through, ask the students to select a partner to time how long it takes to read the text completely. Record the first reading time on a table (see below). Then have students take time each day, in class and/or at home, to read through the same selection. The repetition is for practice to increase speed. After having practiced reading for a week, time the reading selection again and record the difference. Keep track on a graph of the difference in time between the first and the final read-through.

Reading Times	*Week 1*			*Week 2*			*Week 3*			*Week 4*		
Student Name	1st	2nd	Δ*	1st	2nd	Δ	1st	2nd	Δ	1st	2nd	Δ

*The triangle symbol Δ, the Greek letter *delta,* signifies change—the difference in the times from the first to the second reading.

Tip for Parent Involvement

Once students learn how to use and read the above table they can use it at home to track the difference in reading times.

Visualizing/Imagining

Competitive runners take time to visualize and imagine prior to running. They picture the course layout in their minds, and also imagine themselves running at various paces throughout the course. They even imagine the winning moment of breaking the tape at the end of the race. Visualizing and imagining are characteristic strategies of skilled readers as well. Visualizing and imagining contribute to increased comprehension and retention (Sadoski & Quast, 1990).

Visualizing and imagining are two different processes. For the purpose of clarity, *visualizing* is defined as a form of picturing the events of a story in one's mind. *Imagining* is defined as a way to explore one's unique perceptions while reading a story (see Table 14.5).

Graphic Organizers.   Graphic organizers have been shown to be useful tools for visualizing story events (Reutzel & Cooter, 2004; Gordon & Braun, 1983). Consider readers visualizing the layout of a story using a pictorial story ladder. Usually story ladders are developed only on a verbal level. A strategy to increase comprehension across levels of fluency is to represent the actions and events of the story in picture form. Have students collaborate to create a wall-sized, pictorial story ladder. Pairs of students draw selected scenes from a story that lead to a climax and the resulting events of the denouement. Then as a group, they arrange the pictures they draw in a ladder format. Use the following graphic organizer to generate a pictorial story ladder. The pictures are mounted on a bulletin board and connected with yarn or colored string.

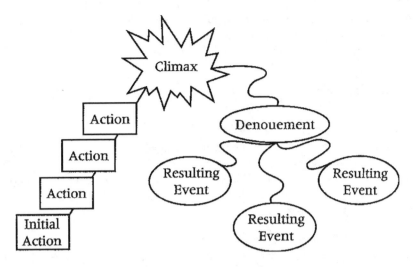

Table 14.5   Visualizing and Imagining

	Beginning	**Early Intermediate and Intermediate**	**Early Advanced and Advanced**
Visualizing	• Work with a more advanced partner to create pictures from story scenes • Collaborate to arrange pictures on a story ladder with assistance	• Identify initial events, connected actions, climax, and resulting events in a story • Draw and arrange pictures on a story ladder.	(Same as prior level) • Differentiate between climax and denouement
Imagining	• Draw a favorite part of the story in a journal • Label significant features and/or events • Draw a picture of yourself in the story	• Maintain an illustrative journal with citations, reflections, and pictures • Write responses to aesthetic questions in a journal • Draw yourself into the story in a variety of places and perspectives	(Same as prior level) • Discuss and/or write about placing yourself in the story from a variety of places in the setting

Students from beginning to advanced levels of fluency can participate in this activity. To facilitate increased comprehension, pair students heterogeneously. By pairing a beginning-level student with an intermediate- or advanced-level student, the higher-level student can more easily refer back to the text to assist the beginner.

Imagining is a different kind of activity; it is more idiosyncratic. To foster imagining, provide ways for students to think creatively about the story. Give them ways to express their own reflections, how they perceive characters, and what they picture in their minds.

This kind of reflective work requires aesthetic questions, illustrative journals, and guided imagery.

Aesthetic Questions.   Aesthetic questions call on the reader to explore what they are thinking as they read, how they feel, how they would change the story. Cox (2004) has developed a series of aesthetic questions based on the reader response theory work of Rosenblatt (1978). Beyond asking questions to recall information about a story, aesthetic questions elicit evocations from a literary work. Following are suggested aesthetic questions to evoke imagining:

What were you thinking as you read the story?
How did you feel when _____ happened?
Which characters are you drawn to? Why?

If you were one of the characters, which would you be? Why?
What would you change if you were in the story?
What do you see in your mind when you read these words?
Does this remind you of any other stories? Which ones? Why?

The above questions are open-ended and will not be appropriate for a beginning-level ELL. Following are some adaptations that can be made to include beginning-level students:

Draw your favorite part of the story.
Point to your favorite character. Draw his or her picture.
Point to what the character does that you like.
Is this character _____ or _____ ? (Provide either/or questions that embed the answer in the question.)
(Show a range of familiar book covers.) Which story is this one most like?

Journaling. There are a variety of ways in which journals are designed to foster reflection about the reading experience. To facilitate imagining, use illustrative journals that involve verbal and pictorial reflection. The unique feature of illustrative journals is the combination of verbal and nonverbal reflection. Each page is a landscape layout with three components. The first is a column for drawing a picture, the second is space for page citations and a name or subtitle of the drawing, and the third is a column for reflective writing about the picture.

Illustrative Journal Page Layout

Draw a picture from the story	Write about the picture
Citation (page and name):	

Tip for Parent Involvement

Use the above journal format as an illustrated home reading log.

Guided Imagery. This technique can be used to help students expand imaginative experience with a story. A significant function of guided imagery is to help students place themselves in the story. Conducting guided imagery is relatively simple. All it requires is a picture from the story that students can see. The picture may come from an illustration in the book, from a teacher-made sketch, or a student drawing. If you create a sketch or ask a student to make a drawing, be sure that it is large enough for the class to see clearly from their seats.

Following is a set of sample directions for guided imagery. In this sample, the guide asks the students to place themselves in the picture of a scene from Beatrix Potter's *The Tale of Peter Rabbit*. Each direction calls the students to an ever closer place in the story picture. You will need to adapt the directions to fit the picture that you select for this activity.

Guided Imagery Sample Directions

1. Look at a picture of this tree. Peter Rabbit lives at the base of this tree.
2. Look at the grass surrounding the tree with Mr. MacGregor's garden in the background.
3. Do you see the road winding by the tree? Picture yourself walking on the road.
4. How do you feel? Warm? Cold? Dry? Wet? Is the wind blowing?
5. Walk up to the tree and look beyond it. Do you see Mr. MacGregor in his garden? What is he doing?
6. Hide behind the tree. Here comes a rabbit. What is it doing?
7. Follow the rabbit through the door at the base of the tree. Can you fit? Squeeze in.
8. How does it look inside the tree? Dark? Light? Are there windows?
9. How big is the inside? As you look around, what do you see?
10. Can you feel the fur of other rabbits? What does it smell like?
11. Peter's mother is serving food and something to drink. What is it? How does it taste?
12. In your illustrative journals, draw a picture of Peter's home and write about your visit there.

Shared Read-Aloud Activities

Shared read-aloud activities can take a variety of forms depending on the teacher's purpose for the activity. By grouping students strategically, teachers address social and instructional needs and avoid placing ELLs at risk of embarrassment by reading aloud to others. Strategic grouping requires knowing the proficiency levels of the students as well as other needs. In order to address social-interactive aspects of reading, group students according to similar reading levels so that they read and discuss the story within a comfort-level group. The purpose of mixed levels is to help address the needs of less proficient readers by partnering them with more proficient reading models.

Tip for Parent Involvement

Give children an assignment to read a short book or a selected passage to as many members of the family as possible. This shares the reading experience, motivates the child, and develops reading fluency.

Identifying the reading level of students requires an assessment tool. There are a number of tools available such as running records (Clay, 1997). For rapid assessment purposes, I recommend a read-aloud rubric. Table 14.6 is a rubric for evaluating how a student reads aloud according to all five levels of proficiency. The rubric evaluates three areas of reading aloud: fluency, expression, and comprehension and critique. Fluency refers to the pacing the student uses while reading. Expression refers to the appropriate use of intonation while reading aloud. Finally, it is possible to memorize a passage and repeat it aloud with fluency and expression without comprehension; however, that would not be reading. Reading by its very definition is a process of making meaning of text (Smith, 1985). Therefore, the rubric includes a component for evaluating comprehension.

Fluency, as described in the rubric, is composed of multiple skills. In this simple rubric three areas make up an evaluation of fluency. Pace, or fluidity, is the first component. The next component is the amount of text, whether it be selected words, sentences, paragraphs, or lengthy selections. Finally, recognition of errors and self-correction are important aspects of fluency. Keep in mind that as the student advances the number of errors decreases; self-correction decreases with increased levels of fluency as well.

Table 14.6 Rubric for Reading Aloud

	Beginning	Early Intermediate	Intermediate	Early Advanced	Advanced
Fluency	• Silent • May recognize some words	• Reads word for word with frequent pauses at unknown words • Reads simple sentences • Little error recognition • Occasional self-correction	• Reads separate sentences fluently (may pause between sentences) • Reads more complex sentences and paragraphs • Recognizes errors and self-corrects	• Fluid, with some errors • Reads multiple paragraphs with relative ease • Rapid self-correction	• Exceptionally fluid with few to no errors • Reads lengthy passages with ease • Little to no need for self-correction
Expression	• No expression in reading	• Little to no change in intonation • May sound monotone or "robotic"	• Changes intonation at exclamation points or question marks	• Reads to an audience • Changes intonation in appropriate places	• Interprets the mood of the text by reading with a range of expression
Comprehension and Critique	• Little to no comprehension	• Identifies story events • Recognizes characters	• Identifies and describes story events • Identifies and describes character traits	• Identifies and describes how story events relate to the overall plot • Compares and contrasts character roles • Establishes an initial critique	• Discusses plot as it relates to previous reading • Describes the author's perspective of characters • Readily provides justification for a critique

Expression, as described in the rubric, is appropriate intonation while reading aloud. This involves changes of intonation as called for by the text. Initially, a reader may sound monotone, or even "robotic," while reading word for word. As proficiency develops, the reader recognizes indicators of change in expression, such as ending punctuation. Advanced readers interpret the mood of text and enhance the reading with a wide range of expression.

Comprehension is a much more involved skill than described in this rubric. The reason for a simple rendering of comprehension here is to make it useful for the rubric assessment. It is my opinion that an overly complex assessment tool will not be useful for rapid assessment. The essential components of comprehension for the purposes of the rubric begin with recognition of story events and characters. It builds on events and characters in terms of increasing depth of understanding of how events and characters relate to the overall plot and other stories. The other area is the development of a personal critique of the story. Advanced readers readily establish a justified critique of the text.

Using the rubric is quite simple. Begin with a reading selection that includes characters and story events. Be sure to select a passage that the student has not read before to ensure the validity of the evaluation. Ask the student to read aloud. Note indicators for levels of fluency and expression in the rubric and match the student's reading to the appropriate level. (A good rule of thumb with rubric evaluation is that when a borderline evaluation occurs, assess the student at the lower level. This is not intended to stigmatize a student, but rather trigger additional assistance. In other words, in order to attain a specific level, the student must clearly demonstrate that level of ability. It does ELLs no favors to be assessed above their ability level.) At the end of the reading, ask the following questions to assess comprehension, and compare the student responses against the criteria for comprehension and critique:

Can you tell me about the story you just read?

What can you tell me about the characters?

(Continue with the following if the student demonstrates considerable comprehension):

Did you enjoy the story? Why?

Same-Level Groupings.   Once the students are assessed according to reading levels, the teacher can make choices about shared reading activities. Same-level students can simply take turns reading selections together as pairs. Less proficient readers would read shorter passages of one sentence to a single paragraph at a time. With more proficient readers, increase the length of the selection from one to more paragraphs. In small group settings, students can read a selection and then call on another student to continue reading. Consider a random reading activity in which students read favorite selections without regard to the order.

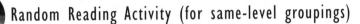

Random Reading Activity (for same-level groupings)

1. Prior to reading, set the parameters of the reading selection (give page numbers or a selection of paragraphs that maintain a theme).
2. Allow a few minutes for students to review the reading.
3. Ask students to choose a favorite passage to share.
4. Ask students to read their favorite passage to a partner as a rehearsal. (Encourage students to help each other pronounce words or to ask for help with difficult words.)
5. Open up the entire group to read their selected passages in the order of their choosing.
6. Ask students. Why was that selection important to you?
7. Ask students to highlight and summarize the important points of the reading selections.
8. Record the summary statements on chart paper so that all can see.
9. Invite students to write about their understanding of the reading in their journals.

Mixed-Level Groupings.   This type of grouping addresses the needs of a less proficient reader by providing a model. The more proficient reader is placed in the role of exemplary reader, which increases their level of attention to the reading task. Reading formats may be either leapfrog reading or model and repeat reading. Leapfrog reading is just as it sounds: The exemplary reader reads one selection and the less proficient reader reads the following selection. The exemplary reader is called on to monitor and to demonstrate how to read difficult words or sentences.

Model and repeat reading is most appropriate when the less proficient reader is a struggling reader. Model and repeat begins with the exemplary reader reading a sentence or paragraph. Then the less proficient reader reads the same passage. If the less proficient reader struggles, they both read the passage again. Avoid rereading too much, which may lead to discouraging both readers. Limit to two rereads and then move on.

Leapfrog and model and repeat strategies are not limited to a single classroom setting. These are also appropriate strategies for cross-age tutoring. Establish a partnership with a classroom at another grade level.

Developing a Love for the Task

A key to reading instruction is to develop a love for the task. Returning to the running analogy, the pleasurable feeling a runner experiences from the release of endorphins is called a "runner's high." The same can be true about reading. Developing a love for the task is a "reader's high." There are a number of ways to develop a love for the task. Reading to children with feeling and enthusiasm, giving ample opportunities to read, and providing students with a wide selection of books are significant

Rules for Leapfrog Reading	*Rules for Model and Repeat Reading*
1. Take turns reading.	1. Teacher assigns partner #1 and partner #2.
2. Listen while your partner is reading.	2. Partner #1 reads first.
3. Always be courteous.	3. Partner #2 follows by reading the same words.
4. What to say to help correct an error:	4. Listen while your partner is reading.
"I read the word like this. . ."	5. Read the same section again if needed.
"Listen to me read the word."	6. Always be courteous.
"Let's read this sentence together."	7. What to say to help correct an error:
"Good job!" "That's right!" "Nice reading."	"I read the word like this. . ."
	"Listen as I read the word."
	"Let's read this sentence together."
	"Good job!" "That's right!" "Nice reading."

Reading Interest Inventory

Name_____   Date:_____

1. List your favorite stories or book titles:
   -
   -
   -

2. List your favorite story characters:
   -
   -
   -

3. Which do you prefer? _____ Fiction _____ Nonfiction

4. Check which genres you have read and circle the ones you like best:

   _____Fantasy   _____Mythology   _____Adventure   _____Historical Fiction

   _____Mystery   _____Horror Stories   _____Poetry   _____Comedy

   _____Biography   _____Historical   _____Scientific   _____Pop Culture

   _____OTHER_____

5. Check which topics interest you:

   ____Exotic Places   ____Animals ____People   ____Technology   ____Jokes

   ____Outer Space   ____Nature ____Cars/Motorcycles   ____Sports   ____Music

   ____Outdoor Adventure   ____Fashion ____Monsters   ____Magic ____Movies

   ____Presidents/Leaders ____OTHER_____

6. What are you reading at this time?_____

   Did you select it?_____Yes_____No

   If so, why?_____

   What is you opinion about it?_____

ways to foster a love of reading. Discussed below are three strategies that contribute to developing a love for the task of reading. First, using a reading interest inventory helps match books to a student's area of interest. Second, utilizing criteria for quality literature helps in selecting wonderful books. Third, teaching the student an easy strategy to avoid choosing a book that is in the frustration level fosters independence in the selection process.

Reading Interest Inventory.   The following is a suggested reading interest inventory. Less proficient ELLs would need assistance in filling it out. More proficient students would be able to complete it in a short period of time.

Rating Quality Books.   The process of selecting quality books requires both a rating instrument and selection criteria. Below is a four-point rating instrument for quality children's books. The reason for a four-point system is to force a decision of whether the book meets criteria or is below criteria. Consider using this rating system for yourself, as teacher, or as an activity for students to do individually or in a group.

The selection criteria listed in the rating instrument address six areas of quality literature: vivid illustrations, character development, engaging story, cultural perspective or diversity, English language development possibilities, and connections to other curricular areas.

Vivid illustrations are essential for ELLs because they contribute to comprehension of the story. Meaningful illustrations provide context and understanding of story events, and also enhance the beauty of the reading experience.

Character development and an engaging story are quality criteria for anyone choosing a book to read. The richness of a good story is dependent on character development and the story's level of engagement. One consideration is that as students mature and change, their notion of an engaging story develops as well.

The cultural perspective or diversity criterion requires some explanation. Identifying a story's cultural perspective—for example, Latino, Anglo, Asian, African American, Persian, Indian, and so forth—is not necessarily to match a story to one's cultural background, but to identify, appreciate, and share cultural insights in our literary world. A distinct cultural perspective provides a reference point for talking about the similarities and differences of one's own culture. Diversity refers to multiple cultural perspectives portrayed in the story as opposed to a single cultural portrayal.

Considering English language development possibilities simply means asking the following question: What can this book teach about English? One book might utilize expansive verbs to show action, another might employ rich descriptive words, and another might use similes for metaphorical thinking. Great books use a wide range of linguistic devices.

Connections to other curricular areas means identifying how a book can contribute to a thematic unit of study. Begin by looking at the setting of story. Is it in a place or time period that is going to be studied in a geography or history lesson? Does the book deal with social science issues? Look for visual and performing arts connections to dance, music, theater, or visual arts.

Rating Instrument for Quality Books:
4 = Exceeds criteria, 3 = Meets criteria, 2 = Below criteria, 1 = Unacceptable or N/A

Selection Criteria	4	3	2	1
Vivid illustrations				
Character development				
Engaging story				
Cultural perspective or diversity				
English language development possibilities				
Connections to other curricular areas. Note curricular area(s):				
Subtotal				
Total ÷**by 6 = Average** _____				

Reviewer's comments:

Using the rating instrument is a matter of reading or previewing a story with the criteria in mind. Place a check in each row under the appropriate number rating. Subtotal and then total the points. Divide the total by six for an average score. Include reviewer comments to highlight unique aspects of a book.

The Five-Finger Test for Self-Selected Reading.   Helping students select books within their reading level is as easy as counting to five. Ask students to select a book and begin to read the first page or a random passage. As they read, tell them to hold up a closed fist lightly and in a comfortable position. Each time the students come across a word they can't read, they hold up a finger. If they get to five fingers before they finish a paragraph, the book is probably at a frustration level. Students who read without raising a finger will either have a readable book, or one that is too easy for their level.

The five-finger test is not a hard and fast rule, nor is it without its exceptions. Sometimes a wonderful book will require work on the part of the reader. There is no harm in encouraging a student to tackle a challenging book. Conversely, we do not want to encourage selecting a book solely because it is an easy read. The five-finger test is limited in its use, but it does give a motivated reader a quick way to assess the level of difficulty the book will pose.

Recording Progress

Reading Logs.   A runner in training logs mileage and a training regime. Readers can track their progress and log reading experiences as well. There are a number of ways to log reading in order to track student progress. The three formats discussed here—training logs, home reading logs, and conversational book reports—are for classroom and/or home use. Using all three might prove to be too much; treat them as a list of suggested tools to choose from.

Training Logs.   Training logs are student-managed logs for classroom reading. A page of a training log will cover a five-day period. Students will record the date, title, author and genre, reading type, page numbers, and the number of minutes each day. At the end of a five-day period the student can total the number of pages and minutes. There is also a comments section for each day where the student can make a notation about the reading experience. Comments may include a highlight in the story, a difficulty, new vocabulary, or a literary response to the reading. The reading type refers to the kind of reading the student is attempting such as an easy read, a tempo read, or a long read.

A reader's training log has several functions. It is used to record reading information. When multiple pages are logged in, the student can compare the number of pages and time spent reading from week to week. This can also be used to develop and monitor reading goals for number of pages and minutes spent reading.

Another function of the log is for planning a reading schedule. The student can fill in several of the columns ahead of time such as title and author, reading type, and minutes. When the day comes, the student can record the date, the number of pages read, and any comments. Planning ahead by using the log can save time in classroom transitions. If a student has the log programmed for a week, little to no time will be spent by the teacher telling the student what to read.

Home Reading Logs.   These are similar to training logs with a few differences. A home reading log is used for a month at a time and is maintained by the student and family members. It requires a signature from a parent or guardian for verification purposes. It also has a section at the bottom for recording total pages and minutes read. Consider maintaining a graph of each student's pages and minutes read at home each week. This will be important data for reporting to parents and school staff. It can also be used as a friendly competition in the classroom to acknowledge and reward persistent reading at home.

Conversational Book Reports.   This activity involves classroom volunteers who assist in the reading progress of each student. Each time a student completes a story or book, he signs up to report to a classroom volunteer. The classroom volunteer takes a three-by-five index card and records the student's name, the date, book title, author, and genre, and then asks the student, "Tell me about the

Reader's Training Log

Date	Title/Author/Genre	Reading Type	Number of Pages	Number of Minutes
Comments:				
Comments:				
Comments:				
Comments:				
Comments:				
Total of pages and minutes				

Home Reading Log

Date	Title/Author/Genre	Number of Pages	Number of Minutes	Signature
Total		pages	minutes	

Tip for Parent Involvement

Initially, maintain home reading logs on a weekly basis. The students turn in their logs each Friday for teacher review and credit. On Mondays send out a new page. Once the rhythm is established, move to a bi-weekly sehedule and then a monthly schedule.

book." The student, in turn, talks about the book, and the volunteer records a summary of what the student says.

The purpose of this report is twofold. First, it gives the student the opportunity to talk about a book with an interested party. The interactive nature of a conversational report is highly motivating for readers. One of the great pleasures of reading is to talk to someone else about the story.

The second purpose is to record the number of books read by individual students and to obtain an aggregate number of books being read by an entire class. The cards can either be filed in a student portfolio or be displayed on a bulletin board showing the total number of books read to date.

Conversational Book report

Student Name _____ Date _____

Book Title _____

Author _____ Genre _____

Oral Report _____

_____

_____

_____

Recorder's Name _____

Tip for Parent Involvement

Parents can involve extended family members in taking conversational book reports. Often an older sibling will do the writing on behalf of a parent who is not literate in English.

Charting Classroom Reading.   Charting classroom reading takes two basic forms: displays and teacher records. Displays can be in the form of a bulletin board class record, a chart in graph form, and/or creative display such as a bookworm.

Displays.   A bulletin board display that I recommend is to show the number of books the class has read by mounting the Conversational Book Report index cards. Divide up the bulletin board into a grid using yarn. Staple the yarn to the bulletin board at intersecting points. Map out the grid so that the name of each student in the classroom is mounted in a square in the grid. Also in each grid square, mount a clip to hold the index cards for each book the student has read. To one side of the bulletin board, mount a large paper cutout of a thermometer with markings for every 100 books read. In the round base of the thermometer, glue a card that records the total number of books read in class. Give the bulletin board a title, such as "Look How Many Books We've Read" or "Can We Read 1,000 Books?" Each time a student completes a Conversational Book Report card, it is clipped next to her name. Each month, students total their cards and a small group of students update the bulletin board and color in the thermometer with the appropriate number of books read to date.

Class reading graphs are a way to show quantitative data about student reading. As mentioned above in "Repetitive reading for time," use the table that records the change in time from the first reading to the second. A longer interval can be recorded so that it displays the difference from one month to the next in number of words read per minute.

Other displays include linear graphs of total number of pages and/or total minutes read each week based upon the data collected from the home reading log or the student training log. They can be recorded by individual or group pages. Consider grouping students into teams and recording total pages read each week in a friendly competition.

Creative classroom displays, like a giant bookworm, is another way to show classroom reading. A giant bookworm is a series of green circles (painted paper plates or colored paper) aligned in a linear fashion with each circle overlapping to give the appearance of the worm's body. The head has a face, but each circle in the body of the worm is a book title. With every book a student reads, a new circle is added to lengthen the body and the worm grows. To increase motivation, the student who read the book has his name displayed on the bookworm by the title.

Teacher Records.   Record keeping is an essential part of charting student progress. Using the read aloud rubric to assess reading levels, the teacher can record a student's level on a trimester basis. At three points during the year, the teacher can listen to a student read and record the level of proficiency using a class record (see sample). The notion is as follows: B = beginning, EI = early intermediate, I = intermediate, EA = early advanced, and A = advanced. Once a student is assessed, the teacher need only record the name of the student and circle the appropriate letter.

Class Record of Level of Proficiency

Student	1st Trimester			2nd Trimester			3rd Trimester		
	B	EI-I	EA-A	B	EI-I	EA-A	B	EI-I	EA-A
	B	EI-I	EA-A	B	EI-I	EA-A	B	EI-I	EA-A
	B	EI-I	EA-A	B	EI-I	EA-A	B	EI-I	EA-A
	B	EI-I	EA-A	B	EI-I	EA-A	B	EI-I	EA-A
	B	EI-I	EA-A	B	EI-I	EA-A	B	EI-I	EA-A
	B	EI-I	EA-A	B	EI-I	EA-A	B	EI-I	EA-A

Another form of record keeping is compiling data from the home reading log. Each month, students turn in a home reading log with total minutes and pages read, and the teacher records the numbers that have been verified in the home log on a class monthly record of reading.

Class Monthly Record of Reading in Total Minutes and Pages

Student		Sept	Oct	Nov	Dec	Jan	Feb	Mar	Apr	May	Jun
	mins										
	pgs										
	mins										
	pgs										
	mins										
	pgs										

APPENDIX: GETTING STARTED WITH POWERPOINT

Creating a New Presentation

1. Open PowerPoint
2. Dialog Box "Create a new presentation"
   -select a design template
   -select a background
   (Navigate with <> arrow keys on the keyboard)
3. Select a title slide from the slide auto layout dialog box.

Text

Adding Text

1. Click in the "click to add title" text box
2. Repeat for the subtitle (Keep statements brief)

Repositioning Text Boxes "Click & Drag"

1. Click inside a text box. When the crossed-arrow cursor appears, hold down the mouse button and drag the text box to the new location.
2. Resize the text box by positioning the cursor on a corner. When the arrow cursor appears, click and drag to size the text box.

Modifying Text

1. Click and drag the cursor over a line of text to select or highlight.
2. Use the toolbar (top of screen) to change font, color, size of text.

Adding Slides

1. Click on new slide icon on the toolbar or "Insert."
2. Select auto layout from the "New Slide" screen. Click OK.

Moving Between Slides

1. Click on the "Slide Sorter View" on the toolbar in the bottom left corner.
2. Select a slide.
3. Repeat #1.

Changing Slide Order

1. Click on the "Slide Sorter View" on the toolbar in the bottom left corner.
2. Move a slide to a different order:
   -Click and drag the selected slide to the desired position
   -Lift the mouse button when in position
3. Exit "Slide Sorter View" by double-clicking on one of the slides.

Adding Clipart

1. Using a slide layout with a "Clipart" box, double click on the "Clipart" icon.
2. Or, add clipart: click on "Insert" on the toolbar, "Picture" and "Clipart."
3. The Clipart Gallery displays a library of pictures for selection.

4. External clipart can be copied and pasted by selecting the picture with a right mouse click on PCs or holding down the mouse button on Macs.
5. Paste the picture on the slide: Hold down the control key and press the "V" key.
6. Reposition clipart using "click & drag" when the crossed-arrow cursor appears.
7. Resize clipart using "click & drag" when the arrow cursor appears on the edge of the picture.

ADDING TRANSITIONS

Multiple Slide Transitions

1. Click on the "Slide Sorter View" on the toolbar in the bottom left corner.
2. Click "Edit" and "Select All" from the upper toolbar menu.
3. Click on the "Transition" icon, far left just under the toolbar.
4. Under "Effect," select the transition(s) you want.
5. Select "Apply to All."
6. View the transitions: Click on "Slide Show View" on the toolbar.
7. Click on the first slide of the presentation.

Single Slide Transition and/or Sounds

1. Click on the "Slide Sorter View" on the toolbar in the bottom left corner.
2. Select the slide you want to create a transition from.
3. Click "Tools," "Slide Transition."
4. Select "Effect," choose a desired effect.
5. Choose whether to activate the transition by mouse click under "Advance."
6. Add sound to the transition by selecting a desired sound from the "Sound Menu." Select "Okay."

Adding Animations

1. Click "Slide Show," "Custom Animation."
2. Click on each graphic or text object you want to animate in the upper left-hand corner of the dialog box.
3. Click and drag to select the "Effect" you desire.
4. Order the appearance of the animations: click on the object and then on the green arrow below.
5. Under "Start Animation," leave it on Mouse Click.
6. Preview the animation by clicking on the preview animation button.

REFERENCES

Clay, M. M. (1997). *Running records for classroom teachers.* Portsmouth, NH: Heinemann.

Cox, C. (2004). *Teaching Language Arts: A child-centered and response-centered approach.* Boston, MA: Allyn & Bacon.

Garcia, G. (2000). Bilingual children's reading. In M. L. Kamil, P. B. Mosenthal, P. D. Pearson, & R. Barr (Eds.), *Handbook of reading research,* Vol. III (pp. 813–834). Mahwah, NJ: Earlbaum.

Gordon, C. J. & Braun, C. (1983). Using story schema as an aid to reading and writing. *The Reading Teacher, 37(2),* 116-121.

Reese, L., Garnier, H., Gallimore, R., & Goldenberg, C. (2000). Longitudinal analysis of the antecedents of emergent Spanish literacy and middle-school English reading achievement of Spanish-speaking students. *American Educational Research Journal, 37(3),* 633–662.

Reutzel, D. R., & Cooter, R. B. (2004). *Teaching children to read: Putting the pieces together.* (4th ed.). Columbus, OH: Pearson/Merrill-Prentice Hall.

Rosenblatt, L. (1978). *The reader, the text, the poem.* Carbondale, IL: Southern Illinois University Press.

Slavin, R., & Cheung, A. (2003). *Effective reading programs for English language learners: A best-evidence synthesis.* Report No. 66. Center for Research on the Education of Students Placed at Risk (CRESPAR), Grant No. R117-D40005 from the Institute of Education Sciences. Baltimore, MD: Johns Hopkins University.

Sadoski, M., & Quast, Z. (1990). Reader response and long-term recall for journalistic text: The roles of imagery, affect and importance. *Reading Research Quarterly, 24*(4), 256–272.

Smith, F. (1988). *Understanding reading.* (4th ed.). Hillsdale, NJ: Erlbaum.

CHAPTER 15

TEACHING WRITING ACROSS PROFICIENCY LEVELS

TESOL GOALS AND STANDARDS

GOAL 3: To use English in socially and culturally appropriate ways

Standard 1: Students will use the appropriate language variety, register, and genre according to audience, purpose and setting

Standard 2: Students will use nonverbal communication appropriate to audience purpose and setting

Standard 3: *Students will use appropriate learning strategies to extend their sociolinguistic and sociocultural competence.*

ALL CHILDREN ARE WRITERS

Simply put, novice writers must write in order to learn to write well. There is no other way. Sit down at a desk. Scratch out ideas individually or as a group. Write for an authentic purpose. Remember that ideas come first and that conventions follow. Don't be afraid to make mistakes; errors are easy to fix. Discuss the writing with other writers. Craft the writing with revisions and editing. Find an outlet to show the work, to make it public, to publish. But the fundamental assumption is that all children are writers.

All children can write. Given the opportunity, they express themselves in written form. The teacher's task, therefore, is to take the unconventional, raw writing and guide the child to craft it into a conventional form.

The purpose of this chapter is to present strategies for teaching the writing process (Graves, 1984) across levels of English language proficiency. The strategies are adapted according to beginning, intermediate, and advanced levels of proficiency. This does not mean that there is no difference between students on an early intermediate and intermediate level or an early advanced and advanced level. It simply means that many of the writing strategies suggested below address multiple levels of proficiency. Often the accommodations for early intermediate or early advanced students are made in terms of the length or complexity of the written product rather than the strategy used for teaching the writing process.

The writing process provides one way to organize strategies for English Language Learners. Graves's (1994) organization outlines prewriting, drafting, revision, editing, and publication. Another way to approach writing is in terms of collaborative, interactive, and individual writing activities. These kinds of activities map onto the writing process and provide strategic ways to help ELLs across levels of proficiency. Collaboration helps the beginning writer to develop entry-level skills in the writing process. Collaboration also creates a social-interactive forum for writing as a team for a singular purpose. Collaborative activities include chart stories, collaborative story interviews, semantic mapping, paragraph coding and outlining, making big books, developing class newsletters, and even composing songs and poems.

Interactive writing is a shared experience like a dialog on paper. Interactive strategies mediate development in writing. Some of the strategies include interactive journals, lap board modeling, and rubric partnering in which a more experienced writer interacts with the novice writer. Vygotsky's (1978) notion of a zone of proximal development is realized in a one-to-one relationship in this kind of interactive arrangement.

Individualized strategies include many of the aforementioned collaborative and interactive strategies done on an individual basis plus dual-entry journal writing, composing poetry, reporting narrative or informational prose, and making personal books. There is overlap to be sure, but collaborative, interactive, and individual strategies can cover multiple skills across all levels of proficiency.

Although writing is referred to as a process, we assess writing as a product in a variety of ways. Assessment of writing can be designed to match the product whether it be collaborative, individual, or across proficiency levels. In this chapter, I will provide several ways to assess writing including a rubric builder for tailoring assessment to a specific writing assignment.

Tip for Parent Involvement

Encourage parents to maintain a writing center at home. A writing center can be as simple as a box of writing materials (pencils, erasers, paper, pencil sharpener, dictionary, thesaurus, and a writing tablet). Having a designated place for writing with sufficient materials can greatly enhance the home-school connection.

THE WRITING PROCESS

The writing process outlines a sequence, or stages, that writers work through. Teaching process writing provides students with essential guidance and tools to craft their writing. It helps establish goals for each writing project. The process appears to be a fixed set of stages, but in reality there is an organic and recursive quality to it. Writers move back and forth between drafting, revising, and editing. Certain revisions may require further prewriting. Also, a change in publishing formats may trigger additional revisions. The writing process, in other words, is deeper and more complex than any single framework can describe.

Prewrite	Draft	Revise	Edit	Publish
• Draw on experiences • Read/listen to stories • Generate ideas • Organize thinking • Talk over ideas • Choose type of writing: journals, letters, expressive writing, articles, literature model • Consider audience	• Rehearse: draw, talk, map, plot, diagram, act out • Put ideas on paper • Focus on meaning over conventions • Experiment • Understand that writing will change • Try out different possibilities • Talk over drafts with others	• Reread during/after writing draft • Rethink what is written • Share with others in a reader's circle • Talk to teacher in editing conference • Change, add to, delete, modify, rearrange paragraphs • Expand ideas	• Proofread revised piece • Talk to the teacher in a writer's conference • Ask for help in peer-editing conference • Rephrase and refine (select a more descriptive word) • Check: spelling, punctuation, capitalization, usage, form, legibility	• Choose the form: -book -display in room -drama -reader's theater -electronic media -letter -big book -newspaper article -poster -advertisement • Share published pieces:

• Brainstorm ideas: list, cluster, quick write	• Rehearse some more		• Identify errors and correct own work	-read aloud to the class -reader's circle -author's chair -writer's workshop

(Graves, 1984)

Prewriting is like preparing the soil before planting a seed. It involves exploring the source of writing such as one's own experiences or events in history, reading resources and listening to stories, researching information, and/or sharing ideas. Ideas tend to germinate and sprout in random ways, so they need an organizer that can be used to quickly get them on paper. Various prewriting organizers will be discussed below in the context of specific activities.

Drafting is the raw, initial writing. The primary focus is getting ideas on paper, with conventions as a secondary focus. This is not to say that conventions are unimportant; it is only to emphasize what comes first. Based on my personal teaching experience, if a child is a frustrated writer, it is often related to a struggle with conventions before developing ideas. The novice writer may need particular help with scripting ideas to be able to continue in the writing process. Once the ideas are germinated and drafted, the conventions can be dealt with in the revisions and editing phases. In other words, develop the notion of drafting ideas with the understanding that the initial draft will change.

(*A note about the use of computers in the classroom.* Encourage students to draft their writing at the computer using a word-processing program. Print out the drafts for revision and editing as a hard copy. Then return to the computer for inputting changes. Many teachers hold off on using computers until the final drafts, but writing initial drafts at the computer will make the other phases of the writing process go so much easier, for example, by moving paragraphs with cut-and-paste features, correcting spelling using a spell-checker, and changing formats, font styles, and layouts. Beginning with word processing from the outset gives the student a wide range of media formats to choose from for publishing at the end of the writing process, as well.)

Revision is the place where the writer takes the audience into account. How to make the writing clearer is of primary concern. The simplest way to initiate revision is to have students read their writing aloud to each other. When students read aloud their writing, they begin to note missing or out-of-order parts, to hear mistakes, and to identify unclear wording that they may have missed while writing. They begin to see flaws because, as they read aloud, they become the audience of their own writing. Reading to a partner provides additional input especially when students are apprised of rubric criteria for the writing ahead of time.

Editing is the easiest phase of the writing process to teach explicitly. It takes a careful reader to edit for grammar, punctuation, spelling, and style; but these corrections can be marked directly on a hard copy. Students participating in a rhythm of writing in a classroom setting learn to expect to get editorial markings on their papers. Editing can be time consuming; however, if students are included in the editing process many of the errors can be addressed prior to the teacher having to review the writing. The students' unedited writing also becomes the source for various mini-lessons that the teacher may give at the beginning of a writing workshop time.

Publishing writing is preparing a work to show in public. There are numerous venues and various media available to teachers to display a student's writing.

The writing process is often viewed as linear. Theoretically, the writer moves lock-step from one stage to the next. The reality, however, is that the type of writing activity one selects dictates the stages of the process. Depending on the intentions of the writer, certain forms of journaling, for example, may not necessarily employ extensive prewriting or revision. The writer's purpose may be more of a free-flowing, "stream of consciousness" style of writing with no intention of it being displayed for publication. Other writing activities such as collaborative story interviewing combine prewriting and drafting simultaneously.

Table 15.1 Writing Activities across Levels of Proficiency

Writing Activities	Beginning	Early Intermediate and Intermediate	Early Advanced and Advanced
Collaborative	• Collaborative story interviews • Graphic organizers—cluster map, tree map • Making big books • Triante poetry frames	(Same as prior level) • Song/poetry word banks and frames • Correspondence centers	(Same as prior level) • Team writing projects • Organizing multiple sections of larger project writing • Edited collections, newsletters, project reports
Interactive	• Interactive journals • Lap board modeling	• Family journals • Pen pals	(Same as prior level) • Web-based discussion boards, or newsgroups
Individual	• Pictorial journals • Making personal illustrated books	(Same as prior level) • Double-entry journals • Informational report frames	(Same as prior level) • persuasive writing

In Table 15.1 various writing activities are organized according to collaborative, interactive, and individual writing. Most of the activities map onto all of the stages of the writing process. They are described according to the sequence of appropriate stages of the writing process.

BEGINNING LEVEL

Collaborative Writing Activities for Beginning Level

Collaborative story interview. This is an activity that is appropriate for beginning-level students, but is easily adapted for all levels. (Adaptations are inserted in parentheses.) In short, a collaborative story interview activity is a group interview of one person. The students ask questions and then tell the teacher what to write on a chart. The teacher facilitates the process by acting as the "scribe" for beginning-level students. This activity also features a coding technique to identify like sentences and order them into paragraphs.

Preparation

1. Materials: Two sheets of lined chart paper, four different colored marking pens, student paper, pencils, and crayons or colored pencils.
2. Choose a student to be interviewed by the class. This may be a star of the week, a random selection, a child playing the role of a story character, or a special guest such as an adult visiting the class.
3. The interviewee chooses who will ask each question. If the interviewee does not wish to respond, she simply says, "pass." An optional rule is that the interviewee alternates fielding questions from boys and girls to ensure gender equity in the process.

Prewriting and Drafting

1. The teacher stands to one side ready to write the students' responses on a large sheet of chart paper. (Early intermediate and intermediate students should be given paper and pencils to write what the teacher models on the chart. Early advanced and advanced students are encouraged to formulate their own sentences.)

2. An important strategy: Instead of writing the students' responses verbatim, the teacher asks the student who posed the question to paraphrase in his own words what the response was. Example:

Interviewer: Where were you born?

Interviewee: In Jalisco, Mexico.

Teacher (asking the interviewer): What do I write?

Interviewer: She was born in Jalisco, Mexico.

3. There are several reasons for having the student paraphrase the responses: (A) Paraphrasing changes the answer from first to third person. This produces a narrative style. (B) Asking students to paraphrase what their fellow students have said teaches them to be active listeners. (C) If an interviewer struggles with how to paraphrase a response, the class becomes involved in negotiating an accurate representation of the response.

4. The teacher writes the paraphrased sentence on the chart paper and the students copy the sentence on their own sheet of paper. (Early intermediate and intermediate students can write the sentence on the chart. To guide the writing, the teacher uses a small white board and dry erase marker to help spell words. If a student makes an error on the chart, cover the mistake with a small piece of white correction tape and write the correction on top of it.)

5. While writing, the teacher uses the student's language to teach punctuation, spelling, and grammatical issues. Features of the writing are highlighted with a different color pen and discussed with the entire class.

Revision

1. At the end of the interview the sentences written on the chart are in random order, so the next step is to group like sentences and order them.

2. Code similar sentences with a symbol, such as a red triangle for sentences concerning family, a blue square for sentences concerning dreams and aspirations, and a green circle for sentences concerning school. Students will color code sentences on their papers.

3. Decide which group should be first in the sequence and number the sentences in order of preference within each coded group. In this way, students begin to see the formation of paragraphs around an idea or theme.

4. Rewrite the interview responses in paragraph form according to the coded and numbered sequence. The teacher rewrites the chart story, and the students rewrite their individual copies as a homework assignment.

Editing

1. When the homework draft is returned, the teacher will ask the students to review a partner's copy for grammar, spelling, and punctuation. Beginning through intermediate students compare their partner's work against the story chart prepared by the teacher. Early advanced through advanced students check work and provide comments.

2. Students rewrite the edited draft for homework.

Publication

1. The large chart story is illustrated by selected students.

2. The finished chart story can be displayed on a bulletin board. Another option is to bind the chart story with other pages to form a collaborative class big book.

Prewriting with graphic organizers for beginners. Graphic organizers are used predominantly in the prewriting stage of the writing process, although they are sometimes displayed within the body of a larger piece to illustrate the relationships between ideas. Organizing writing graphically works to give an overview of the entire piece at a glance. There are any number of ways to organize writing graphically, but two organizers in particular are helpful for process writing with beginners: a cluster map and a tree map. Cluster maps and tree maps work together. The cluster map helps record ideas in random order, while the tree map is used to arrange the clustered ideas in organized categories. Each organizer has its function and adaptations for proficiency levels.

Cluster maps. Also called semantic maps or circle maps, cluster maps are designed to record initial ideas in a random order. Begin with a central idea written or illustrated at the center of a piece of paper. For example, a picture of the main character of the story could occupy the center of the map. The teacher writes the students' words around the center as they identify and describe the main character. Some cluster maps are drawn as two concentric circles. One small circle in the middle contains the central idea, and another large circle functions as a border for the chart. Another way to draw the map is to use a circle in the middle with connecting lines to the center. The lines can show connections of ideas to the center as well as connections among ideas.

Two Types of Cluster Map Designs

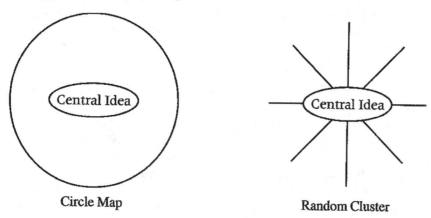

Circle Map   Random Cluster

Four cluster map techniques to use with beginning-level ELLs are questioning strategies, use of meaning sketches, color coding, and movable text clippings.

1. **Questioning strategies.** Beginning-level ELLs cannot respond adequately to open-ended questions such as, "What do we know about this character?" Nevertheless applying appropriate questioning strategies is essential for discussion. Samples of beginning-level questions are:

- yes/no questions: "Is Peter Rabbit trapped?"
- either/or questions: "Is Peter Rabbit trapped in a watering can or a basket?"
- short-answer questions: "What is Peter Rabbit trapped in?"
- call for gestures: "Point to the watering can where Peter Rabbit is trapped."

These types of questions invite the beginning ELL to respond according to ability level. The teacher follows by expanding and elaborating the students' responses and recording a more detailed phrase or complete sentence on the cluster map.

2. **Use of meaningful sketches.** Visual clues are needed with ELLs at all levels and particularly with beginners. Draw meaningful sketches on the cluster map to accompany phrases and sentences.

3. **Color coding.** Identify similar ideas and code them by marking each group of like ideas with a different color. This initiates the process of grouping sentences into paragraphs and foreshadows the use of a tree map graphic organizer.

4. **Movable text clippings.** Consider writing student comments on sticky notes or on separate cut squares of paper. Then place the clippings on the cluster map. This strategy facilitates grouping ideas and transferring them to a tree map. For students who are not writing as yet, movable text clippings allows them to manipulate text into meaningful categories.

Tree maps. The tree map works in consort with the cluster map. The cluster map is used to collect and record random ideas, while the tree map transfers those same ideas to organized categories.

Basic Tree Map Design

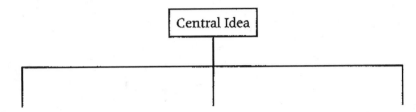

There are two ways to transfer ideas from the cluster map to the tree map. The first way uses the color-coding technique from the cluster map above. Each branch of the tree map corresponds to a color. Students copy the words on the branches according to color and then name the category. An alternative is to use the movable text clippings and simply have students pull them from the cluster map and arrange them in order on the branches of the tree map.

Once the tree map is completed, students can use it in a variety of ways. If the students are writing a single sentence, they can choose from a variety of phrases and sentences arranged on the tree. If they are writing a single paragraph, they can sample a sentence from each of the branches. If they are writing multiple paragraphs, they decide on the order of the branches and use a branch for the content of each paragraph.

Tip for Parent Involvement

Teach parents about the use of semantic maps. Even parents with limited levels of literacy can help their children organize their writing using simple maps. Teach them to expect the child to use a random cluster first, and then follow with a tree map before beginning to write in paragraph form.

Making collaborative big books. Making big books is a whole class project. There are five steps to the process.

Preparation

1. Materials: felt-tipped markers, chart paper, scissors, pencils, crayons or colored pencils, masking tape for binding.
2. Divide the class into pairs. Each pair will get one page of the big book, so you can figure the number of pages you will need according to the number of pairs, plus a cover page and a back page. (More elaborate big books will include a table of contents and authors' page.)
3. Crease chart paper in half. The number of the sheets is based on the number of pairs of students in your class (see #2 above). The folded sheet is a double-sided page. The folded edge is on the outside of the book; the open end is to be taped on the inside, or binding side, of the book.

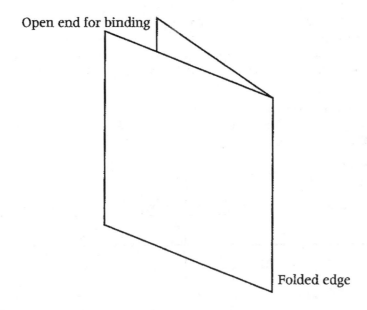

Open end for binding

Folded edge

Prewriting/Arranging

1. Establish a theme to write about. I recommend making a big book about a shared experience such as a recent field trip to the zoo, or a musical concert the class attended.
2. Ask each student to think of a sentence about the shared experience.
3. The teacher records each sentence on a sheet of chart paper for all to see. Avoid repeated ideas. Each sentence should be unique.
4. As a class, decide the order of the sentences from first to last. Number the sentences according to the order established by the students.
5. Slice sentences off of the chart. Use scissors to cut out each numbered sentence.
6. Ask students to sit with their partners.

Drafting/Illustrating

1. Paired students sit side by side. Give each pair of students a sheet of folded chart paper and two sequential sentence strips. Partner group A would get the first and second sentences, partner group B would get the third and fourth sentences, and so forth.
2. Depending on their writing ability, ask the students either to glue the sentence strip or copy it on their side of the folded sheet of paper.
3. Each student then illustrates their side of the paper.

Editing/Proofing

1. Students are responsible for checking their partner's page for accuracy, by comparing the writing against the original sentence strip.
2. The teacher double-checks each page.
3. Once both sides of the sheet are proofed, students may sign their work.
4. Ask students who have finished early to design and illustrate a book cover.

Binding

1. Binding the big book is a two-step process using masking tape. Order the book pages with the folded edges facing out and the open ends on the inside. Open the book as if it were bound and run a line of tape down the middle to bind sequential pages. The book will begin to look like a large accordion as the open, inside edges are taped together.
2. When all inside edges are taped together, close the book. Wrap masking tape around the edges to seal and hold the book together.

Publishing

1. Read the bound book to the whole class.
2. Keep the book on display for self-selected reading.
3. Keep it as a record of shared class experiences.
4. Check with the school librarian about making a section for classroom big books that can be checked out.

Tip for Parent Involvement

Ask parent to listen as their child reads a self-publisher book. Have parents ask the child to read individually to each member of the family to develop fluency and to motivate the child to be an author.

Triante poetry writing with beginners. Poetry writing is a way to express a personal experience, idea, or response to literature. With beginning-level students who speak using one- or two-word utterances, it is useful to provide a simple way to combine words to write a poem. A triante poem format is a triangular-shaped poem that is ideal for this purpose because students collaboratively compose a meaningful cascade of words that do not require attention to conventions of grammar and punctuation.

The writing process requires two scaffold techniques: use of a word bank and transferring selected words to a triante poetry frame. The process can be conducted as a group and then repeated for individual writing.

Prewriting

1. Begin with an experience such as a walk in a garden or selected place around the school.
2. As the students walk, make observations of what you encounter according to the senses of smell, sound, sight, and touch. Use taste only if the experience involves eating.
3. Create a word bank chart to list the words the students come up with under the appropriate sense category.

Triante Poem Word Bank (sample)

Smell	Sound	Sight	Touch
sweet	crackles	huge	fuzzy
like flowers	snaps	bright	soft
spice	whirring	blue	prickly
	hum	clear	smooth
			delicate

Drafting/Revision/Editing

1. Create a triante poem frame to guide drafting, revision, and editing of the poem.

Triante Poem Frame

_____
(Title)

_____ _____
(Smell: 2 words)

_____ _____ _____
(Sound: 3 words)

_____ _____ _____ _____
(Sight: 4 words)

_____ _____ _____ _____ _____
(Touch: 5 words)

2. Using the words that were recorded on the word bank chart, discuss which words should be transferred to the triante poem frame. Discuss selection, order of placement, and spelling and capitalization of each word for the poem. A sample triante poem follows.

Flower

Sweet spice

Hum crackle snaps

Clear blue bright huge

Delicate smooth soft fuzzy prickly

3. Once the words are written on the chart, students may either copy the poem or use the word bank to create their own individual triante poems.

Publish

1. Ask students to rewrite the chart without the drawn lines and word directives. Illustrate the large chart and display on a wall. Have all participants sign the poem.
2. Rewrite individual poems on colorful stationery, and display them on a bulletin board or bind them as a book of poems to make available in the classroom library or school library.

Tip for Parent Involvement

Ask parents to have the child rewrite the poem on stationery. Mail the poem to another member of the family to increase the audience for the published work.

Use this idea for any kind of shape poem, such as a diamond, circle, or hour-glass shape. The possibilities are endless. Each shape can use the same word bank configuration.

Interactive Writing Activities for Beginners

Interactive writing is defined here as writing between a novice and a more experienced writer. The interaction between the two writers creates a zone of proximal development which functions to mediate the development of writing proficiency. Moll (1997) refers to it as a literate and mediated relationship. The following activities are useful at each level of proficiency, but specific adaptive techniques are suggested in order to match the task to the ability level of the beginning English Language Learner.

Interactive journal writing. Interactive journal writing is a way to establish an instructional dialog in written form, with the more experienced writer modeling the language for the novice. The novice writer establishes the theme or content of the writing and the experienced writer models conventions of grammar, punctuation, and spelling. Just as reading with a child fosters fluency and comprehension, journal writing with a novice writer fosters fluency with written expression.

In terms of the writing process, journal writing is not intended to reach the publishing stage; therefore the focus is the initial draft in the journal. Revision and editing stages may not necessarily play a part in the process.

Preparation

1. Provide for each student a notebook, composition book, or a self-made journal with lined and unlined paper for writing and drawing.
2. Plan a time each day to write in journals. I suggest that students journal at the beginning of an instructional period, for example while attendance is being taken and homework collected, or after a recess so that the students know exactly what to do the moment they enter the classroom.
3. Allow ten to fifteen minutes for the journal writing time.
4. Display a sign with directions for journal writing:

Journal Writing

1. What to write about? Write about an event, experience, idea, or response to literature.
2. Spelling questions? Try your best guess; circle the word.
3. Don't know the word? Draw a picture.
4. Read your writing aloud to yourself, then read it to a partner or an adult before bringing it to the teacher.

Responding to Journals

1. Once students have taken time to write in their journals, the teacher or more experienced students respond in writing.
2. Respond to the content written in the journal. Avoid writing bland statement such as "nice writing." If the student writes "I like ice cream," respond with comments such as "I like ice cream too. My favorite flavor of ice cream is strawberry. What is your favorite?" Four techniques are at play here. First, maintain the same content in the response; second, write using many of the same words to model conventions; third, extend the theme with more details; and fourth, ask a question to evoke further written responses.

Managing Journal Writing

1. To avoid drowning in journal writing, don't respond to all journals every day. Consider the following suggestions:

- If you have no helpers, ask students to write in journals for two or more days before you respond to them. Another approach is for students to write Mondays and Wednesdays, to give you two days to respond.
- If you have parent volunteers, involve them in journal writing.

- If you have cross-age tutors, train them to write to your students.
- If you have students who are more experienced writers, designate them as respondents. Give respondents special pens to designate their role. Five respondents can easily write with four other students each to address 20 students total.

2. Organize the class according to a weekly journal-responding calendar. Divide up the class into four groups according to the days of the week. On Monday the teacher responds to group 1, on Tuesday to group 2, and so forth. Leave Fridays open to catch up on students who were absent during the week.

3. Color-code the journals for the day of the week you respond to: for example, red journals on Mondays, blue on Tuesdays, green on Wednesdays, and purple on Thursdays. This facilitates collecting and returning journals. Designate a student from each color group to collect and distribute the completed journals. Store the journals in colored baskets that match their color group.

Lap board model writing. Some essential tools for modeling interactive writing are a small white board with a dry erase marker and eraser, and white correctional tape. Use these tools when developing charts with students.

Procedure

1. When writing a chart story or filling in a word bank, invite the students to write the words. To help the student write conventionally, hold a white board up and ask the other students watching how to spell the key words. Model conventional spelling in dialog with the students. Point out the features of the word as you write it on the board.

2. If the student makes a mistake while writing on a chart in front of the class, provide white correctional tape. Allow the student to cover the misspelling and rewrite the correct word over the taped section.

Individual Writing Activities for Beginners

Individual writing opportunities are limited for beginning-level students. In order for these students to write individually, they must be given the opportunity to visually represent their ideas in a nonverbal way with pictures, such as pictorial journals and personal illustrated books.

Pictorial journals for individual expression. A pictorial journal is a collage of drawings and pasted pictures that represent the weekly events, experiences, and thoughts in a child's life. But it is more than pictures; with assistance, words are also incorporated to facilitate individual writing.

Preparation

1. Provide each student with a three-ring, loose-leaf binder.
2. Collect pictures cut from periodicals. Store and maintain the picture collection in a box.
3. Supply each student with a three-hole-punched piece of paper with a large space for pictures and lines for writing at the bottom of the page. Date the page for the current week.
4. Provide colored pencils or crayons for drawing and glue for pasting.
5. Develop and maintain a bulletin board with high-frequency words to assist in sentence building.

Procedure

1. Schedule time every other day to draw or select pictures from the picture box that represent the student's experience, allowing a day for glue to dry before the picture is placed in a binder.
2. While students are selecting, gluing, and drawing pictures, move from student to student. Ask them, what is in the picture? Label the pictures or drawings with the appropriate names.

3. The next day that pictorial journals are worked on, ask students to use the labeled words to write about the collage they have created.
4. Encourage students to use the high-frequency words on the bulletin board word wall to put together the picture words into complete sentences.
5. Completed pages are placed in the loose-leaf binder. Over time, the pictorial journal will give evidence of writing growth.

Tip for Parent Involvement

Make parents active participants in journal writing on a weekly basis. Encourage them to write their comments in the child's journal. In the case that the parent is illiterate, ask an older sibling to write what the parent dictates and read the entry aloud to the parent.

Making personal illustrated books. Fundamental to writing a story is to sequence story events. For the beginning-level student who may not be able to write more than a few words, making personal illustrated books is a first step in crossing the bridge from solely producing oral language to using print. Drawing story events is the key to making a personal illustrated book. The following directions show how to assist beginning ELLs in making personal illustrated books.

1. Provide the student with a story board frame.

Title _____ Author and Illustrator _____ Date _____	(1)	(2)	(3)
(4)	(5)	(6)	(7)

2. Demonstrate how to draw a sequence of events to tell a story. Use a familiar storybook as a model.
3. Ask the students to draw their own stories in sequence. Suggest that they illustrate a story from their own lives. Encourage them to interview their parents or other family members about an important event in their family's experience.
4. When the storyboard is complete, help the student formulate a title. They write their own name in as author/illustrator. Date the storyboard on the title page.
5. Use scissors to cut the storyboard into individual frames.
6. Collate the pieces into sequential order with the title page on top.
7. Staple at the end to bind the book.

Students can use the book to talk about a significant experience in their lives. An adult or cross-age tutor can write the words on the book pages to give the students practice in reading about themselves. The storyboard format also prepares students for organizing writing and presentations using software such as PowerPoint.

EARLY INTERMEDIATE AND INTERMEDIATE LEVEL

Students at early intermediate and intermediate levels of proficiency are able to write simple sentences and paragraphs. Even though they are able to address conventions of grammar, spelling, and punctuation, students at this level require extensive scaffolding with word banks, writing frames, and graphic organizers. While collaborative, interactive, and individual writing employ all of these kinds of scaffolds, the way they are applied varies with the purpose of the writing project.

Collaborative Writing Activities for Early Intermediate and Intermediate Levels

Collaborative poetry writing. This section addresses three forms of poetry writing that are appropriate for students at the early intermediate and intermediate levels of proficiency: haiku, cinquain, and biopoems. As with the triante poem, there are two components: the word bank and the poetry frame. The design of the word bank and frame is dictated by the specific poetry form, but the writing process for each is essentially the same.

Haiku. Haiku is a Japanese poetry form. There are no hard and fast rules regarding this simplified, children's version of haiku, but it does have several unique features. In Japanese, it is a seventeen-character poetry form, while in English it is a seventeen-syllable form. The syllables generally are arranged in three lines, consisting of five, seven, and five syllables, respectively. The theme is usually nature, but can deal with other areas. Haiku often finishes with a comical or ironic ending.

Prewriting

1. Begin by practicing forming phrases with five or seven syllables.
2. Create an experience such as a nature walk.
3. As the students walk, make observations of what you encounter according to the senses. They are to think about how to express their sensations in five-or seven-syllable phrases.
4. Create a word bank chart in a T-table format to list their phrases (see sample below).

Haiku Poem Word Bank (sample)

5 Syllables	7 Syllables
the lotus flower	floating by the river bank
it smells like perfume	soft and delicate petals
frogs like to see them	decorating the water
bouncing with ripples	bugs are crawling around them
touching the surface	growing in pools of delight
wanting a bouquet	

Drafting/Revision/Editing

1. Create a haiku poetry frame to guide drafting, revision, and editing of the poem as a group:

_____
(5 syllables)

_____
(7 syllables)

_____
(5 syllables)

2. Using the words that were recorded on the word bank chart, discuss which words should be transferred to the poetry frame. Discuss selection, order of placement, and spelling and capitalization of each word for the poem. Write the resulting haiku in the poetry frame, for example:

the lotus flower

decorating the water

wanting a bouquet

3. Once the poem is written, students may either copy it or use the word bank to create their own individual haiku poems.

Publish

1. Ask students to rewrite the chart poem without the drawn lines and word directives. Illustrate the large chart and display on a wall. Have all participants sign the poem.
2. Rewrite individual poems on colorful stationery, display on a bulletin board, or bind as a book of poems to make available in the classroom library or in the school library.

Cinquain. Cinquain comes from the French work cinq, meaning "five." It is a five-line poem that utilizes the same format of a word bank and a frame. In this case, the word bank requires words that are adjectives, verbs, and adverbs. This presents a contextual way to teach parts of speech.

Cinquain Word Bank

Describing Words (Adjectives)	Action Words (Verbs)	Words Feeling (Adverbs)

Cinquain Poetry Frame

(Title)
(3 describing words—adjectives)
(3 action words—verbs)
(3 feeling words—adverbs)
(Refers to title)

Biopoems. Biopoems are a poetic way to describe one's self. The word bank is slightly more complex, but the process is the same. An alternate way to use a biopoem is to apply the format to a character study as literary response and analysis. This only works well if the character being studied is very rich and there is information about parentage and aspirations.

Biopoem Word Bank

Descriptors	Lover of . . .	Who feels . . .	Who needs . . .	Would like to see . . .

Biopoem Frame

First Name _____

4 words that tell about you (or a story character)

_____ _____ _____ _____

Child of _____

Lover of (3 things) _____ _____ _____

Who feels (3 feelings) _____ _____ _____

Who needs (3 ideas) _____ _____ _____

Who would like to see (3 things) _____ _____ _____

Resident of _____

Last Name _____

Collaborative songwriting. The combination of melody, rhythm, and verse appear to make sense to people with a certain ability in music, but to many, song writing is a mysterious process. There is a simple way to involve children collaboratively in writing songs. If you borrow a familiar tune, you no longer need to compose melody and rhythm. What is left to do is manipulate the text so that it fits the melody. This is done by the same format of using an appropriately designed word bank and a song frame. With songs, the word bank and song frame are designed to accommodate the syllable count of each line of the song. It operates just the same way as the haiku poem word bank and frame.

The following songwriting activities use four familiar melodies with accompanying word banks and song frames. The writing process is essentially the same as the poetry sequence described above. The familiar melodies are "Are You Sleeping," "London Bridge," "Twinkle, Twinkle Little Star," and a blues favorite by Jimmy Reed, "You Got Me Up, You Got Me Down." I will describe the writing process for "Are You Sleeping" and then list the other word bank and song frames.

Prewriting

1. Practice forming phrases with four, three, and six counts.
2. Refer to a theme or an experience such as a story, or shared experience such as a field trip.
3. Elicit phrases from students in either four, three, or six syllables.
4. Create a word bank chart to list their phrases as either four, three, or six syllable counts. Note that the order of the chart matches the order of the song frame with the first line of the song being four syllables.

"Are You Sleeping" Word Bank

4 Syllables	*3 Syllables*	*6 Syllables*

Drafting/Revision/Editing

1. Compose a song using a frame to guide drafting, revision, and editing of the lyrics as a group.

"Are you Sleeping" Song Frame

_____
(Title)

_____
(4 syllables)

_____
(4 syllables)

_____
(3 syllables)

_____
(3 syllables)

_____
(6 syllables)

_____
(6 syllables)

_____
(3 syllables)

_____
(3 syllables)

2. Using the words that were recorded on the word bank chart, discuss which words should be transferred to the song frame. Discuss selection, order of placement, and spelling and capitalization of each word for the song.
3. Once the words are written on the song frame, students may either copy the lyrics or use the word bank to create their own individual songs.

Publish

1. Ask students to rewrite the chart song without the drawn lines and word directives. Illustrate the large chart and display on a wall. Have all participants sign the song.
2. Rewrite individual songs on colorful stationery, display on a bulletin board, or bind as a song book to make available in the classroom library or in the school library.
3. Sing the songs together as a class. A song such as "Are You Sleeping" can be sung as a round.

Other Collaborative Song Word Banks and Frames

"Twinkle, Twinkle Little Star" Word Bank

4 Syllables	*3 Syllables*

"Twinkle, Twinkle Little Star" Song Frame

_____
(Title)

_____
(4 syllables)

_____
(3 syllables)

_____
(4 syllables)

_____
(3 syllables)

_____
(4 syllables)

_____
(3 syllables)

_____
(4 syllables)

_____
(3 syllables)

_____
(4 syllables)

_____
(3 syllables)

_____
(4 syllables)

_____
(3 syllables)

"London Bridge" Word Bank

4 Syllables	3 Syllables	6 Syllables

"London Bridge" Song Frame

_____
(Title)

_____
(4 syllables)

_____
(3 syllables)

_____
(3 syllables)

_____
(3 syllables)

_____
(4 syllables)

_____
(3 syllables)

_____
(2 syllables)

_____
(2 syllables)

"You Got Me Up, You Got Me Down" Blues Word Bank

4 Syllables	3 Syllables	2 Syllables	6 Syllables	9 Syllables

"You Got Me Up, You Got Me Down" Song Frame

_____
(Title)

_____
(4 syllables)

_____
(4 syllables)

_____
(3 syllables)

_____
(2 syllables)

_____
(2 syllables)

_____
(6 syllables)

_____
(3 syllables)

_____
(3 syllables)

_____
(9 syllables)

_____
(9 syllables)

Interactive Writing Activities for Early Intermediate and Intermediate Levels

Writing interactively at the early intermediate and intermediate levels includes longer passages and can also involve family members and pen pals. Family journal writing is a five-day cycle of writing that establishes a routine for developing individual writing. Pen pals is not a new idea, but the organization and delivery techniques may prove helpful.

Tip for Parent Involvement

Use the following activity as a means to create a family treasure. Use a large composition book with more than 100 pages to maintain the family journal throughout the entire school year. The child and the parents will cherish this journal for years.

Interactive family journal writing. Inviting the family to participate in journal writing recognizes that literacy begins at home. In some cases the parents may not be able to participate due to low literacy levels in the home language. In that case, the student is encouraged to invite another adult or an older sibling to participate. The graphic organizer techniques used in this activity are described earlier in the chapter.

The following is a five-day journal writing cycle that involves family members. At the beginning of the school year, the teacher will want to model each step explicitly. Once the routine is established, the activity will operate virtually automatically as a regular part of the classroom work.

Our family participated in such a cycle with a journal in Spanish. Here is our daughter Kathryn's third-grade journal.

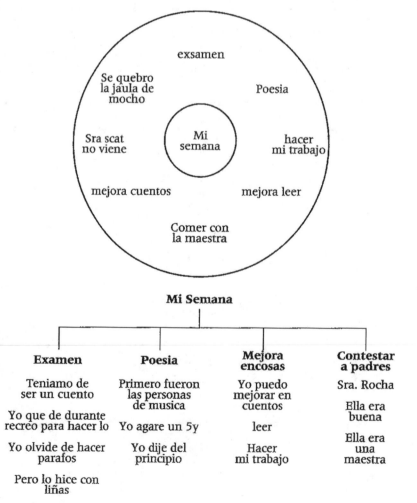

Five-Day Family Journal Writing Cycle

Day 1: On the first page of the journal, make a circle map to brainstorm journal-entry ideas.

Day 2: Transfer the random ideas on the circle map to a simple tree map.

Day 3: Write one or more paragraphs based on the tree map.

Day 4: Take home to read it to an adult. The adult writes a response and poses a question.

Day 5: The child responds to the adult's question. Teacher reads the week's journal entries and posts a comment with a sticky note.

12/2/01
fecha

Querida Mama:

Mi semana era buena. Mi mejor susituta era Sra. Rocha. Ella era mi susituta mas favorito porque, era una buena susituta hablaba español y porque ella era una maestra. Si guste el libro.

Teniamos un exsamen. Teniamos que hacer un cuento. Yo hice de cuando ayude a Corrine en el reporte. Yo no sabia para escribir y quede para recreo y agare una idea. Cuando estaba escridiendo olvide de hacer parafo pero lo ise con liñas.

Isimo la poesa diferente esta semana. Las personas que tenian clase de musica fueron primeros y las personas que no fuero depues. Si dices toda la poema del principio agaras una ☆ y el otro numero que agarastes. Yo agare un 5 y ☆. Lo dije el principio.

Ahora voy a dicir de las cosas que puedo mejoran en, como contar cuentos mejor. Recordar de hacer parafos. Leer y entender que estoy leendo. Algo muy importante es hacer mi trabajo y terminarlo.

Con cariño,
Kathryn

---

el 3 de diciembre 2001

Querida Kathryn,

Ayer me viste llorar. Lloraba porque estaba tratando de expresar mis sentimientos por la directora pre-escolar de Woods-Edgewater que está jubilandose. Tiene que jubilarse porque está muy enferma con cancer. No sabemos si va a vivir en algunos meses. Señorita Betty Woods era una mujer sumamente ejemplar. Ayudaba a muchos niños y sus padres. Dime algo,

☆¿Qué recuerdos tienes de Señorita Betty?

☆¿Qué aprendiste de ella?

Con mucho cariño,
Daddy

Interactive writing with pen pals. Pen pals are pairs of students who commit to corresponding with each other. Two primary considerations dictate the management of pen pals. Are the pen pals local at the school site? Or are they separated by a considerable distance? With pen pals at the same school site, a correspondence center can be created and maintained to facilitate the writing and distribution of the letters. With distant pen pals, consider establishing an "email pals" system.

Local school-site pen pals are easy to set up and maintain.

1. Make a connection with another class at your school that would be willing to participate in a pen pals project.
2. Make a mailbag. Decorate a canvas, two-handle bag with the name of the school and the words "Mail Carrier for Room # __" (Fill in your classroom's room number).
   Designate a classroom "Mail Carrier(s)" to deliver mail daily or every other day. Hang the mailbag by the door of the classroom for easy access.
3. Create a correspondence center: a small portable file box labeled "Correspondence Center" that can be easily stored on a shelf when not in use. Place the following items in the file box:
   • File folders labeled with the students' names, one on each folder
   • A materials folder with stationery and envelopes
   • A cup with pens
   • A laminated card with letter-writing format on one side and mailing directions on the other side
   • A laminated map of the school with room numbers noted
4. On the front of the laminated card, display a standard "friendly" letter-writing format as follows:

(YOUR FULL NAME)

(Classroom Address)

(DATE)
(GREETING) Dear_____
(BODY OF THE LETTER)

_____
_____
_____
_____

(CLOSING) Sincerely
(SIGNATURE)

On the opposite side of the laminated card, outline the pen pal procedure and guidelines.
• Write a friendly letter to your designated pen pal
• Before putting your letter in an envelope, check to make sure you have each component of the letter in place. Did you write your name and classroom address?
• Write your pen pal's name and the classroom number on the front of the envelope.
• Place the letter in the mailbag for the next delivery.

Email pal sites allow students to correspond with students around the world. Setting up email pals is safe and easy with Web-based connection sites. Basically, a Web-based connection site provides the conduit for sending email, matches students according to profiles, and allows correspondents to select the language for writing. One consideration with using a Web-based connection site is that it comes with a nominal price. The following are two Web-based connection sites.

www.epals.com ePALS Classroom Exchange is designed to work with school programs. It offers teachers and students a world-wide, safe, monitored, multilingual email pal system.

A unique feature of the site is that it is developed in compliance with "No Child Left Behind" (NCLB) federal guidelines. Compliance includes parent involvement, seamless education K-16, teacher projects, and Internet safety tips. The program, established in 1976, has safely operated with child participation for almost 30 years. Furthermore, the site is easy to navigate.

www.world-pen-pals.com World Pen Pals is not exclusively for school programs. Originally developed for traditional correspondence over fifty years ago, it offers multiple language correspondence with a secure, monitored system. Picture exchanges are only permitted with participants who are eighteen and older.

Individual Writing Activities for Early Intermediate and Intermediate Levels

Virtually any form of writing can be produced on an individual basis. Although early intermediate and intermediate ELLs are limited in what they can do individually, they can engage in a wide range of writing activities if given scaffolded writing frames. Two activities that are appropriate for this level are double-entry journals and expository writing frames.

Double-entry journals. Double-entry journals are designed to reference reflections, to tie one's reflections to a specific idea or passage in a book. Double-entry journals are composed of a two-column page. In the left column, the writer notes a reference statement. The reference statement could be a title for an idea, a label of a thought, or a citation from a book. In the right column, the writer expands on the idea or reference with a reflective comment.

Double-entry journals are particularly useful for literary response. Students can reference a specific character trait, event, or thought and then write about their perceptions and understandings of the passage. The practice of noting references and citations and then writing a reflective comment is a valuable skill for exploring and recalling one's ideas. It also is a contextual way to teach students note-taking strategies. Below is a format for double-entry journals.

Double-Entry Journal

Name _____	Date _____
Reading Selection _____	No. of Pages _____
References/Citations	**Reflections**

Expository writing frame. Expository writing is standard practice for academic writing. Students need to be proficient in the format to organize topical writing. Intermediate students writing about topics in content areas will benefit from the use of a writing frame for a standard five-paragraph expository essay.

The standard five-paragraph essay employs specific features including a topic sentence highlighting the main points of the essay, transitional sentences leading the reader from one idea to the next, and a conclusion summarizing the ideas discussed in the body of the essay. Below is a frame that can be used to help students organize their expository writing.

Expository Writing Frame

Paragraph #1	Topic sentence: Idea A: Idea B: Idea C:

Paragraph #2	Expand idea A: Transition sentence:

Paragraph #3	Expand idea B: Transition sentence:

Paragraph #4	Expand idea C: Transition sentence:

Paragraph #5	Conclusion (summarize ideas A, B, & C):

EARLY ADVANCED AND ADVANCED LEVEL

Writing at the early advanced and advanced levels incorporates a full range of writing activities. Students at this level write at grade level and often above grade level proficiency due to the fact that they have intentionally and explicitly developed English to a high degree. They also have the advantage of drawing on their own linguistic and cultural diversity which gives them a more complex understanding of their words and their world.

What distinguishes an advanced ELL writer from a native English writer is that there will still be the occasional gap in use of the language that needs to be taught explicitly. Some of the gaps a teacher can anticipate are new vocabulary in specific content areas and/or changes in literary style such as the shift from expository to persuasive writing. This does not limit early advanced or advanced students' writing capacity. What it means is that the teacher needs to be vigilant for the gaps and prepared to address them. When introducing a new concept, the discipline-specific vocabulary must be taught first. Checking for prior knowledge before teaching a new writing style by asking students to paraphrase concepts in their own words is a way to anticipate needed instruction.

Activities for students at advanced levels include refining the use of language, larger writing projects, and more complex forms of writing. Collaborative activities include developing metaphorical thinking with similes in a song, and team writing in which students work on larger projects such as edited collections or newsletters. Interactive writing still includes using journals in formats discussed previously, but students can engage in asynchronous dialog on on-line discussion boards. Individual writing projects increase in complexity and demand that the student offer a critique, state an opinion, or persuade an audience.

Collaborative Writing Activities for Early Advanced and Advanced Levels

Singing similes. "Mr. MacGregor's Garden" is a song I wrote for a group of students to play with the use of simile. The words are easy and the song creates a frame for metaphorical thinking.

Procedure: Sing through the song as a group. Sing through the chorus, "Mr. MacGregor had a very funny garden . . .", a second time. When you get to the verse, "And he grew . . .", call on students to insert fruits or vegetables and state what the color or texture is. Then ask them to make a metaphorical comparison or simile.

Once the group gets the feel for the song, get imaginative. See what ideas and similes the group can come up with that one would not expect to find in a garden. For example, "And he grew <u>snow tires, spiked, snow tires. Snow tires</u> as <u>spiked</u> as <u>a porcupine</u>. . . ."

Mr. MacGregor's Garden

by Dr.BB

Mr. MacGregor had a very funny garden,

a very funny garden,

a very funny garden,

Mr. MacGregor had a very funny garden,

and he worked in it all day long.

And he grew <u>lettuce, green lettuce</u>

<u>Lettuce</u> as <u>green</u> as <u>fresh cut grass</u>

And he grew <u>tomatoes, red tomatoes</u>

<u>Tomatoes</u> as <u>red</u> as <u>a fire truck.</u>

And he grew <u>(fruit or vegetable)</u> , <u>(color or texture)</u> <u>(fruit or vegetable)</u> <u>(fruit or vegetable)</u> as <u>(color or texture)</u> as <u>(simile)</u>

And he grew <u>(fruit or vegetable)</u> , <u>(color or texture)</u> <u>(fruit or vegetable)</u> <u>(fruit or vegetable)</u> as <u>(color or texture)</u> as <u>(simile)</u>

Team writing with larger projects. Team writing projects are for larger works. They can take various forms such as edited collections of writing, newsletters, or content area group reports. They also may be used for media-based productions such as a video-magazine program.

With the team concept, there are several shifts to note in terms of roles and the writing process. First of all, the role of the teacher shifts from the source of information and assignments to that of publisher. The publisher outlines general guidelines, and reviews, monitors, and evaluates the work. The students assume more autonomy with regard to writing assignments, working like an editorial board. As a team, students develop their own projects within the guidelines established by the teacher. They must develop an initial concept and present it in the form of a proposal. They also monitor and edit their own work. This approach expands the writing process, adding a proposal development component within the prewriting stage.

Although the final, written products will vary greatly, the writing team roles remain constant from project to project: the teacher is executive editor, and students take on roles of managing editor, design and layout editor, copy editor, or contributing writer. All team members share in the work as copy editors and contributing writers. This ensures that each student is held responsible to attend to writing conventions and to produce a written piece. No one is allowed to avoid writing and editing text with this rule in place. Each member's role is described in Table 15.2 within the framework of the team.

Even though each team member has one or more specific roles in the writing process, all members are evaluated. Evaluation of the students' writing takes place on two levels: the quality of the whole project, and the individual contributions of each team member. The evaluation is discussed below in the procedure for the Team Writing Process.

Table 15.2 Team Writing Roles and Responsibilities

Roles	Responsibilities
Teacher: Publisher	• Teach team project writing process • Outline writing and publishing guidelines • Assign or recruit managing editors • Consult on and evaluate project proposals • Monitor team writing process • Acquire equipment and materials • Evaluate individual contributions • Evaluate final project
Managing editor(s)	• Act as liaison to the teacher • Recruit team members • Chair team writing meetings • Lead initial concept and proposal development • Ensure consistent project focus • Authorize inclusion of submissions • Handle requests for materials • Write the introduction of the project • Copy editor • Contributing writer
Design and layout editor(s)	• Computer input and organization of writing selections • Merge document files of individual submissions into larger project • Ensure consistent layout of font and formats • Select and edit cover art • Select and edit graphics (clip art, cartoons, icons, maps, illustrations) • Copy editor • Contributing writer
Copy editor(s) **(All team members)**	• Review drafts of writing for conventions of spelling, grammar, and punctuation • Review writing to ensure that the themes and content are consistent with the focus of the larger work • Ensure consistent writing style • Copy editor • Contributing writer
Contributing writers **(All team members)**	• Get a writing assignment from managing editor • Draft writing consistent with the proposal guidelines • Revise drafts • Submit writing as a word-processed document • Copy editor for another contributing writer

Team Writing Proces

Prewriting

1. Guidelines for writing and publishing may vary according to the specific project. The teacher presents guidelines in accordance with content standards and genre. (See rubric language guidelines below in the assessment section.)
2. Writing team recruitment and development should be done initially by the teacher. Once the students understand the process, they can take initiative and form their own teams. The teacher may want to consider guidelines for gender equity, for example, that each team must be made up of equal numbers of boys and girls. Once teams are formed, members decide which roles they will assume.
3. Proposal development requires the use of a Team Writing Proposal Form (see sample). The students decide on a working title, assign themselves to editorial roles, briefly describe the project idea, and present an outline with assigned authors, a calendar for the process, and a list of resources and materials needed.
4. Proposal review is conducted by the teacher. In the right-hand column of the Team Writing Proposal Form, there is a place for inserting comments and providing approval for each part of the project. This is where the teacher monitors who is doing what task and the feasibility of the project. The teacher also verifies if the project meets the established guidelines. Before a project can be started, each component of the proposal must obtain prior approval.
5. Proposal revision and resubmission for review may be required. This is a recursive process. A team may need to rework all or part of a proposal and resubmit it for review. Attention to details and the anticipation of problems at this point can save a writing team hours of work.

Draft

1. An editorial board meeting of the entire team is convened by the managing editor once the proposal is approved. The purpose of the meeting is to review the proposal and publisher comments and to distribute writing assignments and set deadlines for first drafts.
2. Each member of the writing team contributes a piece to be included in the project. Specific guidelines about content and length are clarified at the editorial board meeting.

Revise

1. The editorial board meets again to check writing progress. Agenda items for the meeting may include problems encountered with the original assignments, formatting considerations and fonts, and artwork and graphics to include. Check source material and citations.
2. Each writer shares work and listens to the comments of the group. Changes are suggested and the next deadline for the writing is established.
3. The team provides the managing editor with essential content for writing the introduction to the project.

Edit

1. The editorial board meets for the purpose of reviewing revised drafts for conventions of spelling, grammar, and punctuation.
2. Each member of the team functions as a copy editor at this stage. It is recommended that they all review the writing of each group member so that it gets a maximum number of reviews.
3. Check for placement of graphics and edit cover art.

Team Writing Proposal Form

Project Working Title	Publisher's Comments
	Approved? Y/N
Team Members Managing Editor(s): Design and Layout Editor(s): Copy Editor(s): Contributing Editor(s):	Approved? Y/N
Brief Description of the Project (*What's the big idea?*)	Approved? Y/N
Proposed Outline (*List headings and name each author*) I. II. III. IV. V.	Approved? Y/N

Writing Process Calendar	*Deadlines*	
Initial drafts	Due date:	
Revised drafts	Due date:	
Computer design/layout	Due date:	
Final revisions	Due date:	
Submit as published	Due date:	Approved? Y/N

Resources and Materials Needed		
•	•	
•	•	
•	•	Approved? Y/N

Publish

1. Format each file with the same fonts and styles.
2. Merge each document file into the one file.
3. Insert graphics and apply cover art.
4. Print out hard copies of the work.
5. Compile, bind, and present to the class for display.

Evaluation

1. Individual contributions are evaluated by a self-evaluation and a rubric evaluation of the writing. The self-evaluation is written by each team member describing what was written and

Self-Evaluation of Team Writing

Your Name:	**Date:**
Project Title:	

Role: ____ Managing Editor ____ Design and Layout Editor____ Copy Editor ____ Contributing Writer

What was your strongest contribution?

In what area did you need the most help?

What was the best part of the project?

How would you do the project differently?

other group responsibilities (see sample form). Rubric assessment language is provided at the end of this chapter.

2. Entire project evaluation is done using a rubric that is established in the guidelines at the beginning of the process. Essentially the rubric evaluates the project as a whole for conventions and content. Each team member receives an individual and a group grade.

Interactive Writing Activities for Early Advanced and Advanced Levels

To increase the level of depth and complexity of interactive writing for early advanced and advanced English Language Learners, consider using asynchronous dialog on on-line discussion boards, also known in the vernacular as newsgroups.

Discussion boards. Discussion boards, or newsgroups, are a Web-based way to invite writing dialog about a particular subject. A teacher or group leader posts a message as a prompt. Participants respond directly to the prompt or to another participant's comments.

The string of messages related to a single prompt is called a thread. The term asynchronous dialog describes the way the threads are formed. They do not develop in a linear fashion. A contributor may make an initial comment in response to the prompt and then scroll through the other messages to find an interesting one to respond to.

Caution is advised here. Only engage in discussion boards with children if you have a closed on-line system. Closed on-line systems are course suites designed specifically for classroom use. The site is only available to instructors and students that have been enrolled in the course. A quick search of Web sites that offer discussion boards or newsgroups will tell you that open on-line systems have few safety controls built-in for child protection. A closed network for classroom use is supplied by Web sites such as www.coursecompass.com and www.blackboard.com.

Individual Writing Activities for Early Advanced and Advanced Levels

Early advanced and advanced ELLs should write in a wide range of genres. Numerous forms of writing have already been discussed in this chapter and ELLs at this level can participate in all of them to a greater degree of depth and complexity than those at earlier levels. One form of writing that requires multiple skills is persuasive writing.

Persuasive writing. Persuasive writing, done well, demands evidence and well-reasoned arguments. Building a persuasive writing piece can be a recursive process that calls the writer to revise initial assumptions. A writer begins with an initial opinion, but then sets about to find evidence to support the opinion. Sometimes, after examining the evidence, a writer will change his mind and then become compelled to revise the original opinion.

A "Persuasive Writing Builder" is a format that allows for a recursive process (see sample below). The builder is used in the prewriting stage of the writing process. The balance of the writing would follow a standard writing process format.

1. Write a question that calls for an opinion. Although not the only way to form a question, yes/no and either/or questions do force an opinion. Sample questions would be, "Is chocolate bad for you?" or "Is chocolate good or bad for you?"
2. State an initial opinion. The initial opinion, at this point, gives the writer a direction; it does not have to be fully developed.
3. Research the opinion. Cite the source for each piece of evidence. Note the following in the citation: Author (year), "Title of cited work." Page numbers. City, State: Publisher.
4. Formulate an argument from each piece of evidence. Use phrases such as: "According to . . ." or "Based on . . ." or "Recent studies show . . ."
5. Decide which argument is the strongest. In the "Argument" box, circle A for the strongest argument, B for the next strongest, and C for the least strong argument. This will determine the order of the paragraphs in the persuasive essay.
6. Evaluate your initial opinion. Based on the evidence and the arguments, did the initial opinion change?
7. If so, rewrite the opinion in the final box. If not, keep the initial opinion and begin drafting the persuasive writing piece. Consider revising the opinion to make it stronger.

Persuasive Writing Builder

Write a Yes/No or an Either/Or Question		
State Initial Opinion (What do you think?)		
Source: Evidence:	Argument:	Order: [A B C]
Source: Evidence:	Argument:	Order: [A B C]
Source: Evidence:	Argument:	Order: [A B C]
Evaluate: Did your initial opinion change? Yes? or No? (If yes, rewrite the opinion below.)		
Revised Opinion:		

WRITING ASSESSMENT ACROSS LEVELS OF PROFICIENCY

The purpose of assessment is to evaluate growth of what students know and are able to do, and to report progress to the student, the family, and the educational support community. Part and parcel with assessment is the need to make adjustments in the instruction to match the assessed strengths and needs of the students. Teachers build on identified strengths and address specific needs with instruction.

A number of assessment tools are useful for writing. Below the writing assessment tools are listed according to appropriateness for proficiency levels. At the beginning level, the chart rubrics and journal assessment logs will be useful tools because they record growth over time and involve the students in assessing their own writing from the outset. More complex rubrics and writing conference record sheets are more helpful for students as they begin to demonstrate longer paragraph writing at the intermediate and advanced levels. Each of the assessment tools is helpful for advanced students. At the end of this chapter you will find rubric language for developing rubrics across levels of proficiency and across selected genres of writing.

Writing Assessment	Beginning	Early Intermediate and Intermediate	Early Advanced and Advanced
Tools	• Chart rubric • Journal assessment log	(Same as prior level) • Line item rubrics • Writing conference record sheets	(Same as prior level) • Rubric partners • Self-generated rubrics

Writing Assessment Tools Appropriate for Beginning English Language Learners

Chart rubric. A chart rubric is a displayed rubric to inform and remind students of the level of writing that they are to attain. Chart rubrics can take essentially two forms. One form displays generic criteria for writing in rubric form. The chart functions like a checklist of the highest level of attainment and usually only addresses conventions.

In Your Writing, Did You . . . ?

- Indent all paragraphs
- Write complete sentences
- Use ending punctuation
- Spell all words correctly

A much more powerful way to use a chart rubric is to display writing exemplars at each level. The exemplars are actual children's writing samples, enlarged for easy viewing, that exhibit the criteria for each grading level. A grading level is commonly a four-point scale, with 4 representing the highest level and 1 representing the lowest level. The powerful element of this idea is that students will compare their work to the exemplar chart to make their own assessment. When students begin to assess their own work against exemplary work, they become self-directed in addressing their own needs.

How to develop an exemplars chart rubric. Selecting exemplars takes a certain amount of work ahead of time.

1. Meet with teachers at your grade level.
2. Ask each teacher to a bring a range of student writing samples to evaluate.
3. Separate the student writing samples into graded levels of 1 to 4.
4. As a norming process, come to consensus on what a paper will look like at each level.

5. Select an anchor paper for each level as an exemplar. Often the most difficult one to find is the level 4 paper without errors. If you cannot identify a level 4 paper, consider utilizing a paper from the next grade level up to challenge students to improve their writing.
6. Obtain written permission from the parents of the children to use their papers for exemplars. Specify that the papers will be used anonymously.
7. Photocopy each exemplar in large format for easy display and viewing.
8. Mount the exemplars on a large strip of butcher paper according to their graded level.

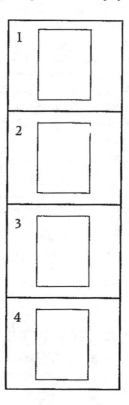

Journal assessment log. Once a month, ask students to write a journal entry for assessment purposes. Instead of writing the entry in the bound composition book or notebook, provide the students with a separate piece of paper which will be collected for assessment.

Use the journal assessment rubric (Table 15.3) to assess the journal writing for punctuation, structure, and grammar and syntax. It is recommended, due to the complex nature of the assessment, to check levels of developmental spelling twice during the school year. Note that content is not assessed in the journals due to the wide variety of topics and material that may be included in a journal.

Some classrooms have a bulletin board on which each student has a place to display the current month's evaluated journal entries. Over time, the journals will show growth and the display will be a way to communicate that growth to the student, family members, and the educational support community.

Writing Assessment Tools Appropriate for Early Intermediate and Intermediate English Language Learners

At the early-intermediate level and above, writing rubrics should address conventions of writing and the content of the writing, as well. Some rubric formats can be cumbersome to manage and difficult to use for assessment, but there is a simple way to address both conventions and content with line-item rubrics. Another assessment tool to use with students who are writing longer and more complex pieces is a writing conference log. The writing conference log records the essential information about a piece of writing and can be used for assessment data. Both tools are described below.

Table 15.3 Rubric for Journal Assessment

Journal Assessment	4	3	2	1
Punctuation (. , ? ! ; : ")	No errors, full usage of punctuation marks	Few errors, most punctuation evident	Many errors with some ending punctuation	Few to no punctuation marks used
Structure (Paragraphs and sentence)	Multiple, indented paragraphs with complete sentences	At least one indented paragraph with complete sentences	1 to 2 sentences, no indentation	Random words or letters with pictures
Grammar and Syntax • Noun/verb agreement • Preposition usage • Word order	No errors	Few errors	Many errors	No grammar or syntax evident
Spelling (See chapter 4 for an assessment)	Conventional	Transitional	Phonetic	Semiphonetic

Journal Assessment Log

Student Roster	Sept	Oct*	Nov	Dec	Jan	Feb	Mar*	Apr	May	June
1.										
2.										
3.										
4.										
5.										
6.										
7.										
8.										
9.										
10.										
11.										
12.										
13.										
14.										

(continued)

Journal Assessment Log (*continued*)

Student Roster	Sept	Oct*	Nov	Dec	Jan	Feb	Mar*	Apr	May	June
15.										
16.										
17.										
18.										
19.										
20.										

* In October and March check for levels of developmental spelling

Line-item rubrics. Think of the times that you have seen student writing that had some wonderful ideas, but was seriously flawed by errors of punctuation, grammar, or spelling. Conversely, think of the writing that appears to be flawless, but is missing the content or lacks any substance.

The way to address both conventions and content is to build what I call a line-item rubric. Line-item rubrics supply multiple criteria for evaluation. Below is a blank frame for a line-item rubric and then a sample rubric for poetry writing. The unique features of line-item rubrics are that criteria statements are listed according to writing conventions and content, a numeric value is provided for quantative data collection, and there is a space for comments and point totals.

The advantages of using this rubric format begin with the ease of developing an assessment tool that is specifically tailored to the needs of the student and the content demands of the genre. The teacher can reference appropriate statements from content standards as criteria. Further, scoring the

Line-Item Rubric Assessment

Assessment Criteria	Evaluation				
Conventions	4	3	2	1	**Points and Comments**
•					
•					
•					
•					
•					
Content	4	3	2	1	**Points and Comments**
•					
•					
•					
•					
•					

Evaluation Key

4 = Outstanding, 3 = Satisfactory, 2 = Needs Improvement, 1 = Incomplete, Off Topic, or Missing

Sample Line-Item Rubric Assessment

Assessment Criteria	Evaluation				
Conventions	**4**	**3**	**2**	**1**	**Points and Comments**
• Spells key words correctly		×			*Check spelling of "turtle, stream, deeply"*
• Appropriate capitalization	×				
• Uses ending punctuation	×				
• Follows poetry form		×			*Be sure to maintain the syllable count on line #6*
Content	**4**	**3**	**2**	**1**	**Points and Comments**
• Meaningful response to a story	×				
• Conveys personal expression	×				*Only one metaphor, consider more use of simile. Need more description, use richer adjectives*
• Creates an image with metaphor			×		
• Uses descriptive words		×			

Evaluation Key

4 = Outstanding, 3 = Satisfactory, 2 = Needs Improvement, 1 = Incomplete, Off Topic, or Missing

rubric requires only a check mark next to the criteria statement, which speeds up the assessment process. This format also facilitates communication with the student by providing a clear indication of the areas of strengths and needs.

Writing conference log. As students engage in process writing, they need to conference with a teacher. Several tasks take place during a writing conference: the teacher reviews the writing for format, content, and errors; consults with the student about the strengths and the needs of the writing; notes next steps to take; and records observations for assessment purposes. The value of a writing conference log is that it facilitates all of the above tasks on a single sheet of paper that is filed with the student's portfolio as a record of consultation for assessment purposes.

The features of the writing conference log are as follows: spaces to identify the student, the working title, and the genre of the writing; a column to record the date of each conference; ample space to write specific comments about the work; and specific rubric criteria for easy reference.

The student keeps the writing conference log clipped to the current draft of the writing. Each time the student meets with the teacher, the date is recorded and comments are added. The rubric space is initially blank so that a uniquely tailored rubric can be developed with the student's input. When the process writing is complete, the teacher takes the writing conference log and keeps it on file in the student's portfolio.

Another function of the writing conference log is as a means of communication with the student's family about work that needs to be done at home. By reviewing the writing conference log, a parent can get a clear idea of the nature of the writing, the rubric requirements, and special instructions from the teacher. Parents can also be invited to write comments on the log to further involve them in their child's writing process. A blank frame is provided below, followed by a sample sheet that is filled in.

Writing Conference Log and Rubric

Student's Name _____

Working Title and Genre _____

Conference Date(s)	Editorial Notes

Assessment Criteria Rubric
Language Conventions
•
•
Content Understanding
•
•

Writing Assessment Tools Appropriate for Early Advanced and Advanced English Language Learners

When students are active participants in the assessment process, they become more self-directed and begin to look at their own writing with a more critical eye. Early advanced and advanced ELLs can benefit from each of the previous assessment tools. They can also benefit from active participation in assessing each other's work with rubric partners and developing rubrics.

Rubric partners. Utilizing rubric partners is a strategy that actively involves students in attending to the criteria of the rubric assessment. This is an efficient way to get all students to help each other improve their writing.

1. Prior to the drafting stage of the writing process, group students with partners. If you have an odd number in your class, group students in small groups of three.
2. Review the criteria statements for conventions and content of the writing.
3. Model how to provide critical feedback. Give the students catchphrases to use such as the following:
    "Note the first criteria statement in the rubric about . . ."
    "Consider . . ."
    "I saw three spelling errors . . ."
    "I would write it this way . . ."
    Remind students to be very courteous at this time. No degrading or insulting remarks are to be tolerated.
4. Set a timer for an allotment of writing time (suggested allotment 15 to 20 minutes).
5. When the timer expires, instruct students to stop writing and meet with their rubric partners.

Sample Writing Conference Log and Rubric

Student's Name _____ Josue V. _____ .
Working Title and Genre "The Knights of Queen Califa"/Fantasy _____

Conference Date(s)	Editorial Notes
7/30	*Your first sentence catches the reader's attention. Consider following with a few sentences that set the location of the story. Think about setting. Provide descriptive details.*
8/2	*The setting is clear and detailed. The characters need some background. Ask yourself these questions: Where did the main character come from? How long has he been a knight? Why is he opposed to the other knights? Who is he related to? What happened in the past to set the knights against each other?*
8/6	*Clearly state the problem that needs to be solved in the fourth paragraph.*
8/9	*Check the marked words for spelling. I see "rescued" misspelled several times.*
8/12	*Take out the marked sentences, they derail the story. Clarify who was saved from the fire. Not all characters are accounted for.*

Assessment Criteria Rubric
Language Conventions
• Interesting lead sentence • Minimum 5 paragraphs • Observes conventions of spelling and grammar
Content Understanding
• Fantasy story with a magical event or creature • Must include a setting/characters/problem/solution story line

6. Ask students to read aloud their unfinished draft to their partner(s).
7. Partners are instructed to refer to the rubric to provide critical feedback about the writing.
8. Once each student has received critical feedback, they return to writing their drafts. (Repeat steps 4 through 8 as needed.)

This strategy has numerous benefits. It reduces the number of times that a teacher must remind students to attend to the criteria for the writing. It utilizes the whole group for assessment. It also prepares students to evaluate their own and each other's work. They practice asking themselves, "Did I meet the rubric criteria? What do I need to do to improve this writing?"

Self-generated rubrics. A very high level of participation in writing assessment is to include the students in generating their own rubrics. Self-generated rubrics is a recommended strategy for students who are highly familiar with the design and function of rubrics. As part of the writing process, consult with students about their own writing and how to evaluate it. Give them a blank rubric frame or a rubric with only a few criteria written in. Their task is to consider what would be important criteria for their own writing, to state that criteria on the rubric in terms of conventions and content, and then to hold themselves accountable to meet their own criteria. The Writing Conference Log is an ideal vehicle for this activity. It provides a frame for writing the rubric and is kept clipped to the student's writing for easy reference. To get specific language for a rubric, refer to the next section on suggested rubric language.

Suggested rubric language. There is no single rubric that can be used for writing assessment. Apart from the standard conventions of spelling, grammar, and punctuation, each genre employs unique formats for conventions and content. Provided below is sample rubric language that can be used across levels of proficiency and with specific genres of writing. The differentiation between early intermediate/intermediate and early advanced/advanced is dictated by two essential factors. The first factor is length and complexity of the writing required by the teacher, such as requiring that early intermediate students write one as opposed to three paragraphs, or that intermediate students use more details. The second factor is whether or not the students had been provided sufficient instruction in one or more of the criteria areas. For example, with narrative writing an early advanced student may need more instruction in establishing a point of view. In that case the teacher could choose to leave the rubric criteria in place, but weigh other criteria more heavily in the evaluation until it was determined that the student could demonstrate sufficient mastery of the requirement.

The following is suggested rubric language across four genres of writing: narrative, expository, biographical, and persuasive. The rubrics provide language for conventions and content with the exception of expository writing in which the content is established according to the selected topic.

Narrative Writing Rubric	Beginning	Early Intermediate/ Intermediately	Early Advanced/ Advanced
Conventions	• Dictates and copies one or more paragraphs • Logical sequence of events • Uses a graphic organizer	• Utilizes story elements (setting, plot, conflict) • One or more paragraphs • Logical sequence of events • Appropriate formats for action and dialog	• Utilizes story elements (setting, plot, conflict) • Multiple paragraphs • Chronological or thematic sequence of events • Appropriate formats for action and dialog
Content	• Identifies a setting • Selects important events • Describes events in order	• Establishes a point of view • Setting described as time and place • Shows, rather than tells, events • Articulates the significance of the experience	• Establishes a point of view • Setting described with rich details • Shows, rather than tells, events • Articulates a lesson learned, moral, or the significance of the experience

Expository Writing Rubric	Beginning	Early Intermediate/ Intermediate	Early Advanced/ Advanced
Conventions (Content varies according to topic)	• Topic sentence • One paragraph dictated or written with assistance • Ideas/events in sequence or chronological order • Concluding sentence	• Topic sentence • Multiple paragraph organization • Ideas/events in sequence or chronological order • Conclusion summarizes ideas	• Topic sentence • Five-paragraph organization • Ideas/events in sequence or chronological order • Provides details and transitions • Conclusion summarizes ideas

Biographical Writing Rubric	Beginning	Early Intermediate/ Intermediate	Early Advanced/ Advanced
Conventions	• Dictates and copies description of a selected person • Begins with a statement about the person • Uses a time line to order events	• Provides an opening sentence • Essay of one or more paragraphs • Chronological or thematic sequence of events • Details supplied • Provides a conclusion	• Captivating opening sentence • Multiple paragraph essay • Chronological or thematic sequence of events • Details supplied • Conclusion is well supported
Content	• Selects a significant person as subject • Identifies important events in person's life • Describes events in order	• Establishes the importance of the person • Cites an information source	• Establishes the importance of the person • Cites sources of information • Takes a stance about the person's contributions or detractions

Persuasive Writing Rubric	Beginning	Early Intermediate/ Intermediate	Early Advanced/ Advanced
Conventions	• Dictates an opinion • Formulates a topic sentence • Uses a graphic organizer to show relationship of evidence to argument for opinion	• Opinion stated in topic sentence • Essay of one or more paragraphs • Evidence and argument(s) match • Provides a conclusion	• Opinion stated in topic sentence • Multiple paragraph essay • Evidence and arguments match • Conclusion is well supported
Content	• Chooses a side given two arguments • States an opinion • Identifies one or more reasons for the opinion	• States an opinion • Supports opinion with one or more arguments • Provides evidence	• Well-founded opinion • Supports opinion with at least three arguments • Each argument is supported by evidence

REFERENCES

Graves, D. (1984). *Writing: Teachers and children at work.* Exeter, NH: Heinemann.

Vygotsky, L. S. (1978). *Mind and society.* Cambridge, MA: Harvard University Press.

CHAPTER 16

PREDICTABLE ROUTINES AND SIGNALS
Reducing Anxiety

This strategy addresses the following TESOL Standards:

Goal 1: To use English to communicate in social settings

> **Standard 3:** Students will use learning strategies to extend their communicative competence

Goal 2: To use English to achieve academically in all content areas

> **Standard 2:** Students will use English to obtain, process, construct, and provide subject-matter information in spoken and written form

Predictable routines and signals in the classroom are among the easiest strategies to implement and yet extremely important in reducing the anxiety of English language learners (Krashen, 1982). Because English language learners do not always understand everything that is said in the classroom, having set patterns, routines, and signals helps them relax and not worry as much about being able to follow the sequence of events and activities during the school day. If they know what to expect, they can focus more of their energy on the instruction and less on what they will be expected to do next. Routines that can be set and predictable include the sequence of the subjects to be taught, places within the classroom where certain things are stored and accessible to students, a certain spot on the chalkboard or bulletin board where reading or homework assignments are posted, a daily list posted that gives the routine in sequence, and hand or flashing light signals that indicate the close of one activity and the beginning of another. See Figure 16.1 for a list of predictable routines and signals that support English language learners in the classroom.

Theory to Practice Connection
Creating a nonstressful environment facilitates languages learning (Krashen & Terrell, 1983).

STEP BY STEP

The steps in implementing predictable routines and signals are the following:

- **Set up your room**—Set up your room with certain areas designated for group activities, free reading, and partner work. Establish these areas with the students by modeling their use and asking questions like, "Will you work with other people in this area?" or "Where will you sit if you want to read a book by yourself?" Use your computer to create large-print, clear, legible signs and graphics to help guide the students.

Routine	Use	Benefit to English Language Learners
Morning sign in	A way of taking role and indicating lunch count	Students feel a part of the class and that their presence is valued
Set activity at the beginning of the school day	A way to engage students immediately. Such things as journal writing, reading library book; tasks such as watering plants, sharpening pencils are appropriate.	Students know what to do immediately. Have a chance to share their evening in writing, sign up to share journal entries, or chat briefly with peers and teacher.
Set place in the room where certain activities occur	Students move to certain areas for group lessons, review, sharing orally	Students know what to expect when moved to a certain area
A list of the day's activities and approximate times are posted in the same place each day	Helps students get their assignments in order and know which books to get out, when homework will be collected	Students have a visual reminder of the day's activities, less reliance on oral directions
Consistent use of modeling and contextualizing of oral directions	Helps students to follow directions	Students waste less energy wondering what to do next
Use of hand signals, light signals	Helps student to redirect their energies, know when activity changes are coming	Students alerted to upcoming events, drawing to a close of activities and events
Posting of assignments, page numbers, long-term assignments, homework	Helps students stay on task	Students are aware of expectations
Set place to submit assignments and get materials	Fosters reliability and self-reliance	Students are aware of expectations

Figure 16.1   Predictable Routines and Signals in the Classroom

- *Establish routines*—Establish a set place for students to turn in assignments; pick up needed materials; and keep their bookbags, lunchboxes, and other personal belongings. Model putting these things in the established places.

- *Model routines*—Model each new routine as it is established and be careful to maintain the routines once they've been established. Anytime a student shows confusion about a classroom routine or expectation, determine if a set routine would lessen the student's confusion.

- *Contextualize directions*—Be consistent about modeling as you give directions. For example, "Take out your math book" should be accompanied by your holding up the math book. "Open to page 21" should be modeled and *page 21* should be written on the board. Modeling, gestures, and demonstrations are all vital ways to contextualize instructions. **Be consistent!**

APPLICATIONS AND EXAMPLES

Mr. Castle's kindergarten students know exactly what to expect when he starts singing, "Time to clean up." They immediately begin to put their materials away. They seem to shift into high gear when they see their teacher pick up a book and go to sit in the rocking chair. They all know it's story time. They quickly clean up and go sit on the carpet. They love to hear Mr. Castle read stories.

Mr. Castle has a set of predictable routines and signals that he uses with his 5-year-olds.

Using consistent and predictable routines is especially effective for his English learners. His students know that when the light on the overhead projector comes on Mr. Castle wants them to quiet down. He has several songs that he sings to give them signals about changing activities and he always puts notices to go home on top of the bookshelf by the door. If Mr. Castle forgets to give out the notices, he hears from 20 youngsters, "You forgot to give us our notes!"

Ms. Newsome teaches high school economics. A number of her students are English language learners so she has set up study partners for them. Ms. Newsome uses a simple routine to signal to her students when an assignment can be done with the study partners. She writes the names of both partners on the top of the assignment page when she determines that the assignment can be done in collaboration. When she thinks that the assignment is one that her English language learners can handle on their own, she doesn't write the names on the assignment paper.

Ms. Newsome has established a set routine that also serves as a signal to her students as to when collaborative work is acceptable. She also has some lessons that she puts on tape and the English language learners are instructed to use the listening station to listen to the tape and follow the directions step by step. Her English language learners know when she wants them to move to the listening station because Ms. Newsome simply hands a tape to Joaquin, which signals that it is his job to go by and tap the others on the shoulder. Ms. Newsome doesn't have to say a word.

CONCLUSION

Predictable routines and signals save a lot of time in the classroom because a short signal or standard routine lets the students know what is expected of them. The signals and routines also serve to lower students' anxiety and help them feel that they are fully participating in the classroom community, especially important for English learners.

STRATEGIES ON VIDEO

Predictable Routines and Signals

Watch Segment 2 of the DVD that accompanies this text as you see predictable routines demonstrated in a kindergarten and a fourth-grade classroom. Ask yourself these questions:

- How do the routines differ in the different grade levels?
- Which of these routines would I use in my own classroom?
- How do the teachers help the students to understand and respond to the routines and signals?
- What did you learn about the teachers as they talked about their classroom routines?

EXAMPLES OF APPROXIMATION BEHAVIORS RELATED TO THE TESOL STANDARDS

K–3 students will:

- restate information given.
- give or ask for permission.

4–8 students will:

- follow directions from modeling.
- associate labeled realia with vocabulary.

9–12 students will:

- ask for information and clarification.
- negotiate solutions to problems.

REFERENCES

Krashen, S. (1982). *Principles and practice in second language acquisition.* Oxford: Pergamon Press.

Krashen, S., & Terrell, T. (1983). *The natural approach: Language acquisition in the classroom.* Oxford: Pergamon Press.

SUGGESTED READING

Diaz-Rico, L., & Weed, K. (2002). *The cross-cultural, language and academic development handbook* (2nd ed.). Needham Heights, MA: Allyn & Bacon.

CHAPTER 17

VISUAL SCAFFOLDING
Providing Language Support Through Visual Images

Visual scaffolding is an approach in which the language used in instruction is made more understandable by the display of drawings or photographs that allow students to hear English words and connect them to the visual images being displayed. To use this strategy, the teacher builds a file of visuals, such as photographs or drawings, that can be easily accessed for teaching. (See Figure 17.1 for suggestions of resources for visuals.)

STEP BY STEP

The steps in planning and implementing visual scaffolding are the following:

- *Identify the vocabulary*—Identify the vocabulary in the lesson to be taught that can be scaffolded with visual images, such as drawings or photographs.
- *Collect visuals*—Find (or make) photos or line drawings that can be used to visually support the vocabulary needed for the students to understand the lesson.

- Internet image resources—for example, *www.google.com* (select *images*) or *www.Altavista.com* (select *image*)
- Teacher-, student-, parent-taken photos
- Illustrations in old textbooks
- Line drawings from old black-line masters or workbooks
- Line drawings from children's coloring books
- Illustrations from big books
- Children's artwork

    (all of the above can be converted to color transparencies)

- Vacation videos
- Commercial videos
- Class-made videos

To make color transparencies from photos or illustrations:
- Scan the picture into your computer using an inexpensive flatbed scanner and print it out. Most printers require special transparency film.
- Take photos using a digital camera, download them to your computer and print them out as hard copy or transparencies. The use of photo-quality printing paper will greatly enhance the quality of the hard copy.
- Download illustrations and photos from the Internet and print out as needed.
- Take standard photos and have them converted to picture CDs at your local photo shop or take them to a local copy and print center to have them converted to color transparencies, posters, calendars, and so on.

Storing transparencies
- A three-ring notebook with clear plastic sleeves can be used to store and organize transparencies. They can be projected without removing them from the sleeve.
- Small transparencies of individual pictures can be stored alphabetically in a shoebox (plastic or otherwise) and be kept near the overhead projector for quick access.
- Digital material may be stored on the hard drive of your classroom computer, on small floppy disks, or on picture CDs for quick, organized access.

Figure 17.1   Visual Scaffolding Resources

- ***Reproduce and organize visuals***—Reproduce the visuals on transparency film and organize them so that they can be easily used during teaching. Sequential order works well for a specific lesson, but you may want to organize your growing picture file alphabetically so that the pictures can be used easily for future lessons. Since pictures to be projected on an overhead projector need not be large, they can be stored in a shoe box on the overhead projector cart.

- ***Engage the students***—Encourage students to use the transparency picture file in their presentations or as a way of asking and answering questions.

- ***Build the file***—Continue to build your file on an ongoing basis.

APPLICATIONS AND EXAMPLES

Visual scaffolding can be used effectively at all grade levels and across curricular areas. In Mr. Chavez's second-grade class he is teaching a social studies unit on community. Because his students all walk to school and their parents often use the city buses for transportation, many of the students have never been more than a few blocks away from the school. Mr. Chavez tries

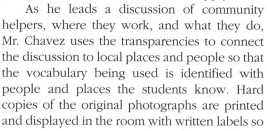

Theory to Practice Connection

Integrating the use of visuals as a part of the lesson plan increases the effectiveness of the lessons for English learners (Genessee, 1999).

to plan the community unit to build the students' sense of pride in their community. Since Mr. Chavez recognizes the importance of visuals for his English learners, he takes digital photographs of local community helpers and institutions such as the post office, postal workers, the neighborhood grocery store, the local grocer, the crossing guard at the corner, a local firefighter, and police officer. These are all places and people with whom his students are familiar. Mr. Chavez then downloads the photographs to his computer and prints them out on special ink jet transparency film from the local office supply store.

As he leads a discussion of community helpers, where they work, and what they do, Mr. Chavez uses the transparencies to connect the discussion to local places and people so that the vocabulary being used is identified with people and places the students know. Hard copies of the original photographs are printed and displayed in the room with written labels so that the students can begin to learn the written forms of the words.

Mr. Chavez and his students then take a field trip into the central part of town where the students are introduced to a supermarket. Mr. Chavez is busy taking pictures with his digital camera and the students join in the discussion back in their classroom as they compare the pictures of the supermarket with the ones of their little neighborhood grocery.

"So many food!" exclaims Mercedes as she looks at the photo of the supermarket produce aisle piled high with fruit and vegetables. "Mr. Santos have only some," she says as she points to the picture of Mr. Santos's small store.

Mercedes's observations are just the beginning of the conversations Mr. Chavez hears among his students during the next few days. He has placed the photos in the writing center and the students are writing about the sights they have seen on their bus trip to the supermarket. The photographs have provided support in the students' understanding of their community. They have also provided a source for verbal stimulation and comparison that lasts for many days.

In Ms. Hammond's high school history class, her students are studying ancient Egypt. Ms. Hammond has transferred her vacation pictures of Egypt onto a picture CD, which she downloads onto her classroom computer and shares with her students. The students are enthralled as she describes her feeling of being extremely small as she stood in front of the pyramids. The students are particularly interested in how the pyramids were built and they listen intently as Ms. Hammond displays transparencies she has scanned from photographs in David McCauley's book *Pyramid* (1976). The students begin a glossary of words they are learning as they study ancient Egypt. They illustrate their glossary using sketches they make of the pictures she displays to support their discussion. As a follow-up to their discussion of the pyramids, the students form groups to research various segments of daily life in ancient Egypt. They add to their glossaries, work together to give oral presentations, and prepare transparencies of their own to demonstrate the facts they are learning about their area of research.

As the students present their reports, Ms. Hammond finds they have followed her example. All of the groups have searched the Internet for pictures and illustrations of costumes, artifacts, and reproductions of Egyptian art to support their presentations. These have been downloaded and reproduced as hard copy or transparencies to share with others in the class. These visuals create a support for English learners as they present their sections of the group report.

CONCLUSION

Although visual scaffolding requires some planning, there is an abundance of resources for visuals and it's a very powerful tool for English learners. Photos can be copied or scanned from books, magazines, and the Internet, and transferred to transparency film to build the picture file for use in scaffolding vocabulary and concept understanding. Photos taken on vacation can often be used in classroom teaching and may even make part of your trip tax deductible. Parents can often contribute photographs that you can copy or scan for your growing file. Send out a request for photos of hard-to-find items to give the parents an opportunity to lend support.

Line drawings, photographs, maps, and realia are not the only visuals that can be used in scaffolding. Video is another visual support that is useful. It is often possible to film brief video clips in advance of a lesson so that students get a moving, real-life scaffold as a topic is discussed. Again, vacation video is a rich source of support.

STRATEGIES ON VIDEO

Visual Scaffolding

Methods for creating color transparencies using visuals from the Internet are demonstrated on Segment 3 of the DVD that accompanies this text. After you view this segment, ask yourself these questions:

- How can I use this technique to improve the quality of one of my lessons?
- How does using visual scaffolding add to vocabulary instruction?
- Why does Dr. Jordan suggest a method for storing visuals?
- What are some of the barriers to using visual scaffolding? How can I overcome these barriers?

EXAMPLES OF APPROXIMATION BEHAVIORS RELATED TO THE TESOL STANDARDS

Pre-K–3 students will:

- retell interesting events.
- ask questions to satisfy personal needs.

4–8 students will:

- work in cooperative groups and follow task roles.

- paraphrase directions given orally or in writing.

9–12 students will:

- use verbal communication to identify expectations for class assigments.
- assist in oral presentations as appropriate.

REFERENCES

Genesee, F. (Ed.). (1999). *Program alternatives for linguistically diverse students.* (Educational Practice Report 1) Santa Cruz, CA & Washington, DC: Center for Research on Education, Diversity, & Excellence.
McCauley, D. (1976). *Pyramid.* Reading, MA: Addison-Wesley.

C H A P T E R

18

REALIA STRATEGIES
Connecting Language Acquisition to the Real World

This strategy addresses the following TESOL Standards:

Goal 2: To use English to achieve academically in all content areas

　　Standard 2: Students will use English to obtain, process, construct, and provide subject-matter information in spoken and written form.

Standard 3: Students will use appropriate learning strategies to construct and apply academic knowledge.

Realia is a term for real things—concrete objects—that are used in the classroom to build background knowledge and vocabulary. Realia is used to provide experiences on which to build and to provide students with opportunities to use all the senses in learning. While using realia in the classroom is not always possible, it is usually the best choice if the student is to learn all they can about a topic. Realia allows the student to see, feel, hear, and even smell the object being explored. If the real thing is not available, the teacher must move down the continuum from the concrete (real thing), to a replica such as a model, to a semiconcrete object such as a photograph or illustration. However, each move down the continuum causes the loss of some sensory information that could be helpful in comprehension. See Figure 18.1 for suggestions of classroom realia that are helpful in the presentation of powerful learning experiences.

STEP BY STEP

The steps in implementing the use of realia are the following:

　　• **Identify opportunities to use realia**—Be aware of opportunities to include realia in lessons as you plan. Preread any stories to be read aloud or used for reading instruction to identify vocabulary that may be unfamiliar to the students and locate realia that will be helpful to their understanding.

　　• **Collect realia**—Begin to collect items that can be stored in the classroom and organize them so that they can be easily accessed for instruction. Plastic tubs or large, clear plastic bags are often used for this purpose. Some items will be used with only one theme or book and should be stored

Category	Realia	Uses
Household items	Eating utensils, kitchen appliances (from different cultures), miniatures such as household furniture, old-fashioned items no longer commonly seen	Active experiences, vocabulary development, role-playing, story reenactment, prereading activities, oral language practice, story problems in math
Food	Fruit, vegetables, unusual items unfamiliar to children; many plastic food items are available for classroom use	Sensory experiences, vocabulary development, acting out stories, grammar activities (singular, plural)
Clothing	Different kinds of hats, gloves, sweaters, jackets, boots, any examples of ethnic clothing to support understanding	Vocabulary development, story reenactment, writing support, oral language practice
Literacy materials	Books, magazines, newspapers, encyclopedia, reference books, checkbooks, bank books	Role-play, vocabulary development, easy access for research, exposure
Farm or occupational items	Rakes, plows, harnesses, tools, baskets, hay, nails, models of barns, silos, scarecrows, wagons, farm carts	Prereading activities, role-playing, vocabulary development, knowledge of size and weight
Flowers and plants	Examples of flowers and plants being studied or read about; unusual plants such as large sunflowers, pumpkins	Vocabulary development, sensory experiences, size comparisons
Animals	Classroom pets, house pets, farm and zoo animals, birds	Sensory experiences, vocabulary development
Crafts	Knitting, crocheting, tatting, sculpting clay, potter's wheel, spinning wheel, loom	Vocabulary development, role-playing, sensory experiences, prereading activities
Ethnic items	Piñatas, chopsticks, wok, tortilla press, tea sets, clothing	Vocabulary development, cross-cultural experiences

Figure 18.1   Realia for Powerful Learning

with the theme materials or book. Yard sales and end-of-season sales at craft stores are good sources of realia for classroom use. Parents can often be helpful in locating and supplying useful items.

• **Build a library of realia**—Collaborate with other teachers at your school or grade level to build a library of realia that can be shared for major theme studies. Locate local merchants, farmers, and other resources for the loan of large items such as farm equipment or animals.

• **Use field trips as realia**—If it's too large to move and your students' learning would benefit by experiencing it, take a field trip. Give your students the opportunity to really understand what they are studying.

APPLICATIONS AND EXAMPLES

Ms. Castaño has found a beautiful little bilingual book, which she wants to use with her third graders. Many of her Hispanic students speak English very well now, but their parents are concerned that they are losing their fluency in Spanish. Ms. Castaño is always looking for ways to encourage the use of their primary language. The book she has found, *My Mexico—México Mio* (Johnson, 1996) is a collection of poetry in English and Spanish. Many of her third graders will be able to read both the English and Spanish versions of the poems and there are many opportunities for active lessons and vocabulary development in both languages.

As Ms. Castaño prepares her lessons for the next week, she also gathers realia to support the students' understanding. Her school is near a little park where she will be able to take the students on a walk to see an adobe wall like the one described in the poem "Adobe Brick." Maybe she can even talk her father into coming to school and demonstrating how to make adobe bricks.

Ms. Castaño has a broom in the classroom and she finds a huge plastic cockroach given to her as a joke years ago that she will use with the broom for the students to reenact the poem "I am Cucaracha." She's smiling to herself now as her preparations for the use of this lovely little poetry book begin to get exciting. Ms. Castaño knows of a market where she can buy some gourds to use in making maracas as described in the poem "Gourds." She knows that her friend Marcella will be glad to bring her loom to school so the children can practice weaving as they read "I Saw a Woman Weaving."

After that experience she can teach the children to weave paper place mats and maybe one of the mothers will come to school to make tortillas as a culminating activity on Friday. She picks up two ears of corn to take to school so the children will understand how the tortilla flour is made.

Ms. Castaño makes a list of new vocabulary words that will be learned this week and is pleased to see many new Spanish and English words on the list. Her native English speakers will be learning a lot from this week's poetry unit, too.

Mr. Millar's sixth graders are exploring survival skills through a combined literature and science study based on several survival stories, *My Side of the Mountain* (George, 1959), *Island of the Blue Dolphins* (O'Dell, 1960), *River Rats, Inc.,* (George, 1979), and *Hatchet* (Paulsen, 1987). The students are working in groups to explore the realia they have found or had relatives send to them from the areas in which the stories took place. In some cases, they have been able to actually taste the berries and boiled twigs that the characters in the books had to eat to survive.

Theory to Practice Connection
Multiple opportunities to explore new vocabulary in different contexts deepens vocabulary knowledge (Nation, 2005).

Mr. Millar has contributed some of the realia used in the study, like some of the more primitive tools that are no longer readily available. In other cases the students have used some of the raw materials described in the books to actually construct the tools and cooking utensils made by the characters in the stories. Now that the students have all read one of the survival stories, they are comparing the survival strategies used in each of the books.

"Most of the tools they made in the stories depended a lot on the wood and stone and other materials that were available in the area," Johan observes.

"That is very true," Mr. Millar agrees. "What else was affected by the location of the story?"

"The problems they had," Susana replies. "Survival in the Canadian wilderness is very different from survival on a Pacific island."

"I thought it was interesting that they had different plants that they used for medicine," Teresa adds.

"The botany books we looked at listed a lot of plants that were edible or used for medicinal purposes," Jacob says. "I never knew that you could eat boiled twigs, either."

"They sure don't taste too great," Teresa says with a grin.

"What could you eat if you were stranded around this area?" Mr. Millar asks.

"Twinkies from the Minute Market," Susana jokes.

"No, seriously," Mr. Millar says. "Are there any local plants you could eat?"

"My grandmother says they used to eat dandelion salad," Johan says. "We could try that. We have a lot of dandelions growing in our yard."

"See whether you can get her recipe," Mr. Millar says with a smile. "We're going to take a survival hike in a few weeks so we need to research the plants that we may have to eat. Mr. Smithson, the botanist at the college, is coming along just to make sure we don't poison ourselves. We will also have to gather indigenous materials from the woods to use as tools and cooking utensils. We have some research to do before we go, though. All we will carry along is a supply of water and some very basic tools like the stone and wood hatchets and a first-aid kit. But first, let's go to the Internet and see if we can find out what kinds of plants are indigenous to our local area and decide if they can be safely eaten or not. Then we will be off to gather our survival feast!"

The students looked at Mr. Millar with a wide assortment of expressions, from excitement to apprehension.

CONCLUSION

The use of realia in the classroom supports English learners in a wide variety of ways. Introducing real objects that can be seen, felt, and manipulated is a powerful way to connect vocabulary to real life. The use of realia is motivating to students because they can actually use the real objects in the way in which they are intended to be used. Realia introduces an authentic hands-on nature to many lessons. The use of real objects conveys meaning in a way that no photograph or illustration can. There is no confusion over the size, weight, texture, or smell of an object, fruit, vegetable, or tool when the real thing is present. In some cases it becomes important to provide several objects in order to see the range of possibilities, such as several different kinds of apples or tiny sunflowers to be compared with the huge examples seen in certain parts of the world.

STRATEGIES ON VIDEO

Realia Strategies

Segment 4 of the DVD that accompanies this text shows realia being used to build vocabulary in a first grade classroom. After you watch this segment, ask yourself these questions:

- How did the teacher connect the objects to the written labels?
- How could she extend the lesson with a writing activity?
- How could you include realia into a lesson you are planning?
- What are some of the barriers you see in implementing the use of realia in the classroom?

EXAMPLES OF APPROXIMATION BEHAVIORS RELATED TO THE TESOL STANDARDS

Pre-K–3 students will:

- associate written symbols and realia.
- represent story sequence with realia.

4–8 students will:

- compare and contrast real objects.
- represent information through the use of realia.

9–12 students will:

- describe change and growth in real things.

REFERENCES

George, J. (1959). *My side of the mountain.* New York: Dutton.

George, J. (1979). *River rats, inc.* New York: Dutton.

Johnson, T. (1996). *My Mexico—México mio.* New York: G. P. Putnam's Sons.

Nation, I. S. P. (2005). In E. Hinkel (Ed.), *Handbook of research on second language teaching and learning* (pp. 581–596). Mahwah, NJ: Lawrence Erlbaum.

O'Dell, S. (1960). *Island of the blue dolphins.* Houghton Mifflin.

Paulsen, G. (1987). *Hatchet.* New York: Aladdin Paperbacks/Simon & Schuster.

CHAPTER 19

LANGUAGE FOCUS LESSONS
Planning Lessons to Support the Acquisition of English Vocabulary and Structures

This strategy addresses the following TESOL Standards:

Goal 1: To use English to communicate in social settings

> **Standard 2:** Students will interact in, through, and with spoken and written English for personal expression and enjoyment.
>
> **Standard 3:** Students will use learning strategies to extend their communicative competence.

Goal 2: To use English to achieve academically in all content areas

> **Standard 1:** Students will use English to interact in the classroom.

Standard 2: Students will use English to obtain, process, construct, and provide subject-matter information in spoken and written form.

Standard 3: Students will use appropriate learning strategies to construct and apply academic knowledge.

Goal 3: To use English in socially and culturally appropriate ways

> **Standard 1:** Students will use the appropriate language variety, register, and genre according to audience, purpose, and setting.

Language focus lessons (Gibbons, 1993) are lessons in which the emphasis is on English vocabulary and usage, rather than the curricular content. These lessons may involve exploration of content such as math, science, or social studies, but the focus of the lesson is on the language being used rather than the content itself. The language selected for language focus lessons is based upon teacher observation and knowledge of the language forms and functions that give English language learners difficulty. Examples of appropriate language for language focus lessons are shown in Figure 19.1.

Language Form	Curricular Connections	Examples
Articles a, an, one, the, this, these	Words that indicate plurals, singular forms	Cloze activities, narratives with articles and numerical indicator left out, which might relate to any subject area
Prepositional phrases, position words in, on, under, beside, in back of	Language arts, science, social studies	Using literature that shows position, such as *Rosie's Walk* Math activities such as placing a certain number of things *beside* others or stacking things *on top of* others using number and position words
Degrees of obligation must, may, might, could, should	Predictions in science, literature, class rules	Discussion of class rules in which situations are discussed, and student choices compared with rules that *must* be followed Science experiments where hypotheses are being tested, students discuss what *might* happen Problem-solving activities in which things that *could* be tried are listed and compared with things that *must* be done
Comparison words smaller, larger, fewer, less, wider, narrower, taller, shorter, greater than, less than, equal to	Mathematics, describing in any subject area	Discussion of size of groups or objects, attributes of anything being compared
Content-related words	Mathematics, science, social studies, reading	Use of content words in context. Scientific terms such as experiment, liquid, solid, gas, presented with realia, multiple examples

Figure 19.1   Suggested Language Forms and Functions for Language Focus Lessons

STEP BY STEP

The steps in teaching a language focus lesson are the following:

- ***Observe and note language errors***—Observe your students and take notes on the types of language that they tend to misuse. Plan time to work with small groups of students who have the same needs for direct instruction in language usage.

- **Gather materials**—Gather realia, visuals, and ideas for hands-on demonstrations of the language usage to be taught.

- **Explain and model language usage**—Introduce the vocabulary and model its use, simultaneously using the language as you model. Give several examples for each term so that students can see when and how the language is used.

- **Practice in active mode**—Give the students an opportunity to actually perform or model a hands-on movement or activity as they use the focus language.

- **Practice for mastery**—Design an activity that allows you to observe the students' mastery of the focus language. If they do not connect the language to the actions correctly, repeat the third and fourth steps.

APPLICATIONS AND EXAMPLES

Mr. Lee is concerned because his second graders often leave off endings of words both orally and in writing. He observes and notes the students who are doing this and plans a language focus lesson for these students. During math the next day, Mr. Lee gathers six students to do an activity with joining sets and writing story problems. Each student is given a laminated picture of a lake with large lily pads and small frogs in green and brown. He instructs the students to pick out 15 green frogs and put them on the lily pads. He then says the following sentence, emphasizing the plural /s/ each time he says it, "There are 15 brown frogs on the lily pads in the lake. Six of them jump into the water to cool off. How many frogs are left on the lily pads?" As the students count out the six frogs he asks, "How many frogs jump into the water?"

The students answer, "Six."

"Yes," Mr. Lee says, "Six frogs jump into the water."

Mr. Lee then asks each student to repeat the words, "Six frogs," emphasizing the final /s/.

"When you add /s/ to the word *frog*, it lets you know there is more than one frog," Mr. Lee explains. "It is very important to pronounce the /s/. One thing you will notice is that when you add the /s/ to the end of the word *frog*, it sounds like a /z/. The 's' at the end of the words sometimes sounds like a /z/ but we still spell it with an 's.' We will make a chart of the words that sound like a /z/ at the end when we add 's' to them.

"We will put the word *frogs* in jail because the 's' doesn't follow the rules and sound like an

Theory to Practice Connection
Focused instruction enables English learners to progress more rapidly and achieve higher levels of language proficiency (Ellis, 2006).

's' should sound," Mr. Lee says as he writes the word *frogs* on a 3-by-5 card and puts it on a bulletin board that has bars on it like a jail cell. "We will put other words in jail whenever we find that they are not following the rules. If you find any more words that are spelled with an 's' at the end but sound like /z/, be sure to tell me so we can put those words in jail."

Next, Mr. Lee has the students write the story problem about the frogs, emphasizing the writing of the "s" on the words *frogs* and *lily pads*.

"Mr. Lee, Mr. Lee!" calls Gustov. "We have to put *pads* in jail too! It sounds like a /z/, just like *frogs*."

"Good for you, Gustov! You're a great word detective," Mr. Lee says as he hands Gustov a blank card and a marker. "Put that word in jail."

"Now, I want you to think of other word problems you can write using the frogs and the lily pads," Mr. Lee says.

After the students have a chance to write some problems, Mr. Lee has them read the problems aloud and the other students work them out using the frogs and the lily pad pictures. Once Mr. Lee sees that the students are adding the "s," both in speaking and in writing, he changes the focus of the lesson to the "ed" ending, using the same materials but emphasizing that the frogs already jumped into the water. Because the "ed" at the end of the word *jumped* sounds like a /t/ instead of /ed/, the children decide that *jumped* must also go to jail.

Jose says, "English is hard, Mr. Lee. There are a lot of rule breakers."

"This is very true," Mr. Lee says with a sigh. "But you are very smart and you will learn to speak English. Just look at the word jail if you need help with a rule breaker. Maybe we need to write the rule that each of the words breaks so we can remember. What should we say about *frogs* and *pads*?"

"They sound like /z/ when they should sound like /s/," Arturo suggests.

"What about *jumped*?" asks Mr. Lee.

"It sounds like /t/ when it should sound like /ed/," Tomas says.

"Let's put them in different cells!" Katey adds.

At the end of the lesson, Mr. Lee teaches the students a signal he will use to remind them when they are leaving off endings in their oral speech and in their written work. The signal he and the students agree on is a pinkie finger touched to the end of the nose. The students and Mr. Lee practice giving this signal to each other to help them to remember to carefully pronounce ending sounds.

Mr. Lee knows that one lesson will not solve the problem of the dropped endings on words, but he will use the pinkie to the nose signal to remind the students to clearly pronounce the /s/ and /ed/ when they are speaking, and to add them in writing. He also signals toward the word jail board to help the students remember how to pronounce the endings.

As the year progresses, Mr. Lee plans to teach more language focus lessons and add the other sounds for the "ed" ending as he sees the need. The children, in the meantime, are looking for more words to put in jail.

Ms. Karras plans to teach a language focus lesson with her sixth-grade English language learners who are having difficulty understanding words that describe the classroom rules. She plans a lesson in which they will review the rules and use examples to help the students understand the meanings of the words *must, may, might, should,* and *could*. To teach this lesson, Ms. Karras will refer to the rules and procedures chart shown in Figure 19.2.

Ms. Karras poses questions based on the statements printed on the chart. As Ms. Karras and the students discuss each item, they make a "requirement line" on the chalkboard, placing each of the "requirement words" from the chart along the line according to its strength. The students decide that *must* is a very strong word that means "every time, no question about it," and they place *must* at the far right of the "requirement line." They place *may* to the far left and discuss the word *could* in relation to *may*. They decide that *could* and *may* are about the same in strength. *Should* is discussed next. The students decide that *should* is not really as strong as *must* but in the classroom both words are often used to mean "It's required. You have to do it."

The lesson continues this way until all the words are placed along the line according to their strength. Ms. Karras then asks the students to think of laws and rules from home and the community that would be examples of each of the words on the chart. Cher suggests, "My dad got a ticket because he didn't stop at a stop sign. Stopping at stop signs goes under *must*."

"Great example!" Ms. Karras says. "The laws are musts. Can you tell me why?"

"Because you can kill someone if you drive a car and don't follow the laws," Cher states solemnly.

"That's true, Cher," Ms. Karras says. "Can you think of an example for *might*?"

"If my mother has time after dinner, she *might* bake a cake," Tina suggests.

1. All students must respect the rights and space of others.
2. When finished with work, students may choose activities from the time management chart.
3. When choosing activities, students must consider any distractions their activities might cause and move away from students who are still completing work.
4. All work should be completed neatly and must be turned in on time.
5. Students must keep their voices low and respectful, being careful to avoid noise that could interfere with the activities of others in the class.

Figure 19.2   Classroom Rules and Procedures

	can		
may	might	should	must

< – >

I _____ go to the movies.   I _____ do my homework.

    I _____ have some candy.   I _____ follow rules.

I _____ go to bed early.   I _____ pick up the trash.

    I _____ give you a pen.   I _____ obey my dad.

I _____ ask my sister.   I _____ copy this over.

    I _____ do that.   I _____ be polite.

Figure 19.3 The Requirement Line and Sample Sentences

"Good example, Tina," Ms. Karras says. "She doesn't have to do it; it's just a possibility. Is there another word you can use in place of *might* in that same sentence?"

"If my mother has time after dinner, she *could* bake a cake," Tina replies.

"Does that mean the same thing?" Ms. Karras asks.

"Not really," Juan comments. "*Might* means she's thinking about it. *Could* means it's something she can do but maybe she's not even thinking about it."

"I think you've got it," Ms. Karras says. "Let's practice some more."

Ms. Karras gives the students cloze sentences written on sentence strips and asks them to take turns reading the sentences and decide which word from the chart completes the sentence best. After they decide on the best word, they have to explain their choice. When they finish this exercise, the chart looks like the one in Figure 19.3.

CONCLUSION

Language focus lessons are appropriate whenever the teacher identifies a mispronunciation or misuse of language that occurs consistently. The lessons can be used with individual students, small groups, or the whole class. However, it is important with young students or those just beginning to risk oral communication, that the lesson not be allowed to interfere with communication. If a student mispronounces or misuses language but the message is clear, it is always important to respond to the request or message. The teacher should note the misuse and the speaker or speakers who misuse the language, and plan a language focus lesson to support English learners in refining their use of English. Language focus lessons are most effective when they are presented in a positive way and the students are encouraged to practice the newly acquired skills in an authentic context.

STRATEGIES ON VIDEO

Language Focus Lessons

Segment 5 of the DVD that accompanies this text shows a middle school–focused language lesson. As you watch this segment, ask yourself these questions:

- How does Ms. Salazar make the purpose of the lesson clear to her students?
- What strategies does she use to get the students actively involved?
- What support does she give the students as they complete the task?
- Why did she decide to teach this lesson?

EXAMPLES OF APPROXIMATION BEHAVIORS RELATED TO THE TESOL STANDARDS

Pre-K–3 students will:

- form and ask questions related to assignments.
- gather and organize materials needed to complete assigned work.

4–8 students will:

- find and use information from several sources to complete assignments.

- edit and revise written assignments.

9–12 students will:

- take and support a position on an assigned topic.
- prepare for and participate in an oral report or debate.

REFERENCES

Ellis, R. (2006). Current issues in the teaching of grammar: An SLA perspective. *TESOL Quarterly, 40*(1), 83–107.

Gibbons, P. (1993). *Learning to learn in a second language.* Portsmouth, NH: Heinemann.

SUGGESTED READINGS

Chamot, A., & O'Malley, J. (1994). *The CALLA handbook.* Reading, MA: Addison-Wesley.

Diaz-Rico, L., & Weed, K. (2002). *The cross-cultural, language, and academic development handbook* (2nd ed.). Needham Heights, MA: Allyn & Bacon.

20

LEVELED QUESTIONS
Adjusting Questioning Strategies to the Language Levels of Students

This strategy addresses the following TESOL Standards:

Goal 2: To use English to achieve academically in all content areas

Standard 1: Students will use English to interact in the classroom.

Standard 2: Students will use English to obtain, process, construct, and provide subject-matter information in spoken and written form.

Standard 3: Students will use appropriate learning strategies to construct and apply academic knowledge.

Leveled questions are used when teachers adapt the way they ask questions so that students can respond to them according to their language acquisition stage (Krashen & Terrell, 1983). To level questions, the teacher must observe the students and note how they interact in English. Once the teacher knows the level at which the student interacts in English, the questions the teacher poses to the student can be adjusted to assure the student's success in answering. This may involve the teacher using gestures, visuals, or slowing the speech slightly while asking the question. The teacher asks the question in a way that encourages the student to answer by pointing to a visual, giving a one-word response, or a complete sentence or explanation depending on the student's level of language acquisition. The teacher's role in using this strategy involves knowing the student's level of English acquisition and providing enough context in the question so that the student can respond, either verbally or nonverbally, with understanding and confidence.

STEP BY STEP

The steps in using leveled questions are the following:

• *Observe and document students' language levels*—Observe your students to determine their current levels of interaction in English. On a class list, indicate whether each student is at the preproduction stage, early production stage, speech emergent stage, or intermediate fluency stage. See Figure 20.1 for a description of students' English proficiency at each of these stages. This list will need to be kept up to date as you work with the students and observe their responses.

Stage	Appropriate Expectations
Preproduction	Nodding, pointing, physically demonstrating
Early production	One- or two-word responses, making choices from given language samples (Is it a whale or a dolphin?)
Speech emergence	Phrase or short sentences (expect grammar errors)
Intermediate fluency	Longer sentences, fewer grammar errors

Figure 20.1 Appropriate Expectations for Students at Different Speech Stages

Adapted from Krashen & Terrell, 1983.

Stage	Question or Cue
Preproduction	"Show me . . . ." "Which of these . . . ?"
Early production	"Is it the _____ one or the _____ one?" Questions that can be answered with one or two words.
Speech emergence	"Did this happen at the beginning or at the end?" "What happened next?" "Where did you find the answer?"
Intermediate fluency	"How did you . . . ?" "What was the character trying to do?"

Figure 20.2 Appropriate Questions for Speech Stages

Adapted from Krashen & Terrell, 1983.

• *Choose and gather materials*—Determine which visuals, artifacts, or gestures you will need to make your meaning clear to the students whose understanding of English is limited. Gather these support materials to use during the presentation of the lesson and your questioning. Remember that English language learners feel more comfortable participating when they have ways to demonstrate their understanding with visuals and support materials.

• *Plan a hierarchy of questions*—Plan a series of questions that will help you involve your students and determine their levels of understanding of the material you will be teaching. In the beginning, it is helpful to plan a series of questions at different levels so that you can move around the room and use levels of questions for appropriate students without too much hesitation or confusion. See Figure 20.2 for suggestions.

- ***Involve all students***—Use the list of students and speech levels as a checklist to make sure that you are involving all the students in discussion and questioning and that you are adapting the levels of your questions to their changing language acquisition levels.

- ***Assess student progress and understanding***—Use the checklist you have created for observation purposes. Observe a few students each day until you have examples of the verbal responses typical for each student. Write these responses into an anecdotal record to include in the student's individual portfolio documenting periodic growth in their abilities to respond to questions in class. These documentation strategies apply to the students' progress in meeting TESOL Standards related to classroom interactions and academic language (Goal 2 at the beginning of this chapter).

- ***Add technology***—Copy and print related visuals from the Internet. Provide them to individual students during the lesson. They can use them for reference, and for responding to questions.

APPLICATIONS AND EXAMPLES

Leveled questions can be used at all grade levels and in all curricular areas. For example, in Ms. Chanis's first-grade class the children are using manipulatives to join sets and build number sentences. As Ms. Chanis moves around the room observing the students at work and asking questions, she varies the way she asks questions according to the language acquisition stages of her students. As she stops at Hnu's table she asks Hnu to show her a set of six objects.

> **Theory to Practice Connection**
> Knowing a student's English language development level and questioning at the level in which the child is comfortable helps to keep students involved and supports student progress (Haley & Austin, 2004).

Because Hnu is functioning at the preproduction stage in English, Ms. Chanis asks, "Show me 6." Hnu quickly counts out six blocks and lines them up on her desk. Ms. Chanis says, "Yes! 1,2,3,4,5,6. You showed me 6." She points to the blocks as she counts them and smiles at Hnu.

By keeping her sentence short and using a sentence form that has been modeled during the lesson introduction, Ms. Chanis is supporting Hnu's successful participation in the math

lesson. As Ms. Chanis moves to other students she adjusts her questions to the language stages of the children. She is keeping track of the students with whom she interacts by checking their names off on a list, which also helps her to keep track of the students' language stages.

Ms. Chanis asks an early production student to tell her how many objects are in the set on his desk. A speech emergence student is asked to give the number sentence for the set of two red blocks added to the set of four green blocks. An intermediate fluency student is asked to tell a story about a picture of a group of two pigs joining a group of four pigs wallowing in the mud.

Each leveled question is followed by a brief modeling of language to help support the students in incorporating more English speech into their verbal interactions. A student responds with one word and then listens as Ms. Chanis models the use of that one word in a short sentence. A student who responds with a short phrase will hear a confirmation that the phrase is correct, but then Ms. Chanis will scaffold that student's response by extending the phrase into a full sentence. Even in math, Ms. Chanis is aware of the need to continually scaffold language for her English language learners.

Leveled questions are appropriate at any grade level as long as there are students who need them to successfully participate in class interactions. In Mr. Burrow's ninth-grade class there are a number of English language learners who need to have leveled questions to participate in class discussions and questioning periods.

As Mr. Burrows reviews the Cuban missile crisis with his students, he wants to discuss the reason for concern at the time. Mr. Burrows structures a series of questions to help his students locate Cuba on the map and recognize the geographic proximity to the United States, which was the reason for concern.

To encourage participation by a preproduction stage student, Mr. Burrows says, "Show me the country of Cuba on the map." The student then uses the map in the classroom to point to Cuba.

Mr. Burrows asks an early production student to go to the map and look at it carefully. He then asks, "What is the name of the ocean or sea in which Cuba is located? Show me where you found that information on the map."

For a speech emergence student he asks, "How far is Cuba from the United States?" He follows up that question with a request to "Show Cuba and Florida on the map."

For an intermediate fluency student, Mr. Burrows asks, "Why was President Kennedy so concerned about the build-up of missiles in Cuba in the early '60s?"

The discussion and questions continue, and the map is used to ensure that the students are able to understand the main points of the discussion. Mr. Burrows models English sentences as he points out the countries on the map and makes it clear that President Kennedy was concerned because the Soviet Union was building up missiles very close to U.S. shores. Mr. Burrows then uses small ship pictures placed on the map to illustrate how the United States blockaded the approaches to Cuba and caused the Soviet ships carrying missiles to return home. Mr. Burrows is aware of the need to provide visuals to support his English language learners' comprehension of English, but he is also aware that their understanding of spoken English is better than their ability to produce English sentences. He finds ways to make himself understood and to actively involve all his students.

CONCLUSION

The use of leveled questions in the classroom requires that the teacher know the stages of language development in which each student is functioning. It also requires that the teacher understand appropriate expectations of students in each stage of language development. Although this knowledge is vital, it is not difficult information to obtain if the teacher is willing to observe the students carefully.

After gathering this knowledge and establishing a method for updating the information regularly, the teacher is ready to use leveled questions to ensure that each student in the class is provided with opportunities to participate fully. The effectiveness of this strategy stems from several sources. The students become more fully engaged in the lessons when their anxiety levels are reduced, their participation supports their understanding, and their self-confidence and language use increases. All of these factors contribute to the reduction of classroom management challenges as well.

STRATEGIES ON VIDEO

Leveled Questions

Segment 6 of the DVD that accompanies this text shows a kindergarten teacher using leveled questions to involve all of her students in a literature lesson. As you view this segment, think about the following:

- Why is it important to know the English language development levels of your students in planning a lesson?
- How does this teacher make sure that all her students can be successful?
- What scaffolding does the teacher provide for her students during this lesson?
- Think about a lesson you are planning and write some leveled questions for it. How does this activity help you to consider the language development levels of your students?

EXAMPLES OF APPROXIMATION BEHAVIORS RELATED TO THE TESOL STANDARDS

Pre-K–3 students will:

- respond to questions appropriate to their level of English language development.
- demonstrate understanding by physical and oral responses.

4–8 students will:

- ask clarification questions.
- demonstrate understanding through physical, verbal, and written replies.

9–12 students will:

- select, connect, and explain information.
- represent information visually and interpret the visual representation orally.

REFERENCES

Haley, M., & Austin, T. (2004). *Content based second language teaching and learning*. Boston: Pearson Education.

Krashen, S., & Terrell, T. (1983). *The natural approach: Language acquisition in the classroom*. Oxford: Pergamon Press.

SUGGESTED READINGS

Diaz-Rico, L. T., & Weed, K. Z. (2002). *The cross-cultural, language, and academic development handbook* (2nd ed.). Needham Heights, MA: Allyn & Bacon.

Gibbons, P. (1993). *Learning to learn in a second language*. Portsmouth, NH: Heinemann.

TESOL. *ESL standards for pre-K–12 students*. Alexandria, VA: Author.

CHAPTER 21

MANIPULATIVE STRATEGIES
Using Objects to Connect Concepts

Manipulatives are concrete devices that students can move and manipulate to support their thinking and learning. Although they are most often used in math and science, they can be very helpful in supporting language understanding in other subject areas. For manipulatives to be used effectively the teacher must demonstrate their use, while simultaneously modeling the connection to academic language. Manipulatives can be concrete representations of the concepts being taught as in models of the human body, which can be disassembled for study, or nonrepresentative manipulatives such as small wooden cubes used for counting and math calculations. The concrete representation manipulatives are often used to support the development of academic vocabulary, while the nonrepresentative manipulatives are used to manipulate an abstract concept such as number. (See Figure 21.1 for suggestions for using manipulatives.)

STEP BY STEP

The steps in the use of manipulatives are the following:

   • *Identify concepts to be taught and ways to represent them*—Identify the concept to be taught and the parts of the concept that could be represented by a concrete object of some kind. Design a teaching plan that allows the demonstration of the concept using the manipulatives as examples.

   • *Demonstrate and explain*—Demonstrate the use of the manipulatives as you explain the concept to the students. Use the demonstration to connect the manipulative, the concept, and any new vocabulary. Model the way you expect the students to use the manipulatives.

Subject Area	Suggested Manipulative Use
Vocabulary	• Miniatures or wooden cut-outs of objects • Colored blocks to teach colors, singular, plural forms • Attribute blocks to teach shapes, sizes, texture, color • Dolls to teach body parts
Mathematics	• Beans for counters • Small props for acting out word problems • Geometric shapes cut into fractional parts • Colored linking cubes for building patterns • Measuring cups and containers for studying measurement
Science	• Human body models • Realia for experiments • Styrofoam balls and toothpicks for construction • Magnets, batteries, iron filings

Figure 21.1   Manipulatives That Might Be Used in Various Subject Areas

• **Provide guided practice**—Provide guided practice in the use of the manipulatives. Walk the students through the procedure to be used, demonstrating how to use the manipulatives and connecting the manipulatives to the vocabulary to be learned.

• **Give students time for additional practice**—Give the students time to use the manipulatives independently while you circulate around the classroom observing, giving feedback, and scaffolding language usage.

• **Celebrate and review**—Celebrate the students' demonstration of learning, again taking the opportunity to connect the manipulatives to the vocabulary and concepts learned.

APPLICATIONS AND EXAMPLES

Mr. Sanchez is using story props to teach his first graders the use of a Venn diagram. Two hula hoops are laid on the floor and the students sit around them. In front of each student are three or four props from one of the two versions of *Stone Soup* that the class has read together in the past few days.

"In the green hoop we will put the props from the newer version of *Stone Soup* (McGovern, 1968) that we read first," Mr. Sanchez says as he places the McGovern version of the book in the center of the green hoop. "In the red hoop we will put the props from the other version of the story," Mr. Sanchez says as he places the Brown (1947) version of the book in the center of the red hoop.

"Now watch what I am going to do," he says as he lifts one hoop and lays it so it overlaps the other one. "Now we have a section of the hoops that overlap. When you see two circles that overlap like this, it is called a Venn diagram. The part that overlaps is where we will put the props that show something that was the same in both versions of the story. Who has something that was in both versions of the story?"

Petra holds up a stone. Mr. Sanchez nods and smiles as he says, "Yes, Petra. There was a stone in each version. That's why it was called *Stone Soup*. Where should we put the stone?"

Petra smiles at Mr. Sanchez but makes no move to place the stone. Mr. Sanchez continues,

"Put the stone in here, Petra," he says as he motions to the overlap in the hoops. "The stone was in the story," he makes a circular motion to indicate the green hoop and points to the first book. "The stone was in the second story," he repeats the motion with the red hoop and the second book. "So we put the stone in here," he points to the overlap and Petra puts the stone in the correct place.

Theory to Practice Connection
By using manipulatives and gestures, teachers can contextualize language, making it more easily understood for English learners (Cummins, 1986).

"Very good! The stone was in both stories," Mr. Sanchez smiles at Petra and points to both books.

The process is repeated with the students making decisions about the proper placement of each of the props in the Venn diagram. As they place the props, the students talk about whether or not they were in both stories. When there is disagreement Mr. Sanchez urges them to look in the book. When all the props have been placed, Mr. Sanchez pairs the students to work together on another Venn diagram. He gives each pair of students a large laminated piece of construction paper with a Venn diagram drawn on it. He gives each pair a set of pictures of the same set of props they have just used. The partners are to reenact the sorting of the props and re-create the Venn diagram they have just done as a class. The only addition to the task is a set of word cards that identify each prop. The partners must read the words and put them into the Venn diagram along with the props. There is a lot of conversation among the pairs, in home languages and English, as the students make decisions about the placement of the props and words. Occasionally a student will come to get one of the versions of the story to prove a point. As the pairs complete their work they raise their hands and Mr. Sanchez comes to them so they can read the words they have placed on the diagram and explain their diagram. Mr. Sanchez uses this time to reinforce word identification skills, their pronunciation of the vocabulary, and their correct use of the Venn diagram.

In this use of manipulatives Mr. Sanchez has used concrete manipulatives, the props. He then moved to semiconcrete manipulatives, the pictures. Finally, he provided abstract manipulatives, the words. He also used partner work to facilitate the use of home languages to communicate and solve problems and supported the students as they reported their results in English.

Older students also benefit from the use of manipulatives in the classroom. As Ms. Yang's fifth graders study the human body, she provides a model of each of the systems of the body that contains removable parts so the students can take the model apart, closely examine the parts, and reassemble the model. They are completing a diagram of each system as a part of a human body notebook they are compiling.

Ms. Yang has put together groups of four students to work cooperatively to disassemble the model, use the parts of the model to help them label their diagrams, and then reassemble the model. The group works together to test each other on the names of the body parts and exactly where the parts fit into the system. Each group includes English learners and every member is expected to help the others to learn each of the body parts, where it fits in the model, how it is spelled, and where the label goes on the diagram in their notebooks.

Everyone knows that the diagrams must be completed again on Friday as a test. Each group that has every member pass the test with at least an 80 percent will get extra recess time on Friday afternoon, so everyone is anxious to help each other learn. No one wants to be sitting inside studying for a human body retest while everyone else is outside playing on Friday afternoon.

CONCLUSION

The use of manipulatives, whether they are real objects that help students to relate language to concepts or representational objects such as blocks, counters, or beans are often supportive to students' understanding and language development. Presenting new concepts in a concrete way, before moving to semiconcrete representations such as pictures, and finally to abstract symbols, helps students make the gradual switch from concrete to abstract thinking. Manipulatives can be used in many ways, but careful thought should be given to connecting the vocabulary, concepts, and thought processes through demonstration, in much the same way vocabulary is introduced to infants. For example, "This is a cup. We drink from a cup," as the cup is being shown and demonstrated.

STRATEGIES ON VIDEO

Manipulative Strategies

As you view Segment 7, Manipulative Strategies, on the DVD that accompanies this text, think about the following:

- How did the teacher use manipulatives to review concepts already taught?
- How did Mr. Workmon incorporate vocabulary instruction with the use of manipulatives?
- What other types of objects can be used as manipulatives?
- How did Mr. Workmon encourage the students to talk during the lesson?

EXAMPLES OF APPROXIMATION BEHAVIORS RELATED TO THE TESOL STANDARDS

Pre-K–3 students will:

- use manipulatives to represent real objects.
- manipulate objects to demonstrate concepts.

4–8 students will:

- use manipulatives to solve problems.

- use manipulatives and verbal explanations to demonstrate problem solutions.

9–12 students will:

- use manipulatives to represent complex interactions.
- use manipulatives to explain concepts to others.

REFERENCES

Brown, M. (1947). *Stone soup*. New York: Aladdin/Macmillan.

Cummins, J. (1986). Empowering minority students: A framework for interaction. *Harvard Review, 56,* 18–36.

McGovern, A. (1968). *Stone soup*. New York: Scholastic.

22

COOPERATIVE LEARNING
Group Interactions to Accomplish Goals

Cooperative learning (Johnson & Johnson, 1984) is a term used for a collection of strategies in which students work together to accomplish a group task.

> K–12 researchers have concluded that, to succeed, group work must be carefully structured; the students must be thoroughly prepared through social skill-building activities; assignments must be open-ended rather than have preset answers; and the task must be such that a group, rather than an individual, is required to accomplish it. (Leki, 2001, p. 41)

The group task is structured so that each member of the group is expected to perform an assigned task. Because of the embedded structure of the unique tasks assigned to each member of the group, cooperative learning is much more effective than ordinary group work usually done in classroom situations. Appropriate training and structure is introduced into the process. These approaches are especially effective for English language learners because the students have more opportunities for verbal interactions in small groups (Kagan, 1989). They are encouraged by the members of the group

Activity	Rules
Arts project	Team members work together to create an artistic display of the team members' names.
Assembly line	Using an arts or crafts project, team members assemble a product in assembly-line fashion. One team member starts the project and passes it to the next member, who adds to it. Each member contributes to the final product.
Brainstorm	Teams work against the clock to try to find three commonalties among the team members. Following the rules for brainstorming accept all ideas, build on other people's ideas—teams try to find a category in which they can all agree—three favorite things that are common among the team, three things they all hate to do, or three movies they all liked, for example. One team member suggests a category, the others quickly give their favorites in that category until they are able to find an area of agreement.
Group task	Group works together to complete a puzzle, word search, or brain teaser.
Line up	Team members work quickly to line themselves up according to a given stipulation such as height, age, birthday, number of brothers and sisters, etc.
Team identity	Team works together to reach consensus on a team name, logo, and motto.

Figure 22.1 Common Team-Building Activities for Cooperative Learning Teams

Adapted from Meyers, 1993.

and can participate at their ability level. English language learners working in cooperative groups must be given assignments according to their levels of English proficiency, which requires the teacher to be aware of their stages of language acquisition. See Chapter 13, Leveled Questions and their levels of ability in English reading and writing.

Cooperative learning activities must be preceded by some team building (see suggestions in Figure 22.1) for the members to understand the value of working together and get to know each other's strengths. In addition, teachers must make their expectations clear if cooperative learning activities are to be successful. Some of the principles of cooperative learning are explained in Figure 22.2.

STEP BY STEP

Steps in using cooperative learning strategies in the classroom are the following:

• ***Assign groups and build a team***—Divide the class into cooperative groups. Provide a team-building activity as "warm-up" for helping students to see the advantages of cooperation and getting to know each other. Each time a new team is formed, there should be a team-building activity to help

Principle	Example	Benefit to English Language Learners
Cooperative tasks are designed so that individuals must work together for the task to be accomplished.	Jigsaw activities involve each member of the team being given a piece of the information so that they must work together or no one will have all the necessary data.	English language learners must be encouraged to participate in the tasks or the whole team will fail to accomplish their assignment.
Positive interactions are developed and encouraged.	The group's evaluation is based on individual and group marks. Group members are rewarded for peer tutoring and supporting weaker students.	Because peer tutoring and group support of individuals are encouraged and rewarded, all students are supported to succeed.
Students have opportunities to work in different teams.	A variety of plans are used for grouping, such as interest groups, random groups, heterogeneous groups, etc.	English language learners have an opportunity to get to know other students in meaningful ways and to demonstrate their competence in a variety of ways.
Social, language, and content skills are all learned in the process of interacting with the group.	Social and academic language interactions in cooperative groups help the students to learn pro-social behaviors as well as content knowledge.	English language learners benefit from the verbal interactions, learning social norms and content-related language.

Figure 22.2   Principles of Cooperative Learning

Adapted from Meyers, 1993.

members become familiar with each other's capabilities. Suggestions for team-building activities are given in Figure 22.1.

• ***Assign roles within the groups***—Give the team members cards that identify their assigned roles and list clear descriptions of their duties. These can be computer-generated and contain graphic images to aid in identifying the role and expectations. Usually one member is designated as the leader, one as note-taker, one as reporter, and one as timekeeper. It is also helpful to give each member a name tag which designates the role to be played so that all members of the group are aware of the roles of all the members. Tasks especially appropriate for English language learners include artist, visual creator (drawing or computer-generated), mime, or translator—providing a physical reenactment or second-language translation of key points for other second-language learners in the classroom.

• ***Assign the task***—Give each team a task to complete and remind each member of the roles they are expected to serve to assist the others in completing the task. The leader keeps everyone working and focused, the note-taker keeps records of the team activity, the reporter shares the information or results with the class at the completion of the activity, and the timekeeper makes sure they are on task and moving toward completion of the task within the time limit.

• *Intervene to ensure full participation*—The teacher's role is crucial in establishing the tone of cooperation and group interaction of its members. Without appropriate team building, expectations, and validation of the contributions of all individuals within the group, cooperative learning exercises might actually be detrimental to the academic and linguistic development of English learners (Leki, 2001). Teachers must carefully monitor group participation and intervene whenever a student is being excluded from the group process or taking over the work of the group (Cohen, 1994). To monitor these behaviors, teachers must listen to make sure every member of the group is being given a chance to talk, watch for physical signs that students are being excluded from the group, and use a variety of strategies to assign status to nonparticipating or excluded members of the group. Teachers can do this by mentioning a personal skill or strength that excluded members can contribute to the task, or by asking questions such as "Is everyone having a chance to talk?" If the teacher's interventions don't correct the problem, a student should be assigned to tally the number of times that each student talks, and be responsible for asking each student his or her opinions in an organized way. If this continues to be a problem, the teacher should schedule more team-building activities before using cooperative learning again.

• *Report back to the class*—Provide an opportunity for the groups to report back to the class at the end of the assigned time. Each group should share their solutions.

• *Debrief and examine the group process*—Give each group an opportunity to debrief, discussing the process and the roles each team member played in the success of the group. Have each group fill out a group report form that focuses on both product and process. A sample group report form is shown in Figure 22.3.

Group Name _____

Task _____ **Date** _____

Group Member	Contributions	New skill practiced? (yes, no, or comment)

Comments

_____

_____

_____

_____

_____

Group Member's Signature

Note: Each group member must fill out a form. The group must agree on the new skill to be practiced. Suggestions: taking turns, sharing materials, staying on task, asking questions, summarizing ideas, encouraging others, restating suggestions, etc.

Figure 22.3 A Cooperative Learning Group Report Form

Adapted from Meyers, 1993.

APPLICATIONS AND EXAMPLES

Ms. Truit's fourth graders are working in cooperative groups to use their math and problem-solving skills to plan a party for the end of the year. Each group of four has been given a budget of $25 to spend and they are to decide on the refreshments, decorations, and games to be played. At the end of the planning period, each group

---

Theory to Practice Connection

One of the important duties of the teacher during cooperative learning is the use of intervention strategies to insure the participation of all students involved in the group projects (Cohen, 1994).

---

will present its plan for the party, complete with a drawing of the decorations, a detailed refreshment list including costs figured from a grocery store price list, and a presentation detailing the process the group used to solve the problems and make decisions. The group with the best

plan will actually get to do the shopping, make the decorations, and be in charge of leading the games. The winning group will have a full school day without other assignments to complete their party preparations.

The groups work diligently to complete their calculations and draw their decorations. The group leaders are encouraging everyone to work together and Ms. Truit is monitoring closely and intervening where necessary to insure full participation by her English learners. The note-takers are in charge of preparing the detailed plans, while the reporters are working along with the others to practice what they will say in their oral presentations. The timekeepers are keeping a close eye on the clock. Motivation and cooperation is high. Everyone wants to have a chance to actually give their party.

Ms. Hill's math students at Mountain High are using their calculators to solve problems related to the state budget. One of the gubernatorial candidates is promising a 12 percent reduction in state income tax if he is elected. He is also promising an increase of 6 percent in state spending for education. Ms. Hill has formed cooperative groups for the purpose of figuring out the answers to some weighty questions.

Each group leader is given a list of line items on the state budget. The group comptroller has been given a detailed list of state income from income taxes, the state education budget, and anticipated revenues for the coming year. Each group secretary has been given a list of bills currently being considered by the state legislature and their anticipated cost. The group calculator has been given the task of making calculations as requested by other members of the group.

The groups have been given the following tasks:

1. Figure the effect of a 12 percent reduction in state income taxes.
2. Figure the effect of a 6 percent increase in state education funding.
3. Figure the cost of new legislation if all of the bills currently being considered are passed, or if only 50 percent of them are passed.
4. Figure by what percentage the state revenues must increase for it to be possible for the gubernatorial candidate to carry out his promises (listed in tasks 1 and 2).
5. Create a visual on transparency film showing your calculations and what combination of factors would make the candidate's promises possible. In this task you may decide which bills could be passed and what the increase in revenues would have to be, on any combination of factors.
6. Watch the clock to make sure the group will be able to complete the task within the time limit. You should be finished and ready to present in 45 minutes.
7. Group reporters will present the results at the end of the class period. They may enlist the help of any (or all) of the group members in making the presentation.

The groups are working hard to make professional presentation visuals, double-check their calculations, and make sure they haven't overlooked any bills that might make a big difference in their calculations. They are learning a lot about calculator math and state government, including vocabulary unfamiliar to a number of them. The teacher is circulating to monitor the group efforts, define unfamiliar words, or refer the students to resources within the room—including the computer online services. She wants to make sure that her English learners have the necessary scaffolding to participate in the activity.

CONCLUSION

Cooperative learning provides an opportunity for communication, planning, research, and oral and visual presentations in the classroom. Quality group cooperation does not occur overnight, however. Taking the time to build teams, monitor the group interactions, and debrief after the activity are all vital pieces of the cooperative learning process. The groups are not just learning content but valuable interpersonal interaction skills, as well. Because there is a definite task to accomplish and support is provided, English learners have a greater opportunity to access the learning. Videotaping the group interactions and having the group watch the video and examine their own behaviors, strengths, and weaknesses is a supportive activity when creating the learning community (Herrell & Fowler, 1997).

STRATEGIES ON VIDEO

Cooperative Learning

A cooperative learning training activity is shown on Segment 8 of the DVD that accompanies this text. As you view this segment, think about the following:

- How does the teacher make her expectations clear?
- How does she provide support and encouragement for the English learners?
- Why do you think the teacher keeps up a running commentary?
- What do you think she would have done if one student was being excluded from the activity?

EXAMPLES OF APPROXIMATION BEHAVIORS RELATED TO THE TESOL STANDARDS

Pre-K–3 students will:

- use social language to request information.
- follow rules to interact in a small group setting.

4–8 students will:

- actively participate in assigned cooperative learning tasks.

- understand and perform a defined cooperative learning group role.

9–12 students will:

- select, connect, and explain information through cooperative group interaction.
- assume a role in the presentation of group outcomes.

REFERENCES

Cohen, E. (1994). *Designing groupwork* (2nd ed.). New York: Teachers College Press.

Herrell, A., & Fowler, J. (1997). *Camcorder in the classroom: Using a video camera to enrich curriculum.* Upper Saddle River, NJ: Merrill/Prentice Hall.

Johnson, D. W., & Johnson, R. T. (1984). *Circles of learning: Cooperation in the classroom.* Alexandria, VA: Association for Supervision and Curriculum Development.

Kagan, S. (1989). *Cooperative learning: Resources for teachers.* San Juan Capistrano, CA: Resources for Teachers.

Leki, I. (2001). A narrow thinking system: Non-native English-speaking students in group projects across the curriculum. *TESOL Quarterly, 35*(1), 39–63.

Meyers, M. (1993). *Teaching to diversity.* Toronto, Canada: Irwin Publishing.

SUGGESTED READING

Chamot, A., & O'Malley, J. (1994). *The CALLA handbook.* Reading, MA: Addison-Wesley.

LESSON PLANNING

Ellis, S. S., & Whalen, S. F. (1990). *Cooperative learning: Getting started.* New York: Scholastic.

Johnson, D. W., & Johnson, R. T. (1985). *Structuring cooperative learning: Lesson plans for teachers.* Edina, MN: Interaction Book Company.

VIDEO

Cooperative learning. (1996). Alexandria, VA: Association for Supervision and Curriculum Development.

CHAPTER 23

MODELED TALK
Showing While You Talk

Modeled talk (Herrell, 1999), the concurrent verbal explanation and physical demonstration of directions or concepts, is one of the simplest and most powerful strategies for use with English language learners. It takes some planning and practice but can soon become a habit for effective teachers. Modeled talk is the use of gestures, visuals, and demonstrations as explanations are made. Gestures and modeling provide examples for learners to follow and lower their anxiety since they know exactly what to do because they have seen the directions or content modeled.

STEP BY STEP

The steps in implementing modeled talk are the following:

• *Identify the lesson and gather materials*—Identify the lesson to be taught and the materials to be used. Think about what you plan to say to explain the lesson and the directions to the students. Prepare the materials the students will use so that you have an example to show and, if necessary, examples in various stages of completion. Design gestures that will help the students understand exactly what will be expected of them without having to rely solely on English vocabulary for understanding.

• *Practice your modeled talk*—Practice your talk in front of a mirror to determine if your instructions, modeling, and gestures convey the message you want the students to understand.

Props	Visuals
Any textbooks to be used Scissors, tape, rulers, pencils, notebooks that will be needed Realia whenever vocabulary will be new Word cards for any new vocabulary to be written Maps, globes, manipulatives, examples of products to be made	Numbered charts showing sequence to be followed Diagrams showing a recap of directions given Standard illustrations for scissors (for directions to cut), crayon (for directions to color), pencil (for directions to write), computer (when it is to be used), ruler (for directions to measure), paintbrush (for directions to paint)

Figure 23.1   Props and Visuals to Support Modeled Talk

• ***Design a visual of directions***—Design a standard visual that will be used regularly if the lesson or directions require that the students follow a sequence of instructions. This will help the students become accustomed to looking for this visual for support in remembering the sequence. Simple numbered drawings work well for this. A set of standard drawings created and saved on the computer, printed, laminated, placed in sequence on the chalkboard, can be used again and again for different activities. A picture of a pair of scissors, for example, always reminds the students that the next step is to cut, while a picture of a crayon reminds them to color.

• ***Review the steps to be taken***—Review the steps the students are to take after you have delivered your modeled talk. Use the visuals you have created to reinforce the students' reference to them for support in remembering what to do. When the students are performing the activities you have explained, refer to the visuals whenever there is a question about what to do next so that the students practice the use of them. See Figure 23.1 for suggestions of props and visuals that support modeled talks.

APPLICATIONS AND EXAMPLES

Ms. Milsovic is using modeled talk to explain the day's learning centers to her kindergarten class of English language learners. She begins by sitting in a small chair with the students sitting on the floor in front of her.

"When I play the music," Ms. Milsovic says as she points to herself and then touches the play button on the tape player so the children hear a short section of the music they use as a signal to change activities, "you (indicates the children) will go to the centers (she motions toward the centers)."

"First (she holds up one finger), you will go to the planning board." As she says this she signals for them to follow her to the planning board. The planning board is made of a large automotive drip pan. It has photographs of each of the centers attached by magnetic tape across the top of it and room for children's names on magnets under each of the center pictures.

"You will look for your name," Ms. Milsovic continues as she shows the children the name cards, which are not yet attached to the board. She reads a few of the names so the children understand what is written on the name cards.

"If Cher's name is under this center," she points to the picture of the Art Center, "she will go to the art center first." She motions for the children to follow Cher to the Art Center.

Theory to Practice Connection
Modeled talk is a powerful application of context-embedded academic language that serves to support English learners in successful classroom participation (Peregoy & Boyle, 2001).

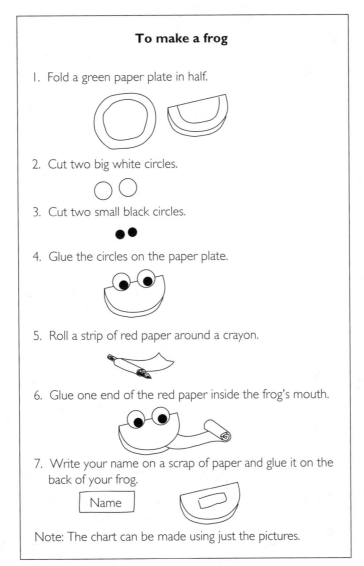

To make a frog

1. Fold a green paper plate in half.

2. Cut two big white circles.

3. Cut two small black circles.

4. Glue the circles on the paper plate.

5. Roll a strip of red paper around a crayon.

6. Glue one end of the red paper inside the frog's mouth.

7. Write your name on a scrap of paper and glue it on the back of your frog.

Name

Note: The chart can be made using just the pictures.

Figure 23.2   Ms. Milsovic's Directions for the Art Center

At the Art Center Ms. Milsovic shows the children exactly what they will do there. She demonstrates each step as she talks about it. On this particular day the children are studying frogs and toads and they are using green paper plates to make frogs with long curled tongues. Ms. Milsovic shows them how to make the frog and posts a visual with drawings that demonstrate what to do first, second, and third. After she demonstrates, she refers to the visual and asks one of the children to tell her what to do at each step. See Figure 23.2 for an example of the visual Ms. Milsovic used.

Each center is carefully modeled and key English vocabulary is taught and practiced.

When all the centers have been explained, the children and Ms. Milsovic return to the planning board and the names of the children are placed on the board so they know where to go first. Once this is done, Ms. Milsovic plays the music on the tape recorder, signaling that it's time to move to the centers. Since the children know what to do at each center and there are visuals available at each center to remind them in case they forget, Ms. Milsovic is able to work with small groups of students at the Writing Center using interactive writing to teach them how to write words describing frogs. The children are secure in their understanding of what is expected of them.

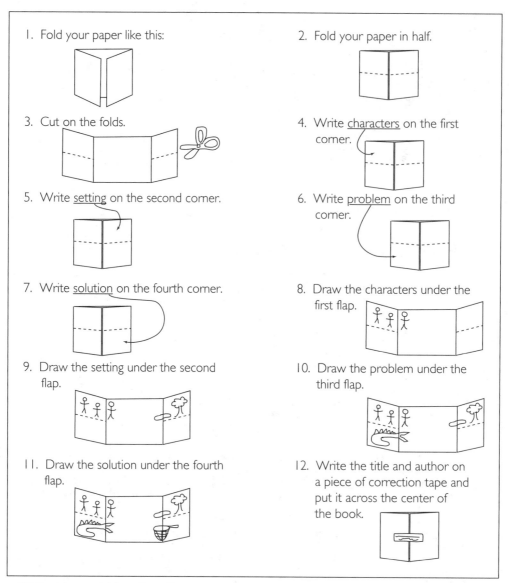

Figure 23.3 How to Make a Four-Corner Book

Ms. Delgado is demonstrating how to make four-corner books for her fifth graders, who are always looking for new ways to celebrate the books they have read. Since the students will be making their books while Ms. Delgado is holding literature discussions, she wants to make sure that they know exactly what to do. She displays a poster that shows each of the steps in their assignment and then she gives a modeled talk demonstrating the steps in the process. Figure 23.3 shows the poster Ms. Delgado displays. She's always careful to use clear instructional illustrations, so that her English learners can easily access the information.

As Ms. Delgado demonstrates the making of a four-corner book, she refers to the steps listed on the poster. "First," she says as she points to the number "1" on the poster, "you fold a piece of paper like this." She demonstrates and then points to the drawing on the poster. Ms. Delgado writes "1" on the chalkboard and puts the sample she has started under the number.

"Second," she continues, as she points to the number "2" on the poster, "you fold the paper in half, this way." She takes a premade sample that was completed in step 1, demonstrates step 2, points to the drawing on the poster, writes the numeral "2" on the chalkboard, and puts the second sample under it.

"Third," she says as she points to the number "3" on the poster, "you cut on the folds you just made." She demonstrates the cutting on an additional sample, makes a "3" on the chalkboard, and puts the third sample under it. At this point she has a sample at each stage of the preparation, sitting along the chalk tray for the students to examine if the need arises.

Next, she takes a premade sample of the four-corner book she has just shown how to make and writes CHARACTERS on one corner. "You write the word *characters* on the first corner," she says as she demonstrates.

Ms. Delgado models each step, adding the word *setting* on the second corner, the word *problem* on the third corner, and the word *solution* on the fourth corner. She then lifts the flap on which the word *characters* is written and demonstrates the drawing of the main characters of her book. She repeats the process with the rest of the four corners.

Last of all, Ms. Delgado takes a piece of wide correction tape and puts it across the middle of her four-corner book and writes the title and author of the book on it. As she does each of these steps she refers the students to the poster and leaves a sample on the chalkboard for them to examine as they are making their own books. Once she has completed the modeled talk, she puts the supplies on a table for the students to use and calls a literature discussion group together. The rest of the class is busily engaged in making four-corner books and her group is not disturbed. They know how to make their books and know they will have an opportunity to share the books after Ms. Delgado finishes working with her groups. This was explained to them as a part of the modeled talk, and it's on the poster.

CONCLUSION

Modeled talk is helpful in lowering students' anxiety because they know what is expected of them. It serves another important function when the teacher uses it consistently. English-speaking students often learn how to model talk and use it when explaining procedures and concepts to English language learners in the classroom. Students' use of modeled talk to other students increases the opportunities for English language learners to interact successfully with their peers and it builds feelings of community within the classroom.

STRATEGIES ON VIDEO

Modeled Talk

As you view Segment 9 on the DVD that accompanies this text, watch how the kindergarten teacher models as she gives directions. Think about the following:

- How does using modeled talk contribute to the studens' abilities to participate successfully in the classroom?
- Does modeling talk require any additional time on the teacher's part?
- How does modeled talk contribute to the students' language acquisition?
- What additional planning is involved in modeling teacher talk?

EXAMPLES OF APPROXIMATION BEHAVIORS RELATED TO THE TESOL STANDARDS

Pre-K–3 students will:

- follow instructions from verbal and nonverbal cues.
- gather and organize materials needed to complete a task.

4–8 students will:

- follow a sequence of instruction based on verbal directions and physical actions.

- generate and ask questions to clarify expectations.

9–12 students will:

- compare and classify information based on verbal instructions and physical modeling.
- construct a chart or visual representation of information gained through oral directions and physical modeling.

REFERENCES

Herrell, A. (1999). Modeling talk to support comprehension in young children. *Kindergarten Education: Research, Theory, and Practice, 3,* 29–42.

Peregoy, S., & Boyle, O. (2001). *Reading, writing, and learning in ESL* (3rd ed.). Boston: Longman.

CHAPTER 24

VOCABULARY ROLE-PLAY
Building Vocabulary Through Dramatization

This strategy addresses the following TESOL Standards:

Goal 1: To use English to communicate in social settings

   Standard 3: Students will use learning strategies to extend their communicative competence.

Goal 2: To use English to achieve academically in all content areas

   Standard 1: Students will use English to interact in the classroom.

   Standard 2: Students will use English to obtain, process, construct, and provide subject-matter information in spoken and written form.

   Standard 3: Students will use appropriate learning strategies to construct and apply academic knowledge.

Goal 3: To use English in socially and culturally appropriate ways

   Standard 2: Students will use nonverbal communication appropriate to audience, purpose, and setting.

Vocabulary role-play (Herrell, 1998) is a strategy used to encourage learners to make connections among their past experiences, the content currently being studied, and vocabulary that is new or being used in an unfamiliar way. Students are introduced to new vocabulary and given an opportunity to discuss and use the vocabulary in context through role-playing. Often several groups of students are given the same vocabulary and asked to write and perform a skit in which the words are used and demonstrated. Since the groups are likely to write and perform skits in which the vocabulary words are used in different contexts, the skits serve to show multiple uses of the same words. In this way, English language learners are given an opportunity to see the vocabulary words used in context, as well as demonstrations of several contexts in which the words may be used appropriately.

STEP BY STEP

The steps in implementing vocabulary role-play are the following:

• *Identify key vocabulary*—Determine the vocabulary words that will be used in a lesson or reading. Make cards with the words written on them.

• *Teach the lesson or read the book*—As you teach the lesson or read the book—either reading aloud or having the students read—stop as you encounter key vocabulary and discuss and act out the words. Pronounce the words carefully and have the students practice pronouncing them, especially if the words contain sounds difficult for them. Be sure to reread the page fluently after the vocabulary is explored. As each word is explored, place it in a pocket chart so students can see it clearly.

• *Connect the vocabulary to past experiences*—After the lesson is complete or the story is read, show the cards to the class, one by one, and ask the students to talk about ways in which they have seen the words used. Use this opportunity to explore multiple meanings of words.

• *Sort the words*—Further explore the words by engaging the students in word sorting. Ask them if any of the words have similar meanings or if any of them are names for things—nouns. Identify the movement words—verbs—and place them together. Review the word meanings in several different ways to help the students remember them. See Figure 24.1 for a typical word sort.

• *Plan ways to use the words*—Leave the words on display in the pocket chart. Use the words in directions during the day. Encourage the students to use the new vocabulary in their writing and celebrate verbally when they do. Involve the students in creating scenes using the new vocabulary by dividing the class into small groups of three to five students and giving each group a set of four or five words. Make sure that each group has at least one member who is a strong reader. Instruct each group to create a scene in which all their words are used.

• *Give the students time to practice*—Give the groups time to work on their scripts and practice performing their scenes. Encourage the groups to make and use simple props.

• *Perform the scenes*—Give each group a chance to perform the scenes that they have written. Discuss how the words were used after each scene is performed, celebrating innovative uses of the new vocabulary.

• *Focus on multiple word meanings*—Compare and contrast the uses of the words by the groups, emphasizing the differing contexts used in the skits, and the similarities and differences in the ways in which the words were used.

Movement Words	Names for Things	Descriptive Words
VERBS	NOUNS	ADJECTIVES/ADVERBS
paraded	ledge	scary
prowled	geranium	slowly
stroked	statue	quickly
winked	puddle	sparkling
stretched	park bench	leisurely

Figure 24.1 A Word Sort Using Words from a Vocabulary Role-Play Lesson

Words taken from *The Third-Story Cat* (Baker, 1987).

APPLICATIONS AND EXAMPLES

Ms. Lee has brought her calico cat, Muffin, to school to visit the children in her first-grade class. Many of the children express fear at the possibility of handling Muffin, but Ms. Lee wants them to become more comfortable with her. She chooses a special book about a calico cat to share with her class. As she sits in the big rocking chair in the corner of the classroom with Muffin sleeping in her lap, Ms. Lee shows the cover of the book she holds, which has no picture on it.

"The title of this book is *The Third-Story Cat* (Baker, 1987)," Ms. Lee says. "There is no picture on the cover to help us guess what it is about. What do you think it might be? What is a third-story cat?"

"Maybe there were two other stories about the cat," Jacob suggests.

> **Theory to Practice Connection**
>
> By acting out words and situations, students are provided with active experiences involving new vocabulary. These experiences provide an opportunity for understanding and internalization of the text (Jordan & Herrrell, 2002).

"That's an idea," Ms. Lee agrees.

"Have you ever heard the expression *third story* before?" she asks.

"I think my uncle lives on the third story," Tony answers tentatively. "You have to go up a lot of stairs to his apartment."

"That's right, Tony. Third story means the same thing as third floor." Ms. Lee opens the book to the title page where the students can see a lovely watercolor painting of an apartment building with three floors. In the apartment on the third floor you can see a calico cat sleeping on the window sill.

"Look up here in the window," Ms. Lee says. "Do you see a cat that looks just like Muffin?"

"O-o-o-h," the students sigh. "It does look like Muffin."

Ms. Lee then uses the illustration of the apartment building to show the meaning of the word *third story*. She sweeps her hand across the first floor of the apartment building in the picture and says, "The people who live on this floor can walk out their doors and be on the sidewalk. This is the first floor or first story." She points to the doors that open onto the sidewalk and to the sidewalk itself as she says the words.

"The people who live on the second floor, or second story, have to go up some stairs to their apartments." Ms. Lee points to the doorway and moves her hand up to the second floor as she explains.

"The people who live on the third story have to go up even more stairs," Ms. Lee explains as she points to the third floor.

"There are a lot of big words in this story," Ms. Lee says. "The author of this book, Leslie Baker, uses a lot of wonderful words to tell us about all the exciting things this cat does one day. Let's read the story and find out what adventures the cat has."

Ms. Lee reads the story aloud to the students, using the beautiful illustrations to help them understand the new vocabulary that is introduced in the story. She stops to demonstrate the meaning of the word *startled* as the cat is surprised by a butterfly flying up out of the geranium box. She has one of the children demonstrate the word *crept* as the cat is balancing along the ledge on the three-story building. As the story is read the children are exposed to a number of new words describing the ways in which cats move: *paraded, prowled, twitched, leaped.* Some other words require some physical practice, like *winked* and *stroked.*

After the story is read, Ms. Lee goes through the new words again and has the children make a large circle. They walk around the room and act out the movements the cats made in the story. They wink, creep, twitch, and parade until they are all very silly. They show the difference between being startled and being frightened, between winking and blinking, between parading and prowling, and between patting and stroking. When they sit back down in the circle, Ms. Lee shows them cards with the new words printed on them and as she holds each card up a child volunteers to act it out.

Ms. Lee leaves the new vocabulary word cards in a part of the room near the pocket chart and shows the children how they can use the cards to fill in the blanks in the pocket chart story.

They are invited to make new sentences with the cards during center time and they even have a new pointer with a calico cat on the end of it to use as they read the sentences they are making. Ms. Lee smiles as she watches the children busily building sentences with the new vocabulary words. One of the children is carrying Muffin around the room with her as she acts out the new words she has learned from *The Third-Story Cat.*

Mr. Valdez's fourth graders are studying Florida history. They are reading about the barefoot mail carriers who brought the mail down the beaches to the first settlements and the ways in which the various people came to Florida to establish permanent residences. Some of the vocabulary is unfamiliar to the students and Mr. Valdez wants to make sure that the words are understood by all his students. Going through the Florida history book, Mr. Valdez selects the words *barefoot, cypress, brackish, humid, Everglades,* and *tidepools,* and writes the words on sentence strips.

After he reads the section from the Florida history book aloud to his class, Mr. Valdez asks the students to talk about the ways in which they have heard the words used before.

Jonah starts the discussion by saying, "I like to go barefoot in the summertime. My mother is always telling me to put my shoes on."

"I know what it means to go barefoot," Katie adds. "I just don't understand why the mail carriers were barefoot."

Mr. Valdez takes the time to explain that since there were very few roads in the early days, the easiest route down the state was walking along the beach and so the mail carriers often got their feet wet. To protect their shoes, they walked barefoot until they came to places where they needed to wear shoes. Then they would stop and put their shoes back on.

Carla talked about brackish water and how her dad is often worried about the salt water at their beach house invading the drinking water. "That's what he calls brackish water," she explains. "It's when the salt water invades the fresh water."

"Yes," Mr. Valdez agrees. "But in some places in the state it's a natural thing for water to be brackish. Some of the rivers empty into the ocean and there is an area in which the salt water and fresh water mix. That's also brackish water."

The discussion continues until each of the words has been discussed. Mr. Valdez then divides the students into groups of three and asks them to write a short skit in which they use as many of the new vocabulary words as they can. One member of the group is assigned as the note-taker and the skits are written. The students are given 15 to 20 minutes to make simple props and each group is given a chance to act out its skit. Some of the groups have one of the members read the script while the other two do the acting. One group chooses to do a charade and asks the class to guess which word they are portraying. Another group has a complete dialogue with each of the speakers emphasizing a few of the new vocabulary words. One of the groups even performs a rap routine using the new words. By the time all six groups perform, all the new words have been demonstrated multiple times in many different contexts. Mr. Valdez is confident that the new vocabulary is thoroughly understood by everyone.

CONCLUSION

Vocabulary role-play provides the link between learning a new word and using the word in context, or multiple contexts. Role-play enables the student to create experiences with which to link the new vocabulary. The study of words, their multiple meanings, and origins can also be effective with the use of vocabulary role-play. Students can add brief videos to illustrate word meaning, create animated computer dictionaries, publish vocabulary books, and illustrate word posters—all of which increase their interactions with and understanding of English vocabulary and multiple meanings.

EXAMPLES OF APPROXIMATION BEHAVIORS RELATED TO THE TESOL STANDARDS

Pre-K–3 students will:

- act out common verbs.
- re-create a scene from a storybook with dialogue and action.

4–8 students will:

- create a scene demonstrating multiple meanings of common words.
- communicate the meanings of words through verbalization and action.

9–12 students will:

- interact with a group to write a script demonstrating word meanings.
- use appropriate language structures to depict a variety of social contexts in dramatic action scenes.

REFERENCES

Baker, L. (1987). *The third-story cat.* Boston: Little, Brown.

Herrell, A. (1998). *Exemplary practices in teaching English language learners.* Fresno: California State University.

Jordan, M., & Herrell, A. (2002). Building comprehension bridges: A multiple strategies approach. *California Reader, 35*(4), 14–19.

CHAPTER 25

WRITING WORKSHOP
Supporting the Acquisition of English Writing Competence

This strategy addresses the following TESOL Standards:

Goal 1: To use English to communicate in social settings

Standard 2: Students will interact in, through, and with spoken and written English for personal expression and enjoyment.

Standard 3: Students will use learning strategies to extend their communicative competence.

Goal 2: To use English to achieve academically in all content areas

Standard 1: Students will use English to interact in the classroom.

Standard 2: Students will use English to obtain, process, construct, and provide subject-matter information in spoken and written form.

Standard 3: Students will use appropriate learning strategies to construct and apply academic knowledge.

Goal 3: To use English in socially and culturally appropriate ways

Standard 1: Students will use the appropriate language variety, register, and genre according to audience, purpose, and setting.

Standard 2: Students will use nonverbal communication appropriate to audience, purpose, and setting.

A **writing workshop** (Graves, 1983) is an approach to teaching writing in which the students choose their own writing topics and move through prewriting, drafting, revising, editing, and publishing their work as though they were professional authors (Tompkins, 1994). writing workshop is especially supportive to English language learners because students are encouraged to discuss their ideas, work with a partner or group in revising and editing, and interact verbally with others (Diaz-Rico & Weed, 2002). The classroom environment in which students work together to support each other as they work through the stages in the writing process provides the support necessary to lower anxiety and motivate students to write. The opportunity to write on self-chosen topics validates each student's experiences. The stages in process writing are shown in Figure 25.1 with suggestions for supporting English language learners.

Writing Process Stage and Definition	**Adaptations for English Language Learners**
Prewriting. Strategies for getting and organizing ideas.	Allow first-language usage if needed. Model more than one strategy using visuals and actual writing ideas being developed. Include realia. Encourage first-language partner or small-group work.
Drafting. Getting some ideas down on paper.	Model putting a draft down on paper using an overhead or chart. Think aloud as you write. Write on every other line to allow for revisions. Model crossing out ideas, writing between lines, making changes as ideas begin to flow. Encourage collaboration and discussion of ideas among students. Allow writing in first language.
Revising. Focusing on the content of the piece, asking questions if parts are not clear, giving suggestions to the writer. This stage can be repeated as needed.	Model a writing group using your writing. Encourage the students to give you feedback and ask questions about the piece of writing you are doing. Work with a small group. Encourage translation to English if the piece is written in another language. Authors can use student translators for both the reading of the piece and feedback and suggestions given. Authors decide which revisions to make based upon the group suggestions.
Editing. Correcting mechanics.	Model the editing process using your own writing. Teach proofreading symbols so that students can work together to correct all spelling, punctuation, capitalization, and other mechanical errors. Encourage partner work. Provide resources such as dictionaries, thesaurures, and English grammar textbooks. After student editing, teacher can serve as final editor.
Publishing. Putting the writing into a final form such as mounting for the bulletin board, binding into a book, creating a shape book, pop-up book, or other novelty form.	Model the publishing of your writing. Introduce the publishing possibilities by modeling each of them. Encourage the students to choose their publishing mode and work with a partner. Take photos of the authors for an "About the Author" page in the book.
Celebration. Sharing the finished work with classmates or others.	Student whose book is published sits in the Author's Chair and reads the newly published book or writing aloud. Principals, other teachers, and parents can be invited.

Figure 25.1   Writing Process Stages Adapted for English Learners

STEP BY STEP

The steps in implementing a writing workshop are the following:

- *Introduce the writing process*—Introduce the writing process stage by stage, modeling each stage with your own writing. Talk about the need for prewriting to get ideas flowing and model a prewriting strategy such as webbing, listing, drawing, or brainstorming. Do your own prewriting using an overhead projector or chart so that the students can see the process and then give them an opportunity to prewrite. Follow this same pattern through each of the subsequent stages in writing, using your own developing piece as an example.

- *Provide daily writing time*—Provide writing materials and time to write each day. As students complete first drafts, schedule writing groups to give them feedback and suggestions. Set the classroom up to encourage interaction among the students as they write, revise, edit, and publish. Provide resources such as dictionaries, thesauruses, and content-area reading for reports.

- *Teach mini-lessons*—As you see the need, teach mini-lessons on skills and additional strategies for each of the stages. These lessons can be whole-group, small-group, or individual. Encourage the students to work at their own pace, writing and publishing on topics that relate to other curricular areas or to their own experiences.

- *Celebrate accomplishments*—As students complete the writing, find ways to celebrate their accomplishments and include their published works in the class library. Always give students an opportunity to share their published works and include their photos and an "About the Author" page in the published books.

- *Add technology*—The word processor is a natural addition to the writing workshop. Students can write their drafts by hand if only one computer is available and when they are ready to produce the final draft, they can type it on the word processor and print the final copy out—looking very professional. If more than one computer is available, students can write their drafts on the word processor. Using the computer for a writing workshop is motivational for a number of students and actually encourages students to write more. Making revisions is easier as well since the whole document does not need to be rewritten.

APPLICATIONS AND EXAMPLES

The fourth graders in Mr. Heil's classroom are using their writing workshop time to write plays for the dragon puppets they have created in art. Since the students are reading fantasy books in reading class, they have decided to write plays about dragons and damsels in distress. To prepare the students to write plays, Mr. Heil

> **Theory to Practice Connection**
> A writing workshop provides multiple opportunities for English learners to interact with English-speaking peers, providing opportunities for building both receptive and productive language (Wong Fillmore, 1982).

has brought in several scripts so the students can see the format they will use. The class brainstorms the elements of fantasy they remember from the stories they are reading and list several possibilities for plays. Mr. Heil organizes the students into groups so that each group has at least one strong writer and the English language learners have a language buddy who can translate for them if needed.

The groups start to work by looking at the puppets they have made and brainstorming a list of characters in their play. Each of the students is assigned an additional puppet to make and the script writing begins.

The students work in groups for several days, producing a rough draft, revising, and editing. Once their script is complete, they bring in the puppets they have made at home and begin to practice their puppet plays. Mr. Heil provides a puppet stage and the groups decide they must have backdrops to make the productions more realistic. At the end of the week, almost all of the groups are ready to perform.

Mr. Heil's class is using a writing workshop to create a collaborative project. They are providing support for the English language learners by working as a group to support the creation of a play. Once the script is complete, all of the group members participate in the performance. Because the script provides a strong scaffold for the oral presentation, all the students are confident reading their parts.

Ms. Martin teaches a senior humanities class in a large high school. She finds the final grading period in the senior year to be difficult since the students are eager to graduate and move on. Ms. Martin decides to try a new project for her senior group. Using a writing workshop format, she suggests that the students look back at the past four years and create a scenario based upon a current event, stage play, or film that will encourage the other seniors to recall something memorable about their high school experience. They begin by brainstorming a list of possibilities and then a list of characters who might be included in the scenarios.

The final lists provide some hilarious suggestions and the students choose topics on which to write. Acknowledging that she has a number of English learners in her class, she allows her students to choose to write alone, in pairs, or in small groups. Since the high school is named Hoover High, the students decide to produce a publication titled, "Hoover History Hash." Their stories change the history of the last four years in slightly wacky ways. One story has the principal as the hero of a local happening in which one of the students drove his car into the river. Mr. Posten, the principal, is hailed as the hero of the story and the events are changed just enough to make the story laughable.

Once the stories are written, Mr. Posten is so impressed with their originality that he chooses five to read over the intercom during the last week of school. The stories are so popular that the student publication is sold out.

CONCLUSION

A writing workshop is a strategy that has many possibilities. Because a writing workshop is intended to simulate the procedures that real authors follow as they prewrite, write, revise, edit, and publish, students have multiple opportunities for context-based verbal interactions as they research, confer, and give and receive feedback on their own and their colleagues' writing. Because the students choose their own topics for writing, students' ideas and experiences are validated. Writing in students' home languages is valued and collaboration to create bilingual (or multilingual) books can contribute to the growing library of such books in the classroom.

For a writing workshop to be effective, students must be given writing time daily. A structure must be set up in the classroom to support all the stages in the writing process and the students must be given instruction in ways to support one another in reading drafts, giving feedback, and editing collaboratively. When the workshop is encouraged and student interaction supported, nothing provides a more collaborative classroom environment than a writing workshop.

STRATEGIES ON VIDEO

Writing Workshop

You visit a first-grade writing workshop in Segment 11 of the DVD that accompanies this text. As you view this segment, think about the following:

- How does Ms. Leonard build on the students's prior experience to create a writing plan?
- What resources are available to the children in the classroom to support their success?
- How does the teacher find time to provide extra support for students who need it?
- How does the celebration circle add to the student's understanding of what constitutes good writing?

EXAMPLES OF APPROXIMATION BEHAVIORS RELATED TO THE TESOL STANDARDS

Pre-K–3 students will:

- use drawings to plan for writing activities.
- use resources in the classroom to support writing.

4–8 students will:

- discuss writing with peers and revise based on the discussion.

- edit writing for correct use of spelling and grammar.

9–12 students will:

- revise writing to enhance and clarify style and fluency.
- create written products based on research.

REFERENCES

Diaz-Rico, L., & Weed, K. (2002). *The cross-cultural, language, and academic handbook.* Boston: Allyn & Bacon.

Graves, D. (1983). *Writing: Teachers and children at work.* Portsmouth, NH: Heinemann.

Tompkins, G. E. (1994). *Teaching writing: Balancing process and product* (2nd ed.). Upper Saddle River, NJ: Merrill/Prentice Hall.

Wong Fillmore, L. (1982). Instructional language as linguistic input: Second language learning in classrooms. In L.C. Wilkinson (Ed.), *Communicating in the classroom* (pp. 283–296). Madison, WI: University of Wisconsin Press.

26

INTERACTIVE WRITING
Developing Writing Skills Through Active Scaffolding

This strategy addresses the following TESOL Standards:

Goal 2: To use English to achieve academically in all content areas

Standard 1: Students will use English to interact in the classroom.

Standard 2: Students will use English to obtain, process, construct, and provide

subject-matter information in spoken and written form.

Standard 3: Students will use appropriate learning strategies to construct and apply academic knowledge.

Interactive writing (Pinnell & McCarrier, 1994) is a form of shared writing or language experience lesson in which the teacher and students compose a story or text and share the pen in writing the words down on a chart or writing paper. The students are supported in using conventional spelling, capitalization, and punctuation. They are encouraged to write the parts of the text they are able to write. The teacher supplies the nonphonetic parts of words as she supports the students' decision making as they practice writing with conventional spelling and mechanics.

Interactive writing provides scaffolding for young children moving from invented spelling into conventional spelling or to older students who are in need of skill- and confidence-building. It is especially appropriate for English language learners because providing an experience about which to write is the first step in interactive writing. While discussing the experience, the students provide the language to be written. The teacher helps them in creating complete English sentences, sounding out the words to be written, and teaching the use of capitalization and punctuation. See Figure 26.1 for texts and skills that can be taught through interactive writing.

STEP BY STEP

The steps in conducting an interactive writing lesson are the following:

• ***Provide an experience on which to focus writing***—Provide an experience to write about. Interactive writing can be done after a field trip, to share daily news, or after reading a book.

Texts	Skills
Labels	Letter formation
Lists	Initial consonants
Daily news	Final consonants
Parent newsletters	Short vowels
Formula poems	Capital letters
Friendly letters	Punctuation
Business letters	Drafting
Reports	Revising
Book reports	Editing
Big books	Alliteration
Alphabet books	Varying word choice
Fact books	Writing dialogue
Autobiographies	Citing sources
New versions of old books	Conventional spelling

Figure 26.1   Texts and Skills Appropriate for Interactive Writing Lessons

The shared experience gives the group something to write about. If the interactive writing is done with an individual, it still works best to have a recent experience to write about.

• *Gather materials*—Display a piece of chart paper on which the text will be written, or a piece of writing paper if the text is to be written with an individual student. Gather markers and correction tape. Inch-wide correction tape is best when the story is written on chart paper.

• *Start the process*—Negotiate a sentence to be written. In the beginning it is best to start with a fairly simple sentence. Have the students help you count the words in the sentence. This helps you remember it and helps the students to see the individual words as they are written.

• *Scaffold the writing*—Say the first word in the sentence slowly, drawing out the sounds. Ask the students what letter they hear at the beginning of the word. Invite one student to come and write the beginning letter, but before it is written ask, "Will you write a lower-case letter or a capital letter?" If the student answers, "Capital," ask, "Why?" The idea is to provide all possible support for success as well as to verbalize the decisions to be made so that all students understand. Then, allow the student to write the letter. Note that with older—or more skilled—students you adjust this step, encouraging them to write whole words, or even phrases, and providing only the support necessary for the students to participate successfully.

• *Reread after each word is added*—After each word is written, go back and reread the sentence so far, pointing to each word as it is read. Continue to compose and support the children in writing the story following the same procedures. Focus on decisions that must be made as the writing is done, such as when to leave spaces, when to use capital letters, commas, periods, and so on. Use the correction tape whenever necessary, but always offer support to the student who made the error and encouragement when the error is corrected.

• *Read the story aloud*—After the text is written, celebrate with the students by having the group read it aloud. Choose a student or two to illustrate it and then display it proudly in the classroom. When completed, an interactive writing lesson should produce a story that is correctly spelled, spaced, punctuated, and capitalized. Every student in the group should be able to read it, pointing to each word as it is read.

APPLICATIONS AND EXAMPLES

Mr. Benning gathers his first-grade students on the carpet at the end of each day. He asks them to tell him about the activities they have enjoyed in school that day. As they talk about their experiences, Mr. Benning conducts an interactive writing lesson. Because he realizes that his students are at varying levels of English language development, each student is encouraged to participate as they are able. Some students can supply beginning letters in words, others can write whole words and even some phrases. Mr. Benning supports the students in sounding out words, leaving spaces, and placing punctuation marks and capital letters. After the text is complete, the students reread it together and talk about information they want to share with their parents. This daily ritual brings closure to their school day and reminds them of stories they want to share with their parents. It also provides a daily model for the uses of writing, conventional spelling, and mechanics. Figure 26.2 shows an example of Mr. Benning's first-grade daily news texts written by students from nine different language backgrounds.

Theory To Practice Connection

Interactive writing combines a number of effective teaching approaches for English learners: repeated practice of writing conventions, creating oral English sentences and writing them down, rereading of familiar text. All of this is supported through the interactive writing process (Tompkins & Collom, 2005).

> Today we went to the zoo.
> We saw lots of animals.
> Jose liked the monkeys the best.
> Paulie liked the elephant.
> We sang songs and ate lunch at the zoo.
> It was fun.

Figure 26.2 Mr. Benning's Daily News (Written Interactively)

Ms. Jacobs teaches eighth-grade English. Her students are reading literature related to the Underground Railroad and she decides that an interactive writing lesson would help the students to summarize their knowledge of the railroad while simultaneously providing an opportunity for her to teach writing mechanics in an authentic way.

Ms. Jacobs provides each student with an individual whiteboard and dry-erase marker. She begins the interactive writing lesson with a question about the book *The Story of Harriet Tubman, Conductor of the Underground Railroad* (McMullan, 1991), which she has been reading aloud to the class. The students help compose a narrative about the book and Tubman's participation in the Underground Railroad. One student is chosen to write on the chart paper provided, but all students are writing the text on their white boards. Ms. Jacobs is monitoring the whiteboards and noting the abilities of the individual students as they write. She also supports the students' composing skills by making observations such as, "We've already started two sentences with 'She.' Maybe we can think of another way to begin this sentence."

Ms. Jacobs' students can write entire sentences as they contribute to the interactive narrative, but she is helping them choose interesting words, complex sentences, and literary forms in their writing.

A fascinating fact comes to light as the students are composing the story and discussing the book. When Ms. Jacobs asks the question, "Where does the Underground Railroad run?" a number of the students answer, "From Mexico to California." This revelation provides an opportunity for Ms. Jacobs to use a United States map to correct a misconception among the students about historical information that she may not have known about if it had not been for the discussion generated by the interactive writing discussion.

The English language learners in the group are participating actively and having great success in composing the story. Because a group is composing the story, the anxiety level is lowered considerably and the peer interactions make writing more enjoyable. The students learn that some of their peers are very good at finding interesting words to use, while others are more adept at deciding on good titles. They are learning to appreciate each other's unique contributions.

CONCLUSION

Interactive writing involves the students in a thought process that is converted to writing. By discussing what they will write, and when and why conventions of writing are used, students are consistently reminded of the rules of writing and spelling in English. Students soon become more confident in their ability to transcribe their thoughts into readable English text because the teacher provides support by asking questions and reminding the students to think about the rules. The conventions and thoughts they practice writing as a group are then transferred to their independent writing.

STRATEGIES ON VIDEO
Interactive Writing

Segment 12 gives you an example of an interactive writing lesson in a kindergarten classroom. As you watch this segment, think about the following:

- How does the teacher support each writer so that they can participate successfully?
- What resources are available to help the students know how to form the letters?
- How are the students involved in creating and remembering the sentence?
- How is reading integrated into an interactive writing lesson?

EXAMPLES OF APPROXIMATION BEHAVIORS RELATED TO THE TESOL STANDARDS

Pre-K–3 students will:

- contribute a letter or word to an interactive writing activity.
- correct writing errors with the teacher's support.

4–8 students will:

- contribute a phrase or a sentence to an interactive writing activity.

- suggest changes in sequence or form to enhance interactive writing products.

9–12 students will:

- contribute ideas and format for interactive writing projects.
- collaboratively revise and restructure an interactive writing project.

REFERENCES

McMullan, K. (1991). *The story of Harriet Tubman, conductor of the Underground Railroad.* New York: Bantam Books.

Pinnell, G., & McCarrier, A. (1994). Interactive writing: A transition tool for assisting children in learning to read and write. In E. Hiebert & B. Taylor (Eds.), *Getting reading right from the start: Effective early literacy interventions* (pp. 149–170). Needham Heights, MA: Allyn & Bacon.

Tompkins, G., & Collom, S. (2005). *Sharing the pen: Using interactive writing in primary classrooms.* Upper Saddle River, NJ: Merrill/Prentice Hall.

SUGGESTED READINGS

Button, K., Johnson, M., & Furgerson, P. (1996). Interactive writing in a primary classroom. *The Reading Teacher, 49,* 446–454.

Fountas, I., & Pinnell, G. (1993). *Guided reading: Good first teaching for all children.* Portsmouth, NH: Heinemann.

CHAPTER 27

GIST
Exploring Tough Text

GIST or **Generating Interaction between Schemata and Text** (Cunningham, 1982) is a strategy for supporting comprehension of informational text. GIST is especially helpful when students are required to read long texts containing a significant amount of new information. Students work in cooperative groups and read sections of the text silently. After each short section is read silently, the members of the group work collaboratively to generate one sentence that summarizes the "gist" of the passage. In some very dense text, this summary sentence is generated paragraph by paragraph. Once a sentence is generated, members of the group write it on their own papers so that each group member ends up with a concise summary of the text. The teacher circulates among the groups to facilitate and provide support. This is a particularly effective strategy for use with English language learners because the group members have a chance to discuss and clarify meaning as they decide on the best summary sentence for the section or paragraph.

STEP BY STEP

The steps in implementing GIST are the following:

- ***Identify appropriate text for GIST***—Identify text that may cause some difficulty for the students. Decide whether the text must be read and summarized paragraph by paragraph or section by section and determine logical stopping or summarizing points.

- ***Group the students***—Divide the class into cooperative groups and identify a leader for each group. Make sure that each group contains a strong English speaker and reader. If possible, group English language learners with other students of the same language background who can provide first-language support if needed. If your main purpose is to facilitate understanding of the text, the discussion of the meaning and the negotiation of the best summary sentence can be done in the students' first languages and later translated to English. If your purpose is facilitating English communication, then the discussion should take place in English with first-language translations made only for the purpose of clarification.

- ***Demonstrate the strategy***—Demonstrate the strategy by discussing background knowledge and informing the students that they will be working in groups to create a summary of the material to be read. Post the summary points, the points in the reading at which each group is to stop, then discuss and summarize. See Figure 27.1 for an example of a summary point chart. Instruct the students to read the passage silently to the first summary point and then stop and write a one-sentence summary of what they read.

- ***Discuss summary sentences***—After the students have completed their summary sentence, ask one of the students to share his/hers with the class. Discuss the sentence as a group and add details that the class thinks will enhance the sentence. Instruct the students to write the summary sentence on their papers. The teacher serves as facilitator and quality controller, making sure that the summary sentences capture the "gist" of the paragraphs. It is important that the quality control be done in a supportive manner through questioning and supporting of the students' understanding of the text.

- ***Read and summarize paragraph by paragraph***—Explain to the class that they will be reading the entire selection in this manner. They will all read to each summary point, as indicated by the chart that is posted. As they wait for the rest of their group to finish reading they should be thinking of the main points in the section and formulating a summary sentence in their minds, or writing it on a scrap piece of paper. The group should then discuss the section and negotiate the best summary sentence they can write. Once the group has decided on a summary sentence, each member of the group writes the sentence on his/her own paper and the process begins again.

- ***Read and compare summary sentences***—Once the selection has been completed, have the groups read and compare their summary sentences. This provides an effective review of the passage read and gives an opportunity to correct any misconceptions. Again, the teacher serves as facilitator and questions the students to lead them to capture the meaning and nuance of the text.

Stop and summarize at these points:
1. Page 3, at the subheading
2. Page 7, at the bottom of the page
3. Page 9, after the chart
4. Page 13, at the subheading
5. Page 18, at the end of the selection

Figure 27.1 Sample of a Summary Point Chart

GROUP	Marcos	Juan	Diana	Carol	Carlos
Listens to others					
Contributes to summary					
Defends own ideas					
Participates verbally					
Takes leadership role					
Presents to class					

Figure 27.2   A Checklist for Documenting Student Interactions and Contributions During GIST Activity

• ***Assess student progress and understanding***—The group work time in this strategy is a perfect opportunity for the teacher to circulate around the room and listen. This is a good time to take anecdotal records, documenting student interactions and writing language samples for inclusion in the student portfolios. It is appropriate to create checklists for documenting specific behaviors exhibited by the students at this time, also. See Figure 27.2 for an example of such a checklist.

APPLICATIONS AND EXAMPLES

The fifth graders in Ms. Menashian's class have been studying the American Revolution. They have read the Jean Fritz biographies of the great men and women who lived at the time of the revolution and the contributions they made. Ms. Menashian wants to conclude the unit of study with the reading of Longfellow's poem "The Midnight Ride of Paul Revere." However, she wants her students to understand the significance of the poem, so she assigns the chapter "A Centennial Celebration" in Augusta Stevenson's biography *Paul Revere: Boston Patriot* (1986).

Ms. Menashian divides the fifth graders into cooperative groups to read and summarize the chapter. Because her class has a number of English language learners, Ms. Menashian makes sure that each group has a strong reader and several students in each group who speak the same home language. She posts a chart of summary points and the students begin reading and summarizing the selection. As she moves among the groups she hears some interesting discussion.

Theory to Practice Connection
Discussions in small groups provide a safe place for English learners to try out their new vocabulary. Group members provide scaffolding for one another (Gibbons, 2002).

"I don't understand this chapter. It says it was 1875," Andre says. "That's a hundred years after Paul Revere's ride."

"I think that's why it's called a centennial celebration. That's a celebration after a hundred years," Juanita says. "I think this chapter is going to talk about how they were still celebrating his ride after a hundred years."

"Oh, I get it," Andre says. "What should we write for our summary sentence?"

"How about this?" Tyra asks. "A hundred years after the famous midnight ride of Paul Revere, the people of Boston were still talking about how brave he was."

"That's good," Margaret says, "but it also said that they were proud of him because of his silverwork too."

"But they were more proud of his patriotism," Juanita says.

"What is patriotism?" Mario asks.

"It's being loyal to your country," Juanita answers. "He risked his life to warn the soldiers that the British soldiers were coming." Juanita says this in English and then repeats the explanation in Spanish.

"OK," Mario says. "So the people of Boston are proud of Paul Revere because he was a great silversmith but more because he was a great patriot."

"That's a good summary sentence," Andre says. "Let's use that one. Say it again, Mario."

As Mario repeats the sentence everyone writes it on their papers, including Mario. The group then reads the next section of the chapter.

When they have completed reading and discussing the chapter, their summary looks like this:

The people of Boston are proud of Paul Revere because he was a great silversmith but more because he was a great patriot.

On April 18, 1775, eight hundred British soldiers were going to Concord to seize the patriot ammunition and guns.

Patriot troops had to be warned that the British soldiers were coming so they could move the powder and guns.

John Hancock and Samuel Adams also needed to be told to leave Lexington before they were arrested and hanged for speaking against the king.

The patriots chose Paul Revere to make the ride to warn the troops that the British were coming.

It was a very dangerous ride because British soldiers and warships were guarding the whole area.

Lanterns in the Old North Church belfry would tell Paul Revere how the British soldiers had gone. There would be two lanterns if they had gone by water, one lantern if they had gone by land.

Paul Revere went to the sexton of the Old North Church and told him to put the lanterns in the church belfry when he knew how the soldiers were coming. Then Paul Revere rowed across the river.

Patriots across the river waited with Paul Revere while they watched for the lanterns.

Paul Revere stopped at all the houses between Boston and Lexington and warned everyone that the British were coming.

The Patriots all grabbed their guns and kept the British from getting to the guns. They also gave John Hancock and Samuel Adams time to escape.

Ms. Menashian was very pleased with the summaries the students wrote about the ride of Paul Revere and about the discussion of the importance of the ride that took place as the groups shared their summaries. As she concluded the study of the Revolution with the reading of the poem, "The Midnight Ride of Paul Revere" (Stevenson, 1986), she was sure that the students really understood the words and the significance of the event to American history.

Some of the reading in Ms. Hughes's 11th-grade literature class is extremely difficult for her students to understand. Although she is sure that her students will enjoy the reading of Mark Twain's most famous works, she is concerned that they will not understand the political significance of his work and its place in history. Because of the difficulty of some of the vocabulary in the biographic readings about Mark Twain, Ms. Hughes decides to encourage her students to work in cooperative groups. Being in groups allows them to discuss the vocabulary, to consider the politics involved at that particular time in history, and to comprehend the nuances in meaning that they might otherwise miss.

Ms. Hughes groups her students for the reading of Bernard de Voto's introductory chapter in *The Portable Mark Twain* (1984). She posts a chart that tells the groups to stop and summarize after each paragraph they read and she walks the class through the steps in the GIST procedure. She explains the double meanings of the term *gist* and the procedure name, which connects schemata and text.

"Who knows what it means to 'get the gist of things'?" Ms. Hughes asks.

"It means that you get the general idea," Leon answers.

"That's exactly right and today you are going to participate in an activity called GIST. You and the rest of your group will work together to figure out what the reading means. Because this introductory chapter is what I call 'tough text,' difficult to read and understand, I want you to stop after each paragraph and discuss the meaning. Your group will write one sentence to summarize each paragraph. When you are finished reading the introductory chapter and writing the summary sentences, you should have a good understanding of Mark Twain and his place in American history. We will talk about the chapter after you have completed the reading."

As the groups work their way through the chapter, Ms. Hughes circulates among the groups and occasionally gets drawn into the discussion. Because there are a number of difficult words in the reading, she also gathers words from the groups to add to the word wall. First-language translations for the new vocabulary are added to the word wall as necessary.

At the end of the period, Ms. Hughes asks the groups to share their summaries and they choose the best sentence for each paragraph to create a class summary of the chapter.

After the groups have read and summarized the introduction to the Mark Twain volume, Ms. Hughes asks the students to think about what they had learned and give an overall summary of the history of the time in which Twain wrote.

After the discussion of the introduction, Ms. Hughes assigns the students the first reading in the Mark Twain anthology and they discuss some vocabulary and background that they will need in order to understand the reading, *The Notorious Jumping Frog of Calaveras County*.

CONCLUSION

Students of all ages and at all stages of language development benefit from the use of collaborative strategies such as GIST. By placing students in heterogeneous groups, with a strong English reader and writer in each group, teachers can encourage discussion of the reading and give students a chance to clarify meaning and vocabulary. The group task of writing a summary sentence for each paragraph that is read provides an authentic assignment that requires the students to discuss the meaning of the paragraph and agree on a sentence that conveys the important information. Once the paragraphs are read and discussed and summary sentences are written and read, each student in the group has a concise summary of the reading assignment.

When several groups read and summarize the same text and then share their summaries, further discussion of the main ideas and supporting details frequently follows. This gives students another chance to hear the information discussed and new vocabulary clarified.

 ## STRATEGIES ON VIDEO

GIST

In Segment 13 you will view a GIST lesson in fourth grade. As you watch this segment, think about the following:

- How did Mr. Workmon make sure that his students understood the process?
- What was Mr. Workmon doing as the students were working?
- What did the teacher do when a group included a misconception in their summary?
- How would using this strategy support students in improving their language abilities?

EXAMPLES OF APPROXIMATION BEHAVIORS RELATED TO THE TESOL STANDARDS

Pre-K–3 students will:

- collaboratively write a summary of a paragraph.
- support their opinions in a group setting.

4–8 students will:

- identify main ideas in text.
- write summary sentences of paragraphs.

9–12 students will:

- discuss nuances of word meanings and negotiate with peers to accurately summarize bodies of text.
- explore specific word meanings related to content in the collaborative summarization of text.

REFERENCES

Cunningham, J. (1982). Generating interactions between schemata and text. In J. A. Niles & L. A. Harris (Eds.), *New inquiries in reading research and instruction* (pp. 42–47). Washington, DC: National Reading Conference.

deVoto, B. (Ed.) (1984). *The portable Mark Twain*. New York: Penguin Books.

Gibbons, P. (2002). *Scaffolding language, scaffolding learning*. Portsmouth, NH: Heinemann.

Stevenson, A. (1986). *Paul Revere: Boston patriot*. New York: Aladdin (Macmillan).

CHAPTER 28

SYNTAX SURGERY
Visually Manipulating English Grammar

This strategy addresses the following TESOL Standards:

Goal 1: To use English to communicate in social settings

Standard 1: Students will use English to participate in social interactions.

Standard 2: Students will interact in, through, and with spoken and written English for personal expression and enjoyment.

Standard 3: Students will use learning strategies to extend their communicative competence.

Goal 2: To use English to achieve academically in all content areas

Standard 1: Students will use English to interact in the classroom.

Standard 2: Students will use English to obtain, process, construct, and provide subject-matter information in spoken and written form.

Standard 3: Students will use appropriate learning strategies to construct and apply academic knowledge.

Goal 3: To use English in socially and culturally appropriate ways

Standard 1: Students will use the appropriate language variety, register, and genre according to audience, purpose, and setting.

Standard 3: Students will use appropriate learning strategies to extend their sociolinguistic and cultural competence.

Syntax surgery (Herrell, 1998) is a strategy that allows students to see the relationship of elements within a sentence that may be confusing to understand. Because English syntax often differs from the word order found in students' home languages, English language learners sometimes encounter difficulty in comprehending sentences they read or confuse word order when speaking or writing in English (Baltra, 1998).

Syntax surgery involves writing a sentence on a sentence strip and then cutting the sentence apart to rearrange it into more understandable pieces. Because the students actually witness the pieces of

352

the sentence being moved, they are more likely to understand and remember the English syntax rules when called on to use them in the future. Syntax surgery is also helpful in refining the students' understanding of the elements of writing and speaking that make their English difficult for others to understand; therefore, the use of this strategy helps them to be more confident in their use of English. Swain (1993) calls this refining of the spoken and written product vital to the development of fluency in her description of output theory.

STEP BY STEP

The steps in implementing syntax surgery are the following:

- ***Identify a problematic sentence***—Identify a sentence that is causing difficulty. It may be a sentence that the student has spoken where the home language word order conflicts with the English word order, or it may be a complex sentence encountered in reading that is causing confusion.

- ***Write the sentence and initiate the "surgery"***—Write the sentence on a sentence strip and reread the sentence aloud with the student or students involved in the speaking or reading activity. For example, if the sentence that was written by the student says, "She was wearing a sweater green," take a pair of scissors and cut the sentence apart in the place or places of difficulty. "She was wearing a sweater green," would be cut before the words *sweater* and *green*.

- ***Rearrange the words***—Rearrange the words in a pocket chart or on the chalk rail in the correct English sequence. Place "She was wearing a green sweater" on the chart and say, "This is the way we say it in English," reading the sentence with the correct English word order. Reaffirm the students' knowledge of the home language by rebuilding the sentence in the original order and say, "This would be the right order of the words in Spanish" (or other language) "but we say it this way in English," and put the words back into the correct order for English. Have the student read the corrected sentence along with you and then explain the difference in the word order as simply as you can.

- ***Practice more sentences with the same pattern***—Write a few more sentences with the same word pattern on sentence strips and have the students read them along with you for additional practice.

- ***Time the lessons***—Be careful not to use this lesson in a way that interrupts communication with the student. If the message the student was conveying was clear, respond to it modeling the correct English syntax. Write the student's sentence down and return at a later time to use the syntax surgery strategy to support the refinement of the student's English. Be observant of other students who might benefit from the explanation and use the opportunity to give instruction to several students at a time.

APPLICATIONS AND EXAMPLES

Ms. Newsome's fifth graders are reading a series of books by Beverly Cleary when one of her English language learners comes to her with a puzzled look on his face. "Ms. Newsome, this sentence doesn't make any sense."

"Let me see, Jorges," Ms. Newsome says. She reads the sentence aloud, "'She pushed her bed out from the wall so that something reaching out from under the curtains or slithering around the wall might not find her.' I see what you mean," Ms. Newsome says. "Let's see if we can figure it out. Let's write the sentence

on a sentence strip." As she writes the sentence on a sentence strip she reads it aloud with Jorges.

"OK, the first part of the sentence says, 'She pushed her bed out from the wall,'" Ms. Newsome says. "Do you understand what 'out from the wall' means?"

Jorges nods, "It means she moved the bed away from the wall."

"Exactly!" Ms. Newsome exclaims and she cuts that part of the sentence away from the rest of it.

"The next part says 'so that,' which means that the next part is going to tell us WHY she moved the bed," Ms. Newsome says as she cuts off the words *so that*.

"Here's where it gets tricky," Ms. Newsome explains. "'Something reaching out from under the curtains or slithering around the wall.' Now did the story say anything about something behind the curtains or on the wall?"

> **Theory to Practice Connection**
> Creating a visual to illustrate parts of a sentence allows the English learner to see the connections. Participating in the creation of the visual gives students opportunities to clarify meaning, as well (Baltra, 1998).

Jorges shakes his head, "No. That's why I'm confused."

"The key is the next word, *might*," Ms. Newsome says. "She's thinking there *might* be something behind the curtains or there *might* be something slithering around the wall. She's scared of things that *might* be in her room."

"Oh," Jorges says. "Now I get it." He takes the scissors and cuts *might* and then *not find her* away from the rest of the sentence. He arranges the sentence again to show the relationships among the clauses. "This makes sense," he says as he looks at the new arrangement.

"The words *something* and *might* are important. They give you clues that this is all in her imagination," Ms. Newsome says as she underlines the two words. "You're really good at this, Jorges," Ms. Newsome says with a smile. See Figure 28.1 to see how Jorges arranged the sentence.

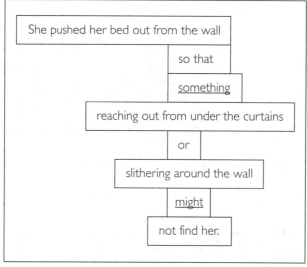

Figure 28.1   Jorges' Arrangement of the Sentence

Mr. Reynolds teaches 10th-grade English in a high school with a large number of Hispanic students. Mr. Reynolds finds that his students enjoy literature but need a lot of support in understanding some of the more formal language in the classic tales they read.

While in the midst of a study of Arthurian legends, Mr. Reynolds shows a video of *King Arthur and His World* and then shares a beautifully illustrated children's story book, *Young Lancelot*, by Robert D. San Souci (1996) to give the students a feel for the history, culture, and language of the times. The students then read *The Lady of the Lake* and *Excalibur* by Sir Thomas Malory, translated by Keith Baines (1996), which is a part of their literary anthology. The students are reading the tale, taking individual parts and trying their best to read with expression so the story will be as exciting as Mr. Reynolds's reading of *Young Lancelot*.

The language is difficult, however, and they often have to stop and discuss the meaning. Mr. Reynolds has used syntax surgery with his students on several occasions and decides to do it in a shortened version during the reading to move the process along so the meaning of the passage doesn't get lost in the analysis. As the students read aloud, Mr. Reynolds writes sections of a sentence on the chalkboard whenever the reading appears to be choppy or without expression. As

brachet (bre – chay) = animal of some kind
pursuing a trail = running along a trail
green marsh = green, wetland
licking his wounds = the knight's wounds
wringing = demonstrating

Is it <u>to him</u> that you will give your sister in marriage.
You will give your sister in marriage to him.

Because he did not see us, Merlin replied. I cast a spell over
him had he done so, you would not have <u>escaped</u> so lightly.
had he not done so = if he had done that

Figure 28.2 Mr. Reynolds's Syntax Surgery Shorthand

Mr. Reynolds writes the phrases or sentences on the board he separates the elements of the sentences that cause difficulty. For example, as a student reads:

> Riding once more through the forest, Sir Lancelot came upon a black brachet, eagerly pursuing a trail. Sir Lancelot followed and soon noticed traces of blood. The brachet kept glancing over its shoulder as if to insure that Sir Lancelot was still there, and finally came to an ancient castle which had been built on a green marsh. The brachet led the way across a shaky bridge and into the hall. A dead knight lay on the floor. The brachet went up to him and started licking his wounds, and then a lady appeared, haggard with grief and wringing her hands. (p. 131)

As the reader is reading this section Mr. Reynolds is writing brief notes on the board. See Figure 28.2 for Mr. Reynolds's notes to the readers. The student watches Mr. Reynolds and rereads the problem sentence using the clues Mr. Reynolds writes. The reading of the Malory tale goes smoothly using this strategy and the students don't lose the meaning in the process.

CONCLUSION

Syntax surgery is a strategy for making English syntax visible to the students. By using written diagrams as Mr. Reynolds does or cutting sentences apart as Ms. Newsome does, the students can both see and hear the differences in the word order in English or separate the thoughts within a complex sentence. By using several avenues to reinforce the English syntax, the students' understanding and memory are supported.

STRATEGIES ON VIDEO

Syntax Surgery

Middle school students perform syntax surgery in Segment 14 of the DVD. As you watch this lesson, think about the following:

- How was the lesson planned so that students addressed the irregular verbs several times?
- Why would cutting out the incorrect verb help the students to remember that they are irregular?
- What other grammar and syntax lesson could be addressed using this strategy?

EXAMPLES OF APPROXIMATION BEHAVIORS RELATED TO THE TESOL STANDARDS

Pre-K–3 students will:

- arrange word cards to create an English sentence.
- add descriptive words to sentences in appropriate places.

4–8 students will:

- expand sentences to include a sequence of adjectives or adverbs in appropriate places within the sentences.

- revise sentences to improve comprehensibility and flow.

9–12 students will:

- visually represent connections between clauses in complex sentences.
- combine sentences with a variety of appropriate connectives.

REFERENCES

Baines, K. (1996). *Malory's Le Morte d'Arthur.* New York: Penguin Books.

Baltra, A. (1998). *Hispanic ESL students reading in English: The language problem.* Unpublished manuscript. Fresno: California State University, Fresno.

Herrell, A. (1998). *Strategies for supporting English language learners as readers.* Manuscript submitted for publication.

San Souci, R. D. (1996). *Young Lancelot.* New York: Doubleday.

Swain, M. (1993). The output hypothesis: Just speaking and writing aren't enough. *The Canadian Modern Language Review, 50,* 158–164.

EFFECTIVE STRATEGIES FOR TEACHING WRITING

Robert C. Dixon, *JP Associates*; Stephen Isaacson, *Portland State University*; Marcy Stein, *University of Washington, Tacoma*

Writing is a highly complex process that writers ultimately apply independently (Bereiter & Scardamalia, 1982). Conceivably, writing is one of the most complex human activities (Bereiter, 1980; Hillocks, 1987; Isaacson, 1989; Scardamalia, 1981.) The inherent complexity of writing suggests that acquiring writing proficiency might prove to be difficult for many students—a speculation borne out both by descriptive research and the experience of many teachers.

For example, two decades ago, Applebee, Langer, and Mullis (1986) reported that students in fourth, eighth, and twelfth grades taking the National Assessment of Educational Progress (NAEP) performed poorly on measures of nonfiction writing: approximately half wrote adequate or better narrative and informative pieces, and only about a third wrote adequate or better persuasive pieces. Eleventh-grade students performed equally as poorly on the 1990 NAEP: they did not write much, and what they did write was of poor quality (Applebee [NAEP], 1990).

Results from the 1998 NAEP were similar (Greenwald, Persky, Campbell, & Masseo [NCES], 1999). There are four levels for reporting writing on the NAEP: below basic, basic, proficient, and advanced. More than half of the students tested scored within the "basic" range. One notable conclusion from the 1998 NAEP is that low-income students score lower than those from better economic backgrounds. The NAEP data and other previous research (Applebee, Langer, Jenkins, Mullis, & Foertsch, 1990; Christenson, Thurlow, Ysseldyke, & McVicar, 1989; Flower & Hayes, 1981) suggest that students in general education experience many writing difficulties. Yet, writing is *important* for so many students (Englert et al., 1988). Writing is not just an end in itself, but a means by which students demonstrate their knowledge within various content areas (Christenson et al., 1989; Graham, 1982; Harris & Graham, 1985).

The students who experience the greatest difficulties with writing are those with learning disabilities and emotional and/or behavioral problems (Englert & Raphael, 1988; Graham, 1982; Graham, Harris, MacArthur, & Schwartz, 1991; Morocco & Neuman, 1986; Montague, Maddux, & Dereshiwsky, 1990; Nodine, Barenbaum, & Newcomer, 1985; Thomas, Englert, & Gregg, 1987). Given the increasing diversity of children in classrooms, there is a need to identify elements of writing instruction that are likely to be most effective at helping teachers improve the writing of the broadest possible range of students. That is, given the practical limitations of the classroom, which characteristics of a *single* writing curriculum are likely to contribute to improved performance for the majority of students?

In this chapter we describe a few fundamental characteristics of writing instruction that can contribute significantly to a single writing curriculum that is effective with a broad range of students at various performance levels. First, we briefly describe some current issues in writing instruction. Then we turn to the specifics of instructional design.

CURRENT ISSUES IN WRITING INSTRUCTION

Opportunity to Learn

We stress a *single* effective writing curriculum because frequently, little or no real writing instruction takes place in regular classrooms (Applebee et al., 1990; Bridge & Hiebert, 1985; Langer & Applebee, 1986). Therefore, it seems quite impractical to advocate the implementation of two or more writing curricula in diverse classrooms as a means of accommodating the needs of diverse learners.

It goes without saying that the minimal requirement for adequate writing achievement is that effective writing instruction be made available to all students. In general, opportunity to learn has long been considered one of the major factors influencing achievement (in addition to pedagogical practice and aptitude; see Carroll, 1963). Students probably will not become better writers if they do not spend a relatively substantial part of most school days engaged in productive writing activities. Graves (1985) states, for example, that students should write for at least 30 minutes a day, at least four days a week, as opposed to a national average of writing one day in eight.

Author versus Secretary, or Author and Secretary

Allocating just any amount of time to "writing" is *not* likely to result in notable writing improvement. For example, neither "free writing" nor instruction on grammar and writing mechanics have proven, by themselves, to be effective means for improving writing performance (Hillocks, 1984). The elements of meaningful, allocated writing time are the principal subject of this chapter. (See Isaacson, 1994, for a full discussion of academic learning time and writing instruction.)

Smith (1982, cited in Isaacson, 1991) characterizes writing as a complex undertaking in which the writer works both as author and secretary throughout the processes of writing. The writer-as-author is concerned primarily with matters of content, including the origination and organization of ideas, levels of diction, and so on. Simultaneously, the writer-as-secretary is concerned with the mechanics of writing. Sometimes the secretary role is characterized as a concern related almost solely to the revision phase of writing, but for students with learning difficulties, mechanical skills such as handwriting and spelling can present severe obstacles to participation in all authoring processes (Graham, 1990).

The author-as-secretary characterization provides a framework for identifying vastly different orientations toward writing instruction. The first is the skills-dominant approach, in which instruction focuses primarily on the mechanics of writing: secretarial concerns. Based on several descriptive studies, this approach has been the predominant one in American schools for many years (Applebee, 1981; Bridge & Hiebert, 1985; Langer & Applebee, 1986; Leinhardt, Zigmond, & Cooley, 1980). Within this approach, composition activities are minimal, often limited to writing short answers or transcribing.

Even less emphasis seems to be placed on composition in skills-dominant approaches used with lower performing students. Such students receive a great deal of skills instruction (Englert et al., 1988; Graham et al., 1991; Isaacson, 1989; Roit & McKenzie, 1985), and even that instruction is poor, because it occurs in isolation and is unconnected with its presumed eventual use (Graves, 1985).

Interestingly, skills-dominant approaches are polemical ghosts, in that they have little if anything to recommend them. To our knowledge, no one advocates skills-dominant approaches in the literature. If there is a rationale for such approaches at all, we can only speculate as to what it might be. Perhaps someone believes that attention to mechanical skills will somehow result in improved composition. Perhaps someone believes that lower performing youngsters are incapable of creating coherent text without first acquiring a full complement of mechanical skills. Or perhaps no rationale for skills-dominant approaches exists at all; for example, a teacher who is not comfortable with his or her own composition ability might inadvertently slight composition instruction in the classroom. We know for certain only that skills-dominated approaches are in widespread use, without the benefit of empirical or theoretical support.

A second, nearly opposite approach to writing may have evolved in reaction to skills-based approaches: the composition-dominant approach, concerned primarily with, authoring aspects of writing. Advocates of this approach generally argue that instruction on mechanics should be restricted to those concerns students raise themselves in connection with the polishing stage of composition (DuCharme, Earl, & Poplin, 1989; Graves, 1983).

We have some general concerns with composition-dominant approaches. First, there is little research to support the hypothesis that the mechanics of writing will take care of themselves in the context of authentic writing experiences. Many of the gains reported anecdotally for students in composition-dominated programs could possibly be the result of maturation. In addition, some measures of collaborative efforts may mask individual achievement, or lack of it.

Second, there is strong evidence that mechanical difficulties can effectively preempt many students from meaningful participation in far more rewarding authoring roles (Graham, 1999; Graham, 1990; Morocco, Dalton, & Tivnan, 1990). The kinds of general difficulties experienced by many students with learning problems strongly suggest such students are not likely to acquire knowledge of any sort casually (Isaacson, 1991). In our well-justified haste to distance ourselves from skills-based approaches to writing, we should be cautious and thoughtful: mechanics are an integral part of writing.

If we envision writing as an interweaving of complexities involving both author and secretary roles, then perhaps parallel instruction is one means for resolving dominance conflicts. Within a parallel framework, instruction includes all aspects of writing from beginning to end—from conceptualization to "publication"—with a concerted focus on the integration of writing knowledge. (See Isaacson, 1989, for an in-depth discussion of this issue.)

Technology

While there have not been any startling, new pedagogical approaches to effective writing instruction in the last 15 years or so, the further proliferation of technology in recent years has had an impact on writing instruction and learning. For instance, the National Writing Project has been experimenting in recent years with professional development courses on how to teach writing, delivered by means of the Internet. Word processing remains a potentially significant tool for the improvement of writing instruction; its influence is greater than ever because more students than ever have access to it.

In recent years, some computer-based products have been developed to directly teach writing to students, integrating word processing, explicit instruction, and stimulating multimedia presentations that can serve as inspirations for writing.

Finally, assistive technology continues to grant access for many to the opportunity to write—many who would have no such access otherwise. For better or for worse, technology is, and is likely to remain for some time, an issue in writing instruction.

Writing Assessment

More than ever before, many individual states administer writing assessments at various grade levels. In some cases, high stakes are associated with such assessments. However, there are serious questions about the technical soundness of these assessments. One serious question is the extent to which the assessments are *fair* for students with disabilities, which is a dimension of *validity*. Some evidence suggests great inconsistencies in the fairness of state writing tests for students with disabilities (Isaacson, 1999).

PRINCIPLES FOR IMPROVING INSTRUCTIONAL STRATEGIES IN WRITING

The implication of time allocated to writing instruction (or the lack of time allocated to writing instruction) is clear and, it seems, unanimously advocated: more time needs to be allocated. Any controversy that exists relates to different approaches to such allocation of time.

In this chapter we apply the six design principles to both the author role and the secretary role of writers. Although we separate the roles for the sake of illustration, we wish to reemphasize that the roles co-exist and intertwine in authentic writing. Although the principles and applications we describe are research-based, we caution readers that much of the substantial research conducted on writing in recent years is descriptive, anecdotal, quasi-experimental, or otherwise questionable as the basis for making broad generalizations about effective writing instruction (Graham et al., 1991). Still, data from a few very good studies, coupled with knowledge of diverse learners and instructional design research, provide the basis for cautiously identifying some important aspects of effective writing instruction for students at diverse levels of writing proficiency.

Designing Instruction Around Big Ideas

Big Ideas and the Author Role in Writing.   In general, big ideas for writing instruction are those that seem to recur across successful writing programs. However, the notion of big ideas in general is not based as much on empirical evidence as on our intuitive analysis of the alternative: teaching small, inconsequential, or marginal aspects of writing.

Writing Process.   One well-known big idea in writing is usually referred to as *the writing process*. The idea that writing instruction should center on the stages through which writers most frequently work goes back more than 35 years, when Herum and Cummings (1970) wrote on the writing process for college students. Those educators may have been ahead of their time, because the widespread acceptance of their approach in public schools is usually credited to Graves (1983).

Although statements regarding the steps in the writing process vary from source to source, the following is representative of discussions on this topic:

1. *Planning*. This step often includes brainstorming, and various graphical or other ways to represent and begin to organize ideas. Sometimes, the initial brainstorming is referred to as "pre-planning," while the early attempts at organization are considered mainstream planning.
2. *Drafting*. Once students have organized their ideas, they can develop their first rough draft. The goal of the draft is to focus upon the *author* role in writing, with little attention paid to the *secretary* role.
3. *Editing/Revising*. These tasks are sometimes viewed as separate operations. Regardless, revising refers primarily to rewriting portions of a draft, while editing now focuses a great deal of attention on the "secretary" role in writing.
4. *Publishing*. Many versions of the writing process include publishing as the final step in the process. Publishing (for peers or others) is thought to give students extra motivation to make their writing as good as they can, and to demonstrate how most writing "ends up" in real-world writing applications.

Presumably, professional writers and those for whom writing is a major part of their profession have always reiteratively planned, drafted, and revised their work, dating back to the classical Greek rhetoricians. Surely it is past time for school children learning to write to be let in on this fairly public "secret" of good writers.

Text Structures. An awareness of the writing process by itself, however necessary to writing instruction, appears to be insufficient for consistent results, particularly for students with learning disabilities and with other learning difficulties (Englert et al., 1991). *Text structure* is another big authoring idea that has resulted in impressive achievement gains when combined with process writing. Each writing genre can be identified by its own set of structural characteristics. Stories, for example, always have a protagonist, a crisis, developing incidents, and a resolution. Students who are unaware of such common recurring elements might write "stories" that are more like rambling narratives or chronologies than true stories.

Several studies have shown solid promise for teaching text structures in conjunction with process writing (Graham & Harris, 1989; Hillocks, 1986; Meyer & Freedle, 1984). The work of Englert et al. (1991) is especially promising in terms of effective writing instruction for diverse learners in that it demonstrates how writing can be effectively taught simultaneously to mainstreamed learners with disabilities and their average-achieving peers.

Englert et al. (1991) also have shown a distinct advantage of focusing on big ideas: their instructional program taught *less*, but students learned *more*. That is, the program they developed taught only two text structures within a school year, but those structures (explanations and compare/contrast) were important to future schooling success, students learned them well, and the results on measures of transference were good. In contrast, our informal analysis of language arts texts reveals that between a dozen and two dozen text structures are typically "taught for exposure" within a single school year. When too much material is "taught for exposure" or merely "covered," many students appear to learn and retain little. The study by Englert et al. (1991) suggests that "less is more" when the content chosen is truly important.

Peer Interaction. Finally, peer interaction appears to be important for improved composition performance. Collaborative work has proven to be an effective instructional tool in many subject matter domains, but it has a particular benefit to writing instruction: When working in cooperative groups, each student has the opportunity to participate in authoring, editing, and revising. Although the act of writing is often a covert and solitary endeavor for mature and able writers, those *learning* to write benefit from many opportunities to talk about writing with peers.

Big Ideas and the Secretary Role in Writing. We can conceive of several potential big ideas related to writing mechanics, ideas that promote understanding and reduce the learning burden for students. Morphology may be a big idea for spelling instruction (Dixon, 1991; Henry, 1988). The idea of combining manuscript and cursive writing into a single system, as in the D'Nealian writing program (Brown, 1984), promises substantial efficiency for teaching writing. Effective keyboarding instruction also might help to reduce the burden of simply setting print to page (Brown, 1984) and promises substantial efficiency in teaching handwriting.

Hillocks's (1984) widely known research review of effective writing practices suggested that although sentence combining alone is not the most effective way to improve writing, it was more effective than other approaches examined (teaching grammar, free writing, using good models of writing). Sentence combining and manipulation, then, might be considered a significant but nondominant big idea for teaching writing mechanics. (We illustrate this possibility more fully in later sections of this chapter.)

The notion of big ideas is less an instructional design characteristic than a foundation on which to build successful instruction. We do not *design* big ideas; we *uncover* them through a careful and complete analysis of content-area literature. Big ideas do not guide us on *how* to teach; they are a major factor in determining *what* to focus on as we design instruction.

Designing Conspicuous Strategies

Conspicuous Strategies and the Author Role in Writing.   Most students with learning difficulties, and many average-achieving students, do not automatically benefit from simply being exposed to big ideas, such as the steps in the writing process or text structures. A substantial body of research has accumulated that supports the teaching of conspicuous strategies for using those ideas (see Deshler & Schumaker, 1986; Pressley, Symons, Snyder, & Cariglia-Bull, 1989).

A teacher once described to the first author of this chapter the difference between the *old* and *new* ways of teaching writing for one of her students: "He used to sit, unable to get started, when trying to write about his summer vacation. Now, he sits, unable to get started, when trying to *plan* what he is going to write."

A conspicuous *planning strategy* could clarify for students some specific steps for starting and successfully completing their planning. The steps in such strategies derive from the best efforts of subject matter specialists to uncover or emulate cognitive processes that are normally employed covertly by experts. However, teaching just any set of steps to follow does not necessarily constitute a good strategy.

The best strategies appear to be those that are *intermediate in generality* (Prawat, 1989). If a strategy is too general, it is not likely to lead to reliable results. For example, "think before you write" is a general strategy and a good idea, but is too general to be of much practical value for many learners. On the other hand, a strategy that is too narrow is likely to result in the rote acquisition of some bit of knowledge with little potential for transference.

Conspicuous strategy instruction has been used with promising results to teach all phases of the writing process: planning (Harris & Graham, 1985), text structure (Englert et al., 1991; Graham &

Harris, 1989), and revising (MacArthur, Graham, & Schwartz, 1991). Such strategies have appeared to meet the intermediate-in-generality criterion.

For example, Graham and Harris (1989) taught students to generate and organize story ideas by asking themselves questions related to the parts of the story: "What does the main character want to do?" (p. 98). On the one hand, the strategy was not narrow: The questions taught in the study all involved parts of stories. On the other hand, the strategy was broad enough: It directed students' attention to the elements common to all stories.

Conspicuous Strategies and the Secretary Role in Writing. Assume that a student is puzzling over the following sentence while attempting to edit and revise a draft:

> *All of we young people seem to like ice cream.*

Is it, the student wonders, *we* or *us* young people? In terms of grammar, the answer can involve a complex array of spiraling knowledge: nominative case, objective case, objects of verbs, objects of prepositions, predicate nominatives, appositives. It is little wonder that many teachers would choose to forgo a grammatical approach in favor of nearly almost any other option, such as telling the student the answer or suggesting that the student rewrite the sentence to make the problem disappear.

Yet the problem can be attacked via conspicuous strategy instruction, with relatively little effort and complexity, and with relatively high potential for transference. The strategy is to decompose or simplify the sentence in question, then examine the results:

> *All young people seem to like ice cream.*
> *All of we/us seem to like ice cream.*

A native speaker of English who does not have a severe language disorder will instantly recognize *us* as the correct choice in the simpler sentence and realize that it is, therefore, the correct choice in the original sentence.

The same general strategy can be applied to far different instances of pronoun case, and to difficulties not involving pronoun case at all.

> *pronoun case: compounds*

> *John gave Mary and I/me a new book.*
> *John gave Mary a new book.*
> *John gave me a new book.*

> *subject/verb agreement*

> *Original sentence: None of the boys was/were on time.*
> *First simplification: Not one of the boys was/were on time.*
> *Second simplification: Not one was on time.*

Designing conspicuous strategies is challenging. We tend to readily recognize good strategies that others have designed, but most instructional designers agree that designing a good strategy from scratch is no simple matter. The best we can do is to suggest that anyone attempting to design conspicuous strategies begin with *something*, then evaluate the early attempts critically, using "intermediate generality" as the principal criterion for analysis. Whenever possible, promising strategies should be field-tested with students.

Designing Mediated Scaffolding

Mediated Scaffolding and the Author Role in Writing. We are using the term "scaffolding" broadly to refer to many kinds of assistance that students may receive as they move toward deeper understanding of what is being taught. Scaffolding may be provided directly by teachers, through guidance and feedback; or it may be provided by peers, through collaboration, or built into instructional materials, through devices that facilitate the successful completion of various tasks.

A primary characteristic of successful conspicuous strategy instruction, discussed above, is scaffolding and guided practice in various forms (Pressley, Harris, & Marks, 1992; Pressley et al., 1989). Two aspects of such scaffolding seem worthy of special note. First, it is provided on an *as-needed* basis and is gradually diminished over time. Second, it includes not only strategies for accomplishing writing goals but provides for self-regulation as well. That is, students are taught to regulate their own thinking about the use of composing strategies. Taken together, these features seem critical to the goal of independence for students with learning difficulties and their average-achieving peers alike.

In addition, collaborative work among students constitutes a form of scaffolding. When students work together on projects, they act as resources for one another for everything from planning a piece of writing to final revision and editing. We should caution, however, that practitioners might be careful to observe the same gradual reduction of scaffolding as advocated by Graham et al. (1991). Otherwise, there is the danger that some students will develop a dependency on collaboration. Put another way, students will fail to achieve self-regulation if scaffolding of any variety is not gradually removed—including the type of scaffolding provided through peer collaboration.

The kinds of scaffolding that are built into tasks are sometimes referred to as *procedural facilitators*. The idea of using procedural facilitation for writing originated with Bereiter and Scardamalia (1982). It is a form of help that assumes students have underlying competencies, but that they are having difficulty implementing them due to the complexity of writing. For example, if a student really *knows* the structure of a given text type, such as a story, but can't effectively plan a draft around that structure because of the complexities involved, then a procedural facilitator could help lessen the cognitive burden of the task.

Graham et al. (1991) caution that the effective use of procedural facilitators is probably dependent on integration with other forms of help whenever the cause of student difficulties is something other than inability to execute complex cognitive demands. That is, if students know how to do something complex, but have trouble using that knowledge, then a procedural facilitator alone might be enough help. But if students have not learned the complex strategy to begin with, then other types of scaffolding are probably necessary. Englert et al. (1991) used procedural facilitation, in conjunction with big ideas, strategies, and other instructional characteristics, to teach writing simultaneously to mainstreamed students with learning disabilities and their nondisabled peers.

Figure 29-1 contains a series of think sheets that illustrate how procedural facilitators for the writing process can enhance the effectiveness of other instructional considerations. All five think sheets are designed to facilitate stages in the writing process (except publication): planning, organizing, revising, and editing.

Figure 29-1A gives students guidance in planning their writing. The potential in such a procedural facilitator is probably most likely to be realized when it is used in conjunction with scaffolded strategy instruction: teacher and student models of planning, frequent discussion with teachers and peers, and frequent monitoring of student work and feedback.

Figure 29-1B specifically facilitates the drafting of one particular text structure: explanations. A different genre, such as a story, requires a different think sheet. An example of a story organization think sheet is given in Figure 29-2.

Figure 29-1C helps students understand the *inner dialogue* role of writers and helps encourage self-regulation. This self-editing think sheet gives students an opportunity to reflect on a draft and to possibly make changes before anyone else reads it.

The Editor's Feedback Worksheet illustrated in Figure 29-1D is based on the assumption that students might not only have difficulty with their own writing, but difficulty giving constructive feedback on the writing of others, as well. We base that assumption less on descriptive research than on the observations of many teachers with whom we have worked.

Finally, Figure 29-1E illustrates a think sheet that could help facilitate revision. In addition to providing guided application of revision strategies, it helps put the role of editors in perspective: that of a valuable resource.

Not only can any given phase of instruction be scaffolded, but instruction on writing a given text structure from beginning to end can be scaffolded as well. Englert et al. (1991), for example, had students write their first explanation as a group project, with a great deal of interaction among students and between teachers and students. Next, students wrote individual papers, but also with substantial support from teachers and other students. Finally, students wrote a *third* explanation in which students were encouraged to write independently, but were given support as needs arose.

Planning Think Sheet

Name of writer _____ Date _____

Topic _____

Who will the audience be? _____

What is my goal? _____

Everything I already know about this topic—anything I can think of:

_____

_____

Possible ways to group my ideas:

_____

_____

Figure 29.1A Think Sheet for Helping Students Plan Their Writing

Organization Think Sheet
Explanation

What am I explaining? _____

What will the reader need (if anything)? Is there any special setting for this?

_____

What can I tell readers at the beginning to get them interested? _____

_____

List the steps:

1. _____
2. _____
3. _____
4. _____
5. _____
6. _____

First   Next   Then   After   Second   Third   Finally

Figure 29.1B Think Sheet for Helping Students Organize an Explanation

Self-Editing Think Sheet
Explanation
My Impressions

The things I like best   The things I like least

_____   _____

A Good Explanation?

Everything is clear.   □

There is a statement saying what is being explained.   □

I've used good key words.   □   The steps are in order.   □

I've added something of special interest to my readers.   □

I've included what is needed, if anything.   □

I've finished with a good summary statement.   □

Questions I would like to ask my editor—friends, teachers, parents—before revision:

1. _____
2. _____

Ideas for Revision

_____   _____

_____   _____

Figure 29.1C Think Sheet for Helping Students Edit Their Own Drafts

Editor's Feedback Worksheet

Title of paper I am editing: _____

Author _____

1. What I like most about this paper: _____

_____

2. Parts I think are not clear: _____

_____

_____

3. Suggestions for improving:

   □ Better introduction   □ Better use of key words

   □ More examples   □ Change organization

   □ Other _____

_____

_____

_____

Figure 29.1D Think Sheet for Helping Students Give Feedback to Other Students

Revision Think Sheet

Suggestions from my Editor

1. Read editor's feedback worksheet carefully.

2. List the suggestions you are interested in using:

_____

_____

Adding Polish

1. At this point, can you think of a good way to get your readers interested right at the beginning of the paper?

_____

2. Does each part of the paper make the reader want to read the next part? _____

_____

3. How is your ending? Any additional ideas for summing everything up neatly?

_____

Revising

Use this page, your self-edit think sheet, and your editor's feedback worksheet as the basis for beginning to revise your draft.

Consider submitting your revision to an editor for further feedback.

Figure 29.1E Think Sheet for Helping Students Revise Their Drafts

That sequence of events can be summarized as *four* extensive opportunities with a single text structure: a complete teacher model of all phases in the writing process as they apply to explanations; the complete development of a class explanation; and two individually written explanations. In the course of the study, students studied explanations extensively, and learned to write them well. This approach is in contrast to that of typical language arts texts, in which a single text structure is taught in a period of a week or less, with little evidence of effectiveness.

Organization Think Sheet
Story

Protagonist? _____

Antagonist? _____

What is the crisis or problem the protagonist must overcome?

_____

_____

Developing incidents

_____

_____

_____

_____

_____

Climax

_____

_____

Ending

_____

_____

Figure 29.2 Think Sheet for Helping Students Organize a Story

Mediated Scaffolding and the Secretary Role in Writing. Few students are likely to fully understand and apply sentence-manipulation strategies, such as those outlined in the last section, without support. Such support can come in a variety of forms, including teacher guidance on the use of procedural facilitators such as those illustrated in Figure 29.3.

In Level 1 tasks, strategies are modeled and heavy scaffolding is provided to ensure that students' first attempts to apply the strategy are successful. At each successive level, a piece of scaffolding is taken away, leading to self-regulated, independent application—at Level 5 in this case. This is in sharp contrast to the approach taken in many textbooks, in which students are given a model, no explicit strategy based on big ideas, and then are expected to complete several application tasks independently.

A straightforward procedure for designing scaffolded tasks is that of beginning at the end. That is, the easiest tasks to design are generally those that represent the final, independent *outcome* that we would like to see students achieve. In the example given in Figure 29-3, the Level 5 task is the outcome task. From here, the designer can work backward, modifying the outcome task slightly by making it slightly easier, then making that task slightly easier, until the designer reaches the beginning: a highly scaffolded task that ensures high success for all or nearly all students.

Designing Strategic Integration

Strategic Integration and the Author Role in Writing. The issue of knowledge integration is crucial at several levels in language arts instruction. At the broadest level, reading and writing instruction can potentially be integrated based on the observation that writers are readers and readers, hopefully, are writers. This relationship between reading and writing has been illustrated by Raphael and Englert (1990).

Also of particular interest is the relationship between writing mechanics and composition. A genuinely holistic view of writing, we believe, must accommodate all those writing elements that in fact intertwine to produce "good writing."

Specific to composition, knowledge of basic text structure should be integrated as a means of efficiently teaching more advanced and complex structures—those used most frequently by expert writers. One major instructional contributor to such integration is cumulative review (discussed in a later section of this chapter).

Level 1: Interactive Model/Heavy Scaffold

Sometimes it is difficult to know when to use words such as *I* and *me* or *she* and *her.* You can usually figure out the right word to use by breaking the sentence into two simpler sentences.

Circle the correct choice in the second simpler sentence. That is the correct choice in the longer sentence.

1. Longer sentence: The doctor gave Elicia and I/me a flu shot.
   Simpler sentences:
   The doctor gave Elicia a flu shot.
   The doctor gave I/me a flu shot.

Level 2: Relatively Heavy Scaffolding

You can usually figure out what word to use by breaking a sentence into two simpler sentences.

For each sentence, one simpler sentence is given for you. First, write the other simpler sentence. Then circle the right word in the longer sentence.

1. Longer sentence: She/Her and John lived next door to us for four years.
   John lived next door to us for four years.

_____

Level 3: Minor Prompting for Scaffolding

For each sentence, write the two simpler sentences. Then circle the right word in the longer sentence.

1. Before going on our camping trip, Melinda and I/me prepared all our supplies.

_____

_____

Level 4: Only Reminder as Scaffold

Circle the correct word in each sentence. Remember, the word that's right in the simpler sentence is also right in the longer sentence.

1. After the team members left, they/them and some other friends went out for burgers.

Level 5: Independent—No Scaffolding

Circle the correct word in each sentence.

1. The movie started before Jaques and I/me arrived.

Figure 29.3 Levels of Scaffolding for a Sentence Manipulation Strategy

The major ingredients of instruction aimed at achieving integration appear to be, first, that students acquire fluency with the knowledge to be integrated, and, second, that instruction deliberately focuses on the integration of such knowledge. All of the instructional characteristics discussed in this chapter potentially contribute to the former: a focus on big ideas, strategies, and so on. In fact, a focus on big ideas alone would tend to encourage knowledge integration because big ideas typically comprise other knowledge realms within a domain.

Strategic Integration and the Secretary Role in Writing. In addition to integrating writing mechanics and composition, we believe that mechanics should be integrated among themselves. The Level 5 task illustrated in Figure 29.3 might be the end of isolated work on pronoun case, but it should be the beginning of integration. When students write, they must discriminately select from among their entire repertoire of writing knowledge. In authentic writing, they are not prompted to use the correct case for pronouns, for instance. Cumulative review serves as a means for making instructional tasks closely emulate the conditions of writing.

Integration is not difficult to design into instruction if the designer keeps one principle in mind: Don't force it. It might be tempting to jump on a knowledge integration bandwagon, but an instructional designer should focus on those aspects of a content area that integrate naturally. For example, if morphology is a big idea in spelling instruction, then spelling, vocabulary, etymology, and even parts of speech interrelate with one another naturally. The morphological parts of the word *alchemist*, for instance, relate to spelling (*al* + *chem* + *ist*), vocabulary (*al-* means "the" and *chem* means "to pour"), word history (the part *al*-comes from the Arabic), and parts of speech (*-ist* means "one who" and forms nouns).

Designing Primed Background Knowledge

Primed Background Knowledge and the Author Role in Writing.   With respect to composition, primed background knowledge is a less critical characteristic of effective instruction relative to other content areas. Learning a given text structure, for example, is not dependent upon a large base of other foundational knowledge. The knowledge that is required to learn text structures can be characterized as the kinds of basic "knowledge of the world" that most school children, other than those with the severest disabilities, are likely to possess.

Primed Background Knowledge and the Secretary Role in Writing.   Primed background knowledge is usually important with respect to the acquisition of writing mechanics skill and knowledge. Relative to grammar and usage, in particular, background knowledge can be of crucial importance, depending on the strategies employed to teach these areas. For example, the traditional approach to teaching pronoun case is through the use of grammatical rules. Those rules, in turn, depend heavily on a broad and deep range of background knowledge, including, possibly, the notion of case, and objects of verbs and of prepositions, subjects, and pronouns.

An instructional designer can determine necessary background knowledge by examining strategies closely. Are there any concepts in the strategy that students might not know fluently? One option for accommodating background knowledge is to test for it. Students who already have prerequisite background knowledge are ready to learn the material. Other students either should not be placed in the instruction, or if they are placed, the instruction should include necessary background knowledge.

Designing Judicious Review

Judicious Review and the Author Role in Writing.   Review in writing instruction has received little attention in the literature. However, the general benefits of review have, been shown across content areas through relatively substantial research. As discussed elsewhere in this book (see Chapter 1), Dempster (1991) summarizes that effective review is adequate, distributed, cumulative, and varied. In addition, there is reason to believe that even excellent writing instruction might be further improved through use of effective review. Graham et al. (1991) point out that we need to "continue to investigate procedures for promoting strategy maintenance and generalization" (p. 103).

The study by Englert et al. (1991) illustrates the potential benefits of *adequate* review. With a complex cognitive process such as composing, it is not surprising to find that a large amount of application opportunity is necessary for mastery.

We are unaware of direct or indirect research on distributed review as it applies to composition. However, the procedures recommended by Englert and her associates (Englert et al. 1991; Raphael & Englert, 1990) tend to strongly support cumulative review, and to a lesser degree, distributed review.

Englert and her associates initially teach distinct text structures, such as explanation and compare and contrast. They teach those structures *thoroughly*: approximately half a school year each for explanations and compare and contrast. Compared with the typical basal "one-topic-per-week" organization, this approach might be thought of as *very* massed practice. However, because scaffolding is gradually reduced as students learn, this approach has some of the attributes of distributed practice as well.

Eventually, students combine basic text structures into more complex writing, scaffolded in part by *expert* think sheets, which are more generic than those for specific text structures. Such practice, in effect, constitutes both a distribution and an accumulation of knowledge.

Finally, in order to promote transference and generalization, review should be varied. With respect to composition specifically, work on a particular text structure can be reasonably varied by simply allowing students to select different topics about which to write. There is evidence, too, of generalization from a set of basic text structures to more complex texts incorporating one or more of the basic structures. For example, in a persuasive essay it is common to find elements of nonfiction narrative, explanation, and comparison and contrast. The crucial prerequisite for such transference appears to be that the "transfer knowledge" (basic text structures) be taught thoroughly to begin with (Englert et al., 1991).

When review is not varied, the result is likely to be a rote-like acquisition of knowledge. The opposite extreme also is possible: review may be so varied that *something else* is actually being reviewed.

Judicious Review and the Secretary Role in Writing.   How much review of sentence-manipulation strategies is adequate? The answer can be found only through field testing with students. However, that amount might be relatively small. First, if the strategy is meaningful, that alone enhances memory (Torgeson, 1988). Second, if the review is well distributed, less total review should be required.

Reviewing cumulatively is critical to full understanding and to realistic integration with composition. In a sense, the Level 5 task shown in Figure 29-3 is still scaffolded to some extent, simply because it applies to only one of many possible applications of sentence-manipulation strategies: first-person plural pronouns in appositives. To learn just how sentence manipulation can be applied to solve a variety of writing mechanics problems, the strategy would need to be applied to those problems cumulatively, as each type is taught (pronouns in compounds, subject-verb agreement, several punctuation applications, etc.).

Finally, the review should include widely varying examples, in order to promote transference of the strategy, but the examples should not vary to the extent that something untaught is being reviewed. We found a lesson in a language arts basal text, for example, that only addressed the pronoun case in compounds, with no instruction on appositives, but then almost immediately gave students practice on pronoun case in appositives.

THE APPLICATION OF INSTRUCTIONAL DESIGN PRINCIPLES

Developing Instructional Tools

Developers should design tools in writing that provide intensive instruction on a small number of text structures in each school year. Instruction should emphasize stages in the writing process, and provide for collaborative work as a means of clarifying the reader-writer relationship. Tools should teach mechanical skills concurrently with composition, focusing upon big ideas such as sentence manipulation to learn usage, or morphology for spelling.

Most critically, developers should provide explicit strategies. However, strategies should not only be explicit, but should be "medium" in terms of generality as well. Such strategies are not simple to develop, but they are between strategies that are too narrow, or too broad. A narrow strategy might be, "Start each paragraph with a topic sentence." A broad writing strategy is "plan before writing."

After students have studied the text structure of a specific writing genre or something else new, their initial work should be supported temporarily by simplified tasks. For instance, think sheets can be provided for each genre and for many mechanics activities. Initially, such aids should lend considerable support to students by virtually *forcing* the appropriate organization of thoughts. Gradually, simplified tasks should be converted into complex, fully self-regulated tasks.

Tools should be designed to purposefully highlight knowledge that naturally integrates to promote more complex knowledge structures. Different text structures (explanations, comparisons, arguments) can and should be integrated into more complex, "expert" structures. Most importantly, in the arena of writing, composition and writing mechanics should be well integrated.

Ideally, instructional tools should include placement tools for determining the extent to which students possess relevant background knowledge. Tools should then provide for those students with gaps in background knowledge by presenting it *relatively* close to the introduction of the target knowledge for which it is prerequisite. For instance, in order for students to write good explanations, they should have some knowledge of words indicating chronology, such as *first, then, next, after, finally,* and so on. Such knowledge is likely to be a part of general background knowledge for many students, but not for some diverse learners. If these students are able to spend time using such words to sequence events prior to the introduction of an explanation text structure, then they will be in a much better position to learn that new structure on a pace with their peers.

The kind of deep understanding required for complex problem solving rarely develops within a short period of time. Review designed according to solid empirical evidence can help students acquire and maintain deep understanding, as well as the kind of fluency required to successfully complete many complex cognitive tasks (such as most writing tasks). If less material but more important material is taught thoroughly (big ideas), then there is plenty of "room" in instructional tools for review that is adequate, distributed, and cumulative. Moreover, *thorough* instruction includes many varied opportunities to apply strategies, which in turn result in better transference of knowledge. This is particularly important with respect to writing, where a given text structure can potentially be used for an nearly unlimited array of purposes.

Selecting Instructional Tools

When selecting instructional tools in writing, evaluate prospective materials to determine the extent to which they focus upon big ideas in composition and mechanics. More time should be allocated to these big ideas than to other, less critical content. Next, identify what explicit strategies, if any, are associated with important, big ideas. The following problems sometimes occur:

1. No explicit strategy can be found.
2. The strategy is explicit, but too narrow or too broad. In general, the strategies used to teach composition tend to be quite broad, and the strategies used to teach writing mechanics tend to be quite narrow.
3. The strategy is explicit and of *medium generality,* but some steps are ambiguous or confusing.

Examine the activities associated with a major topic to see whether scaffolded tasks are routinely provided. One should be able to imagine students "easing in" to full understanding and complete independence as they work from early to later tasks on a given topic. Instructional tools for writing should not, however, go to the extreme of providing scaffolding that is never disassembled. An overzealous dependence upon cooperative work, for example, can effectively prevent many students from achieving individual accountability for their work.

The evaluation of tools can focus to a great extent upon the degree to which important, big ideas are explicitly interrelated. Some tools have emerged in recent years that are excellent in that writing mechanics are not simply *exposed and dropped,* but rather, they accumulate over time to create more and more realistic writing applications. A straightforward method of evaluating materials for integration is to select an instructional unit that would normally be taught in February or March at a given grade level, and then to examine that unit to determine the extent to which earlier topics are integrated in the selected unit.

Instructional tools can be examined to determine the extent to which they accommodate prior knowledge requirements. For example, some review of basic paragraph structure a week or two before the introduction of a new text structure can help diminish differences among students. New strategies associated with big ideas, in particular, should be examined from the viewpoint of a diverse learner to determine whether the strategy assumes crucial background knowledge that some students might not possess.

A "safe" and relatively easy way to evaluate tools for review is, in general, to look for *a lot* of review. Such tools are more likely to be effective, and are the most practical for teachers to use, since eliminating review opportunities is a much simpler matter for teachers than adding them.

Modifying Instructional Tools

To modify instructional tools in writing, identify big ideas in existing materials and plan to allocate more time to them—time "borrowed" by deemphasizing or ignoring less important ideas. Select, for example, just two or three of the most useful text structures presented in materials and teach those thoroughly.

The most difficult modification for teachers or others to make with existing tools is the creation of a strategy where none exists. When strategies are provided, teachers can realistically evaluate them from the point of view of their students and modify those steps that are ambiguous or confusing.

The independent activities provided in tools can be converted to scaffolded activities in either of two major ways. First, independent writing activities can be converted to group activities, wherein students support one another, and teachers provide extensive feedback. Second, tasks can be temporarily simplified. For example, an instructional tool might provide a task in which students proofread text for errors, such as:

> *Rewrite these sentences to make them clearer.*
> *Many stores make empty promises. We put ours in writing.*

Cues can be added to such tasks to increase the likelihood that students will understand them:

> *Did the writer probably mean "our empty promises" or "our promises"?*
> *Change the second sentence to show what the writer probably meant.*
> *We put _____ in writing.*

New activities may be created expressly to promote the integration of knowledge. For example, previously taught text structures can be combined into novel assignments as a means of promoting text structures of greater complexity. If students have mastered a compare-and-contrast text structure as a means of conveying information, and have also mastered a basic argument-and-persuasion text structure, then those two structures can be combined into a more advanced persuasive structure, in which comparing and contrasting is used as a principal means for organizing an argument.

Existing tools can't easily be modified to accommodate background knowledge because such modification implies both the development of new instruction and the "resequencing" of existing instruction. "Better late than never," however, might apply. For example, teachers can diagnose student difficulties to determine if they originate with gaps in background knowledge, and provide instruction on such knowledge as needed. If instruction on particularly crucial background knowledge isn't provided in tools, then teachers may need to identify such knowledge and teach it directly to all students.

Teachers can provide *adequate* review on big ideas by having students write a single text structure, such as an explanation, several times within the same school year. Such basic structures, when learned well to begin with, are then incorporated into more complex structures, which provides distributed review quite naturally. For writing, such a practice is principally a matter of scheduling. A teacher can readily modify a tool that covers several text structures in a year by selecting only two or three of the most important ones, then scheduling repeated assignments involving them. Developing additional review or finding appropriate review supplements is an option for tools that provide minimal review opportunities, particularly with respect to instruction on the mechanics of writing. For instance, many younger students require substantial opportunities to review handwriting in order to become fluent enough that handwriting isn't a major stumbling block to participation in the processes of writing compositions. For writing mechanics, it is most crucial that review be cumulative, in order to closely replicate authentic writing.

SUMMARY

We have looked at designing both composition instruction and instruction on writing mechanics. The research in recent years on teaching composition is heartening and promising for all students, but particularly for students with learning difficulties. Some well-designed studies have shown, for instance, that students with learning disabilities can achieve at a level equal to their average-achieving peers (Englert et al., 1991; Graham & Harris, 1989).

Big ideas in composition instruction appear to be supported strongly, if tacitly, in the work of researchers in the field. The biggest of the big ideas are process writing, text structures, and collaboration. The recommendation of making expert cognitive processes visible through explicit strategy instruction is quite directly supported by research on explicit strategy instruction, as is the scaffolding of instruction.

The effectiveness of teaching explicit strategies depends on the design of good strategies, but is likely to be influenced by students' background knowledge. There is strong research to support the characteristics of effective review, and the need for maintenance and generalization in composition instruction is clear; however, more direct research is needed on the impact of review on composition. Finally, *complete understanding* in any sense implies the full integration of important knowledge—another area that might well benefit from more direct research.

When we turn our backs on instruction in writing mechanics, we are essentially turning our backs on many diverse learners. Without doubt, there exists an endless array of examples of poor—even terrible—writing skills sheets. That does not mean, however, that thoughtful educators, informed by research on composition, cannot find effective ways to teach mechanics and to integrate them smoothly and meaningfully into composition activities. The *principal* prerequisites for this, no doubt, are that effective composition instruction take place on a regular and sustained basis, and that instruction on writing mechanics be reasoned and systematically integrated with composition.

REFLECTION AND APPLICATION: Case Study

Bo is a dually certified general education/special education teacher with a concentration in Reading and English. He's been teaching eighth-grade English for the past two years at Gateway School, which serves children in grades K-8. Through a retirement incentive program, 12 veteran teachers retired last June, five of whom were special educators. Due to budget cuts, the district personnel office tried to save teacher jobs both through the early retirement incentive program and by transferring teachers who currently teach general education, but who hold special education certification, into special education positions. Bo was assigned a position as a grade 4 special education inclusion co-teacher and resource teacher. This position primarily requires Bo to support students in reading and written language, though he may be called upon to help in other areas.

The Gateway School has an integrated approach in grades 3, 4, and 5 in which language arts, science, and social studies are interwoven within thematic units. Grade 4 students study world history within a unit entitled "In Touch With the Past" in which each student becomes a craftsman from the colonial era. The five-month investigation culminates in a reenactment of a working colonial village. As stated in the school handbook, the "integrated theme approach allows students to hone in on written language skills, find voice and develop a personal style as developing authors." The final written project is a lengthy paper representing five months of study, research, and process writing.

Bo was excited to be involved in the "In Touch With the Past" project. Writing was his passion and he particularly enjoyed history and historical fiction. Although this was his first experience in a collaborative inclusion setting, he felt comfortable working with Jenny, his assigned general education co-teacher. Unsure of exactly how the model was intended to work, he found himself doing a lot of "hanging around" in Jenny's classroom during the first few days of school.

Jenny gave the students an overview of the next five months of thematic study and told them that they must "start to do their research," "talk to their parents," and "identify" the craft they wished to focus on for their final project. Each student received a handout with a list of major writing components for the project as well as the dates that they were due. The first component was the introduction for the paper. Over the course of the week, students were, students were directed to work through the steps of the writing process and to hand in the final version of their introductions on Friday. Bo watched Jenny in action with the students. She seemed a master manager; she had the system down.

Bo had five students from Jenny's class on his caseload, each with documented reading and written language disabilities. On Friday, when Bo looked at his students' introductions, it was clear that none of them had anything close to a final product. Moreover, although some of the other students in the class had acceptable introductions, many did not. Bo felt his enthusiasm for "In Touch With the Past" slipping away as he watched Jenny roam the room and enter checks into her green grade book as the students showed her their work folders. If this first assignment was any indication, Bo had serious concerns about whether many students would be able to successfully complete this lengthy long-term writing project without additional support. When Bo shared his concerns with Jenny, she told him that the students already knew the steps of the writing process and should be able to complete each assignment independently.

- If the students did indeed know the steps of the writing process, why might they have had difficulty producing a final version of their introductions by the due date?

- What instructional principles and teaching strategies could Bo utilize to more effectively address the learning needs of his students, as well as the other students in Jenny's class?

The conclusion of the case study can be found later in this chapter.

CONTENT QUESTIONS

1. How does Smith (1982) characterize the writing processes?
2. What has been the predominant approach to writing instruction in American schools?
3. Explain the authors' recommendation for resolving conflicts between skills-dominant and composition-dominant approaches for writing instruction.
4. Identify and describe three big ideas of writing instruction.
5. What are "planning strategies" in writing and why should these strategies be presented conspicuously?
6. Briefly describe the conspicuous strategy that is recommended for addressing grammar problems in sentence writing.
7. Describe three conditions in which scaffolding can be provided to learners.
8. Define the term "procedural facilitators" and describe how it is used for writing instruction. What is the most effective use of procedural facilitators?

REFLECTION AND DISCUSSION

1. What are the potential implications of an approach to teaching writing that emphasizes composition skills at the expense of mechanical writing skills? What are the potential implications of methods that stress writing mechanics at the expense of composition skills? How can principles of effective instruction be used to develop and support a framework of writing instruction that integrates both mechanical and composition skills?

2. The authors note that limited mechanical skills, including handwriting and spelling, may substantially hinder students with learning difficulties from participation in the authoring process. What role might technology, including assistive technology, play in facilitating the development of writing skills among students with learning difficulties?

3. Given the widespread use of procedural facilitators, such as graphic organizers and think sheets, do you think that sufficient instruction and feedback is provided to support students with diverse learning needs in the effective use of these tools?

4. Do you think that the amount of time dedicated to teaching writing is generally commensurate with the inherent complexity of this skill and the emphasis placed on writing in schools and in the workplace?

APPLICATION

1. The authors note that when selecting instructional tools in writing, strategies should be *intermediate in generality*. Evaluate the following two examples of prewriting instructions and identify the appropriateness of the strategy (e.g., too broad or too narrow) for the given task.

2. During our unit "Rocks and Minerals" we have learned many things. Write an essay describing the most important features of the types of rocks we studied in this unit. Remember our writing strategy is "Think-Plan-Write."

3. During our unit "Rocks and Minerals" we have learned many things. Write an essay describing the most important features of the types of rocks we studied in this unit. Remember when we write an essay we always have characters, settings, problems, and an outcome.

4. Parents of fourth graders received the following information in a "Back-to-School Night" handout (see Figure 29-4). Based on your understanding of designing instruction around big ideas, comment on the appropriateness of this schedule for writing instruction. What problems might students with diverse learning needs have with this instructional sequence? What changes would you suggest to the teacher for restructuring the plan for the year?

Case Study (Conclusion)

Bo knew from his training as a special educator and his role as a writing teacher that understanding the steps of the writing process was not sufficient to carry the students successfully through the project. He knew that even strong students need a highly structured, supported, and systematic approach to a long-term writing project.

For each assignment, Bo decided that he would develop procedural facilitators, such as graphic organizers and think sheets to scaffold the students' progress through the writing process. He planned to use overheads of graphic organizers at each step so the students could follow along with him. He would use "think-aloud" procedures to model his thinking while completing the graphic organizers. Following his demonstration, Bo would provide the students with a detailed schedule containing a carefully designed breakdown of necessary steps to successfully accomplish each assignment. He would provide blank copies of the graphic organizers he used in his

---

Writing

This year students will be engaging in the writing process regularly. Research shows that writing instruction and practice must be an ongoing and continuous process to provide students with the opportunities to develop their voice as writers. Regular writing also supports our students in preparing for our state mastery tests. We will cover the following forms of writing this year:

- September: Personal Narratives—"What I Did This Summer"
- October: Creative Writing—A scary creation for the book store contest!
- November: Position Papers—"Why I'm Voting for_____."
- December: Memoir Writing—"My Favorite Holiday Memory"
- January: Poetry—"My Personal Poetry Collection"
- February: Persuasive Writing—"Why I Should Be Able To _____"
- March: Explode the Moment—Descriptive writing
- April: Writing a Thesis Statement—Science curriculum connection
- May: Writing a Research Paper—We'll use April's thesis statement.
- June: State test
- Writer's Celebration: Each student will present his/her favorite piece from a personal portfolio at our "Evening with the Authors."

As you can see, by year's end students will become proficient in various forms of writing. This will prepare them to transition to the middle school for fifth–eighth grades.

Figure 29.4 "Back-to-School Night" Handout

demonstration for the students to use. Bo developed planning sheets for researching, prewriting/planning, drafting, revision, editing, peer conferencing, and publication.

As Bo's students became familiar with the long-term planning guide and graphic organizers, all five displayed a high level of enthusiasm for the work in the "In Touch With the Past" project. Research planning sheets supported their identification of trades and informational resources. The group now included a cooper, wheelwright, saddler, milliner, and founder. Bo continued to model and think aloud, demonstrating his own use of graphic organizers, note cards, and the drafting of his writing piece. After group discussions, he conferenced with individual students to support their learning and progress in the writing process.

In Jenny's classroom, Bo's students were successfully on task. When other students saw the folders with graphic organizers and color-coded index cards that Bo's students were using, they were curious. Bo's students shared their strategies, with pride, excitement, and an impressive and sophisticated level of comprehension. Jenny invited the five "experts" to support their peers in the use of organizers and a detailed project planning sheet. The scaffolded approach that had helped Bo's students seemed to be just what the other students needed. Jenny was also convinced; she decided to incorporate the mediated scaffolding that Bo was using in the resource room systematically into her general education instruction.

- If Bo hadn't spent the time introducing and modeling the use of the detailed planner and the graphic organizers, do you think these materials would have been effective scaffolds? What else might Jenny and Bo decide to do in the future to meet the needs of all learners as they progress in the writing project?
- Many teachers use a thematic approach to instruction in which multiple content areas are integrated within a unit (e.g., writing, math, social studies). What instructional principles should teachers consider when designing such units to ensure the success of students with diverse learning needs?

The Reflection and Application section of this chapter was written by Maureen F. Ruby, and Richard P. Zipoli, Jr., of the University of Connecticut.

REFERENCES

Applebee, A. (1981). *Writing in the secondary school: English and the content areas.* Urbana, IL: National Council of Teachers of English.

Applebee, A. (1990). *The writing report card, 1984–88: Findings from the nation's report card.* (NAEP Report No. 19-W-01). Princeton, NJ: U.S. Department of Education, Office of Educational Research and Improvement.

Applebee, A., Langer, J., Jenkins, L., Mullis, I., & Foertsch, M. (1990). *Learning to write in our nation's schools.* Princeton, NJ: Educational Testing Service.

Applebee, A., Langer, J., & Mullis, I. (1986). *The writing report card: Writing achievement in American schools.* Princeton, NJ: Educational Testing Service.

Bereiter, C. (1980). Development in writing. In L. Gregg, & E. R. Steinberg (Eds.), *Cognitive-processes in writing* (pp. 73–93). Hillsdale, NJ: Erlbaum.

Bereiter, C., & Scardamalia, M. (1982) From conversation to composition: The role of instruction in a developmental process. In R. Glaser (Ed.), *Advances in instructional psychology* (Vol. 2, pp. 1–64). Hillsdale, NJ: Erlbaum.

Bridge, C., & Hiebert, E. (1985). A comparison of classroom writing practices, teachers' perceptions of their writing instruction, and textbook recommendations on writing practices. *Elementary School Journal, 86,* 155–172.

Brown, V. L. (1984). D'Nealian handwriting: What is it and how to teach it. *Remedial and Special Education, 5*(5), 48–52.

Carroll, J. (1963). A model for school learning. *Teacher's College Record, 64,* 723–733.

Christenson, S., Thurlow, M., Ysseldyke, J., & Mcvicar, R. (1989). Writing language instruction for students with mild handicaps: Is there enough quantity to ensure quality? *Learning Disability Quarterly, 12,* 219–229.

Dempster, F. N. (1991). Synthesis of research on reviews and tests. *Educational Leadership, 4,* 71–76.

Deshler, D. D., & Schumaker, J. B. (1986). Learning strategies: An instructional alternative for low-achieving adolescents. *Exceptional Children, 52*(6), 583–590.

Dixon, R. C. (1991). The application of sameness analysis to spelling. *Journal of Learning Disabilities, 24*(5), 285–310.

DuCharme, C., Earl, J., & Poplin, M. S. (1989). The author model: The constructivist view of the writing process. *Learning Disability Quarterly, 12,* 237–242.

Englert, C. S., & Raphael, T. (1988). Constructing well-formed prose: Process, structure, and metacognitive knowledge. *Exceptional Children, 54,* 513–520.

Englert, C. S., Raphael, T., Anderson, L., Anthony, H., Fear, K., & Gregg, S. (1988). A case for writing intervention: Strategies for writing informational text. *Learning Disabilities Focus, 3,* 98–113.

Englert, C. S., Raphael, T., Anderson, L., Anthony, H., Stevens, D., & Fear, K. (1991). Making writing strategies and self-talk visible: Cognitive strategy instruction in writing in regular and special education classrooms. *American Educational Research Journal, 28,* 337–372.

Flower, L., & Hayes, J. (1981). A cognitive process theory of writing. *College Composition and Communication, 32,* 365–387.

Graham, S. (1982). Composition research and practice: A unified approach. *Focus on Exceptional Children, 14*(8), 1–16.

Graham, S. (1990). The role of production factors in learning disabled students' compositions. *Journal of Educational Psychology, 80,* 781–791.

Graham, S. (1999). Handwriting and spelling instruction for students with learning disabilities: A review. *Learning Disability Quarterly, 22*(2), 78–98.

Graham, S., & Harris, K. R. (1989). A components analysis of cognitive strategy instruction: Effects on learning disabled students' compositions and self-efficacy. *Journal of Educational Psychology, 81,* 356–361.

Graham, S., Harris, K. R., MacArthur, C. S., & Schwartz, S. (1991). Writing and writing instruction for students with learning disabilities: Review of a research program. *Learning Disability Quarterly, 14,* 89–114.

Graves, D. (1983). *Writing: Teachers and children at work*. Exeter, NH: Heinemann.

Graves, D. (1985). All children can write. *Learning Disabilities Focus, 1*(1), 36–43.

Greenwald, E. A., Persky, H. R., Campbell, J. R., & Masseo, J. (1999). *NAEP 1998 writing report card for the nation and states*. (NCES 1999–462). Washington, DC: U.S. Department of Education, Office of Educational Research and Improvement.

Harris, K., & Graham, S. (1985). Improving learning disabled students' composition skills: Self-control strategy training. *Learning Disability Quarterly, 8,* 27–36.

Henry, M. K. (1988). Beyond phonics: Integrated decoding and spelling instruction based on word origin and structure. *Annals of Dyslexia, 38,* 258–272.

Herum, J., & Cummings, D. W. (1970). *Writing: Plans, drafts and revisions*. New York: Random House.

Hillocks, G. (1984, November). What works in teaching composition: A meta-analysis of experimental treatment studies. *American Journal of Education, 93,* 133–170.

Hillocks, G. (1986). *Research on written composition*. Urbana, IL: National Conference on Research in English.

Hillocks, G. (1987). Synthesis of research on teaching writing. *Educational Leadership, 44,* 71–82.

Isaacson, S. (1989). Role of secretary vs. author: Resolving the conflict in writing instruction. *Learning Disability Quarterly, 12,* 209–217.

Isaacson, S. (1991). Written expression and the challenges for students with learning problems. *Exceptionality Education Canada, 1*(3), 45–57.

Isaacson, S. (1994). Process, product, and purpose: Written expression and the role of instruction. *Reading Research Quarterly 10*(1), 39–62.

Isaacson, S. (1999). Instructionally relevant writing assessment. *Reading and Writing Quarterly, 15*(1), 29–48.

Langer, J., & Applebee, A. (1986). Reading and writing instruction: Toward a theory of teaching and learning. In E. Rothkopf (Ed.), *Review of research in education* (Vol. 13, pp. 171–194). Washington, DC: American Educational Research Association.

Leinhardt, G., Zigmond, N., & Cooley, W. (1980). *Reading instruction and its effects*. Paper presented at the American Educational Research Association Annual Meeting, San Francisco, CA.

MacArthur, C. A., Graham, S., & Schwartz, S. (1991). Knowledge of revision and revising behavior among students with learning disabilities. *Learning Disability Quarterly, 14,* 61–73.

Meyer, B. J. F., & Freedle, R. O. (1984). Effects of discourse type on recall. *American Education Research Journal, 21,* 121–144.

Montague, M., Maddux, C., & Dereshiwsky, M. I. (1990). Story grammar and comprehension and production of narrative prose by students with learning disabilities. *Journal of Learning Disabilities, 23,* 190–197.

Morocco, C., & Neuman, S. (1986). Word processors and the acquisition of writing strategies. *Journal of Learning Disabilities, 19,* 243–247.

Morocco, C. C., Dalton, B. M., & Tivnan, T. (1990, April). *The impact of computer-supported writing instruction on the writing quality of 4th grade students with and without learning disabilities*. Paper presented at the Annual Meeting of the American Educational Research Association, Boston.

National Assessment of Educational Progress. (1993). *What's wrong with writing and what can we do right now?* (Research Report). Washington, DC: Office of Educational Research and Improvement. (ERIC Document Reproduction Service No. ED 356 477)

Nodine, B., Barenbaum, E., & Newcomer, P. (1985). Story composition by learning disabled, reading disabled, and normal children. *Learning Disability Quarterly, 8,* 167–179.

Prawat, R. S. (1989). Promoting access to knowledge, strategy, and disposition in students: A research synthesis. *Review of Educational Research, 59*(1), 1–41.

Pressley, M., Harris, K. R., & Marks, M. B. (1992). But good strategy instructors are constructivists! *Educational Psychology Review, 4*(1), 3–31.

Pressley, M., Symons, S., Snyder, B. B., & Cariglia-Bull, T. (1989). Strategy instruction research comes of age. *Learning Disability Quarterly, 12,* 16–31.

Raphael, T., & Englert, C. S. (1990, February). Writing and reading: Partners in construction meaning. *The Reading Teacher, 43*(6), 388–400.

Roit, M., & Mckenzie, R. (1985). Disorders of written communication: An instructional priority for LD students. *Journal of Learning Disabilities, 18,* 258–260.

Scardamalia, M. (1981). How children cope with the cognitive demands of writing. In C. H. Frederiksen (Ed.), *Writing: The nature, development, and teaching of written communication. Vol. 2, Writing: process, development, and communication* (pp. 81–103). Hillsdale, NJ: Erlbaum.

Smith, F. (1982). *Writing and the writer.* New York: Holt, Rinehart and Winston.

Thomas, C., Englert, C. C., & Gregg, S. (1987). An analysis of errors and strategies in the expository writing of learning disabled students. *Remedial and Special Education, 8,* 21–30.

Torgeson, J. K. (1988). Studies of children with learning disabilities who perform poorly on memory span tasks. *Journal of Learning Disabilities, 21,* 605–612.

CHAPTER 30

EFFECTIVE STRATEGIES FOR TEACHING MATHEMATICS

Mark K. Harniss, *University of Washington Tacoma;* Douglas W. Carnine, *University of Oregon;* Jerry Silbert, *University of Oregon;* Robert C. Dixon, *JP Associates*

The performance of students in math and science has always been a high priority in the United States, but the successful launching of the Russian satellite *Sputnik* in 1957 mobilized resources in an unprecedented way. In 1958, Congress responded to the perceived threat to American security and competitiveness, by passing the National Defense Education Act to increase support for education in math, science, and languages.

Interestingly, the U.S. Department of Defense (DoD) included 10.3 million dollars in its FY 2006 budget for a new National Defense Education Act (DoD, 2005) and business and community leaders are once again making reference to *Sputnik*. Many have suggested that America needs another "*Sputnik* moment" to rally and focus resources toward improving outcomes in math and science (Leath, 2005). For example, the American Electronics Association recently released a document entitled "Losing the Competitive Advantage: The Challenge for Science and Technology in the United States" (Kazmierczach, James, & Archey, 2005). Their argument broadly addresses U.S. competitiveness in a global economy, but includes the concern that U.S. students will be unable to participate in a technological society without an increased emphasis on math and science. In a similar vein, Bill Gates, chairman of Microsoft, in a speech focused on the failure of American high schools, remarked that

> When I compare our high schools to what I see when I'm traveling abroad, I am terrified for our workforce of tomorrow. In math and science, our 4th graders are among the top students in the world. By 8th grade, they're in the middle of the pack. By 12th grade, U.S. students are scoring near the bottom of all industrialized nations. (Gates, 2005)

Gates is likely referring to the Trends in International Mathematics and Science Studies (National Center for Educational Statistics, 2003). The 1995 TIMSS showed significant performance gaps between American students and, students in other countries (e.g., gaps of 1.5 standard deviations between American students and students in Singapore) with twelfth graders performing significantly below the international average. The 1999 and 2003 administrations of the TIMSS were, conducted only in fourth and eighth grades, in part due to concerns about comparability at the twelfth-grade level across international school systems. The 2003 TIMSS shows American students in the fourth and eighth grades performing above the international average with no change for fourth graders between the 1999 and 2003 administration, but significant improvement for eighth graders.

Another national measure of student performance in math is the National Assessment of Educational Progress (NAEP). There are two types of NAEP assessments. The long-term trend assessment of the NAEP uses a set of questions developed in the early 1970s. In contrast, the main, or national, NAEP assessment is updated every decade to reflect more current classroom expectations. The national NAEP assessment is likely a better reflection of students' performance on contemporary mathematics (National Council of Teachers of Mathematics, 2000); however it does not allow for comparison over time.

Findings from the 2003 NAEP suggest that fourth and eighth graders improved in their mathematics performance and that this result was true for low, middle, and high performers (Braswell, Daane, & Grigg, 2003). Twenty-three percent of fourth graders, and 32 percent of eighth graders performed below basic level for their grades. Thirty-two percent of fourth graders and 29 percent of eighth graders scored at proficient or above.

The long-term trend assessment of the NAEP was administered in 2004 and shows that younger students continue to improve, while older students' scores have remained stable. Specifically, the trend for students at the ages of 9 and 13 has been positive at each measurement point (administered in 1973 and 1999), whereas 17-year-old students' scores have not changed measurably across those years. As Loveless and Diperna (2000) noted, "Clearly, the story is not one of disastrous decline. Slow and steady gains are being made. Nor is it cause for national celebration" (p. 6).

Unlike the area of beginning reading, where research findings have begun to coalesce enough to generate broad consensus (e.g., National Research Council, 1998), mathematics education lacks the research base to provide broadly generalizable answers. High quality research is particularly lacking on the topic of low-achieving learners who struggle to learn math (Baker, Gersten, & Lee, 2002). However, there is an increased focus on mathematics research and practice. For example, the National Research Council has published two summaries of mathematics research (Donovan & Bransford, 2005; Kilpatrick, Swafford, & Findell, 2001). In both documents, the authors reach similar conclusions about the need for a comprehensive approach to supporting students in achieving mathematical proficiency. Kilpatrick et al. (2001) suggest that proficiency develops out of five intertwining strands: (a) conceptual understanding, (b) procedural fluency, (c) strategic competence, (d) adaptive reasoning, and (e) a productive disposition. Donovan and Bransford (2005) condense this to three learning principles for teachers. First, teachers must be aware of students' preconceptions and be willing to activate those preconceptions and link them to new knowledge. Second, teachers need to understand that competence in an area requires both conceptual and factual knowledge. Finally, teachers need to provide assistance to students in developing the metacognitive strategies that support students in monitoring their learning and progress. These frameworks are consonant with the principles described in this book.

This chapter describes considerations for improving instruction for learners at diverse performance levels that are important for all teachers, regardless of the "tradition" they place themselves within. Many of the examples in this chapter are taken from a mathematics program designed to accommodate diverse learners, *Connecting Math Concepts* (Engelmann, Carnine, Kelly, & Engelmann, 1994). Others are taken from Liping Ma's (1999) recent text comparing the practices and knowledge base of American and Chinese educators: *Knowing and Teaching Elementary Mathematics*. Improved instruction alone cannot meet all the challenges that the needs of such learners present. However, the contribution of improved instruction can be enormous and plays a central role in any serious school improvement effort. While these considerations also contribute to the learning of average and above-average students, the considerations are particularly important for diverse learners. The first consideration—organizing content around big ideas—is particularly beneficial for all students, including high-performing students. The focus of this chapter, then, can be thought of as specific recommendations for developing instruction that meets the needs of diverse students.

PRINCIPLES FOR IMPROVING MATH INSTRUCTION STRATEGIES

Designing Instruction Around Big Ideas

Educational tools that are going to facilitate students reaching world-class standards should be organized around big ideas (or fundamental knowledge or root meanings) because these represent major organizing principles, have rich explanatory and predictive power, help frame significant questions, and are applicable in many situations and contexts. In their Principles and Standards in School Mathematics, the National Council of Teachers of Mathematics (NCTM) authors note, "Foundational ideas like place value, equivalence, proportionality, function, and rate of change should have a prominent place in the mathematics curriculum because they enable students to understand other mathematical ideas and connect ideas across different areas of mathematics" (p. 15).

Many of these big ideas are not complex, nor difficult to understand at face value. The difficulty comes in knowing when they apply and how their application changes over time. It is the interweaving of these ideas that provides mathematical power to students. For example, the four operations (addition, subtraction, multiplication, and division) rest upon a limited set of big ideas. These ideas include place value, the distributive, commutative, and associative principles, equivalence, and number sense (primarily the concept of composition and decomposition of numbers in a base 10 system [Ma, 1999]). These big ideas interweave through the teaching and learning of the operations. When they are clearly understood by teacher and student, they serve as the conceptual underpinnings for understanding the operations. In Table 30.1, we define and provide an example of each concept.

When the big ideas described in Table 30.1 are used together, they serve as powerful tools for learners to use in tackling the four basic operations ($+, -, \times$, and $\div$). For example, when students begin adding numbers in addition that require renaming, they engage in the process of composing numbers of higher value. For example, in the following problem students should understand several things. First, when they add the 7 ones from the top number to the 9 ones from the bottom number, they compose a number (i.e., 16) that is made up of one 10 and 6 ones. With their understanding of *place value*, they will know that the one 10 cannot assume the same place (i.e., column) as the 6 ones; rather it must be placed in the tens column. With their understanding of the commutative and associative properties, they will know that they can add the one 10 to the 3 tens in the tens column (i.e., $30 + (7 + 9) = 30 + 16$ and $30 + 16 = (30 + 10) + 6$).

$$\begin{array}{r} 37 \\ +9 \\ \hline 46 \end{array}$$

In subtraction, the inverse is true. In the following question, learners must note that they cannot take 7 ones away from 4 ones, but they can expand the number 34 into 3 tens and 4 ones, decompose the 3 tens by taking one of the tens and adding it to the 4 ones (ideally with an understanding of the associative property, i.e., $(20 + 14) - 7 = 34 - 7$) and finally subtracting 7 ones from 14 leaving 7 ones.

$$\begin{array}{r} 34 \\ -17 \\ \hline 17 \end{array}$$

In multidigit multiplication, these ideas are most powerful in helping learners understand the commonly taught shortcut for multiplying larger numbers. Typically, students might be taught to simply cross multiply without a strong understanding of why they are using this strategy. In fact, in Ma's (1999) study, many U.S. teachers did not understand why the cross multiplication strategy worked. The answer, however, is quite simple if a learner comprehends the underlying concepts. First, learners need to understand the difference between multiplication and the problems they have been previously working in subtraction and addition. Whereas these latter two operations involve the removal of one set of numbers from another set or the combination of two sets together, multiplication is the combination of a number of sets each containing the same number of

Table 30.1 Big Ideas in Operations

Big Idea	Example
Place value: The "place" a number holds . in a sequence of numbers gives information about that number.	In the number 265, the 2 at the beginning of the number is a hundreds number. We know that the placement of the 2 tells us that there are two units of 100, or two 100s, in that number. Similarly, the location of the 6 tells us that there are 6 units of 10 in the number.
Expanded notation: The reduction of a number to its constituent units.	The number 213 is composed of two 100s, one 10, and three 1s, which can be represented in an equation as $100 + 100 + 10 + 1 + 1 + 1 = 213$ or conversely as $200 + 10 + 3 = 213$.
Commutative property: The order in which numbers are placed in the equation can be changed without affecting the outcome. $a + b = b + a$	Addition and multiplication are commutative: In addition, $3 + 4 = 7$ and $4 + 3 = 7$ In multiplication, $4 \times 5 = 20$ and $5 \times 4 = 20$.
	Subtraction and division are not commutative: In subtraction, $5 - 3 = 2$ and $3 - 5 = -2$ In division, $6 \div 3 = 2$ and $3 \div 6 = 0.5$.
Associative property: The groupings in which numbers are placed in the equation can be changed without affecting the outcome. $(a + b) + c = a + (b + c)$	Addition and multiplication are associative: In addition, $(2 + 4) + 5 = 11$ and $2 + (4 + 5) = 11$ In multiplication, $(3 \times 2) \times 5 = 30$ and $3 \times (2 \times 5) = 30$.
	Subtraction and division are not associative: In subtraction, $(15 - 3) - 5 = 7$ and $15 - (3 - 5) = 13$ In division, $(32 \div 8) \div 2 = 2$ and $32 \div (8 \div 2) = 8$.
Distributive property: Numbers in an equation involving multiple operations can be distributed. $a \times (b + c) = (a \times b) + (a \times c)$ You can also distribute numbers in an equation that includes division and subtraction addition. $(a + b) \div c = (a \div c) + (b \div c)$	$5 \times (3 + 2) = (5 \times 3) + (5 \times 2)$ $(8 + 4) \div 2 = (8 \div 2) + (4 \div 2)$
Equivalence: The quantity to the left of the equal sign ($=$) is the same as the quantity to the right.	$32 + 15 = 47$ $16 + 16 + 15 = 47$ $8 + 8 + 8 + 8 + (5 \times 3) = 20 + 20 + 7$ *Note:* Many students interpret the equal sign as an operation (e.g., "when I see the equal sign I add, subtract, etc.") rather than as a relationship (e.g., "when I see the equal sign I know that the quantity on one side must be the same as the other side").
Rate of composition/decomposition (Ma, 1999): A form of number sense. The rate of composition (or decomposition) of sets of numbers in our base 10 system is simply 10.	When you have accumulated 10 ones you have one 10. When you have accumulated 10 tens you have one 100 and so on. This concept is sometimes referred to as *unitizing,* that is creating a tens unit from 10 ones. Similarly, when you remove a 1 from a 10 you have 9 ones, that is you have decomposed the 10.

elements into a larger set. In the problems 345 × 32, a learner is combining 345 sets each containing 32 elements to identify one larger set of items. With smaller numbers, a learner could add the number of elements in a set for the number of sets (for example 3 × 4 = 12 could be translated into 4 + 4 + 4 = 12). But with larger numbers, this approach rapidly becomes tedious. Because each of the 345 sets includes 32 elements, a student cannot simply multiply the number in the ones column vertically as they would have if they were adding them. Multiplying down the columns would result in an answer that would be far too small and inaccurate. With their understanding of place value and expanded notation, they can note that in this problem there are 3 tens and 2 ones in the multiplicand. Their understanding of the distributive property supports them in multiplying (345 × 2) + (345 × 30) or conversely (5 × 2) + (40 × 2) + (300 × 2) + (5 × 30) + (40 × 30) + (300 × 30).

$$
\begin{array}{r}
345 \\
\times 32 \\
\hline
10 \\
80 \\
600 \\
150 \\
1200 \\
+9000 \\
\hline
11040
\end{array}
$$

This strategy can be a helpful transition to the more commonly used multiplication strategy since it highlights the underlying logic of the algorithm. Notice that this strategy removes the need to rename. The more commonly taught algorithm is a simplification of this procedure. Students can use their understanding of the associative property to group the products together before adding them.

$$
\begin{array}{r}
345 \\
\times 32 \\
\hline
690 \\
+10350 \\
\hline
11040
\end{array}
$$

Division, of course, is the inverse of multiplication. Although the form of division problems is different, the underlying big ideas are consistent. Students must learn that division involves separating a larger set into equivalent sized subsets (i.e., measurement division) or conversely separating a larger set into a given number of sets (partitive division) (Stein, Silbert, & Carnine, 1997). In solving even simple multi-digit division problems, students must integrate a number of different big ideas. In the following problem, for example:

$$
\begin{array}{r}
508 \\
9\overline{)4572} \\
45 \\
0 \\
72 \\
-72 \\
\hline
0
\end{array}
$$

The distributive property supports the understanding that (4500 ÷ 9) + (72 ÷ 9) = 508. Students understanding of place value helps them place numbers in the appropriate columns.

The big ideas discussed above are commonly known, although not frequently clearly taught. Often, however, big ideas in mathematics are not at all clear. For example, in geometry, students are typically expected to learn seven formulas to calculate the volume of seven three-dimensional figures:

Rectangular prism: $1 \times w \times h = v$
Wedge: $1/2 \times 1 \times w \times h = v$
Triangular pyramid: $1/6 \times 1 \times w \times h = v$
Cylinder: $\pi \times r^2 \times h = v$

Rectangular pyramid: $1/3 \times 1 \times w \times h = v$
Cone: $1/3 \times \pi \times r^2 \times h = v$
Sphere: $4/3 \times \pi \times r^3 = v$

These equations emphasize rote formulas rather than big ideas. An analysis based on big ideas reduces the number of formulas students must learn from seven to slight variations of a single formula—area of the base times the height (B × h). This approach enhances understanding while simultaneously reducing the quantity of content to be learned, remembered, and applied.

For the regular figures in Figure 30.1 the rectangular prism (box), the wedge, and the cylinder—the volume is the area of the base times the height (B × h). For figures that come to a point—the pyramid with a rectangular base, the pyramid with a triangular base, and the cone—the volume is not the area of the base times the height, but the area of the base times 1/3 of the height (B × 1/3 × h). The sphere is a special case: the area of the base times 2/3 of the height (B × 2/3 × h), where the base is the area of a circle that passes through the center of the sphere and the height is the diameter. This analysis of root meaning fosters understanding of the big idea that volume is a function of the area of the base times some multiple of the height. As Gelman (1986) stated, "a focus on different algorithmic instantiations of a set of principles helps teach children that procedures that seem very different on the surface can share the same mathematical underpinning and, hence, root meanings" (p. 350).

Designing Conspicuous Strategies

When students orchestrate multiple concepts in some fashion, they are executing a strategy. Any routine that leads to both the acquisition and utilization of knowledge can be considered a strategy (Prawat, 1989). While the ultimate purpose of a strategy is meaningful application, acquisition is most reliable for diverse learners when initial instruction explicitly focuses on the strategy itself, rather than its meaningful application.

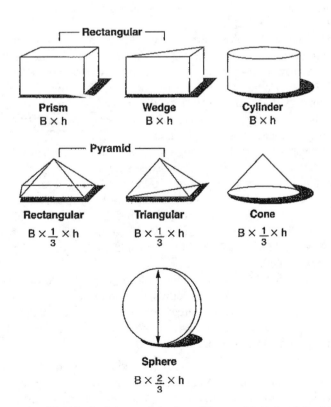

Figure 30.1 Volume as the "Big Idea" of Area of the Base Times a Multiple of the Height

Consider, for example, the following problem, presented to each fifth-grade class in a school:

At lunch, each student can choose a carton of white or chocolate milk. Estimate how many cartons of chocolate and white milk should be ordered for the entire school.

For students to work such problems successfully, they must have both computational ability and well-developed strategies for data gathering, proportions, and probability that are relevant to a broad range, of real mathematical problems.

In contrast to such well-developed strategies, strategies may be so specific and narrow in application that they are little more than a rote sequence for solving a particular problem or a very small set of highly similar problems. For example, in a study by McDaniel and Schlager (1990) on water-jar problem solving, students in one of the teaching conditions learned a rote formula for adding and removing amounts of water with different-sized jars (+1 −2 +1), which, predictably, did not transfer well to solving other water-jar problems.

Too often, mathematics knowledge appears to be rote. Davis (1990) points out that "traditional school practice" tests mainly the ability to repeat back what has been told or demonstrated. There are really two significant problems with the traditional school practice that Davis described. First, such practice is often directed toward *small ideas*—for example, arbitrary procedures such as cross multiplying to solve problems like x/a = b/c. Second, such procedures are frequently "repeated back" for rote recall, effectively preempting the possibility that students will even infer the important mathematical principles underlying them.

At the other extreme, a strategy may be so general that it is little more than a broad set of guidelines. Such strategies may be better than nothing, but they do not dependably lead most students to solutions for most problems. For instance, a broad strategy such as *draw a picture* or *read, analyze, plan, and solve* is probably far too general for reliably leading a majority of students to reasonable solutions for complex problems such as the milk-ordering problem above.

An important goal for strategy instruction is that the strategies taught are *good* in some sense. Some students develop strategies that are too narrow or too broad, while others develop strategies that are *just right*. A major challenge of instruction—perhaps *the* major challenge—is to develop just-right strategies for interventions with those students who do not develop strategies on their own, including, but not limited to, diverse learners.

Based on an exhaustive review of research, Prawat (1989) recommends that efficient strategy interventions should be intermediate in generality. That is, efficient strategies fall somewhere between the extremes of being narrow in application but, presumably, relatively easy to teach successfully, and being broad but not necessarily reliable or easy to teach. This suggests that the principal feature of a good strategy is that it adheres to the Law of Parsimony as it applies to evaluating competing theories: "That theory is best that explains the most in the simplest way" (Mouly, 1978). As applied specifically to evaluating strategies, the Law of Parsimony might read: The best strategy results in the greatest number of students successfully solving the greatest number of problems or completing the broadest range of tasks by applying the fewest possible strategic steps.

When experts implement strategies to acquire and utilize knowledge, only the result is overt; the steps in the strategy the experts follow are covert. The whole purpose of developing, instructional strategies is to explicate expert cognitive processes so that they become visible to nonexpert learners. The research support for explicitly teaching conspicuous strategies is quite strong (Gleason, Carnine, & Boriero, 1990; Leinhardt, 1987; Resnick, Cauzinille-Marmeche, & Mathieu, 1987; Resnick & Omanson, 1987; Tournaki, 2003).

An example of a conspicuous strategy for the volume formula follows. Note that the first step prompts the connection with a more concrete representation of volume in which students can count the cubes in a figure. Step 2 introduces the strategy. In Step 3, the teacher does not assist the students because they have already been taught to compute the area of a rectangle. In contrast, Step 4 calls for a new calculation, so the teacher is more directive.

1. *Linkage to prior knowledge.* "Touch box A. You know how to figure out its volume. Count the cubes and write the volume. What did you write? Yes, 50 cubic meters."
2. *Introduction of new strategy.* "Touch box B. You're going to learn how to calculate the volume by multiplying the area of the base times the height."

3. *Computing the area of the base.* "First calculate the area of the base for box B."
4. *Computing the volume.* "To figure out the volume of the box, you multiply the area of the base times the height. What are the two numbers you will multiply? Yes, 6 × 7."
5. *Writing the complete answer.* Write the answer with the appropriate unit. What did you write? Yes, 42 cubic inches.
   a. Count the cubes:
   b. Multiply the area of the base times the height:

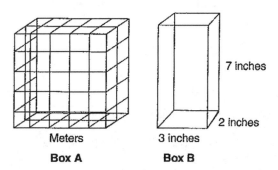

The applicability of the big idea for volume with variations of a single strategy for three-dimensional figures is obvious. In contrast, it is not at all obvious how a single big idea with variations of a strategy could link the following six problems:

1. Five packages of punch mix make 4 gallons. How many gallons of punch can Juan make for the party with 15 packages?
2. How long will it take a train to go 480 miles to Paris if it travels at 120 mph?
3. What is the average rate of a car that goes 450 miles in 9 hours?
4. How many pounds is 8 kilograms?
5. The oil transferred from the storage area has filled 44 tanks. There are 50 tanks. What percentage of the tanks are full?
6. There are 52 cards in a deck. Thirteen of them are hearts. The rest are not hearts. If you took trials (drew a card and then replaced it) until you drew 26 hearts, about how many trials would you expect to take?

However, it is with such seemingly unrelated problem types that a strategy based on a big idea is most valuable, particularly with learners for whom such connections usually remain elusive. The big idea that connects these different problems types is *proportions*. Proportion and ratio have been shown to be foundational concepts that support student learning in fractions, decimals, and percentages (Vergnaud, 1988). The strategy for proportions must be applied to each problem type in a systematic manner, to make clear that the same big idea underlies these very different problems. The application of proportions is most obvious in the first problem:

Five packages of punch mix make 4 gallons. How many gallons of punch can Juan make with fifteen packages?

A medium-level strategy for proportions might first have students map the units:

$$\frac{\text{package}}{\text{gallons}}$$

Next, students insert the relevant information:

$$\frac{\text{package}}{\text{gallons}} \quad \frac{5}{4} = \frac{15}{\Box}$$

Finally, students solve for the missing quantity: *12 gallons*

Rate problems, which are not typically viewed as proportion problems, also can be solved through a proportion strategy. Note that the key to setting up rate problems as proportions is realizing that the ration in the proportion is a number of distance units over a single unit of time. This principle is applicable to solving the second problem:

How long will it take a train to go 480 miles to Paris if it travels at 120 mph?

First, map the units. The abbreviation mph can be represented as:

$$\frac{\text{miles}}{\text{hour}}$$

Next, insert the relevant information:

$$\frac{\text{miles}}{\text{hour}} \quad \frac{120}{1} = \frac{480}{\square}$$

Finally, solve for the answer: *4 hours*

In the next rate problem, students solve for the average rate:

What is the average rate of a car that goes 450 miles in 9 hours?

Map the units:

$$\frac{\text{miles}}{\text{hour}}$$

Insert the relevant information:

$$\frac{\text{miles}}{\text{hour}} \quad \frac{\square}{1} = \frac{450}{9}$$

Solve for the answer: *50 miles per hour*

Another application of proportions occurs with measurement equivalences. The key to this problem type is that students set up a ratio between the two units involved in the equivalence.

How many pounds is 8 kilograms?

Map the units:

$$\frac{\text{pounds}}{\text{kilograms}}$$

Insert the relevant information:

$$\frac{\text{pounds}}{\text{kilograms}} \quad \frac{2.2}{1} = \frac{\square}{8}$$

Solve for the answer: *17.6 pounds*

Similarly, percent problems can be set up as proportions. For percents, the key to treating them as proportions is labeling the second ratio as telling about the percentage and pointing out that the denominator of the percentage ratio, which is almost always unstated, is 100.

The oil transferred from the storage area has filled 44 tanks. There are 50 tanks. What percentage of the tanks are full?

Map the units:

$$\frac{\text{filled tanks}}{\text{total tanks}}$$

Insert the relevant information:

$$\frac{\text{filled tanks}}{\text{total tanks}} \quad \frac{44}{5} = \frac{\overset{\text{percent}}{\square}}{100}$$

Solve for the answer: *88 percent*

With the following, more difficult percentage problem, the proportion strategy makes the problem quite manageable, even for students with learning difficulties.

The oil transferred from the storage area filled 44 tanks. So far, 88% of the oil in the storage area has been transferred into tanks. How many tanks will be filled when all the oil is transferred from the storage area?

Map the units:

$$\frac{\text{filled tanks}}{\text{total tanks}}$$

Insert the relevant information:

$$\frac{\text{filled tanks}}{\text{total tanks}} \frac{44}{\square} = \overset{\text{percent}}{\frac{88}{100}}$$

Solve for the answer: *50 tanks*

The next problem type, illustrating odds and probability, also has a key for typing it to proportions: Setting up a ratio of one type of member to another type or to the total number of members. In the example that follows, the one type of winning trials is related to the total trials.

There are 52 cards in a deck. Thirteen of them are hearts. The rest are not hearts. If you took trials (drew a card and then replaced it) until you drew 26 hearts, about how many trials would you expect to take?

Map the units:

$$\frac{\text{hearts}}{\text{trials}}$$

Insert the relevant information:

$$\frac{\text{hearts}}{\text{trials}} \frac{13}{52} = \frac{26}{\square}$$

Solve for the answer: *104 trials*

The next connection to be illustrated with proportions involves the coordinate system. Proportions can link simple proportion problems—rate, measurement equivalence, percentage, and probability—to the coordinate system. This linkage is illustrated in the graphs for each problem type in Figure 30.2. The concept of functions is also apparent in Figure 30.2. A function table accompanies each graph in the figure.

Finally, let's revisit the milk-ordering problem discussed previously. In this problem, students integrate the advanced proportion strategy with data gathering and probability-statistics strategies. (See Figure 30.3). The students apply data gathering strategies—determining the ratio of chocolate milk to white milk for their class and finding out the total enrollment of the school. The students then invoke the advanced proportions strategy: mapping the relevant information. The fifth graders would need to assume that the preference for types of milk in their class represents the whole school's preference, which entails applying the concept of sampling from statistics and probability. Finally, the concept of missing addends is invoked to solve for the number for white milk.

Many subtle variations are possible with a problem like this, but all are accommodated through the integrated strategies illustrated in Figure 30.3. One variation might be to use average attendance instead of total enrollment, which would cut down on milk ordered (and wasted). In another variation, students might have reason to believe that the preferences in their own class would not be representative of the entire school. The students could gather data from different classes, work the problem, compare the results, and discuss variations in solutions based on different samples. As a final variation, the students could compare results with actual figures on milk ordered to predict shortages or excesses of each type of milk.

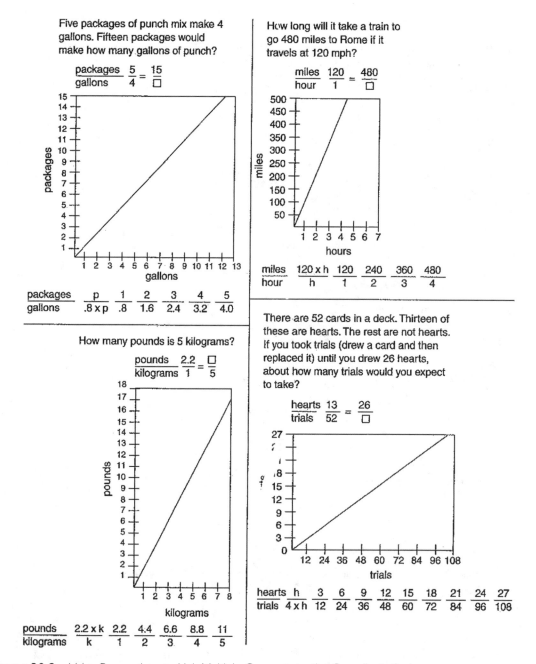

Figure 30.2 Using Proportions to Link Multiple Concepts to the Coordinate System

The milk-ordering problem and its variations illustrate how goals of the NCTM—working together to enhance understanding, engage in conjecture and invention, and connect mathematical ideas—can be effectively met for diverse learners through conspicuous instruction in medium-level strategies based on big ideas. As students discuss their options for selecting a sample group, they are working together to enhance their understanding of mathematics. As they weigh the relative merits of using total enrollment versus average attendance, they are engaging in conjecture and invention. As they link their understandings of various strategies, they are clearly learning to connect mathematical ideas, solve problems, and apply mathematics broadly.

The application of the proportion big idea with variations of a strategy for these problem contexts will deepen the student's understanding not only of proportions but also of rate, measurement equivalencies, percentage, probability, the coordinate system, and functions. One of the most important

Step 1: Data Gathering
The students conduct a survey in their class to determine the preferences for white and chocolate milk. The students also find out from the office the total enrollment for the school.

There are 32 students in the class; 22 prefer chocolate milk and the rest prefer white.

There are 479 students in the school.

Step 2: Advanced Proportions
The students map the units for the advanced proportions strategy and insert the relevant information.

	Fifth-grade class	*Entire school*
Chocolate	22	
White	10	
Total	32	479

Step 3: Probability and Statistics
The students solve a proportion to estimate the number of chocolate milk cartons to purchase for the entire school:

$$\frac{22}{32} = \frac{329}{479}$$

Chocolate	22	329
White	10	
Total	32	479

Step 4: Missing Addends
The students determine the estimate for white milk using their knowledge of missing addends:

$$479 - 329 = 150$$

Chocolate	22	329
White	10	150
Total	32	479

Figure 30.3 Data Gathering, Advanced Proportions, and Probability Statistics Strategies

ways to develop this understanding is through learning how various concepts are linked by a single strategy. In other words, a deep understanding of proportions is constructed by applying the strategy across many contexts. For this reason, the application of a strategy can be thought of as more important in developing understanding and proficiency than how the meaning of a strategy is initially constructed. These applications do far more to develop deep understanding than allowing students to initially construct their own meaning for proportions in authentic activities. Becoming proficient at authentic activities is far more important than starting out with authentic activities.

Designing Mediated Scaffolding

British educator A. J. Romiszowski has characterized traditional mathematics instruction as: "I'll work two on the board, then you do the rest." The "I'll work two" part of that approach can be thought of as a model, and the "you do the rest" is considered immediate testing. It has been said that the problem with learning from experience is that the lessons come too late. The same could be said of this traditional model of instruction. After *doing the rest*, students might receive feedback, ranging from right/wrong, to an explanation of how to do missed problems, and possibly a grade. The feedback is too late and the grade too early.

Scaffolding is a means by which students receive support in various forms along the path to full understanding and doing the rest successfully. Along the way, teachers would remove more bits of scaffolding, but in no instance would they abruptly remove all the scaffolding and, in essence say, "You do the rest." For example, after modeling the formula the teacher would not have the students do the rest. Instead, the teacher would scaffold the steps of the strategy, initially giving students feedback after every step. The steps for a scaffolded volume strategy involving a cone 5 inches tall with a radius of 1.6 inches might take this form:

1. "Write the formula for the volume of the figure."
   Students write: $B \times 1/3 \times h$
2. "Calculate the area of the base for that figure."
   Students write: $3.14 \, (1.6)^2 = 8.04$
3. "Calculate the volume."
   Students write: $8.04 \times 1/3 \times 5 = 13.4$
4. "Write the complete answer with the appropriate unit."
   Students write: 13.4 cubic inches.

This level of scaffolding is specific enough to be useful but general enough to be used flexibly with all three-dimensional figures. One test for flexibility is the degree to which the strategy can be applied to seemingly different problem types, as was illustrated earlier with proportions. This flexibility is also the means by which students come to understand how various big ideas can be linked, such as proportions, functions, and the coordinate system.

Clearly, an important part of scaffolding a task appropriately is to accurately determine students' prerequisite knowledge and target the task toward their instructional level. Vygotsky (1978) uses the term *zone of proximal development* to describe situations in which students' cognitive ability matches the cognitive requirements demanded by an instructional activity. The importance of designing educational strategies scaffolded to match students' zone of proximal development is critical to ensuring that students benefit from instruction and that the instructional experiences enhance the students' self-esteem.

Designing Primed Background Knowledge

In all of the proportion examples given in the conspicuous strategies section, a strategy is applied to a variety of concepts. The concepts to which the proportions strategy is applied—rate, percentage, measurement, probability—are assumed to have been introduced previously. Similarly, when proportions are linked to other big ideas—coordinate system and functions—these big ideas would need to have been taught. Without such prior knowledge, the application of proportions could be a rote activity, extending students' understanding of neither the proportions strategy, nor the concepts to which the strategy is applied, nor the other big ideas to which the strategy is linked. Similarly, the strategy for volume assumes certain prior knowledge on the part of the students: an understanding of the concept of area as well as computational proficiency, e.g., squaring a number and then multiplying by π.

Teachers and curriculum developers should also be aware of the need for important background knowledge to be *primed;* that is, students will need to be reminded of what they know and shown how and when previous knowledge supports the learning of new knowledge. This explicit linking of old to new knowledge is critical in helping students develop rich conceptual networks of mathematical knowledge.

Providing students with both the necessary background knowledge and flexible strategies based on big ideas that can link that knowledge is possibly the best way to prepare diverse learners for the challenges posed by the new NCTM *Standards*. Instruction should purposefully demonstrate a broad range of mathematics applications for students and enable them to successfully engage in such applications by providing the necessary prior knowledge.

Designing Strategic Integration

As the NCTM (2000) notes:

> In planning individual lessons, teachers should strive to organize the mathematics so that fundamental ideas form an integrated whole. Big ideas encountered in a variety of contexts should be established carefully, with important elements such as terminology, definitions, notation, concepts, and skills emerging in the process. (p. 15)

The previous discussion of the big ideas underpinning the four operations (rate, measurement equivalency, percent, and odds and probability) is a good example of how important ideas gain power when students learn how they are applied across the domain of mathematics. Students learn that the idea stays the same, but its implementation and use changes across the four operations.

The same concept is true for students' understanding and use of strategies. Students must not only understand important mathematical strategies as entities, but must also learn the relationships among strategies leading to an integrated, cohesive strategy (Nickerson, 1985; Prawat, 1989; Van Patten, Chao, & Reigeluth, 1986). It is conceivable that a student could learn several "good" strategies but not know when to apply them. However, instruction on individual strategies can be designed to anticipate situations in which several strategies are integrated, a practice also consistent with Piaget's (1973) model of assimilation of the new to the old and accommodation of the old to the new.

For example, if diverse learners are going to have opportunities to successfully engage in solving novel problems, they must not only be able to apply a strategy such as that for proportions but also be able to know when *not* to apply the particular strategy. Understanding involves knowing when a strategy applies and when it does not. Developing such understanding in diverse learners requires integrated teaching, not in the broad sense of interdisciplinary teaching, but within a discipline. Teaching for integration within mathematics can be illustrated with the proportion strategy. Problem A is a fairly straightforward proportion problem:

Problem A. A truck delivers cartons of juice to a store. Two sevenths of the juice is grape. The truck has 8400 cartons of juice. How many are grape juice?

Map the units: $\dfrac{\text{Grape}}{\text{Total}}$

Insert the relevant information: $\dfrac{\text{Grape}}{\text{Total}}$ $\dfrac{2}{7} = \dfrac{\boxed{}}{8400}$

Ratio   *Juice Cartons*

Solve for the answer: *2400 cartons*

If students erroneously apply the same proportion strategy to the numbers in problem B, the answer will also be 2400.

Problem B. A truck delivers cartons of grape and apple juice to a store. Two sevenths of the juice is grape. The truck will deliver 8400 cartons of apple juice. How many cartons of grape juice will the truck deliver?

Map the units: $\dfrac{\text{Grape}}{\text{Total}}$

Insert the relevant information: $\dfrac{\text{Grape}}{\text{Total}}$ $\dfrac{2}{7} = \dfrac{\boxed{2400}}{8400}$

Ratio   *Juice Cartons*

Solve for the answer: *2400 cartons*

For Problem B, the answer 2400 is *incorrect*, of course, because the 8400 does not refer to the total number of cartons, but to apple juice cartons.

With integrated teaching, the students would be less likely to inappropriately apply the basic proportion strategy to problem B because an advanced proportion strategy would have been taught to "accommodate" these more complex problem types that deal with not just two elements (total juice and grape juice), but with three elements (total juice, grape juice, and apple juice). Conversely, the new strategy for three elements must be *assimilated* with the simpler strategy that handles only two elements.

This accommodation and assimilation is accomplished through an advanced proportion strategy for three elements. This strategy illustrated in Figure 30.4.

The advanced proportion strategy in Figure 30.4 is in itself a medium-level strategy that can be flexibly applied to more complex mathematics problems, such as those involving mixtures and discounts. Following is the map for the application of the advanced proportion strategy to a discount problem:

A truck delivers cartons of grape and apple juice to a store. Two sevenths of the juice is grape. The truck will deliver 8400 cartons of apple juice. How many cartons of grape juice will the truck deliver?

		Ratio	Juice Cartons
Step 1: The students map 3 units, not just 2, and insert the relevant information:	Grape	2	☐
	Apple	☐	8400
	Total	7	☐
Step 2: The students use their knowledge of missing addends to come up with the unknown value in the ratio column: $7 - 2 = \boxed{5}$	Grape	2	☐
	Apple	$\boxed{5}$	8400
	Total	7	☐
Step 3: The students write and solve the proportion to determine the number of cartons of grape juice: $\dfrac{2}{5} = \dfrac{\boxed{3360}}{8400}$	Grape	2	$\boxed{3360}$
	Apple	$\boxed{5}$	8400
	Total	7	☐

Figure 30.4 Advanced Proportion Strategy

The application of the complete strategy to a mixture problem is illustrated in Figure 30.5.

Designing Judicious Review

The term "review" can be an emotive one in education, conjuring up images of endless (and, perhaps, mindless) drill and practice. Yet research strongly supports certain review practices as significantly effective (i.e., sufficient, distributed, cumulative, and varied). It can be said that one gets out of review what one puts into it; that is, the quality of instruction—principally in terms of big ideas and strategies—influences the value of review. Regardless of how much review is devoted to "small ideas" or marginally significant material, the ideas remain small and the material, marginally significant. These practices have been discussed in earlier chapters in this book and will not be addressed in detail here.

THE APPLICATION OF INSTRUCTIONAL DESIGN PRINCIPLES

Teachers and instructional developers both play a role in assuring that the tools for teaching mathematics to students are well designed around principles of effective instruction. Teachers primarily engage in the selection and modification of instructional materials. The choices they make in selection of materials and their demands and requests for improved materials create the incentive for those who develop materials to modify and upgrade the materials they produce. The following sections discuss suggestions for developing, selecting, and modifying materials.

Mixture Problem

A mix contains peanuts and almonds in a ratio of 4 to 3. If 35 pounds of mix are made, how many pounds of almonds will be used?

Step 1: The students map the units and write the known values:	Ratio Pounds Peanuts 4 [ ] Almonds 3 [ ] Total [ ] 35
Step 2: The students use their knowledge of missing addends to come up with the unknown value in the ratio column: $4 + 3 = \boxed{7}$	Peanuts 4 [ ] Almonds 3 [ ] Total $\boxed{7}$ 35
Step 3: The students write and solve the proportion to determine the number of pounds of almonds: $\dfrac{3}{7} = \dfrac{\boxed{15}}{35}$	Peanuts 4 $\boxed{20}$ Almonds $\boxed{3}$ $\boxed{15}$ Total 7 35

A shirt was on sale. The discount was $2. The sale price was $18. What percent was the discount?

	Dollars	Percent
Sale Price	18	[ ]
Discount	2	[ ]
Original Price	[ ]	100

Figure 30.5   Application of Advanced Proportion Strategy Applied to a Mixture Problem

Developing Instructional Tools

Instructional tools should be developed to allocate considerable time and space to teaching big ideas crucial to understanding mathematics, as opposed to giving approximately equal resources to the exposure of a multitude of topics or small ideas. Such big ideas would include number families, the identity principle, proportions, volume and area, estimation, and so on. These tools should be developed to provide explicit strategies for learning big ideas. Strategies should not be too narrow because they would likely result in rote learning. Neither should they be too broad, like some common "strategies" for solving verbal problems (e.g., draw a picture).

Some scaffolding, such as peer tutoring or instructional feedback, need not be built into instructional tools, but may instead be part of teachers' professional development training materials. Scaffolded *tasks,* however, should be built into tools. Such tasks are somewhat contrived versions of "outcome" tasks that help students achieve understanding at a reasonable pace. Here is a simple scaffolded task:

$$_____ + 2/3 = /12 + /12 = /$$

This task guides students through the strategy for converting fractions before adding.

Instructional tools that provide strong strategic integration do so by developing tasks and activities with a widespread potential for interrelating otherwise dissimilar-appearing mathematical concepts. For example, a well-designed tool might take a proportion strategy that can be applied variously to verbal problems involving rate, measurement equivalencies, percentages, probability, the coordinate system, and functions. The principal benefit of integrating conceptual knowledge this way is that it fosters deep understanding of problem solving. In addition, integrated tasks and activities are useful in relation to those mathematics topics that predictably cause confusion for students.

Developers should address background knowledge by creating assessment tools that determine whether students possess essential background knowledge for learning the strategies taught in a program and provide instruction on essential background knowledge for students with gaps in such knowledge. For diverse learners, it is risky to assume that material taught last year would be fully retained as essential background knowledge for strategies being taught this year.

Publishers do a great service to teachers when they provide plentiful review with instructional tools, because it is infinitely easier for teachers to simply skip review activities than create additional ones. Programs that include well-distributed review are far more efficient than those that do not, and programs with built-in cumulative review promote strategic integration as just described. Review should also be varied to promote transfer.

Selecting Instructional Tools

Teachers can examine mathematics tools to determine the extent to which the majority of time/space is allocated to teaching big ideas. Teachers should then examine tools to see whether conspicuous strategies exist to teach those big ideas. If conspicuous strategies exist at all, teachers should ask whether they generally appear to be intermediate in generality. Teachers should try to imagine themselves as a diverse learner who has to solve verbal problems presented by the tool based *solely* on the taught strategy.

Teachers can evaluate the extent to which scaffolded tasks are built into instructional tools by examining both *model* or *demonstration* tasks associated with a strategy and the tasks students eventually do independently. Are there "in-between" tasks that will help students gradually achieve independence and understanding?

To determine whether a tool strategically integrates important concepts, teachers can examine the scope and sequence of instructional tools, looking specifically to see whether some chapters (or units or lessons) are designated as "cumulative review" or "integration" or "consolidation." In a well-integrated tool the in-program assessments will include tasks representing all topics taught previously, not just those taught immediately preceding the assessment.

One way for teachers to assess the extent to which a tool relates prior information to new information is to dissect strategies for teaching important mathematics big ideas into their component parts. Then examine about 15 days worth of instruction *preceding* the introduction of the strategy to determine whether and how those components are handled. Ideally, components are taught or reviewed a few lessons preceding the introduction of the new strategy. Also, tools should be checked to determine the extent to which assessment tools are in place to identify important gaps in students' background knowledge. In addition, teachers can determine the extent to which a tool provides adequate review by locating a particularly difficult topic in mathematics, such as solving multistep verbal problems, then tracing the review throughout remainder of the program to determine whether review is plentiful, distributed, cumulative, and appropriately varied.

Modifying Instructional Tools

If a tool needs modification, teachers can identify the most important mathematics concepts and principles in existing tools and reallocate instructional time so that those concepts and principles can be taught thoroughly. Note that valid assessment should focus upon the important mathematics concepts selected for thorough instruction.

Teachers can help students who struggle with concepts and principles they are supposed to discover on their own by developing an explicit strategy for those concepts and principles. When strategies are too narrow, such as the "invert and multiply" rule to solve for x in problems of the form x/a = b/c, clearly and fully explain the underlying principles that make such a rule work. Without consuming too much time, teachers can convert independent tasks into scaffolded tasks by providing hints, cues, or prompts for some of the more difficult steps in the strategies associated with those tasks.

Teachers can also improve the effectiveness of tools by identifying common confusions, such as those identified previously and providing students with additional integrated practice centered on them. For instance, if a tool does not provide practice on a mixture of verbal problem types that have been taught previously, teachers can provide it using problems—or minor modifications of problems—from the instructional tool.

If teachers have the opportunity to analyze important strategies in advance of their introduction to students, they can provide some essential background knowledge based upon that analysis. For example, teachers can review the concept of area and make the connection between area and base before teaching a strategy for understanding volume. Teachers should also examine student errors carefully to determine whether they may be due largely to lack of background knowledge. If necessary, teachers can modify programs to improve the judiciousness of review principally by (a) taking a long set of tasks and distributing them over a period of days, and (b) making review cumulative. However, it can be quite time-consuming for teachers to modify programs to make review *appropriately* varied—that is, varied enough to avoid rote practice, but not so varied that it presses students to perform outside of the limits of strategies they have been taught.

SUMMARY

McCaffrey, Hamilton, Stecher, and Klein's (2001) work shows that teachers who used "reform" practices within traditional curricula were not as successful as teachers who used reform practices within reform curricula. "This finding suggests that efforts to provide professional development for teachers need to consider curriculum and instructional practices in combinations. Simple prescriptions for how to teach are unlikely to be effective" (p. 14). Instructional tools must be developed to assist teachers as they work to develop conceptual learning among students. Teachers who do not leave their preparatory programs with the depth of understanding needed for this task need the support and scaffolding provided by high quality, well-designed instructional materials.

The design considerations for mathematics presented in this chapter have significance for those working directly with students and for those developing and publishing mathematics instructional materials. Specifically, these individuals should develop or select tools for teaching mathematics in which:

- *Big ideas* are explicitly described and manifested through a wide range of appropriate content;
- *Strategies* are of an intermediate level of generality and explicitly described and utilized across a range of problem types;
- Tasks are flexibly *scaffolded* to provide students with support in learning new material and scaffolding is faded over time to lead students to independence;
- Important concepts are strategically *integrated* in ways that show the commonalities and differences between new and old knowledge;
- *Background knowledge* is primed before moving into new learning so students are prepared to make connections;
- *Review* opportunities are appropriately developed to be adequate, distributed, cumulative, and varied.

REFLECTION AND APPLICATION: Case Study

Allison has been hired to teach seventh- and eighth-grade mathematics. She recently completed a teacher training program, and her undergraduate emphasis in mathematics as well as a business background made her a good fit for a recent vacancy at Monroe Middle School. While generally enthusiastic about her new job, she realized that her low-ability, "remedial track" classes would be a challenge.

Half of the students in Math Applications, the lowest math track at Monroe, are mainstreamed special education students. The special education teacher doesn't assist in the instruction, but monitors each student's progress several times throughout the year. Instead, special education services provide Allison with a full-time aide.

The other half of the students in "Math Apps" are in the class for a variety of reasons. Some need just a little extra review before they enter the middle track, pre-algebra classes. Others seem apathetic about math and are taking the class because it is still a required subject. Still others have had a hard time with math since elementary school, but they just don't score low enough to qualify for special education services. As Allison quickly noted, "It really wouldn't make any difference. At this school, they'd still be in my class regardless of whether or not they qualified for special ed."

Allison started her Math Apps class using the district-recommended textbook—a widely marketed commercial basal that begins with a review of basic operations and quickly moves to its main concepts—fractions, decimals and percent, geometry, and negative numbers. In the beginning of the year, Allison thought she'd supplement the text with some daily living applications like learning how to balance a checkbook.

Sequence of District-Recommended Textbook

- Addition/subtraction of whole numbers
- Addition/subtraction of decimals
- Multiplication/division of whole numbers
- Multiplication of decimals
- Division of decimals
- Geometry
- Number theory and equations
- Addition/subtraction of fractions
- Multiplication/division of fractions
- Measurement: Metric units
- Ratio and proportion
- Percent
- Circles and cylinders
- Probability, statistics, and graphs

- Integers
- Measurement: Customary units

By the second week, however, Allison was overwhelmed. The range of academic abilities was too great, and the textbook material moved too quickly. Students were frustrated and bored with the introductory review chapter, and most seemed lost when fractions appeared in chapter 2 of the book. When Allison consulted the special, education teacher, she offered her a highly sequenced set of skills worksheets. They were generally computational problems, from simple multiplication and division through decimals.

When Allison tried the worksheets for the majority of the class at the beginning of the third week, most students complained that the work was babyish and that "they'd seen this stuff before and they knew it already." Neither the prescribed textbook for the class nor a common remedial sequence seemed to be the answer. The text was too demanding cognitively, and the worksheets left students unmotivated and indifferent to mathematics.

Clearly, there was little in Allison's prior training that prepared her to teach these kinds of students. Most importantly, there seemed to be few, if any, resources in the school that could help her adjust the curriculum so that it would adequately meet the needs of her students. When she talked to more experienced faculty about the class, they shared her frustrations and were generally cynical about what could be accomplished with these students. Most felt that students in Math Apps would continue working at the sixth-grade level (at least as measured by district learning objectives) until they graduated from middle school. Allison found the thought of teaching many of these students for three years in a row too depressing.

- In what ways might the textbook have been inappropriate for Allison's students? How might the curriculum be modified to better meet the diverse learning needs of her students?

The conclusion of the case study can be found later in this chapter.

CONTENT QUESTIONS

1. Describe the challenge in providing students with useful strategies.
2. What is the most valuable use of big ideas in mathematics instruction?
3. List seven applications of the proportions strategy.
4. What has been a problem with providing instructional feedback in traditional mathematics instruction?
5. Explain the authors' suggestions for scaffolding mathematics problems.
6. How can instruction prepare diverse learners for the challenges posed by the NCTM standards?
7. What behaviors must diverse learners perform in order to solve novel problems?
8. Name and describe two aspects necessary for the successful integration of problem-solving strategies.

REFLECTION AND DISCUSSION

1. Does there need to be a dichotomy between traditionalists who call for a return to "basics" in mathematics instruction and reformers who call for increased emphasis on conceptual skills, problem solving, and reasoning? What are the implications of these issue positions for students with diverse learning needs?
2. Given the increasing heterogeneity of achievement levels and learning needs in classrooms, how might effective teaching strategies and instructional principles be used to provide access to general education mathematics content for all students, including students with diverse learning needs?
3. A special educator is assigned to co-teach a tenth-grade math class with a general educator. When meeting to discuss the class, the math teacher says, "I'm not sure this will work; teaching math involves a great deal of content knowledge, and you aren't trained in mathematics." How should the special educator respond? What skills does a special educator or other education professional with expertise in instructional principles have that could benefit students in a higher level math class, both those with and without learning difficulties? Does the special educator need the same level of expertise in the content area of mathematics to effectively co-teach the class?

Application

1. Figure 30.6 shows an example of mathematics instruction that was designed using principles of effective instruction. Evaluate the instruction according to the following questions. What big idea does the instruction focus on? How is the instruction conspicuous? How is the instruction scaffolded? What background knowledge do students need to successfully complete the instruction? How could the instruction be extended to provide judicious review?

Case Study (Conclusion)

Allison realized that she was confronted with several challenges. First, the textbook recommended by the district appeared poorly suited to the needs of her mainstreamed special education students and other students with diverse learning needs. It presented a constant barrage of changing concepts that were briefly covered and poorly reviewed. Important ideas, such as proportionality, were not systematically integrated within the textbook and there were few visual displays to support these mathematical concepts.

A related challenge was the lack of adequate time for reorganizing and revising class materials, a problem compounded by the fact that Allison's preservice training had focused primarily on the needs of students with average or above average learning abilities. Additionally, she found that the available opportunities for professional development were not helping her to develop instructional strategies to accommodate the diverse learners in her Math Apps class.

Fortunately, Allison was able to take advantage of a district initiative that offered

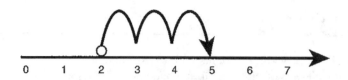

I'll show you how to write the equation for this problem. First, I'll see where the circle started. The circle started at two, so I'll write "2".

2

Now, I'll see how many places the circle moved forward by counting the loops with my finger ...1...2 ...3. So I'll write "plus 3".

2 + 3

Now, I'll see where the circle ended. The circle ended at five so I'll write "equals 5".

2 + 3 = 5

I'll read the whole equation for this problem. "Two plus three equals five."

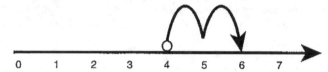

Now it's your turn to write the equation for a problem. First, you'll figure out where the circle started. Where did the circle start? (students respond) That's right! The circle started at four, so you'll write "4".

4

Now, you'll figure out how many places the circle moved forward by counting the loops with your finger. How many places did the circle move forward? (students respond) That's right! So you'll write "plus 2".

4 + 2

Now, you'll figure out where the circle ended. Where did the circle end? (students respond) That's right! The circle ended at six so you'll write "equals 6".

4 + 2 = 6

Read the whole equation for this problem. That's right! "Four plus two equals six."

Figure 30.6 Mathematics Instruction Example

support from educators with extensive experience in adapting curricula to meet the needs of students with diverse learning needs. In collaboration with these specialists, Allison decided that adapting the original math textbook to meet the needs of her Math Apps students would prove too time-consuming. Therefore, the original text was replaced with innovative materials that had previously proven successful with diverse learners. Importantly, the new curriculum was designed around a *few big ideas,* rather than the myriad concepts presented in the old curriculum. The revised curriculum also aligned well with the district's essential learnings and the state framework in mathematics.

Sequence of New Curriculum

1. Proportions
   - Representing common fraction
   - Transforming fractions
   - Understanding decimals
   - Percents
   - Ratios
2. Common measurements
   - Using fractions
   - Metrics
3. Geometry
4. Charting numbers and modeling data

Allison used several instructional strategies to reinforce the big ideas in the new curriculum. Instruction was made more *conspicuous,* for example, by emphasizing graphic displays and other visual supports to illustrate concepts such as fractions and ratios. She explicitly taught steps for solving geometry problems, initially modeling the application of sequential steps for her students. After they had worked through several examples together, Allison utilized *mediated scaffolding* by gradually fading the level of guidance and feedback that she provided for her students.

With the assistance of colleagues available through the district initiative, Allison systematically designed opportunities for *strategic integration, primed background knowledge, and judicious review.* The steps used to find the area of a circle, for example, were reviewed prior to introducing the concept of a cylinder and computation of its volume. Allison was careful to make direct links between the concepts of circles and cylinders, rather than assuming that her students would implicitly make these connections. She also used concrete props to demonstrate how these concepts are similar and different, explaining that the volume of a cylinder represented a measurement of space in three dimensions.

The students in Allison's class responded favorably to this adjusted curriculum. Within a few weeks of initiating these changes, her Math Apps students appeared appropriately challenged by their instruction and demonstrated improved performance on quizzes and homework assignments. Allison eventually decided to apply these instructional principles in her other mathematics classes in order to promote effective learning experiences for *all* of her students.

- How might Allison extend principles of effective instruction to daily living applications, such as balancing a checkbook?
- Would it be realistic to expect all students, including those in upper track math classes, to benefit from the effective teaching strategies that Allison employed successfully in her Math Applications class?
- Would Allison be able to incorporate these instructional strategies in other mathematics classes in the absence of a district initiative and assistance from curriculum specialists?

The Reflection and Application section of this chapter was written by John P. Woodward of the University of Puget Sound and Richard P. Zipoli, Jr. and Maureen F. Ruby from the University of Connecticut.

REFERENCES

Baker, S., Gersten, R., & Lee, D. (2002). A synthesis of empirical research on teaching mathematics to low-achieving students. *Elementary School Journal, 103*(1), 51–73.

Braswell, J., Daane, M., & Grigg W. (2003). *The nation's report card: Mathematics highlights 2003.* Washington, DC: National Center for Education Statistics. Retrieved August 11, 2005 from http://nces.ed.gov/pubsearch/pubsinfo.asp?pubid=2004451

Davis, R. B. (1990). Discovery learning and constructivism. In R. B. Davis, C. A. Maher, & N. Noddings (Eds.), *Constructivist views on the teaching and learning of mathematics.* Reston, VA: National Council of Teachers of Mathematics.

Department of Defense. (2005). *National Defense Act: Ensuring national security tomorrow through education today.* Retrieved October, 11, 2005 from http://www.dod.mil/ddre/text/t_ndea.html

Donovan, M. S., & Bransford, J. D. (2005). *How students learn: History, mathematics, and science in the classroom.* Washington, DC: National Research Council.

Engelmann, S., Carnine, D., Kelly, B., & Engelmann, O. (1994). *Connecting math concepts, A through F.* Columbus, OH: SRA.

Gates, W. (2005). *National Education Summit on High Schools.* Retrieved October 10, 2005 from http://www.gatesfoundation.org/MediaCenter/Speeches/BillgSpeeches/BGSpeechNGA-050226.htm

Gelman, R. (1986). Toward an understanding-based theory of mathematics learning and instruction, or in praise of Lampert on teaching multiplication. *Cognition and Instruction, 3,* 349–355.

Gleason, M., Carnine, D., & Boriero, D. (1990). Improving CAI effectiveness with attention to instructional design in teaching story problems to mildly handicapped students. *Journal of Special Education Technology, 10*(3), 129–136.

Kazmierczach, M. F., James, J., & Archey, W. T. (2005). *Losing the competitive advantage? The challenge for science and technology in the United States.* Retrieved August 16, 2005 from http://www.aeanet.org/publications/idjj_CompetitivenessMain0205.asp.

Kilpatrick, J., Swafford, J., & Findell, B. (Eds.). (2001). *Adding it up: Helping children learn mathematics.* Washington, DC: National Research Council.

Leath, A. T. (2005). Hearing examines science and math education competitiveness, *FYI, The AIP Bulletin of Science Policy News, 84.* Retrieved August, 15, 2005 from http://www.aip.org/fyi/2005/084.html

Leinhardt, G. (1987). Development of an expert explanation: An analysis of a sequence of subtraction lessons. *Cognition and Instruction, 4*(4), 225–282.

Loveless, T., & Diperna, P. (2000). How well are American students learning? Focus on math achievement. *The Brown Center Report on American Education, 1*(1).

Ma, L. (1999). *Knowing and teaching elementary mathematics: Teachers' understanding of fundamental mathematics in China and the United States.* Mahwah, NJ: Erlbaum.

McCaffrey, D. F., Hamilton, L. S., Stecher, B. M., & Klein, S. P. (2001). Interactions among instructional practices, curriculum, and student achievement: The case of standards-based school mathematics. *Journal for Research in Mathematics Education, 32*(5), 493.

McDaniel, M. A., & Schlager, M. S. (1990). Discovery learning and transfer of problem solving. *Cognition and Instruction, 7*(2), 129–159.

Mouly, G. J. (1978). *Educational research: The art and science of investigation.* Boston: Allyn & Bacon.

National Center for Education Statistics. (2003). Trends in International Mathematics and Science Study Retrieved August 11, 2005 from http://nces.ed.gov/timss/Result303.asp

National Center for Educational Statistics. (2005). *NAEP 2004 trends in academic progress three decades of student performance in reading and mathematics.* Retrieved from http://nces.ed.gov/pubsearch/pubsinfo.asp?pubid=2005464

National Council of Teachers of Mathematics. (2000). *NAEP: Understanding the headlines.* Retrieved August 16, 2005 from http://www.nctm.org/news/articles/2000-12naep.htm

National Council of Teachers of Mathematics. (2000). *Principles and standards for school mathematics.* Retrieved August 16, 2005 from http://standards.nctm.org/index.htm

National Research Council. (1998). *Preventing reading difficulties in young children.* Washington, DC: National Academies Press.

Nickerson, R. S. (1985). Understanding. *American Journal of Education, 93,* 201–239.

Piaget, J. (1973). *The child and reality: Problems of genetic psychology.* New York: Viking Press.

Prawat, R. S. (1989). Promoting access to knowledge, strategy, and disposition in students: A research synthesis. *Review of Educational Research, 59*(1), 1–41.

Resnick, L. B., Cauzinille-Marmeche, E., & Mathieu, J. (1987). Understanding algebra. In J. A. Sloboda & D. Rogers (Eds.), *Cognitive proceses in mathematics* (pp. 169–203). Oxford: Clarendon Press.

Resnick, L. B., & Omanson, S. F. (1987). Learning to understand arithmetic. In R. Glaser (Ed.), *Advances in instructional psychology* (pp. 41–95). Hillsdale, NJ: Erlbaum.

Stein, M., Silbert, J., & Carnine, C. (1997). *Designing effective mathematics instruction: A direct instruction approach* (3rd ed.). Upper Saddle River, NJ: Merrill.

Tournaki, N. (2003). The differential effects of teaching addition through strategy instruction versus drill and practice to students with and without learning disabilities. *Journal of Learning Disabilities, 36*(5), 449–458.

Van Patten, J., Chao, C., & Reigeluth, C. M. (1986). A review of strategies for sequencing and synthesizing instruction. *Review of Educational Research, 56*(4), 437–471.

Vergnaud, G. (1988). Multiplicative structures. In J. Hiebert & M. Behr (Eds.), *Number concepts and operations in the middle grades* (pp. 141–161). Reston, VA: NCTM.

Vygotsky, L. S. (1978). *Mind in society: The development of higher psychological processes.* (M. Cole, V. John-Steiner, S. Scribner, & E. Souberman, Eds. & Trans.). Cambridge, MA: Harvard University Press.

EFFECTIVE STRATEGIES FOR TEACHING SCIENCE

Bonnie J. Grossen, *University of Oregon;* Douglas W. Carnine, *University of Oregon;* Nancy R. Romance, *Florida Atlantic University;* Michael R. Vitale, *East Carolina University*

This chapter parallels the other chapters in this book by illustrating the same six key principles in designing educational tools for enabling teachers to accommodate a wide range of students, including diverse learners (children of poverty, children with disabilities, linguistically different and minority children).

The purpose of this chapter is to illustrate the six principles in designing or selecting effective tools in the area of science education. These principles derive from a thorough review of the educational research literature. This chapter is not a research review; it is an illustration of the implications of that research review. The illustrations are directed toward the needs of both educational practitioners (e.g., teachers and supervisors) and designers of new instructional tools (e.g., publishers and developers).

CURRENT ISSUES IN SCIENCE INSTRUCTION

Meeting the needs of all students, including diverse learners, is a purpose that is entirely consistent with recent efforts to reform science education. Two major national efforts to reform science curriculum were initiated in the 1990s: Project 2061 of the American Association for the Advancement of Science (AAAS), and the National Committee on Science Education Standards and Assessment of the National Research Council (1995). The emphasis of both groups was on a commitment to "science for all" that is highly significant for diverse learners. For example, the National Science Education Standards (National Research Council [NRC], 1995) asserts:

> The intent of the *Standards* can be expressed in a single phrase: Science standards for all students. The phrase embodies both excellence and equity. The *Standards* apply to all students, regardless of age, gender, cultural or ethnic background, disabilities, aspirations, or interest and motivation in science. Different students will achieve understanding in different ways, different students will achieve different degrees of depth and breadth of understanding depending on interest, ability, and context. But all students develop the knowledge and skills described in the *Standards,* even as some students go well beyond these levels. (p. 2)

There are a number of common perspectives on problems in teaching science that have bearing on the present chapter. Among the most important are guidelines for teaching the fundamental concepts, principles, facts, laws, and theories that exemplify scientific literacy by providing a foundation for understanding and applying science. The AAAS refers to these fundamental understandings as the "big ideas" of science. In keeping with the NRC standards (1993, p. 4), a big idea is one that:

1. "represents central scientific ideas and organizing principles."
2. "has rich explanatory and predictive power."
3. "motivates the formulation of significant questions."
4. "is applicable to many situations and contexts common to everyday experiences."

The present chapter adopts a curricular emphasis on "big ideas" as a fundamental characteristic for all effective science instructional tools.

Another important concern addressed in the research is the role of textbooks as the most commonly used tool for teaching science, and as the determiners of as much as 70 percent of the instructional activity in science (Raizen, 1988; see also Wood & Wood, 1988). A recent AAAS Project 2061 study examined the most widely used textbooks to determine how well they helped students learn key science ideas in the middle grades and high school (AAAS 1999, 2000). The in-depth study of middle-school texts, including the most recently published "new crop" of texts, found that "most textbooks cover too many topics and don't develop any of them well. All texts include many classroom activities that either are irrelevant to learning key science ideas or don't help students relate what they are doing to the underlying ideas" (AAAS, 1999, p. 1). Not one text was rated satisfactory at any level. The evaluation of high school biology texts found that "Big Biology Books Fail to Convey Big Ideas" (AAAS, 2000, p. 1). Four major problems described are as follows:

1. Research shows that essentially all students—even the best and the brightest—have predictable difficulties grasping many ideas that are covered in the text books. Yet the textbooks fail to take these obstacles into account in designing activities and questions.
2. For many biology concepts, the textbooks ignore or obscure the most important ideas by focusing instead on technical terms and trivial details (which are easy to test).
3. While most of the books are lavishly illustrated, these representations are rarely helpful, because they are too abstract, needlessly complicated, or inadequately explained.
4. Even though several activities are included in every chapter, students are given little guidance in interpreting the results in terms of the scientific concepts to be learned.

Other studies echo these criticisms, including that science texts contain too many concepts, present ideas in a list-like rather than an integrated fashion, have unclear prose and illustrations, and are generally ineffective in effecting conceptual change for meaningful learning (Lloyd, 1989; McCarthy, 2005; Newport, 1990; Osborn, Jones, & Stein, 1985; Smith, Blakeslee, & Anderson, 1993).

Although the admittedly poor design of current science texts has caused many educators to totally reject their value, the view expressed in this chapter is that properly designed (or properly augmented) textbooks can be useful learning tools in science classrooms.

The poor design of science textbooks not only has caused many educators to reject textbooks, but also has led some educators to reject instruction in science subject matter as a reasonable goal for pre-university science instruction (Shaw, 1983; Staver & Small, 1990; Yager & Penick, 1987; Yeany, Yap, & Padilla, 1986). These educators recommend instead that proficiency in science inquiry skills be the primary goal of science education, so that student-directed inquiry methods can be used exclusively, rather than the explicit, teacher-directed presentations that typify textbook-based instruction. Apparently, explicit instruction for content understanding has been denigrated because it is done so poorly in science texts.

However, in keeping with national science standards, stepping back from the challenge of effectively teaching science subject matter would be incompatible with the nation's emerging goals to achieve world-class standards in science. Toward that end, the new science content standards include, along with science inquiry, science subject matter (the concepts and principles of science) as a critical component in both the reform of science education and the achievement of scientific literacy for all students. Two additional goal areas addressed by the new national science education standards are scientific connections and science in human affairs.

The reader should view each of the following design principles as the focus of efforts to develop, select, or enhance instruction so that it accommodates a broad range of students, including diverse learners:

1. Does the instruction focus on teaching the "big ideas" of science?
2. Does it make the strategies for using the big ideas conspicuous?
3. Are important component concepts of big ideas and component steps of strategies taught?
4. Does mediated scaffolding provide a smooth transition to independent success?
5. Is judicious review provided?
6. Is the content strategically integrated for greater efficiency in learning?

In the first part of this chapter, the first three highly interdependent design considerations—big ideas, strategies, component steps and concepts—are discussed, and examples from science inquiry and from subject matter knowledge are given. The sequence of illustrations models the order in which the development of an instructional sequence occurs—starting with the desired student outcome and analyzing back to a reasonable starting point for instruction—rather than the reverse order, which would more closely correspond to the actually teaching of the instructional sequence. In the second part of this chapter, the remaining three considerations—scaffolding, judicious review, and strategic integration—are discussed. These design considerations apply to the design of the communication.

PRINCIPLES FOR IMPROVING INSTRUCTIONAL STRATEGIES IN SCIENCE

Designing Instruction Around Big Ideas in Science Inquiry

Science inquiry—the process of truth-seeking—is perhaps the "biggest" idea of science. The classic approach to science inquiry—the scientific method—consists of several well-accepted steps: observing patterns or discrepancies, forming hypotheses to explain these observed patterns or discrepancies, controlling and manipulating variables, planning investigations to test hypotheses, and interpreting the resulting data.

Science inquiry—the ability to test hypotheses—is a crucial truth-seeking skill in both formal scientific and informal contexts. Kuhn (1993) found that few adults have the minimal truth-seeking skills required to confront their informal beliefs in an honest manner. For example, only 40 percent of her subjects could describe the nature of the evidence that would cause them to falsify their theories for such questions as: What causes prisoners to return to a life of crime after they are released? What causes children to fail in school? What causes unemployment? Many adult subjects claimed that they did not have to consider any evidence because their opinion was their opinion and they were entitled to it.

The processes needed to establish and evaluate everyday beliefs and theories are essentially the same processes used in formal scientific hypothesis testing. For this reason, science inquiry (or the scientific method) is truly a big idea that is relevant to a much larger range of human affairs than simply the domain of science, and is one that connects across a wide range of disciplines.

Component Steps and Concepts in Science Inquiry

One component skill of science inquiry that is also a big idea in the science education of younger children is the ability to identify a pattern in observations. Once a scientist observes a pattern, then the scientist can form a hypothesis to explain or predict the noted pattern. Very young children begin to develop the skill of identifying patterns in their study of the classification system of plants and animals. The common features of the categories represent a pattern in the observations. When teachers make these patterns explicit and engage children in classifying organisms according to the features of the categories, of mammals for example, children are developing their observation skills and their ability to see recurring patterns across several examples or observations.

A second key component of science inquiry is effectively controlling variables (Ross, 1988). As an inquiry skill, controlling variables means that in order to isolate the effect of a variable, students must be able to identify all other relevant variables and then design an experiment that keeps unchanged all but the variable being tested. This critical strategy component—controlling variables—is illustrated in the following section as an example of making a strategy conspicuous.

Designing Conspicuous Strategies in Science Inquiry

A fairly common hypothesis in science education is that "inquiry" instructional methods (also sometimes called nonexplicit, activity-based, student-centered, or discovery methods) are preferable to explicit instructional methods for teaching students how to *do* science inquiry. However, this hypothesis seems generally contradicted by experimental research. Research comparing "inquiry" (nonexplicit) methods with instruction that makes the strategies for carrying out science inquiry explicit finds that the latter results in better learning, especially for students with low academic achievement levels who do not already possess an understanding of inquiry (Klahr & Nigam, 2004; McCleery & Tindal, 1999; Ross, 1988; Rubin & Norman, 1992; Zohar & Aharon-Kravetsky, 2005).

In spite of these findings, the hypothesis that persists is that inquiry instructional methods work better than explicit instruction for teaching science inquiry skills. A second group of studies are often cited to support this hypothesis (e.g., Shymansky, Kyle, & Alport, 1983; Staver & Small, 1990). However, the conclusions from this group of studies are misleading because the "explicit" treatments in these studies teach only scientific principles and do not explicitly teach the skills of science inquiry at all. For example, several studies compare an explicit treatment designed to teach the displacement principle (i.e., the amount of liquid displaced by an object is equal to the volume of the object) with inquiry instruction designed to teach students to derive the principle of displacement through their own inquiry (e.g., Bay, Staver, Bryan, & Hale, 1992). None of the explicit treatment conditions was designed to teach science inquiry skills.

It is not surprising that studies with this design generally find that inquiry teaching methods result in better science inquiry performance than "explicit" instruction (Bredderman, 1983; Shayer & Adey, 1993; Shymansky et al., 1983; Staver & Small, 1990). However, conclusions about explicit instruction for teaching science inquiry cannot be made on the basis of explicit treatments designed to teach only scientific principles. Studies that compare inquiry instruction with instruction designed to make the strategy for science inquiry explicit generally conclude that explicit instruction is more effective. Explicit methods that teach what students are expected to learn usually result in better learning than inquiry (nonexplicit) teaching methods. The conclusions to be drawn from such research are: If students are to learn science inquiry, make the strategy for science inquiry explicit. Similarly, if students are to learn scientific principles, it is important to make the scientific principles explicit.

Our interpretation of this research is that effective instruction makes significant strategies "conspicuous" rather than simply "explicit." We make this distinction because educators often interpret "explicit instruction" to mean simply "verbalized instruction." However, the effective treatments in the first group of studies involved much more than simply teacher verbalization, and, in effect, they made the strategies for science inquiry very conspicuous.

To illustrate a conspicuous strategy that accommodates the needs of *all* learners, we present a modified activity from *Elementary Science Study* (1974), a popular inquiry-based curriculum of the 1970s. In the original inquiry activity, students viewed a row of figures called mellinarks and a second row of figures that were not mellinarks. The students then viewed a third row of mellinarks and nonmellinarks and identified which figures would be classified as mellinarks. The instruction did not model or describe any strategy for controlling variables that the students could use to think about the examples in order to figure out the concept of mellinark. Students continued the activity with similar concepts until they themselves discovered or "self-learned" the inquiry skill needed to derive a concept from examples and nonexamples. Therefore, the instruction was described as an "inquiry" method.

Although this activity may seem quite simple, Lawson et al. (1991) found that only 22 percent of high school chemistry and biology students possess the science inquiry skills to successfully identify a mellinark and other such imaginary concepts. These findings indicate that nearly *all* students would

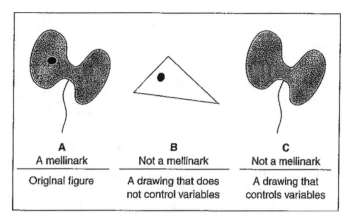

Figure 31.1 Controlling Variables to Define a Concept

benefit from a teacher-directed experiential activity designed to teach a conspicuous strategy for controlling variables.

The instruction begins with the presentation of only one figure, Drawing A in Figure 31.1. The students' goal is to determine with some certainty what it means to be a mellinark by designing (drawing) additional examples, each of which the teacher identifies as mellinark or nonmellinark. For these examples to be most informative, students must control the possible variables; that is, they must design each example so that it is exactly the same as the original figure except for the one feature that students want to test. For example, Drawing B in Figure 31.1 is not very informative because it does not control many variables; that is Drawing B differs from Drawing A in more than one way. On the other hand, Drawing C is quite informative because it controls for all variables except the spot, so the information that Drawing C is not a mellinark would allow students to conclude that a mellinark must have a spot.

The activity continues with students designing more figures that change only one of the other variables listed on the board, or the drawings could test additional variables, such as the range of acceptable sizes for the spot, or even whether more than one spot is possible on a mellinark. The variable list is potentially endless. (This conspicuous strategy with additional scaffolding is illustrated later in this chapter under the topic, scaffolding.)

The steps made conspicuous in the strategy for identifying mellinarks form a generic strategy for controlling variables—a strategy that students can learn and apply not only to the mellinark problem, but to any problem requiring systematic scientific investigation. These elements are: Design the figure (the experiment) so that the new figure (the experimental treatment) differs from the original figure (the control treatment) in only one feature (the independent variable) and all the other features (variables) are kept the same (controlled). Gather information about whether each figure is a mellinark to identify whether the feature that was changed is critical to the figure's being a mellinark (interpret the results).

In the initial instruction, the teacher should not use the sophisticated vocabulary that is normally used to describe these steps (e.g., independent and dependent variable). The teacher's goal should be to make the actual *strategy* conspicuous. Vocabulary words can be taught later, after students have acquired the meanings that go with them. The mellinark activity is easily managed and could readily teach most students, including diverse learners, science inquiry strategies by making them conspicuous to learners.

Designing Instruction Around Big Ideas in Science Subject Matter

As noted earlier, both the NRC and the AAAS science standards emphasize the importance of teaching the big ideas of science subject matter. For purposes of illustration, some significant big ideas in science subject matter include the nature of science, energy transformations, gravity, flow of matter and energy in ecosystems, and the interdependence of life. Such big ideas and their component concepts clearly cut across the science domains (e.g., physics, earth science, biology) and are essential in building a level of scientific literacy among all students that is necessary for understanding and problem solving within the natural and created world.

The AAAS's Project 2061 is analyzing the major big ideas in science in a publication called *Atlas of Science Literacy* (in press). A preview of the contents of this publication can be found on the web at http://www.project2061.org/.

Convection: An Example of a Big Idea.   The principle of convection is a good example of a big idea that both explains and unifies many of the dynamic phenomena that occur within the earth (geology), oceans (oceanography), and atmosphere (meteorology)—three domains of science usually associated with earth science. For example, in the area of geology, plate tectonics, earthquakes, volcanoes, and the formation of mountains are all influenced by convection in the mantle. Global and local convection patterns influence the dynamics of the atmosphere. Similarly, the ocean currents, thermohaline circulation, and coastal upwelling are influenced by global and local convection. In turn, the interaction of these phenomena in the earth and the atmosphere results in the rock cycle, weathering, and changes in landforms. The interaction of these phenomena in the ocean and in the atmosphere influence the water cycle, wind-driven ocean circulation, El Niño, and climate in general.

As is the case for many currently evolving big ideas, alternative and variant explanations for these phenomena have been offered, and the fact that competing theoretical explanations often exist is an aspect of science of which students should be made aware. However, not all the alternative and variant explanations need to be taught, particularly in initial instruction. Figure 31.2 illustrates the core principle of convection and the various phenomena it explains.

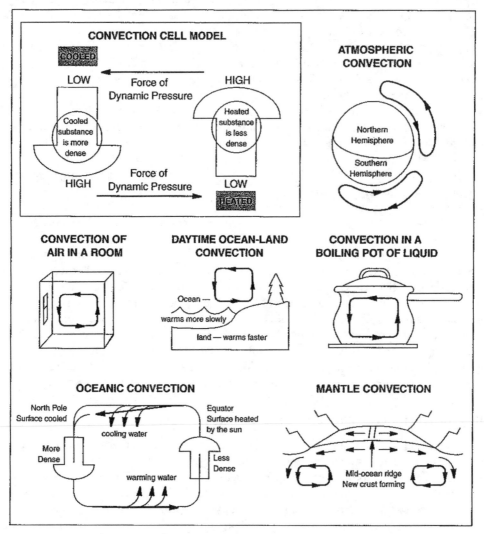

Figure 31.2   The Big Idea of Convection and Simple Visual Maps of Some of Its Applications

Benefits of an Analysis of Big Ideas. By design, big ideas have the potential to transfer or apply more widely to other areas (domains) of science and everyday phenomena than small (or less general) ideas. For example, as discussed previously, the principle of convection can be used to explain dynamic natural phenomena in geology, meteorology, and oceanography. Also, well-designed instruction in big ideas allows for more efficient use of time. Because of the foundational understanding and connections established with big ideas, the teacher can cover a greater amount of meaningful content while teaching fewer principles. And, as students apply big ideas across other domains of science, these big ideas function as prior knowledge within which students can easily assimilate new learning with appropriate elaboration rather than learning everything as if it were new. (While the use of big ideas is an effective and efficient strategy, other characteristics of instructional delivery, such as scaffolding and review, determine the extent to which students actually learn the big idea.)

In general, big ideas represent an adaptive curricular solution that amplifies meaningful understanding in a fashion that is of particular importance to diverse learners, rather than encouraging mere memorization of an array of disconnected facts, as too often occurs. This approach provides diverse learners with the opportunity to learn that scientific concepts and "real world" science phenomena are both understandable and logically related.

Components in Science Subject Matter

Component concepts are essential elements that must be identified when attempting to teach any big ideas, including those identified as benchmarks or standards within the national science reform initiatives of the NRC or AAAS. In order to explain and meaningfully apply a big idea such as convection, for example, students must understand and use its component or underlying concepts. In the case of convection, in-depth understanding depends on students' prior understanding of concepts such as cause-and-effect relationships between and among the phenomena of heating and cooling, density, force, and pressure.

By designing instruction to teach the component concepts conspicuously (in this example, a network of cause-and-effect relationships that underlie the larger causal principle of convection), a deeper understanding of the principle can be achieved by all students rather than a select few. In turn, the knowledge resulting from a deeper understanding of the underlying causes of convection (density, heat, the effect of heat on density and pressure, and so on) provides a meaningful foundation that can be used to explain everyday phenomena as well as more abstract phenomena, such as novas and black holes in the universe.

In fact, unless students have extensive specialized prior scientific knowledge, specific instruction in the component concepts is necessary in order to build understanding of convection. For example, students must understand that heat causes a substance to expand and become less dense, and that substances move from a place of high pressure to a place of low pressure. Simultaneously, in order to understand and apply the underlying component concepts and principle of convection, specific facts about the solar system, the ocean, the solid earth, and the atmosphere must be known. For example, students must know that the sun is the primary external source of heat, that the tilt of the earth as it orbits around the sun causes variations in the amount of heat received in different areas of the earth (i.e., changing seasons), that the core of the earth is hot, that the ocean is very, very deep, and so on.

As students learn to integrate the component concepts with other relevant knowledge, they gain an understanding analogous to a dynamic mental model of a generic convection cell (upper left box in Figure 31.2). By conspicuously teaching component concepts, understanding and application of the convection process becomes accessible to a wider range of diverse students.

Designing Conspicuous Strategies in Science Subject Matter

Better problem solving in the form of applications of scientific knowledge is a major goal of science education reform. To solve problems, students need to learn strategies for using and applying the big ideas of science and their component concepts in a variety of contexts. The big ideas and component concepts represent scientific knowledge that, of necessity, must be brought to bear in the problem-solving process. Thus, the design of instructional tools and classroom instruction around big ideas is a critical dimension underlying the degree to which students can understand and apply the knowledge they have learned. Students should learn important big ideas in a form that optimizes their explanatory and predictive power, along with the kinds of problems to which the big ideas apply.

In fact, the strategies necessary for effective problem solving and learning in science are literally the applications of big ideas. For example, instructional strategies that connect component concepts to a big idea or scientific principle (such as convection) can be applied by students to predict the location of and movement in a substance given the placement of the heat source. Such knowledge becomes dynamic whenever it helps students interpret events in the world or make more accurate predictions about what is likely or not likely to happen. Knowledge of big ideas and their component concepts forms the basis for meaningful conceptual learning and effective problem solving in science. Within this context, science learning for students is analogous to the current problem faced by scientists of predicting earthquakes and volcanoes given prior factual knowledge in conjunction with the conceptual understanding of the location of plates in the earth and their significance.

Building Understanding Through Wide Application of Big Ideas. Once the big idea of convection and the component concepts underlying it are understood in simple forms and are used to explain and predict common experiences, they can then be broadened to explain more abstract phenomena, such as convection in the atmosphere and in the earth's mantle. Given these two applications, the big idea of convection is important to the meaningful understanding of each, for two reasons. First, the common convection models amplify their similarity: The source of heat is at the bottom of the convection cell in both cases because the sun heats the surface of the earth, which causes convection in the atmosphere, and the heated core of earth causes convection in the mantle. Second, aspects of the models amplify their differences: One convection model involves gases, the other involves solids. At a more abstract level, using the convection model to understand that movement in the mantle is similar to movement in the atmosphere and is similar to common experiences prevents a possible misconception that convection does not occur in solids.

Explaining the application of the big idea of convection to the ocean would best be taught after the mantle and atmosphere because it requires more complex understanding beyond convection. In oceans, the source of heat is at the top of the convection cell: The sun heats the surface of the ocean. This is only a minor elaboration of the convection model. However, convection in the ocean also interacts with convection in the atmosphere (i.e., winds), so that the surface currents of the ocean must be explained by both ocean and air convection patterns. Finally, an even more complex process is the interaction of local convection patterns in the atmosphere with global convection in the atmosphere. This interaction can be quite complex, which is why weather prediction is usually very difficult. However, an awareness of the problems involved in using an understanding of convection to make accurate predictions can add a final touch of realism to the instruction.

While other factors are important in these applications (such as the rotation of the earth), the important point is not only that teacher-directed sequences involving the wide application of big ideas can enhance the understanding of big ideas for all students, but also that these forms of adaptation are of great importance in the success of diverse learners in science instruction.

Using Visual Maps to Model Strategies for Organizing Concepts and Big Ideas. Science subject matter content, as represented by big ideas and component concepts, should be presented in such a way that the instruction facilitates the application of big ideas, which often manifest themselves in problem solving. To accomplish this, instruction can use visual maps (i.e., concept maps, pictures, diagrammatic sketches) to emphasize the explanative nature of science and the organization of science's big ideas. This approach will further improve problem-solving performance (Guastello, Beasley, & Sinatra, 2000; Mayer, 1989; Mayer & Gallini, 1990; Woodward, 1994). Ideally, such illustrations should correspond with how an expert organizes and uses the information in applying science concepts to solve problems. This requirement is important because in science, expert problem solvers differ from novice problem solvers in three important ways: Expert problem solvers have more knowledge; the knowledge is better organized in a hierarchical structure; and good problem solvers seem to organize this hierarchy around explanatory principles that function as big ideas.

As an illustration, Figure 31.2 shows a hierarchical organization around an explanative principle: convection. The central concept is a generic convection model (upper left box in Figure 31.2.) The other figures illustrate the various applications or effects of convection. The generic convection model—the big idea—can be used by students to explain everyday occurrences such as the movement of air currents in a room and the movement of water in a heated pan. Each application of the strategy is not unrelated but forms part of a unified, structured schema related to the principle of convection.

In general, visual maps of big ideas add to the overall "considerate" quality of an instruction tool. A considerate tool is one that eases comprehension in a supportive manner (Armbruster, 1984; Armbruster, Anderson, & Ostertag, 1987; Guzzetti, Snyder, Glass, & Gamas, 1993; Yates & Yates, 1990). In addition to visual maps, considerate communication uses cues in the text or textual elements such as headings and signal words to make the structure of the knowledge being communicated as clear and coherent as possible. Considerations of the structure, coherence, unity, and audience appropriateness (Kantor, Anderson, & Armbruster, 1983) and even accuracy (Champagne & Bunce, 1989) have been found to contribute to understanding. Clearly showing useful perspectives on how knowledge is best organized can provide important benefits to diverse learners.

Adding a "Refutational" Aspect to Communication of a Big Idea. In addition to conspicuous strategies for visually representing concept relationships and applications, adding a "refutational" aspect to the communication can further facilitate understanding and conceptual change for students (Guzzetti et al., 1993; Muthukrishna, Carnine, Grossen, & Miller, 1993; Niedelman, 1992; Smith, Blakeslee, & Anderson, 1993). Along with conspicuously presenting a coherent new strategy, a refutational text anticipates common misconceptions and builds into instruction examples that directly confront such misconceptions. Because students have many preconceived notions or misconceptions about science (e.g., "big objects float and small objects sink"), it is important that instruction clearly confront common misconceptions in a conspicuous manner. Many studies have found that a refutational, considerate, explicit text is very successful in achieving conceptual change; some studies have shown that student performance reaches a ceiling of conceptual change (e.g., Guzzetti, 1990). The following example illustrates how conceptually based strategy instruction can be designed to refute misconceptions.

The first step in teaching students to understand density is to have them compare the masses of substances of equal volume and predict which substances will sink when mixed. Two same-sized cubes with differing numbers of dots can be used to teach this step, as in Task 1 in Figure 31.3. In the figure, each dot represents 1 gram of mass. In this case, the more dots there are inside a cube (the greater the mass), the greater the density of the cube.

Next, students can learn to identify equivalent volumes of substances of unequal sizes and predict which will sink when the substances are mixed. In Task 2 of Figure 31.3, figures of different sizes are shown, with empty cubes placed over segments of equal size to confront the misconception that

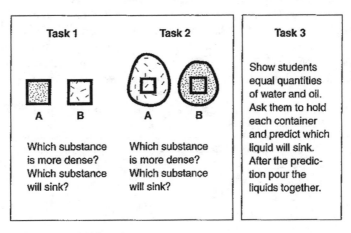

Figure 31.3 Strategy Example with Density

more size means greater density. By looking at the number of dots in the equal-sized cubes, students can tell that substance B is more dense than substance A, although substance B is smaller in size. Students are able to compare the density of a series of substances like those in Task 2 where the size and number of dots varies.

Next, as students form a conceptual understanding of mass and volume, such understanding can provide a foundation for subsequent activities using actual substances in a naturalistic environment in which (in conjunction with appropriate measurement skills) students predict which substance will sink when the substances come together (Task 3 in Figure 31.3).

Research has shown that planned refutations (built-in teaching examples that counter commonly observed misconceptions) were more effective in changing students' naive conceptions to scientific understandings than instruction that left the teacher to provide refutational material spontaneously during instruction. The teachers using the curricular material with planned refutations achieved better learning outcomes than the teachers who introduced refutations spontaneously (Smith et al., 1993).

Because curricular materials are designed before they reach the classroom, they must necessarily incorporate planned refutation if they are to include any refutation at all. As an illustration, Task 2 in Figure 31.3 is a planned example that refutes the common misconception that density is the same as weight. Having all students respond to this example reduces the likelihood that this misconception will occur. By anticipating predictable misconceptions such as this, instruction can be more effective for all students, particularly diverse learners, than instruction that relies on the teacher to respond spontaneously to presumably unpredictable misconceptions that might differ from individual to individual, and then design the teaching examples on the spot.

Providing Relevant Experiential Learning. It is often falsely assumed that if knowledge is conspicuously introduced, it must be in a lecture setting in which the teacher is active (i.e., telling) and the students are passive. Similarly, it is falsely assumed that in order to involve students actively in learning, science instruction must utilize hands-on experiences and the teacher should not communicate information conspicuously. Neither of the preceding assumptions is valid because the initial communication of scientific concepts to naive learners can be very interactive and conspicuous. With this in mind, Table 31.1 contrasts traditional telling methods, inquiry methods, and conspicuous communication methods.

Conspicuous communication methods are interactive and experiential, just as inquiry methods are. However, conspicuous communication methods include only learning experiences that are relevant to understanding big ideas. In this regard, "hands-on" learning experiences may or may not be relevant. Certainly, simple mechanical participation in a hands-on activity without conceptual understanding is analogous to the meaningless memorization of facts. In many cases, it is often impossible to design relevant hands-on activities that effectively communicate underlying causal big ideas. For example, students would have difficulty discovering an acceptable theory of electricity from a pile of wires, batteries, and switches, or from operating the lights and electrical appliances in their homes. Students may believe that a wire that is cut through cannot carry electric current and therefore is safe to touch, when in fact it can still deliver quite a shock if it is still connected to the power source. This is not to say that hands-on activities for applying electricity concepts are inappropriate; they would, for example, be very appropriate for applying strategies about electrical circuits. The important distinction is that students could not be expected necessarily to derive or construct a reliable understanding and explanation of electricity solely from hands-on experiences.

Table 31.1 Features of Traditional Telling Methods and Inquiry Methods Contrasted with Conspicuous Communication Methods for Initially Teaching Naive Learners

Traditional Telling Methods	**Inquiry Methods**	**Conspicuous Communication Methods**
Traditional	Innovative	Innovative
Teacher-directed	Student-directed	Teacher-directed
Nonexperiential	Experiential	Experiential
Noninteractive	Interactive	Interactive

To avoid misconceptions, hands-on activities should be used in initial instruction only when they are concretely relevant to the concept being taught. Hands-on experience would certainly be relevant where physical texture is an important feature of understanding, as it is in most identification and categorization activities, such as the identification of rocks, leaves, or flowers. In most cases, hands-on experience seems to detract from initial learning when texture is not a key feature of meaningful learning, as in learning about electricity, for example (Hider & Rice, 1986).

Designing Mediated Scaffolding in Science Inquiry and Subject Matter Instruction

The Concept of Scaffolding in Instruction.   The emphasis of scaffolding is that, to be effective, instruction must always be adapted to the initial level of student proficiency. It is important to stress that scaffolding addresses and operates on the processes (or means) through which desired instructional goals are accomplished, not on changing (and in particular not simplifying or not limiting) achievement goals. Scaffolding, then, emphasizes dynamic efforts that provide initial learners with substantial support early in learning, support that is then purposively reduced as they gain additional proficiency. Because of its importance in supporting initial learning, scaffolding is also of great importance to ensuring the success of instruction with many diverse learners. The implication of scaffolding is that educators must strive to design, select, or adapt instruction in order to make the goals of science literacy available to all students.

Illustrations in the preceding section characterized ideal initial instruction as being interactive, conspicuous, and teacher-directed. In this context, the notion of scaffolding applied to initial instruction assumes that students are faced with learning instructional content that is new to them. Whenever students experience the key features of a new science concept or inquiry strategy, scaffolding stresses that the initial presentations should strive to make all key features conspicuous through a variety of techniques that include explicit verbal prompts or very clear representational models and examples that provide guidance and support.

When the idea of scaffolding (e.g., through prompts) is combined with other instructional design characteristics, such as a focus on big ideas and conspicuous strategies, the result is effective initial learning in which students are actively and meaningfully involved in experiential learning. In this sense, teacher-directed (or teacher-supported) initial instruction is far more powerful for initial learning than independent, student-directed activities. However, as initial learning activities evolve and students become more proficient, the reduction of support purposefully eliminates teacher direction until learning is, in fact, independent and student-directed. The purpose of scaffolding, thus, is to allow *all* students to become successful in independent activities, not just the select few who do not require initial learning support.

Figure 31.4 shows additional aspects of initial instruction that work to create a supportive learning environment that can enable naive students to enter into new learning successfully. In this sense, the term "scaffolding" is an apt metaphor for describing this dynamically supportive environment. As students, with the support of a scaffold, progress toward proficiency in a learning objective, the scaffolding is removed and the instructional activities become less teacher-directed and more student-driven.

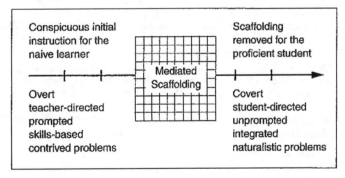

Figure 31.4   Continuum of Effective Instructional Practices as They Relate to the Learner's Level of Performance in the Specific Type of Learning Activity

Understanding the Two Categories of Scaffolding Techniques.   There are at least two distinct ways to scaffold instruction. The first is through teacher assistance and the second is through the design of the examples used in teaching. Both assume that the student is actively involved in learning tasks rather than being a passive learner.

Scaffolding Teacher Talk.   As illustrated in Figure 31.5, the initial presentation of the conspicuous strategy for controlling variables (at the top of the figure) involves more telling, while the later scaffolding (at the bottom of the figure) involves more questioning or scaffolding. In the example, the conspicuous steps of the initial strategy and of the scaffolded strategy are: (1) select one variable (hypothesis) to test; (2) vary the tested variable only and keep the other variables the same;

Initial Conspicuous Strategy Presentation

Step 1: (*Introduction*) You're going to figure out what a mellinark is by drawing pictures that might be mellinarks.

Step 2: (*Generating hypotheses*) This is a mellinark. (Teacher makes Drawing A in Figure 31.1) What variables might be important in determining whether something is a mellinark or not? (As students name possibilities, the teacher lists them on the board: the barbell shape of the body, the curved shape of the body, the presence of a dark spot, the position of the spot, the presence of a tail, the size, the color, and so on, with the list of features [variables] representing a list of hypotheses.)

Step 3: (*Controlling variables*) The best way to figure out what a mellinark is, is to draw a new figure that changes only one variable. The first variable I want to test is whether a mellinark needs a spot. Watch. (Teacher draws Drawing C in Figure 31.1)

Step 4: (*Interpreting data*) This figure is not a mellinark. From that information you can figure out one variable that defines a mellinark. What variable is that? (A spot.) After you draw a figure, I will tell you if it is a mellinark or not. From what I tell you, you should be able to figure out more about the variables that tell about a mellinark.

Later Scaffolded Instruction

Step 1: (*Hypothesis*) (Point to this figure.) This is a glerb. ⎯⎯⎯➤
Pick a feature to test to see if it defines a glerb. What feature did you select?

Step 2: (*Controlling variables*) Draw a figure that allows you to test for that feature.

Step 3: (*Interpret data*) (For example, if the student ⎯⎯⎯➤
drew this figure.)

This is not a glerb. Now, what do you know about glerbs? . . . Yes, they need an opening. (Corrective feedback for drawings that do not control variables, such as this one, for example.) ⎯⎯⎯➤

You did not draw a glerb. But there are a lot of reasons why this is not a glerb. It could be too big; it could be the wrong shape; it could have the wrong number of sides; it could be the wrong color. You can't tell why because you changed too many things from the original figure. When you test a variable, you must keep all the other variables the same.

What variable were you trying to test?   What about the other variables?
Whether it needs straight sides.   *Keep them the same.*

So what variable would you change?
The straight sides.

Figure 31.5   Using Teacher Assistance to Scaffold Instruction

(3) interpret the results. Only the degree of teacher guidance varies. As noted earlier, students will eventually be expected to control variables as they direct their own projects.

Scaffolding Examples. The example presented previously in Figure 31.3 illustrates a way to scaffold instruction through the design of sequences of teaching examples. In the example, each task corresponds to a step in a strategy for applying the concept of density. Task 1 requires students to compare the masses in an equivalent volume and predict which substance will sink. Task 2 requires students to identify equivalent volumes in two unequal-sized substances and predict which substance will sink. Task 3 (with some additional assumptions) requires application of the strategy to real examples.

Because scaffolding is a dynamic process, as learners become more competent, the scaffolding is removed by purposively moving slightly ahead of the learner on the continuum of instructional practice shown in Figure 31.4. As learners grow in competence and independence, effective instruction moves forward on the continuum. This process is illustrated as follows, using activities presented earlier in the chapter.

1. Progress from overt descriptions of the thinking strategies to covert practice of those strategies.
   Example: In initial instruction, the teacher states and/or models overtly the thought process involved in drawing a mellinark to test whether it needs a spot. With covert practice, the teacher says nothing. Students carry out a single step by drawing a figure that changes only one variable.
2. Progress from teacher-directed to student-directed activity.
   Example: When students first begin testing variables, the teacher directs students by telling them which variable to control for (e.g., the spot), how to control for that variable, and so on. When students are proficient, the directions for the activity become more general and students select their own variables (hypotheses) and control for them without assistance.
3. Progress from prompted to unprompted assistance.
   Example: The teacher initially prompts students as they work by giving specific feedback on their mellinark drawings or specific instructions that prompt better control of the next variable. As students become more proficient at controlling variables, the prompts are no longer needed, and students successfully control the variables without teacher prompts.
4. Progress from instruction in component concepts to instruction that integrates the concepts into a whole.
   Example: The instruction in the convection cell begins with instruction in the components of the convection cell, including concepts of density and pressure; understanding of the source of heat; the cause-and-effect relations of heat, density, and pressure; and the effects of these on the movement of cells. Later instruction in the convection cell presumes knowledge of these components and provides an integrated model explaining their interactions.
5. Progress from more contrived problems to naturalistic ones using real objects.
   Example: The density drawings in Tasks 1 and 2 of Figure 31.3 are contrived in order to scaffold the strategy for using density. When students are proficient in the strategy, they can then use it in Task 3 to predict which of two real substances will sink or float.

An example of an activity that incorporates all of these unscaffolded features for students who are more proficient at science inquiry would be a lab activity in which students identify rules that will predict which of various tubes—some made of iron, others aluminum; some hollow, others solid; some short, others long—will roll faster down a ramp (as described in Main & Rowe, 1993). Students will need to apply their knowledge about controlling variables to determine which variables increase the speed of the tubes. The students would need to select appropriate pairs of tubes to roll down the ramp to test possible variables. The variables might include hollow versus solid, large versus small, heavy versus light, short versus long, and so on. Similar experiences with varied unscaffolded applications such as this provide opportunities for details in understanding to be further clarified.

It seems generally that the more the teacher interacts with the students by scaffolding important content, the more effective the instruction. Teacher-directed instruction that is characterized by frequent interactions (i.e., checks for understanding and applications) can scaffold content-specific instruction so that students with learning disabilities acquire an understanding of scientific concepts that Harvard graduates frequently do not have (Muthukrishna et al., 1993).

Designing Judicious Review

Science is a difficult subject for most students. Therefore, review is essential. However, when the instruction focuses on developing an understanding of big ideas, review consists of applications of these big ideas in different contexts, rather than rote recitation of memorized facts. Ample opportunities to apply the concept are necessary if students are to fully understand the relevance and utility of a concept or big idea.

Review can also incorporate new learning as students apply a known concept in a new context. For example, after intensive study of density in a series of introductory lessons, density can be reviewed sporadically as it is applied in the context of learning about pressure, the effects of heat on density and pressure, the effects of changes in density on movement and pressure, and so on.

Over time as a concept is reviewed, the scaffolding is gradually removed and the context of the application becomes more complex, making the application just a bit more challenging each time for the students. From the initial presentation, students can acquire only a basic understanding of concepts. For example, after learning about density, students may not realize that relative density holds for fragments from a piece of substance. Students might predict that a large glob of mercury would sink, but when asked about a tiny ball from that glob, they might predict that it would float. Similarly, after the initial presentation in controlling variables, students will need much more practice in a wide variety of contexts.

Varied practice contributes to students' generating more ideas for solving problems, having higher quality ideas, asking better questions, and more successfully solving problems (Covington & Crutchfield, 1965; Schmidt & Bjork, 1992; Wardrop et al., 1969). When real-world application practice follows instruction using contrived examples, students are able to apply the strategies to different types of problems, and retention improves (Olton & Crutchfield, 1969). When students fail to use knowledge, it is usually associated with very few practice examples (Gick & Holyoak, 1980; Lesgold & Perfetti, 1978) or examples from an overly limited context (Bransford, Vye, Adams, & Perfetti, 1989; Levin, 1979; Nitsch, 1977; Schmidt & Bjork, 1992).

Designing Strategic Integration

In a domain that is hierarchically organized, such as science, review can be designed in such a way that all four of the above review dimensions—sufficient, distributed, varied, and cumulative—are incorporated almost automatically in the design of the curriculum. Instruction can be organized so that new learnings provide a new context for old learnings. In addition, review naturally occurs as subordinate concepts and strategies are incorporated in more complex, integrated concepts and strategies. Figure 31.6 illustrates a strand design that can provide this built-in practice and review. Designing instruction in overlapping strands (topics) facilitates the naturalness of integrated review. The strands that teach the concepts of density, heat, and pressure overlap until they are integrated in the model

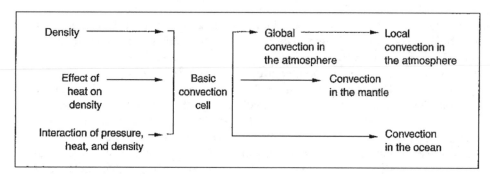

Figure 31.6 A Strand Design

of the basic convection cell. The concept of density is taught first, then the scaffolding is removed and unscaffolded practice using the concept of density is provided in the context of teaching about the effects of heat on density. Similarly, in initial instruction about pressure, unscaffolded practice with density and heat are provided in the context of learning the interaction of heat, density, and static and dynamic pressure. All of these concepts are further reviewed when they are integrated in the basic convection strategy.

This basic strategy is then applied to explain global convection in the atmosphere, the earth's mantle, and the ocean. Each of the applications provide review of the convection cell and its related concepts. In this way, one of the central goals of the new science standards—connectedness—can be achieved.

THE APPLICATION OF INSTRUCTIONAL DESIGN PRINCIPLES

Developing Instructional Tools

One possible application of the six instructional design principles is in developing instructional tools in the area of science education. First, identify the most important scientific principles and reallocate instructional time so that those concepts and principles are taught more thoroughly. For example, rather than simply have students memorize all the different types of rock, have them apply their understanding of the rock cycle (convection) to predict the next form the rock would take.

Teach explicit steps for applying big ideas. Such steps are an approximation of the steps experts follow covertly (and, perhaps, unconsciously) while working toward similar goals. Strategies for using the big ideas of science should initially be made overt and conspicuous for students through the use of visual maps and models that represent expert knowledge and refute common misconceptions. Wide-ranging application of big ideas facilitates strategy acquisition. Experiential application opportunities should be relevant to better understanding of the instructed big idea and its use.

For example, a strategy for using density could require students to:

1. Identify equivalent volumes in two substances
2. Compare the masses within those volumes
3. Predict which substance will sink

The fundamental steps in the strategy for science inquiry are:

1. Identify the variable to test
2. Create a condition that changes that variable
3. Keep the other variables the same
4. Gather data
5. Interpret the outcome

Good strategy instruction starts with teaching a well-organized knowledge base of component concepts and their relationships. Provide specific instruction in difficult component concepts to achieve an in-depth understanding of the big idea or strategy. For example, the component concepts of the relationship between mass and volume are particularly important in understanding convection. Other component concepts of convection that also relate to density include the effect of heat on density and dynamic pressure. Instruction in these component concepts and their cause-and-effect relationships is crucial to an in-depth understanding of convection.

Similarly, the component step of controlling variables is crucial to effective use of the scientific method. This difficult step requires specific, explicit instruction and practice in varying only the variable under examination and keeping all the other relevant variables the same.

Scaffolded practice, which should follow the introduction of big ideas, strategies, and component concepts, provides a systematic transition from the initial teacher-directed, modeled, structured, prompted practice within defined problem types to a more naturalistic environment of student-directed, unstructured, unpredictable problems that vary widely across all problem types.

Scaffolding can be provided through the design of the tasks or examples or through teacher talk. For example, initial scaffolded instruction in controlling variables could model the procedures for controlling for one variable, then direct and prompt students as they control for a second variable, reminding them to change only the variable they are testing and keeping all the others the same. Finally students can control variables on their own.

All of the previous principles of effective instruction can be integrated in such a way that their incorporation seems natural in the development of understanding. Organize the topics for instruction into overlapping strands so that the connections of science are more easily communicated, the big ideas are more easily built, and scaffolding can build new learning on top of a foundation of prior learning.

Selecting Instructional Tools

A second application of the six instructional design principles is in selecting instructional tools in the area of science education. For this purpose, evaluate tools for important big ideas that are well taught. Look for conspicuous models for using scientific principles (and content) and for conspicuous illustrations of the steps students should use in scientific inquiry. More students become proficient in scientific reasoning (i.e., scientific inquiry) when it is explicitly taught. Many currently popular programs use activity-based instruction to teach the scientific method but do not conspicuously focus instruction on this important strategy. The amount of review provided in a text should be appropriate for the slowest learner. From a teacher's standpoint, dropping review is substantially easier than adding review for diverse learners. Review should be distributed rather than massed. (Ten opportunities over ten days can be more effective than ten opportunities within a single class period.) All that is taught in a program should accumulate within review. That is, review should include not only the most recently learned material, but material from throughout the program. This is particularly true for material that is potentially confusing. Examine the initial instruction and the independent application to see if the tool provides "in-between" application tasks that are scaffolded. Finally, review should include new examples, but new examples of the same type as those used during initial instruction.

Many current science materials are organized around units that can be taught in almost any order. While this design allows flexibility in choice of topics, it encourages a fragmented understanding of science content. Curricular materials that use strategic integration to build an integrated understanding around underlying causal principles, such as convection, rather than around more superficial units, such as geology, meteorology, or oceanography, cannot be rearranged so easily.

Researchers and developers affiliated with the University of Oregon have developed some science curricula that exemplify the design principles described in this text. These materials were not evaluated in the AAAS materials evaluations because they are not a full-year curriculum published by a mainstream publisher. The following materials incorporate many of the design principles described in this chapter: *The Earth Science* (1987) and *Understanding Chemistry* (1989) Core Concepts videodisc science programs marketed by BFA Phoenix Film, and *Reasoning and Writing* published by SRA (Engelmann & Grossen, 2001). *Understanding Life Science* (Carnine, Vachon, Carnine, & Shindledecker, 2001), *Understanding Physical Science* (Steely & Carnine, 2001), and *Understanding Earth Science* (Miller & Carnine, 2001), full-year texts either for middle school or for at-risk high school students struggling to meet standards are currently in development but have no publisher as yet.

Modifying Instructional Tools

A third application of the six instructional design principles is in modifying instructional tools. To emphasize big ideas, develop a course or unit outline identifying the 10 most important concepts or principles for students to learn. Focus instruction and testing on these few concepts or principles. To make strategies conspicuous, model each step and verbalize the thinking that accompanies each step.

Teachers can analyze the important big ideas to identify key component concepts. These concepts will answer the question "why?" For example, a thorough understanding of density and its interaction with heat explains in large part "why" convection occurs. Instruction in key concepts requires more than just a teacher explanation. It also requires the other features of instruction described here: mediated scaffolding and judicious review.

After providing the initial model, teachers can provide scaffolding by using prompts and cues borrowed from the model that assist the students in difficult parts of the strategy or concept, gradually removing the prompts and cues until students are able to use the knowledge accurately and without assistance. Such prompting and cueing would be appropriate for any students whose performance on independent tasks indicates that more work is needed before they can successfully perform independently.

Cut back review for students who need less. If not enough review is provided, then design additional review. Consider that the review should be (1) sufficient, (2) distributed, (3) varied, and (4) cumulative.

Sequence topics so that component concepts are taught first and subsequent material builds on earlier learning. Provide the additional instruction to link the old learning with the new learning for deeper understanding.

SUMMARY

This chapter illustrates six instructional design principles that can improve science instruction and result in higher achievement, particularly for diverse learners. Higher achievement for *all* learners is a national goal in four areas of science: science as inquiry, science subject matter, scientific connections, and science and human affairs.

The big ideas of science inquiry can be applied to any domain of study. The big ideas of science subject matter can be linked with the measurement skills of mathematics to add precision to the predictions of science. Furthermore, the relevance of science to human affairs is a fairly natural consequence of selecting big ideas based on their explanative quality, which in part depends on their utility in human affairs. To enable better problem solving, the structure of science knowledge should be clearly communicated using considerate, user-friendly tools, including visual maps, to illustrate the connections of science. Instruction should teach carefully the component concepts that underlie big ideas, build understanding by showing the utility of strategies in problem solving, include examples that confront common misconceptions, and provide relevant experiences.

For initial learning, teacher-directed experiential methods that scaffold the acquisition of meaningful learning are superior to teacher-directed, passive learning methods and also seem superior to student-centered, experiential methods, particularly for diverse learners. As learners become more proficient, scaffolding should be removed. Whether students should work under close teacher direction or independently depends on careful consideration of the learner's proficiency level in the desired learning objective. Review can be organized into overlapping strands so that all the component concepts are consistently reviewed and then integrated into the larger models.

These six principles can be evaluated in the context of student performance using guidelines developed by Romance, Vitale, and Widergren (1996). If the principles illustrated in this chapter are applied to the design of science instruction, better problem solving and higher level thinking for all learners will result. In addition, the instruction can provide the opportunity for diverse learners, not just university-bound students, to acquire a usable knowledge base in the content and reasoning of science. Providing educational opportunities for diverse learners requires more than simply placing these students in a science class typically earmarked for university-bound students and adding a few teaching tips for making the content accessible to diverse learners (Parmar & Cawley, 1993).

If the only instructional methods used are those that seldom work for diverse learners, the opportunity to learn science remains denied. Considerate, user-friendly instruction in the big ideas of science is most likely to open the doors to understanding science. Diverse learners who receive the instruction described previously in convection may not become expert meteorologists, but they will be able to explain scientific principles such as why mountains form or why seasons change (Muthukrishna et al., 1993). Certain aspects of user-friendly tools and approaches that make science accessible to less able students can also make science accessible to more able students. In contrast, an approach that is designed only for more able students is difficult to modify so that less able students can also learn, because the teacher must design and create the needed missing components.

REFLECTION AND APPLICATION: Case Study

Marielle is in her first year as a kindergarten teacher at Marshall Elementary. All of Marshall's classes are characterized by the school as "inclusion classes." Marielle has a kindergarten class of 17 students. Five of the students have IEPs (three children have speech and language concerns, one child has Down's syndrome, and one student is identified with an emotional and behavioral disorder).

Marielle was a biology major and stated in her job interview that her personal goal was to insure that kindergartners learned science. One of her most meaningful learning experiences as a preservice teacher was participating in the New Century Museum of Natural History's "Virtual Science Seminars." These summer seminars were designed to provide elementary science teachers with a deeper understanding of science content through interactive learning experiences.

For example, one unit entitled "Frames of Reference" was designed to support teachers' understanding of Einstein's theory of relativity and the position and motion of objects through hands-on and virtual experiences. During this unit, Marielle observed a computer simulation in which a basketball, which was glowing, was bounced up and down against a dark backdrop by a moving basketball player. Marielle had to answer questions about the relative position of the ball, basketball player, and background by manipulating components of the simulation.

Marielle was eager to use her learning experiences to create a community of "kinderscientists." As an adult learner, she recognized how much she valued the hands-on learning that she was exposed to in Virtual Science Seminars and was determined to design her instruction so that it emphasized student-centered learning. If this was important and successful in her own learning, certainly it was essential for her kindergarten students.

After consulting with the district science frameworks and the state standards, Marielle decided to begin the year by focusing on her state's "Conceptual Theme 2—Properties of Matter." The goal for kindergarten students within this theme was to understand that "objects have properties that can be observed and used to describe similarities and differences." Marielle thought that this "big idea" would be a perfect overarching concept for kindergarten students. Marielle began brainstorming and exploring ways in which she could use this concept as a cohesive thread to organize her first few weeks of school.

A week before school began, Marielle mailed a welcoming letter to her students and their families. In the envelope she included four buttons of different sizes, shapes, colors, and materials. Additionally, she included a small, snack-sized zip-lock baggie with the child's name written on it. The information in the letter, among other things, instructed the children to talk with their family members about the buttons and then place them into the baggie, zip it tightly, and bring it to school for use in an exciting activity.

On the first day of school, Marielle engaged in the typical first day of kindergarten routines. After the children enjoyed some "getting to know you" activities, she asked the children to bring their baggies to morning circle. She then read *The Button Box* by Margaret Reid to the children. Later in the morning Marielle had learning centers set up for the children. Each of the four stations had a bowl of 30 assorted buttons. Marielle instructed the students to bring their buttons to the centers and sort them with the other buttons by how they looked and felt. She set the timer for 7 minutes.

At first, Marielle was encouraged by what she observed. The children went quietly to their stations and began to examine the buttons. However, within a few minutes, many of the children began to play with the buttons and after about four minutes had lapsed, the noise level in the room had risen dramatically. At the end of the seven minutes many of the buttons were on the floor and those that had been sorted into piles seemed to lack any observable organization. When she

questioned her students about the strategy they had used to sort the buttons, only a few were able to answer.

Marielle was surprised by the students' difficulty with this seemingly simple activity. She had done much careful planning in designing similar types of interactive learning activities for her students and hadn't ever considered the possibility that her students might not respond to or learn from this hands-on approach. She felt like she had already failed and was unsure what to do next.

- Why might Marielle's students have had difficulty with this activity? What instructional principles and teaching strategies might Marielle have utilized to make her instruction more likely to result in student success?

The conclusion of the case study can be found later in this chapter.

CONTENT QUESTIONS

1. Describe the big ideas of science according to NRC standards.
2. List four commonly cited criticisms of science texts.
3. Name and describe the steps of the scientific method.
4. What have been the findings of research comparing nonexplicit inquiry strategies with explicit methods of instruction?
5. List five examples of big ideas in science subject matter.
6. What are three benefits of presenting big ideas in science curricula?
7. Provide three examples that contribute to the "considerate" quality of an instructional tool.
8. Describe the continuum of instructional scaffolding in science.
9. List each of the four components of judicious review and their benefits for science students.

REFLECTION AND DISCUSSION

1. Imagine that you are listening to a lecture or discussion or attempting to read an article on a scientific subject that assumes an understanding of essential concepts or sophisticated terms that are beyond your present level of training. How might this affect your learning and your motivation to learn? What are the implications of this thought exercise for all students of science, including those with diverse learning needs?
2. In your opinion, should the goal of science education in the primary through secondary grades be the development of subject matter knowledge, inquiry skills, or both? How can effective teaching strategies be utilized to achieve these goals? How can these strategies be used to support the additional goals of understanding scientific connections in human affairs?
3. Should explicit, teacher-directed instructional methods and science inquiry be seen as mutually exclusive? Please explain your answer.

APPLICATION

1. Review a science textbook with the following questions in mind. Does the textbook focus on big ideas in science or does it cover numerous concepts and details that tend to vary across domains? Are the important ideas clearly presented, well developed, and integrated throughout the book? Are student activities explicitly linked to big ideas in science? Develop an example of how principles of effective instruction might be applied to section of this science textbook in order to better support student learning.

Case Study (Conclusion)

Marielle was exhausted by the time she arrived home after that first day. Determined to identify what went wrong with her lesson, she sat down to peruse the course materials from her science seminar. She reviewed her notes from all of the assignments and activities that initially encouraged her to embark on the hands-on button activity. What had made her own experience so instructionally powerful and engaging? Reflecting upon her own question, she realized that her seminars had set her up for success in the hands-on activities through careful and intentional planning. For example, the course provided background readings outlining foundational concepts that were prerequisites for understanding the simulations. Additionally, instructors provided direct explanations and demonstrations of the processes and strategies that participants would need to use to complete the interactive activities. Finally, the activities were sequenced in such a way that the insights that participants gleaned in the initial activities were directly supportive of the more complex learning that took place later in the summer. The "ah-ha" moments that excited Marielle during her hands-on experiences resulted from the sequential building and mediation of her learning experiences. Her learning experiences was so seamless that she had failed to think through the work that had preceded her connection.

Marielle saw the children's faces in her mind's eye as she replayed the lesson in her head. The children's quiet wandering to the centers may have been a sign of uncertainty or disorientation as they probably had little understanding of the task they faced. The rising noise level was likely additional evidence of their confusion. Marielle realized that the students' inability to articulate any sorting strategies was probably related to her oversight in neglecting to *teach* any strategies conspicuously. Marielle decided to revisit and plan her lesson again.

Marielle realized that in selecting *The Button Box,* she had been distracted by the title. In the book, the boy describes various buttons from the perspective of what he imagines and knows about them in relation to his family history. Marielle decided that her literature introduction should be more closely related to the learning goal of the lesson (i.e., properties of objects). She also decided that for this initial lesson, she should scaffold the instruction so that students would be initially working with only one type of attribute. She hoped that this would help ensure student success and provide a framework for future learning.

She decided to focus first on color. *Is It Red? Is It Yellow? Is It Blue?* by Tana Hoban would be much more supportive to the children in learning about color. After reading the book, and modeling the activity for the children, Marielle would provide them with sets of buttons that were identical in all ways except color. They would engage in sorting buttons by color in their learning centers, followed by a rich discussion designed to process the students' experience with the hands-on activity. It would also allow Marielle to support their developing vocabulary related to sorting and color. Once Marielle was comfortable with the student's grasp of the concept of sorting the buttons by color, she would build upon this understanding and introduce new attributes such as size, shape, and texture. She planned to continue to provide students with interactive learning activities, but not before she was sure that students had the skills and strategies to be successful. Marielle felt more confident that her revised lesson plan would better meet the needs of her students through conspicuous instruction and modeling of effective strategies along with realistic and scaffolded supports for the follow-up hands-on activity.

- How could a teacher who provides conspicuous and scaffolded science instruction respond if a parent expressed concern that students were not being given an "opportunity to discover" science principles on their own?

The Reflection and Application section of this chapter was written by Maureen F. Ruby and Richard P. Zipoli, Jr., both of the University of Connecticut.

REFERENCES

American Association for the Advancement of Science. (1993). *Benchmarks for science literacy: Project 2061*. Washington, DC: Author.

American Association for the Advancement of Science. (1999). *Heavy books light on learning: Not one middle grade science text rated satisfactory by AAAS's Project 2061*. Washington, DC: Author.

American Association for the Advancement of Science. (2000). *Big biology books fail to convey big ideas, reports AAAS's Project 2061*. Washington, DC: Author.

American Association for the Advancement of Science. (in press). *Atlas of science literacy*. Washington, DC: Author.

Armbruster, B. (1984). The problem of "inconsiderate text." In G. G. Duffy, L. R. Roehler, & J. Mason (Eds.), *Comprehension instruction* (pp. 202–217). New York: Longman.

Armbruster, B., Anderson, T. H., & Ostertag, J. (1987). Does text structure/summarization instruction facilitate learning from expository text? *Reading Research Quarterly, 22,* 331–346.

Bay, M., Staver, J., Bryan, T., & Hale, J. (1992). Science instruction for mildly handicapped: Direct instruction versus discovery teaching. *Journal of Research in Science Teaching, 29*(6), 555–570.

Bransford, J. D., Vye, N. J., Adams, L. T., & Perfetti, C. A. (1989). Learning skills and the acquisition of knowledge. In A. Lesgold & R. Glaser (Eds.), *Foundations for a psychology of education* (pp. 199–249). Hillsdale, NJ: Erlbaum.

Bredderman, T. (1983). Effects of activity-based elementary science on student outcomes: A quantitative synthesis. *Review of Educational Research, 53*(4), 499–518.

Carnine, D., Vachon, V., Carnine, L., & Shindledecker, K. (2001). *Understanding life science*. Unpublished manuscript.

Champagne, A., & Bunce, D. (1989, April). *Electricity in 6th grade tests: Too much, too fast*. Paper presented at the American Educational Research Association Conference, San Francisco.

Core Concepts. (1987). *Earth science*. St. Louis, MO: BFA Phoenix Film.

Core Concepts. (1989). *Understanding chemistry*. St. Louis, MO: BFA Phoenix Film.

Covington, M. V., & Crutchfield, R. S. (1965). Facilitation of creative problem solving. *Programmed Instruction, 4,* 3–5, 10.

Elementary Science Study. (1974). *Attribute games and problems: Teacher's Guide*. New York: McGraw-Hill.

Engelmann, Z., & Grossen, B. (2001). *Reasoning and writing*. Blacklick, OH: Science Research Associates.

Gick, M. L., & Holyoak, K. (1980). Analogical problem solving. *Cognitive Psychology, 12,* 306–355.

Guastello, E. F., Beasley, T. M., & Sinatra, R. C. (2000). Concept mapping effects on science content comprehension of low-achieving inner-city seventh graders. *Remedial and Special Education, 21,*(6) 356–365.

Guzzetti, B. J. (1990). Effects of textual and instructional manipulations on concept acquisition. *Reading Psychology, 11,* 49–62.

Guzzetti, B., Snyder, T. E., Glass, G. V., & Gamas, W. S. (1993). Promoting conceptual change in science: A comparative meta-analysis of instructional interventions from reading education and science education. *Reading Research Quarterly, 28*(2), 116–159.

Hider, R. A., & Rice, D. R. (1986). *A comparison of instructional mode on the attitude and achievement of fifth and sixth grade students in science*. Technical research report. Mobile, AL: University of South Alabama.

Kantor, R. N., Anderson, T. H., & Armbruster, B. B. (1983). How inconsiderate are children's textbooks? *Journal of Curriculum Studies, 15,* 6–72.

Klahr, D., & Nigam, M. (2004). The equivalence of learning paths in early science instruction. *Psychological Science, 15*(10), 661–667.

Kuhn, D. (1993). Science as argument: Implications for teaching and learning scientific thinking. *Science Education, 77*(3), 319–557.

Lesgold, A. M., & Perfetti C. A. (1978). Interactive processes in reading comprehension. *Discourse Processes, 1,* 323–336.

Lawson, A., McElrath, C., Burton, M., James, B., Doyle, R. Woodward, S., et al. (1991). Hypothetico-deductive reasoning skill and concept acquisition. Testing a constructivist hypothesis. *Journal of Research in Science Teaching, 28*(10), 953–970.

Levin, T. (1979). Instruction which enables students to develop higher mental processes. *Evaluation in education: An international review series, 3*(3), 174–220.

Lloyd, C. V. (1989, December). *The relationship between scientific literacy and high school biology textbooks.* Paper presented at the annual meeting of the National Reading Conference, Austin, TX.

Main, J., & Rowe, M. (1993). The relation of locus-of-control orientation and task structure to problem-solving performance of sixth-grade student pairs. *Journal of Research in Science Teaching, 30*(4), 401–426.

Mayer, R. E. (1989). Models for understanding. *Review of Educational Research, 59*(1), 43–64.

Mayer, R. E., & Gallini, J. (1990). When is an illustration worth ten thousand words? *Journal of Educational Psychology, 82*(4), 715–726.

McCarthy, C. (2005). Effects of thematic-based, hands-on science teaching versus a textbook approach for students with disabilities, *Journal of Research in Science Teaching, 42*(3) 245–263.

McCleery, J., & Tindal, G. (1999). Teaching the scientific method to at-risk students and students with learning disabilities through concept anchoring and explicit instruction. *Remedial and Special Education, 20*(1), 7–18.

Miller, S., & Carnine, D. (2001). *Understanding earth science.* Unpublished manuscript.

Muthukrishna, A., Carnine, D., Grossen, B., & Miller, S. (1993). Children's alternate frameworks: Should they be directly addressed in science instruction? *Journal of Research in Science Teaching, 30*(3), 233–248.

National Research Council. (1993). *National science education standards: A sampler.* Washington, DC: National Academy Press.

National Research Council. (1995). *National science education standards.* Washington, DC: National Academy Press.

Newport, J. F. (1990). Elementary science texts: What's wrong with them? *Educational Digest, 59,* 68–69.

Niedelman, M. (1992). Problem solving and transfer. In D. Carnine & E. Kame'enui (Eds.), *Higher order thinking: Designing curriculum for mainstreamed students* (pp. 137–156). Austin, TX: Pro-Ed.

Nitsch, K. E. (1977). *Structuring decontextualized forms of knowledge.* Unpublished doctoral dissertation, Vanderbilt University.

Olton, R. M., & Crutchfield, R. S. (1969). Developing the skills of productive thinking. In P. Mussen, J. Langer, & M. Covington (Eds.), *Trends and issues in developmental psychology* (pp. 68–91). New York: Holt, Rinehart and Winston.

Osborn, J. H., Jones, B. F., & Stein, M. (1985). The case for improving textbooks. *Educational Leadership, 42,* 9–16.

Parmar, R. S., & Cawley, J. F. (1993). Analysis of science textbook recommendations provided for students with disabilities. *Exceptional Children, 59*(6), 518–531.

Raizen, S. (1988). *Increasing educational productivity through improving the science curriculum.* Washington, DC: The National Center for Improving Science Education.

Romance, N. R., Vitale, M. R., & Widergren, P. (1996). *Student conceptual understanding in science: Knowledge-based perspectives for enhancing teaching practices.* Monograph series. Washington, DC: National Science Teachers Association.

Ross, J. A. (1988). Controlling variables: A meta-analysis of training studies. *Review of Educational Research, 58*(4), 405–437.

Rubin, R., & Norman, J. (1992). Systematic modeling versus the learning cycle: Comparative effects on integrated science process skill achievement. *Journal of Research in Science Teaching, 29*(7), 715–727.

Schmidt, R., & Bjork, R. (1992). New conceptualizations of practice: Common principles in three paradigms suggest new concepts for training. *Psychological Science, 3*(4), 207–217.

Shaw, T. (1983). The effect of a process-oriented science curriculum upon problem-solving ability. *Science Education, 67*(5), 615–623.

Shayer, M., & Adey, P. (1993). Accelerating the development of formal thinking in middle and high school students IV: Three years after a two-year intervention. *Journal of Research in Science Teaching, 3*(4), 351–366.

Shymansky, J., Kyle, W., & Alport, J. (1983). The effects of new science curricula on student performance. *Journal of Research in Science Teaching, 20*(5), 387–404.

Smith, E., Blakeslee, T., & Anderson, C. (1993). Teaching strategies associated with conceptual change learning in science. *Journal of Research in Science Teaching, 30*(2), 111–126.

Staver, J. R., & Small, L. (1990). Toward a clearer representation of the crisis in science education. *Journal of Research in Science Teaching, 27*(1), 79–89.

Steely, D., & Carnine, D. (2001). *Understanding physical science.* Unpublished manuscript.

Wardrop, J. L., Goodwin, W. L., Klausmeier, R. M., Olton, R. M., Covington, R. S., Crutchfield, et al. (1969). The development of productive thinking skills in 5th-grade children. *Journal of Experimental Education, 37,* 67–77.

Wood, T. L., & Wood, W. L. (1988). Assessing potential difficulties in comprehending fourth-grade science textbooks. *Science Education, 72*(5), 561–574.

Woodward, J. (1994). Effects of curriculum discourse style on eighth graders' recall and problem solving in earth science. *Elementary School Journal, 94*(3), 299–314.

Yager, R. E., & Penick, J. E. (1987). Resolving the crisis in science education: Understanding before resolution. *Science Education, 71*(1), 49–55.

Yates, G. C. R., & Yates, S. (1990). Teacher effectiveness research: Towards describing user-friendly classroom instruction. *Educational Psychology, 10*(3), 225–238.

Yeany, R. H., Yap, K. C., & Padilla, M. J. (1986). Analyzing hierarchical relationships among modes of cognitive reasoning and integrated science process skills. *Journal of Research in Science Teaching, 23*(4), 277–291.

Zohar, A., & Aharon-Kravetsky, S. (2005). Exploring the effects of cognitive conflict and direct teaching for students of different academic levels. *Journal of Research in Science Teaching, 42*(7), 829–855.

EFFECTIVE STRATEGIES FOR TEACHING SOCIAL STUDIES

Donald B. Crawford, *Western Washington University;* Douglas W. Carnine, *University of Oregon;* Mark K. Harniss, *University of Washington;* Keith L. Hollenbeck, *University of Oregon;* Samuel K. Miller, *University of Oregon*

Equal access TO an education should not simply entail using the same instructional strategies with all children; the goal is to use strategies that are effective for every child. This chapter discusses how the six important principles for improving instructional strategies presented in earlier chapters can be applied to social studies education. The six principles are derived from a comprehensive review of the education research literature (National Center to Improve the Tools of Educators, 2001). The chapter purpose is to illustrate how the six principles can be used to modify or develop educational strategies to be effective for teaching social studies to students with diverse learning needs.

CURRENT ISSUES IN SOCIAL STUDIES INSTRUCTION

Current reforms within social studies education require us to begin with a discussion of its fundamental issues. The field of social studies is among the most complex and fractious of all academic fields and classroom subjects. It is based on a loose confederation of disciplines that include anthropology, archaeology, economics, geography, history, law-related education, philosophy, political, science, psychology, religion, and sociology. Educators and curriculum designers have struggled for years over the relative weight to give the various disciplines and over which disciplines to include under the social studies umbrella. The struggle to agree on national standards in the area of history was so contentious that the effort has essentially been abandoned (Ravitch, 2000).

A second struggle over expectations seemingly has been resolved. There is now widespread agreement that competency in social studies is essential for everyone. This goal is exemplified by the recommendation of the Multicultural Education Consensus panel discussing social studies instruction: "Schools should ensure that all students have equitable opportunities to learn and to meet high standards" (Banks et al., 2005, p. 36).

This new emphasis means that social studies teachers face increased expectations for teaching a diverse student population with a wide range of cognitive abilities. The challenge for students is that many of the changes associated with the "new social studies" of the 1960s—inductive teaching, discovery learning, and content drawn from the newer social sciences—continue to influence social studies reform today. These programs were of great interest to scholars and university professors but were not a great success in the classroom and "emphasized the brightest students without much consideration of other students" (Hertzberg, 1981, cited in Brophy, 1990, p. 359). Clearly, yesterday's instructional strategies will not be adequate for teaching today's diverse learners.

In recent years the debate about what social studies education should stress has prompted a series of recommendations from national commissions, task forces, and professional organizations—e.g., the National Council for the Social Studies, the Bradley Commission, the National Commission on Social Studies in the Schools, and the National Center for History in the Schools. The recommendations generally advocate that the purpose of social studies education is to develop well-educated citizens who share a common body of knowledge drawn in a coordinated and systematic way from a range of disciplines and that content knowledge from the social studies should not be treated as knowledge to memorize, but as knowledge through which important questions may be explored.

As an example of these recommendations, the National Council for the Social Studies (NCSS) articulated a set of 10 thematic strands that form the basis of the social studies standards. The scope of the social studies curriculum remains disconcertingly broad, as one can see from the 10 NCSS strands:

Social studies should include experiences that provide for the study of . . .

1. Culture and cultural diversity
2. The ways human beings view themselves in and over time
3. People, places, and environments
4. Individual development and identity
5. Interactions among individuals, groups, and institutions
6. How people create and change structures of power, authority, and governance
7. How people organize for the production, distribution, and consumption of goods and services
8. Relationships among science, technology, and society
9. Global connections and interdependence
10. The ideals, principles, and practices of citizenship in a democratic republic (National Council for the Social Studies, 1994, pp. 365–368)

Developers of state standards for social studies have the difficult task of translating these recommendations into meaningful benchmarks for learning while struggling to reconcile problems associated with content selection and an overloaded curriculum. In general, elementary grade social studies instructional materials are criticized for teaching too little content, and secondary level materials are viewed as two-minute reviews of the earth's history, which emphasize coverage rather than depth. United States history curricula exemplify these problems:

The typical American history survey course . . . comprises everything from Mayans to moon landings. We are, as far as I know, the only country in the Western world that tries to teach the whole of our history to students in a single year. It's just insane. (Gagnon in O'Neil, ASCD Update, 1989, p. 5)

From this discussion it is clear that an ongoing concern about social studies centers on what content is worthwhile to teach and how it can be taught effectively. The challenge of teaching social studies is to provide students with both breadth and depth. In response to this problem, many social studies educators advocate the development of curriculum and instruction around selected concepts, rather than the superficial parade-of-facts approach (Twyman & Tindal, 2005). Some of the national recommendations for teaching social studies reflect a sentiment that can be characterized as "pausing for depth":

There is the ever-present problem of time. Social history, no less than political history, requires careful selection from among the numberless topics available. The sheer scope of the historical record requires the imaginative synthesis of political and social, cultural, economic, and religious history around central, significant themes and questions. (National Center for History in the Schools, 1992, p. 17)

Taking the time to teach depth of knowledge has its cost, and as yet there has been no consensus on content that can be left out to give time for more depth of study. Unfortunately, state officials who write the various state standards do not share the educators' notion of the perspective of "less is more" (Placier, Walker, & Foster, 2002). Students who learned about one particular theme, culture, region, or historical era in depth would likely do poorly on state performance assessments that sample broadly from the lengthy lists of state social studies standards. For this reason teachers feel considerable pressure to cover all of the material listed in the various state social studies standards. This increasing pressure from state level standards-based accountability has overwhelmed any other perspectives on what should be taught in social studies classes. For teachers currently, all instruction must be directly and explicitly aligned with specifics in the state standards (Kauffman, Johnson, Kardos, Liu, & Peske, 2002; Sandholtz, Ogawa, & Scribner, 2004; Twyman & Tindal, 2005). Given that much of this instruction must be designed by the individual teacher, instructional strategies to do so effectively assume ever greater importance.

PRINCIPLES FOR IMPROVING INSTRUCTIONAL STRATEGIES IN SOCIAL STUDIES

One challenge specific to improving the instructional strategies for teaching social studies has to do with how to assist diverse learners in identifying and remembering what is truly important to learn. Social studies teachers widely recognize the difficulties that diverse learners experience when attempting to garner the critical information from textbooks (Twyman & Tindal, 2005). Considerable research has shown that employing a variety of mediators of content such as advance organizers, study guides, interspersed questions, concept maps and other graphic organizers can greatly improve the ability of diverse learners to successfully acquire the essential content. These various forms of content mediation have three basic functions. One, they direct students' attention to the most important ideas in the textbook. Two, they focus attention on the organizational structures of the texts. Three, they require rehearsal by asking students to recite or write down critical information (see Figure 32.1).

Rich, authentic learning experiences are not sufficient for eliminating the difficulties that diverse learners experience in acquiring knowledge by reading textbooks. The same mediators of content needed by diverse learners when they are expected to learn from textbooks are also needed if they are to successfully learn from nontextbook sources such as watching videos, interviewing adult informants, listening to plays, going on field trips, having discussions, or participating in simulations. Even when the source of information is more user friendly than the typical textbook, teachers must still create mediational materials that insure that diverse learners attend to the most important concepts, understand the organization of the information, and have an opportunity to recite or write down the key ideas. Teacher creation of mediational materials that assist diverse learners in acquiring, comprehending, and remembering social studies content demands a critical analysis of the curriculum, and admittedly, can be very time consuming. Ellis and Sabornie (1990) found that teachers trained in creating these kinds of mediational materials were concerned about the extra time required to prepare them. Currently, the demand that all social studies lessons meet specifically delineated state standards has generally relegated textbooks to the status of an occasionally-used reference. Many new teachers attempting to design instruction aligned with state standards, without the ability to rely on a textbook for assistance, are completely overwhelmed (Kauffman et al., 2002).

1. **Direct student's attention** to the most important ideas in the textbook.

2. **Focus attention** on the organizational structures of the text.

3. **Require rehearsal.** Students recite or write down information.

Figure 32.1 Basic Functions of Mediational Materials

A second challenge facing efforts to improve instructional strategies for teaching social studies has to do with how to assess student outcomes. The multiple-choice tests traditionally associated with social studies texts are increasingly coming under attack, as are the somewhat similar multiple-choice national norm-referenced tests in social studies. Recommendations for replacing these with performance assessments of projects, essays, oral reports, simulation activities, and the like have yet to be accompanied by stringent assessment criteria that would help identify students who have not learned what was expected. In addition to lack of stringent assessment criteria, performance assessments have been very difficult to score reliably. Further, when diverse learners lack skills in writing or public speaking, it is often impossible to discern what they have learned from their low scores on performance assessments. Without assessment criteria that can discriminate between successful and unsuccessful student results, teachers receive minimal useful feedback on the effectiveness of their social studies teaching. Without useful feedback on the effectiveness of such teaching efforts, it is very difficult for teachers to improve their instructional strategies.

Designing Instruction Around Big Ideas

Rather than sacrificing breadth of coverage in an effort to make sense of social studies, one approach for bringing order to a breadth of social studies content is to organize it around *big ideas*. Big ideas are important concepts or principles that are more specific than the thematic strands recommended by NCSS and fundamentally different from traditional social studies concepts such as democracy or community. Not all big ideas in social studies are equally useful. Big ideas must be chosen that facilitate efficient and broad acquisition of knowledge. To be instructionally effective, big ideas in social studies must be chosen which enable learners to organize, interrelate, and apply information so that meaningful connections can be made within social studies, and between social studies content and their own lives. Only a few big ideas need to be developed to adequately organize a year's worth of instruction in social studies because these ideas have repeated applicability. Choosing big ideas requires a thorough reading of the material with an eye to recurrent relationships and patterns. The following sections describe several examples of big ideas and discuss their value for preparing meaningful social studies curriculum and instruction. This handful of ideas was enough to organize instruction in U.S. history through the Civil War (Carnine, Crawford, Harniss, & Hollenbeck, 1994).

Problem–Solution–Effect. The problem–solution–effect structure is one example of a big idea. When applied to the study of social studies, it has the potential to help students understand that individuals, groups, and governments tend to react to common problems with identifiable causes and solutions. At the same time, the elements of the problem–solution–effect analysis can have great relevance to the daily lives of students. The structure and examples described are based on a United States history text (Carnine et al., 1994).

Problems. Common problems in social studies can be attributed to the following economic or human rights issues:

1. Economic problems can generally be linked to conditions that create difficulty for people trying to acquire or keep things they need or want. At a basic level, people need and want to maintain the availability of food, clothing, and shelter. In their personal lives students can identify the struggle with economic problems—trying to acquire or keep things they need or want—and have an intuitive understanding of the motivational power of economic issues.
2. Human rights problems in social studies are usually linked to groups of people trying to achieve rights associated with religious freedom, freedom of speech, equal protection under the law, equal rights for women, minorities, different social classes, and so forth. Adolescents are especially concerned about issues related to equal rights and freedom of expression in their own lives.

Solutions. When students can classify common historical problems, they can relate this knowledge to recurring actions people use to solve problems. Recurring solutions to historical problems can be categorized as attempts by individuals or groups to either move, invent, dominate, tolerate, or accommodate. These five solutions are described as follows:

1. *Move.* When people move to solve a problem, they hope to find a new place where the problem does not exist. United States history is filled with examples of immigrants and pioneers who moved in response to problems. While students seldom have the option of moving themselves to solve problems, they all are acquainted with family members or friends who have moved to solve problems as well as the limitations of this type of solution to problems.

2. *Invent.* Throughout history people have tried to solve problems by inventing new ways or abilities to do things they could not do before. For example, people could not farm on the Great Plains because the soil was too heavy to plow. The invention of the steel plow solved this economic problem. Students' experience with inventions rarely extends to seeing them as solutions to problems, but through an examination of historical examples they can develop this understanding.

3. *Dominate.* Another way people historically have solved problems involves controlling or dominating other people. The United States and its allies fought against Germany, Japan, and Italy in World War II. The opposing sides tried to dominate each other in response to economic problems such as inflation, unemployment, and limited natural resources. From personal experience, students know that attempting to dominate others can result in a fight in which both sides lose. Students can apply this knowledge to understand historical events involving domination.

4. *Accommodate.* When people accommodate each other, they adjust or adapt to solve a problem. Historically, people have accommodated each other by negotiating or compromising. For example, delegates from the Northern and Southern states effected a series of compromises that enabled passage of the Constitution despite their serious ideological differences. Young people are aware of the power of negotiations in their dealings with adults and that understanding can be applied to historical situations as well.

5. *Tolerate.* When one group of people decides not to move, invent, dominate, or accommodate, they tolerate a problem. Sometimes this solution is applied because there is no other choice. Before 1863, although many African Americans escaped slavery or fought against it, many others had to tolerate the problems of being slaves and of not having equal rights. Again, students can use their own lives to appreciate the connection between power and one's choice of solution. Adolescents know they only tolerate a situation when they do not have the power to change it.

Understanding the relationship between common problems and solutions can help students view social studies as a dynamic subject. Common solutions to problems in one era often become less viable as times change. Today, moving to solve the problem of acquiring land to grow food is less practical than it was 150 years ago when territory could still be taken from the Native Americans. Moving to acquire land to grow food has been replaced by the invention of new ways to grow more food on land that has already been settled.

Effects. Solutions to problems produce consequences or effects. One effect is that a problem may cease to exist, but an examination of social studies shows that solutions to problems often create new problems. For example, tribes of the Pueblo culture in the Southwest desert solved the problem of building shelters in an environment where wood was hard to find. Their solution was to build the walls of their homes with stones and use logs only to support the roof.

Building the walls with stone had the effect of creating a new problem—the extreme amount of hard work required to carry heavy stones for constructing shelters. The Pueblo tribes solved this problem by eliminating the space between homes so they shared a common wall.

The problem–solution–effect big idea can be useful to teachers as a framework for helping students organize their thinking during oral reading, classroom discussions, and written essays. Such big ideas can be especially useful to students in reading both textbooks and primary source documents.

Figure 32.2 is an excerpt from a social studies textbook (Carnine et al., 1994) which uses the big idea of problem–solution–effect to describe how the Chinook tribe solved problems related to food,

---

The Chinook Culture's Solutions to Basic Problems

The Chinook and the Problem of Food. The Chinook found plenty to eat. The rivers of the Pacific Northwest Coast were a great place to catch fish. The Chinook knew that the best time to catch fish was during the runs when the salmon left the ocean to go up the rivers to spawn. The Chinook would work so hard during the salmon runs that the tribe would catch enough salmon to last all year. They took so many salmon at one time that it was more like harvesting a crop than it was like fishing. The salmon were cleaned and then smoked or dried to preserve them as food for the rest of the year.

In general, Native American tribes had to meet their basic needs by adjusting and adapting to use the natural resources and their environment. The Chinook also had to use the solution of accommodating to their environment in order to survive. The Chinook accommodated to the generous supply of salmon in their environment by making salmon a main staple of their diet.

However, the Chinook wanted to have something to eat besides fish all the time. Another way the Chinook got food was by gathering food from edible plants in the forests, especially blackberries which grow wild in the region.

There was a third way of getting food, besides fishing and gathering, on the Northwest Coast. The men also hunted game, but that was a much less important source of food than fishing.

The Chinook would also go out to sea and bring back other kinds of fish and even whales to eat. The Chinook were the same as the Inuit because they both needed boats of some kind to use to go out to fish in the sea and also travel from village to village. The Chinook were different from the Inuit because they had plenty of trees in their environment. Because they had trees the Chinook did not need to make boats and canoes out of animal skins. The Chinook used the plentiful forests along the Northwest Coast to make their canoes and boats out of wood. The largest boats were 60 to 70 feet long. These huge boats were hollowed out of a single trunk of one of the huge cedar trees in their forests.

The Chinook and the Problem of Clothing. The northernmost tribe in the Northwest Coast, the Tlingit (tling-git, rhymes with fling kit), made use of tailored garments of deerskin, with leggings (pants) and moccasins, a style of clothing that was common throughout North America.

The milder temperature of the rest of the Northwest Coast region meant that the Chinook did not need as much clothing as the Tlingit. South of the Tlingit, the Chinook wore minimal clothing, usually a deerskin leather shirt and breechcloth, which is like the bottom part of a bikini. However, in rainy weather, the deerskin leather clothing became wet and uncomfortable. The Chinook found a way to make use of their plentiful forests to provide clothing that was cooler and more comfortable to wear than deerskin leather. The soft, stringy inner bark of cedar trees was softened and then woven into cloth to make cooler clothes. The tribes south of the Tlingit, where the climate was more rainy and warmer, preferred clothing made of shredded and woven bark. This softened cedar bark was also used to make blankets.

The Chinook and the Problem of Shelter. Because of the plentiful forests in the Northwest Coast region, the Chinook made many things from the trees in the forest. They used wood to construct buildings that were large enough for several families to live in at the same time. The wooden buildings were organized into villages of as many as 1,000 people.

The Effect of the Chinook Solutions. The Chinook accommodated to the plentiful supply of salmon by making salmon their main food. As a result of adapting to their environment the needs of the Chinook were well met. The effect was that the Chinook had more free time for celebrations and for artistic works. The art of the Chinook is still prized today. These are the effects of making good use of the abundant natural resources of the Northwest Coast.

Figure 32.2   Example of Problem–Solution–Effect Passage from Textbook

From: Carnine, D., Crawford, D., Harniss, M., & Hollenbeck, K. (1994). *Understanding U.S. History. Volume 1: Through the Civil War.* Eugene, OR: Considerate Publishing. Reprinted by permission.

clothing, and shelter and the effects of those solutions. Note, however, that a different big idea could have been used to present the same material. For example, an alternate big idea that could be used in this instance is, "People's cultures reflect aspects of their environment."

This narrative is also an example of clearly written text students can easily comprehend. It is important for teachers and authors of instructional materials to understand that improving social studies curricula requires more than simply changing the length of words and sentences. For an

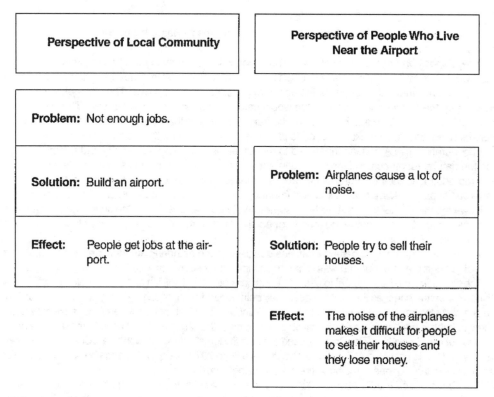

Figure 32.3 Graphic Representation of an Example of Multiple Perspectives

instructional tool to do more than provide information, every aspect of its design must be carefully engineered to bring about understanding.

Multiple Perspectives. Another big idea in social studies is the notion that events can be viewed from more than one perspective and that these different perspectives are important to fully understanding social events. The following discussion of multiple perspectives is placed within the context of the problem–solution–effect big idea.

Something that will be a problem from one perspective may not be a problem from another perspective. In fact, what is a solution from the perspective of one person or group may actually create problems for another person or group. Understanding this relationship can help students recognize that groups of people often have different perspectives about the same event. Figure 32.3 illustrates the big idea of multiple perspectives at an elementary level.

A related big idea that could be used at an elementary level is, "There are always two sides to every story (or argument)." This idea is closely related to multiple perspectives and it could be used both to structure the solving of disagreements and social problems within the classroom as well as to prompt students to look for an opposing point of view when doing research in the newspaper, for example. An instructional tool that consistently presented both sides of each "story" would go a long way toward developing critical thinking skills in students.

Factors of Group Success. Another big idea is that the success of group efforts, such as wars or the establishment of colonies, are frequently associated with the following four factors:

1. *Motivation.* Successful groups have group members or supporters who are committed to a common goal.
2. *Leadership.* Successful groups have highly qualified, knowledgeable, and effective leaders.
3. *Resources.* Successful groups have sufficient resources (usually money) to accomplish their goals.
4. *Capability.* In addition to resources and leadership, successful groups have a sufficient quality of know-how and appropriate tools to accomplish their goals.

These factors can help explain why different groups throughout history either succeeded or failed in reaching their goals. For example, when the Constitution was first proposed, many Americans were reluctant to support its passage. They saw no need to change from the voluntary form of cooperation that had worked for the colonies up to that time. Initially, only wealthy, established leaders known as the Federalists supported establishing the Constitution. The Federalists supported the Constitution because they were convinced a stronger federal government was in their best interest.

The four factors associated with group success can help students understand why the Federalists were able to get the Constitution ratified despite widespread opposition:

1. *Motivation*. The Federalists were motivated to secure passage of the Constitution because they strongly believed it would help protect their considerable business interests. Their desire for success was much greater than that of their opposition, who simply did not like the idea of a federal government.
2. *Leadership*. Both the Federalists and their opponents had capable leaders who were able to persuade followers to support their position.
3. *Resources*. The Federalists had superior monetary resources compared to the anti-Federalists. This gave the Federalists an advantage in organizing and mobilizing their followers.
4. *Capability*. The Federalists had carefully planned and organized how to achieve their goal during, and possibly even prior to, the Constitutional Convention. They knew what they were doing and how to do it. This provided the Federalists with a head start over their opponents and ultimately led to passage of the Constitution.

Problem–solution–effect, multiple perspectives, and the four factors of group success are three examples of big ideas in social studies instruction. When social studies is taught in this way, it becomes possible for students to comprehend historical events as an interrelated network.

Big ideas enable relevance-making activities. At one level big ideas are useful because their explanatory power can help students more easily understand content material. Equally important is that big ideas can help students recognize connections between the content of social studies and their personal lives.

A big idea such as the four factors of group success can provide students with a tool for applying what they learn during social studies to current events and their own lives. Through repeated exposure, students can learn how to use the four factors to analyze the strengths and weaknesses of group efforts in almost any realm. An elementary teacher might use this framework to discuss plans for a fund drive for playground equipment. A high school teacher might use this big idea to lead students to discuss their high school football team in terms of the motivation, leadership, resources, and capability of the team. A political science instructor might use it to analyze and predict the outcome of an upcoming general election.

The problem–solution–effect analysis is another big idea students can apply to their own lives. For example, two eighth-grade boys who had learned this big idea in social studies class got into a fight and were sent to the office. While the boys were awaiting their fate outside the principal's office one of the authors stopped to ask what happened. When they explained they got into a fight, the author remarked, "I guess someone was trying to dominate, eh?" One of the boys replied, "Yeah, next time we ought to try accommodating."

Designing Conspicuous Strategies

Teaching higher order thinking (i.e., problem solving, decision making, analysis, and critical thinking) is another highly valued goal of social studies education reform. Although social studies educators tend to distinguish among the terms *problem solving, decision making, analysis*, and *critical thinking*, they all require students to apply an organizational strategy to understand and apply content knowledge. Extensive empirical evidence suggests that all students benefit from having such organizational strategies made conspicuous for them, and that diverse learners are especially in need of conspicuous presentation of the organization of knowledge. In practice, however, social studies curricula and materials rarely include explicit organizational strategies designed to help students understand and apply content knowledge.

A strategy is a general set of steps used to solve a problem or analyze content. Very often in the social studies, effective strategies are literally the application of a big idea. Higher-performing students are more likely to invent their own useful organizational strategies, given adequate time. The purpose of explicit strategy instruction is to ensure that all learners have equal and timely access to the details that lead to success in solving a problem. The emphasis in social studies on critical thinking provides a natural context for including strategies in instruction on social studies content.

Teaching students to apply the big idea of problem–solution–effect when examining the behavior of groups would be an example of a conspicuous strategy that could be profitably taught initially in the early grades. Problem–solution–effect develops naturally out of the narrative text structure with which students are familiar. Given social studies passages that used problem–solution–effect as an expository text structure, students could learn to anticipate and predict the elements of social studies material as well as they do stories. Looking for the motivating problems, attempts at solutions, and the effects of those attempts could serve as a heuristic strategy for initial efforts at research.

A second strategy for relating historical conditions to group behavior could be taught to students who understand that group cooperation evolves in identifiable developmental stages. Students at a young age can be taught the specific features of this big idea as a strategy for examining group cooperative activities. Figure 32.4 summarizes four common conditions and their relationship to the development of group cooperation.

In a multiyear social studies curriculum designed around big ideas and conspicuous strategies, young learners could begin by learning a basic strategy in social studies of looking for identifiable patterns in human behavior. Then they could be taught the developmental stages of cooperation in the context of a problem they were likely to encounter in their own lives, such as what to do after school. Students could learn the stages of cooperation in the context of a story about how the occasional after-school baseball games of a group of children became more regular and finally became organized into a league with rules. Later, the curriculum could use the stages of group cooperation as a strategy for organizing the study of the how the local city government became organized. In another year it could be applied to the development of the state. Students would learn that the strategy of looking for identifiable patterns of human behavior pays off. The power of a conspicuous strategy in social studies is heuristic—it helps students anticipate what questions to ask and what information is important. At a lower level, students who learned the *two-sides-to-every-story* big idea would know to keep researching until they find the opposing viewpoint.

For example, the application of the strategy of looking for the stages of cooperation can be even more powerful in deriving political science principles from history. The stages of cooperation can help explain why the Second Continental Congress gave almost no power to the central government in the

1. **Gather together and discuss common problems**
   IF some members agree on a solution to a common problem, THEN people will begin occasional voluntary cooperation.

2. **Occasional voluntary cooperation**
   IF cooperative solutions are effective and the problems recur, THEN people will begin to cooperate regularly.

3. **Regular voluntary cooperation**
   IF the need for cooperation continues but voluntary cooperation fails, THEN people may agree to legally binding cooperation.

4. **Legally binding cooperation**
   The group is forced by rules to cooperate.

Figure 32.4 Stages of Group Cooperation

Articles of Confederation. Students often regard the Articles of Confederation as somehow being imperfect because they failed to give the government essential powers needed to run the government. Instructional materials often do not explain that, when the Articles of Confederation were conceived, voluntary cooperation between the states had successfully resulted in the elimination of British taxes and a Revolutionary War victory. Without a strategy for understanding the development of group cooperation, even capable students have difficulty understanding that the weak nature of the Articles and the government were due to the level of cooperation between the states at that time.

However, if students acquire the big idea that groups who regularly cooperate with success are not compelled to adopt legally binding agreements until it is necessary, this knowledge becomes a sophisticated strategy for understanding history and its application to other social sciences at a deeper level. Using the stages of cooperation, students can relate their understanding of the Articles and the weak role of a central government to political science questions, such as the current struggle for cooperation among the republics of the former Soviet Union, rather than being dependent on the teacher for that insight.

Designing Mediated Scaffolding

Temporary assistance along the path to self-regulated learning can help students become independent learners. In social studies this support, or *scaffolding*, is often necessary for diverse learners to comprehend what they read, whether a textbook or primary source document. Ideally, instructional materials should provide carefully designed sequences of tasks that involve concept organizers such as maps, time lines, and study guides. However, if materials do not present such techniques, then the teacher must provide supplemental instruction. Although it is not often provided, scaffolding is also needed for diverse learners to comprehend the critical concepts and ideas of nontextbook sources of social studies information, such as discussions, videos, interviewed informants, and simulation activities. The process of designing scaffolding can be divided into teacher activities done *before, during*, and *after* reading the text, viewing the video, or playing the simulation.

Before Instruction. Supplementing instruction requires a careful analysis of the content aimed at identifying what concepts and ideas are critical for all learners to acquire. Because preparation time for teachers is a scarce commodity, this content analysis should focus on methods for scaffolding instruction that are achievable. One reasonable approach to scaffolding is for a teacher to prepare questions prior to a lesson, which then are interspersed during reading, viewing, or discussing the topic at hand. Interspersed questions prepared in advance can help reduce the number of irrelevant or obscure questions posed by a textbook or by the teacher at the spur of the moment. Carefully chosen questions will help students identify critical information and relationships needed for conceptual understanding. Preparation of graphic organizers that identify the key concepts and fundamental relationships are very helpful. Another important aspect of scaffolding that needs to be accomplished prior to instruction is identifying essential prerequisite information to present to students prior to reading a social studies selection. The value of readings, discussions, video viewings, or simulations that are prefaced in this manner is greatly enhanced for diverse learners, who often have limited background knowledge of common social studies content.

During Instruction. Interspersed questions are more helpful if they are posed in close proximity to the material that answers them. In other words, if a question is widely separated from its answer, the question changes from a facilitator of understanding to a test of memory or a test of searching strategies. It is critical to interrupt reading, lectures, videos, and discussions to intersperse carefully prepared questions that help insure that students capture, express, and summarize the ideas and concepts that they are expected to glean from the activity.

Another useful and common technique for scaffolding students' comprehension of social studies texts is oral reading. When students read the text aloud, it provides an opportunity for teachers to correct decoding and comprehension errors, prevents students from skipping material, and provides sufficient time for all students to process information.

After Instruction. The same graphic organizers, concept maps, and outlines that were used to assist organization of the ideas as presented can be reused as ways to scaffold students' attempts to articulate

---

Introduction to Problem–Solution–Effect

Studying history is like looking back in time through a window. When we look through this window, we can relive important problems and the solutions people used to solve them.

Sometimes these solutions cause positive effects. Often, however, solutions have unintended effects that create new problems.

Problems faced by large numbers of people together are usually *economic problems* or *people's rights* problems. People have problems when they are unable to get things they want or need.

ECONOMIC PROBLEMS

An economic problem involves difficulty in getting and keeping items that people need or want.

- *What is an economic problem?*

   At a basic level, people need three things: (a) food to eat, (b) shelter to keep them dry and out of the weather, and (c) clothing to keep them warm. People require these three basic items to live. For centuries, people have found ways to meet these basic needs.

- *What three basic things must people have to live?*

Figure 32.5   Example of Textbook Introduction to Problem–Solution–Effect

in review the ideas presented. When given the scaffold of the key points to cover, many students are still challenged to write or explain the whole idea. However, far more material is learned and articulated than when students are left on their own to remember and organize the information. Students can eventually be moved into more self-regulated learning by, for example, gradually reducing the quantity of information provided on a graphic organizer. This strategy provides the teacher with a means of taking down the scaffold while still holding students to a high standard of explanation and understanding.

While it is possible for teachers to apply these scaffolding techniques to primary source documents and their existing social studies textbooks, the effort is considerable. Figure 32.5 presents an example appropriate to an elementary text book that carefully presents the big idea of economic problems as a component of the problem–solution–effect big idea. The excerpt supports students' understanding of economic problems through a clearly written narrative and interspersed questions in close proximity to new concepts. Figure 32.6 demonstrates how a middle-school level U.S. history textbook (Carnine et al., 1994) applies the big idea of economic problems to different groups (e.g., families, businesses, governments, and other organizations) and scaffolds the concept by relating it to a graphic model that uses a balance scale. Figure 32.7 shows an example of how an elementary level textbook could conclude its initial presentation of economic problems with scaffolded application questions; i.e., the problem is already set up so the focus is on the implications of the answer rather than on the set-up of the problem.

The amount of scaffolding a teacher or instructional material provides will vary depending on the difficulty level of a concept and the needs of the students. Diverse learners typically require more scaffolding, while more able students are able to develop effective comprehension strategies independently. Regardless of a student's instructional level, scaffolding must be gradually withdrawn over time. It makes little sense to develop learners who can understand social studies only with textbook or teacher-mediated support.

Designing Strategic Integration

Big ideas and strategies related to problem–solution–effect, factors of group success, and the stages of group cooperation should initially be presented as discrete concepts. However, instructional materials should go on to help students integrate this knowledge. The goal of integration is

Over the past 400 years, the way people have met their basic needs has changed dramatically. Four hundred years ago, Native American families grew crops, hunted and killed their own food, helped build their own shelters, and made their own clothes. Now not many people grow their own food, build their own shelters, or make their own clothes. Today, families earn money by working. When members of a family work, they exchange their time and skills for money. The money they earn is spent on food, shelter, clothing, and things such as entertainment. If a family earns more money than it spends, the family will have extra money. When a family saves money, they are accumulating wealth. If a family spends more money than they earn, they would end up in debt. A family that gets too much into debt has an economic problem. They cannot afford the things they want and need.

Larger groups also can have economic problems. Factory owners, for example, earn money by selling their products. Some factories make and sell clothes, while others make and sell computers. A factory spends money for many things, such as paying for materials, machines, buildings, and workers' salaries. Factory owners have economic problems if they spend more money making things than they receive by selling those things.

Governments can have economic problems, too. Governments receive money by collecting taxes from their citizens. Governments spend money to pay for protection by the military, education, social services, and many other services. They have problems if they spend more money than they receive from taxes.

Businesses and governments are like families. When businesses and governments save money, they are accumulating wealth. When they spend more money than they earn, they have economic problems and cannot get all the things they want and need.

The figure below shows three different economic situations that families, businesses, governments, and other organizations may experience.

1. If families, businesses, governments and other organizations earn as much as they spend, they will be **economically balanced.** This situation is shown in box A. For example, if a family earns $4000 a month and spends $4000 a month, then it is economically balanced.

2. If a group earns more than it spends, the group will **accumulate wealth.** This situation is shown in box B. For example, if a business earns $50,000 a month and only spends $30,000 a month, then it is accumulating wealth.

3. If a group spends more than it earns, it will have an **economic problem.** This situation is shown in box C. For example, if a government takes in one billion dollars in taxes a month but spends two billion dollars a month, then it has an economic problem.

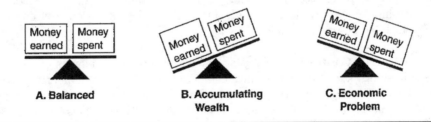

Figure 32.6   Graphic Representation of Economic Problems Analysis

From: Carnine, D., Crawford, D., Harniss, M., & Hollenbeck, K. (1994). *Understanding U.S. History. Volume 1: Through the Civil War.* Eugene, OR: Considerate Publishing. Reprinted by permission.

to help students achieve a deeper understanding of social studies by providing them with opportunities to apply several big ideas and strategies to previously introduced topics. Practice in the application of big ideas and strategies can best be achieved through careful selection and sequencing of material. Following are principles for integrating big ideas and strategies in social studies instruction.

Integrating Several Big Ideas and Strategies. Students can integrate their knowledge of problem–solution–effect and the stages of group cooperation to analyze historical events such as the Federalists' effort to get the Constitution ratified and the resistance to the new Constitution.

Economic Problems Activity

1. Darleen's parents give her $5.00 a week as her allowance. She spends $2.50 a week to buy candy

$$5.00$$
$$- \ 2.50$$

Will Darleen have a balance of money earned and spent, be accumulating wealth, or have an economic problem?

2. Roy earns $2,500.00 a month as a bank teller. He borrows from his parents and spends $2,700.00 a month on car and house payments.

$$2,500.00$$
$$- \ 2,700.00$$

Will Roy have a balance of money earned and spent, be accumulating wealth, or have an economic problem?

3. Larry earns $1,300.00 a month as a radio announcer. He spends $1,300.00 a month on rent and groceries.

$$1,300.00$$
$$- \ 1,300.00$$

Will Larry have a balance of money earned and spent, be accumulating wealth, or have an economic problem?

Figure 32.7   Examples of Math Practice for Learning Economic Problems Analysis

Voluntary cooperation between the states after the Revolutionary War could not prevent interstate taxation, which was limiting trade between the states, nor could it raise a peacetime navy to protect shipping activities or raise enough money to pay off debts incurred by the war. These problems led to economic chaos and a general insurrection in Massachusetts (Shay's Rebellion), which in turn convinced the wealthy colonial establishment that voluntary cooperation defined by the Articles of Confederation needed to be replaced by a stronger central government, via a constitution. Understanding these relationships requires students to apply and integrate their knowledge of problem–solution–effect and the stages of group cooperation.

Integrating Potentially Confusing Concepts. Lower-performing students often become confused when exposed to similar ideas. McKeown and Beck (1990), in a study of elementary students' knowledge of United States history after a year of instruction, found students could no longer discriminate between the Declaration of Independence and the Constitution. The students had a "document stew" level of understanding because the textbook did not anticipate that students would need help remembering important facts about each document.

Thus, well-designed knowledge integration in instructional materials or a teacher presentation involves the initial separation of similar ideas to reduce confusion. Later, however, the potentially confusing concepts must be carefully integrated and explicitly contrasted.

Integrating a Big Idea Across Multiple Contexts. A third aspect of integration involves providing students with opportunities to establish connections between recently and previously introduced topics. An example of this type of integration involves having students throughout all levels of social studies use the four factors of group success to analyze and understand why some group efforts fail. Elementary studies of Roanoke, Jamestown, the Pilgrims, and the Puritans could use the four factors to see why some colonies failed and others succeeded. These factors also can be used to analyze middle-school studies of the changes Britain made during the French and Indian War, which resulted in victory after an initial series of defeats. And, as previously noted, at a high school level the factors can help students analyze the efforts of the Federalists to ratify the Constitution. The application of a big idea across multiple contexts can help students understand their usefulness for comprehending social studies. It also models for students the process of making connections between seemingly diverse content.

Designing Primed Background Knowledge

Research has shown that students with diverse learning needs have less background knowledge of social studies content than their normally achieving peers (Lenz & Alley, 1983). This lack of knowledge impedes comprehension of social studies instructional materials, and the extent of knowledge influences the quality of understanding that a student can construct (McKeown et al., 1992). In order to be effective with diverse learners, instructional tools must provide adequate background knowledge so that all students are able to understand. If not, teachers must provide the requisite information and explanations before students encounter the material.

The components of big ideas and the steps that constitute strategies often require explicit instruction. For example, to understand the following primary source material from the writings of Geronimo, students must have prerequisite knowledge about the world views of the Apache and of Native Americans in general:

> For each tribe of men Usen [Apache word for God] created, He also made a home. In the land created for any particular tribe He placed whatever would be best for the welfare of that tribe.
>
> When Usen created the Apaches He also created their home in the West. He gave them such grain, fruits, and game as they needed to eat. To restore their health when disease attacked them He taught them where to find these herbs, and how to prepare them for medicine. He gave them a pleasant climate and all they needed for clothing and shelter was at hand. (McLuhan, 1971, p. 154)

In preparation for reading this passage, students need to know that Native American tribes had, over thousands of years, evolved very intimate and unique relationships between themselves and their local environments. Far from being one Indian culture, the tribes living in different ecological environments solved their basic needs in very different ways.

This background knowledge would enable students to apply one component of the problem–solution–effect big idea (i.e., Native Americans *accommodated* their environment) to comprehend the deeper meaning of the primary source material. Additionally, having learned the big idea of accommodating versus dominating, students are prepared to understand fundamental differences between how Native Americans and Western cultures relate to the environment. This knowledge can also be used to examine the impact of humans on ecological systems and events associated with the environmental movement's desire of citizens to accommodate the environment.

Without prerequisite knowledge, full application of a big idea or strategy is not possible and students are not prepared to make sophisticated connections between seemingly diverse content.

Designing Judicious Review

A major goal for all students is to remember what they have learned. Retention of social studies content can be especially difficult for diverse learners especially if the instruction they receive covers too many topics superficially. Retention is dependent on the use of effective review practices that are widely supported by research. Reviewing the same or nearly same material ad nauseam promotes rote learning; however, effective review can lead to long-term retention and generalization.

It is easy to confuse the "delivery vehicles" of review—concept maps, mnemonic graphics, study guides, tests—with the attributes of effective review. Social studies programs sometimes include these instructional aids but do not often incorporate effective review principles.

Effective review is achievable when the guidelines pertaining to big ideas, strategies, and scaffolding are inherent in the design of instruction for social studies. In other words, if the presentation (either from the textbook or from a nontextbook source) lacks clarity and coherence, it will also lack a foundation for providing effective review. However, if instructional presentations are designed using big ideas, then principles of effective review can be applied. For example, after the big idea of problem–solution–effect is introduced and subsequently used in a variety of contexts, then the four factors of group success can be introduced and used in a variety of contexts until it too is mastered. Once students learn the four factors that determine group success, the factors can be reviewed through an analysis of various group efforts such as the settlement of Jamestown, the Federalist drive for ratification of the Constitution, and the Civil War. After the two ideas are used separately, then in new contexts both big ideas are reviewed and used together. Varied review of this sort also preempts the possibility of students resorting to shallow, rote recall. Varied review is also linked to big ideas that can be related to current events. In the absence of an understanding of the stages of co-operation, for example, it is difficult for students to recognize connections between events in the former Soviet Union and the events leading up to the adoption of the U.S. Constitution.

THE APPLICATION OF INSTRUCTIONAL DESIGN PRINCIPLES

Developing Instructional Tools

One use of the foregoing six major principles of effective instruction would be to inform the design and development of instructional tools in social studies. Instructional tools could include textbooks, workbooks, video lessons, Web-delivered distance learning, and many other examples. The next section talks about how one could use the six principles of big ideas, conspicuous strategies, mediated scaffolding, strategic integration and judicious review when developing an instructional tool.

One approach for bringing understanding to social studies without sacrificing breadth of content is to develop instructional tools around big ideas. Several of the big ideas applicable to history have been described in this chapter: (a) problem–solution–effect, (b) multiple perspectives, (c) every story (argument) has two sides, (d) four factors of group success, (e) developmental stages of cooperation, and (f) a people's culture is influenced by their environment. Using one or more of these big ideas is a good way to begin developing an instructional tool in social studies. Developing additional big ideas requires fairly extensive reading in the discipline, with an eye for patterns and recurring relationships. However, a developer might only need a handful of big ideas for a year's program. In addition, big ideas are most effective when used repeatedly, rather than relying on new ideas for every topic under examination.

Students with diverse learning needs often have less background knowledge of social studies content than their typically-achieving peers. Therefore, instructional tools that will be used with diverse learners should be designed for students who lack essential background knowledge.

Social studies instructional tools should provide students with scaffolding of key relationships through graphic organizers and explicit explanation of the big ideas until their learning becomes self-regulated. In addition, interspersed questions located close to the content targeted are needed to facilitate identification of important material and ideas during initial input of information.

Instructional tools for use with diverse learners need to provide ample review in a variety of formats. An instructional tool with many review exercises gives teachers the option of using or skipping the exercises depending on the needs of their students. It is far easier for teachers to skip unneeded review exercises than to create additional ones. Integrating such things as graphic organizers, outlines, and semantic webs into the review process enables teachers to incorporate meaningful review. Effective review using big ideas promotes transfer of learning by requiring application of content at different times and in different contexts. Review questions ought to focus on the most important ideas identified. Cumulative review of key material will assist in learning.

Testing materials are most effective when they stimulate study of the material. Production responses such as fill-in-the-blank, short answer, and essay responses require more thorough learning of the material than multiple-choice response formats. Students can more easily remember and make use of more thoroughly learned material. An effective instructional tool in social studies should emphasize knowledge that can be integrated and applied in multiple contexts. The goal is to promote understanding about when to use specific knowledge by providing students with opportunities to apply several big ideas and strategies to new material.

Selecting Instructional Tools

A second use of the six major principles of effective instruction for teaching social studies would be in the process of selecting instructional tools. As noted earlier, teachers who learn how and why to develop strategic supplemental materials to enhance the content of textbooks are critical of publishers' failures to include this essential material in the first place. Once these six principles are learned they can then be used to evaluate the potential for instructional efficacy of textbooks being considered for adoption. The following section describes how this process might occur.

First, examine social studies tools to determine whether the use of big ideas lends cohesion to adequate breadth of coverage. Neither of two extremes is acceptable. Does the tool strike you as a series of unrelated facts rather than an interrelated network of information? Or does the tool strike you as providing depth in only a few areas at the expense of adequate breadth?

Examine several big ideas presented in a tool to assess the degree to which they are explicitly interrelated. This evaluation can be achieved by comparing the development of knowledge presented early in a tool with knowledge presented in subsequent sections.

Examine tools first to see what forms of scaffolding (graphic organizers, concept maps, highlighting, bolded information) are present to help students identify critical information and relationships needed for conceptual understanding. When evaluating a social studies tool for review, *more* is preferable to *less*, provided the review is distributed, cumulative, and varied. It is far easier for teachers not to use the review when it is provided than to prepare the review if it is needed.

Evaluate instructional tools to determine what provisions are made to teach students with limitations in important prerequisite knowledge. If students have gaps in their knowledge, does the tool make provisions to introduce or review important background information several lessons *prior* to introduction of the target knowledge?

Examine instructional tools to determine what explicit strategies associated with the big ideas are described. If strategies are present, determine if they: (1) are clearly described, (2) have narrow or broad application, and (3) are an integral part of the tool or just optional. Try to imagine yourself as a diverse learner who must analyze a problem based solely on a suggested strategy.

Modifying Instructional Tools

The third use of these six major principles of effective instruction, modifying instructional tools, is the biggest chore for the teacher. Modifying instructional tools to make them instructionally effective usually means the teacher will be creating a good deal of supplementary material. This activity must necessarily be extra work, above and beyond normal teaching responsibilities, but can often pay large dividends in the form of increased learning. The following section offers some suggestions on that process.

Identify several big ideas to incorporate into existing instructional materials either through supplemental materials or extensive revision of the tool. Select big ideas that (a) have rich explanatory and predictive power, (b) are a point of departure for posing significant questions, and (c) are generalizable to many situations and contexts.

Preparing interspersed questions in advance can help reduce the number of irrelevant or obscure questions posed in instructional tools or by a teacher on the spur of the moment. Well-chosen questions should help students identify critical information and relationships needed for conceptual understanding. Another example of scaffolding is for students to read social studies material aloud. Oral reading allows teachers to correct decoding and comprehension errors, prevents students from skipping material, and provides sufficient time for all students to process information. Oral reading and interspersed questions can be applied as scaffolding for instructional tools.

Teachers can also provide scaffolding with supplemental materials (e.g., graphics, concept maps, study guides, or outlines). In general, it is difficult for teachers to modify existing tools to accommodate background knowledge. Such modification requires the development of new instruction and affects the sequence of existing instruction. To some extent, teachers can review important big ideas, events, or important prerequisite vocabulary to help students make connections with new information. This requires a thorough analysis of the component skills and concepts needed to understand new knowledge.

Teachers can develop integration activities in which several important concepts are included. Such activities should be preceded by instruction that teaches component concepts first, so the integrated material builds on earlier learning. A more extensive implementation of integration can be achieved through the application of several big ideas to analyze events. Teachers can prepare review activities before instruction begins. This can be accomplished by evaluating the important information presented in a tool that is likely to cause students difficulty. Ask yourself if such information is needed for understanding subsequent material and the extent to which the tool provides sufficient review in anticipated problem areas. Review can also be prepared after instruction takes place and students' knowledge deficiencies become evident. Again, such review should be ample and provide opportunities for practice that can be applied at different times and in different contexts.

SUMMARY

Many of the guidelines for improving instructional strategies for teaching social studies to diverse learners apply to other learners as well. Understanding the guidelines can help teachers determine how best to attempt program modifications and what principles characterize an effective social studies program for diverse learners.

- Organizing social studies curriculum around big ideas is essential to help learners make connections among the facts and concepts they learn in social studies.
- Some big ideas in history are: (a) problem–solution–effect; (b) the developmental stages of group cooperation; (c) multiple perspectives; (d) two sides to every story (argument); (e) a people's culture is influenced by their environment; and (f) the four factors of group success.
- The important ideas that are essential for high-performing students to know are essential for *all* other students.
- Big ideas facilitate the process of making what students learn from content area instruction meaningful and appropriate to their own lives.
- In social studies the strategy is often simply the application of the big ideas to the content.
- Mediated scaffolding in social studies includes oral reading, interspersed questions, concept organizers of various sorts, and application questions.
- Strategically integrated curriculum will offer students an opportunity to successfully integrate several big ideas.
- Big ideas learned in one context must be applicable in multiple contexts.
- Strategic integration of content within the curriculum can help students learn when to use specific knowledge.
- The concepts unified by a big idea or strategy must be explicitly introduced in advance.
- Teachers must make certain that all students possess the requisite background knowledge for deep understanding of the content.
- Effective review of social studies content must be designed to be an integral and meaningful part of later lessons.
- All students require cumulative review to achieve transfer and generalize information.

REFLECTION AND APPLICATION: Case Study

Mario teaches social studies to tenth- and eleventh-grade students in an urban priority school district. His three general World History courses are composed of heterogeneous groups of students, which include several students receiving special education services as well as many other students with diverse learning needs.

Mario recently attended a professional development conference that included presentations and workshops on integrating effective teaching strategies, including big ideas, into social studies curriculums to enhance learning outcomes for all students. Exploring historical events through the framework of problem–solution–effect analysis was among the more prominent big ideas in social studies covered during this training. Mario believed that this strategy was particularly well suited for his Western Civilization courses and he enthusiastically planned to emphasize this important big idea during an upcoming unit.

Shortly after completing the conference, Mario incorporated explicit and clear explanations of problem–solution–effect analysis into a unit on the Age of Revolutions. He demonstrated this process to his students, for example, by applying problem–solution–effect analysis during presentations on Napoleon's invasion of Russia. Mario started with a description of problem–solution–effect analysis, explaining this big idea with language that was clear, concise, and consistent. He then modeled how this analysis could be applied to Napoleon's invasion, using graphic organizers to scaffold instruction.

The results of an examination on this unit were encouraging to Mario. He noted that his best students seemed to demonstrate a deeper understanding of the content than usual. Somewhat more surprisingly, several of his students with diverse learning needs also performed strongly. He also noticed that these students seemed to be more engaged during whole class discussions during the unit.

Based on student success with the problem–solution–effect framework, Mario decided to shift his emphasis to another big idea in social studies during the next unit. He believed that the content in the unit on the Industrial Age was ideal for emphasizing the big idea of environmental influences. Mario continued to provide conspicuous instruction and scaffolding. During an initial presentation, he discussed the importance of environmental influences, and then carefully explained how an increased demand for raw materials contributed to colonialism. Mario also organized a student discussion focusing on the effects that pollution had on ecosystems. In an attempt to scaffold instruction, he posited initial questions and supported student dialogues with occasional comments and feedback.

Once again, Mario's students did well on the exam and were able use the big idea of environmental influences to make meaningful and insightful observations about the unit content. Mario was disappointed, however, that many students failed to apply the problem–solution–effect analysis on one of the examination questions for this unit. He was initially puzzled by the finding that many of his students with diverse learning needs had difficulty utilizing the problem–solution–effect analysis to answer a question on the Industrial Age. Like the other students in his classes, these learners had demonstrated an understanding of this *big idea* during the previous unit on the Age of Revolutions. Moreover, he had used *conspicuous strategies* and *mediated scaffolding* to present this strategy.

- Why might Mario's students have had difficulty applying the big idea of problem–solution–effect to the unit on the Industrial Age? What instructional principles and teaching strategies might Mario have utilized to more effectively address the learning needs of all of the students in his classes?

The conclusion of the case study can be found later in this chapter.

CONTENT QUESTIONS

1. Describe two different struggles over expectations for teaching social studies.
2. What is the purpose of social studies education, according to the recommendations of the National Council for Social Studies (NCSS)?
3. Identify the problems associated with the instructional materials of elementary and secondary level social studies.

4. How are big ideas identified in social studies instruction?
5. Identify three examples of big ideas for social studies curriculum.
6. Describe the components of problem–solution–effect as a big idea in social studies.
7. Define what is meant by a strategy and provide an example of a conspicuous strategy.
8. Provide three examples of content organizers that can be used to scaffold social studies instruction.

REFLECTION AND DISCUSSION

1. Have you ever taken a social studies course in which you felt overwhelmed by having to memorize facts? What was your response to this course? Would your response have been different if the course content had been organized around big ideas?
2. Why might some methods that were utilized for social studies instruction in the past, such as inductive teaching and discovery learning, have been less successful for students with diverse learning needs?
3. Given the variety of disciplines in the field of social studies (e.g., history, economics, philosophy) and the amount of content teachers are expected to cover, how might educators use principles of effective instruction to balance breadth and depth of instruction?

Columbus Discovers America

Marco Polo, a traveling merchant from the city of Venice, ventured from Italy to the East in the late 1200s. He visited China, Japan, and India and returned home with intriguing stories of Asia. These later became his book *The Travels of Marco Polo*. Reading about the riches of the East—perfumes, spices, gold, and silk—enticed European fortune seekers to search for an easier route to Asia than the treacherous land journey Marco Polo had taken.

The sailors and mapmakers of Portugal were students of navigation and cartography. These two sciences deal with the guiding of sea travel and the making of maps. Maps are used in navigation and are often called charts. Prince Henry of Portugal owned the school and directed his men, including Bartholomew Diaz and Vasco de Gama, as they explored the west coast of Africa in the caravels built by his Portuguese navigators. It took years to travel around the southern tip of Africa and arrive in India. Christopher Columbus thought he could find a shorter route.

1271: Marco Polo left Venice
1488: Bartholomew Diaz sails to Cape of Good Hope
1495: *Travels of Marco Polo* published
1498: Vasco de Gama sails to India

Sailors discovered how to make compasses. Compasses use magnetic iron that points to the north by using the earth's magnetic field.

Technology advanced exploration.

Figure 32.8 Columbus Discovers America

APPLICATION

1. In small groups, generate a list of current issues in the news. Design an instructional activity for students in the primary grades that applies the big idea of problem–solution–effect to a current issue. Next design an activity for older students in which the problem–solution–effect analysis is applied to another current issue.

2. Use the six principles of effective instruction to evaluate the following section from a chapter on "Exploration" taken from a fifth-grade social studies textbook (Figure 32.8). How might this section be reorganized or rewritten to reflect effective teaching strategies?

Case Study (Conclusion)

After reviewing notes from the professional development conference, Mario realized that he had not applied the instructional principles of *judicious review* and *strategic integration* during his recent World History classes. Although some students had demonstrated an ability to generalize the problem–effect–solution analysis to the unit on the Industrial Age, many of his students with diverse learning needs had not transferred this big idea in the absence of judicious review and strategic integration. Mario decided to apply these additional instructional strategies during the next several units in an attempt to better meet the needs of his students with diverse learning needs. Specifically, he planned to reinforce the big ideas in social studies that he had already introduced by designing opportunities for judicious review and strategic integration during the next unit, which covered the era of the two world wars.

Prior to discussing the invasion of Russia by Axis troops, Mario reviewed the problem–solution–effect strategy that had previously been used to analyze Napoleon's invasion of Russia. He then guided the students through a discussion of historical parallels between these two invasions, with continued emphasis on the problem–solution–effect framework. During a subsequent class, Mario attempted to facilitate his students' integration of problem–solution–effect analysis with the big idea of environmental influences. He asked the students to discuss the impact of geographic and climatic conditions on Axis troops at the Russian front. Mario was particularly pleased with the responses given by Janet, a student with a learning disability who often appeared withdrawn and unengaged during class discussions. Janet appeared animated and confident when noting how Russia's large land mass and cold winters had also weakened Napoleon's army.

With increased emphasis on judicious review and strategic integration, most of the students with diverse learning needs demonstrated an improved ability to analyze historical events using the problem–solution–effect approach during ongoing class discussions and the unit test. Additionally, Mario was already planning to systematically apply another instructional principle during the next section. The students' recent analysis of two large-scale invasions of Russia would surely afford an excellent opportunity to build on *primed background knowledge* while studying the Cold War.

- Would it be realistic to assume that a teacher could incorporate principles of effective instruction into social studies units after attending a professional development conference? What challenges might a teacher face in attempting to do this? What are potential resources and solutions that could facilitate a teacher's successful integration of instructional principles into his or her social studies teaching?
- Would it be challenging to organize social studies content

around big ideas, such as problem–solution–effect within a social studies textbook or curriculum that was not specifically organized to facilitate these concepts? How might an instructor successfully incorporate these big ideas into a social studies curriculum?

The Reflection and Application section of this chapter was written by Richard P. Zipoli, Jr., and Maureen F. Ruby, both of the University of Connecticut.

REFERENCES

Banks, J. A., Cookson, P., Gay, G., Hawley, W. D., Irvine, J. J., & Nieto, S., et al. (2005). Education and Diversity. *Social Education, 69* (1), 36–40.

Brophy, J. (1990). Teaching social studies for understanding and higher-order applications. In M. Wittrock (Ed.), *The Elementary School Journal, 90*(4), 353–417.

Carnine, D., Crawford, D., Harniss, M., & Hollenbeck, K. (1994). *Understanding U.S. history: Volume 1—Through the Civil War.* Eugene, OR: University of Oregon.

Ellis, E. S., & Sabornie, E. J. (1990). Strategy-based adaptive instruction in content-area classes: Social validity of six options. *Teacher Education and Special Education, 13* (2) 133–144.

Kauffman, D., Johnson, S. M., Kardos, S. M., Liu, E., & Peske, H. G. (2002). "Lost at Sea": New teachers' experiences with curriculum and assessment. *The Teachers College Record, 104* (2), 273–300.

Lenz, B. K., & Alley, G. R. (1983). *The effects of advance organizers on the learning and retention of learning disabled adolescents within the context of a cooperative planning model.* Final research report submitted to the U.S. Department of Education, Office of Special Education, Washington, DC.

McKeown, M. G., & Beck, I. L. (1990). The assessment and characterization of young learners' knowledge of a topic in history. *American Educational Research Journal, 27* (4), 688–726.

McKeown, M. G., Beck, I. L., Sinatra, G. M., & Loxterman, A. (1992). The contribution of prior knowledge and coherent text to comprehension. *Reading Research Quarterly, 27* (4), 78–93.

McLuhan, T. C. (1971). *Touch the earth: A self-portrait of Indian existence.* New York: Promontory Press.

National Center for History in the Schools. (1992). *Lessons from history.* Los Angeles: The National Center for History in the Schools.

National Center to Improve the Tools of Educators. (2001). Retrieved Aug. 10, 2001 from idea.uoregon.edu/~ncite/

National Council for the Social Studies. (1994). Ten thematic strands in social studies. *Social Education, 58* (6) 365–368.

O'Neil, J. (1989). Social studies: Charting a course for a field adrift. *ASCD Curriculum Update,* 1–8.

Placier, M., Walker, M., & Foster, B. (2002). Writing the "show-me" standards: Teacher professionalism and political control in U.S. state curriculum policy. *Curriculum Inquiry, 32*(3), 281–310.

Ravitch, D. (2000). *Left back A century of failed school reforms.* New York: Simon & Schuster.

Sandholtz, J. H., Ogawa, R. T., & Scribner, S. P. (2004). Standards Gaps: Unintended consequences of local standards-based reform. *Teachers College Record, 106* (6), 1177–1202.

Twyman, T., & Tindal, G. (2005). Reaching all of your students in social studies. *Teaching Exceptional Children Plus, 1*(5) Article 1. Retrieved November 1, 2005 from http://escholarship.bc.edu/ education/tecplus/voll/iss5/1

SPECIAL ISSUES

CHAPTER 33

CASTING A WIDER NET
Linking Bilingual and Gifted Education
Jim Granada

In this diverse U.S. society, educators must recognize the educational challenges and make reflective decisions that positively impact the unique needs of students that a diverse population generates. As gifted education and the many variables that impact the delivery of gifted educational services in schools and school districts are considered, special attention must be given to the complexities that impact students who are gifted and potentially gifted and also bilingual and bicultural. In this chapter, the relationship between bilingual and gifted education is examined; the nature and needs of students who are bilingual/bicultural gifted are explored; and methods of identification, programming, and instruction are presented. The chapter concludes with general recommendations for the development of sound gifted bilingual/bicultural programs.

A BRIEF HISTORY OF GIFTED EDUCATION FOR BILINGUAL STUDENTS

Various forms of bilingual education may have been implemented in the United States since its infancy, but federal legislation addressing bilingual education was not passed until the late 1960s. In a political examination of bilingual education, Crawford (1998) reviews significant issues that resulted from the Bilingual Education Act of 1968 and addresses the different perspectives of bilingual education emphasis. Crawford compares a language-as-problem emphasis with that of language-as-resource. In the former, a quick-exit pedagogy focuses on rapid acquisition of English as a priority goal. In the latter, a late-exit enrichment model results from a combination of native-language instruction and English acquisition. The implications of which perspective is adopted by an educational community are extremely significant. Students who are in the "fast lane" toward acquiring a second language may be consistently overlooked for consideration as gifted, particularly if the gifts are not in the area of language acquisition. Those in bilingual programs that emphasize language as resource would appear more likely to have a context in which giftedness in many forms could be identified and nurtured. Bilingual programs with either perspective can connect with gifted education, but they must be approached in very different ways.

Gifted education in the United States has a long history, dating at least back to studies of gifted children in the 1920s. However, gifted education has not received the same level of recognition and funding as have both special education and bilingual education. A national definition of giftedness was outlined in the early 1970s (Marland, 1972), but a gifted education act has proven elusive to advocates of gifted and talented students.

Research in the area of giftedness and bilingual education has been limited. Ernesto Bernal, one of the prominent early researchers on the subject, reported in 1994 that since the first gifted and talented programs began in the 1930s, new understandings about giftedness have led to a more inclusionary view of gifted education. According to Bernal, the field now emphasizes selection over identification and places more value on cultural diversity. In spite of the changing view, bilingual gifted education has proven to be isolated and problematic. Barkan and Bernal (1991) illustrate the shortcomings of bilingual gifted education in the early 1990s: "These children, if they are: 'identified' at all, are typically admitted only after they have mastered English and can receive instruction in an all-English classroom" (p. 144).

School systems on both coasts of the United States and in the Southwest have designed programs targeting bilingual gifted students, with some successful programs organizing as early as the late 1970s. Tucson, Arizona, was the site of one of the programs that was reported in the professional literature. The Tucson Unified School District in 1987 reorganized services for gifted students. The district at that time also used a Title VII bilingual gifted grant to research selection procedures, develop Spanish curriculum materials, and prepare bilingual certified teachers to earn certification in gifted education. Two points focused toward bilingual and gifted education integration were the inclusion of case study approaches and the involvement of language minority communities in identification (Barkan & Bernal, 1991). Additionally, the authors reported that during the 1989–1990 school year, the Tucson school district used a case study procedure that included these elements in the identification of bilingual first-grade gifted students in select schools:

Raven's Coloured Matrices
Teacher checklist of student behaviors
Parent questionnaire
Abbreviated version of the Wechsler Intelligence Scale for Children (WISC)
Rating of self-esteem
Samples of student work

Barkan and Bernal concluded that bilingually competent teachers of the gifted were the key to the education of gifted children who were limited English proficient (LEP). With the shortage of bilingual teachers across the United States, this critical key may prove elusive but should not be forgotten.

CHARACTERISTICS OF POTENTIALLY GIFTED BILINGUAL STUDENTS

Gifted and *potentially gifted* are terms that often lack definitive parameters within the context of their use. This remains true when applying either term to bilingual students. Educators must also consider whether gifted programs for bilingual students are reflective of a bilingual emphasis or a gifted emphasis. I distinguish the bilingual gifted student as one who primarily demonstrates giftedness linguistically, whereas the gifted bilingual student may be gifted in a variety of areas and is also bilingual. Characteristics, identification, and programming must be consistent with the construct if the needs of the gifted student are to be consistently met.

"Both bilingualism and talent development are multidimensional phenomena involving cognitive, affective, cultural, environmental, and situational factors" reports Kloosterman (1997, p. 3). Although this is true, certain distinctions can be made between a student who demonstrates a linguistic giftedness and a student who is gifted in another area but is also bilingual. The bilingual gifted student will be more likely to demonstrate a rapid acquisition of a second language while demonstrating a high degree of manipulation and sophistication in the use of the primary language. This student might be nominated for a gifted program at two different points. He or she may draw attention based on the rapidity in which he or she exits from bilingual or English as a second language (ESL) services, and if criteria are in place to identify verbal giftedness in both languages, the student may qualify early for services. If the student is not identified early, linguistic talents may transfer rapidly to the second language, and the student may demonstrate gifted traits similar to non-second-language peers within a relatively short time, given the fact that traditional gifted students are often verbally gifted and flourish in the highly verbal classrooms of the U.S. educational system. In a 1998 report from the Office of

Educational Research and Improvement of the U.S. Department of Education, reference is made to the argument of some educators that being bilingual is a special ability involving the constant negotiation between two linguistic worlds as well as the problem solving and sophisticated code switching required in such linguistic intelligence. The bilingual gifted student demonstrates this ability much earlier and at a much higher degree than bilingual peers.

The gifted bilingual student, however, may mirror more traditional gifted students, particularly those identified in systems in which multiple areas of giftedness are recognized and served. Giftedness in leadership, the visual and performing arts, and creativity can readily be demonstrated by bilingual students, provided the learning environment in which they are educated allows for experiences to demonstrate these talents as well as nurturing confidence, the lack of which may factor in to the demonstration of high ability. School settings may not always provide the context in which these areas of giftedness are most visible; it may be necessary to move beyond the boundaries of the campus to observe the manifestation of nonacademic gifted behaviors.

More elusive is the bilingual student who is academically gifted. A language-as-resource bilingual education program may be more ideal to recognize the bilingual student who is gifted in math, science, social studies, language arts, technology, or any other content area in which gifted services are provided. Bilingual and ESL programs that provide academic rigor and enrichment in all core areas, rather than focusing predominantly on second-language acquisition, better allow for the demonstration of potential giftedness in content areas. Gifted bilingual students given limited opportunities to demonstrate high levels of content performance in their dominant language may eventually be immersed in English-only classrooms in which the long-term acquisition of a second language may mask the academic talent of the student.

Both bilingual gifted and gifted bilingual students may not demonstrate gifted characteristics found on the many lists that have been designed by gifted education leaders over many years. Cultural traditions and beliefs, heritage, acculturation, and in some cases, poverty, may be critical variables impacting how gifted behaviors are demonstrated. Checklists of characteristics that have proven effective in searching for students for traditional gifted programs may not provide accurate profiles for bilingual students who are also gifted. Alternative characteristics need to be examined if increasing LEP student representation in gifted programs is a priority.

McLean (1995) comments on the first critical variable: culture. "Culture provides the substance and content for attitudes, thought, and action; it allows for a culture-specific idiosyncratic representation of knowledge among its peoples; it determines the kinds of cognitive strategies and learning modes that individuals use for solving complex problems within their society" (p. 8). The traditions that the family and cultural community of a bilingual student follow may provide several indicators of giftedness that are not visible in the culture of the school. These include, among many, storytelling and the oral tradition, depth and breadth of understanding of specific traditions, level of involvement in religious affiliations and community service, and the roles and responsibilities accepted within the family. Also, involvement in artistic endeavors reflecting what is valued in the culture may provide additional evidence of talent.

Educators responsible for gifted programs should also be knowledgeable of how giftedness is defined within a family and culture. Traditional gifted programs are highly representative of middle-class U.S. culture, and programs are often defined based on what is valued as gifted in mainstream society. If a family does not share these mainstream values, then giftedness may be defined in a very different manner. Cultural conflicts can also impact the demonstration of giftedness. For some families, competition and focus on self are not encouraged. Competitive children and those who draw attention to their talents may be more readily identified as potentially gifted in U.S. classrooms than those who have not been raised as such.

Rate of acculturation of a bicultural student may also be considered a possible atypical indicator of giftedness. A student who quickly adapts to the norms of peers in a school setting, which could include mannerisms, fashion, music, and various trends, may be demonstrating both reflective and conceptual thinking, as well as keen observation and analysis of the environment. How well the student adapts among the cultural contexts of the home, the neighborhood, and the school may also indicate a complex level of adaptability few have experienced. Acculturation is not likely to be found in a list of gifted characteristics used to identify gifted students.

Finally, poverty may be a variable impacting some bilingual students, depending on the circumstances surrounding their arrival in the school community. The potentially gifted student who is also living in a poverty situation becomes one of the most difficult students to identify for gifted services. Poverty can impact the demonstration of giftedness dramatically but not always in a negative way. Children of poverty who are creatively gifted may fill their lives with creative, rather than commercial, forms of self-entertainment and may use problem-solving skills to a much higher degree than their peers. Academically gifted children in poverty situations may seek unusual ways to quench an insatiable thirst for knowledge. Intellectually gifted children in poverty settings may apply their intellectual talents to survival or, in a negative sense, may become intellectually manipulative. Impoverished gifted young leaders may focus leadership skills into higher levels of familial responsibility or into neighborhood peer leadership roles. And the artistically gifted child of poverty may channel giftedness into projects of practical construction and design, entertainment, community beautification, or personal writings. A nurturing school environment facilitates some of these manifestations of giftedness becoming obvious, but it is more likely that the outside-of-school setting will provide more opportunities to observe these aspects of giftedness.

IDENTIFICATION RECOMMENDATIONS FOR POTENTIALLY GIFTED BILINGUAL STUDENTS

Prior to embarking on a quest to identify gifted students from a bilingual population, certain questions must be addressed that can then serve as underlying assumptions for program development; identification methods; and curriculum, instruction, and assessment of this target population. These questions are illustrated in Table 33.1.

Research in the area of identification of bilingual gifted students has evolved from broader categorical topics (disadvantaged gifted, minority gifted, Hispanic gifted) to more focused areas of study. The early works of bilingual gifted advocates, such as Ernesto Bernal (1980, 1981), have provided more recent researchers with more discrete variables for the identification of these students. According to Cohen (1990), many school districts now include behavioral checklists, interviews, self-reports, autobiographies, and case histories to assist in the identification of gifted language minority students. The use of multiple criteria continues to be a focus after nearly 20 years of research on the topic of identification.

In a comprehensive look at identification instruments and criteria used to identify Mexican American gifted students, Garcia (1994) cites research showing that intelligence tests and achievement measures are biased against students who are limited English proficient. Expanding beyond the use of these standardized measures with the use of multiple criteria, those involved in identification decisions need to make thoughtful selections.

Garcia cautions that "even when multiple criteria are used, there is often a tendency to ignore qualitative or anecdotal data in favor of test scores such as group-administered intelligence tests and achievement tests" (p. 47). He proposes the use of qualitative instruments, such as portfolios, generic products, culture-specific or culture-sensitive checklists, parent interviews, and jot downs (gifted indicator matrices). In addition, when a student is bilingual, Garcia recommends that proficiency levels of both languages be considered, especially if any English-based measures are used, such as writing samples and verbally loaded standardized instruments.

Qualitative measures, currently popular for use in identification of under-represented gifted populations such as bilingual students, are not the panacea they may initially appear to be. Issues of validity and reliability may cloud the purpose of instruments, such as portfolios, resulting in valuable information being discarded when the issues become a focus (Paulson & Paulson, 1991). Nelson (1982) found behavioral checklists, a popular category of instrument used to identify gifted students, to be inaccurate and ineffective in the identification of gifted students when completed by teachers, unless the teachers received prior training in the use of the checklists. Clarification in the use of qualitative measures is critical if such measures are to maintain credibility in the identification process, and issues such as reliability, validity, and training should be examined when designing systems of identification for all gifted students. Addressing the issues pro-actively helps prevent the loss of the rich data these measures tend to generate.

Table 33.1 Fundamental Considerations for Identification of Potentially Gifted Bilingual Students

Questions to Consider	Implications for Identification	Implications for Services
Will emphasis be placed on identification of students who are gifted linguistically or students who are gifted in multiple areas?	Specific instruments and criteria for selection will differ depending on the area or areas of emphasis. Moving beyond verbal measures requires broader investigation of types of giftedness and methods of identification.	Services for gifted students need to reflect how they were identified for a program. If students are identified using nonverbal or creative ability instruments, they will need services that emphasize what these instruments measure.
What measures are currently in use in either the bilingual or gifted programs that can provide data for selection consideration?	Many instruments used in bilingual programs can provide information on cognitive abilities and achievement, including measurement of gains on certain instruments. Some identification measures used in gifted education do not depend on a student's command of English.	Collaborative efforts can be made between educators of both gifted and bilingual programs to analyze data and recommend not only selection of bilingual gifted students but also to identify intersecting or parallel practices that can be integrated into gifted services for bilingual students.
What variables must be considered in order to change current identification procedures for gifted students to align with best practices outlined in research, including the use of multiple criteria?	Changes in identification methods require extensive information dissemination, involving those families both currently receiving services and those targeted. A comprehensive understanding of the literature on educational change is helpful.	Timelines for changes and implementation will be impacted by these variables. Parallel timelines need to be established in relation to changes in delivery of gifted services, curriculum, and resources used in the program.
What laws or guidelines have been established at the national, state, and district levels that will impact identification decisions?	Certain non-negotiables may need to be established prior to designing or redesigning an identification process.	Gifted programs must remain in compliance with all levels of governance. Adaptations may be required in both programs.
What are the community perspectives regarding gifted and bilingual programs, and how do these perspectives impact services in each?	Level of support for either program can have either positive or negative impacts on changes that impact both programs, including methods of identification and how instruments are used.	Strong support for both programs will not only facilitate full development of new or expanded services but also can decrease levels of criticism during preliminary stages of implementation.
What leadership roles in the district and on campuses will be impacted by the identification of gifted bilingual students?	An implementation of identification changes is only viable if leadership is in place to serve as a catalyst for changes and to orchestrate implementation and evaluation.	Strong leadership is needed in order to bridge concerns of stakeholders in both programs and develop strong networks of communication to ensure success.
What resources are available that reflect the talents that will be discovered through identification of gifted bilingual students?	Identification of students must reflect the curriculum, instruction, and assessment that are provided programmatically.	Teachers may be required to develop new materials, or resources may need to be expanded.

Culture must also be considered when developing identification methods targeting potentially gifted bilingual students. Garcia (1994) points out that cognitive style, which he considers to be a culture-bound attribute, should be considered when screening bilingual students for gifted identification. Scores on instruments may be skewed if there is dissonance between the cognitive style of the student and the style required of the instrument.

Researchers have also focused in the past decade on specific characteristics of bilingual students that could help in gifted identification. Irby and Lara-Alecio (1996), in a study to report gifted attributes of bilingual students as reported by bilingual teachers, developed a list of characteristics organized into 11 clusters: motivation for learning, social and academic languages, cultural sensitivity, familial, collaboration, imagery, achievement, creative performance, support, problem solving, and locus of control. Few of these characteristic clusters would be found in traditional methods of identification.

Reyes, Fletcher, and Paez (1996) conducted a study of a project involving two rural elementary schools on the New Mexico-Texas-Mexico border with an ethnic composition of 97 percent Hispanic and 91 percent at or below the poverty level. The objectives of the project included the establishment of local identification committees to focus on community-valued characteristics; collaboration and involvement of parents, community, and staff; and development of multidimensional identification procedures that reflect a culturally relevant definition of giftedness. Lists of characteristics were identified by parents and community members from which inventories were developed to be completed by teachers, parents, and community contacts. Student self-identification forms, student portfolios, and tests of creative thinking and analogies were also included as part of the identification process. The researchers found that the major challenge to the project was the identification and implementation of nontraditional measures.

Clark and Gonzalez (1998) used a case study approach to examine the interaction of cognition, language, and culture as it relates to the identification of bilingual gifted students. Recommendations based on their findings included the cooperation of parents and teachers in the assessment process and the use of the following instruments: home language survey; parent and teacher ratings of cognitive, linguistic, and social abilities; qualitative use of English and Spanish tasks; cartoon conservation scales; language assessment scales; and the Test of Nonverbal Intelligence–2 (TONI–2). The researchers concluded that the cultural stimuli and perspectives used to interpret student performance were as important as the language used in testing.

One final study to be addressed in this identification overview was completed in 1999. Irby, Lara-Alecio, and Milke conducted a study of 175 Hispanic bilingual students in Texas to determine the degree of correlation between the Hispanic Bilingual Gifted Screening Instrument (HBGSI; Irby & Lara-Alecio, 1996) and the Naglieri Nonverbal Ability Test (NNAT; Naglieri, 1996). The HBGSI is a 78-item observational checklist stemming from an extensive review of the literature related to Hispanic gifted students. The checklist is completed by a student's classroom teacher. The HBGSI was found to significantly correlate with the NNAT. The researchers concluded that the HBGSI, presenting attributes relevant to Hispanic bilingual students, had promise as a referral instrument that would move students to an assessment phase of the identification process. "It is the intent of the HBGSI," state the researchers, "to provide bilingual teachers with a structure to make better referrals for assessment" (p. 20).

The Austin Independent School District in Austin, Texas, developed a system of identification that may prove to be a useful example for school districts addressing the unique demands of creating a system of identification of potentially gifted bilingual students. Directors of the gifted education and bilingual education programs collaborated in the development of a multiple-criteria screening profile that uses a combination of instruments recommended in the literature on bilingual gifted students. The bilingual identification profile parallels the system in place for other students, which helps ensure consistency in both identification and provision of gifted services. Measures include checklists of observed behaviors (academic and gifted characteristics), portfolios (academic traits), and standardized tests (verbal and nonverbal). Texas requires the use of multiple criteria, including data that are both quantitative and qualitative. The Austin district follows this requirement and has also carefully aligned the combination of instruments with the academic focus of its gifted program for students in kindergarten through twelfth grade. This includes the use of the Bilingual Verbal Abilities Test (1998), an instrument included in the identification process to better align bilingual gifted identification with the verbal focus of many services provided in a gifted program with an academic emphasis. The screening profile outlined in Table 33.2 is used by campus selection committees to select students for the gifted program.

Table 33.2 Screening Profile

Criteria	Maximum Score	Target Score	Student Score	Comments
NOMINATION INFORMATION				
Teacher Nomination (required—complete all):				
Adapted/Purdue Academic Scales (language arts)	60	NA		
Adapted/Purdue Academic Scales (math)	60	NA		
Adapted/Purdue Academic Scales (science)	60	NA		
Adapted/Purdue Academic Scales (social studies)	60	NA		
Parent Nomination (required)	45	NA		
Peer/Self-Nomination (circle one—optional)	60	NA		
SCREENING INFORMATION				
Raven's Progressive Matrices	100th percentile	90th percentile		

Traits, Aptitudes, Behaviors

Records score for each characteristic: range is from 2 (weak) to 10 (strong)

Motivation___   Interests___   Communication Skills___

Problem-Solving Ability___   Memory___   Inquiry___

Insight___   Reasoning___   Imagination/Creativity___

Humor___

Narrative comments:

TABS OBSERVATION PERIOD (MINIMUM OF 6 WEEKS):

Bilingual Verbal Abilities Test	Percentile	Age Equivalent	CALP* Level	Comments
Student Scores				
BVAT Narrative Notes:				
Portfolio: *Collect exemplary work in all areas*	**Average**	**Above Average**	**High**	**Comments**
Portfolio (language arts)				
Portfolio (math)				
Portfolio: *Collect exemplary work in all areas*	**Average**	**Above Average**	**High**	**Comments**
Portfolio (science)				
Portfolio (social studies)				
Portfolio Collection Period (minimum of 6 weeks):				

Additional Documented Evidence of Giftedness (Include any additional bilingual measures/documentation)

Criteria/Product/Performance	Comments/Score

*Cognitive academic language proficiency

The identification process using this profile is time consuming but allows for highly reflective selection and placement decisions requiring analysis of data collected from both listed instruments and those used in the bilingual program. Fully initiated during the 2001–2002 school year, the system holds promise in the urban district with a growing Hispanic population.

CURRICULUM, INSTRUCTION, ASSESSMENT, AND THE GIFTED BILINGUAL STUDENT

Once gifted bilingual students have been identified, a new challenge arises: selecting or designing appropriate curriculum, instruction, and assessment resources to meet the complex needs these students bring to the gifted program. Much of the early literature on bilingual gifted education focused on methods of identification. A few researchers have expanded the focus into the areas of program models, curriculum, and instruction. Some early forays into the establishment of bilingual gifted programs explored not only identification methods but also dual language approaches to giftedness with bilingual content enrichment and flexible grouping (Brumberg & Toledo, 1980; Ferguson, 1986; Roby, 1982). These programs recognized the limited availability of curriculum for bilingual gifted learners as well as the need for staff development focusing on curriculum development and instructional strategies.

Emerging research begins to reflect an intersection among best practices in general education, gifted education, and bilingual education. Granada (2002) proposes a comprehensive approach to curriculum development, instructional design, and assessment development that is based on theory and practice in gifted education, bilingual education, and multicultural education. Curriculum in bilingual gifted education should be based in sound theory, developed within a structured framework, and reflective of state and national standards. Infused in the curriculum design are multicultural and linguistic components reflective of the cultures and languages of students being served in the bilingual gifted program. This curriculum also must align with the model or models in place for the delivery of gifted services.

Instruction for the bilingual gifted student must be well designed and purposeful. Teachers of these students must avoid instruction that consists of loosely connected "gifted" activities gleaned from commercial resources or staff development workshops. Cumulative learning experiences are a necessity, particularly those that are child centered and that integrate depth and complexity in content learning and language development. The most exemplary curriculum will be rendered ineffective when paired with poor instruction, and the complex needs of bilingual gifted students do not allow for inefficient use of learning time. Learning experiences that allow bilingual/bicultural gifted students the opportunity to grow linguistically, that celebrate diversity, and that establish an atmosphere conducive to risk taking should be the prioritized instructional goal.

Granada (2002) also recommends that teachers of bilingual gifted students be proficient in multiple methods of assessment, including the use of preassessment tools. Assessment based on clear expectations becomes a cornerstone in the support of student development of advanced products and performances. Assessments should be an integral part of the instructional process, and methods to determine prior content knowledge or skill mastery prior to instruction must be used to avoid unwittingly basing instructional decisions on second-language abilities. When assessments inadvertently focus on a command of the English language, opportunities are lost to develop areas of talent.

THE BILINGUAL GIFTED STUDENT AND CREATIVITY

Gifted students come in all shapes, sizes, and colors, and each is unique. Some gifted students are highly creative, whereas others may have to exert special efforts to generate original ideas or products. The same is true for the bilingual gifted student. A significant difference between this student and his or her mono-lingual English-speaking peers lies in the multiple perspectives associated with being bicultural and the unique mental processes associated with dual language capabilities. According to Lasagabaster (2000), "Concerning the relationship between bilingualism and creativity, most studies coincide in concluding that bilingualism fosters creativity" (p. 2). Creative people are those typically described as having the ability to generate ideas with fluency, think flexibly, produce ideas and products that are original, and elaborate in a variety of ways. Cataldi (1994) indicates that dual language learning "gives rise to mental flexibility, a superiority in concept formation, and a more diversified set of mental abilities" (p. 63).

Creative and intellectual processes may merge through problem solving and allow for metacognitive refinement, which is the ability to understand and verbalize how one thinks in gifted students. Diaz (1985) proposes that knowledge of two languages enhances metalinguistic awareness, serving as a critical component in the development of intelligence. The bilingual gifted student not only can be provided the opportunity to enhance metacognitive abilities but also has the added dimensions of this metalinguistic awareness and multiple cultural perspectives. This combination facilitates rich opportunities to enhance creative thinking, provided the contexts for learning, at school and in the home, encourage creative stimulation of the imagination.

SOCIAL AND EMOTIONAL NEEDS OF THE BILINGUAL GIFTED STUDENT

The best gifted identification system aligned with a well-designed program model that delivers a rich and comprehensive bilingual/multicultural instructional program may still have a void to fill if the social and emotional needs of the students in the program are not addressed and supported. Many gifted students feel disengaged with their peers and recognize that they are different as a result of their giftedness. Asynchronous development may add to frustrations these students may experience, from the young child who reads at a very advanced level but whose hands cannot yet manipulate a pencil with ease to the gifted adolescent who may be a mature thinker but is socially immature and is dealing with the confusion of impending adulthood. Gifted students bring to the classroom very unique social and emotional needs, many of which have been documented in texts for students who are gifted. But what of the gifted student who, in addition to these complex attributes, has to deal with living in a world of two languages and two, if not more, cultures?

The bilingual gifted student faces issues that are difficult for them to understand and accept. The world in which they live in is defined by two languages, two cultures, and a continuum of multiple variables such as talents, norms, and rules. Whereas the mainstream gifted student wrestles with bringing meaning to concepts such as success, individuality, and achievement, the bilingual gifted student must view these same concepts from multiple cultural perspectives, and may struggle with the means to communicate what he or she is experiencing or needing help in understanding.

Bilingual gifted students may, at times, focus their talents on acculturation. Those that quickly adapt to the national culture and the ways of life of their peers may face conflicts with beliefs and traditions of the family and community. Competition, gender roles, and focus on the individual versus the group may increase in importance when examined through a student's multicultural lens.

Formal and informal counseling support for the bilingual gifted student may be the most effective means to address the combination of social and emotional needs of students in a gifted program. Vanderslice (1998) points out the need to provide support to students torn between competing cultures. These students may be caught between the need to demonstrate giftedness and adherence to family patterns and values. Vanderslice recommends that counselors become familiar with cultural backgrounds and values of minority groups to aid in this support. This recommendation should extend to teachers working with the students as well, and a concerted effort should be made to include a strong parental educational component as part of the bilingual gifted program.

SUMMARY AND CONCLUSION

The student who is bilingual, bicultural, and gifted presents a unique and considerable challenge, and research on this population is far from expansive. Researchers and practitioners in gifted education are focusing more and more on issues relative to these students, perhaps as an outgrowth of the projected future demographics of the United States. Reviewing the literature provides some promising recommendations for the successful development of programs to identify and serve the bilingual gifted student population.

Barkan and Bernal (1991) offer the following recommendation: "Programming for bright language minority students must be linguistically and culturally inclusive, building on the assets a child brings to school rather than denigrating the LEP child's first language or implicitly attempting to replace one language and culture with another" (p. 146).

Cohen (1990) makes the following recommendations for improvement of identification and programming for gifted language minority students:

- Broaden the concept of giftedness.
- Expand research on giftedness and minority language students.
- Employ more well-rounded assessment techniques, including the use of multiple criteria.
- Increase staff awareness of their potential for developing a gifted and talented program.
- Explore various program models.
- Increase awareness of different ways giftedness may be manifested in different populations.

A report on talent and diversity (Office of Educational Research and Improvement, 1998) suggests addressing bilingual gifted issues through a learning process.

School staff needs progressive, substantive staff development to supplement and expand their knowledge of other cultural and linguistic groups. They also need support in learning how giftedness manifests itself within cultural norms. This knowledge, when supported with opportunities to pilot new programs geared toward introducing LEP students to high-status knowledge, will aid both in the development of new identification procedures that, while perhaps imperfect, will result in expanding the numbers of LEP students participating in gifted and talented programs. (pp. 14–15)

In addition, the following basic starting points are recommended:

- Establishing a cognitive and philosophical shift that views youth—including youth not yet proficient in English—as high-ability students with outstanding talents that need multi-pronged identification procedures to identify and nurture them.
- Forging a commitment to the long-term social benefit of redesigning gifted education to include and meet the needs of students who are LEP.
- Collaborating across programs; there must be a willingness to negotiate and entertain different points of view.
- Building on strengths and program maturity.
- Establishing a clear and coherent vision of inclusive gifted education.
- Bringing the issue of students who are LEP and gifted education to a heightened level of public awareness.
- Creating an action plan with realistic timelines.
- Securing adequate teacher training and inservice programs, including training in identification procedures for bilingual education teachers. (p. 16)

The identification and program planning for gifted bilingual students is not easy. There is much to learn and researchers and educators have only begun to scratch the surface as they attempt to understand and support these unique individuals. If politics, biases, and lack of knowledge are the guide, failure is destined. However, if solutions are approached with compassion, understanding, and integrity, the path to success will yield endless benefits along the way.

REFERENCES

Barkan, J. H., & Bernal, E. M. (1991). Gifted education for bilingual and limited English proficient students. *Gifted Child Quarterly, 35*(3), 144–147.

Bernal, E. M. (1980). *Methods of identifying gifted minority students.* (ERIC Document Reproduction Service No. ED 204 418)

Bernal, E. M. (1981). *Special problems and procedures for identifying minority gifted students.* Paper presented at the Council for Exceptional Children Conference on The Exceptional Bilingual Child, New Orleans, LA. (ERIC Document Reproduction Service No. ED 203 652)

Brumberg, S. F., & Toledo, V. (1980). *Final evaluation report for the C. S. 211 bilingual gifted and talented program, 1978–1979.* (ERIC Document Reproduction Service No. ED 200 694)

Cataldi, R. J. (1994). Bilingualism and early language acquisition—great assets. *NASSP Bulletin, 78*(564), 62–64.

Clark, E. R., & Gonzalez, V. (1998). Voices and voces: Cultural and linguistic dimensions of giftedness. *Educational Horizons, 77*(1), 41–47.

Cohen, L. M. (1990). *Meeting the needs of gifted and talented minority language students.* ERIC Digest #E480. (ERIC Document Reproduction Service No. ED 321 485)

Crawford, J. (1998). Language politics in the U.S.A.: The paradox of bilingual education. *Social Justice, 25*(3), 50–69.

Diaz, R. M. (1985). *The intellectual power of bilingualism.* Paper presented at a Conference on Early Childhood First and Second Language Acquisition, Fresno, CA. (ERIC Document Reproduction Service No. ED 203 368)

Ferguson, L. (1986). A fair share: Opening doors for the gifted bilingual student. *Equity and Choice, 2*(3), 5–13.

Garcia, J. (1994). Nonstandardized instruments for the assessment of Mexican-American children in gifted/talented programs. In S. B. Garcia (Ed.), *Addressing cultural and linguistic diversity in special education: Issues and trends* (pp. 46–57). Reston, VA: The Council for Exceptional Children.

Granada, A. J. (2002). Addressing the curriculum, instruction, and assessment needs of the gifted bilingual/bicultural student. In J. A. Castellano & E. Diaz (Eds.), *Reaching new horizons: Gifted and talented education for culturally and linguistically diverse students* (pp. 133–153). Boston: Allyn & Bacon/Longman.

Irby, B. L., & Lara-Alecio, R. (1996). Attributes of Hispanic gifted bilingual students as perceived by bilingual educators in Texas. *SABE Journal, 11,* 120–142.

Irby, B. L., Lara-Alecio, R., & Milke, B. (1999). *Assessment from multiple perspectives for second language learners: An analysis of the Hispanic Bilingual Gifted Screening Instrument.* Paper presented at the Annual Meeting of the National Association for Bilingual Education, Denver, CO. (ERIC Document Reproduction Service No. ED 430 404)

Kloosterman, V. I. (1997, Spring). Building a bridge: A combined effort between gifted and bilingual education. *The National Research Center on the Gifted and Talented Newsletter,* 3–6.

Lasagabaster, D. (2000). The effects of three bilingual education models on linguistic creativity. *International Review of Applied Linguistics in Language Teaching, 38*(3/4), 213–228.

Marland, S. P. (1972). *Education of the gifted and talented.* Report to the Congress of the United States by the U.S. Commissioner of Education, Washington, DC: U.S. Government Printing Office. (ERIC Document Reproduction Service No. ED 056 243)

McLean, Z. Y. (1995). History of bilingual assessment and its impact on best practices used today. *New York State Association for Bilingual Education Journal, 10,* 6–12.

Naglieri, J. A. (1996). *Naglieri nonverbal ability test.* San Antonio, TX: Harcourt Brace.

Nelson, H. (1982). The identification of black and Hispanic talented and gifted students—grades K through 6: In search of an educational standard. In *Identifying and educating the disadvantaged gifted/talented: Proceedings from the Fifth National Conference on Disadvantaged Gifted/Talented* (pp. 63–90). Ventura, CA: Ventura County Superintendent of Schools.

Office of Educational Research and Improvement. (1998). *Talent and diversity: The emerging world of limited English proficient students in gifted education.* (MIS Publication No. ORAD-98-1100). Washington, DC: U.S. Department of Education.

Paulson, F. L., & Paulson, P. R. (1991). *The ins and outs of using portfolios to assess performance (rev. ed.).* Paper presented at the Joint Annual Meeting of the National Council of Measurement in Education and the National Association of Test Directors, Chicago, IL. (ERIC Document Reproduction Service No. ED 334 250)

Reyes, E. L., Fletcher, R., & Paez, D. (1996). Developing local multidimensional screening procedures for identifying giftedness among Mexican American border population. *Roeper Review, 18*(3), 208–211.

Roby, W. (1982). *1981–82 project evaluation for Encendiendo Una Llama: A program for bilingual gifted and talented students.* (ERIC Document Reproduction Service No. ED 227 688)

Vanderslice, R. (1998). Hispanic children and giftedness: Why the difficulty in identification? *The Delta Kappa Gamma Bulletin, 64*(3), 18–23.

ESL STUDENTS IN GIFTED EDUCATION

Nilda Aguirre

It is the supreme art of the teacher to awaken joy in creative expression and knowledge.
—Albert Einstein

It is paradoxical that many educators continue to believe that English language proficiency is essential prior to placement in gifted programs. Giftedness is not a trait inherent to native English speakers. Gifted programs must mirror the population of any given community. Therefore, if there has been an increase of minorities in a particular community, there should be a proportionate increase in representation of this same group in gifted education. National studies have repeatedly documented that students who are limited English proficient (LEP) are grossly underrepresented in gifted education.

Population forecasts indicate that the number of language minority student enrollments exceeds projections. The number of students who are LEP has increased dramatically in recent years, by 967,670 in 6 years according to the nation's state education agencies (SEA). In addition, Spanish language students who are LEP represent almost three quarters of the overall population (Fleischman & Hopstock, 1993). According to a report published by the U.S. Department of Education (1988), *Talent and Diversity: The Emerging World of Limited English Proficient Students in Gifted Education,* Hispanic students who are LEP are hindered by current gifted and talented criteria most likely because they come from conditions of poverty. The challenge for the educational system is to establish a cognitive and philosophical shift that will help overcome these barriers without reducing expectations.

Early intervention is crucial if the number of students who are gifted LEP is to increase. A multifaceted identification procedure should be added to the language assessment test that determines language proficiency. Providing adequate assessment of student abilities, strengths and passions will direct the educational plan and ensure that needs are met early.

DISPELLING THE MYTHS

Many myths surround students who are gifted LEP. According to one of the common myths, students who are LEP must exit English for speakers of other language (ESOL) classes before they are tested and placed in the gifted program. Educators, researchers, and policymakers need to design a program for students who are gifted LEP to be placed and served as they acquire English proficiency. This is not a novel idea. Many are implementing this concept and have created "pregifted" classes where potential students who are gifted LEP are nurtured and challenged. The learning environment is demanding and the expectations are high. Students are not held back; they are propelled forward. English language proficiency becomes the byproduct of this innovative approach. Children are exposed to a language rich environment that integrates critical and high-order thinking, as well as the use of multiple intelligences. This concept is explored later in this chapter. There are additional myths that have been associated with students who are gifted LEP, including the following:

- Students who are LEP are less capable and not able to keep up with the other students who are gifted.
- Students who are LEP are different and will have to acculturate before they can understand aspects of giftedness valued by the dominant culture.

- Parents of students who are LEP are not as involved as parents of other children who are gifted.
- Students who are LEP are accustomed to working in groups and will not do well when they have projects that require independent research and work.
- Students who are LEP have accents and limited vocabularies; therefore, they are unable to verbalize or articulate like other children who are gifted.

Bridging the ESL and gifted divide will contribute to dispelling the myths surrounding students who are gifted LEP. Awareness is crucial in order to accomplish this. Current educational reform aims to improve the academic achievement of all students. Access to challenging curriculum and high-quality academic programs are part of the plan. The groundwork has been initiated for educators who have considered certification in both ESOL and gifted education. These teachers now have an opportunity to bridge the divide. The reform must develop from within the fields of ESL and gifted education. Conceptualizing a program to serve students who are both LEP and gifted should be the rule, not the exception.

For some time, educators have expressed frustration at not being able to identify students who are LEP and who demonstrate gifted ability in class. They argue that using standardized intelligence quotient (IQ) tests as primary measures of giftedness does not take into consideration the linguistic and cultural differences of students who are LEP. Renzulli (1978) indicated that "more creative persons come from below the 95th percentile than above it, and if such cut-off scores are needed to determine entrance into special programs, we may be guilty of actually discriminating against persons who have the highest potential for high levels of accomplishment" (p. 1782). Three percent is a conservative estimate of the population that is considered gifted. However, studies indicate that LEP and other minority groups fall below 50 percent of the expected numbers (Chan & Kitano, 1986). Differences in learning styles largely contribute to underrepresentation. Different cultures have different values. That is, they are not automatically aligned with the dominant culture. For example, Hispanic children differ from the dominant culture in that they are raised to value and respect their elders and to respect teachers and authority. This could hinder a student's performance if the teacher is playing devil's advocate and expects students to contradict or challenge him or her. These children are perceived as uncooperative or not participating in the activity, which may result in lower grades. The dominant culture values competition, independence, and initiative. Many minority students possess special talents that are valued within their own culture; however, these special talents are not recognized by the dominant culture as signs of giftedness.

Most of this author's experience with students who are gifted LEP is a result of working with project GOTCHA (Galaxies of Thinking and Creative Heights of Achievement), a former Title VII academic excellence program funded by the Office of Bilingual Education and Minority Language Affairs (OBEMLA) under the U.S. Department of Education. Project GOTCHA was developed to meet the needs of high-ability learners who were not proficient in English. For nine years (1987–1996), project GOTCHA was disseminated in more than 15 states. Project GOTCHA's identification component consisted of a multifaceted approach that took into account parent or community nominations, teacher nominations, analysis of creative ability, Renzulli's Behavioral Checklist (adapted), Torrance Test of Creative Thinking Skills, and leadership ability. The results are recorded on a matrix and the ESL/gifted committee would meet and determine eligibility for placement based on the points obtained. As project disseminator, this author collected the data and interviewed the teachers implementing the program. As a result, a list of characteristics representative of students who are gifted LEP was generated. Table 34.1 presents the list of these characteristics.

ISSUES OF TESTING, EVALUATION, AND ASSESSMENT

Schools systems must examine their current criteria when identifying students who are LEP. Federal law requires screening students who are LEP for English language proficiency when they enter school. Screening is typically done by having parents complete a home language survey during the registration

Table 34.1   Characteristics of Students Who Are Linguistically and Culturally Diverse

- Eagerly shares his/her native culture.
- Shows strong desire to teach peers words from his/her native language.
- Has a strong sense of pride in his/her cultural heritage and ethnic background.
- Eagerly translates for peers and adults.
- Balances appropriate behaviors expected of the native culture and the new culture.
- Possesses advanced knowledge of idioms and native dialects with ability to translate and explain meanings in English.
- Understands jokes and puns related to cultural differences.
- Reads in native language two grades above his/her grade level.
- Functions at language proficiency levels above that of nongifted peers who are LEP.
- Able to code switch.
- Possesses cross-cultural flexibility.
- Has a sense of global community and an awareness of other cultures and languages.
- Learns a second or third language at an accelerated pace (formal or informal).
- Excels in math achievement tests.
- Demonstrates strengths in the creative areas of fluency, elaboration, originality, and flexibility.
- Demonstrates leadership abilities in nontraditional settings: playground, home, church, clubs, and so on.

From *Characteristics of Students Who Are Linguistically and Culturally Diverse*, by N. Aguirre and N. Hernandez, 1999, Baton Rouge, LA: Modern Language Services.

process. At the same time, further assessments should be conducted to determine any other special needs a child might have.

> Where inability to speak and understand the English language excludes national origin minority group children from effective participation in the educational program offered by a school district, the district must take affirmative steps to rectify the language deficiency in order to open its instructional program to these students. Any ability grouping or tracking system employed by the school system to deal with the special language skill needs of national origin minority group children must be designed to meet such language skill needs as soon as possible, and must not operate as an educational dead-end or permanent track. (*Lau v. Nichols*, 414 US 563)

This citation is from the landmark decision by the Supreme Court in the case of *Lau v. Nichols*. It is important to acknowledge that school systems must avoid practices that exclude "national origin minority group children from effective participation in the educational program offered by a school district." *Effective participation* can be interpreted as providing students who are LEP with access to gifted educational programs. Legal history calls for students who are LEP to be served. One question to be asked is, Are teachers only referring bilingual or ESL students to ESL/bilingual or two-way immersion programs? Or, can one interpret that to mean, *all* educational programs available to *all* children. Many have interpreted this ruling to mean special programs that teach English. Think outside the box for a moment. What precludes a school system from developing a program within a program to address the needs of children who are gifted LEP? A deeper understanding is needed of all educational programs to ensure that all the needs of students who are LEP are met. This can be easily accomplished if, as part of the ESL certification requirements imposed by most states, a course is developed that provides in-depth information regarding special services for students who are learning disabled, as well as those who are gifted and talented. ESL certification courses lack information about other needs of children who are LEP. All ESL/bilingual programs should consider a gifted and talented component.

In the quest to find the most appropriate evaluation process to use with students who are LEP and are referred for gifted education, many overlook the obvious: the examiner. The person administering the test is critical in determining whether a student performs at a maximum level, which affects eligibility. Simple nonverbal communication by the test administrator can cause interference, which suggests to the child, "This is too difficult for you; you can't speak English; remember, you only have this one chance." The Kaufman Brief Intelligence Test (K-BIT) is widely used by some systems as a prescreening measure; the instructions clearly state that if a child is not proficient in English he or she should be allowed to answer those items in his or her heritage language. Most examiners will not take the time to provide the opportunity for fair testing. It takes longer and requires a translator. Those who have worked with children who are LEP and have tested them successfully routinely conclude that different methods of assessment are crucial if one is to get a true picture of a child's abilities. The federal government does not mandate criteria for assessing giftedness. This occurs at the state or local level. Those policies need to be reviewed to determine if they are the *best* policies. If a local school system has experienced a growth in the language minority population, it may be time to revise the criteria so they are more inclusive and to cast a wider, deeper net. The results of ignoring these evaluations is potentially devastating to the child and to society. Talents will not be nurtured. Motivation and enthusiasm will be squelched. Creativity will be ignored. And, potentially, children may become discipline problems and possibly drop out of school. We will then conclude that the system has failed them. They have not been challenged or engaged in the educational process. They may gravitate to outside influences, such as gangs, where they can demonstrate gifted behaviors, such as leadership. This is not meant to alarm, but to alert, all that the educational system must tailor programs to meet the needs of the fast-growing minority student population who are also gifted. There is a universal myth that "gifted kids will get it on their own," but nothing is further from the truth!

THE BENEFITS OF PREGIFTED PROGRAMS

The importance of adopting a "pregifted program" for students who are potentially gifted LEP must be recognized. Findings from sites implementing "pregifted programs" affirm the need for these programs and reveal the success of students who were fortunate enough to participate in them. School system leaders who believe in gifted education for children who are LEP have shared some of the ideas that made their programs successful. They suggest the following criteria in order for the program to succeed: (1) ESL teachers who are also certified or knowledgeable about gifted characteristics and strategies, (2) ensuring that all administrators and staff assist students in reaching their maximum potential, (3) a learning climate conducive for academic success, and (4) a collective belief that the myths surrounding students who are gifted LEP are false.

Project GOTCHA advocates pregifted programs as viable solutions for gifted students who are LEP to achieve and have their needs met. Project IGNITE (Identifying Gifted Students in and through ESOL), a Title VII program enhancement grant, has been very successful in placing gifted children who are LEP in gifted classes after 2 years in the pregifted program. More than 34 percent of the students who participated in project IGNITE in the East Baton Rouge Parish School System were eligible for the district's gifted and talented program. School systems that have adopted this concept find that the passage rate of minority students exposed to gifted curriculum and strategies, integrated with ESL methods, far exceeds the traditional approach of waiting for students to exit ESOL prior to referring them for gifted programming. Table 34.2 contains a report of schools that submitted data as a result of having implemented project GOTCHA. It includes cumulative totals of students impacted per state during the years of implementation. The data reflect that 41 percent of the students referred for evaluation met the eligibility criteria set forth by the state. In the early 1990s, the mindset of many in education was to only refer students for gifted programs once they exited the ESOL program. This practice resulted in students who are LEP not being reported as such. Rather, they were reported by ethnicity only.

CURRICULUM AND INSTRUCTION FOR GIFTED LEP STUDENTS

Curriculum and instruction are crucial to the success and achievement of gifted students who are LEP. It is not easy to teach gifted children. They question, challenge, investigate, explore, take risks, and

Table 34.2

States	Schools Implementing GOTCHA	Teachers Trained	Year	Total Students Served	Year	Parents Trained	Year	Evaluated for District's Gifted Program	Students with LEP Meeting Eligibility
Florida	12	28	87–96	2,520	90–96	1,800	94–96	126	48
California	4	5	90–96	360	90–96	150	95–96	30	6
Iowa	1	2	92–96	28	92–96	10	95–96	0	0
Louisiana	3	6	93–96	54	93–96	38	95–96	4	3
Michigan	2	3	93–96	32	93–96	18	95–96	4	3
New York	18	24	92–94	186	92–94	95	93–94	18	15
Georgia	2	2	92–96	18	N/A	0	—	0	0
Nevada	1	1	87–90	8	N/A	0	—	0	0
Texas	5	5	90–92	68	N/A	0	—	9	2
N. Dakota	1	1	95–97	5	N/A	0	—	0	0
Washington	2	2	95–97	5	N/A	0	—	0	0
Illinois	2	2	90–93	43	90–93	35	92–93	5	4
Total Impact	53	81	87–96	3,340	87–96	2,146		196	81

Note: The numbers in column 5 are the total numbers of students who were served during the life of the project.

The number of students referred for evaluation passed the rigorous screening criteria set by their state or local system. Many parents did not give permission for their children to be screened. In some cases the teachers did not refer students until they exited ESOL. Some schools chose not to refer students for gifted and kept the students in the pregifted program.

expect more. Gifted children who are LEP have the same desires as other children but with an added dimension: learning English, and learning it well. Unlike most white middle-class gifted children, many gifted students who are LEP are not perfectionists. This may explain why a gifted child who is LEP does not speak in front of peers but can still achieve straight A's every time he or she takes a test.

Gifted students who are LEP require a curriculum that integrates gifted strategies and provides for accelerated English learning practices. Most gifted programs are accelerated and the curriculum is often compacted to provide opportunities for extensions and enrichment. The same concept holds true for gifted children who are LEP. That is, they acquire English language proficiency twice as fast as their nongifted LEP peers. Findings from project GOTCHA and project IGNITE concur that gifted children who are LEP are capable of completing ESL programs in less time if they are taught using accelerated English instruction combined with gifted strategies. This is substantiated by the results obtained from project IGNITE, where 565 students were screened over a period of 2 years. Ninety-two students were eligible to participate in the program. During the school year, these students were instructed in small groups. Each student served as a catalyst for the other. Project IGNITE provided a forum for acquiring English proficiency in an accelerated academic program that also emphasized creative problem solving, higher-order thinking skills, and academics integrated with the arts. This unique combination not only kept these students engaged but also empowered them to create, inquire, and research on their own. When the program ended 32 students were eligible for participation in the district's gifted and talented programs. The process is not easy. All involved need to support the mission of identifying and instructing gifted students who are LEP.

THE ROLE OF LANGUAGE

Pride in one's cultural heritage and native language is one of the characteristics often found in gifted students who are LEP. In working with gifted children who are LEP, this author found that they sought opportunities to talk about their country, to teach their friends words from their language, and demonstrated interest in learning more about their country through projects. Acceptance of children's culture and language sends a powerful message. Not only does it validate feelings of self-worth but it also teaches them to respect and accept other cultures and languages as well. When children are learning English, there is a period of transition in which they feel empowered by being able to speak a language their parent(s) might not speak or understand. If teachers and peers fail to respect a child's language, the situation could backfire at home where the child chooses only to speak English and not to communicate with parents or other family members. Parents may feel embarrassed that their child negates the culture and language and may try to speak in English, however limited, to the child. This creates two problems: (1) The English spoken by the parent at home may not be standard English and (2) the child will miss out on continued proficiency in his or her native language. The ramifications are damaging to the child, parents, family, and society. The child might have eventually been fluent in two or more languages, thereby having been afforded additional opportunities in the job market as an adult. Parents have expressed their disappointment in teachers and administrators not capitalizing on the strength of the diversity that exists at the school their child attends. Diversity is the strength of the United States. The United States is a tapestry of cultures and languages that form patterns of peace and beauty. Gifted students who are LEP who are taught to value and respect their culture and language contribute to the tapestry.

Ensuring the successful retention of students with English as a second language (ESL) in gifted education depends largely on the support that students receive while they are in the program. Some ESL students lead very unstable lives because parents move to available work locations thereby causing children to change schools. In many instances, the inability to retain gifted ESL students is beyond the parameters of the school. Parental participation is crucial, but so is the involvement of the school in the community. The school and the community must unite to function as an entity. Issues that are important to parents should be brought forth at PTA meetings. The administration needs to work hard at knowing each family and recognizing when a family has problems and might need help. There needs to be a bond between parents, the school, the child, the teacher, and the administration. As the Chinese proverb says, it takes a whole village to educate one child.

The family needs to believe that they are an integral part of the educational system, and they need to understand the benefits that their child will receive in a gifted program. Parent training sessions and conference meetings are essential in keeping parents informed of their child's progress and potential. A caring environment plays an important part in retaining students in programs. Gifted programs are no different. Gifted ESL students must believe that they are accomplishing their goals and fulfilling their needs.

GIFTED LEP STUDENTS: HAVING THEIR SAY

Following are some of the thoughts, comments, suggestions, and warnings offered by students interviewed over the years.

> I love my gifted class. I feel important when I know the answers. I like my teacher. She makes school fun. (Alicia, second grade, Miami-Dade County, Florida)

> I wish my parents would understand what I do in school. They think we play all day. Being gifted means that your teacher thinks up all different ways of doing stuff so we don't get bored. (Thomas, second grade, Dade County, Florida)

> If I could just be in a gifted class that lasts all day. I get so bored in my regular class. The teacher repeats things over and over again. I lose interest many times. I love my gifted class. That's where I belong. (Maria Elena, seventh grade, Lee County, Florida)

> I would like for all teachers to interview us and figure out how we like to learn and what we want to learn. School would be much more interesting. Isn't that what they do in college? (Chamele, fifth grade, Broward County, Florida)

> I love to make puppets, write my own scripts, choose the music, design the stage, create the program, to sum it all up ... I like to do my own thing, and the best thing is that my teacher lets me. (Kemery, third grade, Broward County, Florida)

> Everyone thinks that being gifted means you get straight A's. It's not about grades, it's about what I like to learn. I like my friends in gifted. They don't make fun of how I speak. I have been in America for 2 years and speaking English is very hard for me. That's why I love to write. No one hears me mispronounce words. (Abel, eighth grade, De Anza, California)

> I don't like being in gifted. My teacher goes too fast. I can't understand. My parents say to me that I am smart and will do well, but I am scared of failing. I will try very hard to learn quickly. I just need a little more time. (Mathis, sixth grade, Broward County, Florida)

> When I go to college I want to teach gifted kids like myself. I will know how to understand children who come from Mexico and are gifted. I can make a change for the better. (Melissa, fourth grade, Fabens Independent School District, Texas)

> If I could change one thing in life it would be the following: I would want my parents to have had the opportunity to study so they can get a good job and not have to move all the time. I like being in gifted at this school. I hope papa keeps his job for a long time. (Jaime, sixth grade, Yakima, Washington)

These are testimonials from students who were once served in gifted classes or in pregifted programs. These students are concerned about the future of their families. They crave stability and profess a desire to continue their education. I was inspired by these children to continue disseminating information about gifted education for ESL students. Many educators are concerned with teaching children who are LEP English. I would like to encourage educators to search deeper and allow students' passions to flourish. Learning English should not be the focus of any child's education.

SUMMARY AND CONCLUSION

Identifying gifted students who are LEP is only the tip of the iceberg. Gifted students who are LEP should be provided with an individualized education plan to meet their academic needs. The educational progress of these students depends on educators making the children's educational experiences relevant and meaningful. Gifted and talented individuals have shaped the world: Albert Einstein, Wolfgang Amadeus Mozart, Pablo Picasso, Henry Ford, Simon Bolivar, and Mohandas Gandhi are only a few. Gifted and talented students of today will shape the world of tomorrow. The time has come to combine gifted and ESL programs. Education has seen many changes in the past decade. The "educational revolution," as I like to call it, has intensified the teaching profession, making all reach and teach like never before. Educators and all stakeholders must embrace these challenges and strive to create a community of learners where each child can reach his or her potential.

REFERENCES

Chan, K. S., & Kitano, M. K. (1986). Demographic characteristics of exceptional Asian students. In M. K. Kitano & P. C. Chinn (Eds.), *Exceptional Asian children and youth* (pp. 1–11). Reston, VA: The Council for Exceptional Children.

Fleischman, H., & Hopstock, P. (1993). *Descriptive study of services to limited English proficient students Volume 1: Summary of findings and conclusions*. Arlington, VA: Development Associates.

Lau v. Nichols, 414 U.S. 563 (1974).

Project Ignite. (1999). *Identifying gifted LEP students in and through ESOL*. Title VII Enhancement Grant awarded to East Baton Rouge Parish School System. U.S. Department of Education: Office of Bilingual Education and Language Minority Affairs.

Renzulli, J. S. (1978). What makes giftedness? Re-examining a definition. *Phi Delta Kappan, 60*(3), 180–184, 1782.

U.S. Department of Education. (1998). *Talent and diversity: The emerging world of limited English proficient students in gifted education*. Washington, DC: U.S. Government Printing Office.

Zappia, I. A. (1989). Identification of gifted Hispanic students: A multidimensional view. In C. J. Maker & S. W. Schiever (Eds.), *Defensible programs for gifted students from underserved populations: Cultural and ethnic minorities* (pp. 10–26). Austin: PRO-ED.

CHAPTER 35

GAY, LESBIAN, BISEXUAL, AND TRANSGENDERED (GLBT) DIVERSE LEARNERS

By Ben C. Nworie, Ph.D., M.Div., CRC, LPC
Assistant Professor of Special Education, APU
Dr. Nworie is a Licensed Professional Counselor, a Certified
Rehabilitation Counselor, and a Behavior Specialist.

In the last decade and a half, there has been a significant increase in attention given both in schools and in society to the issue of gay, lesbian, bisexual, and transgendered (GLBT) youth as well as youth who are curious about their sexual identity (Salend, 2005). There have been repeated reports of various forms of unfair treatment against this population of students. Some examples of this unfair, discriminatory treatment include: verbal ridicule such as name calling (for example, such names as "fag", "faggot", or "gay"), damage of their property, bias-related physical assaults, and sometimes alienation by friends and family (Cohn, 2006; Salend, 2005). These harsh treatments against the GLBT young learners are associated with significant adverse consequences in their experience. For example, it is estimated that as a result of their isolation and victimization, nearly 50 to 80% of GLBT youth have had suicidal thoughts while nearly 30 to 40% have had suicidal attempts (Grant & Sleeter, 2007; Salend, 2005).

Significantly higher incidents of depression, hopelessness, and suicidal inclinations are reported among GLBT youth than among their heterosexual peers. Also, GLBT young people are more vulnerable to drug use and abuse, more vulnerable to forced or coerced teenage sexual encounters, and more likely than non-GLBT teens to become victims of sexual assault or assault with a deadly weapon (Grant & Sleeter, 2007; Gutierrez, 2006).

What are the impacts of the anti-homosexual bias, and the GLBT lifestyle, on the educational experiences of the GLBT youth? One obvious negative educational impact is the unequal access by the GLBT young people to social and educational resources. This example from Cohn, (2006) is a pertinent illustration of the point. Regardless of a boy's actual sexual orientation, if he shows extreme giftedness in an area of learning, acting, or caring that is thought to belong predominantly to girls, the boy is likely to hear discouraging comments or rumors from his peers about not being boy enough or being too girlish for them. In the same way, a girl who has extraordinary giftedness in academic skills or endeavors considered to belong mainly to boys, such as mathematical reasoning, engineering, and athletic skills, will in all likelihood quickly learn from her schoolmates that she is on the queer side or that she is not girl enough for them. This is the main focus of this chapter. Overall the chapter seeks to draw attention to the problem, and to promote dialogue from a Christian worldview point on the difficulties which prevent the bridging of the educational disparities.

THE ORIGINS OF HOMOSEXUALITY

In many cultures around the world, people seem to have shown a reluctance or shyness about openly discussing the topic of human sexuality (Sexton, Alexander, & Mease, 2004). It is common knowledge that many parents do not provide their children the sex education they need at home. For example, 66% of girls surveyed in a *Parade* survey felt that they had not been properly taught at home about sex.

This reluctance or wariness about open sexual conversations has certainly been the case until very recently with regard to the open discussion of homosexuality. There have been some recent discussions of the origin of homosexuality which trace it to the human biological systems (Gutierrez, 2006). Some of the studies cited to support this viewpoint did not provide conclusive evidence. That is why Dobson (2001) categorically states that "there are no respected geneticists in the world today who claim to have found a so-called 'gay gene' or other indicators of genetic transmission." Dobson, however, concedes that there may be "some kind of biological predisposition or an inherited temperament that makes one vulnerable to environmental influences" (p. 116). Though there has been a lot of information put out and a lot of effort made to educate the public about the biological origins of, and therefore the irreversibility of, homosexuality, Dobson's contention is that people are not born homosexual. He adds the following points as further evidence that homosexuality is not genetic:

> There is further convincing evidence that it is not. For example, since identical twins share the same chromosomal pattern, or DNA, the genetic contributions are exactly the same within each of the pairs. Therefore, if one twin is "born" homosexual, then the other should inevitably have that characteristic too. That is not the case. When one twin is homosexual, the probability is only 50 percent that the other will have the same condition. Something else must be operating.
>
> Furthermore, if homosexuality were specifically inherited, it would tend to be eliminated from the human gene pool because those who have it tend not to reproduce. Any characteristic that is not passed along to the next generation eventually dies with the individual who carries it.
>
> Not only does homosexuality continue to exist in nations around the world, it flourishes in some cultures. If the condition resulted from inherited characteristics, it would be a "constant" across time. Instead, there have been societies through the ages, such as Sodom and Gomorrah and the ancient Greek and Roman empires, where homosexuality reached epidemic proportions. The historical record tells us that those cultures and many others gradually descended into depravity, as the apostle Paul described in Romans 1, resulting in sexual perversion in all its varieties. That ebbing and flowing with the life cycle of cultures is not the way inherited characteristics are expressed in the human family.
>
> Finally, if homosexuality were genetically transmitted, it would be inevitable, immutable, irresistible, and untreatable. Fortunately, it is not. Prevention is effective. Change is possible. Hope is available. And Christ is in the business of healing. Here again, gay and lesbian organizations and the media have convinced the public that being homosexual is as predetermined as one's race and that nothing can be done about it. That is simply not true. There are eight hundred known former gay and lesbian individuals today who have escaped from the homosexual lifestyle and found wholeness in their newfound heterosexuality.
>
> . . . . I would be less than honest if I didn't admit that homosexuality is not easily overcome and that those who try often struggle mightily. But it would be equally dishonest to say that there is no hope for those who want to change. Credible research indicates otherwise. Psychologist George Rekers says there is considerable evidence that of sexual orientation is possible—with or without psychiatric inter. He wrote, "In a sizable number of cases . . . the gender-identity disorder resolves fully."
>
> Dr. Robert L. Spitzer, a psychiatric professor at Columbia University, created a firestorm in May 2001, when he released the results of his research at a meeting of the American Psychiatric Association. Spitzer, who had spearheaded the APA's decision in 1973 to declassify homosexuality as a mental-health disorder, says his findings "show some people can change from gay to straight, and we ought to acknowledge that."

To further illustrate his points regarding the origin of homosexuality, Dobson quotes from clinical psychologist Dr. Nicolosi's book, entitled *Preventing Homosexuality: A Parents Guide*, the following words:

> There are certain signs of prehomosexuality which are easy to recognize, and the signs come early in the child's life. Most come under the heading of "cross-gender behavior." There are five markers to [diagnose] a child with "gender identity disorder." They are:
>
> 1. Repeatedly stated desire to be, or insistence that he or she is, the other sex.
> 2. In boys, preference for cross-dressing, or simulating female attire. In girls, insistence on wearing only stereotypical masculine clothing.

3. Strong and persistent preference for cross-sexual roles in make-believe play, or persistent fantasies of being the other sex.
4. Intense desire to participate in stereotypical games and pastimes of the other sex.
5. Strong preference for playmates of the other sex.

The onset of most cross-gender behavior occurs during the pre-school years, between the ages of two and four. You needn't worry about occasional cross-dressing. You should become concerned, though, when your little boy continues doing so and, at the same time, begins to acquire some other alarming habits. He may start using his mother's makeup. He may avoid other boys in the neighborhood and their rough-and-tumble activities and prefer being with his sisters instead, who play with dolls and dollhouses. Later he may start speaking in a high-pitched voice. . . . In one study of sixty effeminate boys aged four to eleven, 98 percent of them engaged in cross-dressing, and 83 percent said they wished they had been born a girl.

The fact is, there is a high correlation between feminine behavior in boyhood and adult homosexuality. . . . Perhaps you are concerned about your child and his or her "sexual development." Maybe your son or daughter is saying things like, "I must be gay," or "I'm bisexual." You've found same-sex porn in his room or evidence that he has accessed it on the Internet. You've found intimate journal entries about another girl in her diary. The most important message I can offer to you is that there is no such thing as a "gay child" or a "gay teen." [But] left untreated, studies show these boys have a 75 percent chance of becoming homosexual or bisexual.

It is important to understand, however, that most of my homosexual clients were not explicitly feminine when they were children. More often, they displayed a "nonmasculinity" that set them painfully apart from other boys: unathletic—somewhat passive, unaggressive and uninterested in rough-and-tumble play. A number of them had traits that could be considered gifts: bright, precocious, social and relational, and artistically talented. These characteristics had one common tendency: they set them apart from their male peers and contributed to a distortion in the development of their normal gender identity.

Because most of these men hadn't been explicitly feminine boys, their parents had not suspected anything was wrong, so they had made no efforts at seeking therapy. Many clients have told me, "If only—back then when I was a child—someone had understood the doubts, the feeling of not belonging—and tried to help me." . . .

In my opinion, the father plays an essential role in a boy's normal development as a man . . . . Mothers make boys. Fathers make men. . . .The late Irving Bieber, a prominent researcher, observed that prehomosexual boys are sometimes the victims of their parents' unhappy marital relationship. In a scenario where Mom and Dad are battling, one way Dad can "get even" with Mom is by emotionally abandoning their son. . . .

For a variety of reasons, some mothers also have a tendency to prolong their sons' infancy. A mother's intimacy with her son is primal, complete, exclusive; theirs is a powerful bond which can deepen into what psychiatrist Robert Stoller calls a "blissful symbiosis." But the mother may be inclined to hold onto her son in what becomes an unhealthy mutual dependency, especially if she does not have a satisfying, intimate relationship with the boy's father. She can put too much energy into the boy, using him to fulfill her own needs in a way that is not good for him. In reparative therapy [a psychologist's name for treatment of homosexuals], effeminate boys yearn for what is called "the three A's." They are: their father's affection, attention and approval.

If [a father] wants his son to grow up straight, he has to break the mother-son connection that is proper to infancy but not in the boy's interest after the age of three. In this way, the father has to be a model, demonstrating that it is possible for his son to maintain a loving relationship with this woman, his mom, while maintaining his own independence. In this way, the father is a healthy buffer between mother and son.

. . . "Masculinity is an achievement." . . . growing up straight isn't something that happens. It requires good parenting. It requires societal support. And it takes time. The crucial years are from one and a half to three years old, but the optimal time is before age twelve. Once mothers and fathers recognize the problems their children face, agree to work together to help resolve them, and seek the guidance and expertise of a psychotherapist who believes change is possible, there is great hope.

For his conclusion, Dobson adds:

The bottom line is that homosexuality is not primarily about sex. It is about everything else, including loneliness, rejection, affirmation, intimacy, identity, relationships, parenting, self-hatred, gender confusion, and a search for belonging. This explains why the homosexual experience is so intense—and why there is such anger expressed against those who are perceived as disrespecting gays and lesbians or making their experience more painful. I suppose if we who are straight had walked in the shoes of those in that "other world," we would be angry too . . . another major cause of gender identity disorder . . . results from early sexual abuse. One study indicated that fully 30 percent of homosexuals say they were exploited sexually as a child, many of them repeatedly. That experience can be devastating, and depending on when it occurs, it can be life changing.

HOMOSEXUALITY AND THE CHRISTIAN RESPONSE

Because of the heightened attention to this issue in education as well as society, and because of its relevance to multicultural education, as well as the education of diverse learners, it is necessary to give the topic some attention from a Christian world-view approach. The Bible in several places says homosexuality is wrong (Lev. 18:22; Lev. 20:13; 1 Cor. 6:9–10, Rom. 1:26–28). The Bible, however, also lists a number of other things that are equally wrong such as lying, cheating, committing adultery, covetousness, and others. Christians are not called to throw stones at people who do these wrong things; Christians are all called to be a community of love. The command is to "love our neighbors as we love ourselves." However, love does not mean glamorizing sin, or compromising the Christian witness; it means to be understanding, to be tolerant, and to be accepting of people, not for what they do, but for who they are. Jesus did not condemn the Samaritan woman with a less than perfect sexual history (John 4). He does not condemn those who wrestle with the lifestyle issues that he has not endorsed in his teachings. Instead, he genuinely reaches out to them and makes a difference in their lives.

REFERENCES

Cohn, S. (2006). The gay gifted learner: Facing the challenge of homophobia and antihomosexual bias in schools. In D. Capuzzi & D. Gross (Ed.), *Youth at risk: A prevention resource for counselors, teachers, and parents* (4th ed., pp. 123–134). New Jersey: Prentice Hall.

Dobson, J. (2001). *Bringing up boys: Practical advice and encouragement for those shaping the next generation of men.* Wheaton, IL: Tyndale House Publishers, Inc.

Grant, C. A., & Sleeter, C. E. (2007). *Doing multicultural education for achievment and equity.* New York: Routledge.

Gutierrez, F. J. (2006). Counseling queer youth: Preventing another Matthew Shepard story. In D. Capuzzi & D. Gross (Ed.), *Youth at risk: A prevention resource for counselors, teachers, and parents* (4th ed., pp. 331–371). New Jersey: Prentice Hall.

Salend, S. J. (2005). *Creating inclusive classrooms: Effective and reflective practices* (5th ed.). Upper Saddle River, NJ: Merrill/Prentice Hall.

Sexton, T. L., Alexander, J. F., & Mease, A. L. (2004). Levels of evidence for the models and mechanisms of therapeutic change in family and couple therapy. In M. J. Lambert (Ed.), *Bergin and Garfield's handbook of psychotherapy and behavior change* (5th ed., pp. 590–646). New York: Wiley.

COUNSELING QUEER* YOUTH: PREVENTING ANOTHER MATTHEW SHEPARD STORY

Fernando J. Gutiérrez

Queer adolescents are the least visible of the adolescent minority groups. This invisibility is a significant problem for them because they have to live hidden lives, and clinicians have difficulty identifying struggles these youth may be having as a result of their sexual orientation (O'Connor, 1992). The focus in working with queer adolescents has generally been on assisting these adolescents to cope with and adjust to their sexual orientation, which makes the adolescent the identified "client."

However, to continue addressing only the psychological maladjustment is like treating the symptom rather than the cause. Many of the issues troubling queer youth are the result of living in a society that stigmatizes and marginalizes them (Hersh-berger & D'Augelli, 2000). Hershberger and D'Augelli attributed the source of this stigmatization and marginalization to a motive by some members of society to force queer youth to internalize this disdain so as to force them to rid themselves of their queer feelings and identity and replace them with socially acceptable heterosexuality. Hershberger and D'Augelli concluded that, in counseling queer youth, it is not the queer identity that needs to be repaired but the hostility expressed against it.

The purpose of this chapter is to discuss the prevention needs of queer youth and the interventions that counselors can make at the individual, organizational, and societal levels to change the cultural context of queer youth to prevent more deaths of innocent persons, such as Matthew Shepard, who are victimized because of ignorance and intolerance just for being who they are. (Matthew Shepard, a queer youth from Laramie, Wyoming, was killed by two young assailants because of his sexual orientation. He was taken to a remote location, tied to a fence, beaten and bludgeoned, and left to die.)

Queer teenagers face several problems: deterioration of academic performance, homelessness, substance abuse, arrests for criminal activity, sexual victimization, sexually transmitted diseases, and attempted suicides (Herr, 1997; Remafedi, 1987). As counselors we need to treat these adolescents; however, the problems these adolescents face do not stem from an intrapsychic psychopathology but from adjustment reactions and responses to victimization by society (Hershberger & D'Augelli, 1995; Savin-Williams, 1994).

Other stressors for queer youth are the assumptions of others, such as society, family, and friends, that queer youth are defective; these assumptions result in stigmatization because of perceived deviance (Herdt, 1989). A study of queer youth in a sample from 14 metropolitan communities in the United States found that 80% of queer youth had been victims of verbal insults, 44% had received threats of attack, 23% had property damaged, 33% had objects thrown at them, 30% were chased or followed, 22% had been sexually assaulted, 17% had been physically assaulted, 13% were spat on, and 10% had been assaulted with a deadly weapon (Hershberger & D'Augelli, 1995). Queer youth are also vulnerable to forced or encouraged sexual conduct prior to age 19 (Doll et al., 1992).

---

* The term *queer* is used in this chapter as an acceptable term within the sexual minority communities who have reowned the label that society has placed on these minorities. Reowning the label is a coping mechanism to remove the sting from the attempted insult by society. The term includes lesbian, gay, bisexual, and transgendered persons.

In a sample of 1,925 lesbians, 24% had been beaten or physically abused as they were growing up, 19% were survivors of incest, and 21% were victims of rape or sexual molestation during childhood (Bradford, Ryan, & Rothblum, 1994). In a study of gay and bisexual male youth, almost 60% of the youth interviewed were abusing substances at the time of the interview, and their substance abuse pattern met the clinical criteria for substance abuse. Of these participants, 17% had participated in a chemical dependency treatment program.

Heterosexual adolescents have other visible heterosexual adolescents from whom to learn and emulate, whereas queer youth must remain invisible and, therefore, have become very isolated in navigating the complex adolescent stage of development. Plummer (1989) pointed to the heterosexist and homophobic peer adolescent culture as a contributor in the development of the negative self among queer youth. Coleman and Remafedi (1989) suggested that in addition to positive affirmations of these adolescents' sexual orientation, the counselor must address the following psychological problems resulting from stigmatization: psychological maladjustment, impaired psychosocial development, family alienation, inadequate interpersonal relationships, alcohol and drug abuse, depression and suicidal ideation, and concerns about HIV infection and other sexually transmitted diseases (Coleman, 1988).

Treatment issues should no longer focus on assisting gender-dysphoric individuals in adjusting to their new gender but to reaffirm a new transgendered identity (Carroll, Gilroy, & Ryan, 2002). Carroll et al. suggested that a shift needs to occur from a focus on transforming transgendered clients to a focus on transforming the cultural context in which these clients live. Other counselors have made similar suggestions regarding queer individuals. Dworkin and Gutiérrez (1992) advocated a shift in priorities toward a community counseling approach to the issue of addressing queer issues. Dworkin and Gutiérrez recommended delivering services to the community and not just responding to the onset of pathology. They identified counselor activities recommended by the Boston Conference on the Education of Psychologists for Community Mental Health Committee in 1966, such as active participation in community affairs, preventive intervention at the community level, collaboration with responsible lay-people to reduce community tensions, promoting research that supports sexual minority status as a difference rather than a pathology, working with lawmakers in developing public policy, and educating the public about erroneous queer stereotypes.

PROBLEM DEFINITION

An Underinformed Public

The public at large holds a heterosexual bias based on myths and stereotypes about queer youth. Dworkin and Gutiérrez (1989) stated that "because we do not know the process by which sexual orientation develops, we cope by using methods that are familiar though not always relevant. In the past, when we didn't understand something, we labeled it as a sin or illness" (p. 6).

Money (1987) addressed heterosexual bias when he stated that *sexual preference* is a moral and political term rather than a scientific term, one that implies a voluntary choice. Money pointed out the danger of this heterosexual bias because holding this view gives biased individuals justification to impose heterosexuality on others. If it is a preference, then queer folk could be legally forced to choose heterosexuality or experience punishment.

However, there is legal precedent that such pressure is unconstitutional. In *Skinner v. Oklahoma* (1942), a case in which the state wanted to sterilize habitual criminals, Justice Jackson stated, "There are limits to the extent which a legislatively represented majority may conduct biological experiments at the expense of the dignity and personality and natural powers of a minority—even those who have been guilty of what the majority define as crimes" (p. 541).

Gutiérrez (1994, p. 245) stated, "To force a gay, or lesbian, to behave heterosexually is such an abhorrent experiment conducted by the current legislatively represented majority, which is conducting this experiment at the expense of the dignity and personality of gays and lesbians." Imagine the psychological damage if the reverse were to happen—that heterosexuals be forced to live gay and lesbian lives because a group in power decides that it is the law of the land for everyone to behave homosexually (Hally, 1993).

Why Do We Feel This Way?

There is evidence that sexual orientation and gender variation are biological processes; therefore, to answer, the question, we need to understand the biological process of sexual differentiation. Sexual differentiation proceeds as a result of the influence of the following subsystems: "chromosomal sex, H-Y antigenic sex, gonadal sex, prenatal hormonal sex, internal genital sex, external genital sex, pubertal hormonal sex and rearing, and gender identity/role formation" (Money, 1987, p. 389). These subsystems create sexual differentiation in three major biological systems of the human body: the reproductive tract, the external genitalia, and the brain and central nervous system (Money, 1987).

Reproductive Tract.   Money (1987) stated that the human embryo during the first 8 weeks after conception is actually female. The embryo continues to develop as female unless masculinizing hormones are introduced as a result of the messages sent from the x-y (male) chromosome. The reproductive tract is formed by the differentiation of the gonads into either testes or ovaries. The male hormones prevent the mullerian ducts from developing into the uterus and fallopian tubes, according to Money. Testosterone then allows the wolffian ducts to develop into the prostate gland and seminal vesicles. Sometimes, a male embryo will experience an undescended testicle, for example. This seems to occur because of interference in the message sent to the gonads to differentiate into either a testicle or an ovary.

External Genitalia.   The external genitalia in the fetus forms the labia minora in the female and the clitoris and hood. If the fetus is to be a male, according to Money (1987), the tissues that are the labia minora in the female fuse along the midline of the underside to form the tubular urethra of the penis in the male. The clitoris differentiates into the head of the penis, and the clitoral hood differentiates into the foreskin of the penis. The tissues that would form the labia majora of the vagina in the female fuse along the midline and form the scrotum in the male (Money, 1987). Sometimes, a mutation occurs in the fusing of the tissue of the penis, creating differences in penile formation. For example, in some fetuses that differentiate to male, the opening of the urethra, instead of being at the end and center of the head of the penis, will be underneath the head of the penis along the shaft.

Brain and Central Nervous System.   Money (1987) explained that hormonalization of the brain is ambitypic, meaning that there are two processes going on. If the brain differentiates into a male, the hormones are masculinizing the brain. The converse of this process is not feminization, but demasculinization. At the same time, another process is going on in which the brain, which is differentiating as male, is being defeminized. The converse of this process, according to Money, is feminization of the brain. Money explains that this ambitypic differentiation allows for the coexistence of both feminine and masculine "nuclei and pathways, and the behavior they govern, in some, if not all parts of the brain" (p. 387). Money further explained,

> There are alternative ways in which one side [of the brain] could be rendered masculine and the other feminine to a sufficient degree to constitute bisexuality. Likewise, there are alternative ways in which the brain may be masculinized when the genitals are feminized, or vice versa, so as to constitute homosexuality. (p. 388)

Sexual differentiation generally proceeds in the same direction at every stage; that is, a person develops internal genitalia of the same sex as the external genitalia and the same sex as the brain/central nervous system (Lips, 1978). Lips explained variations in the differentiation process that allow for a person to differentiate as male in one stage and as female in the other stages. A person can have the internal and external genitalia of one sex and the brain formation of the other or both sexes. Thus, a gay man can be clear as to his gender, male, but perceive the world from a more feminine perspective and be sexually attracted to other males because of the specific development of the brain/central nervous system toward this direction.

Sexual orientation is akin to the concept of language formation:

> You do not choose your native language as a preference, even though you are born without it. You assimilate it into a brain prenatally made to receive a native language . . . once assimilated . . . into the

brain, a native language becomes securely locked in—as securely as if it had been phylogenetically preordained to be locked in prenatally by a process of genetic determinism or by the determinism of fetal hormonal or other brain chemistries. (Money, 1987, p. 385)

Money (1987) concluded that

the only scholarly position is to allow that prenatal and postnatal determinants are not mutually exclusive. . . . When nature and nurture interact at critical developmental periods, the residual products may persist immutably. . . . The postnatal determinants that enter the brain through the senses by way of social communication and learning also are biological, for there is biology of learning and remembering. (p. 398)

We have just seen the many steps and complexity of events that create sexual differentiation. In any of these steps, variations can occur to explain differentiations in sexual orientation and gender variations.

Heterosexist Assumptions

Because heterosexuals are a majority in society, there is a tendency to view the world strictly from a heterosexual perspective. The United States is a pluralistic society. A characteristic of a pluralistic society is that it respects the rights and differences of the minority groups in the society and does not impose a "majority view." Levine and Padilla (1980, p. 3) defined pluralistic counseling as "therapy that recognizes the client's culturally based beliefs, values, and behaviors that is concerned with the client's adaptation to his or her particular cultural milieu . . . [and] considers all facets of the client's personal history, family history, and social and cultural orientation." To this definition, sexual orientation and gender variation should be added.

Levine and Padilla (1980) suggested that a pluralistic counselor will be knowledgeable about majority and minority cultures, the points of impact between cultures, and the processes by which cultural elements influence individuals. Counselors can be effective only if their own attitudes toward homosexuality are positive and congruous with the current scientific knowledge about sexual orientation and transgender issues, that is, that these are variations of sexual expression (Coleman & Remafedi, 1989).

For example, Erikson (1968) developed a psychosocial/psychosexual stage of identity development. During the adolescent period, according to Erikson, adolescents must deal with the nuclear conflict between identity and identity confusion. Erikson identified further part conflicts related to this stage, which he defined as the conflict between sexual polarization and bisexual confusion. Erikson made a heterosexual assumption when he described this psychosocial/sexual stage. A queer affirmative interpretation of this stage would view the resolution of the conflict as sexual identity versus sexual identity confusion, without creating a heterosexual bias and assumption that heterosexuality is the preferred mode of resolving the conflict or that bisexuality is a confused state. Erikson's theory, however, acknowledges different potentialities for sexual orientation. His mistake was in assuming that heterosexuality is the ultimate outcome in the resolution of this conflict.

CASE STUDY

Juan is an 18-year-old college freshman dealing with coming out to himself. Juan is a first-generation Hispanic male who immigrated with his parents when he was 11 years old. Juan was born with an undescended testicle, and when he was 8 years old, he received shots to assist the descent of the testicle. At the age of 6, he began to become aware of sexual feelings. Juan would play doctor with a female classmate of his at school. He also learned to masturbate by placing his penis between his legs and squeezing.

When Juan came to the United States, his parents became friends with other people from their country. One of these friends was a body builder who had a picture of himself in a brief bikini-type bathing suit sitting on his nightstand in the bedroom. One day Juan had to go into the bedroom to get something for this friend and saw the picture. Juan became very aroused on seeing the picture.

The next year, Juan entered sixth grade. He had a male teacher who was an attractive, tall, black-haired, sensitive Italian man. Juan developed a secret crush on his sixth-grade teacher. Juan had all these feelings that confused him. He remembered that the school counselor had visited his class, inviting students to speak to him if they needed to talk about anything. Juan also remembered the admonition that his father had given him at the age of 7. His dad had commented in front of Juan that he hoped he would never have a gay son. Having a gay son in the Hispanic culture would mean shame on the family. Juan did not go see the school counselor and continued carrying the confusing feelings with him as he was growing up.

At age 15, Juan had a friend, Carlos, of the same age, from his country, living nearby. This friend was much more sexually sophisticated than Juan and had access to his father's X-rated magazines. Carlos invited Juan to view the X-rated magazines in Carlos's bedroom. They both unbuttoned their pants and began masturbating themselves while looking at the photos. Juan and Carlos did not view this as a homosexual experience, despite the fact that, after a while, the sexual play changed focus from looking at the photos to looking at each other masturbate. Carlos's sister came home shortly after Juan and Carlos were finished. Juan felt a lot of guilt, and when Carlos invited him to do it again on another occasion, Juan declined. Juan gave the excuse that his religious beliefs did not allow him to focus on sex. Juan was still an altar boy at this age.

Juan attended a college preparatory high school for boys. When Juan was in high school, two of his classmates in his homeroom, who appeared quite effeminate, befriended him. One day they made a surprise visit to Juan's house. Juan's mother greeted them. These friends did not know exactly where Juan lived so they stopped at the neighbor's house to ask where Juan's house was. Juan's mother was embarrassed that the neighbors saw these effeminate classmates looking for Juan and that somehow the family would be shamed by the association. Juan himself was not effeminate. When they left, Juan's mother angrily confronted Juan about these friends and forbade Juan to see these friends again or to have them come to the house again.

Juan went through high school having crushes on male teachers and classmates. He felt lonely because he could not talk about his feelings with anyone. He thought about talking to a priest during confession, but he felt attracted to the priest to whom he would confess his sins. Also, giving these feelings a voice would mean that Juan would have to own these homosexual feelings, and he wasn't ready to do that. During his high school years, Juan would deny his gay feelings. He felt much pressure to like girls, so he would fantasize about them with the hopes that he would "straighten out."

Juan did not have much contact with girls because he went to an all boys school. He had to study a lot so he did not have much time for dating anyway. This was a good excuse for Juan to avoid the issue of dating during high school. He did go to the high school prom with the daughter of the family at whose house his two effeminate friends had stopped to ask for directions a couple of years back. Juan felt good that he was somehow covering up that incident by showing interest in the daughter.

Juan felt lonely and isolated during high school. Note that these years are the years for an adolescent to resolve the developmental nuclear conflict of intimacy versus isolation (Erikson, 1968). Juan would cry himself to sleep on many occasions because of the pain he felt about hurting his parents and family if they found out he was gay.

After graduating from high school, Juan went away to college. His decision to go away to school was an unconscious desire to create some psychological distance between him and his family so that he could explore his identity without their intrusion.

Juan did very well during his first semester in college; however, during his second semester, his grades began to slip. He became depressed and lost interest in his extracurricular activities. He decided to go to the counseling center for help. During the counseling sessions, Juan talked about several issues. The counselor noticed that Juan avoided issues of dating and intimacy. The counselor suggested to Juan that Juan might want to talk about his social life for the next session.

When Juan came to his next session, instead of coming into the office from the front door, Juan decided to enter the office on that day from the back door. The counselor opened the session by reminding Juan that they had agreed to discuss Juan's social life. Juan made attempts to talk about prior heterosexual dates. Juan sensed that his counselor knew that he was not being honest. Juan's defense mechanism of denial was no longer working for him. Juan told the counselor, "I know you know. Now somebody else knows." Juan's fear that the counselor would reject him overwhelmed him and he ran out the door. The counselor followed Juan and saw him go into the campus chapel. The counselor called Juan at home later to ensure he was going to be alright.

Juan wrote the counselor the following letter:

Your words have not left my mind since you called. You're right—it is very painful for me (and always has been). But you're wrong. I'm not "O.K."; I am in essence a *freak*! (God, how I wish to be normal . . . why doesn't *He* help me?)! I found out in your office the truth—it was then, that someone *else* knew too!! I don't want it known!—ever!! Ever since my life has collapsed. I'm gripped with the constant fear of my family finding out. (I'm sick.) *Never,* never have I entered a church for help; never have I felt so vacant, so cheap, so hollow, so VULGAR!; and help never came—well *screw you* GOD!

My greatest wish (and has been) to love and be loved, and to love as nature *meant* it to be; all I feel is bitter, apathetic . . . nothing matters any more (school nor music nor myself).

Thank you for caring.

I hurt.

I wish to be alone . . . forever.

J.

P.S. I need time to think.

Bracciale, Sanabria, and Updyke (2003) pointed out that it is important for the counselor not to hurry the client in examining and owning his or her sexual orientation. In Juan's case, Juan felt overwhelmed even at the thought of talking about his social life. Perhaps a better approach by the counselor would have been to ask Juan if he wanted to talk about his social life on the day that they had agreed to talk about it as opposed to reminding Juan that they had agreed to talk about it. This would have given Juan a choice as to whether he wanted to talk about it. By reminding Juan that they had agreed to talk about it, it did not give Juan a choice as to whether to pursue the exploration of his sexual orientation. Juan felt trapped in the situation, and it created a crisis for him that caused him to flee the anxiety-producing situation. Bracciale et al. emphasized the need for the client to set his or her own pace in figuring out his or her sexual orientation. Sometimes the counselor, in his or her eagerness to help the client get there, can push a little too soon.

APPROACHES TO PREVENTION

Individual

The case of Juan illustrates the loneliness and isolation that many queer youth feel. According to Uribe and Harbeck (1992), members of minority groups receive support and acculturation by and from other family members and community resources regarding their status as a member of that minority group. However, the queer teenager is often alone and isolated while dealing with the awareness of his or her newly acquired minority status as queer. "While many minority groups are the target of prejudice (beliefs) and discrimination (actions) in our society, few persons face this hostility without the support and acceptance of their family as do many gay, lesbian, and bisexual youth" (Uribe & Harbeck, 1992, p. 13).

Because a support group did not exist on Juan's high school campus, Juan had to put his developmental growth on hold until he reached college, where there was a program that could assist him in his exploration. Juan had to put on hold the resolution of his part conflict of sexual identity and sexual identity confusion, which, in turn, affected his ability to move on to the next nuclear conflict of intimacy versus isolation. Heterosexual students, however, get to experiment with dating and sexual attraction and behavior in high school, building their psychosocial/sexual skills necessary to move to this next stage of development.

Family

Another approach to prevention for the benefit of queer youth is educating the parents. In general, parental reactions consist of two facets: (a) The parents apply their negative perceptions of homosexual identity to their child and reject the child as a stranger, and (b) the parents feel guilt and failure for fear that somehow they caused their child to become homosexual (Strommen, 1989, p. 40).

For the parent, and members of society at large, a subjective perception is developed that the homosexual is "a member of another species, someone whose essential wants are unrecognizable and different" (Weinberg, 1972, p. 97). This subjective perception turns into prejudice. Sometimes, this prejudice can in turn create hatred, such as the hatred that allowed two individuals to terrorize, torture, and take the life of Matthew Shepard. Therefore, any approach to prevention with the queer community needs to involve the dissemination of state-of-the-art scientific information regarding this population.

School

Uribe and Harbeck (1992) described the formation of Project 10, an in-school counseling program at Fairfax High School in Los Angeles, California, with two purposes: (a) to provide emotional support, information, resources, and referrals to queer youth or individuals who wanted accurate information on the subject of sexual orientation zand (b) to heighten the school community's acceptance and sensitivity to queer issues. This project has grown in impact to the national level as a forum for the expression of the needs of queer teenagers.

In forming Project 10, Uribe and Harbeck (1992) identified three steps that needed to be taken to create a receptive environment to the project:

- break through the wall of silence surrounding the topic of homosexuality to reach the target group
- provide a safe and supportive atmosphere so youth could discuss their sexuality in a non-threatening way
- develop a nonjudgmental posture to serve as a guideline in dealing with queer youth.

Project 10 provided not only counseling support groups for queer students but also education and educational materials, school safety measures, faculty and staff training, human rights advocacy, dropout prevention strategies, and use of community resources.

At the college level, Gutiérrez (1987) discussed the formation of a campus program at a Catholic college based on a campus ecology model. A campus ecology model shifts the focus away from the individual and toward the creation of an environment that facilitates the personal growth and development of the queer students. To do so, the academic institution must examine its implicit and explicit attitudes, rules and regulations, and factors that affect queer youth on campus (Gutiérrez, 1987). The focus is on the individual growth of the queer student, as well as the growth of heterosexual students, faculty, staff, administrators, and the community at large so that they can reach acceptance, not just tolerance, of sexual orientation and gender variational differences.

This college campus program, like Project 10, encouraged counselors, faculty, and staff to deal with their own internalized homophobia because of fear of being seen as homosexual or being discovered as a homosexual. Uribe and Harbeck (1992) pointed out that most minorities cannot hide their status as a member of that minority group. Queer individuals, however, can often hide their homosexuality, giving rise to a socialization process that requires learning to hide (Uribe & Harbeck, 1992). One cannot fight the fight while remaining in the closet.

Community

Approaches to prevention must target different levels of audiences. One must target the affected group (i.e., the queer youth), but one must also target the environment and community that impact this group.

Addressing the needs of queer youth within the schools can be a very political process. For programs to be effective, school districts must work with the community to involve them in the process so that the school districts can obtain the backing of the community. Education must begin with the parents and community leaders to make them aware of the need for the intervention strategies within the school systems.

Other approaches to prevention involve participation in professional organizations that provide the leadership to mold the agenda of the profession to address the needs of queer youth (Dworkin & Gutiérrez, 1992). Research funding to generate studies on issues affecting queer youth is essential, according to Dworkin and Gutiérrez (1992) who stated, "The best weapon to counteract the oppression by specific interest groups is research" (p. 337). Dworkin and Gutiérrez also encouraged counselors to stand up and take action to inform lawmakers and government officials involved in setting public policy regarding the reality of the queer population to avoid decisions from being made on the basis of fears and erroneous stereotypes.

INTERVENTION STRATEGIES

Rappaport (1977, as cited in Banning, 1980, p. 214) identified four intervention strategies from an ecological perspective: individual strategies, group strategies, associational strategies, and institutional strategies. Individual strategies include advising, counseling, or psychotherapy. Group strategies focus on particular groups, such as couples counseling and sensitivity groups. Associational strategies focus on the aspects of an organization that do not adapt to the needs of its members or whose structure impedes the developmental growth of members within the organization. The focus is on organizational dynamics or the operational system of the organization; these include consultation, organizational development, or social organization consultation. Institutional strategies include working to effect change in the attitudes of the organizational administration, faculty, and staff toward the students, as well as the organization's value orientation, policies, and other factors that contribute to a poor ecology for student growth and development (Gutiérrez, 1987).

Individual

Individual strategies, according to Gutiérrez (1987), focus on the coming-out process of queer youth. Recognition of same-sex sexual attraction often occurs at around age 10 (McClintock & Herdt, 1996). For Juan, his awareness to same-sex sexual attraction came even earlier, at age 6. Self-labeling as queer typically occurs at about age 15 (Hershberger & D'Augelli, 1995). This self-labeling can be quite traumatic to individuals. Once a person self-labels as queer, he or she is at the point of no return; the person owns the label and cannot take it back. This awareness can be very frightening to an individual and is the cause of many suicide attempts by queer youth. It is estimated that approximately 30% of suicides among young adults are related to sexual orientation issues (National Center for Health Statistics, 1986).

For Juan, his admission to the counselor that he felt same-sex sexual attraction was the point of no return. Sharing this information with others is even more frightening than admitting it to oneself because to admit it to oneself can be changed by defense mechanisms such as intellectualization, rationalization, and denial, but admitting it to another is harder to deny or take back. Many times, the client will beat around the bush with the counselor. They will say things like "I'm really afraid to say this to you," "I don't know how you will take it," or "I think you will be shocked." A response to these statements can be, "Did you kill somebody?" This response often works to alleviate the anxiety the client feels because the client knows that what he or she is about to reveal is not as serious as murdering somebody and it reduces his or her anxiety level to a more manageable level.

Troiden (1989) described the coming-out process as consisting of four stages:

- *sensitization,* in which the youth develops an awareness of being different from others
- *identity confusion,* in which the youth begins to recognize behaviors and feelings that could be labeled queer
- *identity assumption,* in which the youth begins to own this queer identity
- *commitment,* in which queer becomes a way of being as opposed to a way of behaving.

Juan felt this identity confusion. He needed support in sorting out his feelings and seeing how the queer label fit him. For a client to go through these stages, he or she needs an affirming counselor who can reframe all the negative messages that the client has received about queer orientations. Once these messages have been neutralized and the client receives positive messages, the client can learn to accept who he or she is. For gay youth, it is not a matter of choosing the lifestyle but of accepting who they are without societal value judgments about who they are. When they met again, Juan's counselor talked to Juan about his letter. The counselor pointed out to Juan that, perhaps, God put the counselor in Juan's path, thereby gently challenging Juan's perception of abandonment by God. The counselor assured Juan that he did not perceive Juan as a freak. The counselor pointed out to Juan that his yearning to love and be loved as nature meant it to be can be different for different people. In Juan's case, nature meant him to love and be loved by another man.

For Juan, this acceptance by the counselor was a reenactment of the nuclear conflict of trust versus mistrust (Erikson, 1968). During this nuclear conflict, the child learns to trust himself, his world, and his sense of self in relationship to his parents and significant others. To incorporate this new information into his self-identity, Juan needed to revisit this nuclear conflict and resolve it so that he could learn to trust himself and his world again as a queer person.

After coming out to oneself, the next step is to come out to share this new discovery with a significant other. D'Augelli, Hershberger, and Pilkington (1998) conducted a study with queer youth and found that three quarters of these youth chose a close friend to share this first disclosure. Only 9% chose a parent as the first person to whom to disclose this new identity, and all of these were to their mothers.

Once clients accept their own same-sex attraction, they are now ready to face other people like themselves. Juan asked to meet other students on campus who were going through the same process. The counselor arranged to introduce him to another student on campus, Paul. It was safe for Juan to meet with just another student rather than to join a group. Dealing with the individual differences of another student is not as overwhelming. It also does not involve the peer pressure of being like the other members of the group. This way Juan could compare his situation with that of the other student and could evaluate similarities and differences without the pressure of having to be "politically correct" in his identity.

This stage for Juan was similar to Erikson's (1968) nuclear conflict of autonomy versus shame and doubt. In this stage, children learn that they are separate from their parents and begin to explore their world and assert their own individuality. Juan and Paul could further evaluate the norms and values of the queer world without having to commit to it and accept everything about this world. As in any other, culture, there are variations within the queer culture (Gutiérrez, 1994), and Juan and Paul needed to figure out where they fit in relationship to these variations. As Juan and Paul developed their queer identity, eventually they were ready to join a support group of other students who were dealing with these issues.

Family

Individual strategies can also assist the parents of these youth. On learning of their son's or daughter's queer status, parents often go through similar feelings of shock and isolation (Boxer, Cook, & Herdt, 1995). They go through stages of loss similar to those of someone who experiences a death in the family: denial, anger, bargaining, depression, and acceptance (Kubler-Ross, 1969). Parents may feel that their son or daughter is just going through a phase. They may be angry at whomever "exposed" their son or daughter to this lifestyle. They may become angry at themselves and blame themselves for "causing" their son's or daughter's "queerness." They may even become angry at God, like Juan did in his letter to the counselor.

The queer youth and their parents may go through a bargaining stage, where they bargain with God that if God changes the youth back to "normal" they promise to do x, y, or z. When they see that bargaining is not working for them, they become depressed, and, as they receive more information about the situation, they gradually learn to accept what is going on within themselves or their children and are able to accept themselves or their children as queer.

Robinson, Walters, and Skeen (1989) identified three factors that contribute to a sense of grief by the parents on finding out that their child is queer: (a) an assumption that the child is part of the accepted heterosexual majority and the loss of the dreams of the child's traditional marriage and generation of grandchildren for these parents, (b) the realization that the child is part of a minority group, and (c) the fact that the minority group to which their child belongs has a long history of persecution.

D'Augelli et al. (1998) found that 51% of mothers were accepting of their child's revelation of queer status, 30% were tolerant, 9% were intolerant, and 10% were rejecting. D'Augelli et al. also found that 27% of fathers were accepting of their child's revelation of queer status, 32% were tolerant, 16% were intolerant, and 29% were rejecting. This same study found that 57% of siblings were accepting of their sibling's revelation of queer status, 19% were tolerant, 9% were intolerant, and 15% rejecting.

Although the above figures are encouraging for most queer youth, too many other youth who disclose their queer status to family members risk doing so. D'Augelli et al. (1998) found that mothers verbally abused 38% of daughters and 24% of sons after they revealed their status, 10% of mothers of lesbian daughters and 3% of mothers of gay sons physically threatened their children when they revealed their status, and 10% of mothers of lesbian daughters and 3% of mothers of gay sons physically attacked their children when they revealed their status. In contrast, 19% of fathers abused their revealing daughters and sons, 10% of fathers physically threatened their revealing daughters while only 2% of fathers physically threatened their revealing sons, and 5% of fathers actually physically attacked their revealing daughters while 2% of fathers actually physically attacked their revealing sons. These figures suggest that lesbian youth are more likely to be rejected by both parents and to be victimized by them.

D'Augelli et al. (1998) found that, among revealing lesbians, 19% of brothers and 10% of sisters verbally abused them, 5% of brothers and 14% of sisters physically threatened them, and 0% of brothers and 7% of sisters physically attacked their lesbian sisters. Among revealing gay youth, 22% of brothers and 13% of sisters verbally abused their gay brother, 14% of brothers and 0% of sisters physically threatened them after the revelation, and 7% of brothers and 2% of sisters physically attacked the gay youth after the revelation of their queer status. These figures indicate that lesbian and gay youth receive rejection and are victimized by same-sex siblings more than by opposite-sex siblings.

The grief process for heterosexual parents and family members appears to take 2 years to work through and fully accept the child's sexual orientation (Borhek, 1983), which seems to be the same amount of time associated with the resolution of grief from a divorce or death of a loved one (Robinson et al., 1989).

Although in the majority of the cases, the families of queer youth were either accepting or tolerant, the incidents of abuse, even if verbal, were sufficiently high as to make a queer youth question the risk of revealing their queer status to their families. In Juan's case, the counselor suggested to Juan that he might want to first test his family's reactions to homosexuality in general. Juan might want to have a discussion with his family about Rosie O'Donnell's coming out, for example, to see how receptive or supportive his parents are to learning that someone with whom they are familiar is queer.

Because Juan is away at college, he does not get home very often. The counselor recommended to Juan to wait until the summer break before bringing the subject up with his family. Holidays, which tend to be emotionally charged times of the year when all kinds of issues for families arise, may not be the best time to bring up the subject. Waiting until the summer also gave Juan enough time to continue exploring his sexual orientation in a group and to learn from other members of the group who had already come out to their parents how they approached it, what worked for them, and what didn't.

Another intervention for Juan's parents included the referral of Juan's parents to their local priest. The counselor identified a priest in Juan's family's Catholic parish who was supportive of sexual orientation issues. He then referred Juan's parents to speak to this priest so the priest could provide pastoral guidance around sexual orientation issues. Many religions support pastoral programs that affirm a person's sexual orientation (Gutiérrez, 1987).

School

Group Strategies. Group strategies can consist of counselor-led support groups for queer youth or for their parents. Groups can also be self-help, such as those led by Parents and Friends of Lesbians and Gays (PFLAG). Given the above statistics of family responses to queer youth's disclosures of their queer status, it is imperative that schools, queer youth community centers, and community mental health centers establish programs for family members to be able to explore their reactions to their queer family members' revelations and to educate these family members about the biological as well as psychosocial aspects of queer status.

Counselors need to be aware of the culture of the group with whom they are working. In Juan's case, the counselor must be aware of not only the gay culture but also the Hispanic culture (the ethnic issues are addressed below, in the Adaptations for Diversity section). Juan's counselor could refer Juan to the local lesbian/gay community center and to social groups in which Juan could meet others like himself, such as the local gay/lesbian chorus, bicycle club, runners' group, and so on. Meeting other queer youth in these contexts can give these youth a different picture of who they are as queer youth and what life can be like for them. This process is similar to Erikson's (1968) nuclear conflict of identity versus identity confusion. Of course, certain oppressive elements of society would like queer youth to think that their life is doomed if they continue to live this lifestyle.

With individual and group counseling support, Juan was able, to understand the biological basis for his feelings. His parents were able to stop blaming Juan for being who he is and also stopped blaming themselves for causing Juan's queerness. They learned that they had no control over Juan's status and were able to stop feeling guilty about themselves as parents. For many queer youth, however, there is a sense of a foreshortened future. Feeling that their life is doomed, they turn to the immediate pleasures of life because they do not know what tomorrow will bring. Time perspective for adolescents is very short term. Because adolescents are forced to go underground for their social network, they have very few positive role models and little adult supervision. This situation creates an environment in which substance abuse and high-risk behaviors can flourish. Because the adolescents do not see a future for themselves, why sacrifice and delay gratification?

Paul was able to develop his queer identity; however, unlike Juan, he chose a different path. He did not have the same support from his family that Juan was able to receive from his family. Paul was a strikingly handsome, Swedish-looking, blonde young man. He became unsure of his identity, so he sought validation from other gays by becoming promiscuous. Paul's parents were extremely religious and rejected him after he came out to them. They went as far as throwing him out of the house and cutting off his tuition assistance. Erikson (1968) stated that the counterpart of intimacy is distantiation, or the readiness to repudiate those forces or people whose essence seems dangerous to one's own. Paul's reaction to his parents' religiosity and rejection of him was to reject those forces whose essence was dangerous to his own, his gayness. Erikson warned that youth who are not sure of their identity shy away from interpersonal intimacy and throw themselves into acts that are promiscuous or with self-abandon. These youth develop what Erikson called the negative identity. Although parents of queer youth are not responsible for their child's queer status, they do influence the child's ability to develop a healthy sense of identity. Paul would go to the local gay bar, and because he was not yet of age to enter the bar, he would hang out in the bar's parking lot, offering free oral sex indiscriminately to patrons entering the bar. Paul felt validated for being popular with the bar patrons. Even though he was in college, Paul had no sense of a positive future for himself, so he behaved in a manner that exposed him to sexually transmitted diseases. Paul chose to become a porn movie actor in same-sex pornographic movies. Because of his high-risk behaviors, Paul contracted AIDS and died from it. Because queer youth are vulnerable to substance abuse and high-risk sexual behaviors as a coping mechanism for stressors as a result of their queer status, it is imperative that these youth receive information and support regarding these issues to prevent deaths, such as Paul's, from happening.

Associational Strategies. Hershberger and D'Augelli (1995) cited a study by Gross, Aurand, and Adessa (1988) that showed that in a sample of gay men, 50% of the sample reported victimization in junior high school and 59% in high school; lesbians in the sample reported that 12% of them were victimized in junior high school and 21% in high school. Savin-Williams (1994) cited studies by Remafedi (1987) that showed that over two thirds of gay and bisexual youth had school-related problems; nearly 40% were truant, and 28% dropped out of school. These statistics indicate that schools are not safe places for queer youth.

Uribe and Harbeck (1992) discussed various associational strategies that they implemented at the beginning of Project 10 at Fairfax High School, such as developing an informational brochure that was distributed throughout the community regarding the project and training a core group of teachers, administrators, and counselors. As an organization, the high school was not meeting the needs of gay and lesbian students. The structure of the services in place did not address the needs of these students because the faculty and staff did not have the proper knowledge and training to address these issues. There was a lack of awareness that this was even a problem within the organization. The brochure that was designed and circulated provided a context for the program and educated the high school, the Board of Education, and the community at large as to the problem and the need for the Project 10 program. A training program for staff and faculty bridged the gap of services that were being provided to heterosexual students by training the faculty and staff on the issues facing queer youth and providing these faculty and staff with the skills they needed to address not only the needs of the queer youth but also the heterosexual students' needs in adjusting to the reality of sharing a campus with queer youth. The initial reaction to the program was very positive, according to Uribe and Harbeck. Only 10 negative phone calls were recorded initially.

Gutiérrez (1987) implemented several associational strategies at the college level. He met with his director at the counseling center to obtain approval for the outreach to queer youth on campus. Prior to this point, the counseling center had not made any affirmative efforts to communicate to queer youth that they were welcome in the counseling center and that the staff of the counseling center was knowledgeable, able, and willing to serve the specific needs of queer youth on campus.

The counseling center and the campus ministry office began to explicitly list sexual orientation issues among the issues addressed by the centers, thereby giving sexual orientation visibility as an issue to be addressed on campus. This was done in a queer affirmative way to prevent the wrong impression that these offices were there to "cure" students of their queerness.

The counselor then enlisted the assistance of the Campus Ministry Office and the Women's Center to cosponsor the showing of the movie *Word Is Out* on campus, followed by a discussion afterward. Eighty students attended this showing. The average attendance for workshops sponsored by the counseling center had been 5-8 students. This response was indicative of the yearning for these services by students on campus, queer and heterosexual alike, who were searching for information and support around these issues.

A training workshop was also conducted for resident assistants and hall directors on how to conduct conflict resolution when problems arose in the residence halls regarding sexual orientation. Issues addressed in these trainings could include how to counsel a resident who finds out that his or her roommate is queer, how to counsel a queer resident who is feeling attraction toward his or her roommate who does not reciprocate the feelings, how to diffuse animosity on the floor regarding the presence of a queer student in the residential community, how to conduct educational programming for residents around queer issues, and discussions of safe sex that include queer issues.

The university received two negative phone calls from parents who had found out about the university's new program. These phone calls were fielded to the counselor, who was able to educate the parents regarding the importance of a university education in creating awareness about diversity in our society, which includes queer individuals. The parents were satisfied with the counselor's response, and there were no further complaints.

Institutional Strategies.   Any change in an institution must have the involvement of the policy and decision makers within the institution if effective change is to take place. A study of Oberlin College by Norris (1992) regarding the institutional culture of the college revealed that, although the college has a progressive tradition and was one of the first institutions of higher learning to adopt a nondiscrimination clause based on sexual orientation in 1973, the implementation of the clause has been lacking. Norris suggested that the paradox results from two competing sets of values, one focused on equal rights and the other on a heterosexual orthodoxy. Norris concluded that the inability of the institution to legitimate discussion of sexuality and the concerns of queers on its campus prevents an open airing of issues and concerns.

Gutiérrez (1987) described how the president of Santa Clara University, a Catholic Jesuit institution, obtained the backing of the Board of Trustees before the issue of sexual orientation was addressed on this campus. The president then legitimized the discussion of the issue of sexual orientation by making the issue part of a university-wide Institute on the Family, which was open to the public.

For Project 10, Uribe and Harbeck (1992) obtained the backing of the school board members, administrators, teachers, and students, both queer and heterosexual, as well as members of the community. For example, the City of West Hollywood became involved in providing the funding for library materials, a hotline, incidental costs of publicity, awards, and scholarships sponsored by Project 10. Having such a united front prevents scapegoating of the staff attempting to implement the program as well as shared pride in the success of the program. It also insulates the institution from attacks from opposing groups, because opposing groups can see how much support from the community there is for the program.

The institution must also ground whatever it is doing in research and scholarly rationale. At Santa Clara University, for example, the success of the program was the result of a solid grounding in a theological and pastoral context that was congruous with and not adverse to the religious values of the institution.

When mainstream institutions fail to meet the needs of queer youth, institutions must be formed to meet these needs. Such was the case of the Harvey Milk School in New York City. Most of the students attending this school had dropped out of other New York City public schools primarily because of peer harassment (Martin & Hetrick, 1988). However, this type of institutional strategy should be utilized sparingly, lest we create a world of separate but equal institutions.

The separate but equal method was tried with African Americans in the 1950s, and *Brown v. Board of Education* (1954) held this type of arrangement to be unconstitutional. Other precedents that discourage the separation of individuals who are different from the mainstream are seen in the Individuals With Disabilities Education Act Amendments of 1997. This act prohibits the separation of students with disabilities and requires school districts to mainstream these students and provide a least restrictive environment and a free and appropriate education. So too, queer youth are entitled to a free and appropriate public education free of harassment and free of a hostile environment.

Community

To avoid community criticism and feelings of alienation, the president of Santa Clara University decided to include gays and lesbians in an Institute on the Family that the university was sponsoring during that semester. The institute workshop was open to the community. The counselor assisted with the makeup of the panel, which consisted of a graduate student from a local university, the founders of the local chapter of PFLAG, and a gay male couple from Dignity/San Francisco who were raising one of the partners' 6- and 8-year-old girls. The two girls were also on the panel, and they were the most powerful panelists as they talked about the love they felt from both male parents and the positive experience in their household.

ADAPTATIONS FOR DIVERSITY

Individual Strategies

In working with ethnic minority queer youth, the counselor must be aware that these students are dealing not only with their queer identity but their ethnic identity as well as their personal identity. These identities must be integrated. Therefore, the counselor must become aware of not only the theories of queer identity (Cass, 1979; Troiden, 1989) but also models of minority identity development (Atkinson, Morten, & Sue, 1979; Gutiérrez, 1985; Loiacano, 1989; Parham, 1989).

Chan (1992) identified several factors to look at in the family background of ethnic minority individuals. These include the following: (a) Is the client an immigrant or American born? (b) What is the client's ethnic group? (c) What are the specific values of the ethnic group, the client's family, and the client? (d) How closely does the client follow traditional ethnic customs? (e) What is the client's socioeconomic status? and (f) What is the client's level of bilingualism?

Latinos and Latinas represent a variety of nations, races, and cultures; therefore, they belong to no one group (Morales, 1992). Generally, however, Latinos/Latinas hold the cultural values of familismo, machismo, simpatía, personalismo, and respeto, according to Morales. These values need to be explored as to how they are affected by the superimposed queer context. Ethnic minority groups such as African Americans experience the same racism in the queer culture that they experience in mainstream heterosexual White society, so they are forced to go back to their African American community for support, where they encounter the homophobia that also exists in the White heterosexual mainstream society (Gutiérrez & Dworkin, 1992).

Juan was very transculturated; he was bilingual and bicultural. Juan's ethnic identity was really not an issue for him, but his sexual identity was. Juan held all the internalized homophobic perceptions of seeing himself as a freak and that in order to love as nature meant it to be, he had to love heterosexually. These homophobic values are further magnified in his Hispanic culture, where machismo and Catholicism are so strong. Juan needs to explore how machismo, familismo, respeto, and Catholicism fit into his life as a gay individual.

Juan needs the validation of other Hispanic gays. In many major cities there are gay and lesbian Hispanic organizations that provide emotional and social support within a cultural context. These queer ethnic minority organizations are crucial in preventing the split identified by Gutiérrez and Dworkin (1992) between the racist queer community and the homophobic ethnic minority community. Counselors need to become familiar with these organizations to be able to provide the information to their clients.

Family Strategies

Juan's parents were predominantly Spanish speaking, so they needed referrals to support services that were bilingual and bicultural. For example, earlier, I mentioned that Juan's parents could be referred to a priest who is gay affirming. It would be important for the counselor to investigate a referral for the family with the parish priest who ministers to the Hispanic community. Juan could be helpful to the counselor in identifying this priest.

Another resource for families can be the Metropolitan Community Churches. These churches exist in most major cities in the United States and around the world. The services in these churches are quite similar to a Catholic Mass, except that women are allowed to participate at the altar table. At these churches, queer people often bring family members so that the families can experience the love shared for queer people by these churches. In Fort Lauderdale, for example, attendance at the Sunshine Cathedral reaches over 700 individuals on any given Sunday (although this is an unusually high number, given that Fort Lauderdale is in the Bible Belt and even queer people go to church on Sunday).

Many communities now have PFLAG chapters offering assistance and support in Spanish. Otherwise, PFLAG can assist the counselor in finding an appropriate support network for the family, depending on the family's ethnic or racial background. A support group such as PFLAG can be invaluable in providing families with guidance and role modeling from other parents and family members of the family's ethnic/racial background. It is important to send out the message to all racial/ethnic groups that queer youth exist in all cultures and races.

As family members grow in their acceptance of their children and the issues that their sexual orientation raised for the family, eventually, they could be encouraged to take a leadership role in PFLAG or in the school system or community to advocate for the needs of queer youth and their families for those families who are members of the same ethnic/racial background.

School Strategies

Unless the school holds the value of diversity to begin with, it will be difficult for institutional strategies to be implemented. This is why the involvement of individuals identified under the Community Strategies subsection below is crucial. When school organizers have the group backing of key individuals in the various organizations that make up the community, the task becomes simpler. The more groups the program organizers have behind them, the easier it will be to convince the less supportive members of the community to participate in the project. These leaders can then approach the decision makers of the school to bring them on board to back the programs and to give their blessings to strategies to change the institutional attitudes and values.

Ethnic communities have become accustomed to the White majority making the decisions and excluding ethnic group voices. Therefore, ethnic minorities have become accustomed to the exclusion, and they stay away from the decision-making process. Ethnic minority leaders must be identified and given the power and authority to initiate the dialogue with their communities.

In one recent example, a gay Hispanic leader was invited to attend a meeting of a local politician running for office by the White gay/lesbian campaign committee supporting this politician. A meeting was called to invite Hispanic politicians to attend a meeting with the gay/lesbian community. The gay

Hispanic community leader was not asked to contact the Hispanic politicians, many whom he knew. When the gay Hispanic leader got to the home where the meeting was to be held, he was told that the meeting had been canceled because of lack of response. The organizers had not called him to let him know the meeting had been canceled. The mistake by the White gay/lesbian campaign committee was not to utilize the gay Hispanic leader as a bridge to the two communities. This occurred because of lack of diversity awareness from the political organizers and the gay/lesbian leaders on how to approach ethnic minority communities.

Community Strategies

Uribe and Harbeck (1992) pointed out that the implementation of Project 10 was not successful in predominantly Black and Hispanic schools, suggesting that particular strategies need to be developed to address these populations. What is essential in working with specific groups is that the program designer involve the members of the population one is attempting to reach in the planning of the program. To make Project 10 work in the African American and Hispanic communities, for example, the program organizers need to meet with each community individually.

The organizers can involve queer leaders of the ethnic minority community as bridges to the leaders of the ethnic minority heterosexual communities. It is important that the organizers identify the following from the various groups: the leaders in the ethnic minority churches, both lay and clergy; the leaders of the ethnic minority PTA groups; the political leaders; the ethnic minority members of the school board; the ethnic minority student leaders from the heterosexual community; and the queer ethnic minority student leaders.

Additionally, because machismo tends to be more highly held in the ethnic minority communities, perhaps involvement of athletes who can be seen as leaders and role models who can legitimize the discussion of queerness within ethnic minority schools. Once these group leaders have been identified, they must be trained and sensitized to the issues of queer youth, so that, in turn, they can join the struggle of institutionalizing the programs.

A while back, I was invited by the Cristina Show, the Hispanic Oprah Winfrey, to be the professional guest on a show on gay and lesbian adolescents coming out to their parents. This show is seen by millions of Spanish-speaking television viewers around the world. It was my opportunity to educate millions of Hispanic viewers around sexual orientation. The studio audience was filled with teenagers from various schools who had been bused to be in the audience. When we left the television studio, the audience was waiting for us outside. We were not pelted with stones or insults. Instead we were treated as one would treat a movie star leaving the entertainment venue. We knew that we had done our job of educating these students.

Another powerful community strategy occurred in the recent Miss America Pageant for 2003. Teresa Benitez, Miss Nevada, offered a declamation as her talent portion of the competition. Her declamation consisted of the words of Matthew Shepard's mother during the sentencing phase of Matthew's assailants. It was such an impactful contribution toward the education of millions of television viewers about people who are "different," which was the context of Ms. Benitez's declamation. The Miss America Pageant is a conservative organization, and there were many messages and references to Christianity and "My Savior Jesus Christ" among the contestants. Ms. Benitez's message rang loud and clear within these messages. Ms. Benitez came in as third runner-up in the Miss America competition. She intends to become a U.S. Senator some day. As a Hispanic gay person, I was moved by Ms. Benitez's courage. This is the type of community education that needs to happen.

SUMMARY

According to Uribe and Harbeck (1992),

> Cultural taboos, fear of controversy, and deeply rooted, pervasive homophobia have kept the educational system in the United States blind-folded and mute on the subject of childhood and adolescent homosexuality. The paucity of literature and understanding in this area is a national disgrace. Young men and women

struggling with their sexual orientation during a time of intense physical, social, and developmental change are failed by physicians, educators, mental health professionals, and clergy who breach their ethical and professional obligations by being uninformed and unresponsive to the special problems and need of these youth. (p. 11)

In this chapter, I have defined the problem as the public's lack of scientific knowledge regarding sexual differentiation and the heterosexist assumptions that do not embrace the pluralistic society that forms the fiber of American culture. I have explored the many stressors that queer youth face, such as invisibility, isolation, victimization, suicide potential, substance abuse, and exposure to sexually transmitted diseases because of high-risk behaviors. These unique stressors call for affirmative counseling interventions by culturally sensitive and queer-affirming counselors.

The point was made that while queer youth need to address these stressors, counselors need to shift the focus of treatment to the true client, the community at large, to transform the cultural context in which queer youth live. To create this transformation, an ecological approach needs to be undertaken that would include individual, group, associational, and institutional strategies to effect the societal changes.

We experienced slices of the lives of Juan and Paul with differing outcomes. Both had an affirming counselor who was able to move these individuals toward acceptance of their sexual identity; however, queer youth do not live in a vacuum. They need the love and support of significant others, especially family. Ironically, Paul's family was the more "religious" of the two families. However, being religious does not necessarily translate to the values that many religions profess—love of one's neighbor as one loves oneself. The case of Juan shows how a loving family can go a long way toward a person's self-acceptance and successful resolution of identity crisis. The case of Paul was tragic and could have been averted by the loving guidance of parents who could accept their son as nature made him.

How many more Matthew Shepards must die before society replaces hatred toward queers with understanding and acceptance? Uribe and Harbeck (1992, p. 27) said it best, "The pain and hardship suffered by adolescent, gay lesbian, and bisexual [and transgendered] youth is no longer invisible, and our lack of action is no longer professionally or ethically acceptable."

REFERENCES

Atkinson, D., Morten, G., & Sue, D. (1979). *Counseling American minorities.* Dubuque, IA: Brown.

Banning, J. (1980). The campus ecology manager role. In U. Delworth & G. Hanson (Eds.), *Student services: A handbook for the profession* (pp. 209–227). San Francisco: Jossey-Bass.

Borhek, M. (1983). *Coming out to parents: A two-way survival guide for lesbians and gay men and their parents.* New York: Praeger.

Boxer, A., Cook, J., & Herdt, G. (1995). Double jeopardy: Identity transitions and parent child relations among gay and lesbian youth. In A. D' Augelli & C. Patterson (Eds.), *Lesbian, gay and bisexual identities over the lifespan.* New York: Oxford University Press.

Bracciale, M., Sanabria, S., & Updyke, J. (2003). *Assisting parents of gay and lesbian youth.* Workshop presented at the annual convention of the American Counseling Association, Anaheim, CA.

Bradford, J., Ryan, C, & Rothblum, E. (1994). National lesbian health care survey: Implications for mental health care. *Journal of Consulting and Clinical Psychology, 62,* 228–242.

Brown v. Board of Educ. 347 U.S. 483 (1954).

Carroll, L., Gilroy, P., & Ryan, J. (2002). Counseling transgendered, transexual, and gender-variant clients. *Journal of Counseling & Development, 80,* 131–139.

Cass, V. (1979). Homosexuality identity formation: A theoretical model. *Journal of Homosexuality, 4,* 219–235.

Chan, C. (1992) Cultural considerations in counseling Asian American lesbians and gay men. In S. Dworkin & F. Gutiérrez (Eds.), *Counseling gay men and lesbians: Journey to the end of the rainbow* (pp. 115–124). Alexandria, VA: American Counseling Association.

Coleman, E. (Ed.). (1988). *Psychotherapy with homosexual men and women.* New York: Haworth.

Coleman, E., & Remafedi, G. (1989). Gay, lesbian, and bisexual adolescents: A critical challenge to counselors. *Journal of Counseling & Development, 68,* 36–40.

D'Augelli, A., Hershberger, S., & Pilkington, N. (1998). Lesbian, gay, and bisexual youth and their families: Disclosure of sexual orientation and its consequences. *American Journal of Orthopsychiatry, 68,* 361–371.

Doll, L., Joy, D., Bartholow, B., Harrison, J., Bolan, G., Douglas, J., et al. (1992). Self-reported childhood and adolescent sexual abuse among adult homosexual and bisexual men. *Child Abuse and Neglect, 16,* 855–864.

Dworkin, S., & Gutiérrez, F. (1989). Counselors be aware: Clients come in every size, shape, color, and sexual orientation. *Journal of Counseling & Development, 68,* 6–15.

Dworkin, S., & Gutiérrez, F. (1992). *Epilogue: Where do we go from here?* In S. Dworkin & F. Gutiérrez (Eds.), *Counseling gay men and lesbians: Journey to the end of the rainbow* (pp. 335–339). Alexandria, VA: American Counseling Association.

Erikson, E. (1968). *Identity youth and crisis.* New York: Norton.

Gutiérrez, F. (1985). Bicultural personality development: A process model. In E. Garcia & R. Padilla (Eds.), *Advances in bilingual education research* (pp. 96–124). Tucson: University of Arizona Press.

Gutiérrez, F. (1987). *Managing the campus ecology of gay/lesbian students on Catholic college campuses.* (ERIC Document Reproduction Service No. ED324612).

Gutiérrez, F. (1994). Gay and lesbian: An ethnic identity deserving equal protection. *Law and Sexuality: A Review of Lesbian and Gay Legal Issues, 4,* 195–247.

Gutiérrez, F., & Dworkin, S. (1992). Gay, lesbian, and African American: Managing the integration of identities. In S. Dworkin & F. Gutiérrez (Eds.), *Counseling gay men and lesbians: Journey to the end of the rainbow* (pp. 141–156). Alexandria, VA: American Counseling Association.

Hally, J. E. (1993). *The construction of heterosexuality, fear of a queer planet: Queer politics and social theory.* Minneapolis: University of Minnesota Press.

Herdt, G. (1989). Gay and lesbian youth: Emergent identities and cultural scenes at home and abroad. *Journal of Homosexuality, 17,* 1–42.

Herr, K. (1997). Learning lessons from school: Homophobia, heterosexism and the construction of failure. *Journal of Gay and Lesbian Social Services, 7*(4), 51–64.

Hershberger, S., & D'Augelli, A. (1995). The impact of victimization on the mental health and suicidality of lesbian, gay, and bisexual youths. *Developmental Psychology, 31,* 65–74.

Hershberger, S., & D'Augelli, A. (2000). Issues in counseling lesbian, gay, and bisexual adolescents. In R. M. Perez, K. De Bord, & K. Bieschke (Eds.), *Handbook of counseling and psychotherapy with lesbian, gay, and bisexual clients* (pp. 225–248). Washington, DC: American Psychological Association.

Individuals With Disabilities Education Act Amendments of 1997, 20 U.S.C. § 1400 *et sea.* (Lexis 1998).

Kubler-Ross, E. (1969). *On death and dying.* New York: MacMillan.

Levine, E., & Padilla, A. (1980). *Crossing cultures in therapy: Pluralistic counseling for the Hispanic.* Monterey, CA: Brooks/Cole.

Lips, H. (1978). Sexual differentiation and gender identity. In H. Lips & N. Colwill (Eds.), *The psychology of sex differences* (pp. 52–79). Englewood Cliffs, NJ: Prentice-Hall.

Loiacano, D. (1989). Gay identity issues among Black Americans: Racism, homophobia, and the need for validation. *Journal of Counseling & Development, 68,* 21–25.

Martin, A., & Hetrick, E. (1988). The stigmatization of the gay and lesbian adolescent. *Journal of Homosexuality, 15,* 163–183.

McClintock, M., & Herdt, G. (1996). Rethinking puberty: The development of sexual attraction. *Current Directions in Psychological Science, 5,* 178–183.

Money, J. (1987). Sin, sickness, or status? Homosexual gender identity and psychoneuroendocrinology. *American Psychologist, 42,* 384–399.

Morales, E. (1992). Counseling Latino gays and Latina lesbians. In S. Dworkin & F. Gutiérrez (Eds.), *Counseling gay men and lesbians: Journey to the end of the rainbow* (pp. 125–139). Alexandria, VA: American Counseling Association.

National Center for Health Statistics. (1986). *Vital statistics of the United States: Vol. 2. Mortality, Part A.* Hyattsville, MD: Author.

Norris, W. (1992). Liberal attitudes and homophobic acts: The paradoxes of homosexual experience in a liberal institution. In K. Harbeck (Ed.), *Coming out of the classroom closet* (pp. 81–120). New York: Harrington Park Press.

O'Connor, M. (1992). Psychotherapy with gay and lesbian adolescents. In S. Dworkin & F. Gutiérrez (Eds.), *Counseling gay men and lesbians: Journey to the end of the rainbow* (pp. 3–21). Alexandria, VA: American Counseling Association.

Parham, T. (1989). Cycles of psychological nigrescence. *The Counseling Psychologist, 17,* 187–226.

Plummer, K. (1989). Lesbian and gay youth in England. *Journal of Homosexuality, 17,* 195–223.

Remafedi, G. (1987). Adolescent homosexuality: Medical and psychological implications. *Pediatrics, 79,* 331–337.

Robinson, B., Walters, L., & Skeen, P. (1989). Response of parents to learning that their child is homosexual and concern over AIDS: A national study. *Journal of Homosexuality, 18,* 59–80.

Savin-Williams, R. (1994). Verbal and physical abuse as stressors in the lives of lesbian, gay male, and bisexual youths: Associations with school problems, running away, substance abuse, prostitution, and suicide. *Journal of Consulting and Clinical Psychology, 62,* 261–269.

Skinner v. Oklahoma, 316 U.S. 535 (1942).

Strommen, E. (1989). You're a what?: Family member reaction to the disclosure of homosexuality. *Journal of Homosexuality, 18,* 37–57.

Troiden, R. (1989). The formation of homosexual identities. *Journal of Homosexuality, 17*(1/2), 43–73.

Uribe, V., & Harbeck, K. (1992). Addressing the needs of lesbian, gay, and bisexual youth: The origins of Project 10 and school-based intervention. In K. Harbeck (Ed.), *Coming out of the classroom closet: Gay and lesbian students, teachers, and curricula* (pp. 9–28). New York: Harrington Park Press.

Weinberg, G. (1972). *Society and the healthy homosexual.* New York: St. Martin's Press.

B I B L I O G R A P H Y

For Chapters 1–5

Ada, A. (1989). Los libros mágicos. *California Tomorrow, 42–44.*

Adams, T. L. (2003). Reading mathematics: More than words can say. *The Reading Teacher, 56*(8), 786–795.

Adamson, H. (1993). *Academic competence.* New York: Longman.

Addison, A. (1988, November). Comprehensible textbooks in science for the nonnative English-speaker: Evidence from discourse analysis. *The CATESOL Journal, 1*(1), 49–66.

Adger, C. (2000). School/community partnerships to support language minority student success. *CREDE Research Brief #5.* Santa Cruz, CA: Center for Research on Education, Diversity and Excellence. Retrieved January 26, 2005, from www.crede.org/products/print/research_briefs/rb5.shtml.

Agar, M. (1980). *The professional stranger: An informal introduction to ethnography.* Orlando, FL: Academic Press.

Aladjem, P. (2000). *A suggested guide to the special education pre-referral process for bilingual learners.* Washington, DC: National Clearinghouse for Bilingual Education. Retrieved February 1, 2005, from www.ncela.gwu.edu/pubs/voices/aladjem.pdf.

Alexander v. Sandoval. (2001). 532 US 275, Docket No. 99-1908.

Alexander, S. (1983). *Nadia, the willful.* New York: Dial.

Allan, K. K., & Miller, M. S. (2005). *Literacy and learning in the content areas* (2nd ed.). Boston: Houghton Mifflin.

Allen, E., & Vallette, R. (1977). *Classroom techniques: Foreign languages and English as a second language.* San Diego: Harcourt Brace Jovanovich.

Alvarez, J. (2007). My English. In R. Spack (Ed.), *Guidelines: A cross-cultural reading/writing text* (pp. 30–35). New York: Cambridge University Press.

American Educational Research Association. (2004). English language learners: Boosting academic achievement. *Research Points, 2*(1).

American Psychological Association. (1991). *APA guidelines for providers of psychological services to ethnic, linguistic, and culturally diverse populations.* Retrieved February 10, 2005, from www.apa.org/pi/oema/guide.html.

Amselle, J. (1999). Dual immersion delays English. *American Language Review, 3*(5), 8.

Anderson, L. (2004). From mechanics to meaning through formative peer feedback. *Essential Teacher, 1*(5), 54–56.

Andrews, L. (2001). *Linguistics for L2 teachers.* Mahwah, NJ: Erlbaum.

Anstrom, K. (1996). Federal policy, legislation, and education reform: The promise and the challenge for language minority students. *NCBE Resource Collection Series No. 5.* Washington, DC: NCBE. Retrieved January 28, 2005, from www.ncela.gwu.edu/pubs/resource/fedpol.htm.

Anstrom, K. (1999a). Preparing secondary education teachers to work with English language learners: Mathematics. *NCBE Resource Collection Series No. 13.* Washington, DC: National Clearinghouse for Bilingual Education. Retrieved July 12, 2008, from www.ncela.gwu.edu/pubs/resource/ells/math.htm.

Anstrom, K. (1999b). Preparing secondary education teachers to work with English language learners: Social studies. *NCBE Resource Collection Series No. 12.* Washington, DC: National Clearinghouse for Bilingual Education. Retrieved July 12, 2008, from www.ncela.gwu.edu/pubs/resource/ells/social.htm.

Anti-Defamation League (2004). *The "December dilemma": December holiday guidelines for public schools.* Retrieved May 27, 2008, from www.adl.org/issue_education/december_dilemma_2004.

Aoki, E. (1992). Turning the page: Asian Pacific American children's literature. In V. J. Harris (Ed.), *Teaching multicultural literature in grades K–8* (pp. 109–135). Norwood, MA: Christopher-Gordon.

Appiah, K. A., & Gates, H. L. (2003). *Africana.* New York: Perseus.

Arab American Institute Foundation. (n.d.). *Quick facts about Arab Americans.* Washington, DC: Author. Retrieved January 13, 2005, from www.aaiusa.org/educational_packet.htm.

Arias, I. (1996). *Proxemics in the ESL classroom.* Retrieved September 2, 2004, from http://exchanges.state.gov/forum/vols/vol34/no1/p32.htm.

Artiles, A. J., & Trent, S. C. (1994). Overrepresentation of minority students in special education: A continuing debate. *Journal of Special Education, 27*(4), 410–437.

Asher, J. (1982). *Learning another language through actions: The complete teachers' guidebook.* Los Gatos, CA: Sky Oaks.

Au, K., & Jordan, C. (1981). Teaching reading to Hawaiian children: Finding a culturally appropriate solution. In H. Trueba, G. Guthrie, & K. Au (Eds.), *Culture and the bilingual classroom: Studies in classroom ethnography* (pp. 139–152). Rowley, MA: Newbury House.

August, D., Hakuta, K., & Pompa, D. (1994). *For all students: Limited English proficient students and Goals 2000.* Washington, DC: National Clearinghouse for Bilingual Education.

August, D., & Pease-Alvarez, L. (1996). *Attributes of effective programs and classrooms serving English language learners.* Santa Cruz, CA: Center for Research on Cultural Diversity and Second Language Learning.

Babbitt, N. (1976). *Tuck everlasting.* New York: Bantam Books.

Baca, L., & Cervantes, H. T. (1984). *The bilingual special education interface.* Columbus, OH: Merrill.

Baca, L., & de Valenzuela, J. S. (1994). *Reconstructing the bilingual special education interface.* Retrieved February 9, 2005, from www.ncela.gwu.edu/pubs/pigs/pig20.htm.

Baker, C. (2001). *Foundations of bilingual education and bilingualism* (3rd ed.). Clevedon, Eng.: Multilingual Matters.

Balderrama, M. V., & Díaz-Rico, L. T. (2006). *Teacher performance expectations for educating English learners.* Boston: Allyn & Bacon.

Bandlow, R. (2002). Suburban bigotry: A descent into racism and struggle for redemption. In F. Schultz (Ed.), *Annual editions: Multicultural education 2002–2003* (pp. 90–93). Guilford, CT: McGraw-Hill/Dushkin.

Banks, C. (2004). Families and teachers working together for school improvement. In J. Banks & C. Banks (Eds.), *Multicultural education: Issues and perspectives* (5th ed., pp. 421–442). Hoboken, NJ: Wiley.

Banks, J. (1994). *An introduction to multicultural education.* Boston: Allyn & Bacon.

Barna, L. M. (2007). Intercultural communication stumbling blocks. In R. Spack (Ed.), *Guidelines: A cross-cultural reading/writing text* (pp. 66–74). New York: Cambridge University Press.

Barr, R., Blachowicz, C. L. Z., Bates, A., Katz, C. & Kaufman, B. (2007). *Reading diagnosis for teachers: An instructional approach.* Boston: Pearson.

Barrett, J. (1978). *Cloudy with a chance of meatballs.* New York: Scholastic Books.

Beck, M. (2004). *California standards assessment workbook.* White Plains, NY: Longman.

Beeghly, D. G., & Prudhoe, C. M. (2002). *Litlinks: Activities for connected learning in elementary classrooms.* Boston: McGraw-Hill.

Bennett, C. (2003). *Comprehensive multicultural education: Theory and practice* (5th ed.). Boston: Allyn & Bacon.

Bermúdez, A., & Márquez, J. (1996). An examination of a four-way collaborative to increase parental involvement in the schools. *Journal of Educational Issues of Language Minority Students, 16.* Retrieved January 28, 2005, from www.ncela.gwu.edu/pubs/jeilms/vol16/jeilms1601.htm.

Bernstein, D. K. (1989). Assessing children with limited English proficiency: Current perspectives. *Topics in Language Disorders, 9,* 15–20.

Bielenberg, B., & Wong Fillmore, L. (2004/2005). The English they need for the test. *Educational Leadership, 62*(4), 45–49.

Bigelow, B. (2007). Rethinking the line between us. *Educational Leadership, 64*(6), 47–61.

Bilingual Education Act, Pub. L. No. (90-247), 81 Stat. 816 (1968).

Bilingual Education Act, Pub. L. No. (93-380), 88 Stat. 503 (1974).

Bilingual Education Act, Pub. L. No. (95-561), 92 Stat. 2268 (1978).

Bilingual Education Act, Pub. L. No. (98-511), 98 Stat. 2370 (1984).

Bilingual Education Act, Pub. L. No. (100-297), 102 Stat. 279 (1988).

Bilingual Education Act, Pub. L. No. (103-382) (1994).

Birdwhistell, R. (1974). The language of the body: The natural environment of words. In A. Silverstein (Ed.), *Human communication: Theoretical explorations* (pp. 203–220). Hillsdale, NJ: Erlbaum.

Bitter, G. G., & Legacy, M. E. (2006). *Using technology in the classroom.* Boston: Pearson.

Bitter, G. G., & Pierson, J. M. (2006). *Using technology in the classroom.* Boston: Pearson.

Black, P., Harrison, C., Lee, C., Marshall, B., Wiliam, D. (2004). Working inside the black box: Assessment for learning in the classroom. *Phi Delta Kappan, 86*(1), 9–21.

Bonilla-Silva, E. (2003). *Racism without racists: Color-blind racism and the persistence of racial inequality in the United States.* Lanham, MD: Rowman & Littlefield.

Bourdieu, P. (with Passeron, J.). (1977). *Reproduction in society, education, and culture.* Los Angeles: Sage.

Brahier, D. J. (2009). *Teaching secondary and middle school mathematics* (3rd ed.). Boston: Pearson.

Brandt, R. (1994). On educating for diversity: A conversation with James A. Banks. *Educational Leadership, 51,* 28–31.

Brass, J. J. (2008). Local knowledge and digital movie composing in an after-school literacy program. *Journal of Adolescent & Adult Literacy, 51*(5), 464–473.

Bratt Paulston, C. (1992). *Sociolinguistic perspectives on bilingual education.* Clevedon, Eng.: Multilingual Matters.

Brewer, D., García, M., & Aguilar, Y. F. (2007, September 7). Some children left behind. *Los Angeles Times,* A29.

Brinton, D. (2003). Content-based instruction. In D. Nunan (Ed.), *Practical English language teaching* (pp. 199–224). New York: McGraw Hill.

Brisk, M. E. (1998). *Bilingual education: From compensatory to quality schooling.* Mahwah, NJ: Erlbaum.

Brown, D. (1987). *Principles of language learning and teaching* (2nd ed.). Englewood Cliffs, NJ: Prentice Hall.

Brown, D. (2000). *Principles of language learning and teaching* (4th ed.). Englewood Cliffs, NJ: Prentice Hall.

Bruder, M. B., Anderson, R., Schultz, G., & Caldera, M. (1991). *Ninos especiales* program: A culturally sensitive early intervention model. *Journal of Early Intervention, 15*(3), 268–277.

Brusca-Vega, R. (2002). Disproportionate representation of English language learners in special education. In *Serving English language learners with disabilities: A resource manual for Illinois educators.* Retrieved February 9, 2005, from www.isbe.state.il.us/spec-ed/bilingualmanual2002.htm.

Buckmaster, R. (2000, June 22–28). First and second languages do battle for the classroom. *(Manchester) Guardian Weekly (Learning English* supplement), 3.

Buell, M. Z. (2004). Code-switching and second-language writing: How multiple codes are combined in a text. In C. Bazerman & P. Prior (Eds.), *What writing does and how it does it* (pp. 97–122). Mahwah, NJ: Erlbaum.

Buettner, E. G. (2002). Sentence-by-sentence self-monitoring. *The Reading Teacher, 56*(1), 34–44.

Bunting, E. (1990). *How many days to America? A Thanksgiving story.* New York: Clarion.

Burgstahler, S. (2008). *Creating video products that are accessible to people with sensory impairments.* Retrieved October 27, 2008, from www.washington.edu/doit/Brochures/Technology/vid_sensory.html.

Burgstahler, S. (2002). *Universal design of instruction.* Retrieved January 25, 2005, from www.washington.edu/doit/Brochures/Academics/instruction.html.

Burke, J. (1999). *The English teacher's companion: A complete guide to classrooms, curriculum, and the profession.* Portsmouth, NH: Boynton Cooke.

Burnette, J. (2000). *Assessment of culturally and linguistically diverse students for special education eligibility.* ERIC Clearinghouse on Disabilities and Gifted Education (ED #E604).

Bursuck, W. D., Polloway, E. A., Plante, L., Epstein, M. H., Jayanthi, M., & McConeghy, J. (1996). Report card grading and adaptations: A national survey of classroom practices. *Exceptional Children, 62,* 301–318.

Caine, R. N., Caine, G., McClintic, C., & Klimek, K. (2004). *Brain/mind learning principles in action: The fieldbook for making connections, teaching, and the human brain.* Thousand Oaks, CA: Sage.

Caine, R., & Caine, G. (1994). *Making connections: Teaching and the human brain*. Menlo Park, CA: Addison Wesley.

Calderón, M. (2007). Adolescent literacy and English language learners: An urgent issue. *ESL Magazine, 56*, 9–14.

Calderón, M., & Slavin, R. (2001). Success for all in a two-way immersion school. In D. Christian & F. Genesee (Eds.), *Bilingual Education*. Alexandria, VA: Teachers of English to Speakers of Other Languages.

California Department of Education (CDE). (1992). *Handbook for teaching Korean-American students*. Sacramento: Author.

California Department of Education (CDE). (1994). *Physical education framework*. Retrieved October 18, 2004, from www.cde.ca.gov/ci/cr/cf/allfwks.asp.

California Department of Education (CDE). (1995). Educational Demographics Unit. *Language census report for California public schools*. Sacramento: Author.

California Department of Education (CDE). (1998a). *English-language arts content standards*. Retrieved March 17, 2005, from www.cde.ca.gov/be/st/ss/engmain.asp.

California Department of Education (CDE). (1998b). *Visual and performing arts standards*. Retrieved October 18, 2004, from www.cde.ca.gov/be/st/ss/vamain.asp.

California Department of Education (CDE). (1999). *Reading/language arts framework for California public schools*. Sacramento: Author. Retrieved September 10, 2004, from www.cde.ca.gov/cdepress/lang_arts.pdf.

California Department of Education (CDE). (2002). *English language development standards*. Sacramento: Author. Retrieved September 10, 2004, from www.cde.ca.gov.

California State Code of Regulations. (1998). *Title 5, Division 1, Chapter 11: English language learner education. Subchapter 4. English language learner education*. Retrieved May 16, 2001, from www.cde.ca.gov/prop227.html.

Canale, M. (1983). From communicative competence to communicative language pedagogy. In J. Richards & R. Schmidt (Eds.), *Language and communication* (pp. 2–27). New York: Longman.

Carkin, G. (2004). Drama and pronunciation. *Essential Teacher, Compleat Links, 1*(5). Retrieved January 27, 2005, from www.tesol.org/s_tesol/sec_document.asp?CID=724&DID=3021.

Carnuccio, L. M. (2004). Cybersites. *Essential Teacher, 1*(3), 59.

Carr, J., & Lagunoff, R. (2006). *The map of standards for English learners, Grades K–5 and Grades 6–12 versions* (5th ed.). San Francisco: WestEd. Retrieved May 30, 2008, from www.wested.org/cs/we/view/rs/796.

Carrasquillo, A., & Rodríguez, V. (2002). *Language minority students in the mainstream classroom*. Clevedon, Eng.: Multilingual Matters.

Cartagena, J. (1991). English only in the 1980s: A product of myths, phobias, and bias. In S. Benesch (Ed.), *ESL in America: Myths and possibilities* (pp. 11–26). Portsmouth, NH: Boynton/Cook.

Casey, J. (2004). A place for first language in the ESOL classroom. *Essential Teacher, 1*(4), 50–52.

Casteñada v. Pickard, 648 F.2d 989 (5th Cir. 1981).

CATESOL. (1998). *CATESOL position statement on literacy instruction for English language learners, grades K–12*. Retrieved September 14, 2004, from www.catesol.org/literacy.html.

Cavanaugh, C. (2006). *Clips from the classroom: Learning with technology*. Boston: Allyn & Bacon.

Cazden, C. (1986). ESL teachers as language advocates for children. In P. Rigg & D. S. Enright (Eds.), *Children and ESL: Integrating perspectives* (pp. 9–21). Alexandria, VA: Teachers of English to Speakers of Other Languages.

Center for Advanced Research on Language Acquisition. (2001). *K–12 less commonly taught languages*. Retrieved January 12, 2005, from http://carla.acad.umn.edu:591/k12.html.

Center for Research on Education, Diversity, & Excellence. (2002). *Instructional conversation*. Retrieved October 24, 2008, from http://crede.berkeley.edu/Standards/5inst_con.shtml.

Center for Research on Education, Diversity, and Excellence (CREDE). (2004). *Observing the five standards of practice*. Retrieved April 8, 2005, from www.cal.org/crede/pubs/rb11.pdf.

Chamot, A. U., Barnhardt, S., El-Dinary, P. B., & Robbins, J. (1999). *The learning strategies handbook*. White Plains, NY: Longman.

Chamot, A., & O'Malley, J. M. (1994). *The CALLA handbook: Implementing the cognitive academic language learning approach*. Reading, MA: Addison-Wesley.

Chan, L. (2004). The inexorable demand for qualified ESL teachers. *Language Magazine, 3*(6), 30–31.

Chandler, D. (2005). *Semiotics for beginners*. Retrieved January 27, 2005, from www.aber.ac.uk/media/Documents/S4B/semiotic.html.

Chang, B., & Au, W. (2007–2008). Unmasking the myth of the model minority. *Rethinking Schools, 22*(2), 14–19.

Chang, J-M. (2005). *Asian American children in special education: Need for multidimensional collaboration*. Retrieved February 2, 2005, from www.dinf.ne.jp/doc/english/Us_Eu/ada_e/pres_com/pres-dd/chang.htm.

Chesterfield, R., & Chesterfield, K. (1985). Natural order in children's use of second language learning strategies. *Applied Linguistics, 6,* 45–59.

Children's Defense Fund. (2004a). *Defining poverty and why it matters for children*. Retrieved January 15, 2005, from www.childrensdefense.org/family income/childpoverty/default.asp.

Children's Defense Fund. (2004b). *Each day in America*. Retrieved January 15, 2005, from www.childrensdefense.org/data/eachday.asp.

Children's Defense Fund. (2004c). *2003 facts on child poverty in America*. Retrieved January 13, 2005, from www.childrensdefense.org/familyincome/childpoverty/basicfacts.asp.

Cho Bassoff, T. (2004). Compleat Links: Three steps toward a strong home–school connection. *Essential Teacher, 1*(4). Retrieved February 8, 2005, from www.tesol.org/s_tesol/sec_document.asp?CID=658 &DID=2586.

Chomsky, N. (1959). Review of B. F. Skinner "Verbal Behavior." *Language, 35,* 26–58.

Christensen, L. (2000). *Reading, writing, rising up: Teaching about social justice and the power of the written word*. Milwaukee, WI: Rethinking Schools.

Civil Rights Act, Pub. L. No. (88-352), 78 Stat.(1964).

Clark, B. (1983). *Growing up gifted: Developing the potential of children at home and at school* (2nd ed.). Columbus, OH: Merrill.

Cloud, N., Genesee, F., & Hamayan, E. (2000). *Dual language instruction*. Boston: Heinle and Heinle.

Cohen, E., Lotan, R., & Catanzarite, L. (1990). Treating status problems in the cooperative classroom. In S. Sharon (Ed.), *Cooperative learning: Theory and research* (pp. 203–229). New York: Praeger.

Coiro, J. (2003). Exploring literacy on the Internet. *The Reading Teacher, 56*(5), 458–460.

Cole, K. (2007). Pressures and promise in the mainstream classroom. In K. Cole, C. Collier, & S. Herrera (Eds.), *Making the right investments: Strengthening the education of English language and bilingual learners: Research conference proceedings* (pp. 3–11). Harrisburg, PA: Center for Schools and Communities.

Cole, M. (1998, April 16). *Cultural psychology: Can it help us think about diversity?* Presentation at the annual meeting of the American Educational Research Association, San Diego.

College Entrance Examination Board. (2003). *National report on college-bound seniors, by race/ethnicity: Selected years, 1986–87 to 2002–03*. Retrieved March 20, 2005, from http://nces.ed.gov/programs/digest/d03/tables/dt131.asp.

Collier, L. (2008). The importance of academic language for English language learners. *The Council Chronicle, 17*(3), 10–13.

Collier, V. (1987). Age and rate of acquisition of second language for academic purposes. *TESOL Quarterly, 21*(4), 617–641.

Collier, V. P. (1995). Acquiring a second language for school. *Directions in Language & Education*. Retrieved April 8, 2005, from www.ncela.gwu.edu/pubs/directions/04.htm.

Conchas, G. Q. (2006). *The color of success: Race and high-achieving urban youth*. New York: Teachers College Press.

Conley, M. W. (2008). *Content area literacy: Learners in context*. Boston: Allyn & Bacon.

Connell, B., Jones, M., Mace, R., Mueller, J., Mullick, A., Ostroff, E., Sanford, J., Steinfield, E., Story, M., & Vanderheiden, G. (1997). *The principles of universal design (Version 2.0)*. Retrieved January 25, 2005, from www.design.ncsu.edu.8120/cud/univ_ design/principles/udprinciples.htm.

Connor, M. H., & Boskin, J. (2001). Overrepresentation of bilingual and poor children in special education classes: A continuing problem. *Journal of Children and Poverty, 7*(1), 23–32.

Cook, V. (1999). Going beyond the native speaker in language teaching. *TESOL Quarterly, 33*(2), 185–209.

Copeland, L. (2008, March 3). Cold realities take back seat in this classroom. *USA Today,* 9D.

Corson, D. (1990). *Language policy across the curriculum.* Clevedon, Eng.: Multilingual Matters.

Corson, D. (1999). *Language policy in schools: A resource for teachers and administrators.* Mahwah, NJ: Erlbaum.

Cortés, C. (1993). Acculturation, assimilation, and "adducation." *BEOutreach, 4*(1), 3–5.

Cotton, K. (1989). *Expectations and student outcomes.* Retrieved April 6, 2005, from www.nwrel .org/scpd/sirs/4/cu7.html.

Coutinho, M. J., & Oswald, D. P. (2004). *Dispropor–tionate representation of culturally and linguistically diverse students in special education: Measuring the problem.* National Center for Culturally Responsive Educational Systems. Retrieved July 12, 2008, from www.nccrest.org/publications.html.

Cox, K. B. (2008, May 14). Reading a little more closely. Letter to the editor, *Los Angeles Times,* A20.

Crago, M. (1993). Communicative interaction and second language acquisition: An Inuit example. *TESOL Quarterly, 26*(3), 487–506.

Craig, B. A. (1996). Parental attitudes toward bilingualism in a local two-way immersion program. *Bilingual Research Journal, 10*(3 & 4), 383–410.

Crawford, J. (1997). *Best evidence: Research foundations of the Bilingual Education Act.* Retrieved April 8, 2005, from www.ncela.gwu.edu/pubs/reports/bestevidence.

Crawford, J. (1998). *Ten common fallacies about bilingual education.* Retrieved April 8, 2005, from www.cal.org/resources/digest/crawford01.html.

Crawford, J. (1999). *Bilingual education: History, politics, theory, and practice* (4th ed.). Los Angeles: Bilingual Educational Services.

Crawford, J. (2003). *Language legislation in the U.S.A.* Retrieved March 19, 2005, from http://ourworld .compuserve.com/homepages/JWCRAWFORD/
langleg.htm.

Crawford, J. (2004a). *Educating English learners: Language diversity in the classroom* (formerly *A bilingual education: History, politics, theory, and practice*). Los Angeles: Bilingual Educational Services.

Crawford, J. (2004b). Has two-way been oversold? *Bilingual Family Newsletter* (Multilingual Matters), *21*(1), 3.

Crawford, L. (1993). *Language and literacy learning in multicultural classrooms.* Boston: Allyn & Bacon.

Criston, L. (1993, May 23). Has he stepped out of the shadow? *Los Angeles Times Calendar,* pp. 6, 70, 72.

Cronin, J., Dahlin, M., Adkins, D., & Kingsbury, G. G. (2007). *The proficiency illusion.* Thomas B. Fordham Institute. Retrieved June 27, 2008, from www.edexcellence.net/detail/news.cfm?news_ id=376.

Cummins, J. (1979). Cognitive/academic language proficiency, linguistic interdependence, the optimum age question and some other matters. *Working Papers on Bilingualism, 19,* 121–129.

Cummins, J. (1980). The cross-lingual dimensions of language proficiency: Implications for bilingual education and the optimal age issue. *TESOL Quarterly, 14*(2), 175–187.

Cummins, J. (1981a). Age on arrival and immigrant second language learning in Canada: A reassessment. *Applied Linguistics 2*(2), 132–149.

Cummins, J. (1981b). The role of primary language development in promoting educational success for language minority students. In *Schooling and language minority students: A theoretical framework* (pp. 3–49). Sacramento: California State Department of Education.

Cummins, J. (1984). *Bilingualism and special education: Issues in assessment and pedagogy.* San Diego: College-Hill.

Cummins, J. (1986). Empowering minority students: A framework for intervention. *Harvard Educational Review, 56*(1), 18–36.

Cummins, J. (1989). *Empowering minority students.* Sacramento: California Association for Bilingual Education.

Cummins, J. (2001). *Negotiating identities: Education for empowerment in a diverse society*. Los Angeles: California Association for Bilingual Education.

Cummins, J. (2003). Reading and the bilingual student: Fact and friction. In G. García (Ed.), *English learners reaching the highest level of English literacy* (pp. 2–33). Newark, DE: International Reading Association.

Cummins, J. (2008). *The role of culture in reading instruction*. Presentation at the annual conference of the Teachers of English to Speakers of Other Language.

Cunningham, C. A., & Billingsley, M. (2006). *Curriculum webs: Weaving the web into teaching and learning*. Boston: Pearson.

Curtain, H., & Dahlberg, C. A. (2004). *Language and children—Making the match: New languages for young learners, grades K–8*. Boston: Allyn & Bacon.

Cushner, K. (1999). *Human diversity in action*. Boston: McGraw-Hill.

Dale, T., & Cuevas, G. (1987). Integrating language and mathematics learning. In J. Crandall (Ed.), *ESL through content-area instruction: Mathematics, science, social studies*. Englewood Cliffs, NJ: Regents/Prentice Hall.

Dale, T., & Cuevas, G. (1992). Integrating mathematics and language learning. In P. Richard-Amato & M. Snow (Eds.), *The multicultural classroom* (pp. 330–348). White Plains, NY: Longman.

Dalle, T. S., & Young, L. J. (2003). *PACE yourself: A handbook for ESL tutors*. Alexandria, VA: Teachers of English to Speakers of Other Languages.

Darder, A. (1991). *Culture and power in the classroom*. New York: Bergin and Garvey.

Day, F. A. (1994). *Multicultural voices in contemporary literature: A resource for teachers*. Portsmouth, NH: Heinemann.

Day, F. A. (1997). *Latina and Latino voices in literature for children and teenagers*. Portsmouth, NH: Heinemann.

Day, F. A. (2003). *Latina and Latino voices in literature: Lives and works*. Westport, CT: Greenwood Publishers.

De la Paz, S. (2007). Best practices in teaching writing to students with special needs. In S. Graham, C. A. MacArthur, & J. Fitzgerald (Eds.), *Best practices in writing instruction* (pp. 308–328). New York: Guilford.

Delgado-Gaitan, C., & Trueba, H. (1991). *Crossing cultural borders: Education for immigrant families in America*. London: Falmer Press.

Denver Public Schools. (2002). *Newcomer centers*. Denver, CO: Author.

dePaola, T. (1981). *Now one foot, now the other*. New York: Putnam's.

Derman-Sparks, L., & Anti-Bias Curriculum Task Force. (1988). *Anti-bias curriculum: Tools for empowering young children*. Washington, DC: National Association for the Education of Young Children.

Dewitz, P., & Dewitz, P. K. (2003). They can read the words, but they can't understand: Refining comprehension assessment. *The Reading Teacher, 56*(3), 422–435.

Diamond, B., & Moore, M. (1995). *Multicultural literacy*. White Plains, NY: Longman.

Díaz-Rico, L. (1993). From monocultural to multicultural teaching in an inner-city middle school. In A. Woolfolk (Ed.), *Readings and cases in educational psychology* (pp. 272–279). Boston: Allyn & Bacon.

Díaz-Rico, L. T. (2000). Intercultural communication in teacher education: The knowledge base for CLAD teacher credential programs. *CATESOL Journal, 12*(1), 145–161.

Díaz-Rico, L. T. (2008). *Strategies for teaching English learners*. Boston: Allyn & Bacon.

Díaz-Rico, L. T. (2008). *Teaching English learners*. Boston: Allyn & Bacon.

Díaz-Rico, L. T., & Dullien, S. (2004). *Semiotics and people watching*. Presentation at the regional conference of the California Teachers of English to Speakers of Other Languages regional conference, Los Angeles.

Dicker, S. (1992). Societal views of bilingualism and language learning. *TESOL: Applied Linguistics Interest Section Newsletter, 14*(1), 1, 4.

Digest of Education Statistics. (2003a). *College enrollment and labor force status of 2001 and 2002 high school completers, by sex and race/ethnicity: October 2001 and October 2002* (Table 382). Retrieved January 28, 2005, from http://nces.ed.gov/programs/digest/d03/tables/dt382.asp.

Doggett, G. (1986). *Eight approaches to language teaching.* Washington, DC: Center for Applied Linguistics/ERIC Clearinghouse on Languages and Linguistics.

Domenech, D. (2008). Upholding standards. *Language Magazine, 7*(8), 24–26.

Dresser, N. (1993). *Our own stories.* White Plains, NY: Longman.

Dryfoos, J. (1998). *Safe passage: Making it through adolescence in a risky society.* New York: Oxford University Press.

Dudley-Marling, C., & Paugh, P. (2004). *A classroom teacher's guide to struggling readers.* Portsmouth, NH: Heinemann.

Dudley-Marling, C., & Searle, D. (1991). *When students have time to talk.* Portsmouth, NH: Heinemann.

Duran, B. J., Dugan, T., & Weffer, R. E. (1997). Increasing teacher effectiveness with language minority students. *High School Journal, 80*(4), 238–246.

Dutro, S., & Moran, C. (2003). Rethinking English language instruction: An architectural approach. In G. García (Ed.), *English learners reaching the highest level of English literacy* (pp. 227–258). Newark, DE: International Reading Association.

Dyson, M. E. (1996). *Between God and gangsta rap: Bearing witness to black culture.* New York: Oxford University Press.

Echevarria, J., & Graves, A. (2007). *Sheltered content instruction: Teaching English language learners with diverse abilities.* Boston: Allyn & Bacon.

Echevarria, J., Vogt, M. E., & Short, D. (2004). *Making content comprehensible for English language learners: The SIOP model* (2nd ed.). Boston: Allyn & Bacon.

Eckert, A. (1992). *Sorrow in our heart.* New York: Bantam.

Edmonson, M. (1971). *Lore: An introduction to the science of fiction.* New York: Holt, Rinehart and Winston.

EdSource (2008, March). *English learners in California: What the numbers say.* Mountain View, CA: Author.

Egbert, J. (2004). Access to knowledge: Implications of Universal Design for CALL environments. *CALL_EJ Online, 5*(2). Retrieved October 27, 2008, from www.tell.is.ritsumei.ac.jp/callejonline/journal/5–2/egbert.html.

Egbert, J., & Hanson-Smith, E. (2007). *CALL environments: Research, practice, and critical issues* (2nd ed.). Alexandria, VA: Teachers of English to Speakers of Other Languages.

Ehri, L. C. (1995). Phases of development in learning to read words by sight. *Journal of Research in Reading, 18,* 116–125.

Ellis, R. (1988). *Classroom second language development.* New York: Prentice Hall.

Enright, D., & McCloskey, M. (1988). *Integrating English: Developing English language and literacy in the multilingual classroom.* Reading, MA: –Addison-Wesley.

Equal Educational Opportunities Act of 1974, Pub. L. No. (93-380), 88 Stat. 514 (1974).

Erickson, F. (1977). Some approaches to inquiry in school-community ethnography. *Anthropology and Education Quarterly, 8*(2), 58–69.

Escalante, J., & Dirmann, J. (1990). The Jaime Escalante math program. *Journal of Negro Education, 59*(3), 407–423.

Fairclough, N. (1989). *Language and power.* New York: Longman.

Fairclough, N. (1997). *Critical discourse analysis: The critical study of language.* Reading, MA: Addison-Wesley.

Faltis, C. J., & Coulter, C. A. (2008). *Teaching English learners and immigrant students in secondary schools.* Upper Saddle River, NJ: Pearson Merrill Prentice Hall.

Farrell, T. S. C. (2006). *Succeeding with English language learners: A guide for beginning teachers.* Thousand Oaks, CA: Corwin.

Feagin, J., & Feagin, C. (1993). *Racial and ethnic relations* (4th ed.). Englewood Cliffs, NJ: Prentice Hall.

Feng, J. (1994). Asian-American children: What teachers should know. *ERIC Digest,* ED 369577.

Figueroa, R. A. (1989). Psychological testing of linguistic minority students: Knowledge gaps and regulations. *Exceptional Children, 56*(2), 145–152.

Figueroa, R. A. (1993). The reconstruction of bilingual special education. *Focus on Diversity, 3*(3), 2–3.

Figueroa, R., Fradd, S. H., & Correa, V. I. (1989). Bilingual special education and this issue. *Exceptional Children, 56,* 174–178.

Finders, M. J., & Hynds, S. (2007). *Language arts and literacy in the middle grades: Planning, teaching, and assessing learning.* Upper Saddle River, NJ: Pearson.

Finnan, C. (1987). The influence of the ethnic community on the adjustment of Vietnamese refugees. In G. Spindler & L. Spindler (Eds.), *Interpretive ethnography of education: At home and abroad* (pp. 313–330). Hillsdale, NJ: Erlbaum.

Fisher, M. (2005). From the coffee house to the schoolhouse: The promise and potential of spoken word poetry in school contexts. *English Education, 37,* 115–131.

Fitzgerald, J. (1999). What is this thing called "balance"? *Reading Teacher, 53*(2), 100–107.

Fitzgerald, J., & Amendum, S. (2007). What is sound writing instruction for multilingual learners? In S. Graham, C. A. MacArthur, & J. Fitzgerald (Eds.), *Best practices in writing instruction* (pp. 289–307). New York: Guilford.

Florida Department of Education. (2003). *Inclusion as an instructional model for LEP students.* Retrieved February 10, 2005, from www.firn.edu/doe/omsle/tapinclu.htm.

Flynt, E. S., & Cooter, R. B. (1999). *The English–Español reading inventory for the classroom.* Upper Saddle River, NJ: Merrill Prentice Hall.

Ford, D. Y. (1998). The underrepresentation of minority students in gifted education: Problems and promises in recruitment and retention. *Journal of Special Education, 32*(1), 4–14.

Foucault, M. (1979). *Discipline and punish: The birth of the prison.* New York: Vintage Books.

Foucault, M. (1980). *Power/knowledge: Selected interviews and other writings 1971–1977.* New York: Pantheon Books.

Frank, A. (1997). *The diary of Anne Frank* (O. Frank and M. Pressler, Eds.; S. Massotty, Trans.). New York: Bantam.

Freeman, D. E., & Freeman, Y. S. (2004). *Essential linguistics: What you need to know to teach.* Portsmouth, NH: Heinemann.

Freeman, R. (2004). *Building on community bilingualism.* Philadelphia: Caslon.

Freeman, Y., & Freeman, D. (1998). *ESL/EFL teaching: Principles for success.* Portsmouth, NH: Heinemann.

Freire, P. (1985). *The politics of education* (D. Macedo, Trans.). New York: Bergin and Garvey.

Frey, N., & Fisher, D. (2007). *Reading for information in the elementary school: Content literacy strategies to build comprehension.* Upper Saddle River, NJ: Pearson.

Friend, M., & Bursuck, W. D. (2006). *Including students with special needs: A practical guide for classroom teachers* (4th ed.). Boston: Allyn & Bacon.

Friend, M., & Cook, L. (1996). *Interactions: Collaboration skills for school professionals.* White Plains, NY: Longman.

From the Classroom. (1991). Teachers seek a fair and meaningful assessment process to measure LEP students' progress. *Teacher Designed Learning, 2*(1), 1, 3.

Fromkin, V., Rodman, R., & Hyams, N. (2003). *An introduction to language* (7th ed.). Boston: Heinle and Heinle.

Fuller, M., & Olson, G. (1998). *Home-school relations: Working successfully with parents and families.* Boston: Allyn & Bacon.

Funaki, I., & Burnett, K. (1993). *When educational systems collide: Teaching and learning with Polynesian students.* Presentation at the annual conference of the Association of Teacher Educators, Los Angeles.

Furey, P. (1986). A framework for cross-cultural analysis of teaching methods. In P. Byrd (Ed.), *Teaching across cultures in the university ESL program* (pp. 15–29). Washington, DC: National Association of Foreign Student Advisors.

Gaitan, C. D. (2006). *Building culturally responsive classrooms.* Thousand Oaks, CA: Corwin.

Galindo, R. (1997). Language wars: The ideological dimensions of the debates on bilingual education. *Bilingual Research Journal, 21*(2 & 3). Retrieved February 5, 2005, from http://brj.asu.edu/archives/23v21/articles/art5.html#issues.

Gándara, P. (1997). *Review of research on instruction of limited English proficient students.* Davis: University of California, Linguistic Minority Research Institute.

García, E. (2004). The many languages of art. In M. Goldberg (Ed.), *Teaching English language learners through the arts: A SUAVE experience* (pp. 43–54). Boston: Pearson.

García, E. E., & Jensen, B. (2007). Helping young Hispanic learners. *Educational Leadership, 64*(6), 34–39.

García, S. B., & Ortiz, A. A. (2004). *Preventing disproportionate representation: Culturally and linguistically responsive prereferral interventions.* National Center for Culturally Responsive Educational Systems. Retrieved January 25, 2005, from www.nccrest.org/publications.html.

Gardner, H. (1983). *Frames of mind: The theory of multiple intelligences.* New York: Basic Books.

Gardner, R., & Lambert, W. (1972). *Attitudes and motivation in second language learning.* Rowley, MA: Newbury House.

Gass, S. (2000, March 15). *Roundtable on interaction in classroom discourse.* Presentation at the annual meeting of the Teachers of English to Speakers of Other Languages, Vancouver, Canada.

Gass, S., & Selinker, L. (2001). *Second language acquisition.* Mahwah, NJ: Erlbaum.

Gay, G. (1975, October). Cultural differences important in education of black children. *Momentum, 30–32.*

Genesee, F. (Ed.). (1999). *Program alternatives for linguistically diverse students.* Santa Cruz, CA: Center for Research on Education, Diversity and Excellence. Retrieved April 8, 2005, from www.cal.org/crede/pubs/edpractice/Epr1.pdf.

Gibbons, P. (2006). Steps for planning an integrated program for ESL learners in mainstream classes. In P. McKay (Ed.), *Planning and teaching creatively within a required curriculum* (pp. 215–233). Alexandria, VA: Teachers of English to Speakers of Other Languages.

Gibson, M. (1991). Minorities and schooling: Some implications. In M. Gibson & J. Ogbu (Eds.), *Minority status and schooling. A comparative study of immigrant and involuntary minorities* (pp. 357–381). New York: Garland.

Gilbert, J. B. (2006). *Clear speech: Pronunciation and listening comprehension in North American English.* New York: Cambridge University Press.

Gillett, P. (1989a). *Cambodian refugees: An introduction to their history and culture.* Available from New Faces of Liberty/SFSC, P.O. Box 5646, San Francisco, CA 94101.

Gillett, P. (1989b). *El Salvador: A country in crisis.* Available from New Faces of Liberty/SFSC, P.O. Box 5646, San Francisco, CA 94101.

Giroux, H. (1983). Theories of reproduction and resistance in the new sociology of education: A critical appraisal. *Harvard Educational Review, 53,* 257–293.

Giroux, H., & McLaren, P. (1996). Teacher education and the politics of engagement: The case for democratic schooling. *Harvard Educational Review, 56*(3), 213–238.

Glaser, S., & Brown, C. (1993). *Portfolios and beyond: Collaborative assessment in reading and writing.* Norwood, MA: Christopher-Gordon.

Goals 2000: Educate America Act Pub. L. No. (103-227), (1994).

Gollnick, D. M., & Chinn, P. C. (2006). *Multicultural education in a pluralistic society* (7th ed.). Upper Saddle River, NJ: Merrill Prentice Hall.

Gómez v. Illinois State Board of Education, 811 F. 2d 1030 (7th Cir. 1987).

González, V. (1994). Bilingual special voices. *NABE News, 17*(6), 19–22.

Good, T., & Brophy, J. (1984). *Looking in classrooms* (3rd ed.). New York: Harper & Row.

Goodman, K. (1986). *What's whole in whole language?* Portsmouth, NH: Heinemann.

Gopaul-McNicol, S., & Thomas-Presswood, T. (1998). *Working with linguistically and culturally different children.* Boston: Allyn & Bacon.

Gordon, M. (1964). *Assimilation in American life.* New York: Oxford University Press.

Gorman, A., & Pierson, D. (2007, September 13). Not at home with English. *Los Angeles Times,* A1, A17.

Gottlieb, M. (1995). Nurturing student learning through portfolios. *TESOL Journal, 5*(1), 12–14.

Gottlieb, M. (2006). *Assessing English language learners.* Thousand Oaks, CA: Corwin.

Gottlieb, M. (2007). *Teacher's manual for Rigby ELL assessment kit.* Orlando, FL: Harcourt Achieve.

Gottlieb, M. (Prin. Writer). (n.d.). *The language proficiency handbook.* Illinois State Board of Education. Retrieved January 7, 2005, from www.isbe.net/assessment/PDF/lang_pro.pdf.

Graham, C. (1978). *Jazz chants*. New York: Oxford University Press.

Graham, C. (1992). *Singing, chanting, telling tales*. Englewood Cliffs, NJ: Regents/Prentice Hall.

Graham, S., & Harris, K. H. (2005). Improving the writing performance of young struggling writers: Theoretical and programmatic research from the Center on Accelerating Student Learning. *Journal of Special Education, 39,* 19–33.

Gramsci, A. (1971). *Selections from the prison notebooks of Antonio Gramsci* (Q. Hoare & G. N. Smith, Trans. and Eds.). New York: International Publishers.

Grant, C. A., & Sleeter, C. (1986). *After the school bell rings*. Philadelphia: Falmer Press.

Greaver, M., & Hedberg, K. (2001). Daily reading interventions to help targeted ESL and non-ESL students. Retrieved September 17, 2004, from www.fcps.k12.va.us/DeerParkES/TR/reading/reading.htm.

Green, A. (2007, March 12). This class is learning to its own beat. *Los Angeles Times,* B3.

Greene, J. P. (1998). *A meta-analysis of the effectiveness of bilingual education*. Claremont, CA: Tomas Rivera Policy Institute.

Griffin, J., & Morgan, L. (1998). Physical education—WRITE ON! *Strategies, 11*(4), 34–37.

Grognet, A., Jameson, J., Franco, L., Derrick-Mescua, M. (2000). *Enhancing English language learning in elementary classrooms study guide*. McHenry, IL: Center for Applied Linguistics and Delta Systems.

Guillarme, A. M. (2008). *K–12 classroom teaching: A primer for professionals* (3rd ed.). Upper Saddle River, NJ: Pearson Merrill Prentice Hall.

Gunning, T. G. (2005). *Creating literacy: Instruction for all students* (5th ed.). Boston: Allyn & Bacon.

Guth, N. (2002). Community Literacy Day: A new school develops community support. *The Reading Teacher, 56*(8), 234–235.

Hadaway, N. L., Vardell, S. M., & Young, T. A. (2002). *Literature-based instruction with English language learners, K–12*. Boston: Allyn & Bacon.

Hakuta, K. (1986). *Mirror of language*. New York: Basic Books.

Hakuta, K., Butler, Y. G., & Witt, D. (2000). *How long does it take English learners to attain proficiency?* Santa Barbara: University of California Linguistic Minority Research Institute Policy Report 2000–2001.

Hall, E. (1959). *The silent language*. New York: Anchor Books.

Halliday, M. (1975). *Learning how to mean: Explorations in the development of language*. London: Edward Arnold.

Halliday, M. (1978). *Language as a social semiotic*. Baltimore: University Park Press.

Hamayan, E. (1994). Language development of low-literacy students. In F. Genesee (Ed.), *Educating second language children* (pp. 278–300). Cambridge: Cambridge University Press.

Hammond, J. (2006). The potential of peer scaffolding for ESL students in the mainstream class. In P. McKay (Ed.), *Planning and teaching creatively within a required curriculum* (pp. 149–170). Alexandria, VA: Teachers of English to Speakers of Other Languages.

Han, Z. (2004). *Fossilization in adult second language acquisition*. Clevedon, Eng.: Multilingual Matters.

Hancock, C. (1994). Alternative assessment and second language study: What and why? *ERIC Digest*. ED376695.

Hankes, J. E., & Fast, G. R. (Eds.). (2002). *Changing the face of mathematics: Perspectives on indigenous people of North America*. Reston, VA: National Council of Teachers of Mathematics.

Hansen, J. W. (2000). Parables of technological literacy. *Journal of Engineering Technology, 17*(2), 29–31.

Hanson-Smith, E. (1997). *Technology in the classroom: Practice and promise in the 21st century*. Alexandria, VA: Teachers of English to Speakers of Other Languages.

Hardt, U. (1992, Spring). Teaching multicultural understanding. *Oregon English Journal, 13*(1), 3–5.

Harris, P. (2006). Teaching English language learners. *The Council Chronicle* (NCTE) *16*(1), 1, 5–7.

Harris, V. (1997). *Teaching multicultural literature in grades K–8*. Norwood, MA: Christopher-Gordon.

Hart, L. (1975). *How the brain works: A new understanding of human learning, emotion, and thinking*. New York: Basic Books.

Hart, L. (1983). *Human brain, human learning.* New York: Longman.

Hayasaki, E. (2004, December 3). Cultural divide on campus. *Los Angeles Times,* A1, A36–A37.

Haycock, K. (2001). Closing the achievement gap. *Educational Leadership, 58*(6), 6–11.

Hayes, C. (1998). *Literacy con cariño: A story of migrant children's success.* Portsmouth, NH: Heinemann.

Haynes, J. (2004, Winter). What effective classroom teachers do. *Essential Teacher, 1*(5), 6–7.

Haynes, J. (2007). The December dilemma and English language learners. *Essential Teacher, 4*(4), 6–7.

Heath, S. (1983a). Language policies. *Society, 20*(4), 56–63.

Heath, S. (1983b). *Ways with words.* Cambridge, Eng.: Cambridge University Press.

Heide, F., & Gilliland, J. (1990). *The day of Ahmed's secret.* New York: Lothrop, Lee, & Shepard.

Heilman, A. W. (2002). *Phonics in proper perspective* (9th ed.). Upper Saddle River, NJ: Merrill Prentice Hall.

Helfand, D. (2005, March 24). Nearly half of Blacks, Latinos drop out, school study shows. *Los Angeles Times,* A1, A26.

Henderson, D., & May, J. (2005). *Exploring culturally diverse literature for children and adolescents.* Boston: Pearson.

Henwood, D. (1997). Trash-o-nomics. In M. Wray, M. Newitz, & A. Newitz, (Eds.), *White trash: Race and class in America* (pp. 177–191). New York: Routledge.

Hernández, B. (2005, January 12). Numerical grades help schools to measure progress. *Los Angeles Times,* B2.

Hernandez, H. (2001). *Multicultural education: A teacher's guide to linking context, process, and content* (2nd ed.). Upper Saddle River, NJ: Merrill Prentice Hall.

Herrell, A. (2000). *Fifty strategies for teaching English language learners.* Upper Saddle River, NJ: Merrill.

Hibbard, K. L., & Moutes, M. (2006). *Instructor's resource manual and test bank for Friend and Bursack's* Including students with special needs. Boston: Allyn & Bacon.

Hibbing, A. N., & Rankin-Erickson, J. L. (2003). A picture is worth a thousand words: Using visual images to improve comprehension for middle school struggling readers. *The Reading Teacher, 56*(8), 758–770.

Hinton, L., & Hale, K. (Eds.). (2001). *The green book of language revitalization in practice.* Burlington, MA: Elsevier.

Hispanic Concerns Study Committee. (1987). *Hispanic concerns study committee report.* Available from National Education Association, 1201 Sixteenth Street NW, Washington, DC 20036.

Hispanic Dropout Project. (1998). *No more excuses: The final report of the Hispanic Dropout Project.* Washington, DC: U.S. Department of Education, Office of the Under Secretary. Retrieved July 12, 2008, from www.ncela.gov/edu/pubs/hdp/.

Hopstock, P. J., & Stephenson, T. (2003). *Descriptive study of services to LEP students and LEP students with disabilities.* Washington, DC: U.S. Department of Education. Retrieved July 12, 2008, from www.ncela.gwu.edu/resabout/research/descriptivestudyfiles.

Howard, G. R. (2007). As diversity grows, so must we. *Educational Leadership, 64*(6), 16–22.

Hruska-Riechmann, S., & Grasha, A. F. (1982). The Grasha-Riechmann Student Learning Scales: Research findings and applications. In J. Keefe (Ed.), *Student learning styles and brain behavior* (pp. 81–86). Reston, VA: National Association of Secondary School Principals.

Hughes, J. (2004). On bridge making. *Essential Teacher, 1*(1), 8–10.

Hymes, D. (1961). The ethnography of speaking. In T. Gladwin & W. Sturtevant (Eds.), *Anthropology and human behavior* (pp. 13–53). Washington, DC: Anthropological Society of Washington.

Idaho Migrant Council v. Board of Education, 647 F. 2d 69 (9th Cir. 1981).

Improving America's Schools Act (IASA). 1994 (P.L. 103-382).

Institute for Education in Transformation. (1992). *Voices from the inside: A report on schooling from inside the classroom.* Available from the Institute for Education in Transformation, Claremont Graduate School, 121 East Tenth St., Claremont, CA 91711-6160.

Ishii, S., & Bruneau, T. (1991). Silence and silences in cross-cultural perspective: Japan and the United States. In L. Samovar & R. Porter (Eds.), *Intercultural communication: A reader* (6th ed., pp. 314–319). Belmont, CA: Wadsworth.

Jacobs, V., Goldberg, M., & Bennett, T. (2004). Experiencing science through the arts. In M. Goldberg (Ed.), *Teaching English language learners through the arts: A SUAVE experience* (pp. 87–98). Boston: Pearson.

Jenks, C., Lee, J. O., & Kanpol, B. (2002). Approaches to multicultural education in preservice teacher education: Philosophical frameworks and models for teaching. In F. Schultz (Ed.), *Annual editions: Multicultural education 2002–2003* (pp. 20–28). Guilford, CT: McGraw-Hill/Dushkin.

Jensen, E. (1998). *Teaching with the brain in mind.* Alexandria, VA: Association for Supervision and Curriculum Development.

Jesness, J. (2004). *Teaching English language learners K–12.* Thousand Oaks, CA: Corwin.

Jewell, M. (1976). Formal institutional studies and language. In W. O'Barr & J. O'Barr (Eds.), *Language and politics* (pp. 421–429). The Hague, Netherlands: Mouton.

Jitendra, A. K., & Rohena-Diaz, E. (1996). Language assessment of students who are linguistically diverse: Why a discrete approach is not the answer. *School Psychology Review, 25*(1), 40–56.

Johnson, D. W., & Johnson, R. T. (1979). Conflict in the classroom: Controversy and learning. *Review of Educational Research, 49*(1), 51–70.

Johnson, D. W., & Johnson, R. T. (1987). *Learning together and alone.* Englewood Cliffs, NJ: Prentice Hall.

Johnson, D. W., & Johnson, R. T. (1994). Constructive conflict in the schools. *Journal of Social Issues, 50*(1), 117–137.

Johnson, D. W., & Johnson, R. T. (1995). Why violence prevention programs don't work—and what does. *Educational Leadership, 52*(5), 63–68.

Johnson, D. W., Johnson, R. T., Dudley, B., & Acikgoz, K. (1994). Effects of conflict resolution training on elementary school students. *Journal of Social Psychology, 134*(6), 803–817.

Jonassen, D. H. (2006). *Modeling with technology: Mindtools for conceptual change* (3rd ed.). Upper Saddle River, NJ: Pearson/Merrill/Prentice Hall.

Jones, J. (1981). The concept of racism and its changing reality. In B. Bowser & R. Hunt (Eds.), *Impacts of racism on white Americans* (pp. 27–49). Beverly Hills, CA: Sage.

Julian, L. (2007, October 28). TAKS: Bar set so low, it hurts kids. *Houston Chronicle,* E1, E4.

Jussim, L. (1986). Self-fulfilling prophecies: A theoretical and integrative review. *Psychological Review, 93*(4), 429–445.

Kagan, S. (1986). Cooperative learning and sociocultural factors in schooling. *Beyond language: Social and cultural factors in schooling language minority students* (pp. 198–231). Los Angeles: Evaluation, Dissemination and Assessment Center, California State University, Los Angeles.

Kagan, S. (2007). *Differentiated instruction* (smart card). San Clemente, CA: Kagan Publishing.

Kamberelis, G., & de la Luna, L. (2004). Children's writing: How textual forms, contextual forces, and textual politics co-emerge. In C. Bazerman & P. Prior (Eds.), *What writing does and how it does it* (pp. 239–277). Mahwah, NJ: Erlbaum.

Kandel, W., & Cromartie, J. (2004). *New patterns of Hispanic settlement in rural America.* Retrieved January 16, 2005, from www.ers.usda.gov/publications/rdrr99.

Kang, H-W., Kuehn, P., & Herrell, A. (1996). The Hmong literacy project: Parents working to preserve the past and ensure the future. *The Journal of Educational Issues of Language Minority Students, 16.* Retrieved March 20, 2005, from www.ncela.gwu.edu/pubs/jeilms/vol16/jeilms1602.htm.

Karchmer-Klein, R. (2007). Best practices in using the Internet to support writing. In S. Graham, C. A. MacArthur, & J. Fitzgerald (Eds.), *Best practices in writing instruction* (pp. 222–241). New York: Guilford.

Kaufman, P., Alt, M. N., & Chapman, C. D. (2004). *Dropout rates in the United States: 2001.* Washington, DC: National Center for Education Statistics.

Kea, C., Campbell-Whatley, G. D., & Richards, H. V. (2004). *Becoming culturally responsive educators: Rethinking teacher education pedagogy.* National Center for Culturally Responsive Educational Systems. Retrieved January 29, 2005, from www.nccrest.org/publications.html.

Keefe, M. W. (1987). *Learning style theory and practice.* Reston, VA: National Association of Secondary School Principals.

Kessler, C., Quinn, M., & Fathman, A. (1992). Science and cooperative learning for LEP students. In C. Kessler (Ed.), *Cooperative language learning*(pp. 65–83). Englewood Cliffs, NJ: Regents/Prentice Hall.

Keyes v. School District Number One, Denver, Colorado, 576 F. Supp. 1503 (D. Colo. 1983).

Kim, E. Y. (2001). *The yin and yang of American culture.* Yarmouth, ME: Intercultural Press.

Kleinfeld, J. (1988, June). Letter to the editor. *Harvard Education Letter, 4*(3).

Klentschy, M. (2005). Science notebook essentials. *Science and Children, 43*(3). 24–27.

Kluge, D. (1999). A brief introduction to cooperative learning. (ERIC Document Reproduction Service No. ED 437 840). Retrieved April 6, 2005, from www.eric.ed.gov.

Kohn, A. (2007, June 1). Too destructive to salvage. *USA Today,* 7A.

Kopan, A. (1974). Melting pot: Myth or reality? In E. Epps (Ed.), *Cultural pluralism* (pp. 37–55). Berkeley, CA: McCutchan.

Kottler, J. A. (1997). *What's really said in the teacher's lounge: Provocative ideas about cultures and classrooms.* Thousand Oaks: Corwin Press.

Krashen, S. (1981). Bilingual education and second language acquisition theory. In C. F. Leyba (Ed.), *Schooling and language minority students: A theoretical framework* (pp. 51–79). Los Angeles: Evaluation, Dissemination and Assessment Center, California State University, Los Angeles.

Krashen, S. (1982). *Principles and practice in second language acquisition.* Oxford: Pergamon.

Krashen, S. (1985). *The input hypothesis: Issues and implications.* New York: Longman.

Krashen, S. (2006). *Bilingual education accelerates English language development.* Takoma Park, ND: Institute for Language and Education Policy. Retrieved May 16, 2008, from www .elladvocates.org/issuebriefs/Kranshen_bilingual.pdf.

Krashen, S., & Terrell, T. (1983). *The natural approach: Language acquisition in the classroom.* Oxford: Pergamon.

Krashen, S. D. (1996). *Under attack: The case against bilingual education.* Culver City, CA: Language Education Associates.

Kress, G. R., & Van Leeuwen, T. (1995). Reading images: The grammar of visual design. London: Routledge.

Kress, J. (1993). *The ESL teacher's book of lists.* West Nyack, NY: Center for Applied Research in Education.

Kroll, B. (1991). Teaching writing in the ESL context. In M. Celce-Murcia (Ed.), *Teaching English as a second or foreign language* (2nd ed., pp. 245–263). New York: Newbury House.

Labbe, J. R. (2007, September 1). Losing literacy. *The [Riverside, CA] Press-Enterprise,* B11.

Labov, W. (1972). *Sociolinguistic patterns.* Philadelphia: University of Pennsylvania Press.

Lambert, W. (1984). An overview of issues in immersion education. In California Department of Education, *Studies on immersion education* (pp. 8–30). Sacramento: California Department of Education.

Lapkoff, S., & Li, R. M. (2007). Five trends for schools. *Educational Leadership, 64*(6), 8–15.

Laturnau, J. (2001). Standards-based instruction for English language learners. Retrieved April 9, 2005, from www.prel.org/products/pc_standards-based.htm.

Lau v. Nichols. (1974). 414 U.S. 563.

Leathers, N. (1967). *The Japanese in America.* Minneapolis: Lerner Publications.

Lee, H. (1960). *To kill a mockingbird.* New York: Lippincott.

Lee, J. (2000). Success for all? *American Language Review, 4*(2), 22, 24.

Lemberger, N. (1999). Factors affecting language development from the perspectives of four bilingual teachers. In I. Heath & C. Serrano (Eds.), *Annual editions: Teaching English as a second language* (2nd ed., pp. 30–37). Guilford, CT: Dushkin/McGraw-Hill.

Lenneberg, E. (1967). *Biological foundations of language.* New York: Wiley.

Lessow-Hurley, J. (2009). *The foundations of dual language instruction* (5th ed.). Boston: Allyn & Bacon.

Levine, D., & Adelman, M. (1982). *Beyond language: Intercultural communication for English as a second language.* Englewood Cliffs, NJ: Prentice Hall.

LeVine, J. E. (2002). Writing letters to support literacy. *The Reading Teacher, 56*(8), 232–234.

Lin, S. (2002). *Remembering the contributions and sacrifices Chinese Americans have made to America: A time to give back.* Retrieved October 27, 2007, from www.scanews.com/spot/2002/august/s623/memory/ca.html.

Lindholm, K. (1992). Two-way bilingual/immersion education: Theory, conceptual issues and pedagogical implications. In R. Padilla & A. Benavides (Eds.), *Critical perspectives in bilingual education research* (pp. 195–220). Tucson, AZ: Bilingual Review/Press.

Linquanti, R. (2008). Assessing language proficiency of California's English learners and what it means for accountability. *University of California Linguistic Minority Research Institute (LMRI) Newsletter, 17*(2), 1–3.

Lockwood, A. T. (2000). *Transforming education for Hispanic youth: Broad recommendations for teachers and program staff.* Washington, DC: National Clearinghouse for Bilingual Education, 4. Retrieved January 28, 2005, from www.ncela.gwu.edu/pubs/issuebriefs/ib4.html.

Lockwood, A. T., & Secada, W. G. (1991). *Transforming education for Hispanic youth: Exemplary practices, programs, and schools.* Accessed July 12, 2008, from http://citeseer.ist.psu.edu/lockwood99 transforming.html.

Loewen, J. (1995). *Lies my teacher told me.* New York: Touchstone.

Loop, C., & Barron, V. (2002). *Which states have statewide ELD standards and language proficiency assessments?* Retrieved March 22, 2005, from www.ncela.gwu.edu/expert/faq/eldstandardsdraft.htm.

Lopez, E. C. (2002). *Tips for the use of interpreters in the assessment of English language learners.* Retrieved February 14, 2005, from http://66.102.7.104/search?q=cache:8COtfXfYi-IJ:www.nasponline.org/culturalcompetence/recommend.pdf +working+with+an+interpreter&hl=en.

Los Angeles Times. (2008). Letters. January 6, p. M2.

Los Angeles Unified School District. (1993). *Sheltered instruction teacher handbook: Strategies for teaching LEP students in the elementary grades* (Publication No. EC-617). Los Angeles: Author.

Lucas, T., & Wagner, S. (1999). Facilitating secondary English language learners' transition into the mainstream. *TESOL Journal, 8*(4), 6–13.

Lund, R. J. (1990). A taxonomy for teaching second-language listening. *Foreign Language Annals, 23,* 105–115.

Lyons, C. A., & Clay, M. M. (2003). *Teaching struggling readers: How to use brain-based research to maximize learning.* Portsmouth, NH: Heinemann.

Maceri, D. (2007). America's languages: Tower of Babel or asset? *Language Magazine, 6*(8), 15.

Maciejewski, T. (2003). *Pragmatics.* Retrieved August 31, 2004, from www.lisle.dupage.k12.il.us/maciejewski/social.htm.

Macmillan, D. L., & Reschly, D. J. (1998). Overrepresentation of minority students: The case for greater specificity or reconsideration of the variables examined. *Journal of Special Education, 32*(1), 15–24.

Majors, P. (n.d.). *Charleston County School District, Charleston, SC, sample standards-based lesson plan.* Retrieved September 29, 2004, from www.cal.org/eslstandards/Charleston.html.

Malavé, L. (1991). Conceptual framework to design a programme intervention for culturally and linguistically different handicapped students. In L. Malavé & G. Duquette (Eds.), *Language, culture and cognition* (pp. 176–189). Clevedon, Eng.: Multilingual Matters.

Malkina, N. (1996). Fun with storytelling. In V. Whiteson (Ed.), *New ways of using drama and literature in language teaching* (pp. 41–42). Alexandria, VA: Teachers of English to Speakers of Other Languages.

Mandlebaum, L. H., & Wilson, R. (1989). Teaching listening skills in the special education classroom. *Academic Therapy, 24,* 451–452.

Manning, M. L. (2002). Understanding diversity, accepting others: Realities and directions. In F. Schultz (Ed.), *Annual editions: Multicultural education 2002/2003* (pp. 206–208). Guilford, CT: McGraw-Hill/Dushkin.

March, T. (2007). The new WWW: Whatever, whenever, wherever. In F. Schultz (Ed.), *Annual editions 10/08: Education* (pp. 213–216). Dubuque, IA: McGraw-Hill Contemporary Learning Series.

Marinova-Todd, S., Marshall, D., & Snow, C. (2000). Three misconceptions about age and L2 learning. *TESOL Quarterly, 34*(1), 9–34.

Marshall, C., & Oliva, M. (2006). *Leadership for social justice: Making revolutions in education.* Boston: Pearson.

Martin, B., & Ringham, F. (2006). *Key terms in semiotics.* London: Continuum.

McDaniel, E., & Wilde, K. (2008). Candidate assessment. In C. E. Feistritzer (Ed.), *Building a quality teaching force* (pp. 88–109). Upper Saddle River, NJ: Pearson.

McGovern, A. (1969). *If you sailed on the Mayflower in 1620.* New York: Scholastic.

McIntosh, P. (1996). White privilege and male privilege: A personal account of coming to see correspondences through work in women's studies. In M. Anderson & P. Collins (Eds.), *Race, class, and gender: An anthology* (2nd ed., pp. 76–87). Belmont, CA: Wadsworth.

McKay, J. (2000). Building self-esteem in children. In M. McKay & P. Fanning, *Self-esteem* (3rd ed., pp. 279–313). New York: Barnes and Noble Books.

McKeon, D. (1994). When meeting common standards is uncommonly difficult. *Educational Leadership, 51*(8), 45–49.

McLaughlin, B. (1987). *Theories of second-language learning.* London: Arnold.

McLeod, B. (1996). *School reform and student diversity: Exemplary schooling for language minority students.* Retrieved March 20, 2005, from www.ncela.gwu.edu/pubs/resource/schref.htm.

McVey, D. C. (2007). Helping ESL students improve their grammar. *ESL Magazine, 56,* 16–18.

Mehan, H., Hubbard, L., Lintz, A., & Villanueva, I. (1994). *Tracking untracking: The consequences of placing low-track students in high-track classes.* Santa Cruz, CA: National Center for Research on Cultural Diversity & Second Language Learning. Retrieved April 8, 2005, from www.ncela.gwu.edu/pubs/ncrcdsll/rr10.

Mercer, N. (2000). *Words and minds: How we use language to think together and get things done.* London: Routledge.

Merino, B. (2007). Identifying critical competencies for teachers of English learners. *University of California Linguistic Minority Research Institute (LMRI) Newsletter, 16*(4), 1–7.

Mermelstein, L. (2006). *Reading/writing connections in the K–2 classroom.* Boston: Pearson.

Meyer v. Nebraska, 262 U.S. 390 (1923).

Meyer, E. F. (2008, May 9). Many immigrants are motivated to learn English. Letter to the Editor, *USA Today,* 20A.

Migration Policy Institute. (2004). *A new century: Immigration and the U.S.* Retrieved January 15, 2005, from www.migrationinformation.org/Profiles/display.cfm?ID=6.

Milambiling, J. (2002). Good neighbors: Mainstreaming ESL students in the rural Midwest. In E. P. Cochran, *Mainstreaming* (pp. 21–30). Alexandria, VA: Teachers of English to Speakers of Other Languages.

Miller, G. (1985). Nonverbal communication. In V. Clark, P. Eschholz, & A. Rosa (Eds.), *Language: Introductory readings* (4th ed., pp. 633–641). New York: St. Martin's Press.

Miller, W. H. (1995). *Alternative assessment techniques for reading and writing.* West Nyack, NY: Center for Applied Research in Education.

Mills, S. C. (2006). *Using the Internet for active teaching and learning.* Upper Saddle River, NJ: Pearson/Merrill/Prentice Hall.

Mintz, E., & Yun, J. T. (1999). *The complex world of teaching: Perspectives from theory and practice.* Cambridge, MA: Harvard Educational Review.

Molina, R. (2000). Building equitable two-way programs. In N. Cloud, F. Genesee, & E. Hamayan (Eds.), *Dual language instruction* (pp. 11–12). Boston: Heinle and Heinle.

Monroe, R. J. (2008). Standardized testing in the lives of the ESL students: A teacher's firsthand account. *Institute for Language and Education Policy.* Accessed July 28, 2008, from www.elladvocates.org/documents/nclb/Monroe_Standardized_Testing_for_ELLs.pdf.

Moore, M. S., & Panara, R. F. (1996). *Great deaf Americans* (2nd ed.). New York: DeafLife Press.

Moran, R. F. (2004). Undone by law: The uncertain legacy of *Lau v. Nichols. UC-LMRI Newsletter, 13*(4), 1, 3.

Morey, A., & Kilano, M. (1997). *Multicultural course transformation in higher education: A broader truth.* Boston: Allyn & Bacon.

Morley, J. (2001). Aural comprehension instruction: Principles & practices. In M. Celce-Murcia (Ed.), *Teaching English as a second or foreign language* (3rd ed.). Boston: Heinle and Heinle.

Nash, P. (1991). ESL and the myth of the model minority. In S. Benesch (Ed.), *ESL in America* (pp. 46–55). Portsmouth, NH: Boynton/Cook.

National Center for Education Evaluation and Regional Assistance (2008). *Reading First impact study: Interim report*. Washington, DC: Author.

National Center for Education Statistics. (2001). *States using minimum-competency testing, by grade levels assessed, and expected uses of standards: 1998–99*. Retrieved March 22, 2005, from http://nces.ed.gov/programs/digest/d01/dt155.asp.

National Center for Education Statistics (NCES). (2002). *Percentage distribution of enrollment in public elementary and secondary schools, by race/ethnicity and state: Fall 1986 and fall 2000*. Retrieved January 14, 2005, from nces.ed.gov/programs/digest/d02/dt042.asp.

National Center for Education Statistics (NCES). (2003a). *College enrollment and enrollment rates of recent high school completers, by race/ethnicity: 1960 to 2001*. Retrieved March 20, 2005, from http://nces.ed.gov/programs/digest/d03/tables/dt185.asp.

National Center for Education Statistics (NCES). (2003b). *Employees in degree-granting institutions, by race/ethnicity, primary occupation, sex, employment status, and control and type of institution: Fall 2001*. Retrieved March 20, 2005, from http://nces.ed.gov/programs/digest/d03/tables/dt228.asp.

National Center for Education Statistics (NCES). (2007). *Status and trends in the education of racial and ethnic minorities*. Retrieved October 24, 2008, from http://nces.ed.gov/pubs2007/minoritytrends/ind_4_16.asp.

National Clearinghouse for English Language Acquisition (NCELA). (1996). *Ask NCELA #7 What court rulings have impacted the education of language minority students in the U.S.?* Retrieved March 19, 2005, from www.ncela.gwu.edu/expert/askncela/07court.htm.

National Clearinghouse for English Language Acquisition (NCELA). (2002). *Ask NCELA #3 How has federal policy for language minority students evolved in the U.S.?* Retrieved March 19, 2005, from www.ncela.gwu.edu/expert/faq/03history.htm.

National Clearinghouse for English Language Acquisition and Language Instruction Educational Programs (2007). *2005–2008 Poster*. Retrieved July 3, 2008, from http://www.ncela.gwu/stats/2_nation.htm.

National Commission on Teaching and America's Future. (1996). *What matters most: Teaching and America's future*. New York: Author.

National Council for the Social Studies (NCSS). (1994). *Expectations for excellence: Curriculum standards for social studies*. Washington, DC: Author.

National Council of Teachers of English (NCTE) & International Reading Association (IRA). (1996). *Standards for the English language arts*. Urbana, IL & Newark, DE: Authors.

National Council of Teachers of Mathematics (NCTM). (2000). *Principles and standards for school mathematics*. Reston, VA: Author.

National Council of Teachers of Mathematics (NCTM). (2007). *Mathematics teaching today: Improving practice, improving student learning* (2nd ed., T. Martin, Ed.). Reston, VA: Author.

National Research Council. (1996). *The national science education standards*. Washington, DC: National Academy Press.

Navarrete, C., & Gustke, C. (1996). *A guide to performance assessment for linguistically diverse students*. Retrieved February 2, 2005, from www.ncela.gwu.edu/pubs/eacwest/performance.

Nelson, B. (1996). *Learning English: How school reform fosters language acquisition and development for limited English proficient elementary school students*. Santa Cruz, CA: National Center for Research on Cultural Diversity & Second Language Learning. Retrieved April 8, 2005, from www.ncela.gwu.edu/pubs/ncrcdsll/epr16.htm.

Nelson, C. (2004). Reclaiming teacher preparation for success in high-needs schools. *Education, 124*(3), 475–480.

Nelson-Barber, S. (1999). A better education for every child: The dilemma for teachers of culturally and linguistically diverse students. In Mid-continent Research for Education and Learning (McREL) (Ed.), *Including culturally and linguistically diverse students in standards-based reform: A report on McREL's Diversity Roundtable I* (pp. 3–22). Retrieved April 8, 2005, from www.mcrel.org/PDFConversion/Diversity/rt1chapter2.htm.

Nemmer-Fanta, M. (2002). Accommodations and modifications for English language learners. In *Serving English language learners with disabilities: A resource manual for Illinois educators*. Retrieved February 9, 2005, from www.isbe.state.il.us/spec-ed/bilingualmanual2002.htm.

Newman, C. M. (2006). *Strategies for test-taking success: Reading*. Boston: Thompson Heinle.

Newman, J. M. (1985). What about reading? In J. M. Newman (Ed.), *Whole language: Theory in use* (pp. 99–100). Portsmouth, NH: Heinemann.

Newman, J. R. (1956). Srinivasa Ramanujan. In J. R. Newman (Ed.), *The world of mathematics, Vol. 1* (pp. 368–376). New York: Simon and Schuster.

Nichols, S. L. (1999). Gay, lesbian, and bisexual youth: Understanding diversity and promoting tolerance in schools. *The Elementary School Journal, 99*(5), 505–519.

Nieto, S., & Bode, P. (2008). *Affirming diversity* (5th ed.). Boston: Allyn & Bacon.

Nilsen, A. P., & Donelson, K. E. (2009). *Literature for today's young adults* (8th ed.). Boston: Pearson.

No Child Left Behind Act of 2001. (2002). Retrieved October 14, 2004, from www.ed.gov/policy/elsec/leg/esea02/index.html.

Nolan, J. F., & Hoover, L. A. (2008). *Teacher supervision & evaluation* (2nd ed.). Hoboken, NJ: Wiley.

Nunan, D. (1989). *Designing tasks for the communicative classroom*. Cambridge, Eng.: Cambridge University Press.

O'Malley, J. M., & Pierce, L. V. (1996). *Authentic assessment for English language learners*. Menlo Park, CA: Addison-Wesley.

O'Malley, J., Chamot, A., Stewner-Manzanares, G., Kupper, L., & Russo, R. (1985a). Learning strategies used by beginning and intermediate ESL students. *Language Learning, 35*(1), 21–40.

O'Malley, J., Chamot, A., Stewner-Manzanares, G., Kupper, L., & Russo, R. (1985b). Learning strategy applications with students of English as a second language. *TESOL Quarterly, 19*(3), 557–584.

Oakes, J. (1985). *Keeping track: How schools structure inequality*. New Haven, CT: Yale University Press.

Oakes, J. (1992). Can tracking research inform practice? Technical, normative, and political considerations. *Educational Researcher, 21*(4), 12–21.

Oakes, J., & Lipton, M. (2007). *Teaching to change the world* (3rd ed.). Boston: McGraw-Hill.

Ogbu, J. (1978). *Minority education and caste: The American system in crosscultural perspective*. New York: Academic Press.

Ogbu, J., & Matute-Bianchi, M. (1986). Understanding sociocultural factors: Knowledge, identity, and school adjustment. In *Beyond language: Social and cultural factors in schooling language minority students* (pp. 73–142). Los Angeles: Evaluation, Dissemination and Assessment Center, California State University, Los Angeles.

Oh, J. (1992). The effects of L2 reading assessment methods on anxiety level. *TESOL Quarterly, 26*(1), 172–176.

Olsen, L. (1988). *Crossing the schoolhouse border: Immigrant students and the California public schools*. San Francisco: California Tomorrow.

Olson, S., & Loucks-Horsley, S. (2000). *Inquiry and the national science education standards*. Washington, DC: National Academy Press.

Ong, M. F., & Murugesan, V. (2007). *Teaching English to young learners: Trainer's handbook*. Santa Fe Springs, CA: Compass.

Ong, W. (1982). *Orality and literacy*. London: Methuen.

Open Court Reading series. (2003). New York: McGraw-Hill/SRA.

Orfield, T., & Lee, C. (2005). *Why segregation matters: Poverty and educational inequality*. Retrieved March 20, 2005, from www.civilrightsproject.harvard.edu/research/deseg/deseg05.php.

Ortiz, A. A. (2002). Prevention of school failure and early intervention for English language learners. In A. J. Artiles & A. A. Ortiz (Eds.), *English language learners with special education needs: Identification, assessment, and instruction* (pp. 31–63). Washington, DC: Center for Applied Linguistics and Delta Systems Co.

Osgood, K. W. (2002). It takes a class to teach a child: The challenge program. In E. P. Cochran, *Mainstreaming* (pp. 43–51). Alexandria, VA: Teachers of English to Speakers of Other Languages.

Ovando, C., & Collier, V. (1998). *Bilingual and ESL classrooms: Teaching in multicultural contexts*. Boston: McGraw-Hill.

Oyama, S. (1976). A sensitive period for the acquisition of nonnative phonological system. *Journal of Psycholinguistic Research, 5,* 261–284.

Padilla, E. (1998). *Hispanic contributions to the United States.* Retrieved January 10, 2005, from http://members.aol.com/pjchacon/aims/contributions.html.

Pappamihiel, N. E. (2002). English as a second language students and English language anxiety: Issues in the mainstream classroom. *Research in the Teaching of English, 36,* 327–355.

Parade Magazine. (2007, October 28). Making a profit off kids, 10.

Paradis, M. (2005). *Neurolinguistics of bilingualism and the teaching of languages.* Retrieved January 23, 2005, from www.semioticon.com/virtuals/talks/paradis_txt.htm.

Parla, J. (1994). Educating teachers for cultural and linguistic diversity: A model for all teachers. *New York State Association for Bilingual Education Journal, 9,* 1–6. Retrieved February 7, 2005, from www.ncela.gwu.edu/pubs/nysabe/vol9/model.htm.

Pasternak, J. (1994, March 29). Bias blights life outside Appalachia. *Los Angeles Times,* A1, A16.

Payan, R. (1984). Language assessment for bilingual exceptional children. In L. Baca & H. Cervantes (Eds.), *The bilingual special education interface* (pp. 125–137). St. Louis, MO: Times Mirror/Mosby.

Pearson, R. (1974). *Introduction to anthropology.* New York: Holt, Rinehart and Winston.

Peñalosa, F. (1980). *Chicano sociolinguistics, a brief introduction.* Rowley, MA: Newbury House.

Pennycook, A. (1994). *The cultural politics of English as an international language.* New York: Longman.

Penrod, D. (2008). Web 2.0, meet Literacy 2.0. *Educational Technology, 48*(1), 50–52.

Peregoy, S., & Boyle, O. (2008). *Reading, writing, and learning in ESL* (5th ed.). Boston: Pearson.

Pérez, B., & Torres-Guzmán, M. (2002). *Learning in two worlds* (3rd ed.). New York: Longman.

Perkins, C. (1995). *Equity in mathematics assessment for English as a second language students.* Retrieved January 20, 2005, from http://jwilson.coe.uga.edu/EMT705/EMT705Perkins.html.

Philips, S. (1972). Participant structures and communicative competence: Warm Springs children in community and classroom. In C. Cazden, V. John, & D. Hymes (Eds.), *Functions of language in the classroom* (pp. 370–394). New York: Teachers College Press.

Phillips, J. (1978). College of, by, and for Navajo Indians. *Chronicle of Higher Education, 15,* 10–12.

Pierangelo, R., & Giuliani, G. A. (2001). *What every teacher should know about students with special needs.* Champaign, IL: Research Press.

Pinnell, G. S. (1985). Ways to look at the functions of children's language. In A. Jaggar & M. Smith-Burke (Eds.), *Observing the language learner* (pp. 57–72). Newark, DE: International Reading Association.

Plyler v. Doe, 457 U.S. 202, 102 S. Ct. 2382 (1982).

Pope, D. (2002). *Doing school: How we are creating a generation of stressed-out, materialistic, and miseducated students.* New Haven, CT: Yale University Press.

Porter, P., & Taylor, B. P. (2003). Experience is the best teacher: Linking the MA pedagogical grammar course with the ESL grammar classroom. In D. Liu & P. Master, *Grammar teaching in teacher education* (pp. 151–164). Alexandria, VA: Teachers of English to Speakers of Other Languages.

Porter, R. (1990). *Forked tongue: The politics of bilingual education.* New York: Basic Books.

Porterfield, K. (2002). *Indian encyclopedia wins Colorado book award.* Retrieved October 27, 2008, from www.kporterfield.com/aicttw/articles/award.html.

Potowski, K. (2007). *Language and identity in a dual immersion school.* Clevedon, Eng.: Multilingual Matters.

Pransky, K. (2008). *Beneath the surface: The hidden realities of teaching culturally and linguistically diverse young learners, K–6.* Portsmouth, NH: Heinemann.

Prothrow-Smith, D. (1994, April). Building violence prevention into the classroom. *The School Administrator, 8*(12), 8–12.

Pruitt, W. (2000). Using story to compare, conclude, and identify. In B. Agor (Ed.), *Integrating the ESL standards into classroom practice: Grades 9–12* (pp. 31–54). Alexandria, VA: Teachers of English to Speakers of Other Languages.

Pryor, C. B. (2002). New immigrants and refugees in American schools: Multiple voices. In F. Schultz (Ed.), *Annual editions: Multicultural education 2002/2003* (pp. 185–193). Guilford, CT: McGraw-Hill/Dushkin.

Public Schools of North Carolina. (2004). *The North Carolina competency tests: A handbook for students in the ninth grade for the first time in 2001–2002 and beyond*. Raleigh: Author. Retrieved February 2, 2005, from www.ncpublicschools.org/accountability/testing/competency.

Qualls-Mitchell, P. (2008). Reading enhancement for deaf and hard-of-hearing children through multicultural empowerment. *The Reading Teacher, 56*(1), 76–84.

Quinn, Q. (2007). Motivating reading. *Language Magazine, 6*(10), 24–26.

Quinones, S. (2008, February 25). A different kind of home schooling. *Los Angeles Times,* B4.

Rahilly, M. K., & Weinmann, A. (2007). *An overview of Title III programs*. Presentation at the annual conference of the Teachers of English to Speakers of Other Languages, Seattle.

Raimes, A. (Ed.). (1996). *Identities: Readings from contemporary culture*. Boston: Houghton Mifflin.

Ramírez, J. (1992, Winter/Spring). Executive summary, final report: Longitudinal study of structured English immersion strategy, early-exit and late-exit transitional bilingual education programs for language-minority children. *Bilingual Research Journal, 16*(1 & 2), 1–62.

Rance-Rooney, J. (2008). Digital storytelling for language and culture learning. *Essential Teacher, 5*(1), 29–31.

Ray, B., & Seely, C. (1998). *Fluency through TPR storytelling: Achieving real language acquisition in school* (2nd ed.). Berkeley; CA: Command Performance Language Institute.

Reckendorf, K., & Ortiz, F. W. (2000). *English and ESL inclusion model*. Unpublished article. Amherst, MA: Amherst Regional Middle School.

Reese, D. (2007). Proceed with caution: Using Native American folktales in the classroom. *Language Arts, 84*(3), 245–256.

Reese, S. (2006). When foreign languages are not seen or heard. *The Language Educator, 1*(2), 32–37.

Reeves, D. B. (2002). *Making standards work*. Denver, CO: Center for Performance Assessment.

Reid, J. (2006). New census data shows 1.3 million children have fallen into poverty since 2000. Children's Defense Fund. Retrieved May 16, 2008, from www.childrensdefense.org/site/News2?page=NewsArticle&id=7887.

Richard-Amato, P. (2003). *Making it happen* (3rd ed.). White Plains, NY: Longman.

Richards, H. V., Brown, A. E., & Forde, T. B. (2004). *Addressing diversity in schools: Culturally responsive pedagogy*. National Center for Culturally Responsive Educational Systems. Retrieved January 21, 2005, from www.nccrest.org/publications.html.

Richards, J., & Gipe, J. (1995). What's the structure? A game to help middle school students recognize common writing patterns. *Journal of Reading, 38*(8), 667–669.

Rico, H. (2000). *Programs for English learners: Overview of federal and state requirements*. Retrieved February 22, 2001, from www.cde.ca.gov/ccpdiv/eng_learn/ccr2000-el/index.htm.

Ríos v. Read. 75 Civ. 296 (U.S. District Ct. Ed. NY, 1977).

Rivera, C. (2008, March 10). Strife and solutions at school conferences. *Los Angeles Times,* B1, B 6.

Roberts, C. (1995, Summer/Fall). Bilingual education program models. *Bilingual Research Journal, 19*(3 & 4), 369–378.

Robinson, G. (1985). *Crosscultural understanding*. New York: Pergamon Institute of English.

Rodríguez, R., Prieto, A., & Rueda, R. (1984). Issues in bilingual/multicultural special education. *Journal of the National Association for Bilingual Education, 8*(3), 55–65.

Rolstad, K., Mahoney, K., & Glass, G. V. (2005). The big picture: A meta-analysis of program effectiveness research on English language learners. *Educational Policy, 19*(4), 572–594.

Rose, C. (1987). *Accelerated learning*. New York: Dell.

Rowan, T., & Bourne, B. (1994). *Thinking like mathematics*. Portsmouth, NH: Heinemann.

Rubel, A., & Kupferer, H. (1973). The myth of the melting pot. In T. Weaver (Ed.), *To see ourselves: Anthropology and modern social issues* (pp. 103–107). Glenview, IL: Scott Foresman.

Rueda, R. (1987). Social and communicative aspects of language proficiency in low-achieving language minority students. In H. Trueba (Ed.), *Success or failure? Learning and the language minority student* (pp. 185–197). Cambridge, MA: Newbury House.

Ruíz, R. (1984). Orientations in language planning. *NABE Journal, 8*(2), 15–34.

Runner, J. (2000). *"I don't understand" in over 230 languages.* Retrieved April 8, 2005, from www.elite.net/~runner/jennifers/understa.htm.

Russell, M. (2008). Solving the crisis of the male teacher shortage. *Teachers of Color, 3*(1), 12–14.

Ryan, M. (2008). *Ask the teacher: A practitioner's guide to teaching and learning in the diverse classroom.* Boston: Pearson.

Ryder, M. (2005). *Semiotics.* Retrieved January 23, 2005, from http://carbon.cudenver.edu/~mryder/itc_data/semiotics.html.

Sales, F. (1989). *Ibrahim.* New York: Lippincott.

Sánchez, F. (1989). *What is primary language instruction?* Hayward, CA: Alameda County Office of Education.

Sands, D. J., Kozleski, E. B., & French, N. K. (2000). *Special education for the twenty-first century: Making schools inclusive communities.* Belmont, CA: Wadsworth.

Saslow, J., & Ascher, A. (2006). *Top Notch 2 Copy & go.* White Plains, NY: Pearson Longman.

Sasser, L., Naccarato, L., Corren, J., & Tran, Q. (2002). *English language development progress profile.* Alhambra, CA: Alhambra School District.

Sattler, J. (1974). *Assessment of children's intelligence.* Philadelphia: W. B. Saunders.

Saunders, W., & Goldenberg, C. (2001). Strengthening the transition in transitional bilingual education. In D. Christian & F. Genesee (Eds.), *Bilingual education* (pp. 41–56). Alexandria, VA: Teachers of English to Speakers of Other Languages.

Schachter, J. (2003). *Migration by race and Hispanic origin: 1995 to 2000.* Retrieved January 16, 2005, from www.census.gov/prod/2003pubs/censr-13.pdf.

Schifini, A. (1994). Language, literacy, and content instruction: Strategies for teachers. In K. Spangenberg Urbschat & R. Pritchard (Eds.), *Kids come in all language: Reading instruction for ESL students* (pp. 158–179). Newark, DE: International Reading Association.

Schifini, A., Short, D., & Tinajero, J. V. (2002). *High points: Teacher's edition.* Carmel, CA: Hampton Brown.

Schildroth, A., & Hotto, S. (1994). Inclusion or exclusion: Deaf students and the inclusion movement. *American Annals of the Deaf, 139,* 239–243.

Schmidt, P. (2008, February 20). Asians, not whites, hurt most by race-conscious admissions. *USA Today,* 13A.

Schultz, J., & Theophano, J. (1987). Saving place and marking time: Some aspects of the social lives of three-year-old children. In H. Trueba (Ed.), *Success or failure* (pp. 33–48). Cambridge, MA: Newbury House.

Schumann, J. (1978). The acculturation model for second-language acquisition. In R. Gringas (Ed.), *Second language acquisition and foreign language teaching* (pp. 27–50). Washington, DC: Center for Applied Linguistics.

Schumann, J. (1994). Emotion and cognition in second language acquisition. *Studies in Second Language Acquisition, 16,* 231–242.

Scieszka, J., & Smith, L. (1992). *The stinky cheese man and other fairly stupid tales.* New York: Viking Juvenile.

Scollon, R., & Scollon, S. W. (2003). *Discourses in place: Language in the material world.* London: Routledge.

Scribner, S., & Cole, M. (1978). Literacy without schooling: Testing for intellectual effects. *Harvard Educational Review, 48,* 448–461.

Seelye, H. (1984). *Teaching culture.* Lincolnwood, IL: National Textbook Company.

Selinker, L. (1972). Interlanguage. *International Review of Applied Linguistics, 10*(3), 209–231.

Selinker, L. (1991). Along the way: Interlanguage systems in second language acquisition. In L. Malavé & G. Duquette (Eds.), *Language, culture and cognition* (pp. 23–35). Clevedon, Eng.: Multilingual Matters.

Seng, C. (2005). *Teaching English to blind students.* Retrieved February 2, 2005, from www.teachingenglish.org.uk/think/methodology/blind.shtml.

Serna v. Portales Municipal Schools, 499 F. 2d 1147 (10th Cir. 1972).

Shade, B., & New, C. (1993). Cultural influences on learning: Teaching implications. In J. Banks & C. Banks (Eds.), *Multicultural education: Issues and perspectives.* Boston: Allyn & Bacon.

Short, D. (1998). Secondary newcomer programs: Helping recent immigrants prepare for school success. *ERIC Digest.* Retrieved January 28, 2005, from http://searcheric.org/scripts/seget2.asp?db=ericft&want=http://searcheric.org/ericdc/ED419385.htm.

Short, D., & Echevarria, J. (1999). The sheltered instruction observation protocol: A tool for teacher-researcher collaboration and professional development. *ERIC Digest.* Retrieved January 28, 2005, from http://searcheric.org/scripts/seget2.asp?db=ericft&want=http://searcheric.org/ericdc/ ED436981 .htm.

Shukoor, A. (1991). What does being bilingual mean to my family and me? *NABE Conference Program.* Washington, DC: National Association for Bilingual Education.

Shuter, R. (1991). The Hmong of Laos: Orality, communication, and acculturation. In L. Samovar & R. Porter (Eds.), *Intercultural communication: A reader* (6th ed., pp. 270–276). Belmont, CA: Wadsworth.

Siccone, F. (1995). *Celebrating diversity: Building self-esteem in today's multicultural classrooms.* Boston: Allyn & Bacon.

Siegel, J. (1999). Stigmatized and standardized varieties in the classroom: Interference or separation? *TESOL Quarterly, 33*(4), 701–728.

SIL International. (2000). *Geographic distribution of living languages, 2000.* Retrieved August 24, 2004, from www.ethnologue.com/ethno_docs/distribution.asp.

Sindell, P. (1988). Some discontinuities in the enculturation of Mistassini Cree children. In J. Wurzel (Ed.), *Toward multiculturalism.* Yarmouth, ME: Intercultural Press.

Singleton, D., & Ryan, L. (2004). *Language acquisition: The age factor* (2nd ed.). Clevedon, Eng.: Multilingual Matters.

Siskind Susser. (n.d.). *The ABC's of immigration—grounds for asylum and refuge.* Retrieved January 16, 2005, from www.visalaw.com.

Skinner, B. (1957). *Verbal behavior.* New York: Appleton, Century, Crofts.

Skutnabb-Kangas, T. (1981). *Bilingualism or not: The education of minorities* (L. Malmberg & D. Crane, Trans.). Clevedon, Eng.: Multilingual Matters.

Skutnabb-Kangas, T. (1993, February 3). *Linguistic genocide and bilingual education.* Presentation at the annual conference of the California Association for Bilingual Education, Anaheim.

Skutnabb-Kangas, T. (2000). *Linguistic genocide in education—or worldwide diversity and human rights?* Mahwah, NJ: Erlbaum.

Slater, J. (2000, May 12). *ELD standards.* Presentation at the Linguistic Minority Research Institute Conference, Irvine, CA.

Sleeter, C. E. (1986). Learning disabilities: The social construction of a special education category. *Exceptional Children, 53*(1), 46–54.

Smilkstein, R. (2002). *We're born to learn: Using the brain's natural learning process to create today's curriculum.* Thousand Oaks, CA: Sage.

Smith, F. (1983). *Essays into literacy.* Portsmouth, NH: Heinemann.

Smith, S. L., Paige, R. M., & Steglitz, I. (1998). Theoretical foundations of intercultural training and applications to the teaching of culture. In D. L. Lange, C. A. Klee, R. M. Paige, & Y. A. Yershova (Eds.), *Culture as the core: Interdisciplinary perspectives on culture teaching and learning in the language curriculum* (pp. 53–91). Minneapolis: Center for Advanced Research on Language Acquisition, University of Minnesota.

Smith, T. E. C., Polloway, E. A., Patton, J. R., & Dowdy, C. A. (2003). *Teaching children with special needs in inclusive settings* (4th ed.). Boston: Allyn & Bacon.

Snow, C., & Hoefnagel-Hoehle, M. (1978). The critical period for language acquisition: Evidence from second language learning. *Child Development, 49,* 1114–1118.

Snow, C., Burns, S., & Griffin, P. (Eds.). (1998). *Preventing reading difficulties in young children.* Washington, DC: National Academy Press.

Snow, D. (1996). *More than a native speaker.* Alexandria, VA: Teachers of English to Speakers of Other Languages.

Sonbuchner, G. M. (1991). *How to take advantage of your learning styles.* Syracuse, NY: New Readers Press.

Southern Poverty Law Center. (1999). *Youth at the edge.* Retrieved April 8, 2005, from www.splcenter .org/intel/intelreport/article.jsp?pid=537.

Spandel, V., & Hicks, J. (2006). *WriteTraits advanced sample*r. Wilmington, MA: Houghton-Mifflin.

Spinelli, E. (1994). *English grammar for students of Spanish.* Ann Arbor, MI: Olivia and Hill Press.

Spring, J. (2001). The new Mandarin society? Testing on the fast track. *The Joel Spring Library.* Retrieved April 8, 2005, from www.mhhe.com/socscience/education/spring/commentary.mhtml.

Stahl, S. A., Duffy-Hester, A. M., & Stahl, K. (1998). Everything you wanted to know about phonics (but were afraid to ask). *Reading Research Quarterly, 33*(3), 338–355.

Stainback, W., & Stainback, S. (1984). A rationale for the merger of special and regular education. *Exceptional Children, 51*(2), 102–111.

Strehorn, K. (2001). The application of Universal Instructional Design to ESL teaching. *Internet TESL Journal.* Retrieved January 25, 2005, from http://iteslj.org/Techniques/Strehorn-UID.html.

Suina, J. (1985). . . . And then I went to school. *New Mexico Journal of Reading, 5*(2). (Reprinted in *Outlook, 59,* 20–26).

Suleiman, M. (Ed.). (1999). *Arabs in America: Building a new future.* Chicago, IL: Kazi.

Sutherland, D. E. (1989). *The expansion of everyday life 1860–1876.* New York: Harper & Row.

Swanson, C. B. (2008). *Cities in crisis.* America's Promise Alliance. Retrieved May 27, 2008, from www.americaspromise.org/APA.aspx.

Swartz, S. L., Shook, R. E., Klein, A. F., Moon, C., Bunnell, K., Belt, M., & Huntley, C. (2003). *Guided reading and literacy centers.* Carlsbad, CA: Dominie Press.

Takahashi, E., Austin, T., & Morimoto, Y. (2000). Social interaction and language development in a FLES classroom. In J. K. Hall & L. S. Verplaetse (Eds.), *Second and foreign language learning through classroom interaction* (pp. 139–162). Mahwah, NJ: Erlbaum.

Tannen, D. (n.d.). *Discourse analysis.* Linguistic Society of America, "Fields of Linguistics." Retrieved March 13, 2005, from www.lsadc.org.

Tateishi, C. A. (2007–2008). Taking a chance with words. *Rethinking Schools, 22*(2), 20–23.

Taylor, D. (2000). Facing hardships: Jamestown and colonial life. In K. Samway (Ed.), *Integrating the ESL standards into classroom practice* (pp. 53–81). Alexandria, VA: Teachers of English to Speakers of Other Languages.

Teachers of English to Speakers of Other Languages (TESOL). (2001). *Scenarios for ESL standards-based assessment.* Alexandria, VA: Author.

Teachers of English to Speakers of Other Languages (TESOL). (2006). *PreK–12 English language proficiency standards in the core content areas.* Alexandria, VA: Author.

Teaching Mathematics to ESL students. (n.d.). Retrieved September 29, 2004, from www.eduweb.vic.gov.au/curriculumatwork/esl/es_maprim.htm.

Teske, M., & Marcy, P. (2007). *Step up: Listening, speaking, and critical thinking.* Boston: Houghton Mifflin.

Tharp, R. (1989a). Culturally compatible education: A formula for designing effective classrooms. In H. Trueba, G. Spindler, & L. Spindler (Eds.), *What do anthropologists have to say about dropouts?* (pp. 51–66). New York: Falmer Press.

Tharp, R. (1989b, February). Psychocultural variables and constants: Effects on teaching and learning in schools. *American Psychologist, 44*(2), 349–359.

Thomas, W., & Collier, V. (1997). *School effective-ness for language minority students.* Retrieved April 8, 2005, from www.ncela.gwu/pubs/resource/effectiveness/index.htm.

Thonis, E. (2005). *The English-Spanish connection.* Miami: Santillana.

Tikunoff, W., Ward, B., Romero, M., Lucas, T., Katz, A., Van Broekhuisen, L., & Castaneda, L. (1991, April). *Addressing the instructional needs of the limited English proficient student: Results of the exemplary SAIP descriptive study.* Symposium at the annual meeting of the American Educational Research Association, Chicago.

Tileston, D. W., & Darling, S. K. (2008). Why culture matters. *Teachers of Color, 3*(1), 58, 60.

Tinker Sachs, G., & Ho, B. (2007). *ESL/EFL cases: Contexts for teacher professional discussions.* Hong Kong: City University of Hong Kong Press.

Tollefson, J. W. (1991). *Planning language, planning inequality*. London: Longman.

Tollefson, J. W. (Ed.). (1995). *Power and inequality in language education*. Cambridge, Eng.: Cambridge University Press.

Tollefson, J. W. (Ed.). (2002). *Language policies in education: Critical issues*. Mahwah, NJ: Erlbaum.

Tompkins, G. (2005). *Literacy for the 21st century: A balanced approach* (4th ed.). Upper Saddle River, NJ: Merrill.

Toppo, G. (2004). An answer to standardized tests. *USA Today*. Retrieved April 8, 2005, from www.usatoday.com/news/education/2004–10–12-tests-usat_x.htm.

Torres-Guzmán, M. E., Abbate, J., Brisk, M. E., & Minaya-Rowe, L. (2002). Defining and documenting success for bilingual learners: A collective case study. *Bilingual Research Journal, 26*(1). Retrieved April 9, 2005, from http://brj.asu.edu/v261/articles/art3.html#intro.

Triandis, H. C. (1995). *Individualism & collectivism*. Boulder, CO: Westview Press.

Trueba, H. (1989). *Raising silent voices*. Boston: Heinle and Heinle.

Trueba, H., Cheng, L., & Ima, K. (1993). *Myth or reality: Adaptive strategies of Asian Americans in California*. Washington, DC: Falmer Press.

Tunnell, M. O., & Jacobs, J. S. (2000). *Children's literature, briefly* (2nd ed.). Upper Saddle River, NJ: Merrill Prentice Hall.

Ukpokodu, N. (2002). Multiculturalism vs. globalism. In F. Schultz (Ed.), *Annual editions: Multicultural education 2002–2003* (pp. 7–10). Guilford, CT: McGraw-Hill/Dushkin.

U.S. Census Bureau. (2003). *USA Quickfacts*. Retrieved January 25, 2005, from http://quickfacts.census.gov/qfd/states/00000.html.

U.S. Census Bureau. (2004a). *Educational attainment in the U.S.: 2003*. Retrieved January 12, 2005, from www.census.gov/population/www/socdem/educ-attn.html.

U.S. Census Bureau. (2004b). *Health insurance data*. Retrieved January 12, 2005, from www.census.gov/hhes/www/hlthins/hlthin03/hlthtables03.html.

U.S. Census Bureau. (2004c). *Poverty tables 2003*. Retrieved January 12, 2005, from www.census.gov/hhes/poverty/poverty03/tables03.html.

U.S. Department of Education. (2008). *Reading First*. Retrieved June 24, 2008, from www.ed.gov/programs/readingfirst/index.html.

U.S. Department of State, Bureau of Consular Affairs. (2004). *Visa Bulletin, 8*(76). Washington, DC: Author. Retrieved January 18, 2005, from http://travel.state.gov/visa/frvi/bulletin/bulletin_1343.html.

U.S. Government Accounting Office. (2002). *Per-pupil spending differences between selected inner city and suburban schools varied by metropolitan area*. Retrieved January 14, 2005, from www.gao.gov/new.items/d03234.pdf.

U.S. Office for Civil Rights. (1970). *May 25 memorandum*. Retrieved March 19, 2005, from www.ed.gov/about/offices/list/ocr/docs/lau1970.html.

U.S. Office for Civil Rights. (1976). Office for Civil Rights guidelines: Task force findings specifying remedies available for eliminating past educational practices ruled unlawful under *Lau v. Nichols*. In J. Alatis & K. Twaddell (Eds.), *English as a second language in bilingual education* (pp. 325–332). Washington, DC: Teachers of English to Speakers of Other Languages.

U.S. Office for Civil Rights. (1999). *Programs for English language learners*. Retrieved from www.ed.gov/offices/OCR/ELL.

University of Texas at Austin. (1991, Spring). Individuals with Disabilities Education Act challenges educators to improve the education of minority students with disabilities. *Bilingual Special Education Perspective, 10*, 1–6.

Unrau, N. (2008). *Content area reading and writing: Fostering literacies in middle and high school cultures*. Upper Saddle River, NJ: Merrill Prentice Hall.

Uribe, D. (2008). Crazed on phonics. *Language Magazine, 7*(8), 37.

Urow, C., & Sontag, J. (2001). Creating commuity—*un mundo entero*: The Inter-American experience. In D. Christian & F. Genesee (Eds.), *Bilingual education*. Alexandria, VA: Teachers of English to Speakers of Other Languages.

Valdes, A. (2007). Top 10 immigration myths. *Colors[NW] Magazine, 6*(12), 21–32, 43.

Valencia, R. R., & Villareal, B. J. (2003). Improving students' reading performance via standards-based school reform: A critique. *The Reading Teacher, 56*(7), 612–621.

Valles, E. C. (1998). The disproportionate representation of minority students in special education: Responding to the problem. *Journal of Special Education, 32*(1), 52–54.

Veeder, K., & Tramutt, J. (2000). Strengthening literacy in both languages. In N. Cloud, F. Genesee, & E. Hamayan (Eds.), *Dual language instruction* (p. 91). Boston: Heinle and Heinle.

Veltman, C. (1988). *The future of the Spanish language in the United States.* Washington, DC: Hispanic Policy Development Project.

Verdugo Hills High School. (2004). *Redesignated students.* Retrieved February 2, 2005, from www .lausd.k12.ca.us/Verdugo_HS/classes/esl/redes.htm.

Villa, R. A., Thousand, J. S., & Nevin, A. I. (2004). *A guide to co-teaching.* Thousand Oaks, CA: Corwin.

Villaseñor, V. (1992). *Rain of gold.* New York: Dell.

Villaume, S., & Brabham, E. (2003). Phonics instruction: Beyond the debate. *The Reading Teacher, 56*(5), 478–482.

Villegas, A. M., & Lucas, T. (2002). Preparing culturally responsive teachers: Rethinking the curriculum. *Journal of Teacher Education, 53*(1), 20–32.

Villegas, A. M., & Lucas, T. (2007). The culturally responsive teacher. *Educational Leadership, 64*(6), 28–33.

Vygotsky, L. (1978). *Mind in society.* Cambridge, MA: Harvard University Press.

Wadsworth, D., & Remaley, M. H. (2007). What families want. *Educational Leadership, 64*(6), 23–27.

Waggoner, D. (1995, November). Are current home speakers of non-English languages learning English? *Numbers and Needs, 5.*

Wallach, G. P., & Miller, L. (1988). *Language intervention and academic success.* Boston: Little, Brown.

Walqui, A. (1999). Assessment of culturally and linguistically diverse students: Considerations for the 21st century. In Mid-continent Research for Education and Learning (McREL) (Ed.), *Including culturally and linguistically diverse students in standards-based reform: A report on McREL's Diversity Roundtable I* (pp. 55–84). Retrieved March 17, 2005, from www.mcrel.org/topics/productDetail .asp?topicsID=3&productID=56.

Ward, A. W., & Murray-Ward, M. (1999). *Assessment in the classroom.* Belmont, CA: Wadsworth.

Weaver, C. (1988). *Reading process and practice.* Portsmouth, NH: Heinemann.

Weber, A. (2001). An international school in Indiana, USA. In D. Christian & F. Genesee (Eds.), *Bilingual education* (pp. 151–165). Alexandria, VA: Teachers of English to Speakers of Other Languages.

Weber, E. (2005). *MI strategies in the classroom and beyond.* Boston: Pearson.

Weber, G. (2008). A proud history: New African-American curriculum helps students realize cultural pride. *Teachers of Color, 3*(1), 44–45.

Weed, K., & Ford, M. (1999). Achieving literacy through multiple meaning systems. In E. Franklin (Ed.), *Reading and writing in more than one language* (pp. 65–80). Alexandria, VA: Teachers of English to Speakers of Other Languages.

Weiler, J. (2000). Recent changes in school desegregation. ERIC Clearinghouse on Urban Education. Retrieved April 8, 2005, from http://niusi.edreform.net/resource/5816.

Wells, M. C. (1996). *Literacies lost: When students move from a progressive middle school to a traditional high school.* New York: Teachers College Press.

West, J. F., & Idol, L. (1990). Collaborative consultation in the education of mildly handicapped and at-risk students. *Remedial and Special Education, 11*(1), 22–31.

Wiese, A. M., & García, E. (1998). The Bilingual Education Act: Language minority students and equal educational opportunity. *Bilingual Research Journal, 22*(1). Retrieved April 9, 2005, from http:// brj.asu.edu/v221/articles/art1.html.

Wiggins, G. (2005). What is understanding by design? *Understanding by design.* Retrieved March 23, 2005, from www.grantwiggins.org/ubd.html.

Willard, N. E. (2007). *Cyberbullying and cyberthreats: Responding to the challenge of online social aggression, threats, and distress.* Champaign, IL: Research Press. 367C.

Williams, B. T. (2007). Standardized students: The problems with writing for tests instead of people. In Schultz, F. (Ed.), *Annual editions 10/08: Education* (pp. 71–75). Dubuque, IA: McGraw-Hill Contemporary Learning Series.

Willig, A. C. (1985). A meta-analysis of selected studies on the effectiveness of bilingual education. *Review of Educational Research, 55,* 269–317.

Wilner, L. K., & Feinstein-Whitaker, M. (2008). Accenting the positive. *Language Magazine, 7*(8), 34.

Wilson, W. (1984). The urban underclass. In L. Dunbar (Ed.), *Minority report*. New York: Pantheon Books.

Wilton, D. (2003). *How many words are there in the English language?* Retrieved August 30, 2004, from www.wordorigins.org/number.htm.

Wolfenbarger, C. D., & Sipe, L. R. (2007). A unique and literary art form: Recent research on picture books. *Language Arts, 84*(3), 273–280.

Wollenberg, C. (1989). *The new immigrants and California's multiethnic heritage.* Available from New Faces of Liberty/SFSC, P.O. Box 5646, San Francisco, CA 94101.

Woolfolk, A. (2007). *Educational psychology* (10th ed.). Boston: Allyn & Bacon.

Woolfolk, A., & Brooks, D. (1985). The influence of teachers' nonverbal behaviors on students' perceptions and performance. *Elementary School Journal, 85,* 514–528.

Worthen, B., & Spandel, V. (1991). Putting the standardized test debate in perspective. *Educational Leadership, 48*(5), 65–69.

Worthy, J., Moorman, M., & Turner, M. (1999). What Johnny likes to read is hard to find in school. *Reading Research Quarterly, 14,* 12–27.

Wray, M., & Newitz, A. (1997). *White trash: Race and class in America.* New York: Routledge.

Yamauchi, L., & Wilhelm, P. (2001). *e Ola Ka Hawai'i I Kona 'Olelo:* Hawaiians live in their language. In D. Christian & F. Genesee (Eds.), *Bilingual education* (pp. 83–94). Alexandria, VA: Teachers of English to Speakers of Other Languages.

Yao, E. (1988). Working effectively with Asian immigrant parents. *Phi Delta Kappan, 70*(3), 223–225.

Yates, S. (1996). English in cyberspace. In S. Goodman & D. Graddol (Eds.), *Redesigning English: New texts, new identities* (pp. 106–140). London: Routledge.

Yep, L. (1975). *Dragonwings.* New York: Harper & Row.

Young, M., & Helvie, S. (1996). Parent power: A positive link to school success. *Journal of Educational Issues of Language Minority Students, 16.* Retrieved April 8, 2005, from www.ncela.gwu.edu/pubs/jeilms/vol16/jeilms1611.htm.

Zacarian, D. (2004a). Keeping Tren in school. *Essential Teacher, 1*(2), 12–13.

Zacarian, D. (2004b). The road taken: "I was lost before the end of the first minute." *Essential Teacher, 1*(3), 11–13.

Zanger, V. V. (1994). "Not joined in": The social context of English literacy development for Hispanic youth. In B. M. Ferdman, R.-M. Weber, & A. G. Ramírez (Eds.), *Literacy across languages and cultures* (pp. 171–198). Albany: SUNY Press.

Zarate, M. E., Bhimji, F., & Reese, L. (2005). Ethnic identity and academic achievement among Latino/a adolescents. *Journal of Latinos in Education, 4*(2), 93–114.

Zehler, A., Hopstock, P., Fleischman, H., & Greniuk, C. (1994). *An examination of assessment of limited English proficient students.* Arlington, VA: Special Issues Analysis Center. Retrieved April 8, 2005, from www.ncela.gwu.edu/pubs/siac/lepasses.htm.

Zeiler, H. (2007). Successful interventions. *Language Magazine, 6*(9), 32–35.

Zemach, D. (2007). Picture this. *Essential Teacher, 4*(2), 12–13.

For Chapter 6

Adams, M. J. (1990). *Beginning to read: Thinking and learning about print.* Cambridge, MA: MIT Press.

Adamson, H.D. (1993). *Academic competence.* New York Longman.

Addison, A. (1988, November). Comprehensible text books in science for the nonnative English-speaker: Evidence from discourse analysis. *The CATESOL Journal 1*(1), 49–66.

Adger, C. (2000). School/community partnerships to support language minority student success. *CREDE Research Brief #5.* Santa Cruz, CA: Center for Research on Education, Diversity and Excellence. Accessed July 7, 2006, from www.crede.org/products/print/research_briefs/rb5.shtml

Af Trampe, P. (1994). Monitor theory: Application and ethics. In R. Barasch & C. James (Eds.), *Beyond the monitor model* Boston: Heinle and Heinle.

Agar, M. (1980). *The professional stranger: An informal introduction to ethnography.* Orlando, FL: Academic Press.

Agor, B. (Ed.). (2000). *Integrating the ESL standards into classroom practice: Grades 9–12.* Alexandria, VA: Teachers of English to Speakers of Other Languages (TESOL).

Alcaya, C, Lybeck, K., Mougel, P., & Weaver, S. (1995). *Some strategies useful for speaking a foreign language.* Unpublished manuscript, University of Minnesota.

Alexander, S. (1983). *Nadia, the willful.* New York: Dial.

Altman, L. J. (1993). *Amelia's road.* New York: Lee and Low Books.

Allen, E., & Vallette, R. (1977). *Classroom techniques. Foreign languages and English as a second language.* San Diego, CA: Harcourt Brace Jovanovich.

Allport, G. (1954). *The nature of prejudice.* Garden City, NY: Doubleday Anchor.

Amselle, J. (1999). Dual immersion delays English. *American Language Review, 3*(5), 8.

Andersen, J., & Powell, R. {1991). Intercultural communication and the classroom. In L. Samovar & R. Porter (Eds.), *Intercultural communication: A reader* (6th ed.). Belmont, CA: Wadsworth.

Anderson, J., & Gunderson, L. (2004). You don't *read* a science book, you *study* it: An exploration of cultural concepts of reading. Accessed July 24, 2006, from www.readingonline.org/electronic/elec_index.asp?HREF=anderson/index.html

Antuñez, B. (2002). *Reading and English language learners.* Accessed July 25, 2006, from www.colorincolorado.org/articles/antunez_readindandells.php

Anyon, J. (1994). The retreat of Marxism and socialist feminism: Postmodern and poststructural theories in education. *Curriculum Inquiry, 24,* 115–133.

Aoki, E. (1992). Turning the page: Asian Pacific American children's literature. In V. J. Harris (Ed.), *Teaching multicultural literature in grades K–8.* Norwood, MA: Christopher-Gordon Publishers.

Arvizu, S. (1992). Home-school linkages: A cross-cultural approach to parent participation. In M. Saravia-Shore & S. Arvizu (Eds.), *Cross-cultural literacy: Ethnographies of communication in multi-ethnic classrooms.* New York: Garland.

Asher, J. (1982). *Learning another language through actions: The complete teachers' guidebook.* Los Gatos, CA: Sky Oaks.

Asian Pacific Fund. (2003, Fall/Winter). *Asian outlook: Bay area people in need.* San Francisco: Author. Accessed August 2, 2006, from www.asianpacificfund.org/resources

Au, K., & Jordan, C. (1981). Teaching reading to Hawaiian children: Finding a culturally appropriate solution. In H. Trueba, G. Guthrie, & K. Au (Eds.), *Culture and the bilingual classroom: Studies in classroom ethnography.* Rowley, MA: Newbury House.

Babbitt, N. (1976). *Tuck Everlasting.* New York: Bantam Books.

Baker, C. (1993). *Foundations of bilingual education and bilingualism.* Clevedon, UK: Multilingual Matters.

Baker, C. (2001). *Foundations of bilingual education and bilingualism* (3rd ed.). Clevedon, UK: Multilingual Matters.

Balderrama, M. V., & Díaz-Rico, L. T. (2006). *Teacher performance expectations for educating English learners.* Boston: Allyn & Bacon.

Bandlow, R. (2002). Suburban bigotry: A descent into racism & struggle for redemption. In F. Schultz (Ed.), *Annual editions: Multicultural education 2002—2003* (pp. 90–93). Guilford, CT: McGraw-Hill/Dushkin.

Banks, J. (1991.). A Curriculum for empowerment, action, and change. In G. Sleeter (Ed.), *Empowerment through multicultural education.* Albany: State University of New York Press.

Banks, J. (1994). *An introduction to multicultural education.* Boston: Allyn & Bacon.

Barbe, W. B., Wasylyk, T. M., Hackney, C. S., and Braun, L. A. (1984). *Zaner-Bloser creative growth in handwriting (grades K-8).* Columbus, OH: Zaner-Bloser.

Barks, D., & Watts, P. (2001). Textual borrowing strategies for graduate-level ESL students. In D. Belcher and A. Hirvela (Eds.), *Linking literacies: Perspectives on L2 reading-writing connections* (pp. 246–267). Ann Arbor, MI: The University of Michigan Press.

Barr, R. & Johnson, B. (1997). *Teaching reading and writing in elementary classrooms* (2nd ed.). New York: Longman.

Bartolomé, L. I. (1994). Beyond the methods fetish: Toward a humanizing pedagogy. *Harvard Educational Review, 64*(2), 173–194.

Barton, D., Hamilton, M., & Ivanič, R. (2000). Introduction. In D. Barton, M. Hamilton, & R. Ivanič (Eds.), *Situated literacies* (pp. 1–15). London and New York Routledge.

Bartram, M., & Walton, R. (1994). *Correction: A positive approach to language mistakes.* Hove, UK: Language Teaching Publications.

Bassano, S., & Christison, M. A. (1995). *Community spirit: A practical guide to collaborative language learning.* San Francisco: Alta Book Center.

Bell, C. (2002). Secondary level report—Explaining SDAIE to colleagues. *CATESOL News, 34*(3), 15.

Belmont, J. M. (1989). Cognitive strategies and strategic learning: The socioinstructional approach. *American Psychologist, 44,* 142–148.

Bembridge, T. (1992). A MAP for reading assessment *Educational Leadership, 49*(8), 46–48.

Bennett, C. (1990). *Comprehensive multicultural education: Theory and practice* (2nd ed.). Boston: Allyn & Bacon.

Bennett, C. (2003). *Comprehensive multicultural education: Theory and practice* (5th ed.). Boston: Allyn & Bacon.

Benson, V. A. (1999). Syl/la/bles and linking. In N. Shameem & M. Tickoo (Eds.), *New ways in using communicative games* (pp. 18–19). Alexandria, VA: Teachers of English to Speakers of Other Languages.

Bergman, J. L., & Schuder, T. (1993). Teaching at-risk students to read strategically. *Educational Leadership, 50*(54), 19–23.

Berk, L. E., & Winsler, A. (1995). *Scaffolding children's learning: Vygotsky and early childhood education.* Washington, DC: National Association for the Education of Young Children.

Bermúdez, A., & Márquez, J. (1996). An examination of a four-way collaborative to increase parental involvement in the schools. *The Journal of Educational Issues of Language Minority Students, 16.* Accessed July 7, 2006, from www.ncela.gwu.edu/pubs/jeilms/voll6/jeilms1601.htm

Bielenberg, B., & Wong Fillmore, L. (2004/2005). The English they need for the test. *Educational Leadership, 62*(4), 45–49.

Birdwhistell, R. (1974). The language of the body: The natural environment of words. In A. Silverstein (Ed.), *Human communication: Theoretical explorations.* Hillsdale, NJ: Erlbaum.

Bitter, G., Pierson, M., & Burvikovs, A. (2004). *Using technology in the classroom* (6th ed.). Boston: Allyn & Bacon.

Blair, R.W. (Ed.). (1982). *Innovative approaches to language teaching.* Boston: Heinle & Heinle.

Bliatout, B., Downing, B., Lewis, J., & Yang, D. (1988). *Handbook for teaching Hmong-speaking students.* Folsom, CA: Folsom Cordova Unified School District, Southeast Asia Community Resource Center.

Bloch, J. (2001). Plagiarism and the ESL student: From printed to electronic texts. In D. Belcher & A. Hirvela (Eds.), *Linking literacies: Perspectives on L2 reading-writing connections* (pp. 209–228). Ann Arbor: The University of Michigan Press.

Bosher, S. (1997). Language and cultural identity: A study of Hmong students at the postsecondary level. *TESOL Quarterly, 31*(3), 593–603.

Bourdieu, P. (1977). *Reproduction in society, education, and culture* (with J. Passeron). Los Angeles: Sage.

Boyd-Batstone, P. (2006). *Differentiated early literacy for English language learners: Practical strategies.* Boston: Pearson.

Bradley, K. S., & Bradley, J. A. (2004). Scaffolding academic learning for second language learners. Accessed July 31, 2006, from http://iteslj.org/Articles/Bradley-Scaffolding/

Brandt, R. (1994). On educating for diversity: A conversation with James A. Banks. *Educational Leadership, 51,* 28–31.

Brend, R. M. (1975). Male-female intonation patterns in American English. In B. Thorne & N. Henley (Eds.), *Language and sex: Differences and dominance.* Rowley, MA: Newbury House.

Brinton, D. (2003). Content-based instruction. In D. Nunan (Ed.), *Practical English language teaching*. New York: McGraw-Hill.

Brinton, D., & Master, P. (Eds.). (1997). *New ways in content-based instruction*. Alexandria, VA: Teachers of English to Speakers of Other Languages (TESOL).

Brisk, M. E., & Harrington, M. M. (2000). *Literacy and bilingualism*. Mahwah, NJ: Erlbaum.

Bromberg, M., Liebb, J., & Traiger, A. (2005). *504 absolutely essential words* (5th ed.). Hauppage, NY: Barron's.

Bromley, K. D. (1989). Buddy journals make the reading-writing connection. *The Reading Teacher, 43*(2), 122–129.

Brown, D. (1987). *Principles of language learning and teaching* (2nd ed.). Englewood Cliffs, NJ: Prentice Hall.

Brown, D. (2000). *Principles of language learning and teaching* (4th ed.). Englewood Cliffs, NJ: Prentice Hall.

Bruner, J. (1986). *Actual minds, possible worlds*. Cambridge: Harvard University Press.

Brutt-Griffler, J., & Samimy, K. K. (1999). Revisiting the colonial in the postcolonial: Critical praxis for the nonnative-English-speaking teachers in a TESOL program. *TESOL Quarterly, 33*(3), 413–431.

Buchanan, K., & Helman, M. (1997). Reforming mathematics instruction for ESL literacy students. *ERIC Digest*. Retrieved Oct. 15, 2004, from www.cal.org/resources/digest/buchan01.html

Bunch, G. C, Abram, P. L, Lotan, R. A., & Valdes, G. (2001). Beyond sheltered instruction: Rethinking conditions for academic language development. *TESOL Journal, 10(2/3),* 28–33.

Bunting, E. (1988). *How many days to America?* New York: Clarion.

Burgstahler, S. (2002). *Universal design of instruction*. Retrieved July 7, 2006, from www.washington.edu/doit/Brochures/Academics/instruction.html

Burely-Allen, M. (1995). *Listening: The forgotten skill*. New York: John Wiley & Sons.

Byrd, P., & Benson, B. (1994). *Problem-solution: A reference for ESL writers*. Boston: Heinle & Heinle.

Caine, R. N., Caine, G., McClintic, C., & Klimek, K. (2004). *Brain/mind learning principles in action: The fieldbook for making connections, teaching, and the human brain*. Thousand Oaks, CA: Sage.

California Department of Education. (1992). *Handbook for teaching Korean-American students*. Sacramento: Author.

California Department of Education. (1997). *English/language arts standards*. Sacramento: Author. Accessed July 18, 2006, from www.cde.ca.gov/be/st/ss/engmain.asp

California Department of Education. (1999). *English language development standards*. Sacramento: Author. Online at www.cde.ca.gov/statetests/eld/eld_grd_span.pdf

California Department of Education. (2004a). *Physical education model content standards for California public schools*. Sacramento: Author.

California Department of Education. (2004b). *English learner students*. Accessed August 4, 2006, from www.cde.ca.gov/re/pn/fb/yr04english.asp

California Department of Education. (2006a). *Reading/language arts framework for California public schools* (draft). Sacramento: Author. Accessed July 18, 2006, from www.cde.ca.gov/ci/rl/cf/index.asp

California Department of Education (CDE). (2006b). *Number of English learners by language*. Accessed May 11, 2006, from http://datal.cde.ca.gov/dataquest/LEPbyLangl.asp

California Department of Education (CDE). (2006c). *The science content standards for kindergarten through grade five*. Accessed August 4, 2006, from www.cde.ca.gov/re/pn/fd/sci-frame-dwnld.asp

Cameron, A. (1988). *The most beautiful place in the world*. New York: Random House.

Campbell, C. (1998). *Teaching second language writing: Interacting with text*. Pacific Grove, CA: Heinle & Heinle.

Canale, M. (1983). From communicative competence to communicative language pedagogy. In J. Richards & R. Schmidt (Eds.), *Language and communication*. New York: Longman.

Cantlon, T. L. (1991). *Structuring the classroom successfully for cooperative team learning*. Portland, OR: Prestige Publishers.

Carnuccio, L. M. (2004). Cybersites. *Essential Teacher, 1*(3), 59.

Carrasquillo, A., & Rodríguez, V. (2002). *Language minority students in the mainstream classroom*. Clevedon, UK: Multilingual Matters.

Cary, S. (2000). *Working with second language learners: Answers to teachers' top ten questions.* Portsmouth, NH: Heinemann.

Casey, J. (2004). A place for first language in the ESOL classroom. *Essential Teacher, 1*(4), 50–52.

CATESOL. (1998). *CATESOL position statement on literacy instruction for English language learners, grades K–12.* Retrieved July 24, 2006, from www.catesol.org/literacy.html

Celce-Murcia, M., & Olshtain, E. (2001). *Discourse and context in language teaching.* Cambridge: Cambridge University Press.

Center for Educational Reform. (2000). *National charter school directory* (7th ed.). Washington, DC: Author.

Chambers, J.,& Parrish, T. (1992). *Meeting the challenge of diversity: An evaluation of programs for pupils with limited proficiency in English: Vol. 4. Cost of programs and services for LEP students.* Berkeley, CA: BW Associates.

Chamot, A. U., & O'Malley, J. (1994). *The CALLA handbook: Implementing the cognitive academic language learning approach.* Boston: Addison-Wesley.

Chan, L. (2004). The inexorable rise in demand for qualified ESL teachers. *Language, 3*(6), 30–31.

Chandler, D. (2005) *Semiotics for beginners.* Retrieved June 27, 2006, from www.aber.ac.uk/media/Documents/S4B/semiotic.html

Chaney, A. L., & Burk, T. L. (1998). *Teaching oral communication in grades K-8.* Boston: Allyn & Bacon.

Chard, D. J., Pikulski, J. J., & Templeton, S. (n.d.). prom phonemic awareness to fluency: Effective decoding instruction in a research-based reading program. Accessed July 24, 2006, from www.eduplace.com/state/pdf/author/chard_pik_temp.pdf

Cheng, L. (1987). English communicative competence of language minority children: Assessment and treatment of language "impaired" preschoolers. In H. Trueba (Ed.), *Success or failure? Learning and the language minority student.* Boston: Heinle and Heinle.

Chesterfield, R., & Chesterfield, K. (1985). Natural order in children's use of second language learning strategies. *Applied Linguistics, 6,* 45–59.

Children's Defense Fund. (2005). *The state of America's children.* Retrieved August 2, 2006, from http://cdf.convio.net/site/PageServer?pagename=research_publications

Cho Bassoff, T. (2004). Compleat Links: Three steps toward a strong home-school connection. *Essential Teacher, 1*(4). Retrieved August 3, 2006, from www.tesol.org/s_tesol/sec_document.asp?CID=65&DID=2586

Christensen, L. (2000). *Reading, writing, rising up: Teaching about social justice and the power of the written word.* Milwaukee, WI: Rethinking Schools.

Chung, H. (1989). *Working with Vietnamese high school students.* San Francisco: New Faces of Liberty/SFSC.

Cipollone, N., reiser, S. H., & Vasishth, S. (1998). *Language files* (7th ed.). Columbus: Ohio State University Press.

Clark, B. (1983). *Growing up gifted: Developing the potential of children at home and at school* (2nd ed.). Columbus, OH: Merrill.

Cloud, N., Genesee, F., & Hamayan, E. (2000). *Dual language instruction.* Boston: Heinle & Heinle.

Cockcroft, J. D. (1995). *Latinos in the struggle for equal education.* Danbury, CT: Franklin Watts.

Coehlo, E., Winer, L., & Olsen, J. W-B. (1989). *All sides of the issue: Activities for cooperative jigsaw groups.* Hayward, CA: Alemany Press.

Cogan, D. (1999). What am I saying? In N. Shameem & M. Tickoo (Eds.), *New ways in using communicative games* (pp. 22–23). Alexandria, VA: Teachers of English to Speakers of Other Languages.

Cohen, E. (1994). *Designing groupwork: Strategies for the heterogeneous classroom.* New York: Teachers College Press.

Cohn, D., & Bahrampour, T. (2006, May 10). Of U.S. children under 5, nearly half are minorities. *Washington Post,* A01.

Cole, K. (2003, March). *Negotiating intersubjectivity in the classroom: Mutual socialization to classroom conversations.* Presentation at the American Association for Applied Linguistics annual conference, Arlington, VA.

Cole, M. (1998). *Cultural psychology: Can it help us think about diversity?* Presentation, annual meeting, American Educational Research Association, San Diego.

Collie, J., & Slater, S. (1987). *Literature in the language classroom.* Cambridge: Cambridge University Press.

Collier, V. (1987). Age and rate of acquisition of second language for academic purposes. *TESOL Quarterly, 21*(4), 617–641.

Collier, V. P. (1995). Acquiring a second language for school. *Directions in Language & Education, National Clearinghouse for Bilingual Education, 1*(4). Accessed July 7, 2006, from www.ncela.gwu.edu/pubs/directions/04.htm

Contra Costa County Office of Education. (2006). Curriculum and instruction: Standards implementation. Accessed August 4, 2006, from www.cccoe.kl2.ca.us/edsvcs/assessmenthtml

Cook, V. (1999). Going beyond the native speaker in language teaching. *TESOL Quarterly, 33*(2), 185–209.

Corley, M. A. (2003). *Poverty, racism, and literacy.* ERIC Clearinghouse on Adult, Career, and Vocational Education. ERIC Digest #243.

Cortés, C. (1993). Acculturation, assimilation, and "adducation." *BEOutreach, 4*(1), 3–5.

Costa, A. L., & Garmston, R. J. (2002). *Cognitive coaching: A foundation for renaissance schools* (2nd ed.). Norwood, MA: Christopher-Gordon.

Cotton, K. (1989). *Expectations and student outcomes.* Retrieved August 3, 2006, from www.nwrel.org/scpd/sirs/4/cu7.html

Crago, M. (1993). Communicative interaction and second language acquisition: An Inuit example. *TESOL Quarterly, 26*(3), 487–506.

Crawford, J. (1999). *Bilingual education: History, politics, theory, and practice* (4th ed.). Los Angeles: Bilingual Educational Services.

Crawford, J. (2004). *Educating English learners: Language diversity in the classroom* (5th ed.). Los Angeles: Bilingual Educational Services, Inc.

Crawford, J. (2006). National language amendment: Political blunder by Republicans. Accessed July 6, 2006, from http://ourworld.compuserve.com/homepages/JWCrawford/

Cummins, J. (1976). The influence of bilingualism on cognitive growth: A synthesis of research findings and explanatory hypothesis. *Working Papers on Bilingualism, 9,* 1–43.

Cummins, J. (1979). Linguistic interdependence and the educational development of bilingual children. *Review of Educational Research, 49*(2), 222–251.

Cummins, J. (1980). The cross-lingual dimensions of language proficiency. Implications for bilingual education and the optimal age issue. *TESOL Quarterly, 14*(2), 175–187.

Cummins, J. (1981a). Age on arrival and immigrant second language learning in Canada: A reassessment. *Applied Linguistics, 2*(2), 132–149.

Cummins, J. (1981b). The role of primary language development in promoting educational success for language minority students. In *Schooling and language minority students: A theoretical framework.* Sacramento: California State Department of Education.

Cummins, J. (1984). *Bilingualism and special education: Issues in assessment and pedagogy,* San Diego: College-Hill

Cummins, J. (1989). *Empowering minority students.* Sacramento: California Association for Bilingual Education.

Cummins, J. (1996). *Negotiating identities: Education for empowerment in a diverse society.* Los Angeles: California Association for Bilingual Education.

Cummins, J. (2000a). Beyond adversarial discourse: Searching for common ground in the education of bilingual students. In P. McLaren & C. J. Ovando (Eds.), *The politics of multiculturalism and bilingual education* (pp. 126–147). Boston: The McGraw-Hill Companies.

Curtain, H., & Dahlberg, C. A. (2004). *Language and children—Making the match: New languages for young learners, grades K–8.* Boston: Allyn & Bacon.

Cushner, K. (1999). *Human diversity in action*. Boston: McGraw-Hill.

Daloğlu, A. (2005). Reducing learning burden in academic vocabulary development *Teachers of English to Speakers of Other Languages EFLIS Newsletter, 5*(1).

Dale, P., & Poms, L. (2005). *English pronunciation made simple*. White Plains, NY: Pearson/ Longman.

Dale, T., & Cuevas, G. (1992). Integrating mathematics and language learning. In P. Richard-Amato & M. Snow (Eds.), *The multicultural classroom*. White Plains, NY: Longman.

Danesi, M. (1985). *A guide to puzzles and games in second language pedagogy*. Toronto: Ontario Institute for Studies in Education.

Darder, A. (1991). *Culture and power in the classroom*. New York: Bergin and Garvey.

Davies, A., Cameron, C., Politano, C., & Gregory, K. (1992). *Together is better: Collaborative assessment, evaluation, and reporting*. Winnepeg, CAN: Peguis.

Day, F. A. (1994). *Multicultural voices in contemporary literature: A resource for teachers*. Portsmouth, NH: Heinemann.

Day, F. A. (1997). *Latina and Latino voices in literature for children and teenagers*. Portsmouth, NH: Heinemann.

Day, F. A. (2003). *Latina and Latino voices in literature: Lives and works*. Westport, CT: Greenwood Publishers.

De Boinod, A-J. (2006). *The meaning of tingo*. New York: Penguin.

DeGeorge, G. (1987–1988, Winter). Assessment and placement of language minority students: Procedures for mainstreaming. *NCBE Occasional Papers #3*. Retrieved March 23, 2005, from www .ncela.gwu.edu/pubs/classics/focus/03mainstream.htm

Delgado-Gaitan, C., & Trueba, H. (1991). *Crossing cultural borders: Education for immigrant families in America*. London: Falmer Press.

dePaola, T. (1981). *Now one foot, now the other*. New York: G. P. Putnam's Sons.

deUnamuno, M. (1925). *Essays and soliloquies*. New York: Knopf.

Diamond, B., & Moore, M. (1995). *Multicultural literacy*. White Plains, NY: Longman.

Díaz, R. M., Neal, C. J., & Vachio, A. (1991). Maternal teaching in the zone of proximal development: A comparison of low- and high-risk dyads. *Merrill-Palmer Quarterly, 37,* 83–108.

Díaz-Rico, L. T. (2004). *Teaching English learners: Strategies and methods*. Boston: Allyn & Bacon.

Díaz-Rico, L. T., & Dullien, S. (2004). *Semiotics and people watching*. Presentation, California Teachers of English to Speakers of Other Languages regional conference, Los Angeles, CA.

Díaz-Rico, L. T., & Weed, K. Z. (2006). *Crosscultural, language, and academic development handbook* (3rd ed.). Boston: Allyn & Bacon.

Dicker, S. (1992). Societal views of bilingualism and language learning. *TESOL: Applied Linguistics Interest Section Newsletter, 14*(1), 1, 4.

Donato, R. (1997). *The other struggle for equal schools: Mexican Americans during the Civil Rights Era*. New York: State University of New York Press.

Dudley-Marling, C., & Seare, D. (1991). *When students have time to talk*. Portsmouth, NH: Heinemann.

Dumont, R. (1972). Learning English and how to be silent: Studies in Sioux and Cherokee classrooms. In C. Caz-den, V. John, & D. Hymes (Eds.), *Functions of language in the classroom*. New York: Teachers College Press.

Dunkel, P., & Lim, P. L. (1994). *Intermediate listening comprehension: Understanding and recalling spoken English*. Boston: Heinle & Heinle.

Dunkel, P. A., Pialorsi, F., & Kozyrev, J. (1996). *Advanced listening comprehension: Developing aural and note-taking skills*. Boston: Heinle & Heinle.

Dryfoos, J. (1998). *Safe passage: Making it through adolescence in a risky society*. New York Oxford.

Echevarria, J., Vogt, M. E., & Short, D. (2004). *Making content comprehensible for English language learners: The SIOP model* (2nd ed.). Boston: Allyn & Bacon.

Ediger, A., & Pavlik, C. (1999). *Reading connections: Skills and strategies for purposeful reading*. New York: Oxford University Press.

Edmonson, M., (1971). *Lore: An introduction to the science of fiction*. New York: Holt, Rinehart and Winston.

Education Trust, The. (1998). *Education watch: The Education Trust 1998 state and national data book*. Washington, DC: Author.

Egan, K., & Gajdamaschko, N. (2003). Some cognitive tools of literacy. In A. Kozulin, B. Gindis, V. S. Ageyev, & S. M. Miller (Eds.), *Vygotsky's educational theory in cultural context* (pp. 83–98). Cambridge: Cambridge University Press.

Egbert, J. (2004). Access to knowledge: Implications of Universal Design for CALL environments. *CALL_EJ Online, 5*(2). Retrieved July 7, 2006, from www.tell.is.ritsumei.ac.jp/callejonline/journal/5–2/egbert.html

Egbert, J., & Hanson-Smith, E. (1999). *CALL environments: Research, practice, and critical issues*. Alexandria, VA: Teachers of English to Speakers of Other Languages.

Ehri, L. (1997). Learning to read and learning to spell are one and the same, almost. In C. Perfetti, L. Rieben, & M. Fayol (Eds.), *Learning to spell: Research, theory, and practice across languages* (pp. 237–269). Mahwah, NJ: Erlbaum.

Ellis, R. (1986). *Understanding second language acquisition*. Oxford: Oxford University Press.

Ellis, S. S., & Whalen, S. F. (1992). Keys to cooperative learning: 35 ways to keep kids responsible, challenged, and most of all, cooperative. *Instructor, 101(6),* 34–37.

Erickson, F. (1977). Some approaches to inquiry in school-community ethnography. *Anthropology and Education Quarterly, 8*(2), 58–69.

Escalante, J., & Dirmann, J. (1990). The Jaime Escalante math program. *Journal of Negro Education, 59*(3), 407–423.

Faber, J. E., Morris, J. D., & Lieberman, M. G. (2000). The effect of note taking on ninth grade students' comprehension. *Reading Psychology, 21,* 257–270.

Faltis, C. (1993). Critical issues in the use of sheltered content instruction in high school bilingual programs. *Peabody Journal of Education, 69*(1), 136–151.

Faltis, C. (2001). *Joinfostering* (3rd ed.). Upper Saddle River, NJ: Prentice Hall.

Farr, M. (1994). En los dos idiomas: Literacy practices among Chicago Mexicanos. In B. Moss (Ed.), *Literacy across communities* (pp. 1–9). Cresskill, NJ: Hampton Press.

Feng, J. (1994). Asian-American children: What teachers should know. *ERIC Digest*. Champaign, IL: Clearing-house on Elementary and Early Childhood Education. Online at http://ericps.ed.uiuc.edu/eece/pubs

Feuerstein, T. & Schcolnik, M. (1995). *Enhancing reading comprehension in the language learning classroom*. San Francisco, CA: Alta.

Finnan, C. (1987). The influence of the ethnic community on the adjustment of Vietnamese refugees. In G. & L. Spindler (Eds.), *Interpretive ethnography of education: At home and abroad*. Hillsdale, NJ: Erlbaum.

Fischer, B., & Fischer, L. (1979, January). Styles in teaching and learning. *Educational Leadership, 36*(4), 245–251.

Fisher, D., Brozo, W. G., Frey, N., & Ivey, G. (2007). *50 content area strategies for adolescent literacy*. Upper Saddle River, NJ: Merrill/Prentice Hall.

Flood, J., Lapp, D., Tinajero, J., & Hurley, S. (1997). Literacy instruction for students acquiring English: Moving beyond the immersion debate. *The Reading Teacher,* 356–358.

Florida Department of Education. (2003). *Inclusion as an instructional model for LEP students*. Retrieved February 10, 2005, from www.firn.edu/doe/omsle/tapindu.htm

Flower, L. (1994). *The construction of negotiated meaning: A social cognitive theory of writing*. Carbondale and Edwardsville, IL: Southern Illinois University Press.

Flynn, K.(1995). *Graphic organizers . . . helping kids think visually*. Cypress, CA: Creative Thinking Press.

Flynt, E. S., & Cooter, R. B. (1999). *The English-Espanõl reading inventory for the classroom*. Upper Saddle River, NJ: Merrill/Prentice Hall.

Folse, K. S. (1996). *Discussion starters*. Ann Arbor: The University of Michigan Press.

Fosnot, C. T. (1989). *Enquiring teachers, enquiring learners: A constructivist approach for teaching*. New York: Teachers College Press.

Foucault, M. (1979). *Discipline and punish: The birth of the prison*. New York: Vintage Books.

Foucault, M. (1980). *Power/knowledge: Selected interviews and other writings 1971–1977.* New York: Pantheon Books.

Fraser, N., & Nicholson, L. (1988). Social criticism without philosophy: An encounter between feminism and postmodernism. In A. Ross (Ed.), *Universal abandon? The politics of postmodernism* (pp. 83–94). Minneapolis: University of Minnesota Press.

Freeman, R. (2004). *Building on community bilingualtsm.* Philadelphia: Caslon.

Freire, P. (1970). *Pedagogy of the oppressed.* New York: Seabury Press.

Frey, N., & Fisher, D. (2007). *Reading for information in elementary school: Content literacy strategies to build comprehension.* Upper Saddle River, NJ: Merrill/Prentice Hall.

Friend, M., & Bursuck, W. D. (2002). *including students with special needs: A practical guide for classroom teachers.* Boston: Allyn & Bacon.

Friend, M., & Cook, L. (1996). *Interactions: Collaboration skills for school professionals.* White Plains, NY: Longman.

From the Classroom. (1991). Teachers seek a fair and meaningful assessment process to measure LEP students' progress. Fountain Valley, CA: *Teacher Designed Learning, 2*(1), 1, 3.

Fu, D. (2004). Teaching ELL students in regular class-rooms at the secondary level. *Voices from the Middle, 11*(4), 8–15.

Fuller, B. (2003). Educational policy under cultural pluralism. *Educational Researcher, 32*(9), 15–24.

Funaki, I., & Burnett, K. (1993). *When educational systems collide: Teaching and learning with Polynesian students.* Presentation, annual conference, Association of Teacher Educators, Los Angeles.

Furey, P. (1986). A framework for cross-cultural analysis of teaching methods. In P. Byrd (Ed.), *Teaching across cultures in the university ESL program.* Washington, DC: National Association of Foreign Student Advisors.

Gamrel, L. B., & Bales, R. J. (1986). Mental imagery and the comprehension-monitoring performance of fourth- and fifth-grade poor readers. *Reading Research Quarterly, 21,* 454–464.

Gándara, P. (1997). *Review of research on instruction of limited English proficient students.* Davis, CA: University of California, Linguistic Minority Research Institute.

Gándara, P., Maxwell-Jolly, J., Garía, E., Asato, J., Gutierrez, K., Stritkus, T., & Curry, J. (2000). *The initial impact of Proposition 227 on the instruction of English learners.* Davis, CA: University of California Linguistic Minority Research Center.

Gaouette, N. (2006, May 10). Latinos boost U.S. population. *Los Angeles Times,* A04.

García, S. B., & Ortiz, A. A. (2004). *Preventing disproportionate representation: Culturally and linguistically responsive prereferral interventions.* National Center for Culturally Responsive Educational Systems. Retrieved August 4, 2006, from www.nccrest.org/publications.html

García, E. (2000). *The best of times and the worst of times: Proposition 227 aftermath in California.* Tenth Annual Bilingual Education Institute, Arizona State University West, Phoenix.

Gardner, H. (1983). *Frames of mind: The theory of multi-ple intelligences.* New York: Basic Books.

Gardner, R., & Lambert, W. (1972). *Attitudes and motivation in second language learning.* Rowley, MA: Newbury House.

Garrison, D. (1990). Inductive strategies for teaching Spanish–English cognates. *Hispania, 73*(2), 508–512.

Gascoigne, C. (2002). *The debate on grammar in second language acquisition: Past, present, and future.* Lewiston, NY: Edwin Mellen Press.

Gass, S. (2000). *Interaction in classroom discourse.* Presentation, annual meeting, Teachers of English to Speakers of Other Languages, Vancouver, Canada.

Gass, S., & Selinker, L. (2001). *Second language acquisition.* Mahwah, NJ: Erlbaum.

Gay, G. (1975, October). Cultural differences important in education of Black children. *Momentum,* 30–32.

Genesee, F. (Ed.). (1999). *Program alternatives for linguistically diverse students.* Santa Cruz, CA: Center for Research on Education, Diversity and Excellence. Online at www.cal.org/crede/pubs/edpractice/Eprl.pdf

Gibson, M. (1987). Punjabi immigrants in an American high school. In G. & L. Spindler (Eds.), *Interpretive ethnography of education: At home and abroad.* Hillsdale, NJ: Erlbaum.

Gillett, P. (1989a). *Cambodian refugees: An introduction to their history and culture.* San Francisco, CA: New Faces of Liberty/SFSC.

Gillett, P. (1989b). *El Salvador: A country in crisis.* San Francisco, CA: New Faces of Liberty/SFSC.

Giroux, H. (1983). Theories of reproduction and resistance in the new sociology of education: A critical appraisal. *Harvard Educational Review, 53,* 257–293.

Giroux, H. A. (1988). *Teachers as intellectuals: Toward a pedagogy of critical learning.* New York: Bergin & Garvey.

Giroux, H., & McLaren, P. (1996). Teacher education and the politics of engagement: The case for democratic schooling. *Harvard Educational Review, 56*(3), 213–238.

Glaser, S., & Brown, C. (1993). *Portfolios and beyond: Collaborative assessment in reading and writing.* Norwood, MA: Christopher-Gordon.

Goldenberg, C. (2001, January 25). These steps can help us teach Johnny to read. *Los Angeles Times,* B11.

Goldenberg, C., & Gallimore, R. (1991). Changing teaching takes more than a one-shot workshop. *Educational Leadership, 49*(3), 69–72.

Gollnick, D. M., & Chinn, P. C. (2002). *Multicultural education in a pluralistic society* (6th ed.). Upper Saddle River, NJ: Merrill Prentice Hall.

Gombert, J. E. (1992). *Metalinguistic development.* Chicago: The University of Chicago Press.

González, N. E., Moll, L., & Amanti, C. (Eds.). (2005). *Funds of knowledge: Theorizing practices in households, communities, and classrooms.* Mahwah, NJ: Erlbaum.

Good, T., & Brophy, J. (1984). *Looking in classrooms* (3rd ed.). New York: Harper and Row.

Goodman, K. (1986). *What's whole in whole language?* Portsmouth, NH: Heinemann.

Goodwin, J., Brinton, D., & Celce-Murcia, M. (1994). Pronunciation assessment in the ESL/EFL curriculum. In J. Morley (Ed.), *Pronunciation pedagogy theory: New views, new directions.* Alexandria, VA: Teachers of English to Speakers of Other Languages.

Gopaul-McNicol, S., & Thomas-Presswood, T. (1998). *Working with linguistically and culturally different children.* Boston: Allyn & Bacon.

Gottlieb, M. (1995). Nurturing student learning through portfolios. *TESOL Journal, 5*(1), 12–14.

Graham, C. (1988). *Jazz chant fairy tales.* New York: Oxford University Press.

Graham, C. (1992). *Singing, chanting, telling tales.* Englewood Cliffs, NJ: Regents/Prentice Hall.

Grasha, A. F. (1990). Using traditional versus naturalistic approaches to assess learning styles in college teaching. *Journal on Excellence in College Teaching, 1,* 23–38.

Graves, K. (1996). Teaching opposites through music: Lesson plan. Online at www.lessonplanspage .com/MusicOpposites.htm

Greaver, M., & Hedberg, K. (2001). Daily reading interventions to help targeted ESL and non-ESL-students. Retrieved July 24, 2006, from www.fcps.k12.va.us/DeerParkES/TchrResearch.html

Gregory, G. (2003). *Differentiating instructional strategies in practice: Training, implementation, and supervision.* Thousand Oaks, CA: Corwin.

Gregory, G. H., & Kuzmich, L. (2005). *Differentiated literacy strategies for student growth and achievement in grades 7–12.* Thousand Oaks, CA: Corwin.

Grognet, A., Jameson, J., Franco, L., Derrick-Mescua, M. (2000). *Enhancing English language learning in elementary classrooms study guide.* McHenry, IL: Center for Applied Linguistics and Delta Systems.

Grossberg, L. (1988). Putting the pop back into postmodernism. In A. Ross (Ed.), *Universal abandon? The politics of postmodernism* (pp. 167–190). Minneapolis: University of Minnesota Press.

Groves, M. (2000, January 26). Vast majority of state's schools lag in new index. *Los Angeles Times,* pp. 1, 14.

Groves, M. (2001, August 20). "Direct instruction" paying off. *Los Angeles Times,* B1, B8.

Gunning, T. G. (2005). *Creating literacy: Instruction for all students* (5th ed.). Boston: Allyn & Bacon.

Guthrie, J., & Wigfield, A. (2000). Engagement and motivation in reading. In M. Kamil, P. Mosenthal, P. D. Pearson, & R. Barr (2002). *Handbook of reading research* (Vol. 3, pp. 403–422). Mahwah, NJ: Erlbaum.

Gutierrez, A. S., & Rodríguez, A. P. (2005). *Latino student success (K-20): Local community culture and context*. Spring 2005 Colloquium of the Maryland Institute for Minority Achievement and Urban Education, Baltimore, MD.

Hadaway, N. L., Vardell, S. M., & Young, T. A. (2002). *Literature-based instruction with English language learners, K–12*. Boston: Allyn & Bacon.

Hafernik, J. J., Messerschmitt, D. S., & Vandrick, S. (2002). *Ethical issues for ESL faculty*. Mahwah, NJ: Erlbaum.

Hakuta, K. (1986). *Mirror of language*. New York: Basic Books.

Hakuta, K., Butler, Y. G., & Witt, D. (2000). *How long does it take English learners to attain proficiency?* Santa Barbara: University of California Linguistic Minority Research Institute Policy Report 2000–1.

Hall, E. (1959). *The silent language*. New York: Anchor Books.

Halliday, M. (1975). *Learning how to mean: Explorations in the development of language*. London: Edward Arnold.

Halliday, M. (1978). *Language as a social semiotic*. Baltimore, MD: University Park Press.

Hamayan, E. (1994). Language development of low-literacy students. In F. Genesee (Ed.), *Educating second language children*. Cambridge: Cambridge University Press.

Hamers, J. F., & Blanc, M. A. H. (1989). *Bilinguality and bilingualism*. Cambridge: Cambridge University Press.

Han, Z. (2004). *Fossilization in adult second language acquisition*. Clevedon, UK: Multilingual Matters.

Hancock, C. (1994). Alternative assessment and second language study: What and why? *ERIC Digest*. Online at www.cal.org/ericcll/digest/hancoc01.html

Harel, Y. (1992). Teacher talk in the cooperative learning classroom. In C. Kessler (Ed.), *Cooperative language learning*. Englewood Cliffs, NJ: Prentice Hall.

Harris, T. L., & Hodges, R. E. (1995). *The literacy dictionary: The vocabulary of reading and writing*. Newark, DE: International Reading Association.

Harris, V. (1997). *Teaching multicultural literature in grades K–8*. Norwood, MA: Christopher-Gordon.

Hatfield, M. M., Edwards, M, T., Bitter, G., & Morrow, J. (2004). *Mathematics methods for elementary and middle school teachers*. Hoboken, NJ: John Wiley & Sons.

Hayasaki, E. (2004, December 3). Cultural divide on campus. *Los Angeles Times,* A1, A36, A37. Teacher, *1*(5), 6–7

Haycock, K., Jerald, C., & Huang, S. (2001). *Thinking K–16, closing the gap: Done in a decade*. Washington, DC: The Education Trust.

Haynes, J. (2004). What effective classroom teachers do. Essential Teacher, *1*(5), 6–7.

Heath, S. B. (1999). *Ways with words: language, life and work in communities and classrooms* (2nd ed.). Cambridge: Cambridge University Press.

Heide, F., & Gilliland, J. (1990). *The day of Ahmed's secret*. New York: Lothrop, Lee, & Shepard.

Heinle & Heinle. (2002). *Launch into reading, Level I: Teacher's resource book*. Boston: Author.

Heilman, A. W. (2002). *Phonics in proper perspective*. Upper Saddle River, NJ: Merrill Prentice Hall.

Henwood, D. (1997). Trash-o-nomics. In M. Wray, M. Newitz, & A. Newitz, (Eds.), *White trash: Race and class in America* (pp. 177–191). New York and London: Routledge.

Henderson, D., & May, J. (2005). *Exploring culturally diverse literature for children and adolescents*. Boston: Pearson.

Herrell, A. L. (2000). *Fifty strategies for teaching English language learners*. Upper Saddle River, NJ, and Columbus, OH: Merrill Prentice Hall.

Herring, S. (1996). *Computer-mediated communication: Linguistic, social, and cross-cultural perspectives*. Amsterdam/Philadelphia: John Benjamins Publishing.

Hetherton, G. (1999). Headline news. In N. Shameem & M. Tickoo (Eds.), *New ways in using communicative games* (67–68). Alexandria, VA: Teachers of English to Speakers of Other Languages.

Hispanic Dropout Project (1998). *No more excuses: The final report of the Hispanic Dropout Project*. Washington, DC: U.S. Department of Education, Office of the Under Secretary. Online at www.senate.gov/~bingaman/databw.pdf

Hodgkinson, H. L. (1998). Demographics of diversity for the 21st century. *The Education Digest, 64*(1), 4–7.

Hopstock, P. J., & Stephenson, T. (2003). Descriptive study of services to LEP students and LEP students with disabilities. Washington, DC: U.S. Department of Education. Retrieved August 4, 2006, from www.ncela.gwu.edu/resabout/research/descriptivestudyfiles/native_languages1.pdf

Horwitz, E., Horwitz, M., & Cope, J. (1991). Foreign language classroom anxiety. In E. Horwitz & D. Young (Eds.), *Language anxiety: From theory and research to classroom implications* (pp. 27–36). Englewood Cliffs, NJ: Prentice Hall.

Hudelson, S. (1984). Kan yu ret an rayt in Ingles: Children become literate in English as a second language. *TESOL Quarterly, 18,* 221–238.

Hughes, J. (2004). On bridge making. *Essential Teacher, 1*(1).

Huizenga, J., & Thomas-Ruzic, M. (1992). *All talk: Problem solving for new students of English.* Boston: Heinle & Heinle.

Huntley, H. (2006). *Essential academic vocabulary: Mastering the complete academic word list.* Boston: Houghton Mifflin.

Hymes, D. (1972). On communicative competence. In J. Pride & J. Holmes (Eds.), *Sociolinguistics.* Harmondsworth, UK: Penguin.

International Reading Association. (1997). *The role of phonics in reading instruction:. A position statement of the International Reading Association.* Newark, DE: Author.

Irujo, S. (Ed.). (2000). *Integrating the ESL standards into classroom practice: Grades 6–8.* Alexandria, VA: Teachers of English to Speakers of Other Languages (TESOL).

Irvine, J. J. (1990). *Black students and school failure.* Westport, CT: Greenwood Press.

Ishii, S., & Bruneau, T. (1991). Silence and silences in cross-cultural perspective: Japan and the United States. In L. Samovar & R. Porter (Eds.), *Intercultural communication: A reader* (6th ed.). Belmont, CA: Wadsworth.

Jametz, K. (1994). Making sure that assessment improves performance. *Educational Leadership, 51*(6), 55–57.

Jasmine, J. (1993). *Portfolios and other assessments.* Huntington Beach, CA: Teacher Created Materials.

Jenks, C., Lee, J. O., & Kanpol, B. (2002). Approaches to multicultural education in preservice teacher education: Philosophical frameworks and models for teaching. In F. Schultz (Ed.), *Annual editions: Multicultural education 2002–2003* (pp. 20–28). Guilford, CT: McGraw-Hill/Dushkin.

Jensen, E. (1998). *Teaching with the brain in mind.* Alexandria, VA: Association for Supervision and Curriculum Development.

Johns, K. (1992). Mainstreaming language minority students through cooperative grouping. *The Journal of Educational Issues of Language Minority Students, 11,* Boise, ID: Boise State University Press.

Johnson, D. W., & Johnson, R. (1994). Cooperative learning in second language classes. *The Language Teacher, 18,* 4–7.

Johnson, D. W., & Johnson, R. T. (1995). Why violence prevention programs don't work—And what does. *Educational Leadership, 52*(5), 63–68.

Johnson, D. W., Johnson, R., & Holubec, E. (1993). *Circles of learning: Cooperation in the classroom* (3rd ed.). Edina, MN: Interaction Book Company.

Johnson, D. W., Johnson, R. T., Dudley, B., & Acikgoz, K. (1994). Effects of conflict resolution training on elementary school students. *The Journal of Social Psychology, 134*(6), 803–817.

Jones, L. T. (1991). *Strategies for involving parents in their children's education.* Bloomington, IN: Phi Delta Kappa Educational Foundation.

Jordan, C., Tharp, R., & Baird-Vogt, L. (1992)."Just open the door": Cultural compatibility and classroom rapport. In M. Saravia-Shore & S. Arvizu (Eds.), *Cross-cultural literacy.* New York & London: Garland.

Josephs, K. M. (2004). African American language styles in Afrocentric schools. Accessed August 1, 2006, from www.swarthmore.edu/SocSci/Linguistics/papers/2004/josephs.doc

Jussim, L. (1986). Self-fulfilling prophecies: A theoretical and integrative review. *Psychological Review, 93,* 429–445.

Kagan, S. (1998). *Cooperative learning smart card.* Kagan Cooperative Learning. Online at kaganonline.com

Kagan, S. (1999). *Teambuilding smart card*. Kagan Cooperative Learning. Online at kaganonline.com

Kame'enui, E. J., & Simmons, D. C. (2000). *Planning and evaluation tool for effective schoolwide reading programs*. Eugene, OR: Institute for the Development of Educational Achievement.

Kandel, W., & Cromartie, J. (2004). *New patterns of Hispanic settlement in rural America*. Retrieved January 16, 2005, from www.ers.usda.gov/publications/rdrr99/

Kang, H-W., Kuehn, P., & Herrell, A. (1996). The Hmong literacy project Parents working to preserve the past and ensure, the future. Retrieved July 7, 2006, from www.ncela.gwu.edu/pubs/jeilms/vol16/jeilms1602.htm

Kaufman, P., Alt, M. N., & Chapman, C. (2004). *Dropout rates in the United States: 2001* (NCES 2005–046). U.S. Department of Education. National Center for Education Statistics. Washington, DC: U.S. Government Printing Office. Retrieved August 4, 2006, from www.nces.ed.gov/pubs/205/2005046.pdf

Kea, C., Campbell-Whatley, G. D., Richards, H. V. (2004). *Becoming culturally responsive educators: Rethinking teacher education pedagogy*. National Center for Culturally Responsive Educational Systems. Retrieved January 29, 2005, from www.nccrest.org/publications.html

Kealey, J., & Inness, D. (2007). *Shenanigames: Grammar-focused interactive ESL/EfL activities and games*. Brattleboro, VT: Prolingua.

Keefe, M. W. (1987). *Learning style theory and practice*. Reston, VA: National Association of Secondary School Principals.

Kehe, D., & Kehe, P. D. (1998). *Discussion strategies*. Brattleboro, VT: Prolingua Associates.

Kelley, M. L. (1990). *School-home notes: Promoting children's classroom success*. New York: Guilford Press.

Kessler, C., Quinn, M., & Fathman, A. (1992). Science and cooperative learning for LEP students. In C. Kessler (Ed.), *Cooperative language learning* (pp. 65–83). Englewood Cliffs, NJ: Regents/Prentice Hall.

Kim, E. Y. (2001). *The yin and yang of American culture*. Yarmouth, ME: Intercultural Press.

Kluge, D. (1999). A brief introduction to cooperative learning. ERIC Document Service (ED437840). Accessed August 4, 2006, from www.eric.ed.gov

Kozyrev, J. R. (1998). *Talk it up! Oral communication for the real world*. Boston: Houghton Mifflin.

Krashen, S. (1981). Bilingual education and second language acquisition theory. In *Schooling and language minority students: A theoretical framework*. Los Angeles, CA: Evaluation, Dissemination and Assessment Center, California State University, Los Angeles.

Krashen, S. (1982). *Principles and practice in second language acquisition*. Oxford: Pergamon.

Krashen, S. (1985). *The input hypothesis: Issues and implications*. New York: Longman.

Krashen, S. (2003). *Explorations in language acquisition and language use: The Taipei lectures*. Portsmouth, NH: Heinemann. Quote accessed on July 20, 2006, from www.coas.uncc.edu/linguistics/courses/6163/should_we_teach_grammar.htm

Krashen, S., & Terrell, T. (1983). *The natural approach: Language acquisition in the classroom*. Oxford: Pergamon.

Kress, G. (2000). *Early spelling: Between convention and creativity*. London and New York: Routledge.

Kress, G. R., & Van Leeuwen, T. (1995). *Reading images: The grammar of visual design*. London: Routledge.

Laberge, D., & Samuels, S. J. (1974). Toward a theory of automatic information processing in reading. *Cognitive Psychology, 6,* 293–323.

Laufer, B. (1989). What percentage of text-lexis is essential for comprehension? In C. Lauren & M. Nordman (Eds.), *Special language: From humans thinking to thinking machines* (pp. 316–323). Clevedon, UK: Multilingual Matters.

Laufer, B., & Paribakht, S. (1998). The relationship between passive and active vocabularies: Effects of language learning contexts. *Language Learning, 48,* 365–391.

Lave, J., & Wenger, E. (1991). *Situated learning: Legitimate peripheral participation*. New York: Cambridge University Press.

Law, B., & Eckes, M. (2000). *The more-than-just-surviving handbook* (2nd ed.). Winnipeg, Canada: Peguis.

Leathers, N. (1967). *The Japanese in America*. Minneapolis: Lerner Publications.

LeCompte, M. (1981). The Procrustean bed: Public schools, management systems, and minority students. In H. Trueba, G. Guthrie, & K. Au (Eds.), *Culture and the bilingual classroom: Studies in class-room ethnography*. Rowley, MA: Newbury House.

Lee, O. (2005). Science education with English language learners: Synthesis and research agenda. *Review of Educational Research, 75*(4), 491–530.

Leistyna, P., Woodrum, A.,& Sherblom, S. (Eds.). (1996). Glossary. In P. Leistyna, A. Woodrum, & S. A. Sherblom (Eds.), *Breaking free: The transformative power of critical pedagogy* (pp. 301–331). *Harvard Educational Review* Reprint Series #27. Cambridge, MA: Harvard University Press.

Leki, I. (1992). *Understanding ESL writers*. Portsmouth, NH: Boynton/Cook.

LeLoup, J., & Ponterio, R. (2000). *Enhancing authentic language learning experiences through Internet technology*. ERIC Digest; Online at www.cal.org/ericcll/digest/0002enhancing.html

Lemberger, N. (1999). Factors affecting language development from the perspectives of four bilingual teachers. In I. Heath & C. Serrano (Eds.), *Annual editions: Teaching English as a second language* (2nd ed.). Guilford, CT: Dushkin/McGraw-Hill.

Lenneberg, E. (1967). *Biological foundations of language*. New York: John Wiley & Sons.

LePage, R. B., & Tabouret-Keller, A. (1985). *Acts of identity: Creole-based approaches to language and ethnicity*. Cambridge: Cambridge University Press.

Levine, D., & Adelman, M. (1982). *Beyond language: Intercultural communication for English as a second language*. Englewood Cliffs, NJ: Prentice Hall.

Levine, L. N. (2000). The most beautiful place in the world. In K. D. Samway (Ed.), *Integrating the ESL standards into classroom practice: Grades 3–5* (pp. 109–131). Alexandria, VA: Teachers of English to Speakers of Other Languages (TESOL).

Levstik, L. S., & Barton, K. C. (2001). Doing history: Investigating with children in elementary and middle schools (2nd ed.). Mahwah, NJ: Erlbaum.

Lewis, G., & Bedson, G. (1999). *Games for children*. Oxford: Oxford University Press.

Lewis, M. (1997). *New ways in teaching adults*. Alexandria, VA: Teachers of English to Speakers of Other Languages.

Lindholm, K. (1994). Promoting positive cross-cultural attitudes and perceived competence in culturally and linguistically diverse classrooms. In R. A. DeVillar, C. Faltis, and J. Cummins (Eds.), *Cultural diversity in schools: From rhetoric to practice* (pp. 189–206). Albany: SUNY Press.

Lindholm-Leary, K. (2000). *Biliteracy for a global society: An idea book on dual language eEducation*. Washington, DC: National Clearinghouse for Bilingual Education.

Linse, C. (2006). Using favorite songs and poems with young learners. *English Teaching Forum, 44*(2), 38–40.

Linn, R. L. (2000). Assessments and accountability. *Educational Researcher, 29*(2), 4–26.

Lippi-Green, R. (1997). *English with an accent*. London and New York: Routledge.

Lipton, L, & Hubble, D. (1997). *More than 50 ways to learner-centered literacy*. Arlington Heights, IL: Skylight Professional Development.

Lockwood, A. T. (2000). *Transforming education for Hispanic youth: Broad recommendations for teachers and program staff*. Washington, DC: National Clearing-house for Bilingual Education, 4. Retrieved January 28, 2005, from www.ncela.gwu.edu/pubs/issuebriefs/ib4.html

Lockwood, A. T., & Secada, W. G. (1999). *Transforming education for Hispanic youth: Exemplary practices, programs, and schools. NCELA Resource Collection Series, 12*. Accessed August 3, 2006, from www.ncela.gwu.edu/pubs/resource/hispanicyouth/hdp.htm

Long, M. H. (1987). Listening comprehension: Approach, design, procedure. In M. H. Long & J. C. Richards (Eds.), *Methodology in TESOL: A book of readings* (pp. 161–176). New York: Newbury House.

Long, M. (1980). *Input, interaction, and language acquisition*. Unpublished PhD dissertation, University of California, Los Angeles.

Losen, D., & Wald, J. (2005). *Confronting the graduation rate crisis in California*. Cambridge, MA: Final report, Harvard Civil Rights Project.

Lu, M-L. (2000). *Language development in the early years*. Bloomington, IN: ERIC Clearinghouse on Reading, English, and Communication Digest #154.

Lucas, T., & Wagner, S. (1999). Facilitating secondary English language learners' transition into the mainstream. *TESOL Journal, 8*(4), 6–13.

Lyons, C. A., & Clay, M. M. (2003). *Teaching struggling readers: How to use brain-based research to maximize learning*. Portsmouth, NH: Heinemann.

Macedo, D., & Freire, A. M. A. (1998). Foreword. In P. Freire (Ed.), *Teachers as cultural workers* (pp. ix–xix). Boulder, CO: Westview Press.

Maciejewski, T. (2003). *Pragmatics*. Retrieved August 4, 2006, from www.lisle.dupage.k12.il.us/maciejewski/social.htm

McCarty, T. L. (Ed.). (2005). *Language, literacy, and power in schooling*. Mahwah, NJ: Erlbaum.

McKenna, M. C., & Robinson, R. D. (1997). *Teaching through text: A content literacy approach to content area reading* (2nd ed.). New York: Longman.

McLaren, P. (1995). Critical multiculturalism, media literacy, and the politics of representation. In J. Frederickson (Ed.), *Reclaiming our voices: Bilingual education, critical pedagogy, and praxis* (pp. 99–138). Ontario, CA: California Association for Bilingual Education. New York: Longman.

McLaughlin, B. (1987). *Theories of second-language learning*. London: Arnold.

McLaughlin, B. (1990). "Conscious" versus "unconscious" learning. *TESOL Quarterly, 24*(4), 617–634.

McLeod, B. (1995). *School reform & student diversity: Lessons learned—Educating students from diverse linguistic and cultural backgrounds*. Retrieved January 28, 2005, from www.ncela.gwu.edu/pubs/ncrcdsll/srsd/schoolorg.htm

Maculaitis, J. (1988). *The complete ESL/EFL resource book: Strategies, activities, and units for the classroom*. Lincolnwood, IL: National Textbook Company.

Mahoney, D. (1999a). Shadow tableaux. In N. Shameem & M. Tickoo (Eds.), *New ways in using communicative games* (pp. 13–14). Alexandria, VA: Teachers of English to Speakers of Other Languages.

Mahoney, D. (1999b). Stress clapping. In N. Shameem & M. Tickoo (Eds.), New *ways in using communicative games* (pp. 20–21). Alexandria, VA: Teachers of English to Speakers of Other Languages.

Majors, P. (n.d.). Charleston County School District, Charleston, SC, Sample Standards-Based Lesson plan. Retrieved August 4, 2006, from www.cal.org/eslstandards/Charleston.html

Malavé, L. (1991). Conceptual framework to design a programme intervention for culturally and linguistically different handicapped students. In L. Malavé & G. Duquette (Eds.), *Language, culture and cognition* (pp. 176–189). Clevedon, UK: Multilingual Matters.

Mandlebaum, L. H., & Wilson, R. (1989). Teaching listening skills in the special education classroom. *Academic Therapy, 24,* 451–452.

Manning, M. L. (2002). Understanding diversity, accepting others: Realities and directions. In F. Schultz, (Ed.), *Annual editions: Multicultural education 2002/2003*. Guilford, CT: McGraw-Hill/Dushkin.

Mansour, W. (1999). Give me a word that In N. Shameem & M. Tickoo (Eds.), *New ways in using communicative games* (pp. 103–104). Alexandria, VA: Teachers of English to Speakers of Other Languages.

Marinova-Todd, S., Marshall, D., & Snow, C. (2000). Three misconceptions about age and L2 learning. *TESOL Quarterly, 34*(1), 9–34.

Marlowe, B. A., & Page, M. L. (1999). Making the most of the classroom mosaic: A constructivist perspective. *Multicultural Education, 6*(4), 19–21.

Marton, W. (1994). The antipedagogical aspects of Krashen's theory of second language acquisition. In R. Barasch & C. James (Eds.), *Beyond the Monitor Model*. Boston: Heinle and Heinle.

Marzano, R. J. (1994). Lessons from the field about outcome-based performance assessments. *Educational Leadership, 51*(6), 44–50.

May, F. B., & Rizzardi, L. (2002). *Reading as communication* (6th ed.). Upper Saddle River, NJ: Merrill Prentice Hall.

Medina, M., Jr., & Escamilla, K. (1992). Evaluation of transitional and maintenance bilingual programs. *Urban Education, 27(3),* 263–290.

Mehan, H. (1979). *Learning lessons*. Cambridge, MA: Harvard University Press.

Mehan, H. (1981). Ethnography of bilingual education. In H. Trueba, G. Guthrie, & K. Au (Eds.), *Culture and the bilingual classroom: Studies in classroom ethnography*. Rowley, MA: Newbury House.

Mehan, H., & Hubbard, L. (1999). *Tracking untracking: Evaluating the effectiveness of an educational innovation*. Santa Cruz, CA: The National Center for Research on Cultural Diversity & Second Language Learning. Online at www.cal.org/crede/pubs/ResBreef3.pdf

Mehrabian, A. (1969). Communication without words. In *Readings in Psychology Today*. Del Mar, CA: CMR Books.

Migration Policy Institute. (2004). *A new century: Immigration and the US*. Accessed January 15, 2005, from www.migrationinformation.org/Profiles/display.cfm?ID=6

Miller, G. (1985). Nonverbal communication. In V. Clark, P. Eschholz, & A. Rosa (Eds.), *Language: Introductory readings* (4th ed.). New York: St. Martin's Press.

Miller, W. H. (1995). *Alternative assessment techniques for reading and writing*. West Nyack, NJ: The Center for Applied Research in Education.

Miller, L. (2004). Developing listening skills with authentic materials. Accessed July 21, 2006, from www.eslmag.com/modules.php?name=News&file=article&sid=20

Molina, H., Hanson, R. A., & Siegel, D. F. (1997). *Empowering the second-language classroom: Putting the parts together*. San Francisco: Caddo Gap Press.

Moll, L. C. (1992). Bilingual classroom studies and community analysis: Some recent trends. *Educational Researcher, 21(2)*, 20–24.

Monroe, S. (1999). Multicultural children's literature: Canon of the future. Reprinted in *Annual editions 99/00: Teaching English as a second language*. Guilford, CO: Dushkin/McGraw-Hill.

Mora, J. K. (2000). Staying the course in times of change: Preparing teachers for linguistically diverse classrooms. *Journal of Teacher Education, 51*(5), 345–357.

Mora, J. K. (2002). Proposition 227's second anniversary: Triumph or travesty? Accessed June 30, 2006, from http://coe.sdsu.edu/people/jmora/Prop227/227YearTwo.htm

Morey, A., & Kilano, M. (1997). *Multicultural course transformation in higher education: A broader truth*. Boston: Allyn & Bacon.

Morgan, B. (1998). *The ESL classoom: Teaching, critical practice, and community development*. Toronto: University of Toronto Press.

Morgan, R. (1992). Distinctive voices—Developing oral language in multilingual classrooms. In P. Pinsent (Ed.), *Language, culture, and young children* (pp. 37–46). London: David Fulton Publisher.

Morley, J. (1999). Current perspectives on improving aural comprehension. *ESL Magazine, 2*(1), 16–19.

Moskowitz, G. (1978). *Caring and sharing in the foreign language classroom*. Cambridge, MA: Newbury House.

Moxley, J. M. (1994). *Becoming an academic writer: A modern rhetoric*. Lexington, MA: D.C. Heath.

Murray, D. E. (2000). Protean communication: The language of computer-mediated communication. *TESOL Quarterly, 34*(3), 397–421.

Nagy, W. E. (1997). On the role of context in first- and second-language vocabulary learning. In N. Schmitt & M. McCarthy (Eds.), *Vocabulary: Description, acquisition, pedagogy* (pp. 64–83). Cambridge, UK: Cambridge University Press.

Nagy, W. E., García, G. E., Durgunoglu, A., & Hancin-Bhatt, B. (1993). Spanish-English bilingual students' use of cognates in English reading. *Bilingual Research Journal, 18*, 83–97.

Nash, P. (1991). ESL and the myth of the model minority. In S. Benesch (Ed.), *ESL in America*. Portsmouth, NH: Boynton/Cook.

Natheson-Mejia, S. (1989). Writing in a second language. *Language Arts, 66*(5), 516–526.

Nation, I. S. P. (1990). *Teaching and learning vocabulary*. New York: Newbury House.

Nation, P. (1994). *New ways in teaching vocabulary*. Alexandria, VA: Teachers of English to Speakers of Other Languages.

National Center for Culturally Responsive Educational Systems, 2006. *Cultural pluralism*. Accessed July 31, 2006, from http://nccrest.edreform.net/subject/culturalpluralism

National Center for Education Statistics (NCES). (2000). *NAEP 1999 trends in academic progress: Three decades of student performance*. Washington, DC: U.S. Department of Education.

National Center for Education Statistics. (2002). *Percentage distribution of enrollment in public elementary and secondary schools, by race/ethnicity and state: Fall 1986 and fall 2000.* Retrieved August 3, 2005, from http://nces.ed.gov/programs/digest/d02/dt042.asp

National Center for Education Statistics. (2003). *Employees in degree-granting institutions, by race/ethnicity, primary occupation, sex, employment status, and control and type of institution: Fall 2001.* Accessed March 20, 2005, from http://nces.ed.gov/programs/digest/d03/tables/dt228.asp

National Center for Education Statistics (NCES). (2005). *Postsecondary participation rates by sex and race/ethnicity: 1974–2003.* Washington: Author.

National Clearinghouse for English Language Acquisition & Language Instruction Programs (NCELA). (2004). *ELLs and the No Child Left Behind Act.* Accessed August 2, 2006, from www.ncela.gwu.edu/about/lieps/5ellnclb.html

National Commission on Teaching and America's Future. (2002). Teacher shortage question unraveled: NCTAF challenges the nation to address the teacher retention crisis. Washington, DC: Author.

National Education Association. (1975). *Code of ethics of the education profession.* Washington, DC: Author.

Nelson-Barber, S. (1999). A better education for every child: The dilemma for teachers of culturally and linguistically diverse students. In Mid-continent Research for Education and Learning (McREL). (Ed.). *Including culturally and linguistically diverse students in standards-based reform: A report on McREL's Diversity Roundtable I* (pp. 3–22). Aurora, CO: Author.

Nemmer-Fanta, M. (2002). Accommodations and modifications for English language learners. In *Serving English language learners with disabilities: A resource manual for Illinois educators.* Retrieved February 9, 2005, from www.isbe.state.il.us/speced/bilingualmanual2002.htm

Nero, S. J. (1997). English is my native language . . . or so I believe. *TESOL Quarterly, 31*(3), 585–593.

Newman, J. M. (1985). What about reading? In J. M. Newman (Ed.), *Whole language: Theory in use* (pp. 99–100). Portsmouth, NH: Heinemann.

Nieto, S. (2004). *Affirming diversity* (4th ed.). New York: Longman.

No Child Left Behind (NCLB). (2001). Title III, Part A, Sec. 3102. Purposes (1). Accessed August 4, 2006, from www.ncela.gwu.edu/about/lieps/5_ellnclb.html

Nunan, D. (1989). *Designing tasks for the communicative classroom.* Cambridge: Cambridge University Press.

Nunan, D. (1991). *Language teaching methodology: A textbook for teachers.* New York: Prentice Hall.

Oakes, J. (1985). *Keeping track: How schools structure inequality.* New Haven, CT: Yale University Press.

Oakes, J. (1992). Can tracking research inform practice? Technical, normative, and political considerations. *Educational Researcher, 21*(4), 12–21.

O'Barr, W. M., & Atkins, B. K. (1980). Women's language or powerless language. In S. McConnell-Ginet, R. Borker, & N. Furman (Eds.), *Women and language in literature and society* (pp. 93–110). New York: Praeger.

O'Connor, T. (2004). Understanding discrimination against Asian-Americans. Accessed August 4, 2006, from http://faculty.ncwc.edu/toconnor/soc/355lect10.htm.

Odlin, T. (1989). *Language transfer: Cross-linguistic influence in language learning.* Cambridge: Cambridge University Press.

Office of English Language Acquisition, Language Enhancements and Academic Achievement for Limited English Proficient Students (OELA). (2003). *The growing numbers of limited English proficient students 1991/2–2001/02.* Washington, DC: Author.

Ogbu, J. (1978). *Minority education and caste: The American system in crosscultural perspective.* New York: Academic Press.

Ogbu, J., & Matute-Bianchi, M. (1986). Understanding sociocultural factors: Knowledge, identity, and school adjustment. In *Beyond language: Social and cultural factors in schooling language minority students.* Los Angeles: Evaluation, Dissemination and Assessment Center, California State University, Los Angeles.

Olmedo, I. M. (1993, summer). Junior historians: Doing oral history with ESL and bilingual students. *TESOL Journal, 2*(4), 7–9.

Omaggio, A. (1978). *Games and simulations in the foreign language classroom*. Washington, DC: Center for Applied Linguistics.

Omaggio, A. C. (1986), *Teaching language in context*. Boston: Heinle & Heinle.

O'Malley, J. M., & Pierce, L. V. (1996). *Authentic assessment for English language learners*. Menlo Park, CA: Addison-Wesley.

Ong, W. (1982). *Orality and literacy*. London: Methuen.

Orfield, T., & Lee, C. (2005). Why segregation matters: Poverty and educational inequality. Retrieved August 6, 2006, from www.civilrightsproject.harvard.edu/research/deseg/deseg05.php

Ortiz, A. A. (2002). Prevention of school failure and early intervention for English Language Learners. In A. J. Artiles & A. A. Ortiz (Eds.), *English language learners with special education needs: Identification, assessment, and instruction* (pp. 31–63). Washington, DC: Center for Applied Linguistics and Delta Systems.

Ortiz, F. (1988). Hispanic-American children's experiences in classrooms: A comparison between Hispanic and non-Hispanic children. In L. Weis (Ed.), *Class, race, and gender in American education*. Albany: State University of New York Press.

Ouk, M., Huffman, F., & Lewis, J. (1988). *Handbook for teaching Khmer-speaking students*. Sacramento: Spilman Printing.

Ovando, C., & Collier, V. (1998). *Bilingual and ESL class-rooms: Teaching in multicultural contexts*. Boston: McGraw-Hill.

Oyama, S. (1976). A sensitive period for the acquisition of nonnative phonological system. *Journal of Psycholinguistic Research, 5,* 261–284.

Packer, N.H., J & Timpane, (1997). *Writing worth reading: The critical process* (3rd ed.). Boston: Bedford Books.

Paige, R. M. (1999). Theoretical foundations of intercultural training and applications to the teaching of culture. In R. M. Paige, D. L. Lange, & Y. A. Yershova (Eds.), *Culture as the core: Integrating culture into the language curriculum* (pp. 21–29). Minneapolis: Center for Advanced Research on Language Acquisition, University of Minnesota.

Palinscar, A. S., & Brown, A. L. (1984). Reciprocal teaching of comprehension-fostering and comprehension-monitoring activities. *Cognition and Instruction, 1,* 117–175.

Pappas, C. C. Kiefer, B. Z., & Levstik, L. S. (2006). *An integrated language perspective in the elementary school* (4th ed.). Boston: Allyn & Bacon.

Parks, S., & Black, H. (1990). *Organizing thinking: Graphic organizers*. Pacific Grove, CA: Critical Thinking Press & Software.

Pasternak, J. (1994, March 29). Bias blights life outside Appalachia. *Los Angeles Times,* A1, A16.

Pearson, R. (1974). *Introduction to anthropology*. New York: Holt, Rinehart and Winston.

Peim, N. (1993). *Critical theory and the English teacher*. London and New York: Routledge.

Pennycook, A. (1998). Text, ownership, memory, and plagiarism. In V. Zamel & R. Spack (Eds.), *Negotiating academic literacies: Teaching and learning across languages and cultures* (pp. 265–292). Mahwah, NJ: Erlbaum.

Peregoy, S., & Boyle, O. (2005). *Reading, writing, and learning in ESL* (4th ed.). Boston: Pearson.

Pérez, B., & Torres-Guzmán, M. (2002). *Learning in two worlds* (3rd ed.). New York: Longman.

Philips, S. (1972). Participant structures and communicative competence: Warm Springs children in community and classroom. In C. Cazden, V. John, & D. Hymes (Eds.), *Functions of language in the classroom*. New York: Teachers College Press.

Phillips, J. (1978). College of, by and for Navajo Indians. *Chronicle of Higher Education, 15,* 10–12.

Pinnell, G. S. (1985) Ways to look at the functions of children's language. In A. Jaggar & M. Smith-Burke (Eds.), *Observing the language learner*. Newark, DE: International Reading Association.

Porter, R. (1990). *Forked tongue: The politics of bilingual education*. New York: Basic Books.

Pratt, C., & Nesdale, A. R. (1984). Pragmatic awareness in children. In W. E. Tunmer, C. Pratt, & M. L. Herriman (Eds.), *Metalinguistic awareness in children* (pp. 105–125). Berlin: Springer Verlag.

Pridham, F. (2001). *The language of conversation*. New York and London: Routledge.

Prothrow-Smith, D. (1994, April). Building violence prevention into the classroom. *The School Administrator, 8*(12), 8–12.

Pruitt, W. (2000). Using story to compare, conclude, and identify. In B. Agor (Ed.), *Integrating the ESL standards into classroom practice: Grades 9–12* (pp. 31–49). Alexandria, VA: TESOL.

Pryor, C. B. (2002). New immigrants and refugees in American schools: Multiple voices. In F. Schultz (Ed.), *Annual editions: Multicultural education 2002/2003* (pp. 185–193). Guilford, CT: McGraw-Hill/Dushkin.

Raimes, A. (Ed.). (1996). *Identities: Readings from contemporary culture*. Boston: Houghton Mifflin.

Raphael, T. E. (1986). Teaching question answer relationships, revisited. *The Reading Teacher, 39,* 516–523.

Ramírez, J. (1992, winter/spring). Executive summary, final report: Longitudinal study of structured English immersion strategy, early-exit and late-exit transitional bilingual education programs for language-minority children. *Bilingual Research Journal,* 16(l&2), 1–62.

Rasinski, T., & Fredericks, A. (1989). Dimensions of parent involvement. *The Reading Teacher, 43*(2), 180–182.

Reid, J. M. (1993). *Teaching ESL writing*. Englewood Cliffs, NJ: Prentice Hall Regents.

Reid, J. M. (1995). Preface. In J. Reid (Ed.), *Learning styles in the ESL/EFL classroom* (pp. viii–xvii). Boston: Heinle and Heinle.

Remillar, J. T., & Cahnmann, M. (2005). Researching mathematics teaching in bilingual-bicultural classrooms. In T. L. McCarty (Ed.), *Language, literacy, and power in schooling* (pp. 169–187). Mahwah, NJ: Erlbaum.

Ricento, T. (1995). Language policy in the United States: An overview. In M. Herriman & B. Burnaby (Eds.), *Language policy in English dominant countries: Six case studies*. Clevedon, UK: Multilingual Matters.

Richard-Amato, P. (2003). *Making it happen* (3rd ed.). White Plains, NY: Longman.

Richard-Amato, P., & Snow, M. (1992). Strategies for content-area teachers. In P. Richard-Amato & M. Snow (Eds.), *The multicultural classroom*. White Plains, NY: Longman.

Riles, G. B. & Lenarcic, C. (2000). Exploring world religions. In B. Agor (Ed.), *Integrating the ESL standards into classroom practice: Grades 9–12* (pp. 1–29). Alexandria, VA: Teachers of English to Speakers of Other Languages (TESOL).

Rinvolucri, M. (1984). *Grammar games: Cognitive, affective and drama activities for EFL students*. Cambridge: Cambridge University Press.

Rivera, C. (2006, June 9). Charter school fights back. *Los Angeles Times*. Accessed July 7, 2006, from www.latimes.com/news/local/lame-charter9jun09,1,4660030.story?ctrack=1&cset=true

Robin, R. (2006). *Should we teach grammar?* Accessed July 20, 2006, from www.coas.uncc.edu/linguistics/courses/6163/should_we_teach_grammar.htm

Robinson, G. (1985). *Crosscultural understanding*. New York: Pergamon Institute of English.

Rodby, J. (1999). Contingent literacy: The social construction of writing for nonnative English-speaking college freshman. In L. Harklau, K. M. Losey, & M. Siegal (Eds.), *Generation 1.5 meets college composition: Issues in the teaching of writing to U.S.-educated learners of ESL* (pp. 45–60). Mahwah, NJ: Erlbaum.

Rose, C. (1987). *Accelerated learning*. New York: Dell.

Rosebery, A. S., Warren, B., & Conant, F. R. (1992). Appropriating scientific discourse: Finding from language minority classrooms. *Journal of the Learning Sciences, 21,* 61–94.

Rowan, T., & Bourne, B. (1994). *Thinking like mathematics*. Portsmouth, NH: Heinemann.

Rumbaut, R. G. (1995). The new Californians: Comparative research findings on the education progress of immigrant children. In R. G. Rumbaut & W. A. Cornelius, *California's immigrant children: Theory, research, and implications for educational policy* (pp. 17–70). San Diego, CA: University of California, San Diego Center for U.S.-Mexican Studies.

Runner, J. (2000). *"I don't understand" in over 230 languages*. Accessed August 2, 2006, from www.elite.net/~runner/jennifers/understa.htm

Sadker, M. P., & Sadker, D. M. (2003). Questioning skills. In J. Cooper (Ed.), *Classroom teaching skills* (7th ed., pp. 101–147). Boston: Houghton-Mifflin.

Sales, F. (1989). *Ibrahim*. New York: Lippincott.

Samway, K. D. (Ed.). (2000). *Integrating the ESL standards into classroom practice: Grades 3–5*. Alexandria, VA: Teachers of English to Speakers of Other Languages (TESOL).

Samway, K. D., & McKeon, D. (1999). *Myths and realities: Best practices for language minority students*. Portsmouth, NH: Heinemann.

Santa Ana, O. (2004). Giving voice to the silenced. *Language, 3*(8), 15–17.

Sato, C. (1982). Ethnic styles in classroom discourse. In M. Hines and W. Rutherford (Eds.), *On TESOL 81*. Washington, DC: TESOL.

Scarcella, R. (1990). *Teaching language minority students in the multicultural classroom*. Englewood Cliffs, NJ: Prentice Hall.

Scarcella, R., & Rumberger, R. W. (2000). Academic English key to long-term success in school. *University of California Linguistic Minority Research Institute Newsletter, 9*(4), 1–2.

Schifini, A., Short, D., & Tinajero, J. V. (2002). *High point*. Carmel, CA: Hampton-Brown.

Schultz, J., & Theophano, J. (1987). Saving place and marking time: Some aspects of the Social lives of three-year-old children. In H. Trueba (Ed.), *Success or failure?* Cambridge, MA: Newbury House Publishers.

Schumann, J. (1978). The acculturation model for second-language acquisition. In R. Gringas (Ed.), *Second language acquisition and foreign language teaching*. Washington, DC: Center for Applied Linguistics.

Schumann, J. (1994). Emotion and cognition in second language acquisition. *Studies in Second Language Acquisition, 16*, 231–242.

Scollon, R., & Scollon, S. W. (2003). *Discourses in place: Language in the material world*. London and New York: Routledge.

Selinker, L. (1972). Interlanguage. *IRAL, 10*(3), 209–231.

Selinker, L. (1991). Along the way: Interlanguage systems in second language acquisition. In L. Malavé & G. Duquette (Eds.), *Language, culture and cognition*. Clevedon, UK: Multilingual Matters.

Shade, B., & New, C. (1993). Cultural influences on learning: Teaching implications. In J. Banks & C. Banks (Eds.), *Multicultural education: Issues and perspectives*. Boston: Allyn & Bacon.

Shaffer, D. R. (1999). *Developmental psychology: Childhood & adolescence* (5th ed.). Pacific Grove, CA: Brook Cole Publishing Company.

Shannon, S. (1994). Introduction. In R. Barasch & C. James (Eds.), *Beyond the Monitor Model*. Boston: Heinle & Heinle.

Shoemaker, C., & Polycarpou, S. (1993). *Write ideas: A beginning writing text*. Boston: Heinle & Heinle.

Sholley, D. (2006). Two culture, one unique talent. *The Sun-San Bernardino County,* July 20, U1-U2.

Short, D. (1998). Secondary newcomer programs: Helping recent immigrants prepare for school success. *ERIC Digest*.Retrieved January 28, 2005, from http://searcheric.org/scripts/seget2.asp?db= ericft&want=http://searcheric.org/ericdc/ED419385.htm

Short, D. J., & Boyson, B. A. (2004). *Creating access: Language and academic programs for secondary school newcomers*. Santa Cruz, CA: Center for Research on Education, Diversity, & Excellence.

Short, D. J., & Echevarria, J. (1999). The sheltered instruction observation protocol: A tool for teacher-researcher collaboration and professional development. *ERIC Digest*. Retrieved January 28, 2005, from http://searcheric.org/scripts/seget2.asp?db=ericf&want=http://searcheric.org/ericdc/ED436981.htm

Shuit, D., & McConnell, P. (1992, January 6). Calculating the impact of California's immigrants. *Los Angeles. Times,* A1, A19.

Siccone, F. (1995). *Celebrating diversity: Building self-esteem in today's multicultural classrooms*. Boston: Allyn & Bacon.

SIL International. (2000). *Geographic distribution of living languages, 2000*. Accessed May 17, 2006, from www.ethnologue.com/ethno_docs/distribution.asp

Silver, H. F., Strong, R. W., & Perini, M. J. (2000). *So each may learn: Integrating learning styles and multiple intelligences*. Alexandria, VA: Association for Supervision and Curriculum Development.

Sindell, P. (1988). Some discontinuities in the enculturation of Mistassini Cree children. In J. Wurzel (Ed.), *Toward multiculturalism*. Yarmouth, ME: Intercultural Press.

Singleton, D. M., & Ryan, L. (2004). *Language acquisition: The age factor*. Clevedon, UK: Multilingual Matters.

Skutnabb-Kangas, T. (1981). *Bilingualism or not: The education of minorities.* (L. Malmberg & D. Crane, Trans.) Clevedon, UK: Multilingual Matters.

Slavin, R. E. (1991). A synthesis of research on cooperative learning. *Educational Leadership, 48,* 71–82.

Smallwood, B. A. (Ed.). (2000). *Integrating the ESL standards into classroom practice: Grades Pre-K-2.* Alexandria, VA: Teachers of English to Speakers of Other Languages (TESOL).

Smilkstein, R.(2002) *We're born to learn: Using the brain's natural learning process to create today's curriculum.* Thousand Oaks, CA: Sage Publications.

Smith, F. (1982). *Writing and the writer.* New York: Holt, Rinehart, & Winston.

Smith, F. (1983). *Essays into literacy.* Portsmouth, NH: Heinemann.

Smith, S. L., Paige, R. M., & Steglitz, I. (1998). Theoretical foundations of intercultural training and applications to the teaching of culture. In D. L. Lange, C. A. Klee, R. M. Paige, and Y. A. Yershova (Eds.), *Culture as the core: Interdisciplinary perspectives on culture teaching and learning in the language curriculum* (pp. 53–91). Minneapolis: Center for Advanced Research on Language Acquisition, University of Minnesota.

Smith, T. E. C., Polloway, E. A., Patton, J. R., & Dowdy, C. A. (2003). *Teaching children with special needs in inclusive settings* (4th ed.). Boston: Allyn & Bacon.

Snow, C., & Hoefhagel-Hoehle, M. (1978). The critical period for language acquisition: Evidence from second language learning. *Child Development, 49,* 1114–1118.

Snow, C. E., Burns, S. M., & Griffin, P. (Eds.). (1998). *Preventing reading difficulties in young children.* Washington, DC: National Academy Press.

Snow, D. (1996). *More than a native speaker.* Alexandria, VA: TESOL.

Snow, M. A. (1993). Discipline-based foreign language teaching: Implications from ESL/EFL. In M. Krueger & F. Ryan (Eds.), *Language and content. Discipline-and content-based approaches to language study* (pp. 37–56). Lexington, MA: D.C. Heath.

Snow, M. A., & Brinton, D. M. (1988). Content-based language instruction: Investigating the effectiveness of the adjunct model. *TESOL Quarterly, 22*(3), 201–217.

So, H. (2006, April 28). School interpreters' goal: Being word perfect. *Los Angeles Times,* B2.

Sonbuchner, G. M. (1991). *How to take advantage of your learning styles.* Syracuse, NY: New Readers Press.

Southern Poverty Law Center. (1999). *Youth at the edge.* Montgomery, AL: Author. Accessed. August 2, 2006, from www.splcenter.org/intel/intelreport/article.jsp?aid=302

Spears, R. A. (1992). *Common American phrases.* Lin-cblnwood, IL: National Textbook Company.

Spellmeyer, K. (1989). A common ground: The essay in the academy. *College English, 51,* 262–276.

Spinelli, E. (1994). *English grammar for students of Spanish* (3rd ed.). Ann Arbor, M: The Olivia and Hill Press.

Spring, J. (2001). The new Mandarin society? Testing on the fast track. *The Joel Spring Library* Accessed July 31, 2006, from www.mhhe.com/socscience/education/spring/commentary.mhtml

Stahl, N.A., King, J.R., & Herik, W. A. (1991). Enhancing students' notetaking through training and evaluation. *Journal of Reading, 34*(8), 614–622.

Stanovich, K. (1986). Matthew effects in reading: Some consequences in individual differences in the acquisition of literacy. *Reading Research Quarterly, 21,* 360–407.

Strehorn, K. (2001). The application of Universal Instructional Design to ESL teaching. *Internet TESL Journal.* Accessed July 7, 2006, from http://iteslj.org/Techniques/Strehorn-UID.html

Suid, M., & Lincoln, W. (1992). *Ten-minute whole language warm-ups.* Palo Alto, CA: Monday Morning Books.

Suina, J. (1985) And then I went to school. New *Mexico Journal of Reading V(2).*

Sunal, C. S., & Haas, M. E. (2005). *Social studies for elementary and middle grades: A constructivist approach.* Boston: Allyn & Bacon.

Suresh, B. (2003). Get'em hooked on books—Start an ESL book club. *CATESOL News, 30*(2), 14.

Suzuki, B. (1989, November/December). Asian Americans as the "model minority." *Change, 21,* 12–19.

Swartz, S., Klein, A. F., & Shook, R. E. (2002). *Interactive writing & interactive editing: Making connections between writing and reading.* Carlsbad, CA: Dominie Press.

Swartz, S. L., Shook, R. E., Klein, A. F., Moon, C., Bunnell, K., Belt, M., & Huntley, C. (2003). *Guided reading and literacy centers.* Carlsbad, CA: Dominie Press.

Swerdlow, J. L. (2001). Changing America. *National Geographic Magazine, 200*(3), 42–61.

Takahashi, E., Austin, T., & Morimoto, Y. (2000). Social interaction and language development in an FLES classroom. In J. K. Hall & L. S. Verplaetse (Eds.), *Second and foreign language learning through classroom interaction* (pp. 139–162). Mahwah, NJ: Lawrence Erlbaum.

Taylor, B. P. (1987). In M. H. Long and J. C. Richards (Eds.), *Methodology in TESOL: A book of readings* (pp. 45–60): New York: Newbury House.

Taylor, D. (2000). Facing hardships: Jamestown and colonial life. In K. Samway (Ed.), *Integrating the ESL Standards into classroom practice* (pp. 53–55). Alexandria, VA: TESOL.

Tannen, D. (2001). *Discourse analysis.* In Linguistic Society of America, "Fields of Linguistics." Online at www.lsadc.org/web2/ftdcont.html

Tharp, R. (1989). Culturally compatible education: A formula for designing effective classrooms. In H. Trueba, G. Spindler, & L. Spindler (Eds.), *What do anthropologists have to say about dropouts?* New York: Falmer Press.

Tharp, R., & Gallimore, R. (1991). *The instructional conversation: Teaching and learning in social activity.* Washington, DC: National Center for Research on Cultural Diversity and Second Language Learning.

Thernstrom, A., & Thernstrom, S. (2003). *No excuses: Closing the racial gap in learning.* New York: Simon & Schuster.

Thomas, W., & Collier, V. (1997). *School effectiveness for language minority students.* Accessed August 4, 2006, from www.ncela.gov.edu/pubs/resource/effectiveness/

Thonis, E. (1983). *The English-Spanish connection.* Los Angeles: Santillana.

Tresaugue, M. (2002, January 31). Back to the basics. *Riverside Press-Enterprise,* A1, A8.

Trueba, H. (1989). *Raising silent voices.* Boston: Heinle & Heinle.

Tunmer, W., & Nesdale, A. (1985). Phonemic segmentation skill and beginning reading. *Journal of Educational Psychology, 77,* 417–427.

Tinajero, J. V., & Schifini, A. (1997). *Into English.* Carmel, CA: Hampton-Brown.

Trueba, H. (1989). *Raising silent voices.* Boston: Heinle & Heinle.

Trueba, H., Cheng, L., & Ima, K. (1993). *Myth or reality:. Adaptive strategies of Asian Americans in California.* Washington, DC: Falmer Press.

Tunmer, W. E., Herriman, M. L., & Nesdale, A. R. (1988). Metalinguistic abilities and beginning reading. *Reading Research Quarterly, 23*(2), 134–158.

Ukpokodu, N. (2002). Multiculturalism vs. globalism. In F. Schultz (Ed.), *Annual editions: Multicultural education 2002–2003* (pp. 7–10). Guilford, CT: McGraw-Hill/Dushkin.

U.S. Census Bureau. (2000). Hispanic population in the United States: Population characteristics. Accessed August 4, 2006, from www.census.gov/population/www/socdemo/hispanic/ho00.html

U.S. Census Bureau. (2001a). *The Asian and Pacific Islander population in the United States: March 1999* (Update) (PPL-131). Online at www.census.gov/population/www/socdemo/race/api99.html

U.S. Census Bureau. (2001b). *Census 2000 Supplementary Survey.* Washington, DC: Author.

U.S. Census Bureau. (2001c). *Census 2000 Supplementary Survey.* Washington, DC: Author.

U.S. Census Bureau. (2003). *Language use, English ability, and linguistic isolation for the population 5 years and over by state, 2000* (Summary File 3, Tables P19, PCT13, and PCT14). Washington, DC: Author.

U.S. Census Bureau. (2004a). Educational attainment in the U.S.: 2003. Accessed August 2, 2006, from www.census.gov/population/www/socdemo/educ-attn.html

U.S. Census Bureau. (2004b). Poverty tables 2003. Accessed August 2, 2006, from www.census.gov/hhes/poverty/poverty03/tables03.html

U.S. Department of Education. (1998). *Fall staff survey.* Online at http://nces.ed.gov/pubs2000

U.S. Government Accounting Office. (2002). Per-pupil spending differences between selected inner city and suburban schools varied by metropolitan area. Accessed August 2, 2006, from www.gao.gov/new.items/d03234.pdf

Valenzuela, J. S., & Baca, L. (2004). Procedures and techniques for assessing the bilingual exceptional child. In L. M. Baca & H. T. Cervantes (Eds.), *The bilingual special education interface* (4th ed., pp. 184–203). Upper Saddle River, NJ: Pearson Merrill/Prentice Hall.

Veeder, K., & Tramutt, J. (2000). Strengthening literacy in both languages. In N. Cloud, F. Genesee, & E. Hamayan (Eds.), *Dual language instruction*. Boston: Heinle & Heinle.

Verdugo Hills High School. (2004). *Redesignated students*. Accessed February 2, 2005, from www.Iausd.k12.ca.us/Verdugo_HS/classes/esl/redes.htm

Villegas, A. M., & Lucas, T. (2002). Preparing culturally responsive teachers: Rethinking the curriculum. *Journal of Teacher Education, 53*(1), 20–32.

Vygotsky, L. (1981). The genesis of higher mental functions. In J. V. Wertsch (Ed.), *The concept of activity in Soviet psychology*. Armonk, NY: Sharpe.

Wallraff, B. (2000). What global language? *The Atlantic Monthly, 286*(5), 52–66.

Walqui, A. (1999). Assessment of culturally and linguistically diverse students: Considerations for the 21st century. In Mid-continent Research for Education and Learning (McREL) (Ed.), *Including culturally and linguistically diverse students in standards-based reform: A report on McREL's Diversity Roundtable I* (pp. 55–84). Aurora, CO: Author (online at http://www.mcrel.org/topics/productDetail.asp?topicsID=3&productID=56)

Ward, A. W, & Murray-Ward, M. (1999). *Assessment in the classroom*. Belmont, CA: Wadsworth.

Warren, B., Ballenger, C, Ogonowski, M., Rosebery, A., & Hudicourt-Barnes, J. (2001). Rethinking diversity in learning science: The logic of everyday language. *Journal of Research in Science Teaching, 38*(5), 529–552.

Warschauer, M. (1995). *E-mail for English teaching*. Alexandria, VA: Teachers of English to Speakers of Other Languages.

Warschauer, M., Shetzer, H., & Meloni, C. (2000). *Internet for English teaching*. Alexandria, VA: Teachers of English to Speakers of Other Languages.

Watahomigie, L. (1995). The power of American Indian parents and communities. *Bilingual Research Journal, 19*(1), 99–115.

Weatherly, S. D. (1999). I'll buy it! In R. E. Larimer & L. Schleicher (Eds.), *New ways in using authentic materials in the classroom* (pp. 73–80). Alexandria, VA: Teachers of English to Speakers of Other Languages.

Weaver, C. (1988). *Reading process and practice*. Portsmouth, NH: Heinemann.

Weber, E. (2005). *MI strategies in the classroom and beyond*. Boston: Pearson.

Weiler, J. (1998). Recent changes in school desegregation. *ERIC Digest. Clearinghouse on Urban Education, ED#419029*. Accessed August 4, 2006, from www.ericfacility.net/ericdigests/ed419029.htm

Weiss, I. R., & Pasley, J. D. (2004, February). What is high-quality instruction? *Educational Leadership*, 24–28.

Wells, C. G. (1981). *Learning through interaction: The study of language development*. Cambridge: Cambridge University Press.

Wells, G. (1998). Using the tool-kit of discourse in the activity of learning and teaching. From Wells, G. (Ed.), *Dialogic inquiry* (pp. 231–266). Cambridge: Cambridge University Press.

Wells, G., & Chang-Wells, G. L. (1992). *Constructing knowledge together: Classrooms as centers of inquiry and literacy*. Portsmouth, NH: Heinemann.

Westling, D. L., & Koorland, M. A. (1988). *The special educator's handbook*. Boston: Allyn & Bacon.

Wexler, E., & Huerta, K. (2002). An empowering spirit is not enough: A Latino charter school struggles for leadership. In B. Fuller (Ed.), *Inside charter schools: The paradox of radical decentralizaion* (pp. 98–123). Cambridge, MA: Harvard University Press.

Whisler, N., & Williams, J. (1990). Literature and cooperative *learning: Pathway to literacy*. Sacramento: Literature Co-op.

Whitman, E. L. (1994). *Miss Nell fell in the well*. Kissim-mee, FL: Learning Pyramid.

Wiese, A. M., & García, E. (1998). The Bilingual Education Act: Language minority students and equal educational opportunity. *Bilingual Research Journal, 22*(1). Retrieved on June 21, 2005, from http://brj.asu.edu/v221/artides/art1.html

Wiggins, G. P., & McTighe, J. (1998). *Understanding by design*. Alexandria, VA: Association for Supervision and Curriculum Development.

Wilson, W. (1984). The urban underclass. In L. Dunbar (Ed.), *Minority report*. New York: Pantheon Books.

Wilton, D. (2003). How many words are there in the English language? Retrieved May 19, 2006, from www.wordorigins.org/number.htm

Wink, J. (2000). *Critical pedagogy: Notes from the real world*. New York: Addison Wesley.

Witte, K. (1991). The role of culture in health and disease. In L. Samovar & R. Porter (Eds.), *Intercultural communication: A reader* (6th ed.). Belmont, CA: Wadsworth.

Wolfe, P., & Poynor, L. (2001). Politics and the pendulum: An alternative understanding of the case of whole language as educational innovation. *Educational Researcher, 30*(1), 15–20.

Wolfram, W. (1991). *Dialects and American English*. Englewood Cliffs, NJ: Prentice Hall.

Wolfram, W. (1995). Reexamining dialect in TESOL. *TESOL Matters, 5*(2), 1, 22.

Wong, M. S. (1998). *You said it! Listening/speaking strategies and activities*. New York: St. Martin's Press.

Woolfolk, A. (2003). *Educational psychology* (9th ed.). Boston: Allyn & Bacon.

Woolfolk, A., & Brooks, D. (1985). The influence of teachers' nonverbal behaviors on students' perceptions and performance. *Elementary School Journal, 85,* 514–528.

Wray, M., & Newitz, A. (1997). *White trash: Race and class in America*. New York and London: Routledge.

Yao, E. (1988). Working effectively with Asian immigrant parents. *Phi Delta Kappan, 70*(3), 223–225.

Yep, L. (1975). *Dragonwings*. New York: Harper and Row.

Young, M., & Helvie, S. (1996). Parent power: A positive link to school success. *Journal of Educational Issues of Language Minority Students, 16*. Accessed July 7, 2006, from www.ncela.gwu.edu/pubs/jeihns/voll6/jeilms1611.htm

Zacarian, D. (2004). I was lost before the end of the first minute. *Essential Teacher, 2*(3), 11–13.

Zacarian, D. (2005). Rainforests and parking lots. *Essential Teacher, 2*(1), 10–11.

Zacarian, D. (2006). Testing, testing. *Essential Teacher, 3*(2), 10–12.

Zahar, R., Cobb, T., & Spada, N. (2001). Acquiring vocabulary through reading: Effects of frequency and contextual richness. *Canadian Modern Language Review, 57*(4). Accessed July 24, 2006, from www.utpjournals.com/product/cmlr/574/574-Zahar.html

Zelman, N. (1996). *Conversational inspirations: Over 2000 conversation topics*. Battleboro, VT: Pro Lingua Associates.

Zimmerman, C. (1997). Do reading and interactive vocabulary instruction make a difference? An empirical study. *TESOL Quarterly, 31*(1), 121–140.

For Chapter 7

Adams, K. L., & Brink, D. T. (Eds.). (1990). *Perspectives on official English: The campaign for English as the official language of the USA*. Berlin: Mouton de Gruyter.

Ambert, A. N., & Melendez, S. E. (1985). *Bilingual education: A sourcebook*. New York: Teachers College Press.

American Bible Society. (1995). *De good nyews bout Jedus Christ wa Luke write*. New York: Author.

American Speech-Language-Hearing Association. (1983). Committee on Language Report, *ASHA, 25*(6).

Amoriggi, H. D., & Gefteas, D. J. (1981). *Affective considerations in bilingual education: Problems and solutions*. Rosslyn, VA: National Clearinghouse for Bilingual Education.

Andrews, L. (2001). *Linguistics for L2 teachers*. Mahwah, NJ: Lawrence Erlbaum.

Aratani, L. (1998, January 22). High school leads the way in single-sex classes. *San Jose Mercury News*, pp. 1B, 4B.

Arons, S. (1983). *Compelling belief: The culture of American schooling*. New York: McGraw-Hill.

Artiles, A. J., Rueda R., Salazar, J. J., & Higareda, I. (2002). English-language learner representation in California urban school districts. In D. J. Losen & G. Orfeld (Eds.), *Racial inequity in special education* (pp. 117–136). Cambridge, MA: Harvard University Press.

Arvizu, S. F., Snyder, W. A., & Espinosa, P. T. (1980). *Demystifying the concept of culture: Theoretical and conceptual tools*. Los Angeles: Evaluation, Dissemination and Assessment Center, California State University, Los Angeles.

Asher, J. J. (1982). The total physical response approach. In R. W. Blair (Ed.), *Innovative approaches to language learning* (pp. 54–66). Rowley, MA: Newbury House.

Asher, J. J. (1986). *Learning another language through actions: The complete teacher's guidebook.* Los Gatos, CA: Sky Oaks Productions.

Aspira of New York v. Board of Education of the City of New York, Civ. No. 4002 (S.D. N.Y. consent agreement, August 29, 1974).

Association of Northern California Chinese Schools. (2003). Member schools. Retrieved June 5, 2003, from www.anccs.org.

Au, K. H., & Jordan, C. (1981). Teaching reading to Hawaiian children: Finding a culturally appropriate solution. In H. T. Trueba, C. P. Guthrie, & K. H. Au (Eds.), *Culture and the bilingual classroom: Studies in classroom ethnography* (pp. 139–152). Rowley, MA: Newbury House.

Baca, L. M., & Cervantes, H. T. (1998). *The bilingual special education interface* (3rd ed.). Upper Saddle River, NJ: Merrill.

Baetens, B. H. (1993). *European models of bilingual education.* Clevedon, UK: Multilingual Matters.

Baker, C. (2006). *Foundations of bilingual education and bilingualism* (4th ed.). Clevedon, UK: Multilingual Matters.

Baker, K. A., & de Kanter, A. A. (1981, September 25). *Effectiveness of bilingual education: A review of the literature.* Washington, DC: Office of Planning, Budget and Evaluation, U.S. Department of Education.

Bancroft, W. J. (1978). The Lozanov method and its American adaptations. *Modern Language Journal, 62,* 167–174.

Banks, J. A. (1977). *Multiethnic education: Practices and promises.* Bloomington, IN: Phi Delta Kappa Educational Foundation.

Barinaga, M. (1997, August 1). New insights into how babies learn language. *Science,* 641.

Baron, D. (1990). *The English-only question: An official language for Americans?* New Haven, CT: Yale University Press.

Battle in Spain on teaching in Spanish. (1993, November). *The New York Times,* p. A4.

Beardsley, T. (1995, January). For whom the bell curve really tolls. *Scientific American, 272*(1), 14, 16–17.

Bell, L. A. (1991). Changing our ideas about ourselves: Group consciousness raising with elementary school girls as a means to empowerment. In C. E. Sleeter (Ed.), *Empowerment through multicultural education* (pp. 229–249). Albany: State University of New York Press.

Benderson, A. (1983). *Foreign languages in the schools.* Princeton, NJ: Educational Testing Service (ERIC Document Reproduction Service No. ED 239 516).

Bereiter, C., & Engelmann, S. (1966). *Teaching disadvantaged children in the preschool.* Englewood Cliffs, NJ: Prentice-Hall.

Bialystok, E. (Ed.). (1991). *Language processing in bilingual children.* Cambridge, UK: Cambridge University Press.

Bialystok, E., & Hakuta, K. (1994). *In other words: The science and psychology of second language acquisition.* New York: Basic Books.

Bilingual Education Act, as amended, 20 U.S.C. sec. 3221 et seq.

Bilingual programs in Sweden are truly so. (1985). *The Reading Teacher, 39,* 213.

Blair, R. W. (Ed.). (1982). *Innovative approaches to language teaching.* Rowley, MA: Newbury House.

Block, L. (1992). *A walk among the tombstones.* New York: William Morrow.

Bloom, L., & Lahey, M. (1978). *Language development and language disorders.* New York: John Wiley & Sons.

Bloomfield, L. (1933). *Language.* New York: Holt, Rinehart, and Winston.

Boisson, S. (2006). When America sent her own packing. *American History, 41,* 20–27.

Boyd, S. (1999). Sweden: Immigrant languages. In B. Spolsky (Ed.), *Concise encyclopedia of educational linguistics* (pp. 73–74). Oxford, UK: Elsevier Science.

Boykin, A. W. (1984). Reading achievement and the social-cultural frame of reference of Afro-American children. *Journal of Negro Education, 53,* 464–473.

Brecht, R. D., & Rivers, W. P. (2000). Language and national security in the 21st century: The role of Title VI/Fulbright-Hays in supporting national language capacity. Dubuque, IA: Kendall/Hunt.

Brown, H. D. (1980). *Principles of language learning and teaching*. Englewood Cliffs, NJ: Prentice-Hall.

Brown, H. D. (1987). *Principles of language learning and teaching* (2nd ed.). Englewood Cliffs, NJ: Prentice-Hall.

Brown, J. E. (Ed.). (1972). *The North American Indians: A selection of photographs by Edward S. Curtis*. Millerton, NY: Aperture.

Brown, R., Cazden, C., & Bellugi, U. (1973). The child's grammar from I to III. In C. Ferguson & D. Slobin (Eds.), *Studies of child language development* (pp. 295–333). New York: Holt, Rinehart, & Winston.

Brown v. Board of Education of Topeka, 347 U.S. 483 (1954).

Bryson, B. (1994). *Made in America: An informal history of the English language in the United States*. New York: William Morrow.

Butler-Pascoe, M. E., & Wiburg, K. M. (2003). *Technology and teaching English language learners*. New York: Pearson.

Butterfield, F. (1986, August 3). Why Asians are going to the head of the class. *The New York Times*, Sec. XII, pp. 18–19.

Butterfield, F. (1994, December 30). Programs seek to stop trouble before it starts. *The New York Times*, p. A11.

California Department of Education. (2003). *Number of English learners in California public schools by language and grade*. Retrieved 2003 from Dataquest: www.cde.ca.gov/dataquest.

California Department of Education (Ed.). (2007). Number of English Learners by Language, 2006–2007. Retrieved January 7, 2008 from dq.cde.ca.gov/dataquest.

California State Department of Education (Ed.). (1984). *Studies on immersion education: A collection for United States educators*. Sacramento, CA: Office of Bilingual Bicultural Education.

California State Department of Education (Ed.). (1986). *Beyond language: Social and cultural factors in schooling language minority students*. Los Angeles: Evaluation, Dissemination and Assessment Center, California State University, Los Angeles.

California State Department of Education (Ed.). (1994). *Schooling and language minority students: A theoretical framework* (2nd ed.). Sacramento, CA: Bilingual Education Office.

Campbell-Jones, S. (Producer). (1985). *Baby talk* [video]. San Diego, CA: Media Guild.

Canale, M., & Swain, M. (1980). Theoretical bases of communicative approaches to second language teaching and testing. *Applied Linguistics, 1,* 1–47.

Capps, R., Fix, M. E., & Passel, J. S. (2002). The dispersal of immigrants in the 1990's. Washington, DC: The Urban Institute. Retrieved January 7, 2008, from www.urban.org/publications/410589.html.

Carle, E. (1969). *The very hungry caterpillar*. New York: World Publishing.

Carter, T. P. (1970). *Mexican Americans in school: A history of educational neglect*. New York: College Entrance Examination Board.

Castañeda v. Pickard, 648 F.2d 989 (5th Cir. 1981).

Castellanos, D. (1983). *The best of two worlds: Bilingual-bicultural education in the U.S.* Trenton, NJ: New Jersey State Department of Education.

Center for Applied Linguistics. (2007). *Directory of two-way immersion programs in the U.S.* Retrieved September 4, 2007, from www.cal.org/twi/directory.

Chaika, E. (1989). *Language: The social mirror* (2nd ed.). Rowley, MA: Newbury House.

Chamot, A. U., & O'Malley, J. M. (1987). The cognitive academic language learning approach: A bridge to the mainstream. *TESOL Quarterly, 21,* 227–249.

Chamot, A. U., & O'Malley, J. M. (1994). *The CALLA handbook: Implementing the cognitive academic language learning approach*. New York: Addison-Wesley.

Chavez, L. (1987, January 29). Struggling to keep Spanish in the U.S. pure. *The New York Times*, Section II, p. l.

Chen, E. (1995). Implications of "Official English" Legislation. http://archive.aclu.org/congress/chen.html.

Cheng, L. L. (1987). *Assessing Asian language performance: Guidelines for evaluating limited-English-proficient students*. Rockville, MD: Aspen Publishers.

Chomsky, N. (1968). *Language and mind.* New York: Harcourt, Brace & World.

Civil Rights Act of 1964, 42 U.S.C. sec. 2000(d).

Cohen, A. D. (1980). *Testing language ability in the classroom.* Rowley, MA: Newbury House.

Cohen, E. G. (1986). *Designing groupwork: Strategies for the heterogeneous classroom.* New York: Teachers College Press.

Collier, V. P. (1987). The effect of age on acquisition of a second language for school. *New Focus, 1*(2).

Commission of the European Communities. (2003). *Promoting language learning and linguistic diversity: An action plan 2004–2006.* Brussels: Author.

Conklin, N., & Lourie, M. (1983). *A host of tongues: Language communities in the United States.* New York: The Free Press.

Consentino de Cohen, C., & Chu Clewell, B. (2007). *Putting English language learners on the map.* Washington, DC: Urban Institute.

Contín, M. (1995, February 1). U.S. Ninth Circuit Court reverses Arizona English-only. *NABE News,* p. 1.

Corballis, M. C. (2002). *From hand to mouth: The origins of language.* Princeton, NJ: Princeton University Press.

Corson, D. (1995). The learning and use of academic English words. *Language Learning, 47,* 671–718.

Cortés, C. E. (1986). The education of language minority students: A contextual interaction model. In California State Department of Education (Ed.), *Beyond language: Social and cultural factors in schooling language minority students* (pp. 3–33). Los Angeles: Evaluation, Dissemination and Assessment Center, California State University, Los Angeles.

Cortés, C. E. (1990, March/April). Multicultural education: A curricular basic for our multiethnic future. *Doubts and Certainties, 4*(78), 1–5.

Council of Chief State School Officers. (1990). *School success for limited English proficient students: The challenge and state response.* Washington, DC: Author.

Crawford, J. (1986, April 23). Immersion method is faring poorly in bilingual study. *Education Week,* pp. 1, 10.

Crawford, J. (1989). *Bilingual education: History, politics, theory, and practice.* Trenton, NJ: Crane.

Crawford, J. (1992a). *Hold your tongue: Bilingualism and the politics of "English only."* Reading, MA: Addison-Wesley.

Crawford, J. (1992b). *Language loyalties: A source book on the official English controversy.* Chicago: University of Chicago Press.

Crawford, J. (1997). *Best evidence: Research foundations of the Bilingual Education Act.* Washington, DC: NCBE.

Crawford, J. (2007, June 6). A diminished vision of civil rights: No Child Left Behind and the growing divide in how educational equity is understood. Retrieved January 6, 2008 from ourworld .compuserve.com/homepages/JWCrawford/home.htm.

CREDE. (2003). *Research brief #10: A national study of school effectiveness for language minority students' long-term academic achievement.* Berkeley, CA: Center for Research on Education, Diversity and Excellence.

Crystal, D. (1987). *The Cambridge encyclopedia of language.* Cambridge, UK: Cambridge University Press.

Crystal, D. (1997). *The Cambridge encyclopedia of language* (2nd ed.). Cambridge, UK: Cambridge University Press.

Crystal, D. (2000). *Language death.* Cambridge, UK: Cambridge University Press.

Crystal, D. (2001). *Language and the internet.* Cambridge, UK: Cambridge University Press.

Cummins, J. (1981). The role of primary language development in promoting educational success for language minority students. In California State Department of Education (Ed.), *Schooling and language minority students: A theoretical framework* (pp. 3–49). Los Angeles: Evaluation, Dissemination and Assessment Center, California State University, Los Angeles.

Cummins, J. (1984). Linguistic minorities and multicultural policy in Canada. In J. Edwards (Ed.), *Linguistic minorities, policies and pluralism* (pp. 81–105). London: Academic Press.

Cummins, J. (1989). *Empowering minority students.* Sacramento, CA: California Association of Bilingual Education.

Cummins, J. (1994). Primary language instruction and the education of language minority students. In California State Department of Education (Ed.), *Schooling and language minority students: A theoretical framework* (2nd ed.) (pp. 3–46). Los Angeles: Evaluation, Dissemination and Assessment Center, California State University, Los Angeles.

Cummins, J. (1996). *Negotiating identities: Education for empowerment in a diverse society.* Ontario, CA: California Association for Bilingual Education.

Cummins, J., & Swain, M. (1986). *Bilingualism in education.* White Plains, NY: Longman.

Curran, C. A. (1982). Community language learning. In R. W. Blair (Ed.), *Innovative approaches to language teaching* (pp. 118–133). Rowley, MA: Newbury House.

Dalby, A. (2003). *Language in danger: The loss of linguistic diversity and the threat to our future.* New York: Columbia University Press.

Danoff, M. N., Coles, G. J., McLaughlin, D. H., & Reynolds, D. J. (1977a). *Evaluation of the impact of ESEA Title VII Spanish/English bilingual education programs, Volume I: Study design and interim findings.* Palo Alto, CA: American Institutes for Research.

Danoff, M. N., Coles, G. J., McLaughlin, D. H., & Reynolds, D. J. (1977b). *Evaluation of the impact of ESEA Title VII Spanish/English bilingual education programs, Volume II: Project descriptions.* Palo Alto, CA: American Institutes for Research.

Danoff, M. N., Coles, G. J., McLaughlin, D. H., & Reynolds, D. J. (1978). *Evaluation of the impact of ESEA Title VII Spanish/English bilingual education programs, Volume III: Year two impact data, educational process, and in-depth analysis.* Palo Alto, CA: American Institutes for Research.

Day, E. C. (1981). Assessing communicative competence: Integrative testing of second language learners. In J. U. Erickson & D. R. Omark (Eds.), *Communication assessment of the bilingual bicultural child: Issues and guidelines* (pp. 179–197). Baltimore, MD: University Park Press.

Day, E. C., McCollum, P. A., Cieslak, V. A., & Erickson, J. G. (1981). Discrete point language tests of bilinguals: A review of selected tests. In J. G. Erickson & D. R. Omark (Eds.), *Communication assessment of the bilingual bicultural child: Issues and guidelines* (pp. 129–161). Baltimore, MD: University Park Press.

DeAvila, E., Duncan, S., & Navarrete, C. (1987). *Finding Out/Descubrimiento.* Northvale, NJ: Santillana.

de la Luz Reyes, M. (2001). Unleashing possibilities: Biliteracy in the primary grades. In M. de la Luz Reyes & J. J. Halcón (Eds.), *The best for our children: Critical Perspectives on literacy for Latino students* (pp. 96–121). New York: Teachers College Press.

de la Luz Reyes, M., & Halcón, J. J. (Eds.). (2001). *The best for our children: Critical perspectives on literacy for Latino students.* New York: Teachers College Press.

Del Valle, S. (2003). *Language rights and the law in the United States: Finding our voices.* Clevedon, UK: Multilingual Matters.

de Villiers, P. A., & de Villiers, J. G. (1979). *Early language.* Cambridge, MA: Harvard University Press.

Diana v. State Board of Education, C-70-37 RFP, N. D. Cal, Jan. 7, 1970, and June 18, 1972.

Dicker, S. J. (1996). *Languages in America: A pluralist view.* Clevedon, UK: Multilingual Matters.

Diller, K. C. (1978). *The language teaching controversy.* Rowley, MA: Newbury House.

Dillon, S. (2003, March 19). Suddenly, a seller's market in Arabic studies. *The New York Times,* p. A24.

Doerner, W. R. (1987, September 14). Troubles of a tongue en crise. *Newsweek,* p. 49.

Dunbar, R. (1996). *Grooming, gossip, and the evolution of language.* Cambridge, MA: Harvard University Press.

Echevarria, J. & Graves, A. (2007). *Sheltered content instruction: Teaching English language learners with diverse abilities* (3rd ed.). Boston: Pearson.

Education Trust. (2003). *ESEA: Myths versus realities: Answers to common questions about the new No Child Left Behind Act.* Washington, DC: Author.

Education Week. Retrieved August 24, 2007, from www.edweek.org.

Edwards, J. (1998). *Language in Canada.* Cambridge, UK: Cambridge University Press.

Eggen, D. (2006, October 11). FBI agents still lacking Arabic skills. *Washington Post,* p. A01.

Elford, G., & Woodford, P. (1982). *A study of bilingual instructional practices in nonpublic schools: Final report.* Princeton, NJ: Educational Testing Service. (ERIC Document Reproduction Service No. ED 240 855).

Ellis, R. (1988). Theories of second language acquisition. In P. A. Richard-Amato (Ed.), *Making it happen: Interaction in the second language classroom, from theory to practice* (pp. 319–329). White Plains, NY: Longman.

English First. (2007). Retrieved July 19, 2007, from www.English-first.org.

Equal Educational Opportunities Act of 1974, 20 U.S.C. 1703(f).

Erickson, J. G., & Omark, D. R. (Eds.). (1981). *Communication assessment of the bilingual bicultural child: Issues and guidelines.* Baltimore, MD: University Park Press.

Ervin-Tripp, S. M. (1976). Language development. *Psychological Documents, 6,* 4. (Ms. No. 1336).

Escamilla, K. (1980). German-English bilingual schools 1870–1917: Cultural and linguistic survival in St. Louis. *Bilingual Journal, 5*(2), 16–20.

Escamilla, K. (1993). Promoting biliteracy: Issues in promoting English literacy in students acquiring English. In J. V. Tinajero & A. Flor Ada (Eds.), *The power of two languages* (pp. 220–233). New York: Macmillan/McGraw-Hill.

Ferguson, C. A. (1978). Language and global interdependence. In E. M. Gerli, J. E. Alatis, & R. I. Brod (Eds.), *Language in American life: Proceedings of the Georgetown University Modern Language Association Conference October 6–8, 1977, Washington, DC* (pp. 23–31). Washington, DC: Georgetown University Press.

Ferguson, C. A., & Heath, S. B. (Eds.). (1981). *Language in the USA.* New York: Cambridge University Press.

Feuerstein, R. (1978). The dynamic assessment of retarded performers: The learning potential assessment device, theory, instruments, and techniques. Baltimore, MD: University Park Press.

Fincher, B. H. (1978). Bilingualism in contemporary China: The coexistence of oral diversity and written uniformity. In B. Spolsky & R. L. Cooper (Eds.), *Case studies in bilingual education* (pp. 72–87). Rowley, MA: Newbury House.

Fishman, J. A. (1981). Language policy: Past, present and future. In C. A. Ferguson & S. B. Heath (Eds.), *Language in the USA* (pp. 516–526). New York: Cambridge University Press.

Fishman, J. A. (1985). *Ethnicity in action: The community resources of ethnic languages in the United States.* Binghamton, NY: Bilingual Press/Editorial Bilingüe.

Fishman, J. A. (Ed.). (2001). *Can threatened languages be saved? Reversing language shift revisited: A 21st century perspective.* Clevedon, UK: Multilingual Matters.

Fishman, J. A., Gertner, M. H., Lowy, E. G., & Milan, W. G. (Eds.). (1985). *The rise and fall of the ethnic revival: Perspectives on language and ethnicity.* Berlin: Mouton de Gruyter.

Fishman, J. A., & Keller, G. D. (Eds.). (1982). *Bilingual education for Hispanic students in the United States.* New York: Teachers College Press.

Fleischman, H. L., & Staples-Said, M. (1994). *Descriptive study of services to limited English proficient students.* Arlington, VA: Development Associates.

Flor Ada, A. (1988). The Pajaro Valley experience: Working with Spanish-speaking parents to develop children's reading and writing skills through the use of children's literature. In T. Skutnabb-Kangas & J. Cummins (Eds.), *Minority Education: From Shame to Struggle.* Clevedon, UK: Multilingual Matters.

Foley, D. E. (1994). Reconsidering anthropological explanations of minority school failure. In F. Schultz (Ed.), *Multicultural Education 94/95.* Guilford, CT: Dushkin.

Fordham, S. (1991). Peer-proofing academic competition among black adolescents: "Acting White" black American style. In C. E. Sleeter (Ed.), *Empowerment through multicultural education* (pp. 69–93). Albany: State University of New York Press.

Foreman, G. (1938). *Sequoyah.* Norman, OK: University of Oklahoma Press.

Frederickson, J. (1995). *Reclaiming our voices: Bilingual education, critical pedagogy & praxis.* Los Angeles: California Association for Bilingual Education.

Freeman, D. E., & Freeman, Y. S. (2001). *Between worlds: Access to second language acquisition* (2nd ed.). Portsmouth, NH: Heinemann.

Freeman, D. E., & Freeman, Y. S. (2004). *Essential linguistics: What you need to know to teach reading, ESL, spelling, phonics, grammar.* Portsmouth, NH: Heinemann.

Freire, P. (1970). *Pedagogy of the oppressed.* New York: The Seabury Press.

Garcia, E., & Figueroa, R. A. (Fall, 1994). Issues in testing students from culturally and linguistically diverse backgrounds. *Multicultural Education, 2*(1), 10–19.

Gargan, E. A. (1997, December 24). Move to Cantonese in schools shakes up Hong Kong. *The Mercury News,* p. 11A.

Garnica, O. K. (1977). Some prosodic and paralinguistic features of speech to young children. In C. E. Snow & C. A. Ferguson (Eds.), *Talking to children* (pp. 63–88). New York: Cambridge University Press.

Gass, S. M., & Selinker, L. (1994). *Second language acquisition: An introductory course.* Hillsdale, NJ: Lawrence Erlbaum.

Genesee, F. (1987). *Learning through two languages: Studies of immersion and bilingual education.* Cambridge, MA: Newbury House.

Genesee, F. (Ed.). (1994). *Educating second language children: The whole child, the whole curriculum, the whole community.* Cambridge, UK: Cambridge University Press.

Genesee, F., & Hamayan, E. V. (1994). Classroom-based assessment. In F. Genesee (Ed.), *Educating second language children: The whole child, the whole curriculum, the whole community.* Cambridge, UK: Cambridge University Press.

Gingrich, N. (1995). *To Renew America.* New York: HarperPaperbacks.

Giroux, H. (1988, March). *Teacher empowerment and the struggle for public life.* Paper presented at San Jose State University, San Jose, CA.

Givón, T. (1985). Function, structure, and language acquisition. In D. I. Slobin (Ed.), *The crosslinguistic study of language acquisition: Vol. 2. Theoretical issues* (pp. 1005–1027). Hillsdale, NJ: Lawrence Erlbaum.

Gleason, J. B. (1973). Code switching in children's language. In T. E. Moore (Ed.), *Cognitive development and the acquisition of language* (pp. 159–167). New York: Academic Press.

Gleason, J. B. (1985). Studying language development. In J. B. Gleason (Ed.), *The development of language* (pp. 1–35). Columbus, OH: Merrill.

Gleason, P. (1984). Pluralism and assimilation: A conceptual history. In J. Edwards (Ed.), *Linguistic minorities, policies and pluralism* (pp. 221–257). London: Academic Press.

Glod, M. (2006, August 8). Schools Try Elementary Approach to Teaching Foreign Languages. *Washington Post.*

Goldhor Lerner, H. (September, 1993). Good advice. *New Woman,* p. 40.

Gomez v. Illinois State Board of Education, 811 F.2d 1030 (7th Cir. 1987).

Gonzalez, A., & Guerrero, M. (1983). *A cooperative/interdependent approach to bilingual education.* Hollister, CA: Hollister School District.

Gonzalez, G., & Maez, L. F. (1980). To switch or not to switch: The role of code-switching in the elementary bilingual classroom. In R. V. Padilla (Ed.), *Ethnoperspectives in bilingual education research: Theory in bilingual education* (pp. 125–135). Ypsilanti, MI: Eastern Michigan University.

Gonzalez, V., Brusca-Vega, R., & Yawkey, T. (1997). *Assessment and instruction of culturally and linguistically diverse students with or at-risk of learning problems: From research to practice.* Boston: Allyn & Bacon.

Goodenough, W. (1971). *Culture, language, and society.* Reading, MA: Addison-Wesley.

Gray, P. (Fall, 1993). Teach your children well [Special Issue]. *Time,* pp. 69–71.

Grittner, F. M. (1969). *Teaching foreign languages.* New York: Harper & Row.

Grosjean, F. (1982). *Life with two languages.* Cambridge, MA: Harvard University Press.

Growth of a nation. (1985, July 8). *Newsweek,* pp. 34–35.

Guido, M. (1995, March 16). Model escuela: Two-way language immersion program to be emulated by schools in other regions. *San Jose Mercury News,* pp. 1A, 22A.

Gumperz, J. J. (1981). Conversational inference and classroom learning. In J. L. Green & C. Wallat (Eds.), *Ethnography and language in educational settings* (pp. 3–23). Norwood, NJ: Ablex.

Hadaway, N. L., Vardell, S. M., & Young, T. A. (2002). *Literature-based instruction with English language learners.* Boston: Allyn and Bacon.

Hakuta, K. (1985, December). Bilingualism and its potential impact on the nation's schools. *CABE Newsletter,* pp. 1, 5, 13.

Hakuta, K. (1986). *Mirror of language: The debate on bilingualism.* New York: Basic Books.

Hakuta, K., & Gould, L. J. (1987). Synthesis of research on bilingual education. *Educational Leadership, 44*(6), 38–45.

Hall, E. T. (1959). *The silent language.* Garden City, NY: Doubleday.

Hall, E. T. (1966). *The hidden dimension.* Garden City, NY: Doubleday.

Hamayan, E., & Damico, J. (Eds.). (1991). *Limiting bias in the assessment of bilingual students.* Austin, TX: Pro-ed.

Hamayan, E. V., & Perlman, R. (1990, Spring). *Helping language minority students after they exit from bilingual/ESL programs: A handbook for teachers.* Rosslyn, VA: National Clearinghouse for Bilingual Education.

Harman, S. (1991). One more critique of testing—with two differences. In C. Edelsky (Ed.), *With literacy and justice for all: Rethinking the social in language and education.* London: The Falmer Press.

Haugen, E. (1987). *Blessings of Babel: Bilingualism and language planning.* Berlin: Mouton de Gruyter.

Hayes, C. W., Ornstein, J., & Gage, W. W. (1977). *ABC's of language and linguistics: A practical primer to language science in today's world.* Silver Spring, MD: Institute of Modern Languages.

Heath, S. B. (1983). Language policies. *Society, 20*(4), 57–63.

Here they come, ready or not. (1986, May 14). *Education Week,* pp. 14–39.

Hernandez-Chavez, E., Burt, M., & Dulay, H. (1978). Language dominance and proficiency testing: Some general considerations. *NABE Journal, 3*(1), 41–54.

Higgs, T. V. (1991). Research on the role of grammar and accuracy in classroom-based foreign language acquisition. In B. F. Freed (Ed.), *Foreign language acquisition research and the classroom* (pp. 46–53). Lexington, MA: D. C. Heath and Company.

Hudelson, S. (1994). Literacy development of second language children. In F. Genesee (Ed.), *Educating second language children: The whole child, the whole curriculum, the whole community* (pp. 129–158). Cambridge, UK: Cambridge University Press.

Idaho Migrant Council v. Board of Education, 647 F.2d 69 (9th Cir. 1981).

Igoa, C. (1995). *The inner world of the immigrant child.* New York: St. Martin's Press.

Immigration Project of the National Lawyers Guild. (1981). *Immigration law and defense* (2nd ed.). New York: Clark Boardman.

International School of the Peninsula. Mission and accreditations. Palo Alto, CA: International School of the Peninsula. Retrieved June 5, 2003, from www.istp.org.

Iowa State University. (2006, December 12). The national K–12 Foreign Language Resource Center receives $1.3 million grant. Press release. Retrieved September 4, 2007, from www.hs.iastate.edu/news/release/view.php?article=63.

Jacobson, R. (1987). *Allocating two languages as a key feature of a bilingual methodology.* Paper presented at the meeting of the National Association for Bilingual Education, Denver, CO.

Jensen, A. R. (1969). How much can we boost IQ and scholastic achievement? *Harvard Educational Review, 39,* 1–123.

Jernudd, B. H. (1999). Language education policy—Asia. In B. Spolsky (Ed.), *Concise encyclopedia of educational linguistics* (pp. 116–122). Oxford, UK: Elsevier Science.

Jespersen, O. (1922). *Language: Its nature, development and origin.* London: George Allen & Unwin.

Kagan, S. (1986). Cooperative learning and sociocultural factors in schooling. In California State Department of Education (Ed.), *Beyond language: Social and cultural factors in schooling language minority students* (pp. 231–298). Los Angeles: Evaluation, Dissemination and Assessment Center, California State University, Los Angeles.

Kamin, L. J. (1995, February). Behind the curve. *Scientific American,* pp. 99–103.

Karst, K. L. (1986). Paths to belonging: The Constitution and cultural identity. *North Carolina Law Review, 64,* 303–377.

Kaufman, D. (2003, April). Letters for the people. *Language Magazine, 7,* 24–26.

Keller, G. D., & Van Hooft, K. S. (1982). A chronology of bilingualism and bilingual education in the United States. In J. A. Fishman & G. D. Keller (Eds.), *Bilingual education for Hispanic students in the United States* (pp. 3–19). New York: Teachers College Press.

Kelley, T. (1998, April 30). It is for you defective day of hats, no? *The New York Times,* pp. D1, D7.

Kester, E. S., & Pena, E. D. (2002). Limitations of current language testing practices for bilinguals. (ERIC Document Reproduction Service No. ED 470 203).

Keyes v. School District No. 1, Denver, 380 F. Supp. 673 (D. Colo. 1974).

Khubchandani, L. M. (1978). Multilingual education in India. In B. Spolsky & R. L. Cooper (Eds.), *Case studies in bilingual education* (pp. 88–125). Rowley, MA: Newbury House.

Kilpatrick, J. F. (1965). *Sequoyah of earth & intellect.* Austin, TX: The Encino Press.

Kim, K. H. S., Relkin, N. R., Lee, K., & Hirsch, J. (1997). Distinct cortical areas associated with native and second languages. *Nature, 388,* 171–174.

Kindler, A. L. (2002, October). *Survey of the states' limited English proficient students and available educational programs and services: 2000–2001 summary report.* Washington, DC: NCELA.

Kinzer, S. (1998, January 26). Nehru spoke it, but it's still 'foreign.' *The New York Times,* p. A4.

Kirkland, R. I., Jr. (1988, March 14). Entering a new age of boundless competition. *Fortune,* pp. 40–42, 46, 48.

Kjolseth, R. (1976). Bilingual education programs in the United States: For assimilation or pluralism? In F. Cordasco (Ed.), *Bilingual schooling in the United States: A sourcebook for educational personnel* (pp. 122–140). New York: McGraw-Hill.

Kjolseth, R. (1983). Cultural politics and bilingualism. *Society, 20*(4), 40–48.

Kloss, H. (1977). *The American bilingual tradition.* Rowley, MA: Newbury House.

Kondracke, M. (1979, March 31). The ugly American redux. *The New Republic,* pp. 55–62.

Kotlowitz, A. (2007, August 5). Our Town. *New York Times,* Section 6, pp. 30–37, 52, 57.

Krashen, S. D. (1981). Bilingual education and second language acquisition theory. In California State Department of Education (Ed.), *Schooling and language minority students: A theoretical framework* (pp. 51–79). Los Angeles: Evaluation, Dissemination and Assessment Center, California State University, Los Angeles.

Krashen, S. D. (1996). *Under attack: The case against bilingual education.* Culver City, CA: Language Education Associates.

Krashen, S. D. (December 1997/January 1998). Bridging inequity with books. *Educational Leadership, 55*(4), 18–22.

Krashen, S. D. (2003). *Explorations in language acquisition and use: The Taipei lectures.* Portsmouth, NH: Heinemann.

Krashen, S. D., & Biber, D. (1988). *On course: Bilingual education's success in California.* Sacramento, CA: California Association for Bilingual Education.

Krashen, S. D., & Terrell, T. D. (1983). *The natural approach: Language acquisition in the classroom.* San Francisco: Alemany.

Krauss, C. (2003, April 13). Quebec seeking to end its old cultural divide: Getting along in English and en Francais. *The New York Times,* p. A6.

Krauss, M. (1992). The world's languages in crisis. *Language, 68,* 6–10.

Labov, W. (1970). *The study of nonstandard English.* Champaign, IL: National Council of the Teachers of English.

Labov, W. (1995). The logic of nonstandard English. In D. Benett Durkin (Ed.), *Language issues: Readings for teachers.* New York: Longman. [Reprinted from *Report of the twentieth annual round table meeting on linguistics and language studies,* Monograph Series on Language and Linguistics, Alatis, J. P. (Ed.), 1979].

Lambert, W. E., & Taylor, D. M. (1987). Language minorities in the United States: Conflicts around assimilation and proposed modes of accommodation. In W. A. Van Horne & T. V. Tonnesen (Eds.), *Ethnicity and language* (pp. 58–89). Milwaukee: The University of Wisconsin System Institute on Race and Ethnicity.

Langer, J. A. (1991). Literacy and schooling: A sociocognitive perspective. In E. H. Hiebert (Ed.), *Literacy for a diverse society: Perspectives, practices, and policies* (pp. 9–27). New York: Teachers College Press.

Larsen-Freeman, D., & Long, M. H. (1991). *An introduction to second language research*. White Plains, NY: Longman.

Lau v. Nichols, 414 U.S. 563 (1974).

Legarreta-Marcaida, D. (1981). Effective use of the primary language in the classroom. In California State Department of Education (Ed.), *Schooling and language minority students: A theoretical framework* (pp. 83–116). Los Angeles: Evaluation, Dissemination and Assessment Center, California State University, Los Angeles.

Lemberger, N. (1997). *Bilingual education: Teachers' narratives*. Mahwah, NJ: Lawrence Erlbaum Associates.

Lenneberg, E. (1967). *Biological foundations of language*. New York: John Wiley & Sons.

Lessow-Hurley, J. (1977). *Como ellos lo ven: Migrant children look at life in Longmont*. Boulder, CO: Western Interstate Commission on Higher Education.

Levine, R. (1997). *A geography of time: The temporal misadventures of a social psychologist, or how every culture keeps time just a little bit differently*. New York: Basic Books.

Lewis, E. G. (1976). Bilingualism and bilingual education: The ancient world to the Renaissance. In J. A. Fishman (Ed.), *Bilingual education: An international sociological perspective* (pp. 150–200). Rowley, MA: Newbury House.

Lewis, M. (1972). Parents and children: Sex-role development. *School Review, 80,* 229–240.

Lieberman, P. (1998). *Eve Spoke*. New York: W. W. Norton.

Liebowitz, A. H. (1971). *Educational policy and political acceptance: The imposition of English as the language of instruction in American schools*. Washington, DC: Center for Applied Linguistics. (ERIC Document Reproduction Service No. ED 047 321).

Liebowitz, A. H. (1978). Language policy in the United States. In H. LaFontaine, B. Persky, & L. H. Golubehick (Eds.), *Bilingual Education* (pp. 3–15). Wayne, NJ: Avery.

Lightbown, P., & Spada N. (1993). *How languages are learned*. Oxford, UK: Oxford University Press.

Lindholm, K. J. (1994). Promoting positive cross-cultural attitudes and perceived competence in culturally and linguistically diverse classrooms. In R. A. DeVillar, C. J. Flatis, & J. P. Cummins (Eds.), *Cultural diversity in schools: From rhetoric to practice* (pp. 189–206). Albany: State University of New York Press.

Lindholm, K. J., & Molina, R. (1998). Learning in dual language education classrooms in the U.S.: Implementation and evaluation outcomes. *Proceedings of the III European Conference on Immersion Programmes*.

Lippi-Green, R. (1997). *English with an accent*. London and New York: Routledge.

Long, M. H., & Porter, P. A. (1985). Group work, interlanguage talk, and second language acquisition. *TESOL Quarterly, 18,* 207–227.

Losen, D. J., & Orfeld, G. (Eds.). (2002). *Racial inequity in special education*. Cambridge, MA: Harvard University Press.

Lozanov, G. (1982). Suggestology and Suggestopedia. In R. W. Blair (Ed.), *Innovative approaches to language teaching* (pp. 146–159). Rowley, MA: Newbury House.

Macaulay, R. (1980). *Generally speaking: How children learn language*. Rowley, MA: Newbury House.

Macías, R. F., & Kelly, C. (1996). *Summary report of the survey of the states' limited English proficient students and available educational programs and services 1994–1995*. Washington, DC: National Clearinghouse for Bilingual Education.

Mackey, W. F. (1972). *Bilingual education in a binational school*. Rowley, MA: Newbury House.

Mackey, W. F. (1978). The importation of bilingual education models. In J. E. Alatis (Ed.), *Georgetown University round table on languages and linguistics 1978* (pp. 1–18). Washington, DC: Georgetown University Press.

Marin, C., & Macgregor-Scott, P. (Producers). (1987). *Born in East L. A.* [Film]. Universal City, CA: Universal Pictures.

Mayer, J. (May/June 2002). The promise of ESEA, Title III. *Multilingual News, 25*(6), 1, 6–7, 9.

McCarty, T. L., & Zepeda, O. (1995, Winter). Indigenous Language Education and Literacy. *Bilingual Research Journal, 19*(1).

McCollum, P. A., & Day, E. C. (1981). Quasi-integrative approaches: Discrete point scoring of expressive language samples. In J. G. Erickson & D. R. Omark (Eds.), *Communication assessment of the bilingual bicultural child: Issues and guidelines* (pp. 163–177). Baltimore, MD: University Park Press.

McCrum, R., Cran, W., & MacNeil, R. (1986). *The story of English*. New York: Elizabeth Sifton Books (Viking).

McDermott, R. P. (1997). Achieving school failure (1972–1997). In G. D. Spindler (Ed.), *Education and cultural process: Anthropological approaches* (3rd ed., pp. 110–135). Prospect Heights, IL: Waveland Press.

McDermott, R. P., & Gospodinoff, K. (1981). Social contexts for ethnic borders and school failure. In H. T. Trueba, G. P. Guthrie, & K. H. Au (Eds.), *Culture and the bilingual classroom: Studies in classroom ethnography* (pp. 212–230). Rowley, MA: Newbury House.

McFadden, B. J. (1983). Bilingual education and the law. *Journal of Law and Education, 12,* 1-27.

McMurrer, J. (2007). *Choices, changes, and challenges: Curriculum and instruction in the NCLB era.* Washington, DC: Center on Education Policy.

McWhorter, J. (2001). *The power of Babel: A natural history of language.* New York: W. H. Freeman.

Menendez, R., Musca, T., & Olmos, E. J. (Producers). (1988). *Stand and deliver* [Film]. Burbank, CA: Warner Bros.

Menken, K. (2008). *English learners left behind: Standardized testing as language policy.* Clevedon, UK: Multilingual Matters.

Mercer, J., & Lewis, J. F. (1979). *System of multicultural pluralistic assessment.* New York: The Psychological Corporation.

Met, M. (1994). Teaching content through a second language. In F. Genesee (Ed.), *Educating second language children: The whole child, the whole curriculum, the whole community.* Cambridge, UK: Cambridge University Press.

Meyer v. Nebraska, 262 U.S. 390 (1923).

Miller, H., & Miller, K. (1996). Language policy and identity: The case of Catalonia. *International Studies in Sociology of Education, 6,* 113–128.

Miller, J. (1983). *Many voices: Bilingualism, culture and education.* London: Routledge & Kegan Paul.

Miller, T. (2007). *How I learned English.* Washington, DC: National Geographic.

Mohatt, G. V., & Erickson, F. (1981). Cultural differences in teaching styles in an Odawa school: A sociolinguistic approach. In H. T. Trueba, G. P. Guthrie, & K. H. Au (Eds.), *Culture and the bilingual classroom: Studies in classroom ethnography* (pp. 105–119). Rowley, MA: Newbury House.

Morris, D. (1977). *Manwatching: A field guide to human behavior.* New York: Harry N. Abrams.

Murray, C., & Herrnstein, R. (1994). *The bell curve: The reshaping of American life by differences in intelligence.* New York: The Free Press.

National Clearinghouse for English Language Acquisition. (2007). NCELA FAQ: Which states offer certification or endorsement in Bilingual Education or ESL? Retrieved January 5, 2008, from www.ncela.gwu.edu/expert/faq/09certif.htm.

National Defense Education Act. (1958). 20 U.S.C. sec. 401 et seq., P.L. 85-864, 72 Stat. 1580.

National Public Radio. (March 7, 1995). *Morning Edition.* Washington, DC.

NCELA. (2003). Poster. The growing numbers of LEP students 2001–2002. Retrieved 2003 from www.ncela.gwu.edu/states/stateposter.pdf.

New York Times Magazine (1997, July 20), advertisement on p. 31.

Nieto, S. (1992). *Affirming diversity: The sociopolitical context of multicultural education.* White Plains, NY: Longman.

Nunberg, G. (2001). *The way we talk now: Commentaries on language and culture.* Boston: Houghton Mifflin.

Office of Bilingual Bicultural Education, California State Department of Education. (1984). *Studies on immersion education: A collection for United States educators.* Sacramento: California State Department of Education.

Ogbu, J. U. (1978). *Minority education and caste: The American system in cross-cultural perspective.* New York: Academic Press.

Ogbu, J. U. (1992). Understanding cultural diversity and learning. *Educational Researcher, 21*(8), 5–14.

Ogbu, J. U. (1994). Racial stratification and education in the United States: Why inequality persists. *Teachers College Record, 96,* 264–298.

Ogbu, J. U., & Matute-Bianchi, M. E. (1986). Understanding sociocultural factors: Knowledge, identity, and school adjustment. In California State Department of Education (Ed.), *Beyond language: Social and cultural factors in schooling language minority students* (pp. 73–142). Los Angeles: Evaluation, Dissemination and Assessment Center, California State University, Los Angeles.

Okazaki, S. (Director). (1987). *Living on Tokyo time* [Film]. Los Angeles: Skouras Pictures.

Olsen, L. (1997). *Made in America: Immigrant students in our public schools.* New York: The New Press.

Olsen, L. et al. (1994). *The unfinished journey: Restructuring schools in a diverse society.* San Francisco: California Tomorrow.

O'Malley, J. M., & Valdez Pierce, L. (1991, November). Portfolio assessment: Using portfolio and alternative assessment with LEP students. *Forum, 15*(1), pp. 1–2.

O'Malley, J. M., & Valdez Pierce, L. (1992, Spring). *Performance and portfolio assessment for language minority students.* Washington, DC: National Clearinghouse for Bilingual Education.

O'Riagain, P. (1997). *Language policy and social reproduction: Ireland 1893–1993.* New York: Oxford University Press.

O'Riagain, P. (2001). Irish language production and reproduction 1981–1996. In J. Fishman (Ed.), *Can threatened languages be saved? Reversing language shift, revisited: A 21st century perspective* (pp. 195–214). Clevedon, UK: Multilingual Matters.

Ovando, C. J., & Collier, V. P. (1985). *Bilingual and ESL classrooms.* New York: McGraw-Hill.

Owens, R. E. (1984). *Language development: An introduction.* Columbus, OH: Merrill.

Patinkin, M. (1998). *Mamaloshen* [CD]. New York: Nonesuch. 1998.

Perea, J. F. (Ed.). (1997). *Immigrants out! The new nativism and the anti-immigrant impulse in the United States.* New York: New York University Press.

Peregoy, S. F., & Boyle, O. F. (2005). *Reading, writing, & learning in ESL: A resource book for K–8 teachers* (4th ed.). White Plains, NY: Longman.

Pérez, B. (Ed.). (1998). *Sociocultural contexts of language and literacy.* Mahwah, NJ: Lawrence Erlbaum.

Pérez, B., & Torres-Guzmán, M. (1992). *Learning in two worlds: An integrated Spanish/English biliteracy approach.* White Plains, NY: Longman.

Perssons, L. (1993). *Parent handbook: Kokopelli's flute.* (Unpublished classroom materials).

Peske, H. G., & Haycock, K. (2006). *Teaching inequality: How poor and minority students are shortchanged on teacher quality.* Washington, DC: Education Trust.

Peters, A. M. (1985). Language segmentation: Operating principles for the perception and analysis of language. In D. I. Slobin (Ed.), *The crosslinguistic study of language acquisition: Vol.?2. Theoretical issues* (pp. 1029–1067). Hillsdale, NJ: Lawrence Erlbaum.

Pfeiffer, J. (1988, January). How not to lose the trade wars by cultural gaffes. *Smithsonian,* pp. 145–146, 148, 150–152, 154–155.

Philips, S. U. (1983). *The invisible culture: Communication in classroom and community on the Warm Springs Indian Reservation.* White Plains, NY: Longman.

Piatt, B. (1986). Toward domestic recognition of a human right to language. *Houston Law Review, 23,* 885–906.

Piatt, B. (1990). *¿Only English? Law and language policy in the United States.* Albuquerque: University of New Mexico Press.

Pinker, S. (1994). *The language instinct.* New York: William Morrow.

Plessy v. Ferguson, 163 U.S. 537 (1896).

Portes, A., and Rumbaut, R. G. (2006). *Immigrant America: A portrait* (3rd ed.). Berkeley: University of California Press.

Postman, N. (1995). *The end of education: Redefining the value of school.* New York: Alfred A. Knopf.

Pringle, I. (1999). Canadian Language Policy. In B. Spolsky (Ed.), *Concise encyclopedia of educational linguistics* (pp. 81–83). Oxford, UK: Elsevier Science.

Pufahl, I., Rhodes, N. C., & Christian, D. (2000). *Foreign language teaching: What the United States can learn from other countries.* Washington, DC: Center for Applied Linguistics.

Quebec seeking to end its old cultural divide. (2003, April 13). *The New York Times,* p. A6.

Ramírez, A. G. (1995). *Creating contexts for second language acquisition: Theory and methods.* White Plains, NY: Longman.

Ramírez, D., Yuen, S. D., & Ramey, D. R. (1991). *Final report: Longitudinal study of English immersion strategy, early-exit and late-exit transitional bilingual education programs for language-minority children.* (Department of Education Contract No. 300-87-0156.) San Mateo, CA: Aguirre International.

Ramírez, M., & Castañeda, A. (1974). *Cultural democracy, bicognitive development, and education.* New York: Academic Press.

Reacting to *The Bell Curve.* (1995, January 11). *Education Week,* pp. 29–32.

Rheingold, J. (1988). *They have a word for it.* Los Angeles: Jeremy P. Tarcher.

Richard-Amato, P. A. (1988). *Making it happen: Interaction in the second language classroom from theory to practice* (2nd ed.). White Plains, NY: Longman.

Richard-Amato, P. A., & Snow, M. A. (1995). *The multicultural classroom: Readings for content-area teachers* (2nd ed.). White Plains, NY: Longman.

Riches, C., & Genesee, F. (2006). Literacy: Crosslinguistic and crossmodal issues. In F. Genesee, K. Lindholm-Leary, W. M. Saunders, & D. Christian (Eds.), *Educating English language learners: A synthesis of research evidence* (pp. 64–108). Cambridge, UK: Cambridge University Press.

Riggs, P. (1991). Whole language in TESOL. *TESOL Quarterly, 25,* 521–542.

Rodriguez, R. (1982). *Hunger of memory: The education of Richard Rodriguez.* Boston: David R. Godine.

Rossell, C., & Baker, K. (1996). The educational effectiveness of bilingual education. *Research in the Teaching of English, 30,* 7–74.

Roth Pierpont, C. (1997, February 17). A society of one. *The New Yorker,* 80–86.

Rubin, J. (1972). Bilingual usage in Paraguay. In J. A. Fishman (Ed.), *Readings in the sociology of language* (pp. 512–530). The Hague, Neth.: Mouton.

Sachs, J. (1985). Prelinguistic development. In J. B. Gleason (Ed.), *The development of language* (pp. 37–60). Columbus, OH: Merrill.

Saravia-Shore, M., & Arvizu, S. F. (1992). *Cross-cultural literacy: Ethnographies of communication in multiethnic classrooms.* New York: Garland.

Saville-Troike, M. (1976). Bilingual children: A resource document. In F. Cordasco (Ed.), *Bilingual schooling in the United States: A sourcebook for educational personnel* (pp. 165–188). New York: McGraw-Hill.

Saville-Troike, M. (1982). *The ethnography of communication: An introduction.* Oxford, UK: Basil Blackwell.

Schieffelin, B. B. (1985). The acquisition of Kaluli. In D. I. Slobin (Ed.), *The cross-linguistic study of language acquisition: Vol. 1. The data* (pp. 525–593). Hillsdale, NJ: Lawrence Erlbaum.

Schmemann, S. (1996, January 31). A word handed down, but not set in stone. *The New York Times,* pp. A1, A4.

Schmidley, A. D., & Robinson, J. G. (October 2003). Measuring the foreign-born population in the United States with the current population survey: 1994–2002. *Population Division Working Paper No. 73.* Washington, DC: Population Division, U.S. Bureau of the Census.

Sedaris, D. (1997, May). The ashtray is on the table today . . . and other misadventures of a would-be French speaker. *Travel & Leisure,* 70–73.

Seliger, H. (1977). Does practice make perfect? A study of interaction patterns and L2 competence. *Language Learning, 27*(2), 263–278.

Serna v. Portales Municipal Schools, 499 F.2d 1147 (10th Cir. 1974).

Short, D. J. (Spring, 2002). Language learning in sheltered social studies classes. *TESOL Journal, 11*(1), 18–24.

Siguan, M. (1991). The Catalan language in the educational system of Catalonia. *International Review of Education, 37,* 87–98.

Simon, P. (1980). *The tongue-tied American.* New York: Continuum.

Skutnabb-Kangas, T. (1981). *Bilingualism or not: The education of minorities.* Clevedon, UK: Multilingual Matters.

Skutnabb-Kangas, T. (1998, March). *Linguistic education: A national perspective.* Paper presented at the San Jose Unified School District, San Jose, CA.

Skutnabb-Kangas, T., & Phillipson, R. (Eds.). (1994). *Linguistic human rights: Overcoming linguistic discrimination.* Berlin: Mouton de Gruyter.

Snow, C. (1977). The development of conversation between mothers and babies. *Journal of Child Language, 4,* 1–22.

Snow, M. A., Met, M., & Genesee, F. (1989). A conceptual framework for the integration of language and content in second/foreign language instruction. *TESOL Quarterly, 23*(2), 201–217.

Solano-Flores, G. , & Trumbull, E. (2003). Examining language in context: The need for new research and practice in the testing of English-language learners. *Educational Researcher 32*(2), 1–13.

Speech therapist who gives and takes accents. (1993, August 11). *The New York Times,* p. A10.

Spolsky, B. (1986). *Language and education in multilingual settings.* San Diego, CA: College-Hill Press.

Spolsky, B. (1995). *Measured words: The development of objective language testing.* Oxford, UK: Oxford University Press.

Spolksy, B. (2004). *Language policy.* Cambridge, UK: Cambridge University Press.

Spradley, J. P. (Ed.). (1972). *Culture and cognition: Rules, maps, and plans.* San Francisco: Chandler.

Sridhar, K. K. (1993). Meaning, means, and maintenance. In J. E. Alatis (Ed.), *Georgetown University round table on languages and linguistics 1992: Language, communication, and social meaning* (pp. 56–65). Washington, DC: Georgetown University Press.

Stockwell, P. (2002). *Sociolinguistics: A resource book for students.* London: Routledge.

Strength through wisdom: A critique of U.S. capability. (1980). *Modern Language Journal, 64,* 9–57.

Study reveals teachers' superstitious beliefs. (1988, September 11). *San Jose Mercury News,* p. 20A.

Suárez-Orozco, M. M. (2005). Everything you ever wanted to know about assimilation but were afraid to ask. In M. M. Suárez-Orozco, C. Suárez-Orozco, & D. Baolian Qin (Eds.), *The new immigration: An interdisciplinary reader* (pp. 67–83). New York: Routledge.

Suarez-Orozco, M. M., & Suarez-Orozco, C. E. (1993). Hispanic cultural psychology: Implications for teacher education and research. In P. Phelan & A. Locke Davidson (Eds.), *Renegotiating cultural diversity in American schools.* New York: Teachers College Press.

Sue, S., & Padilla, A. (1986). Ethnic minority issues in the United States: Challenges for the educational system. In California State Department of Education (Ed.), *Beyond language: Social and cultural factors in schooling language minority students* (pp. 36–72). Los Angeles: Evaluation, Dissemination and Assessment Center, California State University, Los Angeles.

Swain, M. (1985). Communicative competence: Some roles of comprehensible input and comprehensible output in its development. In S. Gass & C. Madden (Eds.), *Input in second language acquisition* (pp. 235–253). Rowley, MA: Newbury House.

Swain, M. (1991). French immersion and its offshoots: Getting two for one. In B. F. Freed (Ed.), *Foreign language acquisition research and the classroom* (pp. 91–103). Lexington, MA: D. C. Heath and Company.

Tannen, D. (1990). *You just don't understand: Women and men in conversation.* New York: Morrow.

Temple-Raston, D. (2007, July 30). FBI recruiting class shows language diversity. San Francisco: KQED.

Terrell, T. D. (1981). The natural approach in bilingual education. In California State Department of Education (Ed.), *Schooling and language minority students: A theoretical framework* (pp. 117–146). Los Angeles: Evaluation, Dissemination and Assessment Center, California State University, Los Angeles.

Thiong'o, N. (2004). Recovering the original. In W. Lesser (Ed.), *The genius of language* (pp. 102–110). New York: Pantheon.

Thomas, R. M., Jr. (1998, February 1). Carl Gorman, code talker in World War II, dies at 90. *The New York Times,* p. A31.

Thomas, W., & Collier, V. (1997). Two languages are better than one. *Educational Leadership, 55*(4), 23–26.

Thonis, E. (1983). *The English-Spanish connection*. Northvale, NJ: Santillana.

Todd, L. (2001). Pidgins and creoles: An overview. In R. Mesthrie (Ed.), *Concise encyclopedia of sociolinguistics*, (pp. 534–530). Oxford, UK: Elsevier Science.

Tollefson, J. W. (2002). *Language policies in education*. Mahwah, NJ: Lawrence Erlbaum.

Tomlinson, E. H., & Eastwick, J. F. (1980). Allons enfants. *Independent School, 40*(1), 23–31.

Trasvina, J. (1981, August 7). Bilingual elections safeguard rights of linguistic minorities. *The Denver Post*.

Trueba, H. T., Guthrie, G. P., & Au, K. H. (Eds.). (1981). *Culture and the bilingual classroom: Studies in classroom ethnography*. Rowley, MA: Newbury House.

Tse, L. (2001). *Why don't they learn English? Separating fact from fallacy in the U.S. language debate*. New York: Teachers College Press.

Tyack, D. B. (1974). *The one best system: A history of American urban education*. Cambridge, MA: Harvard University Press.

U.S. Bureau of the Census (1997). Statistical Abstract of the United States: 1997 (117th ed.) Washington, DC: U.S. Bureau of the Census.

U.S. Department of Education, Office of the Secretary. (1992). *The condition of bilingual education in the nation: A report to congress and the president, June 30, 1992*. Washington, DC: Government Printing Office.

U.S. Department of Education, Office of Educational Research and Improvement. (1997). *Digest of Education Statistics*. Washington, DC: U.S. Government Printing Office.

U.S. Department of Justice, Civil Rights Division. (2004, September 21). Executive order 13166, Limited English proficient resource document: Tips and tools from the field. Washington, DC: Author.

U.S. Department of State. (2006, January 5). *National Security Language Initiative fact sheet*. Retrieved January 5, 2008, from www.state.gov/r/pa/prs/ps/2006/58733.htm.

U.S. English. (2007). Retrieved July 19, 2007, from www.us-english.org/inc/about.

U.S. General Accounting Office. (1987a). *Bilingual education: A new look at the research evidence* (GAO/PEMD-87-12BR). Washington, DC: Government Printing Office.

U.S. General Accounting Office. (1987b). *Bilingual education: Information on limited English proficient students* (GAO/HRD-87-85BR). Washington, DC: Government Printing Office.

U.S. General Accounting Office. (January, 2002). *Foreign languages: Human capital approach needed to correct staffing and proficiency shortfalls*. (GAO-02-375). Washington, DC: Author.

Valdés, G. (2001). *Learning and not learning English*. New York: Teachers College Press.

Valdés, G., & Figueroa, R. A. (1994). *Bilingualism and testing: A special case of bias*. Norwood, NJ: Ablex Publishing.

Valdes, J. M. (Ed.). (1986). *Culture bound: Bridging the cultural gap in language teaching*. New York: Cambridge University Press.

Van Horne, W. A., & Tonnesen, T. V. (Eds.). (1987). *Ethnicity and language*. Milwaukee: The University of Wisconsin System Institute on Race and Ethnicity.

Ventriglia, L. (1982). *Conversations with Miguel and Maria: How children learn English as a second language: Implications for classroom teaching*. Reading, MA: Addison-Wesley.

Viadero, D. (1997, July 9). Two different worlds, *Education Week*, pp. 31–35.

Villarreal, A. (1999). Rethinking the education of English language learners: Transitional bilingual education programs. *Bilingual Research Journal 23*(1). Washington DC: National Association for Bilingual Education.

Voting Rights Act of 1965, as amended, 42 U.S.C. sec. 1973 et seq.

Wang, P. C. (1986). A bilingual education lesson from China. *Thrust, 16*(1), 38–39.

Wardhaugh, R. (1993). *Investigating language: Central problems in linguistics*. Oxford, UK: Blackwell.

Warren-Leubecker, A., & Bohannon J. N. III. (1985). Language in society: Variation and adaptation. In J. B. Gleason (Ed.), *The development of language* (pp. 331–367). Columbus, OH: Merrill.

Wasserman, J. (1973). Immigration law and practice. Philadelphia: American Law Institute.

Weinberg, M. (1977). *A chance to learn: A history of race and education in the United States*. New York: Cambridge University Press.

Weiner, R., and Pristoop, E. (2006). *How states shortchange the districts that need the most help*. Washington, DC: Education Trust.

Welles, E. (2004). Foreign language enrollments in United States institutions of higher education, Fall 2002, *ADFL Bulletin 35*(2–3): 7–26.

Wells, S. (1986, July 28). Bilingualism: The accent is on youth. *U.S. News & World Report,* p. 60.

Wesman, A. G. (1969). Intelligent testing. *American Psychologist, 23,* 267–274.

When a snow day is more than just play. (2003, April 17). *The New York Times.* p. A14.

Wilbur, R. (1980). The linguistic description of American sign language. In H. Lane & F. Grosjean (Eds.), *Recent perspectives on American sign language* (pp. 7–31). Hillsdale, NJ: Lawrence Erlbaum Associates.

Williams, J. D., & Capizzi Snipper, G. (1990). *Literacy and bilingualism.* White Plains, NY: Longman.

Williams, S. W. (1991). Classroom use of African American language: Educational tool or social weapon? In C. E. Sleeter (Ed.), *Empowerment through multicultural education* (pp. 199–215). Albany: State University of New York Press.

Willig, A. C. (1985). A meta-analysis of selected studies on the effectiveness of bilingual education. *Review of Educational Research, 55,* 269–317.

Wineburg, S. S. (1987). When good intentions aren't enough. *Phi Delta Kappan, 68,* 544–545.

Wolcott, H. F. (1997). The teacher as an enemy. In G. D. Spindler (Ed.), *Education and cultural process: Anthropological approaches* (3rd ed.) (pp. 77–92). Prospect Heights, IL: Waveland Press.

Wolfram, W., & Ward, B. (Eds.). (2006). *American voices: How dialects differ from coast to coast.* Oxford, UK: Blackwell.

Wolfson, N., & Manes, J. (Eds.). (1985). *Language of inequality.* Berlin: Mouton de Gruyter.

Wong Fillmore, L. (1979). Individual differences in second language acquisition. In C. J. Fillmore, D. Kempler, & Wang, S. Y. William (Eds.), *Individual differences in language ability and language behavior.* New York: Academic Press.

Wong Fillmore, L. (1985). Second language learning in children: A proposed model. In National Clearinghouse for Bilingual Education (Ed.), *Issues in English language development* (pp. 33–42). Rosslyn, VA: National Clearinghouse for Bilingual Education.

Wong Fillmore, L. (1991). Second-language learning in children: A model of language learning in social context. In E. Bialystok (Ed.), *Language processing in bilingual children* (pp. 49–69). Cambridge, UK: Cambridge University Press.

Woolard, K. A. (1985). Catalonia: The dilemma of language rights. In N. Wolfson & J. Manes (Eds.), *Language of inequality* (pp. 91–107). Berlin: Mouton de Gruyter.

Wurm, S. A. (Ed.). (1996). *Atlas of the world's languages in danger of disappearing.* Paris/Canberra: UNESCO Publishing/Pacific Linguistics.

Zehr, M. A. (2007, August 1). Students get taste of "national security languages." *Education Week,* pp. 5, 12.

INDEX